Red Hat® Linux® Fedora™ All-in-One Desk Reference For Dummies®

Cheat Sheet

Bash Shell

- Pipe:
  - command1 | command2
- Redirections:
  - command > file (output goes to file)
  - command < file (input from file)
  - command >> file (append to file)
  - command 2> file (errors go to file)
- Commands:
  - alias (Defines shortcut for a long command)
  - apropos (Searches the manpages for keywords)

- history (Displays most recent commands)
- locate (Finds files)
- whereis (Finds executable files for a command)
- which (Shows full pathname ___ ___ and)
- ma ___
- pr ___ bles)
- Environ ___
  - HO ___
  - PA ___)
  - TER ___ (Name of terminal type)

File System

- Key directories in the file system:
  - / Root directory (base of file system)
  - /bin (Executable programs)
  - /boot (Linux kernel and boot loader)
  - /dev (Special device files)
  - /etc (System configuration files)
  - /home (Home directories of all users)
  - /lib (Library files for programs)
  - /mnt (Mount points for CD-ROM, floppy)
  - /root (Home directory of the root user)
  - /sbin (System-administration commands)
  - /tmp (Temporary directory)
  - /usr (Many important programs)
  - /var (Various system files, such as logs)
- Commands:
  - cat — Copies a file to the standard output
  - cd — Changes current directory
  - chmod — Changes file permissions
  - chown — Changes file ownerships
  - cp — Copies files
  - dd — Copies blocks of data
  - df — Reports disk space usage by device
  - diff — Compares two text files
  - du — Reports disk space usage by directory
  - file — Displays the type of data in a file
  - find — Finds files based on specified criteria

- grep — Searches for text in a file
- ln — Links a file name to a link name
- ls — Displays the contents of a directory
- mkdir — Creates a directory
- more — Displays a text file, one page at a time
- mount — Mounts a file system
- mv — Renames or moves file
- pwd — Displays the current directory
- rm — Deletes files
- rmdir — Deletes directories
- sort — Sorts lines in a text file
- split — Splits a file into smaller parts
- umount — Unmount a file system
- wc — Counts words and lines in a file
- File permissions:
  - rwxrwxrwx 3 groups of rwx, leftmost is for owner, middle for group, rightmost for others; rwx stands for read (r), write (w), execute (x); dash (-) means no permission
  - rwx------ Only owner can read, write, execute
  - rw-r--r-- Everyone can read, owner can write
  - rw------- Only owner can read and write
  - r--r--r-- Read-only file (everyone can read)

Red Hat® Linux® Fedora™ All-in-One Desk Reference For Dummies®

Cheat Sheet

Red Hat Linux Installation

1. Resize disk partition using partitioning tool such as PartitionMagic or get a second hard disk.
2. Boot PC from first CD-ROM or create boot disk and boot from the boot disk.
3. Go through graphical installation steps.
4. Configure other hardware when system first boots up.

GNOME and KDE Desktops

- Click the Main Menu button in GNOME or KDE and then select applications to run
- Always right-click for a pop-up menu of options
- Right-click on the GNOME panel to add applets to the panel
- To run OpenOffice.org applications: Main Menu⇨Office

Red Hat Linux Configuration

- Run graphical Red Hat configuration tools from Main Menu⇨System Settings
- To configure the X Window System, run

  `redhat-config-xfree86`

- Printer setup: Main Menu⇨System Settings⇨Printing
- Sound card setup: Main Menu⇨System Settings⇨Soundcard Detection

System Administration

Manage user accounts: Main Menu⇨ System Settings⇨Users and Groups

Manage packages: Main Menu⇨System Settings⇨Add/Remove Applications

Configure services: Main Menu⇨System Settings⇨Server Settings⇨Services

Install RPM packages: `rpm -ivh` *packagefile*

Check if RPM is installed: `rpm -q` *rpmname*

Unpack compressed tar files: `tar zxvf` *filename*.tgz

Unpack bz2 compressed files: `bzip2 -d` *filename*.bz2

Network Configuration

- **Network configuration:** Main Menu⇨System Tools⇨Network Device Control
- **Internet connection:** Main Menu⇨System Tools⇨Internet Configuration Wizard

Commands:

- `ping`   Checks network connectivity
- `ifconfig` Configures network interface
- `iwconfig` Configures wireless network interface
- `netstat`   Displays network status

For Dummies: Bestselling Book Series for Beginners

Red Hat® Linux® Fedora™

ALL-IN-ONE DESK REFERENCE

FOR DUMMIES®

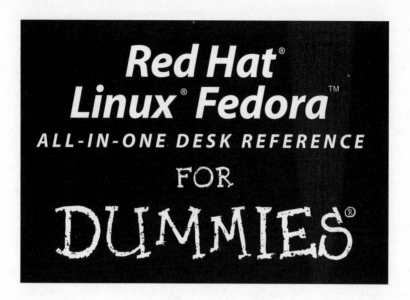

Red Hat® Linux® Fedora™
ALL-IN-ONE DESK REFERENCE
FOR
DUMMIES®

by Naba Barkakati

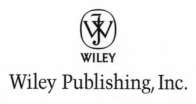

WILEY

Wiley Publishing, Inc.

Red Hat® Linux® Fedora™ All-in-One Desk Reference For Dummies®

Published by
Wiley Publishing, Inc.
111 River Street
Hoboken, NJ 07030

www.wiley.com

WILEY   is a trademark of Wiley Publishing, Inc.

About the Author

Naba Barkakati is an electrical engineer and a successful computer-book author who has experience in a wide variety of systems, ranging from MS-DOS and Windows to UNIX and Linux. He bought his first personal computer — an IBM PC-AT — in 1984 after graduating with a PhD in electrical engineering from the University of Maryland at College Park. While pursuing a full-time career in engineering, Naba dreamed of writing software for the emerging PC software market. As luck would have it, instead of building a software empire like Microsoft, he ended up writing successful computer books. Currently, Naba is a Senior Level Technologist at the Center for Technology and Engineering in the U.S. General Accounting Office.

Over the past 15 years, Naba has written over 25 computer books on a number of topics ranging from Windows programming with C++ to Linux. He has authored several best-selling titles, such as The Waite Group's Turbo C++ Bible, Object-Oriented Programming in C++, X Window System Programming, Visual C++ Developer's Guide, Borland C++ 4 Developer's Guide, and Linux Secrets. His books have been translated into many languages, including Spanish, French, Polish, Greek, Italian, Chinese, Japanese, and Korean. Naba's most recent book is *Red Hat Linux 9 Secrets*, also published by Wiley Publishing, Inc.

Naba lives in North Potomac, Maryland, with his wife Leha, and their children, Ivy, Emily, and Ashley.

Dedication

I would like to dedicate this book to my wife Leha, and daughters Ivy, Emily, and Ashley.

Author's Acknowledgments

I am grateful to Terri Varveris for getting me started on this book — a set of nine quick reference guides on all aspects of Red Hat Linux. As the project editor, Nicole Sholly guided me through the manuscript-submission process and kept everything moving. I appreciate the guidance and support that Terri and Nicole gave me during this project.

I would like to thank Jason Luster for reviewing the manuscript for technical accuracy and providing many useful suggestions for improving the book's content.

Thanks to everyone at Wiley Publishing for transforming my raw manuscript into this well-edited and beautifully packaged book.

Of course, there would be no reason for this book if it were not for Linux. For this, we have Linus Torvalds and the legions of Linux developers around the world to thank. Thanks to Red Hat for providing beta copies of Red Hat Linux and the publisher's edition CDs that are bundled with this book.

Finally, and as always, my greatest thanks go to my wife, Leha, and our daughters, Ivy, Emily, and Ashley — it is their love and support that keeps me going. Thanks for being there!

Publisher's Acknowledgments

We're proud of this book; please send us your comments through our online registration form located at `www.dummies.com/register/`.

Some of the people who helped bring this book to market include the following:

Acquisitions, Editorial, and Media Development

Associate Project Editor: Nicole Sholly

Acquisitions Editor: Terri Varveris

Senior Copy Editor: Barry Childs-Helton

Technical Editor: Jason Luster

Editorial Manager: Kevin Kirschner

Permissions Editor: Laura Moss

Media Development Specialist: Angela Denny

Media Development Manager: Laura VanWinkle

Media Development Supervisor: Richard Graves

Editorial Assistants: Amanda Foxworth, Virginia Sanders

Cartoons: Rich Tennant (`www.the5thwave.com`)

Production

Project Coordinator: Regnia Snyder

Layout and Graphics: Seth Conley, Joyce Haughey, Stephanie D. Jumper, Jacque Schneider, Julie Trippetti, Shae Wilson, Melanee Wolven

Proofreaders: John Greenough, Andy Hollandbeck, Susan Moritz, Linda Quigley

Indexer: Infodex Indexing Services Inc.

Publishing and Editorial for Technology Dummies

    Richard Swadley, Vice President and Executive Group Publisher

    Andy Cummings, Vice President and Publisher

    Mary C. Corder, Editorial Director

Publishing for Consumer Dummies

    Diane Graves Steele, Vice President and Publisher

    Joyce Pepple, Acquisitions Director

Composition Services

    Gerry Fahey, Vice President of Production Services

    Debbie Stailey, Director of Composition Services

Contents at a Glance

Table of Contents

Introduction

Red Hat continues to improve its version of Linux. The recently released Red Hat Linux comes with many new system components including the Linux 2.4.22 kernel, XFree86 4.3.0, GNOME 2.4, KDE 3.1, GCC 3.3 compiler, and the glibc 2.3.2 system libraries. This version supports many new features such as Advanced Configuration and Power Interface (ACPI), Bluetooth wireless connections, and a graphical boot screen that shows system startup messages in a user-friendly screen.

Red Hat Linux also includes the OpenOffice.org office suite. To top it off, Red Hat Linux comes with a graphical installation program that makes installation easy!

Finally, starting with this version, the Red Hat Linux *product* is becoming the Fedora *project* — a collaborative development project open to all who have the skills and interest to participate and contribute. With this new model of development, the original developers (instead of Red Hat developers) will maintain control of various packages that make up Red Hat Linux.

Note: At press time, Red Hat renamed its Linux product the Fedora Project. Throughout the course of this book, I refer to the product as Red Hat Linux or simply as Red Hat. You'll probably see the product referred to as the Fedora Project in the news, on the Web, and elsewhere, but you can rest assured that the different terms, as used in this book, are referring to the same product.

About Red Hat Linux Fedora All-in-One

Red Hat Linux Fedora All-in-One Desk Reference For Dummies follows the successful model of the All-in-One Desk Reference and gives you nine different quick-reference guides in a single book. Taken together, these nine minibooks provide detailed information on installing, configuring, and using Red Hat Linux.

What you'll like most about this book is that you don't have to read it sequentially chapter by chapter, or, for that matter, even the sections in a chapter. You can pretty much turn to the topic you want and quickly get the answer to your pressing questions about Red Hat Linux, be it about using the OpenOffice.org word processor or setting up the Apache Web server.

Here are some of the things you can do with this book:

✦ Install and configure Red Hat Linux from the DVD included with the book.

✦ Connect the Red Hat Linux PC to the Internet through a DSL or cable modem.

✦ Set up dial-up networking with PPP.

✦ Get tips, techniques, and shortcuts for specific uses of Red Hat Linux, such as

- Setting up and using Internet services such as Web, Mail, News, FTP, NFS, NIS, and DNS

- Setting up a Windows server using Samba

- Using Red Hat Linux commands

- Using Perl, shell, and C programming on Red Hat Linux

- Using the OpenOffice.org office suite and other applications that come with Red Hat Linux

- Understanding the basics of system and network security

- Performing system administration tasks

Conventions Used in This Book

I use a simple notational style in this book. All listings, filenames, function names, variable names, and keywords are typeset in a `monospace` font for ease of reading. I italicize the first occurrences of new terms and concepts and then provide a definition right there. The output of commands follows the typed command and the output is shown in a monospace font.

What You Don't Have to Read

Each mini reference book zeros in on a specific task area such as using the Internet or running Internet servers and then provides hands-on instructions on how to perform a series of related tasks. You can jump right to a section and read about a specific task. You don't have to read anything but the few paragraphs or the list of steps that relate to your question. Use the Table of Contents or the Index to locate the pages that are relevant to your question.

You can safely ignore text next to the Technical Stuff icons as well as the sidebars.

Who Are You?

I assume that you are somewhat familiar with a PC — you know how to turn it on and off and you have dabbled a bit with Windows. Considering that most new PCs come preloaded with Windows, this should be a safe assumption, right?

When it comes to installing Red Hat Linux on your PC, if you want to retain your Windows 2000 or Windows XP installations intact, I assume you won't mind investing in a good disk-partitioning tool such as PowerQuest's PartitionMagic, available at `www.powerquest.com/partitionmagic` (no, I don't have any connections with PowerQuest).

I also assume that you are willing to accept the risk that when you try to install Red Hat Linux, some things may not quite work. This can happen if you have some uncommon types of hardware. If you are afraid of ruining your system, try finding a slightly older spare Pentium PC that you can sacrifice and then install Red Hat Linux on that PC.

How This Book Is Organized

Red Hat Linux Fedora All-in-One Desk Reference For Dummies has nine mini-books, each of which focuses on a small set of related topics. If you are looking for information on a specific topic, check the book names on the spine or consult the Table of Contents.

This desk reference starts with a mini-book that explains the basics of Red Hat Linux and guides you through the installation process (this is a unique aspect of this book because you typically do not purchase a PC with Red Hat Linux preinstalled). The second minibook serves as a user's guide to Red Hat Linux — it focuses on exploring various aspects of a Red Hat Linux workstation, including the GNOME and KDE GUIs and many of the applications that come bundled with Red Hat Linux. The third minibook is a user's guide to the OpenOffice.org office applications. The fourth minibook covers networking and Book V goes into using the Internet. Book VI introduces system administration. The seventh minibook turns to the important subject of securing a Red Hat Linux system and its associated network. Book VIII teaches how to run a variety of Internet servers from mail to Web server. The ninth and final minibook introduces you to programming.

Here's a quick overview of the nine books and what they contain:

Book I: Fedora Basics: What is Red Hat Linux? Installing, configuring, and troubleshooting Red Hat Linux. Taking Red Hat Linux for a test drive.

Book II: Workstations and Applications: Exploring GNOME and KDE. Learning how to use the shell (what's a shell anyway?). Learning to navigate the Red Hat Linux file system. Exploring the applications such as multimedia software as well as the text editors (vi and Emacs).

Book III: OpenOffice.org: Writing with OpenOffice.org Writer. Preparing spreadsheets with OpenOffice.org Calc. Making presentations with OpenOffice.org Impress. Preparing drawings with OpenOffice.org Draw.

Book IV: Networking: Connecting the Red Hat Linux PC to the Internet through a dial-up connection or a high-speed always-on connection such as DSL or cable modem. Configuring and managing TCP/IP networks, including wireless Ethernets.

Book V: Internet: Using various Internet services such as e-mail, Web surfing, and reading newsgroups. Transferring files with FTP.

Book VI: Administration: Learning to perform basic system administration. Managing user accounts and the file system. Installing applications. Working with devices and printers. Using USB devices. Upgrading and customizing the Linux kernel.

Book VII: Security: Understanding network and host security. Learning the techniques to secure the host and the network. Performing security audits.

Book VIII: Internet Servers: Managing the Internet services. Configuring the Apache Web server. Setting up the FTP server (including anonymous FTP). Configuring the mail and news servers. Providing DNS and NIS. File sharing with NFS. Using Samba to set up a Windows server.

Book IX: Programming: Learning the basics of programming. Exploring the software development tools in Red Hat Linux. Writing shell scripts. Learning C and Perl programming.

Appendix: About the DVD: Summarizes the contents of the book's companion DVD.

Sidebars

I use sidebars throughout the book to highlight interesting, but not critical, information. Sidebars explain concepts you may not have encountered before or give a little insight into a related topic. If you're in a hurry, you can safely skip the sidebars.

What's on the DVD?

The DVD contains Red Hat Linux from Red Hat, Inc. You may use the DVD in accordance with the license agreements accompanying the software. To learn more about the contents of the DVD, please consult the appendix.

Icons Used in This Book

Following the time-honored tradition of the *All-in-One Desk Reference For Dummies* series, I use icons to help you quickly pinpoint useful information. The icons include the following:

The Remember icon marks a general interesting fact — something that I thought you'd like to know and remember.

The Tip icon marks things that you can do to make your job easier.

The Warning icon highlights potential pitfalls. With this icon, I'm telling you: "Watch out! This could hurt your system!"

The Technical Stuff icon marks technical information that could be of interest to an advanced user (or those of us aspiring to be advanced users).

Where to Go from Here

It's time to get started on your Red Hat Linux adventure. Take out the DVD and install Red Hat Linux. Then, turn to a relevant chapter and let the fun begin. Use the Table of Contents and the Index to figure out where you want to go. Before you know it, you'll become an expert at Red Hat Linux!

If you want to participate in the Red Hat Linux project, visit the project's Web site at `rhl.redhat.com` for more information.

I hope you enjoy consulting this book as much as I enjoyed writing it!

Book I

Fedora Basics

"I don't care what your E-Mail friends in Europe say, you're not having a glass of Chianti with your bologna sandwich."

Contents at a Glance

Chapter 1: Introducing Red Hat Linux

In This Chapter

✔ Explaining what Red Hat Linux is

✔ Going over what Red Hat Linux includes

✔ Discovering how Red Hat Linux helps you manage

✔ Getting started

I bet you've heard about Linux, and you probably know the Red Hat name as well. If you're wondering what exactly Red Hat Linux is and what it can help you do, this chapter is all about answering those questions. Here I provide a broad-brushstroke picture of Red Hat Linux and tell you how you can start using it right away. I also briefly mention the Fedora project.

By the way, this book covers Red Hat Linux Fedora for Intel 80x86 and Pentium processors (basically any PC that can run any flavor of Windows).

What Is Red Hat Linux?

Trying to describe Red Hat Linux is a bit like that story of six blind men trying to describe an elephant. You know the one — one blind man touches the elephant's side and says the elephant is like a wall, another checks out the tusk and concludes that an elephant is like a spear, and so on. Along those lines, Red Hat Linux appears to be many different things depending on what you experience. You can think of it as the graphical user interface or just a PC to run your e-mail program, but, at its heart, it's an operating system. The following sections explain what I mean by this statement.

Operating systems and Linux

You know that your PC is a bunch of *hardware* — things you can touch, like the system box, monitor, keyboard, and mouse. The system box contains the most important hardware of all — the *central processing unit* (CPU), the microchip that runs the *software* (any program that tells the computer how to do your bidding) — which you actually *can't* touch. In a typical Pentium 4 PC, the Pentium 4 microprocessor is the CPU. Other important hardware in the system box includes the memory (RAM chips) and the hard drive — and one program has to run all this stuff and get it to play nice: the operating system.

The *operating system* is software that manages all the hardware and runs other software at your command. You, the user, provide those commands by clicking menus and icons or by typing some cryptic text. Linux is an operating system — as are UNIX, Windows 98, Windows 2000, and Windows XP. The Linux operating system is modeled after UNIX; in its most basic, no-frills form, it also goes by the name *Linux kernel*.

The operating system is what gives a computer — any computer — its personality. For example, you can run Windows 98 or Windows XP on a PC — and on that same PC, you can *also* install and run Linux. That means, depending on which operating system is installed and running, *the same PC* can be a Windows 98, Windows XP, or Linux system.

The primary job of an operating system is to load software (computer programs) from the hard disk (or other permanent storage) into the memory and get the CPU to run those programs. Everything you do with your computer is possible because of the operating system; so if the operating system somehow messes up, the whole system freezes up. You know how infuriating it is when your favorite operating system — maybe even the one that came with your PC — suddenly calls it quits just as you were about to click the Send button after composing that long e-mail to your friend. You try the three-finger salute (Ctrl+Alt+Del), but nothing happens. Then it's time for the Reset button (provided your computer's builders were wise enough to include one). Luckily, that sort of thing almost never happens with Linux — it has a reputation for being a very reliable operating system.

Does Linux really run on any computer?

Linux runs on many different types of computer systems — and it does seem able to run on nearly any type of computer. Linus Torvalds and other programmers originally developed Linux for the Intel 80x86 line of processors. Nowadays, Linux is also available for systems based on other processors — such as those with Intel's new 64-bit IA-64 architecture (known as Itanium processors); the Motorola 68000 family; Alpha AXPs; Sun SPARCs and UltraSPARCs; Hewlett-Packard's HP PA-RISC; the PowerPC and PowerPC64 processors; and the MIPS R4x00 and R5x00. More recently, IBM has released its own version of Linux for its S/390 mainframe. This book covers Red Hat Linux for Intel 80x86 and Pentium processors (these have in common a basic physical structure known as *IA-32 architecture*).

In technical mumbo jumbo, Linux is a *multiuser, multitasking operating system*. All this means is that Linux enables multiple users to log in, and Linux can run more than one program at the same time. Nearly all operating systems are multiuser and multitasking these days, but when Linux first started in 1994, *multiuser* and *multitasking* were big selling points.

Linux distributions

Red Hat Linux is a specific *Linux distribution* — essentially a package of features. Red Hat Linux consists of the Linux *kernel* (the operating system) and a collection of applications, together with an easy-to-use installation program.

There are many Linux distributions, and each includes the standard Linux operating system:

✦ **The XFree86 X Window System:** This is the graphical user interface.

✦ **One or more graphical desktops:** Among the most popular are GNOME and KDE.

✦ **A selection of applications:** Linux programs come in the form of ready-to-run software, but the *source code* (the commands we humans use to tell the computer what to do, but you don't need the source code to run the operating system or any applications) is included, as is its documentation.

  Current Linux distributions include a huge selection of software — so much that it requires multiple CD-ROMs or a single DVD (which this book includes).

Like many other Linux distributions, Red Hat Linux is a commercial product that you can buy in computer stores and bookstores. If you have heard about Open Source and the GNU (*GNU's Not UNIX*) license, you may assume that no one can sell Linux for profit. Luckily for companies such as Red Hat, the GNU license — also called the GNU General Public License (GPL) — does allow commercial, for-profit distribution, but requires that the software be distributed in source-code form, and stipulates that anyone may copy and distribute the software in source-code form to anyone else. This means that my publisher may include the Red Hat Linux DVD with this book and you may make as many copies of the DVD as you like.

Making sense of version numbers

Both the Linux kernel and Red Hat Linux have their own version numbers, not to mention the many other software programs (such as GNOME and KDE) that come with Red Hat Linux. The version numbers for the Linux kernel and Red Hat Linux are unrelated, but each has particular significance.

Linux-kernel version numbers

After Linux kernel version 1.0 was released on March 14, 1994, the loosely knit Linux development community adopted a version-numbering scheme. Version numbers such as 1.$X.Y$ and 2.$X.Y$, where X is an even number, are considered to be the stable versions. The last number, Y, is the patch level, which is incremented as problems are fixed. For example, 2.4.21 is a typical, stable version of the Linux kernel. Notice that these version numbers are in the form of three integers separated by periods — *Major.Minor.Patch* — where *Major* and *Minor* are numbers denoting the major and minor version numbers, and *Patch* is another number representing the patch level.

Version numbers of the form 2.$X.Y$ with an odd X number are beta releases for developers only; they may be unstable, so you should not adopt such versions for day-to-day use. For example, when you look at version 2.5.75 of the Linux kernel, notice the *5* — that tells you it's a beta release. Developers add new features to these odd-numbered versions of Linux.

You can find out about the latest version of the Linux kernel online at www.kernel.org.

Red Hat Linux version numbers

Red Hat assigns the Red Hat Linux version numbers, such as 7.3 or 8.0. They are of the form $X.Y$, where X is the major version and Y the minor version. Nowadays if the minor version number is zero, it's simply dropped — as in Red Hat Linux 9. Unlike with the Linux-kernel version numbers, there's no special meaning associated with odd and even minor versions. Each version of Red Hat Linux includes specific versions of the Linux kernel and other major components, such as GNOME, KDE, and various applications.

Red Hat releases new versions of Red Hat Linux on a regular basis. For example, Red Hat Linux 7.0 came out in September 2000, 7.3 in May 2002, 8.0 in September 2002, and Red Hat Linux 9 on March 31, 2003. Typically, each new major version of Red Hat Linux provides significant new features.

Transitioning to the Fedora Project

In late September 2003, Red Hat announced the Fedora Project — an open-source project sponsored by Red Hat where the developer community can participate and continue to evolve what used to be the Red Hat Linux product. The new product goes by the name *Fedora Core* and the project is expected to have Fedora Core releases every four to six months. Red Hat will continue to participate in the Fedora Project and help prepare the Fedora Core releases, but everything will be done with involvement of the open source community under a public release schedule. As you might expect, Fedora Core will be available freely, just as Red Hat Linux used to be, and you can expect books such as this one to include Fedora Core on DVD or CDs.

What is the GNU Project?

GNU is a recursive acronym that stands for *GNU's Not UNIX.* The GNU Project was launched in 1984 by Richard Stallman to develop a complete UNIX-like operating system. The GNU Project developed nearly everything needed for a complete operating system except for the operating system kernel. All GNU software was distributed under the GNU General Public License (GPL). GPL essentially requires that the software is distributed in source-code form and stipulates that any user may copy, modify, and distribute the software to anyone else in source-code form. Users may, however, have to pay for their individual copies of GNU software.

The Free Software Foundation (FSF) is a tax-exempt charity that raises funds for work on the GNU Project. To find out more about the GNU Project, visit its home page at `www.gnu.org`. There you can find information about how to contact the Free Software Foundation and how to help the GNU Project.

Red Hat continues to sell its commercial Linux distribution — called Red Hat Enterprise Linux. Red Hat anticipates that new technologies and enhancements that first appear in Fedora Core would eventually find their way into Red Hat Enterprise Linux. In this way, the Fedora Project should serve as an incubator and testing ground for future Linux development.

To learn more about the Fedore Project, visit `fedora.redhat.com`.

What Red Hat Linux Includes

Red Hat Linux comes with the Linux kernel and a whole lot more software. These software packages include everything from the graphical desktops to Internet servers and programming tools to create new software. In this section, I briefly describe some major software packages that come bundled with Red Hat Linux. Without this bundled software, Red Hat Linux wouldn't be as popular as it is today.

GNU software

I start with a collection of software that came from the GNU Project. You get to know these GNU utilities only if you use your Red Hat Linux system through a text terminal (or a graphical window that mimics one) — a basic *command-line interface* that puts nothing much on-screen but a prompt at which you type in your commands. The GNU software is one of the basic parts of Red Hat Linux.

As a Red Hat Linux user, you might not realize the extent to which Red Hat Linux (and, for that matter, all Linux distributions) relies on GNU software.

Nearly all tasks you perform in a Red Hat Linux system involve one or more GNU software packages. For example, the GNOME graphical user interface (GUI) and the command interpreter (that is, the Bash shell) are both GNU software programs. By the way, the *shell* is the command-interpreter application that accepts the commands you type and runs programs in response to those commands. If you rebuild the kernel or develop software, you do so with the GNU C and C++ compiler (which is part of the GNU software that accompanies Red Hat Linux). If you edit text files with the ed or Emacs editor, you're again using a GNU software package. The list goes on and on.

Table 1-1 lists some of the well-known GNU software packages that come with Red Hat Linux. I show this table only to give you a feel for all the different kinds of things you can do with GNU software. Depending on your interests, you may never need to use many of these packages, but it's good to know they are there in case you ever need them.

Table 1-1	Well-Known GNU Software Packages
Software Package	*Description*
Autoconf	Generates shell scripts that automatically configure source-code packages
Automake	Generates `Makefile.in` files for use with Autoconf
Bash	The default shell — command interpreter — in Red Hat Linux
Bc	An interactive calculator with arbitrary precision numbers
Binutils	A package that includes several utilities for working with binary files: `ar`, `as`, `gasp`, `gprof`, `ld`, `nm`, `objcopy`, `objdump`, `ranlib`, `readelf`, `size`, `strings`, and `strip`
Coreutils	A package that combines three individual packages called Fileutils, Shellutils, and Textutils and implements utilities such as: `chgrp`, `chmod`, `chown`, `cp`, `dd`, `df`, `dir`, `dircolors`, `du`, `install`, `ln`, `ls`, `mkdir`, `mkfifo`, `mknod`, `mv`, `rm`, `rmdir`, `sync`, `touch`, `vdir`, `basename`, `chroot`, `date`, `dirname`, `echo`, `env`, `expr`, `factor`, `false`, `groups`, `hostname`, `id`, `logname`, `nice`, `nohup`, `pathchk`, `printenv`, `printf`, `pwd`, `seq`, `sleep`, `stty`, `su`, `tee`, `test`, `true`, `tty`, `uname`, `uptime`, `users`, `who`, `whoami`, `yes`, `cut`, `join`, `nl`, `split`, `tail`, `wc`, and so on
Cpio	Copies file archives to and from disk or to another part of the file system.
Diff	Compares files, showing line-by-line changes in several different formats.
Ed	A line-oriented text editor
Emacs	An extensible, customizable full-screen text editor and computing environment
Findutils	A package that includes the `find`, `locate`, and `xargs` utilities
Finger	A utility program designed to enable users on the Internet to get information about one another

Software Package	Description
Gawk	The GNU Project's implementation of the AWK programming language
GCC	Compilers for C, C++, Objective C, and other languages
Gdb	Source-level debugger for C, C++ and Fortran
Gdbm	A replacement for the traditional `dbm` and `ndbm` database libraries
Gettext	A set of utilities that enables software maintainers to internationalize (that means make the software work with different languages such as English, French, Spanish, etc.) a software package's user messages
Ghostscript	An interpreter for the Postscript and Portable Document Format (PDF) languages
Ghostview	An X Window System application that makes Ghostscript accessible from the GUI, enabling users to view Postscript or PDF files in a window
The GIMP	The GNU Image Manipulation Program is an Adobe Photoshop–like image-processing program
GNOME	Provides a graphical user interface (GUI) for a wide variety of tasks that a Linux user might perform
GNU C Library	For use with all Linux programs
Gnuchess	A chess-playing program
Gnumeric	A graphical spreadsheet (similar to Microsoft Excel) that works in GNOME
grep package	Includes the `grep`, `egrep`, and `fgrep` commands that are used to find lines that match a specified text pattern
Groff	A document-formatting system similar to `troff`
GTK+	A GUI toolkit for the X Window System (used to develop GNOME applications)
Gzip	A GNU utility for compressing and decompressing files
Indent	Formats C source code by indenting it in one of several different styles
Less	A page-by-page display program similar to `more`, but with additional capabilities
Libpng	A library for image files in the Portable Network Graphics (PNG) format
m4	An implementation of the traditional UNIX macro processor
Make	A utility that determines which files of a large software package need to be recompiled, and issues the commands to recompile them
Mtools	A set of programs that enables users to read, write, and manipulate files on a DOS file system (typically a floppy disk)
Ncurses	A package for displaying and updating text on text-only terminals
Patch	A GNU version of Larry Wall's program to take the output of diff and apply those differences to an original file to generate the modified version

(continued)

Table 1-1 *(continued)*

Software Package	Description
RCS	The Revision Control System; used for version control and management of source files in software projects
Sed	A stream-oriented version of the ed text editor
Sharutils	A package that includes `shar` (used to make shell archives out of many files) and `unshar` (to unpack these shell archives)
Tar	A tape archiving program that includes multivolume support; the capability to archive sparse files, handle compression and decompression, and create remote archives; and other special features for incremental and full backups
Texinfo	A set of utilities that generates printed manuals, plain ASCII text, and online hypertext documentation (called Info), and enables users to view and read online Info documents
Time	A utility that reports the user, system, and actual time that a process uses

GUIs and applications

Let's face it — typing cryptic Linux commands on a terminal is boring. For average users like us, it's much easier to use the system through a *graphical user interface* (*GUI*, pronounced "gooey") that gives us pictures to click and windows (small *w*) to open. This is where the X Window System, or X, comes to our rescue.

X is kind of like Microsoft Windows, but the underlying details of how X works is completely different from Windows. Unlike Windows, X provides the basic features of displaying windows on-screen, but it does not come with any specific look or feel for graphical applications. That look and feel comes from GUIs, such as GNOME and KDE, which make use of the X Window System.

Red Hat Linux comes with the X Window System in the form of XFree86 — an implementation of X Window System for 80x86 systems. XFree86 works with a wide variety of video cards available for today's PCs.

As for the GUI, Red Hat Linux includes two powerful GUI desktops: KDE (K Desktop Environment) and GNOME (GNU Object Model Environment). If both GNOME and KDE are installed on a PC, you can choose which desktop you want as the default — or switch between the two. KDE and GNOME provide desktops similar to those of Microsoft Windows and the Macintosh OS. GNOME also comes with the Nautilus graphical shell that makes it easy to find files, run applications, and configure your Red Hat Linux system. With GNOME or KDE, you can begin using your Red Hat Linux workstation without having to learn cryptic Linux commands. However, if you should ever need to use those commands directly, all you have to do is open a terminal window and type them at the prompt.

Red Hat Linux also comes with many graphical applications. The most note-worthy program is GIMP (GNU Image Manipulation Program, also known as "*The* Gimp"), a program for working with photos and other images. GIMP's capabilities are on a par with Adobe Photoshop.

Providing common productivity software — such as word processing, spread-sheet, and database applications — is an area in which Linux used to be lack-ing. This situation has changed, though. Red Hat Linux comes with the OpenOffice.org office-productivity applications. In addition, you may want to check out these prominent, commercially available office-productivity appli-cations for Linux that are not included on the companion DVD:

+ Applixware Office — now called Anyware Desktop for Linux — is a good example of productivity software for Linux. You can find it at `www.vistasource.com`.

+ StarOffice from Sun Microsystems (`www.sun.com/staroffice`) is another well-known productivity-software package.

+ CrossOver Office, from CodeWeavers (`www.codeweavers.com/ products/office/`), enables you to install your Microsoft Office applications (only Office 97 or Office 2000, not Office XP) in Linux.

As you can see, there's no shortage of Microsoft Office-compatible office applications for Linux.

Networks

Red Hat Linux comes with everything needed to use the system in networks so that the system can exchange data with other systems. On networks, computers that exchange data have to follow well-defined rules or proto-cols. A *network protocol* is a method that the sender and receiver agree upon for exchanging data across a network. Such a protocol is similar to the rules you might follow when you're having a polite conversation with someone at a party. You typically start by saying hello, exchanging names, and then taking turns talking. That's about the same way network protocols work. The two computers use the protocol to send bits and bytes back and forth across the network.

One of the most well-known and popular network protocols is Transmission Control Protocol/Internet Protocol (*TCP/IP*). TCP/IP is the protocol of choice on the Internet — the "network of networks" that now spans the globe. Red Hat Linux supports the TCP/IP protocol and any network applications that make use of TCP/IP.

Internet servers

Some popular network applications are specifically designed to deliver infor-mation from one system to another. When you send electronic mail (e-mail) or visit Web sites using a Web browser, you use these network applications (also called Internet services). Here are some common Internet services:

+ Electronic mail (e-mail) that you use to send messages to any other person on the Internet using addresses like `joe@someplace.com`.

+ World Wide Web (or simply, Web) that you browse using a Web browser.

+ News services, where you can read newsgroups and post news items to newsgroups with names such as `comp.os.linux.networking` or `comp.os.linux.setup`.

+ File-transfer utilities that you can use to download files.

+ Remote login that you can use to connect to and work with another computer (the remote computer) on the Internet — assuming you have the required user name and password to access that remote computer.

Any Red Hat Linux PC can offer these Internet services. To do so, the PC must be connected to the Internet and it must run special server software that we call the *Internet servers*. Each of the servers uses a specific protocol for transferring information. For example, here are some common Internet servers that you'll find in Red Hat Linux:

+ `sendmail` is the mail server for exchanging e-mail messages between systems using SMTP *(Simple Mail Transfer Protocol)*.

+ Apache `httpd` is the Web server for sending documents from one system to another using HTTP *(Hypertext Transfer Protocol)*.

+ `vsftpd` is the server for transferring files between computers on the Internet using FTP *(File Transfer Protocol)*.

+ `innd` is the news server for distribution of news articles in a store-and-forward fashion across the Internet using NNTP *(Network News Transfer Protocol)*.

+ `in.telnetd` allows a user on one system to log in to another system on the Internet using the TELNET protocol.

Software development

Red Hat Linux is particularly well suited to software development. Straight out of the box, it's chock-full of software development tools such as the compiler and libraries of code needed to build programs. If you happen to know UNIX and the C programming language, you will feel right at home programming in Red Hat Linux.

As far as the development environment goes, Red Hat Linux has the same basic tools (such as an editor, a compiler, and a debugger) that you might use on other UNIX workstations, such as those from IBM, Sun Microsystems, and Hewlett-Packard (HP). What this means is that if you work by day on one of these UNIX workstations, you can use a Red Hat Linux PC in the evening at home to duplicate that development environment at a fraction of the cost. Then you can either complete work projects at home or devote your time to software you write for fun and to share on the Internet.

Just to give you a sense of Linux's software-development support, here's a list of various features that make Linux a productive software development environment:

✦ GNU C compiler, gcc, can compile ANSI-standard C programs.

✦ GNU C++ compiler (g++) supports ANSI-standard C++ features.

✦ The GNU Java compiler (gcj) can compile programs written in the Java programming language.

✦ The GNU make utility enables you to compile and link large programs.

✦ The GNU debugger, gdb, enables you to step through your program to find problems and to determine where and how a program has failed. (The failed program's memory image is saved in a file named core; gdb can examine this file.)

✦ The GNU profiling utility, gprof, enables you to determine the degree to which a piece of software uses your computer's processor time.

✦ Concurrent Versions System (CVS) and Revision Control System (RCS) maintain version information and control access to the source files so that two programmers don't modify the same source file inadvertently.

✦ The GNU Emacs editor prepares source files and even launches a compile-link process to build the program.

✦ Perl is a scripting language you can use to write scripts to accomplish a specific task, tying together many smaller programs with Linux commands.

✦ The Tool Command Language and its graphical toolkit (Tcl/Tk) enable you to build graphical applications rapidly.

✦ Python is an interpreted programming language comparable to Perl and Tcl (the Red Hat Linux installation program, called anaconda, is written in Python).

✦ Dynamically linked shared libraries allow your actual program files to be much smaller because all the library code that several programs may need is shared — with only one copy loaded in the system's memory.

Online documentation

As you become more adept at using Red Hat Linux, you may want to look up information quickly — without having to turn the pages of (ahem) this great book, for example. Luckily, Red Hat Linux comes with enough online information to jog your memory in those situations when you vaguely recall a command's name, but can't remember the exact syntax of what you're supposed to type.

If you use Linux commands, you can view the manual page — commonly referred to as the *man page* — for a command by using the `man` command. (You do have to remember that command in order to access online help.)

You can also get help from the GUI desktops. Both GNOME and KDE desktops come with help viewers to view online help information. In GNOME, choose Main Menu⇨Help. You then see two broad categories of information:

✦ **GNOME - Desktop** is information on how to use the GNOME desktop and some GNOME applications.

✦ **Additional documents** includes online documentation for the GNU software (primarily for the software development tools) and the set of online manual pages (called man pages for short).

You can then browse the information by clicking the links on the initial help window. Figure 1-1 shows a typical help file in GNOME.

In KDE desktop, you can start KDE Help by choosing Main Menu⇨Help. The KDE Help application looks similar to the GNOME help browser (Figure 1-2).

Figure 1-1: Here's a typical sample of online help in the GNOME desktop.

Figure 1-2:
The KDE
Help Center
provides
online help
in the KDE
desktop.

You can then click the links to view specific online help information. There are links to learn how to use KDE and obtain information about the KDE Project. Another set of links provides access to the man pages and GNU info pages, just as the GNOME Help browser does.

What Red Hat Linux Helps You Manage

As an operating system, Red Hat Linux acts as the intermediary through which you, as the "lord of the system," manage all the hardware. The hardware includes the system box, the monitor, the keyboard, the mouse, and anything else connected to the system box. The catch-all term *peripheral* refers to any equipment attached to the system. If you use a laptop computer, all of your hardware is packaged into the laptop.

Inside that system box is the system's brain — the microprocessor (Intel Pentium 4, for example) or the central processing unit (CPU) — that performs the instructions contained in a computer program. When the microprocessor is running a computer program, that program's instructions are stored in the memory or RAM. RAM stands for *Random Access Memory* (that means any part of the memory can be accessed randomly — in arbitrary order).

The system box has another crucial component — the hard disk or hard drive, as it is sometimes called. The hard disk is the permanent storage space for computer programs and data. It's permanent in the sense that the contents don't disappear when you power off the PC. The hard disk is organized into files, which are in turn organized in a hierarchical fashion into directories and subdirectories (somewhat like organizing paper folders into the drawers in a file cabinet).

To keep a Red Hat Linux system running properly, you or someone else has to make sure the hardware is working properly and the files are backed up regularly. There is also the matter of security — making sure only legitimate people can access and use the system. These tasks are what we call *system administration*.

If you are using Red Hat Linux at a big facility with many computers, there's probably a full-time system administrator who takes care of all system administration tasks. On the other hand, if you are running Red Hat Linux on a home PC, you are the system administrator. Don't let the thought frighten you. You don't have to learn any magic incantations or prepare cryptic configuration files to be a system administrator. Red Hat Linux includes many graphical tools such as GNOME's Nautilus graphical shell that makes system administration a "point-and-click" job just like running any other application.

So what kinds of things do you do to manage the hardware and files? Let's take a look.

Disks, CD-ROMS, and DVD-ROMs

Red Hat Linux comes on two or more CD-ROMs or a single DVD. After installation, the Linux kernel and all the applications are stored on your hard drive — which is where your PC will look first when you tell it to do something.

Typically, the hard drive is prepared to use Red Hat Linux during the installation process. After that, you usually leave the hard drive alone except to back up the data stored there or (occasionally) to install new applications.

Using CD-ROMs or DVD-ROMs, in Red Hat Linux is easy. While you are logged in at the GNOME or KDE desktop, just pop in a CD or DVD-ROMs, in the drive and the CD or DVD's contents should automatically appear in a window. This whole process of accessing the files on a CD or DVD from Red Hat Linux is called *mounting the CD or DVD*.

Besides the hard drive and DVD/CD-ROM drive, of course, your PC may have other drives, such as a floppy-disk or Zip drive, and using those disks in Red Hat Linux is also simple: You insert a disk and double-click the icon that represents the disk drive on the GUI desktop. Doing so mounts the disk so you can begin using it.

Peripheral devices

Anything connected to your PC is a peripheral device, and so are some components like sound cards that are installed inside the system box. You can configure and manage these peripheral devices in Red Hat Linux.

One of the common peripherals is a printer, typically hooked up to the parallel port of your PC. (Red Hat Linux comes with a graphical Printer Configuration tool that you can use to configure the printer.)

Another peripheral device that needs configuration is the sound card. Unlike Windows, Red Hat Linux requires you to perform a configuration step before the sound will work. Again, you can run a graphical sound card detection utility to test the sound card (choose Main Menu⇨System Settings⇨Soundcard Detection from the graphical desktop).

Red Hat Linux configures other peripheral devices such as the mouse and keyboard at the time of installation. You can pretty much leave them alone after installation.

Nowadays PCs come with a USB (Universal Serial Bus) interface and many devices, such as printers and scanners, plug into a PC's USB port. One nice feature of USB devices is that you can plug them into the USB port and unplug them at any time — the device does not have to be connected when you power up the system. This is what people call *hot plug* because you can plug in a device when the system is hot, meaning while it's running. Red Hat Linux supports many hot plug USB devices. When you plug in a device into the USB port, Red Hat Linux loads the correct driver and makes the device available to applications.

File systems and sharing

The whole organization of directories and files is called the *file system*. You can, of course, manage the file system using Red Hat Linux. When you browse the files from the GNOME or KDE graphical desktop, you work with the familiar folder icons.

A key task in caring for a file system is to back up important files. In Red Hat Linux you can use the `tar` program to archive one or more directories on a floppy or a Zip drive. You can even back up files on a tape (if you have a tape drive). If you have a CD burner, you can also burn a CD with the files you want to back up or save for posterity.

Red Hat Linux can also share parts of the file system with other systems on a network. For example, you can use the Network File System (NFS) to share files with other systems on the network. To a user on the system, the remote system's files appear to be in a directory on the local system.

Red Hat Linux also comes with the Samba package, which supports file sharing with Microsoft Windows systems. Samba makes a Red Hat Linux system work just like a Windows file or print server.

Network

Now that most PCs are either in a local area network or connected to the Internet, you need to manage the network as well. Red Hat Linux comes with a Network Configuration tool to set up the local area network. For connecting to the Internet using a modem, you use the Internet Configuration Wizard (choose Main Menu⇨System Tools⇨Internet Configuration Wizard).

If you connect to the Internet using DSL (that's the fast Internet connection from the phone company) or cable modem, then you need a PC with an Ethernet card that connects to the cable or DSL. It also means you have to set up a local area network and configure the Ethernet card. But fortunately, these steps are typically a part of Red Hat Linux installation. If you want to do the configurations later, you can — by using the Network Configuration tool (choose Main Menu⇨System Settings⇨Network).

Red Hat Linux also includes tools for configuring a *firewall,* a protective buffer that helps keep your system relatively secure from anyone trying to snoop over your Internet connection. You can configure the firewall by running the Firewall Configuration tool (choose Main Menu⇨System Settings⇨Security Level from the graphical desktop).

How Do I Get Started?

Based on my personal experience in learning new subjects, I prescribe a four-step process to get started with Red Hat Linux:

1. **Install** Red Hat Linux on your PC.
2. **Configure** Red Hat Linux so that everything works to your liking.
3. **Explore** the GUI desktops and the applications.
4. **Learn** the details of specific subjects such as Internet servers.

In the following sections, I explain this prescription a bit more.

Install

Microsoft Windows comes installed on your new PC, but Red Hat Linux usu-ally doesn't. So your first hurdle is to get Red Hat Linux onto your PC.

After you overcome that initial human fear of the unknown, I'll bet you find Red Hat Linux fairly easy to install — but where do you *get* it in the first place? Well, the good news is that it's free — available just for the download-ing. For example, you can visit the Linux Online Web site at `www.linux.org` and click the Download button.

Because the complete distribution is HUGE — it takes up several CDs or a single DVD — your best bet is to buy a book (such as this one) that comes with Red Hat Linux on DVD. You can then do the installation by following the instructions in the book.

Just to pique your curiosity, installation involves creating space on the hard disk for both Windows and Linux. Then there is a step to create the Linux partitions and install Red Hat Linux from the DVDs. Along the way, you con-figure many items from the Ethernet card (if any) to the X Window System.

Configure

When you've finished installing Red Hat Linux, the next step is to configure individual system components (for example, the sound card and the printer) and tweak any needed settings that weren't configured during installation.

If you aren't getting a graphical login screen, for example, Red Hat Linux comes with tools that help you troubleshoot that problem (typically by configuring the X Window System).

You also want to configure your GUI desktop of choice — GNOME or KDE. Each has configuration tools. You can use these tools to adjust the look and feel of the desktop (background, title fonts, even the entire color scheme).

After you're through with the configuration step, all the hardware on your system and the applications should be running to your liking.

Explore

With a properly configured Red Hat Linux PC at your disposal, you'll be ready to explore Red Hat Linux itself. You can begin the exploration from the GUI desktop that you get after logging in.

Explore the GUI desktops — GNOME and KDE — and the folders and files that make up the Linux file system. You can also try out the applications from the desktop. You'll find office and multimedia applications and databases to explore.

You should also try out the `shell` — open up a terminal window and type some Linux commands in that window. You can also explore the text editors that work in text mode. It's good to know how to edit text files without the GUI just in case the GUI is not available. At least you won't be helpless.

Learn

After you have explored the Red Hat Linux landscape and know what is what, you can then dig in deeper and learn specific subject areas. For example, you may be interested in setting up Internet servers. You can then learn the details of setting up individual servers, such as sendmail for e-mail, Apache for Web server, and the INN server for news.

There are many more areas you can choose to learn about, such as security, programming, and system administration.

Of course, you can expect this step to go on and on, even after you have your system running the way you want it — for now. After all, learning is a lifelong journey.

Bon voyage!

Chapter 2: Installing Red Hat Linux

In This Chapter

✔ Making a list of your PC's hardware

✔ Creating a Red Hat install boot disk

✔ Setting aside disk space for Red Hat Linux

✔ Starting the Red Hat Linux installation

✔ Creating hard disk partitions for Red Hat Linux

✔ Setting up key system parameters

✔ Selecting packages to install

*P*Cs come with Microsoft Windows preinstalled. If you want to use Red Hat Linux, first you have to install it. This book comes with the Red Hat Linux DVD — all you have to do to install it is follow the steps explained in this chapter.

You may feel worried about installing a new operating system on your PC. You may feel that it's like brain surgery — or, rather, more like grafting on a new brain because you can install Red Hat Linux in addition to Microsoft Windows. When you install two operating systems like that, you can choose to start one or the other as you power up the PC. The biggest headache in adding Red Hat Linux to a PC with Windows is creating a new *disk partition* — basically setting aside a part of the disk — for Red Hat Linux. The rest of the installation is fairly routine, just a matter of following the instructions. I explain everything in this chapter.

Following the Installation Steps

Installing Red Hat Linux involves a number of steps — and I want to walk you through them briefly, without the details. Then you can follow the detailed steps and install Red Hat Linux from this book's companion DVD.

The very first step is to take a quick inventory of some key hardware components in your PC and make sure that everything works in Red Hat Linux.

If you're buying a new PC, make sure its components are Linux-friendly before you buy. If you plan to install Red Hat Linux on an older PC, gather information about the hardware (makers, model numbers, and so on) and check it against the list of hardware that Red Hat Linux supports (this list is available on the Web at `hardware.redhat.com/hcl`). If some of the old PC's components won't work in Red Hat Linux — and it won't run without them — then don't install Red Hat Linux on that PC.

The second step — if your PC can't boot up from the DVD-ROM drive — is to prepare a Red Hat *installation boot disk* — a floppy disk you can use to boot the PC when you start the installation. You can prepare the boot disk in Windows, using a program designed for the purpose (included on the companion DVD-ROM).

The third step is to make room for Red Hat Linux on your PC's hard disk. If you're running Microsoft Windows, this step can be easy or hard, depending on whether you want to *replace* Windows with Red Hat Linux or keep *both* Windows and Red Hat Linux.

If you want to install Red Hat Linux without removing (or disturbing) Windows, remember that your existing operating system — which is, I assume, Windows 95, 98, Me, NT, 2000, or XP — is currently using the entire hard disk. That means you have to *partition* (divide) the hard disk so Windows can live on one part of it and Red Hat Linux can live on the other. Doing so can be a scary step because you run the risk of ruining the hard disk and wiping out whatever is on the disk.

Before you create a new place on your hard drive that the Red Hat Linux installation program can use, you may want to preserve your peace of mind by using a program to help you create the partition. If your version of Windows is NT, 2000, or XP, consider investing in a commercial hard-drive partitioning product such as PartitionMagic. For Windows 95/98/Me systems, you can use a program called FIPS (included on this book's DVD).

After you set aside a hard-drive partition for Red Hat Linux, you can begin the final step — boot the PC from your Red Hat installation boot disk and start the Red Hat Linux installation. There are quite a few steps during installation, but, when you've come this far, it should be smooth sailing. Just go through the installation screens and you should be done in an hour or two. The Red Hat installer brings up a graphical user interface (GUI) and guides you through all the steps. One key step involves partitioning the hard disk again, but this time you simply split the extra partition you created earlier. After a few configuration steps, such as setting up the network and the time zone, you select the software packages to install and then let the installer complete the remaining installation chores.

Checking Your PC's Hardware

Before you do anything else, you first need to check to see whether your PC's hardware works with Red Hat Linux. You could jump right in and begin installing, but if Red Hat Linux fails to recognize some hardware in your PC, the installation may not be successful. So check out the hardware for compatibility with Red Hat Linux *before* you begin installation.

Note: Not *every* piece of hardware has to be compatible with Red Hat Linux — only the ones you want to use with it. For example, you can install Red Hat Linux on a PC with an unsupported sound card — as long as you don't care about playing any audio CDs in Red Hat Linux.

Here, then, is a short list of PC hardware that *must* work in Red Hat Linux or else you can't proceed:

✦ Processor (also known as the central processing unit, or CPU)

✦ Hard drive

✦ DVD-ROM drive (if you have only a CD-ROM drive, you have to use the coupon at the back of this book to order Red Hat Linux on CD-ROMs)

✦ Keyboard

All of these must be compatible with Red Hat Linux. For the GUI desktops such as GNOME and KDE to work, the PC must also have a compatible mouse, video card, and monitor.

Making a list, checking it twice

Before you can check whether Red Hat Linux supports the hardware in your PC, you have to find out what's in your PC. To make a list of your PC's hardware, follow these steps:

1. **From Windows (any version), open the Control Panel and double-click the System icon.**

The System Properties window appears. The initial window shows some important information, such as the version of Windows, the processor type (for example, GenuineIntel Pentium II Processor), and the amount of memory (for example, 128.0MB RAM). Write down that information.

2. **In Windows 95/98/Me, click the Device Manager tab. In Windows NT/2000/XP, click the Hardware Tab and then click the Device Manager button.**

Information about all the PC's devices appears.

3. **Browse the information from the treelike hierarchical organization that shows the devices by type.**

   For example, you'll see labels such as CDROM, Disk drives, Display adapters, and so on. Click the plus sign (+) next to a label to see the details for that device type. For example, when I click the plus sign next to Display adapters, I see ATI Xpert98 AGP 2X, the model name of the display adapter (video card) on my PC.

4. **Write down the make, model, and any other information about the following devices to create your hardware inventory:**

   - DVD/CD-ROM drive

   - Disk drives

   - Video card

   - Monitor

   - Keyboard

   - Mouse

   - Any network card, SCSI controller, sound card, and modem

After you complete these steps, you need to install Red Hat Linux. To summarize, you typically need to gather information about some or all of the following key components in your PC before you start the Red Hat installation:

✦ **Processor:** A 400 MHz Pentium II or better is best. The processor speed, expressed in MHz (megahertz) or GHz (gigahertz), is not that important as long as it's over 400 MHz, but the faster the better. Red Hat Linux can run on other Intel-compatible processors such as AMD K5, K6, and Cyrix and IBM processors.

✦ **RAM:** This is the amount of memory your system has. As with processing speed, the more RAM, the better. You need at least 128MB to install Red Hat Linux and run a GUI desktop. (Okay, I confess. I have installed Red Hat Linux on a 233 MHz Pentium II PC with 64MB of RAM and it works fine, but everything — from the installation to daily use — is painfully slow. At least it works!)

✦ **DVD/CD-ROM:** The exact model doesn't matter. What matters is how the DVD/CD-ROM drive is connected to the PC. Most new PCs have DVD/CD-ROM drives that connect to the hard disk controller (called IDE for *integrated drive electronics*). Any IDE DVD/CD-ROM works in Red Hat Linux.

✦ **Hard drives:** If you see the word *IDE* in the disk drive's name, then it's an IDE drive and should work in Red Hat Linux. Another type of hard disk controller is SCSI (Small Computer System Interface), which Red Hat Linux also supports. You also need to know the size of the hard disk. To find the disk size, double-click the My Computer icon on the

Windows desktop and then right-click the disk drive icon (for example, labeled C:), and choose Properties from the pop-up menu. A window then shows information about the disk drive, including the total capacity and the amount of free space. To comfortably install and play with Red Hat Linux, you need about 4GB of disk space.

✦ **Keyboard:** All keyboards should work with Red Hat Linux. All you need to write down is the type of keyboard (such as Standard 101/102-key keyboard).

✦ **Mouse:** You need the type of mouse (such as PS/2 or USB) and model (such as Microsoft Intellimouse) to configure the X Window System.

✦ **Video card:** You need the make and model of the video card (also known as *display adapter*) to configure the X Window System. Red Hat Linux works fine with all video cards in text mode, but if you want the GUI, then you need a video card that works with the X Window System.

✦ **Monitor:** The kind of monitor is not particularly critical except that it must be capable of displaying the screen resolutions that the video card uses. The screen resolution is expressed in terms of the number of picture elements (pixels), horizontally and vertically (for example, *1024 x 768*). Write down the make and model of the monitor (which you can find on the back of the monitor).

✦ **Network card:** Not all PCs have network cards, but if yours does, jot down the make and model (such as *Linksys LNE100TX Fast Ethernet Adapter*). If the installation program fails to detect the network card, you need this information to set up the network.

✦ **SCSI controller:** Some high-performance PCs have SCSI controllers that connect disk drives and other peripherals to a PC. If your PC happens to have a SCSI controller, write down the name of the controller.

✦ **Sound card:** If your PC has a sound card and you want to have sound in Red Hat Linux, you have to know the make and model of the sound card and make sure it's compatible. You can configure the sound card after successfully installing Red Hat Linux.

✦ **Modem:** If you plan to dial out to the Internet, you need modem model information (such as *Sportster 56k*).

In addition to this hardware, you should also find out the make and model of any printer you plan to use in Red Hat Linux.

Checking for Red Hat compatibility

With your hardware inventory in hand, visit Red Hat's Web site at `hardware.redhat.com/hcl`. Click the Hardware Compatibility List (HCL) link. From the search form on that Web page you can look up your hardware to see whether it's supported.

Red Hat lists the status of each hardware component, using one of the following:

✦ **Certified:** Hardware has been tested and certified by Red Hat. This type of hardware is fully supported. The installation program automatically detects certified hardware and installs the appropriate drivers.

✦ **Compatible:** Hardware has been reviewed by Red Hat and is supported. Such hardware is generally known to work, but Red Hat has not certified the hardware. The installation program should be able to detect and use compatible hardware.

✦ **Community Knowledge:** Hardware is not tested or supported by Red Hat. To use this hardware, you may perform some explicit steps, such as manually loading the driver and editing configuration files.

✦ **Not Supported:** Hardware has been tested by Red Hat and found not to work properly in Red Hat Linux.

If you're lucky, most of your PC's hardware (such as video card, monitor, and network card) will be certified or compatible.

Creating the Red Hat Install Boot Disk

To boot your PC and start the Red Hat Linux installation program, you need a Red Hat install *boot disk* (you can skip this step if your PC can boot directly from the DVD). You prepare the boot disk in Windows, using the program on the first of this book's companion DVD.

To create the boot disk, follow these steps:

1. **In Windows 95/98/Me, open an MS-DOS Prompt window by choosing Start⇨Run and then typing the word** Command **in the text field. Click OK or press Enter to run the program.**

2. **In Windows NT/2000/XP, choose Start⇨Run. Then type the word** Command **in the text field and press Enter or click OK to run that program.**

3. **Put the DVD in the DVD-ROM drive. Then type the following commands in the window you opened in Step 1 or 2 (my comments are in parentheses, and your input is in boldface):**

```
d:    (use the drive letter for your DVD-ROM drive)
cd \dosutils
rawrite
Enter disk image source filename: \images\bootdisk.img
Enter target diskette drive: a
Please insert a formatted diskette into drive A: and
  press -ENTER- :
```

As instructed, put a formatted disk into your PC's A drive and then press Enter. That disk will become the Red Hat install boot disk.

4. **When you see the command prompt again, take the Red Hat installa-tion boot disk out of the A drive and (if you haven't done so already) label it or mark it so you know what that disk is, and put it aside.**

Setting Aside Space for Red Hat Linux

In a typical Windows PC, Windows is sitting on a big partition, taking over the whole disk. You want to shrink that partition and create room for Linux. During Linux installation, the installation program uses that free space for the Linux partitions.

The challenge is to resize the current partition without destroying anything on the hard disk. I cover tools that help you resize the partition, but first you have to make sure that all used areas of the disk are *contiguous*, or as tightly packed as possible. This is where defragmenting comes in.

Defragmenting your hard disk

"Defrag your disk" is the magic chant of many a help desk. It's the help desk's prescription for all PC ailments. Well, for once they're right — you *do* need to defragment your hard disk to make room for Red Hat Linux. What defragmenting does is move all the files to the beginning of the partition and pack them tight. The result is free space at the end of the partition, so the partition can be shrunk without destroying any data.

To defragment the hard disk, follow these steps:

1. **Double-click My Computer from the desktop, right-click the disk icon, and then select Properties from the pop-up menu.**

2. **In the Properties window, click the Tools tab and then click the Defragment Now button.**

3. **Wait. And wait. And wait.**

   You'll hear lots of noise from the disk drive while it moves files around. After a couple of hours, the defragmenting should be complete.

There are some *gotchas* with these instructions. First, don't use your PC or other programs while defragmenting the hard disk. Close all programs, including the ones in the system tray. One good way to do so is to press Ctrl+Alt+Del (which calls up the Task Manager), click which program you want to stop, and then click the End Task button.

The second *gotcha* is that the defragmenter does not move hidden files — and there are plenty of such files in your system. You don't see them in the folders because (guess what) they're hidden. You may have to manually find the hidden files and see whether you can delete the ones that seem to be junk. (Don't worry; a how-to is coming right up.)

You can find all the hidden files in your PC with a simple command. Open a Command Prompt window and then type the following commands:

```
scd \
dir /a:h /s > hidden.txt
```

After the command is finished, you'll have a list of all hidden files in the text file called `hidden.txt`. Open the file in Microsoft Word or just type **edit hidden.txt** to browse that file in a text editor. When I tried this, I noticed a whole lot of files with names like `~WRL0004.TMP` — and they clearly seemed to be temporary files, created by some Microsoft software (probably Word). Who knows why they were hidden? Anyway, I had to change the file attribute by using MS-DOS incantations like `ATTRIB -H ~WRL0004.TMP` and then typing **ERASE ~WRL0004.TMP** to finally delete the file. I had to repeat this for many more junk files. What a bummer — but it's worth taking your time and doing it carefully!

Another option for dealing with the hidden files is to just unhide them and then run the defragmenter. To unhide all files in the PC, type the following command in an MS-DOS window:

```
attrib -h *.* /s
```

Sit back. After a long time, this command unhides all files. *Then* you can run the defragmenter.

Resizing your hard disk partition

After defragmenting the hard disk, you're ready to shrink the existing hard disk partition. You want to do this without damaging the current contents of the hard disk. You have two choices:

✦ **PartitionMagic:** This is a commercial product that can resize hard-drive partitions and create new partitions for any version of Microsoft Windows.

✦ **FIPS:** This is a free program that runs in MS-DOS mode and can split an existing partition into two. FIPS works only with Windows 95/98/Me systems. More accurately, FIPS does *not* work with the NTFS file system that's often used in Windows NT/2000/XP systems. For those systems, your best bet is PartitionMagic.

I'll quickly go over repartitioning with both PartitionMagic and FIPS.

Repartitioning with PartitionMagic

PartitionMagic, from PowerQuest, can resize and split disk partitions in all Microsoft operating systems from Windows 95/98/Me to Windows NT/2000/XP. It's a commercial product, so you have to buy it to use it. At the time I'm writing this, the list price of PartitionMagic 8.0 is $69.95. You can read about it and buy it at www.powerquest.com/partitionmagic.

Resizing the disk partition always involves the risk of losing all data on the hard disk. Therefore, before you resize hard disk partitions using a disk-partitioning tool such as PartitionMagic, you should *back up your hard drive*. After making your backup — and before you do *anything* to the partitions — please make sure that you can restore your files from the backup.

When you run PartitionMagic, it shows the current partitions in a window. If you're running Windows XP, your hard disk typically has two partitions: one small, hidden partition that contains Windows XP installation files, and a huge second NTFS partition that serves as the C drive. You have to reduce the size of the existing C drive. Doing so creates unused space following that partition. Then, during Red Hat Linux installation, the installation program can create new Linux partitions in the unused space.

To reduce the size of the Windows partition, follow these steps:

1. **In the partition map in PartitionMagic's main window, right-click the partition and select Resize/Move from the menu.**

   The Resize Partition dialog box appears.

2. **In the Resize Partition dialog box, click and drag the right edge of the partition to a smaller size.**

   For a large hard disk (anything over 10GB), reduce the Windows partition to 5GB and leave the rest for Red Hat Linux.

3. **Click OK and then Apply to apply the changes. After PartitionMagic has made the changes, click OK.**

4. **Reboot the PC.**

5. **Choose Start⊏⊃Programs⊏⊃Accessories⊏⊃System Tools⊏⊃ScanDisk to run ScanDisk.**

You don't have to do anything with the disk space left over after shrinking the partition that used to be the C drive. During installation, the Red Hat installer uses that free space to install Red Hat Linux.

Repartitioning with FIPS

The companion DVD includes a utility program called FIPS (the *First Nondestructive Interactive Partition Splitting Program*) that can split an existing disk partition into two partitions. FIPS cordons off the unused part of a hard disk and makes a new partition out of that unused part without destroying any existing data. FIPS cannot split partitions with the NTFS file system that's often used in Windows NT/2000/XP systems.

Some words of caution before you proceed to repartition your hard disk with FIPS. In the words of the FIPS author Arno Schaefer, "FIPS is still somewhat experimental, although it has been used by many people successfully and without serious problems." That tells you in a nutshell that you're on your own when it comes to using FIPS. Neither the publisher nor I can accept responsibility or liability for damages resulting from the use or misuse of FIPS. There is a chance that FIPS could damage your hard disk, making it unusable. You should try FIPS only after making sure that you've backed up everything on the hard drive and that your backup is usable. Also, before you use FIPS, check your hard disk to make sure it's ready:

✦ Your hard drive should have only a FAT or FAT32 partition to start with.

✦ The drive should have enough free space available for a useful Red Hat Linux installation — and that means 3 to 4 gigabytes (3–4GB) of free space.

✦ The drive must be defragmented before you can use FIPS.

✦ The drive must not be in use. You can't partition the hard drive while you're using it, which means (among other things) that you can't run FIPS from inside Windows. You have to shut down Windows, boot from a startup disk, and run FIPS by itself.

When you're ready to use FIPS, follow these steps (use FIPS only if you are running Windows 95/98/Me):

1. **Open the Control Panel by choosing Start➪Settings➪Control Panel.**

2. **Double-click the Add/Remove Programs icon in the Control Panel window.**

3. **Click the Startup Disk tab, click the Create Disk button, and follow the instructions.**

4. **Insert this book's DVD-ROM in the DVD-ROM drive.**

5. **Use Explorer to view the contents of the DOSUTILS folder. Then copy FIPS.EXE and RESTORRB.EXE to the startup disk in the A drive.**

   FIPS.EXE is the program that splits partitions. RESTORRB.EXE is a program that can restore parts of your hard drive from a backup of the areas created by FIPS (you use RESTORRB if something goes wrong).

6. **Go to the FIPSDOCS folder that's inside the DOSUTILS folder on the DVD. Copy the ERRORS.TXT file to the startup disk.**

ERRORS.TXT is a list of FIPS error messages. Consult this list for an explanation of any error messages displayed by FIPS.

7. Leave the startup disk in the A drive, and restart the PC.

The PC boots from the A drive and displays the A:\> prompt.

8. Type FIPS.

The FIPS program runs, showing you information about your hard disk. FIPS gives you an opportunity to save a backup copy of important disk areas before you proceed. After that, FIPS displays the first free *cylinder* (section of the disk) where a new partition can start — as well as the size of the partition, in megabytes. Ignore the cylinder number and focus on the number of megabytes. You'll need 3 to 4 thousand of them (that is, 3 to 4 gigabytes).

9. Use the left and right arrow keys to adjust the size of the new partition — the one that results from splitting the existing partition.

Pressing the left arrow shrinks the existing partition; pressing the right arrow leaves more room in the existing partition, but reduces the size of the new partition you are creating.

10. When you're satisfied with the size of the new partition, press Enter.

FIPS displays the modified partition table and prompts you to press *C* to continue or *R* to reedit the partition table.

11. Press *C* to continue.

FIPS displays some information about the disk and asks whether you want to write the new partition information to the disk.

12. Press *Y*.

FIPS writes the new partition table to the hard disk and then exits.

13. Remove the disk from the A drive and reboot the PC.

When the system comes back up, everything on your hard drive should be intact, but the C drive will be smaller. That's because you've created a new partition from the unused parts of the old C drive.

14. Choose Start➪Programs➪Accessories➪System Tools➪ScanDisk to run ScanDisk.

Running this program ensures that Windows gets adjusted to the new size of the C drive.

You needn't do anything with the newly created partition under DOS. Later, during Red Hat Linux installation, you'll create two or more Linux partitions out of this new partition.

After you use FIPS, Windows may assign different drive letters to other disk and DVD/CD-ROM drives on your PC. (For example, your D drive may become E.) FIPS does make sure, however, that the C drive remains C, so you should be able to boot your system after FIPS splits the partitions. Remember those different drive names (for example, E instead of D) when you want to get to programs and files on drives other than C. Keeping a list of them couldn't hurt, at least until you get used to them.

Starting the Red Hat Linux Installation

To install Linux, insert the DVD in the DVD drive, put the Red Hat install boot disk in your A drive, and restart your PC (in Windows choose Start⇨ Shutdown and then select Restart from the dialog box). The install boot disk contains a smaller version of the Linux kernel and the installation program.

If your PC can boot from the DVD drive, you don't need the boot disk. Most new PCs can boot directly from the DVD drive, but some PCs may require intervention from you. To set up a PC to boot from the DVD drive, you have to go into SETUP as the PC powers up. The exact steps for entering SETUP and setting the boot device vary from one PC to the next, but typically they involve pressing a key such as F2. As the PC powers up, a brief message should tell you what key to press to enter SETUP. When you're in SETUP, you can designate the DVD drive as the boot device. After your PC is set up to boot from the DVD drive, simply put the DVD in the DVD drive and restart your PC.

After your PC powers up, it loads the Linux kernel from the boot disk and the Linux kernel starts running the Red Hat installation program. For the rest of the installation, you work with the installation program's GUI screens.

If you're using a Red Hat installation boot disk and the DVD is not in the drive when you reboot the PC, the installer starts in text mode and prompts you for the DVD. Only then will it start the X Window System and switch to a graphical installation screen.

After a few moments, the text screen displays a welcome message and a `boot:` prompt. The welcome message tells you that help is available by pressing one of the function keys F1 through F5. To start installing Red Hat Linux immediately, press Enter. You then get a chance to test the DVD media for any problems. Press Enter to perform the media check. After the media check, you can continue with the installation.

Installing Red Hat Linux from the companion DVD on a fast (400MHz or better) Pentium PC should take about an hour, if you install nearly all packages.

The Red Hat installation program *probes* — attempts to determine the presence of — specific hardware and tailors the installation steps accordingly. For example, if the installation program detects a network card, the program automatically displays the screens needed to configure your PC to work with the network in Linux. You may see a different sequence of screens from what I show in this chapter; the exact sequence depends on your PC's specific hardware configuration.

If you run into any problems during the installation, please turn to Chapter 3 of this mini-book. That chapter shows how to troubleshoot common installation problems.

Selecting Keyboard, Mouse, and Installation Type

This is the first phase of the installation where you go through a number of steps before moving on to create the disk partitions for Red Hat Linux. Here are the steps in the first phase:

1. **The installation program displays a list of languages that you can use for the rest of the installation. Use your mouse to select the language you want from the list displayed and then click Next to proceed to the next step.**

   Each screen has online help available on the left side of the screen. You can read the help message to learn more about what you're supposed to do in a specific screen.

2. **The installation program displays a list of keyboard layouts, as shown in Figure 2-1.**

   Select a keyboard layout suitable for your language's character set (for example, U.S. English in the United States).

3. **The installation program displays a screen (see Figure 2-2) from which you can configure the mouse in your system.**

   A treelike list shows the mouse types, organized alphabetically by manufacturer. You should know your mouse type and whether it's connected to the PC's serial port or the PS/2 port (the small, round connector). If the name of your mouse appears in the list, select it. Otherwise select a generic mouse type. Most new PCs have a PS/2 mouse. Finally, for a two-button mouse, select the Emulate 3 Buttons option. Because many X applications assume you're using a three-button mouse, you should select this option. (On a typical two-button mouse, you can simulate a middle-button click by pressing both buttons simultaneously. On a Microsoft Intellimouse, the wheel acts as the middle button.)

Figure 2-1:
Select a
keyboard
configu-
ration from
this screen.

Figure 2-2:
Configure
your mouse
in this
screen.

If you select a mouse with a serial interface, you have to specify the serial port where the mouse is connected. For COM1, specify /dev/ttyS0 as the device; for COM2, the device name is /dev/ttyS1.

The installer tries to detect the monitor and displays a screen with the results, whether or not it detects correctly (see Figure 2-3).

4. **If the Red Hat installer displays a wrong monitor or a generic one as the choice, scroll through the list and pick the correct name of your monitor from the list.**

(One good thing about monitors is that you can always easily look up the make and model number on the back of the monitor.)

5. **The installation program displays a screen asking whether you want to install a new system or upgrade an older Red Hat installation. For a new Red Hat Linux installation, click Install. Then a screen (see Figure 2-4) prompts you for the installation type.**

For a new installation, you have to select the installation type — Personal Desktop, Workstation, Server, or Custom. The Personal Desktop, Workstation, and Server installations simplify the installation process by partitioning the disk in a predefined manner. The Personal Desktop installation creates a Red Hat Linux system for home, laptop, or desktop use. A graphical environment is installed along with productivity applications.

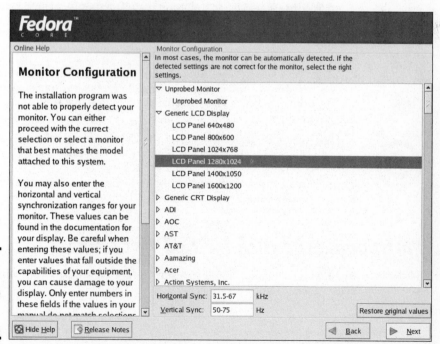

Figure 2-3: Select your monitor type from this screen.

Figure 2-4:
Select what
type of
installation
you want.

A Workstation-class installation installs a graphical environment as well as software development tools. This type of installation also deletes all currently existing Linux-related partitions, creating a set of new partitions for Linux.

A Server-class installation deletes *all* existing disk partitions, including any existing Windows partitions, and creates a whole slew of Linux partitions. Server-class installation does not install the graphical environment.

For maximum flexibility, select the Custom installation. That way you can select only the packages you want to try out.

The next major phase of installation involves partitioning the hard disk for use in Red Hat Linux.

Partitioning the Disk for Red Hat Linux

The Red Hat installer displays a screen (see Figure 2-5) from which you can select a partitioning strategy.

The screen gives you the following options for partitioning and using the hard disk:

✦ **Automatically partition:** This option (the one most users choose) causes the Red Hat installation program to create new partitions for installing Linux according to your chosen installation type, such as workstation or server. After the automatic partitioning, you get a chance to customize the partitions.

✦ **Manually partition with Disk Druid:** With this option, you can use the Disk Druid program that lets you partition the disk and, at the same time, specify which parts of the Linux file system to load, and on which partition(s).

From the disk-partitioning strategy screen (refer to Figure 2-5), select the first option to have the installer automatically partition the disk for you. The Red Hat installer then displays another screen (see Figure 2-6) that asks how you want the automatic partitioning to be done.

You can select from three options:

✦ **Remove all Linux Partitions on this system:** This option causes the Red Hat installer to remove all existing Linux partitions and create new partitions for installing Red Hat Linux. You can use this option if you already have any version of Linux installed on your PC and want to wipe it out and install the latest version of Red Hat Linux.

✦ **Remove all partitions on this system:** This option is similar to the first option, except that the installation program removes all partitions, including those used by other operating systems such as Microsoft Windows. *Use this only if you want Red Hat Linux as the only operating system for your PC.*

✦ **Keep all partitions and use existing free space:** If you've created space for Linux by using PartitionMagic or the FIPS utility, select this option to create the Linux partitions using the free space on the hard disk. If you are installing Red Hat Linux on a new PC after resizing the partition, this is the option to choose.

Select the appropriate option and click Next. For example, if you select the first option, the Red Hat Linux installation program displays a dialog box to confirm your choice and to point out that all data in the existing Linux partitions will be lost. Click Yes to continue. The installation program shows the partitions it has prepared, as shown in Figure 2-7. The exact appearance of this screen depends on your hard disk's current partitions.

This Disk Setup screen displays a list of disk drives and the current partition information for one of the drives. If you want to accept these partitions as is, click Next to proceed.

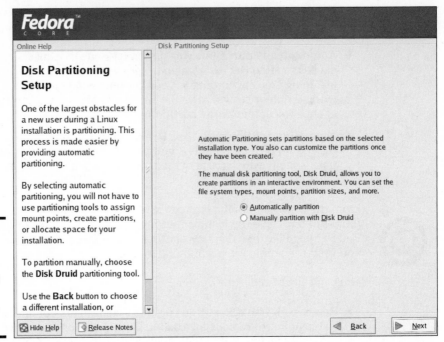

Figure 2-5:
Select
a disk-
partitioning
strategy
from this
screen.

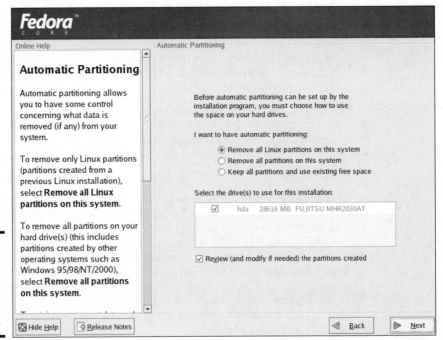

Figure 2-6:
Select an
automatic
partitioning
option from
this screen.

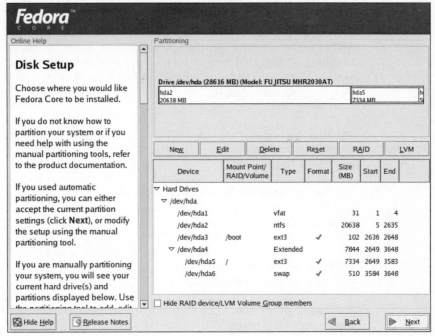

Figure 2-7:
Disk
partitions
created by
the Red Hat
installer.

If your PC doesn't have enough memory (typically less than 128MB), the installer asks if it can write the partition table and activate the swap partition. After you do this, your hard disk partitions will be changed. Click Yes *only* if you are committed to the new partitions and definitely want to install Red Hat Linux.

Setting Up Key System Parameters

With the disk partitioning out of the way, you're almost ready to begin installing the software packages. First, the Red Hat installer prompts you to set up some key system parameters. Specifically, you have to do the following:

✦ Install the boot loader

✦ Configure the network

✦ Configure the firewall

✦ Select languages to support

✦ Set the time zone

✦ Set the root password

You can go through these steps fairly quickly.

Installing the boot loader

You can install one of two boot loaders — GRUB or LILO. GRUB stands for *GRand Unified Bootloader*, and LILO stands for *Linux Loader*. The *boot loader* is a tiny program that resides on the hard disk and starts an operating system when you power up your PC. If you have Windows on your hard disk, you can configure the boot loader to load any other installed operating systems as well.

The Red Hat installer displays the boot loader installation screen (shown in Figure 2-8) that prompts you to select the boot loader you want to install — and where to install it.

The top part of the screen explains that GRUB is the default boot loader and that it's installed by default. If you want, click Change Boot Loader to select the older LILO boot loader. You can also skip the boot loader installation entirely. If you choose not to install any boot loader, you should definitely create a boot disk later on. Otherwise, you won't be able to start Red Hat Linux when you reboot the PC. You get a chance to create the boot disk at the very end of the installation.

The middle of the boot loader installation screen lists the disk partitions from which you can boot the PC. A table lists the Linux partition and any other partitions that may contain another operating system (such as Windows XP or 2000). Each entry in that table is an operating system that the boot loader can load and start. Any Windows operating system appears with a DOS label. The default operating system is the one with a check mark in the Default column shown in Figure 2-8 (in this case, Red Hat Linux is the default operating system).

For greater security (so no one can boot your system without a password), select the Use a Boot Loader Password check box. The installer displays a dialog box in which you can specify a password for GRUB.

If you select the Configure Advanced Boot Loader Options check box (Figure 2-8) and click Next, the next screen gives you the option to install the boot loader in one of two locations:

✦ *Master Boot Record* (MBR), which is located in the first sector of your PC's hard drive (the C drive)

✦ First sector of the Linux boot partition

You should install the boot loader in the Master Boot Record unless you are using another operating system loader, such as BootMagic or Windows NT/2000/XP Boot Manager. After making your selections, click Next to continue.

Figure 2-8:
Indicate
whether to
install a
boot loader
and where
to install it.

Configuring the network

Assuming the Linux kernel detected a network card, the Red Hat installer
displays the network configuration screen (as in Figure 2-9).

From this screen, you can set up your network card's IP address (so other
PCs in the network can talk to your PC). This screen displays a list of the
network devices (for example, Ethernet cards) installed in your PC. For each
network device, you can indicate how the IP address is set. Click the Edit
button next to the list and a dialog box appears (as in Figure 2-10); there you
can specify the options.

You have two choices for specifying the IP (Internet Protocol) address for
the network card:

✦ **Configure using DHCP:** Enable this option if your PC gets its IP address
and other network information from a *Dynamic Host Configuration
Protocol* (DHCP) server. This is often the case if your PC is connected to
a DSL or cable modem router.

✦ **Activate on boot:** Enable this option to turn on the network when your
system boots.

Figure 2-9:
Configure
the network
options from
this screen.

Figure 2-10:
Configure
each
network
interface
from a
dialog box
like this one.

Select DHCP only if a DHCP server is running on your local area network. If you choose DHCP, your network configuration is set automatically, and you can skip the rest of this section.

If you do not select the Configure Using DHCP option, you have to provide an IP address and other network information. Do so by entering the requested parameters in the text-input fields that appear in the dialog box (refer to Figure 2-9). Make the appropriate selections and click OK to close the dialog box.

In the rest of the Network Configuration screen (Figure 2-8), you specify how to set the host name. You have two options:

✦ **automatically via DHCP:** Enable this option to assign a host name automatically using DHCP (the name is of the form `dhcppc1`, `dhcppc2`, and so on).

✦ **manually:** Use this option if you want to manually specify a host name and type the name in the text field next to the radio button.

Enter the requested parameters and click Next to continue.

Configuring the firewall

In this step, select a predefined level of security from the Firewall Configuration screen (see Figure 2-11) and customize these security levels to suit your needs.

From this screen, you can set the security levels of your Red Hat Linux PC. You have to select from one of the following options:

✦ **No firewall** means your system accepts all types of connections and does not perform any security checking. Use this option only if your system runs in a trusted network or if you plan to set up a firewall configuration later on (the sooner the better).

✦ **Enable firewall** means you want to set up a firewall. You can then select services such as Mail and FTP that are allowed to pass through the firewall. You can also enter port numbers that are allowed through the firewall. You can also allow all traffic from a specific NIC.

When you're done configuring the firewall, click Next to continue.

Selecting languages to support

In this step, select one or more languages that your Red Hat Linux system must support when the installation is complete. These are the languages that the system will support when you reboot the PC after completing your Red Hat Linux installation. From the Language Support Selection screen, select one or more languages to support. You must also select a default language. Then click Next to continue.

Setting the time zone

After completing the network configuration, select the time zone — the difference between the local time and the current time in Greenwich, England, which is the standard reference time (also known as *Greenwich Mean Time* or GMT as well as UTC or *Universal Coordinated Time*). The installer shows you a screen (as in Figure 2-12) from which you can select the time zone, in terms of a geographic location.

As you move the mouse over the map, the currently selected location's name appears in a text field. If you want, you can also select your location from a long list of countries and regions. If you live on the East Coast of the United States, for example, select America/New_York. (Of course, the easiest way is to simply click a location nearest to your city in the eastern United States on the map.)

After you select your time zone, click Next to continue.

Setting the root password

The installer displays the Set Root Password screen (see Figure 2-13) from which you can set the root password. Earlier versions of the Red Hat installer enabled you to add one or more user accounts at this step, but now you get a chance to add user accounts when the system boots for the first time (see Chapter 4 of this mini-book).

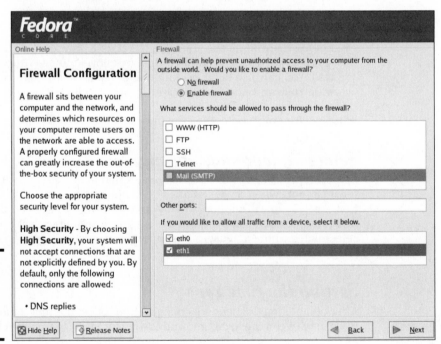

Figure 2-11: Select a security level from this screen.

Figure 2-12:
Select your
time zone in
terms of a
geographic
location.

Figure 2-13:
Set the root
password
from this
screen.

The *root user* is the *superuser* in Linux — the one who can do anything in the system. You're better off reserving that account for your own exclusive use. You should assign a password that you can remember but that others cannot guess easily. Make the password at least eight characters long, include a mix of letters and numbers, and (for good measure) throw in some special characters, such as + or *.

Type the password on the first line and re-enter the password on the next line. Each character in the password appears as an asterisk (*) on the screen. You have to type the password twice, and both entries must match before the installation program accepts it. This feature ensures that a mistyped (or guessed) password won't work.

You must enter the `root` password before you can proceed with the rest of the installation. After you have done so, click the Next button to continue with the installation.

Selecting and Installing the Package Groups

After you set up the key system parameters, the installer displays a screen from which you can select Red Hat Linux package groups to install. After you have selected the package groups, you can take a coffee break and let the Red Hat installation program get busy formatting the disk partitions and copying all your selected files to those partitions.

A *package group* is made up of several Red Hat packages. Each Red Hat package, in turn, includes many files that make up specific software.

Figure 2-14 shows the screen with the list of package groups (in effect the software components) you can choose to install. An icon, a descriptive label, and a check-box prefix identify each package group.

Some package groups are already selected, as indicated by the check marks in the check boxes. Think of the selected package groups as the minimal set of packages recommended by Red Hat for the class of installation (workstation, server, or custom) you've chosen. You can, however, choose to install any or all components. Use the mouse to move up and down in the scrolling list, clicking a check box to select or deselect each package group as appropriate.

In an actual production installation of Red Hat Linux, you would install exactly the package groups you need. However, when you're trying to learn everything about Red Hat Linux, you need many different packages. If you have enough disk space (at least 6GB) for the Linux partition, select the package group labeled `Everything` — this installs all the package groups so you can try out the whole nine yards.

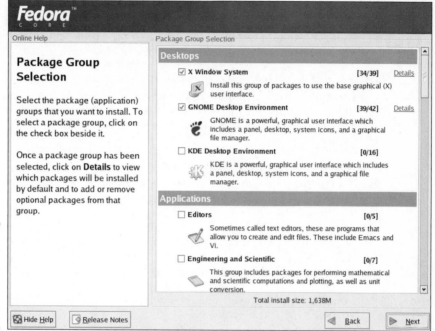

Figure 2-14:
Select the
package
groups to
install from
this screen.

In addition to the package groups that you select from the screen shown in
Figure 2-14, the Red Hat installer automatically installs a large number of
packages needed to run the Linux kernel and the applications you select.
Even if you don't select a single package group from this screen, the installation program installs a plethora of packages — and they're all needed simply
to run the core Linux operating system and a minimal set of utilities.

Each package group requires specific packages to run. The Red Hat installation program automatically checks for any package dependencies and
shows you a list of any required packages you haven't selected. In this case,
you should install the required packages.

After you have selected the package groups you want to install, click Next to
continue.

The installer then displays a screen informing you that installation is about
to begin. Click Next to proceed with the installation. The Red Hat installer
formats the disk partitions and installs the packages. As it installs packages,
the installation program displays a status screen to show the progress of
the installation, including information such as total number of packages to
install, number installed so far, estimated amount of disk space needed, and
estimated time remaining until the installation is complete.

The hard disk formatting and installation can take quite a bit of time — so you can take a break and check back in 15 minutes or so. When you come back, you should be able to get a sense of the time remaining from the status screen, which updates continuously.

After all the packages are installed, the installation program displays a screen (Figure 2-15) that asks you to insert a blank floppy into your PC's A drive. This floppy is the boot disk that you can use to start Red Hat Linux if something happens to the hard drive (or if you have not installed the boot loader).

Insert a blank floppy into your PC's A drive and click Next (note that all data on the floppy is destroyed). The installation program copies the Linux kernel and some other files to the floppy.

After you finish creating the boot disk, the installer displays a message informing you that installation is complete and tells you to visit the Red Hat Web site at `www.redhat.com/errata` for information on any updates and bug fixes. Click the Exit button to reboot your PC.

Congratulations! You're now the owner of a brand new Red Hat Linux system!

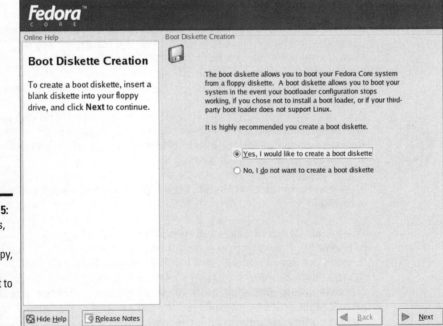

Figure 2-15:
Select Yes,
insert a
blank floppy,
and then
click Next to
create a
boot disk.

Chapter 3: Troubleshooting and Configuring Red Hat Linux

In This Chapter

✔ Troubleshooting the installation

✔ Configuring X

✔ Setting up printers

✔ Turning on sound

✔ Adding user accounts

✔ Managing CD-ROMs

✔ Installing RPM packages

During Red Hat Linux installation, the installer attempts to detect key hardware components such as the SCSI controller and network card. Then, according to what it detects, the program takes you through a sequence of installation steps. For example, if the installer cannot detect the network card, it skips the network configuration step.

Another installation problem crops up when you restart the PC and, instead of a graphical login screen, you get a text terminal — which means there's something wrong with the X Window System (or X) configuration.

Also, Red Hat normally keeps the installation simple and doesn't include configuration procedures for every piece of hardware in your PC system. For example, the installation does not set up printers or configure the sound card.

In this chapter, I show you some alternative ways to install Red Hat Linux so that you can force it to configure some key hardware such as the network card and the SCSI controller (if you have one). I show you how to reconfigure X and do a few other configuration steps, such as adding a user account, setting up a printer, and configuring the sound card.

You may also have to install additional software packages from the companion DVD. I show you how to install Red Hat Packages (RPMs) — the format in which you get the most from this software.

Using Text Mode Installation

The Red Hat installer attempts to use a minimal X Window System (X) to display the graphical user installation screens. If the installer fails to detect a video card, X does not start. If — for this reason or any other reason — it fails to start X, you can always fall back on a text mode installation. Then you can specify the video card manually.

To use text mode installation, type **text** at the `boot:` prompt after you start the PC from the Red Hat install boot floppy. From then on, the basic sequence of installation is similar to that of the graphical installation that I describe in Chapter 2 of this mini-book. You should be able to respond to the prompts and perform the installation.

In text mode, if the installer fails to detect the video card, it displays a list of video cards from which you can select one. By selecting the video card, you make it more likely that X will work when you reboot the PC. If it doesn't, you can configure X by using the Xconfigurator program (which I show later in this chapter).

Using the linux noprobe Command

If the Red Hat installer does not detect the SCSI controller or network card, you can specify these devices manually by typing **linux noprobe** at the `boot:` prompt.

To see whether the installer deleted the hardware, look for any indication of SCSI or network devices in the messages the Linux kernel displays as it boots. To view these messages during installation, press Ctrl+Alt+F4. This switches the display to a text mode virtual console on which the messages appear. (A *virtual console* is a screen of text or graphical information stored in memory that you can view on the physical screen by pressing a specific key sequence.)

Another sign of undetected hardware is when the installation program skips a step. For example, if the Linux kernel does not detect the network card, the installation program skips the network configuration step.

To manually install devices, follow these steps:

1. **Type** linux noprobe **at the** `boot:` **prompt in the initial text screen.**

The installer then displays a dialog box that gives you the opportunity to add devices.

2. **Press Tab to highlight the Add Device button; then press Enter.**

   The installer displays a dialog box that prompts you for the type of device — SCSI or Network.

3. **If you have any SCSI device, such as an SCSI hard drive, select SCSI and press Enter.**

   The installer displays a list of SCSI controllers. When you select the one on your system and press Enter, the installer then loads the appropriate driver module. The SCSI driver automatically probes and determines the SCSI controller's settings.

   After you add any SCSI controllers, you're back at the initial dialog box — and from there you can add network cards.

4. **If you select Network from the list and press Enter, the installation program displays a list of network cards from which you can select your network card.**

   When you press Enter, the installation program loads the driver module for the selected network card. That driver then probes and determines the network card settings.

5. **[Optional] If you need a Linux device driver that does not come with Red Hat Linux, try checking the vendor's Web site or a search engine (such as Google —** `www.google.com`**).**

   Many hardware vendors provide Linux device drivers for download, just as they do Windows drivers.

   After you finish adding the SCSI controllers and network cards, the installer switches to graphics mode and guides you through the rest of the installation.

Troubleshooting X

I have this problem on an older PC every time I install Red Hat Linux: During installation, the GUI installation works fine — but when I reboot the PC for the first time after installation, the graphical login screen does not appear. Instead, the boot process seems to hang just as it starts `firstboot`. If this happens to you, here's how you can troubleshoot the problem.

That `firstboot` process happens to be a special step where, if all went well, the Red Hat Setup agent would start and enable you to perform one-time setups (such as date and time configuration) and install programs from any other CDs. The reason `firstboot` may get stuck is because the graphical X environment isn't working on your system. You have to get around the firstboot process and configure X again before you can continue the normal course of events that Red Hat has planned for you. Here's what you should do:

1. **Press Ctrl+Alt+F1 to get back to the boot screen.**

   You see the text display with the boot messages that stop at a line displaying information about firstboot.

2. **Press Ctrl+Alt+Del to reboot the PC.**

   The PC starts to boot and you get to a screen where the GRUB boot loader prompts you to press Enter to boot Red Hat Linux.

3. **Press *A* to add an option for use by the Linux kernel.**

   The GRUB boot loader then displays a command line for the Linux kernel and prompts you to add what you want.

4. **Type a space followed by the word** single **and then press Enter.**

   The Linux kernel boots in a single-user mode and displays a prompt that looks like the following:

   ```
   sh-2.05b#
   ```

   Now you're ready to configure X.

X uses a configuration file, called XF86Config, to figure out the type of display card, monitor, and the kind of screen resolution you want. The Red Hat installer prepares the configuration file, but sometimes the configuration isn't correct.

To quickly create a working XF86Config file, follow these steps:

1. **Type the following command:**

   ```
   /usr/X11R6/bin/XFree86 -configure
   ```

   The screen goes blank and then XFree86 exits after displaying some messages. The last line of the message says the following:

   ```
   To test the server, run 'XFree86 -xf86config
       //XF86Config.new'
   ```

2. **Try the new configuration file by typing the following command:**

   ```
   /usr/X11R6/bin/XFree86 -xf86config //XF86Config.new
   ```

   If you see a blank screen with a X-shaped cursor, the configuration file is probably working fine.

3. **Press Ctrl+Alt+Backspace to kill the X server.**

4. **Copy the new** XF86Config **file to the** /etc/X11 **directory with the following command:**

```
cp //XF86Xonfig.new /etc/X11/XF86Config
```

That should provide a working X configuration file.

Reboot the PC by pressing Ctrl+Alt+Del or typing reboot.

If all goes well, you'll go through the normal Red Hat Linux initial setup
screens and (finally) get the graphical login screen.

The XF86Config file created by using the -configure option of the X
server does not display at the best resolution possible. To fine-tune the
configuration file, you should run the Display Settings utility (choose Main
Menu⇨System Settings⇨Display) after you reboot the system. By using that
utility you can configure the video card, monitor, and display settings
through a graphical user interface.

Resolving Other Installation Problems

I'm sure I haven't exhausted all the installation problems that are lurking out
there. Nobody can. There are so many different combinations of components in Intel x86 PCs that Murphy's Law practically requires some combination of hardware to exist that the installation program can't handle. This
section lists a few known problems. For others, I would advise you to go to
Google Groups (groups.google.com) and type in some of the symptoms of
the trouble. Assuming that others are running into similar problems, you
should get some indication of how to troubleshoot your way out of your particular predicament.

Unable to boot from boot disk

Sometimes the PC doesn't boot with the Red Hat installation boot disk. If
this happens to you, try creating another boot disk — using a fresh floppy
disk — and see whether that takes care of the problem. Otherwise you
might need updated *boot images* (a small program that runs the Linux kernel
and then loads the Red Hat installation program from the DVD to get things
going). New boot images, if any, should be available at the Red Hat support
Web site (www.redhat.com/apps/support/errata/). After you download
the image file, save it on your Windows system, give it a short name such as
new.img, and then create a new boot disk by following the steps explained
in Chapter 2 of this mini-book. Remember to specify the new boot image file
in response to the question that asks for the image source filename.

The fatal signal 11 error

Some people get a fatal `signal 11 error` message during installation — and it stops the process cold. This usually happens past the initial boot screen as the `anaconda` installer is starting its GUI or text interface. The most likely cause of a `signal 11 error` during installation is a hardware error related to memory or the cache associated with the CPU (microprocessor).

Signal 11, also known as SIGSEGV (short for Segment Violation Signal), can occur in other Linux applications. A *segment violation* occurs when a process tries to access a memory location that it's not supposed to access. The operating system catches the problem before it happens and stops the offending process by sending it a signal 11. When that happens during installation, it means `anaconda` made an error while accessing memory, and the most likely reason is some hardware problem. A commonly suggested cure for the signal 11 problem is to turn off CPU cache in the BIOS. To do so, you have to enter setup while the PC boots (by pressing a function key such as F2) and then turn off the CPU cache from the BIOS setup menus.

If the problem is due to a hardware error in memory (in other words, the result of bad memory chips), you could try swapping the memory modules around in their slots. You may also consider replacing an existing memory module with another memory module, if you have one handy.

You can read more about the signal 11 problem at `www.bitwizard.nl/ sig11/`.

Setting Up Printers

The Red Hat installer does not include a printer configuration step, but you can easily configure a printer from a graphical utility program. To set up printers, follow these steps:

1. **From the graphical login screen, log in as** `root`.

   If you're not logged in as `root`, proceed to the next step and the printer configuration tool will prompt you for the `root` password.

2. **From the GNOME or KDE desktop, choose Main Menu⇨System Settings⇨Printing.**

   The Printer Configuration tool is called `redhat-config-printer`. Figure 3-1 shows its main window.

Figure 3-1:
Configure
and manage
printers
from the
Printer
Configur-
ation tool.

3. **Click the New button to configure a new printer.**

This starts Red Hat's Printer Configuration Wizard. The initial screen
displays a message that assures you that nothing will be changed until
you click the Apply button at the end of all the steps. Click Forward to
continue.

4. **In the next screen (see Figure 3-2), enter the name for the print queue
and a short description of the print queue; then click Forward.**

You should use some systematic approach when naming the print
queue. For example, if I have a HP Laserjet 5000 printer on the second
floor in Room 210, I might name the queue Room210HPLJ5000 because
this makes it easy to find the printer. Sometimes system administrators
choose cute names such as kermit, piggy, elmo, cookiemonster, and
so on, but after you have too many printers, such cute schemes don't
work well. It's best to provide a clue about the printer's location as well
as the make and model in the print queue's name.

Figure 3-2:
Enter the
print queue
name and
description.

5. **In the next screen (see Figure 3-3), select a queue type from the drop-down selection box; then click Forward.**

Figure 3-3:
Select the
print queue
type from
this window.

Select the print queue type that applies to your situation. For example, if you want to print on a shared Windows printer, select the Windows Printer check box.

To set up a printer connected to your PC's parallel port, select Locally-connected.

The following types of print queues are available:

- **Locally-connected:** Refers to a printer connected directly to the serial, parallel, or USB port of your PC.

- **Networked CUPS (IPP):** Refers to a Common UNIX Printing System (CUPS) print queue at another server on the network. (IPP refers to the Internet Printing Protocol used to communicate with the remote CUPS server.)

- **Networked UNIX (LPD):** Refers to a print queue managed by the LPD server on another UNIX system on the local network. (LPD refers to Line Printer Daemon — another print spooler for UNIX systems.)

- **Networked Windows (SMB):** Refers to a printer connected to another PC on the local network and that uses the Server Message Block (SMB) protocol, the underlying protocol in Windows file and print sharing.

- **Networked Novell (NCP):** Refers to a printer connected to a Novell Netware server on the local network.

- **Networked JetDirect:** Refers to a HP JetDirect printer that's connected directly to the local network.

6. **If you select the Local Printer, the next screen displays information about the detected parallel port; click Forward to continue.**

For other options, you get a screen that prompts you to identify the network printer. The way you specify a network printer depends on the network type. For example, to use a networked CUPS printer on a host with the IP address 192.168.0.8 on your local area network, you have to type a name such as **http://192.168.0.8:631/printers/HPLaserjetRoom210** where *HPLaserjetRoom210* is the name of the networked printer.

7. **Select the make and model of your printer from the screen shown in Figure 3-4 and then click Forward.**

**Book I
Chapter 3**

**Troubleshooting
and Configuring
Red Hat Linux**

Figure 3-4:
Select your
printer's
make and
model from
this window.

Click the drop-down list (above the scrolling list) to display a list of printer manufacturers. When you choose a printer manufacturer from this list, the scrolling list displays the names of different printer models from that manufacturer, as shown in Figure 3-4 (for HP). If you have a PostScript printer, you can simply go to the Generic list (Generic is one of the choices in the manufacturer list) and select PostScript printer.

The last screen (Figure 3-5) shows information about the new print queue.

Figure 3-5:
Check the
information
for
accuracy.

8. **Review all information to make sure it's correct and then click Finish to create the print queue.**

9. **When a dialog box appears, asking whether you want to print a test page, click Yes.**

   Doing so applies all changes and restarts the print-scheduler program that takes care of printing. The printer should now print a test page, after which a message box appears and asks you to check the test page.

10. **Click OK to dismiss the message box.**

    The new print queue should appear in the printer configuration window, and you should be able to submit print jobs to this queue.

11. **Quit the printer configuration tool.**

    You can do so by choosing Action⇨Quit, or by closing the printer configuration window (click the X button in the upper-right corner of the window's frame).

Turning On Sound

Your PC must have a sound card and speakers to play audio CDs. If your PC has a sound card, hook up the speakers according to the instructions from the PC's manufacturer.

When you first boot your PC with Red Hat Linux, a utility called Kudzu detects the sound card and installs the driver. If you've gone through that step, you're set to try out the sound card. Otherwise you can set up the sound card by following these steps:

1. **At the graphics login screen, log in as** root.

2. **When you get to the GNOME desktop, choose Main Menu⇨System Settings⇨Soundcard Detection.**

   This runs the Red Hat sound card configuration utility.

   The sound card configuration utility gets information about the sound cards from another program called Kudzu and displays information about the detected sound card (Figure 3-6).

3. **Click the Play Test Sound button to play a test sound clip.**

   If all goes well, you should hear the sound.

4. **Click OK to quit the sound card configuration utility.**

After you configure the sound card, you can play audio CDs and other sound files in Red Hat Linux.

Figure 3-6:
The sound
card config-
uration
utility
displays
information
about the
sound card.

Adding User Accounts

When you start Red Hat Linux for the first time, you get the chance to add a
personal user account. If you didn't add a user account during the first boot
as described in Chapter 4 of this mini-book (or if you want to add more user
accounts for family members or coworkers), you can do so at any time by
using the Red Hat User Manager.

Setting up a personal user account other than root is a good idea. The
problem with root is the absolute power of that superuser account — you
can literally do anything, even destroy critical system files, with ease. It's
better to log in as an ordinary user. When you must do something as root,
simply type the su - command. You'll be prompted for the root password;
after you enter that password you'll become root. When you're finished
with your superuser duties, type **exit** to return to your mere mortal self.

To add user accounts with the Red Hat User Manager, follow these steps:

1. **Choose Main Menu⇨System Settings⇨Users and Groups from the
GNOME desktop.**

If you're not logged in as root, the Red Hat User Manager prompts you
for the root password (see Figure 3-7), which you have to enter to run
the manager.

Figure 3-7:
Enter the
root
password
here.

Query

You are attempting to run "redhat-config-users" which
requires administrative privileges, but more
information is needed in order to do so.

Password for root   [************************]

✗ Cancel   ✔ OK

2. **Enter the password and click OK.**

   The Red Hat User Manager window (shown in Figure 3-8) features two tabs: Users and Groups. The Users tab displays the current list of user accounts. The Groups tab lists your current groups. Figure 3-8, for example, lists the users on my Red Hat Linux system; the list will be different on your system.

3. **To add a new user, click the Add User button on the toolbar.**

   The Create New User dialog box appears, as shown in Figure 3-9.

4. **Fill in the requested information, and then click OK.**

   The new user now appears in the list on the Users tab in the Red Hat User Manager window.

Figure 3-8:
The Red
Hat User
Manager
window
shows the
current user
accounts.

Figure 3-9:
Entering
information
about a
new user
account.

5. **Repeat Steps 3 and 4 to add as many user accounts as you want.**

6. **When you're done, choose File⇨Exit to quit the Red Hat User Manager.**

To edit existing user account information, select the user name from the list in the Users tab and then click the Properties button on the toolbar. The selected user's information appears in a User Properties dialog box, where you can then edit it; click OK to make the changes.

If you want to remove a user account, click the user name in the Users tab. Then click the Delete button on the toolbar.

Managing CD-ROMs

The GNOME desktop makes it easy to use CD-ROMs in Red Hat Linux. Just place a CD-ROM in the drive, and an icon appears on the desktop. Behind the scenes a special utility called Magicdev is always running, waiting to detect when a CD-ROM is inserted or removed. When you insert a CD that has an autorun file, Magicdev asks whether you want to run that file (Figure 3-10).

Figure 3-10:
The
Magicdev
prompt.

Typically, running the autorun file starts an installer program that can install the software on the CD.

Magicdev also automatically starts the Nautilus file manager, which shows the contents of the CD-ROM (as in Figure 3-11).

Finally, Magicdev puts a CD-ROM icon on the GNOME desktop. You can then use the CD, either through the Nautilus file manager or through the icon on the desktop. To access the files and folders, you simply double-click the icons in the Nautilus window.

The CD-ROM icon is your best bet for certain tasks such as ejecting the CD when you're done with it. If you right-click the CD-ROM icon, a pop-up menu appears, listing the things you can do with the CD-ROM (as in Figure 3-12).

Figure 3-11:
When you
insert a CD,
Nautilus
displays
the CD's
contents.

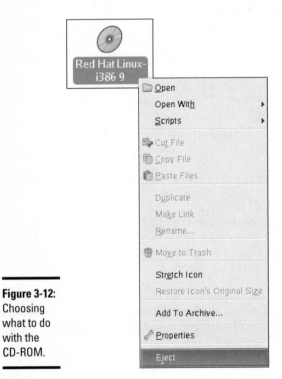

Figure 3-12:
Choosing
what to do
with the
CD-ROM.

When you're done with the CD, choose Eject from the pop-up menu to eject the CD-ROM from the drive. Doing so automatically removes the icon.

TIP

If there is a CD in the CD-ROM drive and you don't see a CD-ROM icon on the GNOME desktop, just eject the CD (by pressing the Eject button on the CD-ROM drive). Insert the CD again and Magicdev should recognize the CD.

The KDE desktop also automatically opens a CD-ROM's contents in a file manager called Konqueror. For example, Figure 3-13 shows the result of inserting a CD in the KDE desktop.

Figure 3-13: KDE automatically displays a CD's contents in the Konqueror file manager.

Installing RPM Packages

Sometimes you have to install or remove software to troubleshoot or configure your Red Hat Linux system. Most Red Hat Linux software comes in the form of Red Hat Package Manager (RPM) files. An RPM file is basically a single package that contains everything — all the files and configuration information — needed to install a software product. This section shows you how to install RPM packages.

From the GNOME desktop, use Add and Remove Software utility — a graphical utility for installing and uninstalling RPMs. Follow these steps:

1. **Choose Main Menu⇨System Settings⇨Add/Remove Applications.**

If you're not logged in as root, a dialog box prompts you for the root password.

2. **Type in the root password and press Enter.**

The Add and Remove Software utility starts and gathers information about the status of packages installed on your system. After it sorts through the information about all the installed packages, the utility displays a list of all the packages (Figure 3-14). The left side of the window has two large buttons: Install Software and Remove Software. By default the Install Software button is selected.

Figure 3-14:
The Add
and Remove
Software
utility shows
information
about the
package
groups.

The utility displays information about the packages organized into package groups such as Desktops and Applications (a *package group* is a collection of related RPMs). Each package group has a graphical icon, a label such as X Window System or GNOME Desktop Environment, and a brief description as well. For each package group, the utility displays how many packages are installed. If a package group has any uninstalled packages, the utility displays an Install hyperlink.

3. **To install any uninstalled package, click the <u>Install</u> hyperlink next to that package.**

   A dialog box appears with details of what you're about to install and how much disk space the new packages would require. Figure 3-15 shows the result of clicking the <u>Install</u> hyperlink next to the KDE Desktop Environment in Figure 3-14.

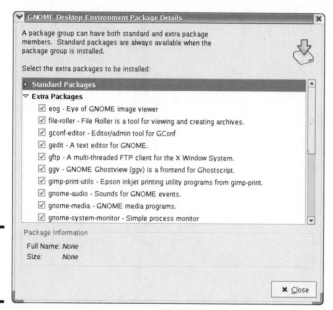

Figure 3-15:
A package
group's
details.

4. **Click Install Packages to install the selected package.**

   To remove one or more package groups, click the Remove Software button on the left panel in the Add and Remove Software window. Now the Add and Remove Software window shows the installed packages with a <u>Remove</u> hyperlink. To remove packages from a package group, click the <u>Remove</u> hyperlink next to that package group. A dialog box pops up listing the packages you can remove. Click Remove Packages and those packages are history!

Chapter 4: Trying Out Red Hat Linux

In This Chapter

✔ **Booting Red Hat Linux**

✔ **Logging in**

✔ **Checking out the GUI desktops**

✔ **Playing with the shell**

✔ **Shutting down**

You're sitting in front of your PC about to turn it on. You know that the PC has Red Hat Linux installed (maybe you did the installing yourself, but who's keeping track?). You're wondering what to expect when you turn it on and what you should do afterward. Not to worry. If this is your first time using Red Hat Linux, this chapter shows you how to log in, check out the graphical desktops, try out some cryptic Linux commands, and finally, shut down the PC.

Those of you who already know something about Red Hat Linux, flip through the pages to see if anything here looks new. You never know what you may not know!

Booting Red Hat Linux

When you power up the PC, it goes through the normal power-up sequence and loads the boot loader — GRUB or LILO, depending on which one was selected during Red Hat Linux installation. The *boot loader* is a tiny computer program that loads the rest of the operating system from disk into the computer's memory. These programs are now called *boot loaders* (once known as bootstrap loader). The whole process of starting up a computer is called *booting*.

Whether the boot loader is LILO or GRUB doesn't matter much. In either case, a graphical screen appears with the names of operating systems that the boot loader can load. For example, if your PC has Windows and Red Hat Linux, you see both names listed. You can then use the Up and Down arrow keys to select the operating system you want to use. If the PC is set up to load Red Hat Linux by default, wait a few seconds and then the boot loader starts Red Hat Linux. To be more precise, the boot loader loads the *Linux kernel* — the core of the Linux operating system — into the PC's memory.

As the Linux kernel starts, you should see a long list of opening messages often referred to as the *boot messages* (you can see these messages at any time by typing the **dmesg** command in a terminal window). These messages include the names of the devices that Linux detects. One of the first lines in the boot messages reads

```
Calibrating delay loop... 2955.67 BogoMIPS
```

BogoMIPS is Linux jargon (explained here in a handy sidebar) for a measure of time. The number that precedes BogoMIPS depends on your PC's processor speed, whether it's an old 200MHz Pentium or a new 4GHz Pentium 4. The kernel uses the BogoMIPS measurement when it has to wait a small amount of time for some event to occur (like getting a response back from a disk controller when it's ready).

After the boot messages, Red Hat Linux switches to a graphical boot screen that shows information about the progress of system startup. Specifically, you see information such as servers being started and hardware being probed.

When you boot Red Hat Linux for the first time after installation, you get the Red Hat Setup Agent that displays a welcome screen and then the Fedora Core license agreement. You must read and accept the agreement before the Setup Agent will take take you through date and time setup (Figure 4-1), user account setup, sound card check, and give you a chance to register with Red Hat Network and install programs from any additional CDs.

What is BogoMIPS?

As Red Hat Linux boots, you get a message that says Calibrating delay loop... 421. 23 BogoMIPS, with some number before the word *BogoMIPS*. BogoMIPS is one of those words that confounds new Linux users, but it's just jargon with a simple meaning.

BogoMIPS is Linus's invention (yes, the same Linus Torvalds who started Linux), and it means *bogus MIPS*. As you may know, MIPS is an acronym for *millions of instructions per second* — a measure of how fast your computer runs programs. Unfortunately, MIPS isn't

a very good measure of performance; the MIPS measurements of different types of computers are difficult to compare accurately. BogoMIPS is basically a way to measure the computer's speed that's independent of the exact processor type. Linux uses the BogoMIPS number to calibrate a *delay loop*, in which the computer keeps running some useless instructions until a specified amount of time has passed. Of course, the reason for killing valuable processor time like this is to wait for some slowpoke device to get ready for work.

Figure 4-1:
Configure
date and
time from
this screen
in Red Hat
Setup
Agent.

If the screen goes dark and there is no activity, the first time configuration utility may be having trouble starting the X Window System. Unfortunately, you cannot try out Red Hat Linux without fixing this problem. Sometimes the graphical environment fails even though the graphical interface seems to work fine during installation. There are ways to fix this problem. Go to Chapter 3 of this mini-book for more information on how to troubleshoot this problem.

The Red Hat Setup Agent's first configuration step is for date and time setup. You can set the date and time from the Date and Time window (refer to Figure 4-1) and then click Next.

If your system is connected to the Internet, select the Enable Network Time Protocol check box and then select a server from the Server drop-down list. That way the system gets its time values directly from one of the super-accurate time servers on the Net. The Red Hat Setup Agent's second configuration step is for setting up a user account. Enter the account information in the screen shown in Figure 4-2.

After entering the user account information, click Next. The Red Hat Setup Agent then displays information about the sound card and gives you an opportunity to play a test sound. Click Next to continue. The Red Hat Setup Agent prompts you to register with Red Hat Network (Figure 4-3). To register, click Next and respond to the requested information. After that step is done, click Next again.

Figure 4-2:
Set up
a user
account
from this
window.

Figure 4-3:
You get an
opportunity
to register
with
Red Hat
Network.

The Red Hat Setup Agent then displays a window from which you can install programs from additional CDs (Figure 4-4). If you have additional CDs to install, click the appropriate icon. Otherwise, click Forward.

When you're done with the Red Hat Setup Agent, you're really done for good because it runs only once when you boot for the first time. If, for some reason, you want to go through these steps again (perhaps you want to set the time or register with Red Hat Network — although you can do these things without having to run the Setup Agent), here's the scoop on how to run the Red Hat Setup Agent again:

Log in as `root` and type the following commands in a terminal window (to open a terminal window, choose Main Menu⇨System Tools⇨Terminal):

```
rm /etc/sysconfig/firstboot
chkconfig --level 5 firstboot on
```

That's it! Next time you reboot the PC, you'll have the pleasure of meeting the Red Hat Setup Agent again. If you want to run `firstboot` interactively from GNOME or KDE, you can do so by logging in as `root` and typing the following commands in a terminal window:

```
rm /etc/sysconfig/firstboot
firstboot
```

When you're through with the Red Hat Setup Agent, you should get the graphical login screen (shown in Figure 4-5).

The login window in the middle of the screen displays a welcome message with your PC's name — it's called the *host name*. The name is assigned when the network is configured. If the network isn't configured, `localhost.localdomain` is the host name. If your PC gets its network address (the IP address) from a Dynamic Host Configuration Protocol (DHCP) server, then that server provides a cryptic host name for your PC. The login window also has a text input field that prompts you for your user name.

Figure 4-4:
You can install any other CDs you may have.

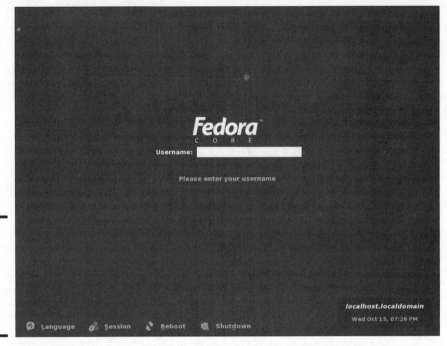

The login window in the middle of the screen displays a text input field that prompts you for your username. The lower-right corner of the screen shows your PC's name — it's called the *host name*. The name is assigned when the network is configured. If the network isn't configured, localhost.localdomain is the host name. If your PC gets its network address (the IP address) from a Dynamic Host Configuration Protocol (DHCP) server, that server provides a cryptic host name for your PC.

For example, to log in as user spiderman, type **spiderman** in the first text field and press Enter (move the mouse over the login dialog box before you begin typing). Then type spiderman's password and press Enter. You should then see the initial graphical user interface (GUI — pronounced *gooey* for short) appear. What you get depends on your choice of GUI — GNOME or KDE. If someone made the choice for you, don't worry, GNOME and KDE are both quite good and versatile.

Exploring GUI Desktops

Red Hat Linux comes with two GUI desktops — GNOME and KDE. If you have installed both, you can try each GUI. It's easy to select one of these desktops just before you log in to the system — and here's where I show you how.

GNOME is typically the default GUI in Red Hat Linux, so you can start with GNOME. Then log out and log back in, but select KDE as the GUI. That way you can try out both desktops.

GNOME

GNOME stands for *GNU Network Object Model Environment* (and GNU, as you probably know, stands for *GNU's Not UNIX*). GNOME is a graphical user interface (GUI) and a programming environment. From the user's perspective, GNOME is like Microsoft Windows. Behind the scenes, GNOME has many features that allow programmers to write graphical applications that can work well together. In this chapter, I point out only some key features of the GNOME GUI, leaving the details for you to explore on your own at your leisure.

If you're curious, you can always find out the latest information about GNOME by visiting the GNOME home page at www.gnome.org.

Typically, GNOME is the default in Red Hat Linux. After you log in, you see the GNOME GUI desktop. Figure 4-6 shows the GNOME desktop after I log in with my user name naba.

When you log in as root, you could accidentally damage your system because you can do anything when you're root. Always log in as a normal user.

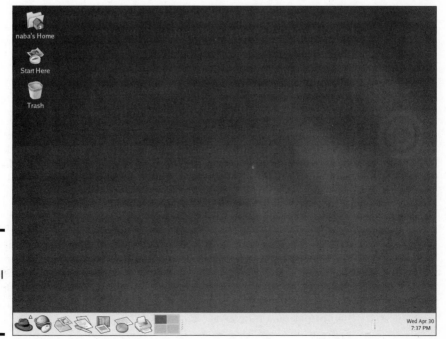

Figure 4-6:
Initial
GNOME GUI
desktop
after
logging in.

The exact appearance of the GNOME desktop depends on the current *session* (the set of applications that is running at that time). As you can see, the initial GNOME desktop, shown in Figure 4-6, is very similar to the Windows desktop. It has the GNOME panel, or simply the panel (similar to the Windows taskbar) along the bottom and icons for folders and applications appear directly on the desktop. This is similar to the way you can place icons directly on the Windows desktop.

You can move and resize the windows just as you do in Microsoft Windows. Also, as in the window frames in Microsoft Windows, the right-hand corner of the window's title bar includes three buttons. The leftmost button reduces the window to an icon, the middle button maximizes the window to fill up the entire screen, and the rightmost button closes the window.

The GNOME panel

The GNOME panel is a key feature of the GNOME desktop. The panel is a separate GNOME application. As Figure 4-7 shows, it provides a display area for menus and small panel applets. Each panel applet is a small program that is designed to work inside the panel. For example, the clock applet on the panel's far right displays the current date and time.

Figure 4-7:
The GNOME panel.

The panel includes several other applets besides the clock applet at the far right edge:

+ **The GNOME Pager applet:** Provides a virtual desktop that's larger than the physical dimensions of your system's screen. In Figure 4-7, the pager displays four pages in a small display area. Each page represents an area equal to the size of the display screen. To go to a specific page, click that page in the pager window. The GNOME Pager applet displays buttons for each window being displayed in the current virtual page.

+ **Launcher applets:** The buttons to the right of the Red Hat icon are launcher applets. Each of these applets displays a button with the icon of application. Clicking a button starts (launches) that application. Try clicking each of these buttons to see what happens. The mouse and earth button launches the Mozilla Web browser whereas clicking the pen and paper icon opens the OpenOffice.org Writer word processor. Move the mouse over an icon and a small help message appears with information about that icon.

✦ **The GNOME weather applet:** Displays the local weather. You don't see this applet until you start it. You can start it from the menu that appears when you right-click in an empty area of the panel window.

The Main Menu button, or the "Red Hat Logo"

In Figure 4-6, the leftmost edge of the panel shows a button with the familiar Red Hat logo. That "red hat" is the Main Menu button — the most important part of the GNOME panel. Just like the Start button in Microsoft Windows, you can launch applications from the menu that pops up when you click the red hat. Figure 4-8 shows a typical view of the Main Menu on a Red Hat Linux PC.

Typically, the Main Menu and its submenus list items that start an application. Some of the menu items have an arrow; move the mouse pointer on an item with an arrow and another menu pops up. In Figure 4-8, the menu selection is Main Menu⇨System Settings⇨Server Settings⇨Services. Notice that when you point to a menu selection, a balloon help pops up with information about that selection.

Figure 4-8:
Click the red hat (Main Menu) and move the mouse pointer from menu to menu to start the program you want.

TIP

You can start applets such as the weather applet from the menu that appears when you right-click the GNOME panel. To start the weather applet, right-click the panel and choose Add to Panel⇨Accessories⇨Weather Report (Figure 4-9). In the Add to Panel menu, you find many more categories of applets you can try.

Figure 4-9:
Right click
the panel
and click
Add to
Panel to
see the
available
applets.

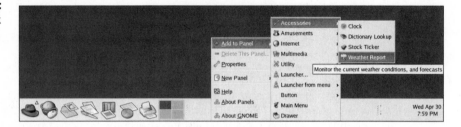

Explore all the items in the Main Menu to see all the tasks you can perform from this menu. In particular, move the mouse pointer over the Main Menu⇨Preferences item to see your options (Figure 4-10) for changing the appearance of the desktop. For example, you can change the desktop's background from this menu.

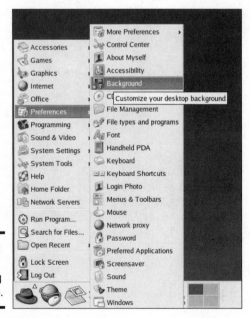

Figure 4-10:
Options for
customizing
the desktop.

Customizing GNOME

By now you may be itching to do a bit of decorating. No one likes to stick to the plain blue GNOME desktop. After all, it's your desktop. You should be able to set it up any way you want it. You can configure most aspects of the GNOME desktop's *look and feel* — the appearance and behavior — by choosing various options from the Main Menu⇨Preferences menu.

Changing the background

To see how the desktop decorating business works, start by choosing Main Menu⇨Preferences⇨Background and a dialog box appears, as shown in Figure 4-11.

Figure 4-11:
Changing
the GNOME
desktop's
background.

From this dialog box, you can select a background of solid color or a color gradient background or pick *wallpaper* (an image to be used as the background). A *color gradient* background starts with one color and gradually changes to another color. The gradient can be in the vertical direction (top to bottom) or horizontal (left to right).

To select a horizontal color gradient, try these steps:

1. **From the Background Style drop-down box — the one that currently says Solid color (see Figure 4-11) — choose Horizontal gradient.**

2. **Click the button that shows a color next to the label Left Color.**

   This brings up a color selection dialog box (shown in Figure 4-12) from which you can pick a color.

3. **Repeat the same process to select the right color.**

Figure 4-12:
The Pick a Color dialog box.

After you complete these steps, the image of the monitor in the dialog box shows you a preview of the new background color.

If you want to use an image as wallpaper, click the Select Picture box in the upper-left corner of the dialog box. A dialog box displays the contents of the /usr/share/backgrounds/images directory. That directory has the default.png file with the default wallpaper you see on the GNOME desktop. For more wallpaper images, change to the directory /usr/share/backgrounds/wallpapers and select an image you want. As you click an image file's name, you see a preview of the image (Figure 4-13). You can select any *Joint Photographic Experts Group* (JPEG) or *Portable Network Graphics* (PNG) format image file as wallpaper. After selecting an image, click OK.

Figure 4-13:
Select an image to use as wallpaper from this dialog box.

The new wallpaper should immediately appear on the desktop (as in Figure 4-14). When you're done making the changes, click the OK button to close the dialog box and apply the changes.

Figure 4-14:
The newly
selected
wallpaper.

Selecting a theme

Another more exciting customization is to select a new theme for the entire
user interface. A *theme* refers to a collection of appearance and behavior
(look and feel) for all the user interface components: buttons, check boxes,
scroll bars, and so on.

To try out some new themes, choose Main Menu⇨Preferences⇨Theme.
From the Theme Preferences dialog box (see Figure 4-15), you can try
different themes and select one that you like. The default theme is called
Bluecurve. To try another theme, select the theme from the list and the
desktop's appearance changes to match the theme.

Go ahead and try some of the available themes. When you select a theme,
you can see the results in the desktop and the Theme Preference window
itself. If you like a theme, click the Close button to use that theme.
Otherwise, select the Bluecurve theme before clicking Close.

Logging out of GNOME

If you want to try the KDE GUI, you have to log out first. Choose Main Menu⇨
Log out. Click Yes when a dialog box asks whether you really want to log out.

Figure 4-15:
Selecting a
new theme
for the
desktop.

KDE

KDE stands for the *K Desktop Environment*. The KDE project started in October 1996 with an intent to develop a common GUI for UNIX systems that use the X Window System. The first beta version of KDE version was released a year later in October 1997. KDE version 1.0 was released in July 1998; KDE 2.0 on October 23, 2000; KDE 3.0 was released on April 3, 2002; and the latest version — KDE 3.1.2 — was released on May 19, 2003.

From the user's perspective, KDE provides a graphical desktop environment that includes a window manager, the Konqueror Web browser and file manager, a panel for starting applications, a help system, configuration tools, and many applications, including the OpenOffice.org office suite, image viewer, PostScript viewer, and mail and news programs.

From the developer's perspective, KDE has class libraries and object models for easy application development in C++. KDE is a large development project with many collaborators.

You can always find the latest information about KDE by visiting the KDE home page at `www.kde.org`.

To try the KDE GUI, you have to have KDE installed on your system. If you don't have KDE installed, you probably did not want the KDE GUI in the first place. If your system has only KDE installed, you get the KDE GUI as soon as you log in.

If you have both GNOME and KDE installed on your system, you can select the GUI just before you log in. From the login window, click Session and from the pop-up dialog box (see Figure 4-16), choose KDE for a KDE session and then log in as usual. A dialog box asks whether you want to make KDE the default for future sessions. Click Yes or No depending on what you prefer.

When you log in after selecting a KDE session, you get the KDE desktop for this session. The next time you log in, the system continues to use KDE until you switch back to GNOME.

After you select KDE as the GUI for the session and then log in, you should see an initial KDE desktop similar to the one shown in Figure 4-17. The initial KDE session includes a window showing a helpful tip. That's the only part that makes this desktop look different from the one you get in GNOME.

Figure 4-16:
Choosing
a KDE
session.

Figure 4-17:
The initial
KDE
desktop for
a typical
user.

You will find that KDE is very easy to use and is similar in many ways to the Windows GUI. You can start applications from a menu that's similar to the Start menu in Windows. As in Windows, you can place folders and applications directly on the KDE desktop.

KDE panel

The KDE panel appearing along the bottom edge of the screen is meant for starting applications. The right end of the panel shows an arrow pointing to the right. You can click this arrow to hide the panel and make more room on the desktop for applications. When the panel is hidden, it still shows a small bar with an arrow. To view the entire panel again, click that arrow and the panel slides out.

The most important component of the panel is the Red Hat button on the left-hand side of the panel. (In default KDE installations, the menu appears as a large letter K, but Red Hat has replaced it with the Red Hat logo.) That button is like the Start button in Windows. When you click the Red Hat button, a pop-up menu appears. From this menu, you can get to other menus by moving the mouse pointer over items that display a rightward-pointing arrow. For example, Figure 4-18 shows a typical menu selection for changing the desktop background.

Figure 4-18: Click the Red Hat (Main Menu) button and then move the mouse pointer from menu to menu to open the KDE menus.

You can start applications from this menu. That's why the KDE documentation calls the Red Hat button (of course, the KDE documentation refers to the button as the K button) the *Application Starter*.

Next to the Red Hat button, the panel includes many more buttons. If you don't know what a button does, simply move the mouse pointer over the button; a small pop-up window displays a brief message about that button.

Table 4-1 gives you an idea of what happens when you click each of the major buttons on the KDE panel. When you have some time, try these buttons one by one to get a feel for what you can do in KDE.

Table 4-1	KDE Panel Buttons
When You Click This	*It Does This*
	Shows the application menu from which you can start any application.
	Starts the Mozilla Web browser.
	Starts the Ximian Evolution e-mail and calendaring software.
	Runs OpenOffice.org Writer, a Microsoft Word–like word processor.
	Runs the OpenOffice.org Impress slide presentation program that's similar to Microsoft PowerPoint.
	Runs OpenOffice.org Calc, a Microsoft Excel–like spreadsheet program.
	Runs Print Manager, a utility that enables you to set up and monitor print queues.
	Switches to the desktop whose number you have clicked.
	Runs Klipper, the KDE clipboard utility for cutting and pasting information.
20:42	Displays the current time. Click to view the current month's calendar. Right-click the menu to adjust date and time.

Customizing the KDE desktop

KDE makes it very easy to customize the look and feel of the KDE desktop. Everything you have to decorate the desktop is in one place: the KDE Control Center. To start the KDE Control Center, choose Main Menu⇨ Control Center.

When the KDE Control Center starts, it displays the main window with a tree menu on the left side and some summary information about your system in the workspace to the right, as shown in Figure 4-19.

Figure 4-19: Initial window of the KDE Control Center.

The KDE Control Center tree menu shows the items that you can customize with this program. The tree menu is organized into categories such as Appearance & Themes, Internet & Network, Peripherals, Security & Privacy, and so on. Click the plus sign (+) to the left of an item to view the subcategories for that item. To change an item, go through the tree menu to locate the item and then click it. That item's configuration options then appear in a tabbed dialog box on the right side of the window.

Changing the background

To change the desktop's background, choose Appearance & Themes⇨ Background. A tab appears (as in Figure 4-20) that shows the options for customizing the desktop's background.

If you want to change the background of a specific desktop, deselect the Common Background check box (to remove the check mark). Then, from the list of desktops, you can select the desktop whose background you want to change.

Book I
Chapter 4

Trying Out
Red Hat Linux

You can select either a solid color background with a variety of gradients (meaning the color changes gradually from one color to another) or wallpaper (an image used as a background). For solid color backgrounds, you can select the gradient from the Mode drop-down menu. You can then pick the two colors by clicking the Color 1 and Color 2 color buttons. After making your selections, click Apply to try out the background. (If you don't like what you get, click Reset to revert back to the previous background.)

If you want to use wallpaper as background, click the Wallpaper tab for the wallpaper selections. Then click the Browse button. This brings up a dialog box showing the JPEG images in the `/usr/share/backgrounds/wallpapers` directory. You can select any one of these images and click OK. Then click the Apply button in the KDE Control Center to apply this wallpaper to the desktop. If you don't like the appearance, click Reset.

Selecting a theme

As you can see from the menu items in the Appearance & Themes category of the KDE Control Center (refer to Figure 4-20), you can customize a number of aspects of look and feel, from colors and fonts to icons. I won't go through all the items here, but you should experiment with some of them to see what you want for your KDE desktop.

One quick and easy way to select a packaged look and feel is to use one of the themes offered by the Theme Manager. To pick a theme, choose Appearance & Themes➪Theme Manager. This brings up the Theme Manager selections from which you can click the name of a theme and see a preview of that theme, as shown in Figure 4-21.

Figure 4-20:
Changing the desktop background with the KDE Control Center.

Figure 4-21:
Selecting
and
previewing
a theme in
the KDE
Control
Center.

To try a theme, click Apply. If you don't like it, click Reset to revert back to the current look and feel.

Logging out of KDE

When you're done exploring KDE, log out. To log out of KDE, choose K⇨Logout. You can also right-click empty areas of the desktop and choose Logout from the pop-up menu that appears.

Playing with the Shell

Red Hat Linux is basically UNIX, and UNIX just doesn't feel like UNIX unless you can type cryptic commands in a text terminal. Although GNOME and KDE have done a lot to bring us into the world of *w*indows, *i*cons, *m*ouse, and *p*ointer (affectionately known as *WIMP* :-), sometimes you're stuck with nothing but a plain text screen with a prompt that looks like this (when you log in as root):

```
[root@dhcppc4 etc]#
```

This is most often the case when something is *wrong* with the X Window System, which is essentially the machinery that runs the windows and menus you normally see. In those cases, you have to work with the shell and learn some of the cryptic Linux commands.

You can prepare for unexpected encounters with the shell by trying out some Linux commands in a terminal window while you're in the GNOME or KDE GUI. After you get the hang of it, you might even keep a terminal window open, just so you can use one of those cryptic commands simply because it's faster than trying to point and click (those two-letter commands do pack some punch!).

Starting the Bash shell

Simply put, the *shell* is the Linux *command interpreter* — a program that reads what you type, interprets that text as a command, and does what the command is supposed to do.

Before you start playing with the shell, open a terminal window. In either GNOME or KDE, choose Main Menu⇨System Tools⇨Terminal. What appears is a window with a prompt, like the one shown in Figure 4-22. That's a terminal window, and it works just like an old-fashioned terminal. A shell program is running and ready to accept any text that you type. You type text, press Enter, and something happens (depending on what you typed).

Figure 4-22:
You can type Linux commands at the shell prompt in a terminal window.

The prompt that you see depends on the shell that runs in that terminal window. The default Linux shell is called *Bash*.

Bash understands a whole host of standard Linux commands with which you can look at files, go from one directory to another, see what programs are running (and who else is logged in), and a whole lot more.

In addition to the Linux commands, Bash can run any program stored in an executable file. Bash can also execute *shell scripts*, text files that contain Linux commands.

Understanding shell commands

Because a shell interprets what you type, it's important to know how the shell figures out the text that you enter. All shell commands have this general format:

```
command option1 option2 ... optionN
```

Such a single line of commands is commonly called a *command line*. On a command line, you enter a command followed by one or more optional parameters (or *arguments*). Such *command-line options* (or command-line arguments) help you specify what you want the command to do.

One basic rule is that you have to use a space or a tab to separate the command from the options. You also must separate options with a space or a tab. If you want to use an option that contains embedded spaces, you have to put that option inside quotation marks. For example, to search for two words of text in the password file, I enter the following grep command (grep is one of those cryptic commands used to search for text in files):

```
grep "Font Server" /etc/passwd
```

When grep prints the line with those words, it looks like this:

```
xfs:x:43:43:X Font Server:/etc/X11/fs:/sbin/nologin
```

If you created a user account in your name, go ahead and type the grep command with your name as an argument, but remember to enclose the name in quotes.

Trying a few Linux commands

While you have the terminal window open, try a few Linux commands just for fun. I guide you through some random examples to give you a feel for what you can do at the shell prompt.

To see how long the Red Hat Linux PC has been up since you last powered it up, type the following. (*Note:* I show the typed command in bold, followed by the output from that command.)

```
uptime
```

```
    7:13pm  up 29 days, 55 min,  3 users,  load average: 1.00,
       1.00, 1.00
```

The part up 29 days, 55 min tells you that this particular PC has been up for nearly a month. Hmmm . . . can Windows do that?

To see what version of Linux kernel your system is running, use the `uname` command like this:

```
uname -srv
```

```
Linux 2.4.21-20.1.2024.2.1.nptl #1 Fri Jul 11 06:04:52 EDT 2003
```

In this case, the system is running Linux kernel version 2.4.21.

To read a file, use the `more` command. Here's an example:

```
more /etc/passwd
```

```
root:x:0:0:root:/root:/bin/bash
bin:x:1:1:bin:/bin:/sbin/nologin
daemon:x:2:2:daemon:/sbin:/sbin/nologin
adm:x:3:4:adm:/var/adm:/sbin/nologin
... lines deleted ...
```

To see a list of all the programs that are currently running on the system, use the `ps` command, like this:

```
ps ax
```

```
PID TTY       STAT   TIME COMMAND
   1 ?          S     0:04 init
   2 ?          SW    0:00 [keventd]
   3 ?          SW    0:00 [kapmd]
   4 ?          SWN   0:00 [ksoftirqd_CPU0]
   5 ?          SW    0:44 [kswapd]
   6 ?          SW    0:00 [bdflush]
   7 ?          SW    0:00 [kupdated]
   8 ?          SW    0:00 [mdrecoveryd]
  12 ?          SW    0:17 [kjournald]
  91 ?          SW    0:00 [khubd]
 194 ?          SW    0:00 [kjournald]
 604 ?          S     0:04 syslogd -m 0
 609 ?          S     0:00 klogd -x
 629 ?          S     0:00 portmap
 657 ?          S     0:00 rpc.statd
... lines deleted ...
```

Amazing how many programs can run on a system even when there's only you logged in as a user, isn't it?

As you can guess, you can do everything from a shell prompt, but it does take some getting used to.

Shutting Down

When you're ready to shut down Red Hat Linux, you must do so in an orderly manner. Even if you're the sole user of a Red Hat Linux PC, several other programs are usually running in the background. Also, operating systems such as Linux try to optimize the way that they write data to the disk. Because disk access is relatively slow (compared with the time needed to access memory locations), data generally is held in memory and written to the disk in large chunks. Therefore, if you simply turn off the power, you run the risk that some files won't be updated properly.

Any user (you don't even have to be logged in) can shut down the system from the desktop or from the graphical login screen. Choose Main Menu⇨ Log Out. A Logout dialog box appears that provides the options for rebooting or halting the system or simply logging out. To shut down the system, simply select Shutdown, and click OK. The system then shuts down in an orderly manner.

If you're at the graphical login screen, click the Shutdown label in the bottom part of the screen. Then another dialog box asks you to confirm that you really want to halt the system. Click the Yes button. The system then shuts down in an orderly manner.

As the system shuts down, you see messages about processes being shut down. You may be surprised at how many processes there are, even when no one is explicitly running any programs on the system. If your system does not automatically power off on shutdown, you can manually turn off the power.

Note that it does *not* require `root` access to shut down or reboot the system in this manner. Make sure that physical access to the console is protected adequately.

Book II

Workstations and Applications

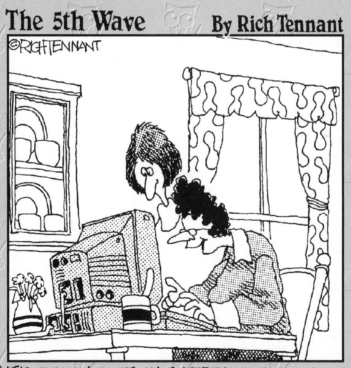

The 5th Wave   By Rich Tennant

©RICHTENNANT

"IT'S REALLY QUITE AN ENTERTAINING PIECE OF SOFTWARE. THERE'S ROLLER COASTER ACTION, SUSPENSE AND DRAMA, WHERE SKILL AND STRATEGY ARE MATCHED AGAINST WINNING AND LOSING. AND I THOUGHT MANAGING OUR BUDGET WOULD BE DULL."

Contents at a Glance

Chapter 1: Exploring GNOME

In This Chapter

✔ **Taking stock of GNOME**

✔ **Using the GNOME panel**

✔ **Examining the Main Menu**

✔ **Running applets**

✔ **Using the Nautilus shell**

✔ **Configuring GNOME**

GNOME (pronounced *Guh-NOME*) is a GUI for Red Hat Linux. GNOME is similar to Microsoft Windows, but does have its differences. Unlike Microsoft Windows, you can pick your GUI in Red Hat Linux. If you don't like GNOME, just log out and log back in with the KDE, the other GUI. Try doing that with Microsoft Windows!

The best way to get a feel for GNOME is to explore it as a user. I give you a brief guided tour of GNOME in this chapter. Then you can continue to explore and learn more as you continue to use GNOME.

By the way, GNOME is developed independently of Linux. In fact, GNOME runs on other UNIX operating systems besides Linux. Visit the GNOME home page at www.gnome.org to learn the latest about GNOME.

Taking Stock of GNOME

When you use GNOME, all that you see and experience is the GUI desktop. There is, however, much more to GNOME than the GUI desktop. For example, here are some key facts about GNOME:

✦ GNOME provides a development environment for GUI applications. It comes with a programming toolkit that programmers can use to create GUI applications.

✦ GNOME supports an object model — it defines the structure of software components so that they can communicate with one another.

✦ The GNOME GUI is modular, so it works with any window manager designed for the X Window System. For example, Red Hat Linux comes with several window managers such as Metacity, MWM, and TWM. Each window manager has its own look and feel. GNOME works with any of these window managers.

✦ All GNOME documentation is written using the *Standard Generalized Markup Language* (SGML). This means that you can view the manual for a GNOME application on any Web browser.

✦ GNOME comes with a set of office applications called OpenOffice.org. It includes the Writer word processor, the Calc spreadsheet, the Impress presentation program, and the Draw drawing program. See Book III for more about OpenOffice.org.

Okay, I think you get the idea. GNOME is a mighty workhorse underneath that pretty exterior.

GNOME desktop

Typically, GNOME is the default GUI in Red Hat Linux; you get the GNOME desktop if you log in without selecting a specific GUI.

If you have both GNOME and KDE installed on your system, you can select which GUI you want just before you log in. From the graphical login window, choose Session⇨GNOME to select a GNOME session and then log in as usual.

The initial GNOME desktop (shown in Figure 1-1) looks like any other popular GUI such as Microsoft Windows or the Apple desktop on a Mac.

The desktop shows icons for your folder, the trashcan for deleted files, and an icon for any CD-ROM in the CD-ROM drive. Double-clicking the Start Here icon starts the Nautilus file manager.

The other major feature of the GNOME desktop is the bar along the bottom, which is called the *GNOME panel* or just *the panel*. The panel is similar to the Windows task bar. It has buttons on the left (shortcuts to various programs) and a date and time display to the right. The middle part of the panel shows buttons for applications you may be running.

Desktop pop-up menus

Right-click a clear area on the GNOME desktop and a menu pops up (as in Figure 1-2).

You can use these menu options for a number of tasks — from opening a Nautilus window to changing the desktop background. Table 1-1 explains what each menu option does. The menu items that don't apply are grayed out. Go ahead and give some of these menu options a try.

Figure 1-1:
The GNOME desktop looks like other popular GUI desktops.

Figure 1-2:
Right-click on the GNOME desktop for this pop-up menu.

Table 1-1	GNOME Desktop Menu Options
When You Select This Option	*It Does the Following*
Open New Window	Opens a new Nautilus window that shows your home directory (folder).
Open New Terminal	Opens a terminal window where you can type Linux commands.
Create Folder	Creates a new folder on the desktop and waits for you to edit the folder's name.

(continued)

Table 1-1 *(continued)*

When You Select This Option	It Does the Following
Create Launcher	Brings up a dialog box from where you can set up a new launcher — an icon the desktop that acts as a shortcut to an application.
Clean Up by Name	Arranges the desktop icons alphabetically by name.
Keep Aligned	When selected, aligns the icons on the desktop.
Paste Files	Pastes a file onto the desktop (where the icon then appears).
Disks	Brings up a menu of removable drives and CD-ROM drives from which you can select a drive to access.
Use Default Background	Resets the desktop background to the default.
Change Desktop Background	Brings up a dialog box from which you can select a new background.

Icon pop-up menus

Right-clicking any desktop icon causes another menu to appear. This pop-up menu has some options that are the same for any icon, but the last option depends on the icon being clicked. For example, Figure 1-3 shows the menu that appears when you right-click the trashcan icon.

Figure 1-3: Right-click an icon on the GNOME desktop for this type of pop-up menu.

Notice that the last option is Empty Trash, which is appropriate for the trashcan icon. Table 1-2 gives an overview of the common menu options in the icon pop-up menus. As you'd expect, the menu items that don't apply to an icon are grayed out.

Table 1-2	GNOME Icon Menu Options
When You Select This Option	**It Does the Following**
Open	Opens the file (usually in a Nautilus window).
Open With	Opens the file with a viewer or an application (you choose).
Cut File	Cuts selected files.
Copy File	Copies selected files.
Make Link	Creates a link to that icon (a link is a shortcut).
Rename	Renames the icon (you have to enter the new name).
Move to Trash	Moves the icon to the trash.
Stretch Icon	Stretches the icon (you have to drag the mouse to indicate the new size).
Restore Icon's Original Size	Returns the icon to its earlier size.
Add To Archive	Displays a dialog box that enables you to add the items in trash to an archive by using the GNOME File Roller application (appears only when you click a file or folder icon).
Properties	Displays information about the icon.
Empty Trash	Permanently deletes items in the trash (you get a chance to say yes or no) — this item appears only when you right-click the trashcan icon.

Book II Chapter 1

Exploring GNOME

Okay. Do you see the pattern here? I bet you do. Whenever you're exploring GNOME (or, for that matter, any GUI), always right-click before you pick. You'll be amazed at all kinds of things you can do from the menus that pop up when you right-click!

Using the GNOME Panel

The GNOME panel, or simply *the panel*, is the long rectangular window that stretches across the bottom of the GNOME desktop. Figure 1-4 shows a typical view of the panel.

Figure 1-4:
This is a
typical view
of the
GNOME
panel.

The panel is a parking place for icons. Some of them start programs when you click them. Some show status (such as what programs are currently running), as well as information such as date and time.

Starting at the left, the Red Hat icon is GNOME's Main Menu button — it's like the Start button in Microsoft Windows. Then come a few icons that start various programs. Table 1-3 briefly explains what these icons do.

By the way, if you move the mouse pointer on top of an icon, a small help balloon pops up and gives you a helpful hint about the icon.

Table 1-3	Icons on the GNOME Panel
When You Click This Icon	*It Does the Following*
	Brings up the Main Menu from which you can select applications to run.
	Runs the Mozilla Web browser.
	Starts the Ximian Evolution e-mail and calendar software.
	Runs OpenOffice.org Writer, a Microsoft Word–like word processor.
	Runs the OpenOffice.org Impress slide presentation program (which is similar to Microsoft PowerPoint).
	Runs the OpenOffice.org Calc, a Microsoft Excel–like spreadsheet program.
	Runs GNOME Print Manager, from which you can set up and monitor printers.

To the right of these icons, a workspace-switcher icon shows four rectangular areas, each representing a virtual desktop. You can click one of these rectangles to switch to a different virtual desktop. This feature seems to offer four separate desktops to work with. To be honest, I seem to stay stuck in one virtual screen, but it's nice to know the other virtual desktops are there, if I ever need them.

The area to the right of the pager icon displays buttons for the programs you have started so far. This area is blank if you have not yet started any programs.

There may be other icons next to the pager, but the date and time is what always appear at the rightmost edge of the panel.

Now for a little bit of technical detail about these icons on the panel. The panel itself is a GNOME application; each icon is a program called an *applet* (for little application). These panel applets can do things like launch other programs or display the date and time.

If you right-click any icon or anywhere on the panel, you get a pop-up menu from which you can learn more or perform some task. For example, if you right-click the second icon from the left, the menu shown in Figure 1-5 pops up. As you can see, you can perform tasks such as remove the icon from the panel, move the icon on the panel, and look at its properties from the pop-up menu. If you right-click an empty area of the panel, you can even access the menus to start any program.

Main Menu

As with any self-respecting GUI, GNOME is about convenience and ease of use. In fact, it offers one place where you can find — and launch — everything you want to run in Red Hat Linux.

The Red Hat icon on the GNOME panel is the Main Menu button for Red Hat Linux. I am not going to bore you with a lengthy listing of everything in the Main Menu; rather, I provide an overview and point out some interesting items. You can do the exploring yourself.

Figure 1-5:
Right-click an icon on the GNOME panel to view its pop-up menu.

Click the Main Menu button to bring up the initial menu. Then move the pointer to an arrow next to a menu item to bring up the next menu, and so on. You can go through a menu hierarchy and make selections from the final menu. If you position the cursor on a menu item, a small help balloon may give you more information about that item. Figure 1-6 shows a typical menu hierarchy, showing the selection of the Web browser. Note the balloon help that appears in the small rectangular window next to the Mozilla Web Browser menu item.

You'd have guessed it anyway, but here goes. I use the notation Main Menu⇨ Internet⇨Mozilla Web Browser to denote the menu selection sequence that you use to select the Web browser, as shown in Figure 1-6.

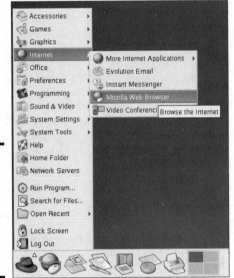

Figure 1-6:
Click the
Main Menu
button and
mouse over
to view the
program
menus.

As the first menu in the hierarchy, the Programs item gives you access to all the applications and utilities in Red Hat Linux. These are organized into the menu categories you see in the next menu pane:

✦ **Accessories:** This menu gives you access to utilities such as a calculator, dictionary, a file archive manager, text editor, and a tool for synchronizing with a Palm or Handspring personal digital assistant (PDA).

✦ **Games:** This menu has a selection of — what else? — games.

✦ **Graphics:** This menu has programs such as The GIMP (an Adobe Photoshop–like program), a digital camera interface, a scanner interface, and an Adobe Acrobat viewer.

✦ **Internet:** This menu is for Internet applications such as the Mozilla Web browsers, the Ximian Evolution e-mail and personal information-management (PIM) software, and the Gaim AOL Instant Messenger client.

✦ **Office:** This menu brings up a menu of the OpenOffice.org office applications that include Write word processor, Calc spreadsheet, Draw drawing program, Impress slide presentation program, and several other applications.

✦ **Preferences:** This menu has utilities that you can use to configure various aspects of the GNOME desktop.

✦ **Programming:** This menu lets you start some software-development tools, such as a programmer's editor (Emacs).

✦ **Sound & Video:** This menu has multimedia applications, such as CD player, sound recorder, and volume control.

✦ **System Settings:** This menu has system configuration utilities that you can use to perform many system administration tasks, such as add user accounts and set the date and time.

System Settings also gives you access to the Server Settings submenu; here you can configure and manage the servers — such as the Web server, Domain Name System (DNS) server, and Network File System (NFS) server. You can also configure various servers to start automatically at system startup.

✦ **System Tools:** This is the menu where you find system-management utilities, such as floppy formatter, system monitor, Internet configuration wizard, system log viewer, and a terminal.

The other menu items on Main Menu are for some commonly performed tasks. Here's what they do:

✦ Main Menu➪Help brings up the GNOME help browser.

✦ Main Menu➪Home Folder opens your home directory in the Nautilus file manager.

✦ Main Menu➪Network Servers displays your network servers in the Nautilus file manager. You can access any Windows servers on your network from this Nautilus window.

✦ Main Menu➪Run Program displays a dialog box where you can enter the name of a program to run and then click Run to start that program.

✦ Main Menu➪Search for Files runs a search tool from which you can search for files.

✦ Main Menu➪Lock Screen starts the screen saver and locks the screen.

✦ Main Menu➪Log Out logs you out (you get a chance to confirm whether you really want to log out or not).

Okay. That's all I'm telling you. You'll use the Main Menu a lot as you use Red Hat Linux. Even if it seems too much initially, it'll all become very familiar as you spend more time with Red Hat Linux.

Applets

Applets are small programs that run inside the GNOME panel. What that means is that the applets do some useful tasks and then display some interesting information on the panel. For example, the date and time display on the right edge of the panel is the output of the Clock applet. You can launch an applet from the menus that appear when you right-click an empty area of the panel. Applets are really handy when you want to monitor some information or just want a convenient way to run some application.

One of the interesting utility applets is Weather Report. Assuming that your Red Hat Linux PC has an Internet connection, this applet downloads the weather and displays it. You can set up your geographic location in the applet.

To add the Weather Report applet to the panel, right-click an empty area of the panel and select Add to Panel⇨Accessories⇨Weather Report. Figure 1-7 shows the menu from which you select the GNOME Weather Report.

Figure 1-7:
You can
select
applets
by right-
clicking on
the GNOME
panel and
choosing
Add to
Panel.

After the Weather Report applet runs, it initially appears in the middle of the empty area in the panel. Right-click the icon and select Move. Then you can position it where you want it on the panel.

To set the geographic location in the Weather report applet, right-click and select Preferences. The Weather Preferences menu appears, as shown in Figure 1-8.

Figure 1-8:
Set the geographic location from the Weather Preferences menu.

Book II
Chapter 1

Exploring GNOME

For U.S. locations, scroll down to your state and click the plus sign. Then select your location from the list and click OK. Then right-click the GNOME Weather Report applet icon and select Update. The applet should now display the weather for your location. Figure 1-9 shows a typical weather display by the Weather Report applet.

Figure 1-9:
The Weather Report applet displays weather information on the panel.

If you don't want the applet anymore, right-click and choose Remove from Panel from the menu.

GNOME has many more applets (over 20, in fact) to try out. There is almost a cottage industry of applets. For example, refer to Figure 1-7: The first menu shows five categories of applets and a number of button applets such as the Log Out button and the Lock button. Table 1-4 gives you an overview of the applets in these categories.

If any applet listed in Table 1-4 strikes your fancy, go ahead and try it out. To find an applet, right-click an empty area of the panel, choose Add to Panel, and then look in the appropriate category menu.

Table 1-4	GNOME Applets
Applet	*What It Does*
Accessories	
Clock	Displays the current time (and date, when you mouse over the applet).
Dictionary Lookup	Displays a small text input area and a Lookup button so you can type a word and look up its meaning by using the GNOME Dictionary program.
Stock Ticker	Displays stock quotes in a scrolling stock ticker.
Weather Report	Displays weather information.
Amusements	
Fish	Displays a small fish.
Geyes	A pair of eyes that follows your mouse around the screen.
Internet	
Inbox Monitor	Checks for e-mail and lets you know when you have new mail.
Modem Lights	Provides an interface for dialing out with the modem and viewing status information about the modem when you're using it.
Terminal Server Client	Runs an application that can connect as a client to Microsoft Windows 2000 Terminal Server and display a remote desktop from that server (available only if you install the `tsclient` package).
Wireless Link Monitor	Displays the status of your PC's wireless link, provided you have a wireless link up and running.
Multimedia	
CD Player	Provides the user interface for a CD player.
Volume Control	Provides an interface for controlling sound volume and launching an audio mixer application.
Utility	
Battery Charge Monitor	Displays the charge status of your laptop's battery (so this applet is for laptops only).
Character Palette	Shows accented versions of a character (you type the character) so that you can copy and paste it into documents.
Command Line	Adds a small command line where you can type Linux commands.
Disk Mounter	Displays a disk drive icon that you can click to access a drive.
Keyboard Layout Switcher	Displays an icon through which you can switch the keyboard layout from one country to another.

Applet	What It Does
Utility	
Notification Area	Sets up an area where notification icons appear.
Pilot Applet	Displays an icon for synchronizing your Palm Pilot with the Red Hat Linux system.
Show Desktop Button	Displays a button that lets you hide all windows and show the desktop.
System Monitor	Shows you how busy your PC is.
Window List	Displays buttons for each of the running applications.
Workspace Switcher	Displays a rectangle that contains four small rectangular areas, each representing a virtual desktop that you can click to switch to that virtual desktop.
Launchers	
Launcher...	Brings up a dialog box from where you can set up a new launcher — an icon on the panel that acts as a shortcut to an application.
Launcher from menu	Provides access to the entire Main Menu hierarchy from which you can pick a program and create a launcher for that program on the panel.
Other	
Button	Brings up a list from which you can select a button to add to the panel (the buttons enable the user to perform specific tasks such as log out, lock the screen, take a screenshot, perform a search, and run a command).
Main Menu	Adds a Main Menu button to the panel (this is the Red Hat button from which you can access the entire menu hierarchy and start any application).
Drawer	Adds a drawer, which acts as a storage area for other applets (it looks like a real drawer — you can open and close it by clicking).

**Book II
Chapter 1**

Exploring GNOME

Using the Nautilus Shell

The Nautilus file manager, or more accurately *graphical shell*, is intuitive to use — it's similar to the Windows Active Desktop. You can manage files and folders and also manage your system with Nautilus.

Viewing files and folders

When you double-click a file or a folder, Nautilus starts automatically. For example, double-click the home icon in the upper-left corner of the GNOME desktop. Nautilus runs and displays the contents of your home directory (think of a *directory* as a folder that can contain other files and folders). If you want to see the folders you're browsing, choose View⇨Side Pane from the Nautilus menu. Figure 1-10 shows a typical user's home directory in the Nautilus file manager after you choose View⇨Side Pane.

With the side pane open, the Nautilus window is vertically divided into two parts. The left window shows different views of the file system and other objects that you can browse with Nautilus. The right window shows the files and folders in the currently selected folder in the left window. Nautilus displays icons for files and folders. For image files, it shows a thumbnail of the image.

The Nautilus window's title bar shows the name of the currently selected folder. The Location text box along the top of the window shows the full name of the directory in Linuxspeak — in this case, Figure 1-10 is showing the contents of the /home/naba directory.

If you have used Windows Explorer, you can use Nautilus in a similar manner. To view the contents of another directory, do the following:

1. **Choose Tree from the Information drop-down menu (located in the left window).**

   A tree menu of directories appears in that window. Initially the tree shows the root directory as a folder labeled /.

2. **Click the right arrow next to the / folder; in the resulting tree view, locate the directory you want to browse.**

   For example, to look at the /etc directory, click the right arrow next to the /etc directory. This causes Nautilus to display the subdirectories in /etc and to change the right arrow to a down arrow. X11 is one of the subdirectories in /etc that you'd view in the next step.

3. **To view the contents of the X11 subdirectory, click X11.**

   The window on the right now shows the contents of the /etc/X11 directory, as shown in Figure 1-11.

Nautilus displays the contents of the selected directory using different types of icons. Each directory appears as a folder, with the name of the directory shown underneath the folder icon. Ordinary files, such as XF86Config, appear as a sheet of paper. The file named X is a link to an executable file. The prefdm file is another executable file.

The Nautilus window has the usual menu bar and a toolbar. Notice the View as Icons button in Figure 1-11 on the right side of the toolbar. That means Nautilus is displaying the directory contents using large icons. Click the button, and a drop-down list appears. Select View as List from the list; this causes Nautilus to display the contents by using smaller icons in a list format, along with detailed information, such as the size of each file or directory and the time when each was last modified, as shown in Figure 1-12.

Figure 1-10:
You can view files and folders in Nautilus.

Figure 1-11:
The Nautilus file manager shows the contents of the /etc/X11 directory.

Figure 1-12:
The Nautilus file manager shows a list view of the /etc/X11 directory.

If you click any of the column headings — File Name, Size, Type, or Date Modified — along the top of the list view, Nautilus sorts the list according to that column. For example, click the Date Modified column heading. Nautilus now displays the list of files and directories sorted according to the time of their last modification. Clicking the File Name column heading sorts the files and folders alphabetically.

Not only can you move around different folders using Nautilus, you can also do things like move a file from one folder to another or delete a file. I won't outline each step because they are intuitive and similar to what you'd do in any GUI such as Windows or Mac. Here are some of the things you can do in Nautilus:

✦ To move a file to a different folder, drag and drop the file's icon on the folder where you want the file.

✦ To copy a file to a new location, select the file's icon and choose Edit⇨Copy File from the Nautilus menu. You can also right-click the file's icon and choose Copy File from the pop-up menu. Then move to the folder where you want to copy the file and choose Edit⇨Paste Files.

✦ To delete a file or directory, right-click the icon, and choose Move to Trash from the pop-up menu (you can do this only if you have permission to delete the file). To permanently delete the file, right-click the Trash icon on the desktop, and choose Empty Trash from the pop-up menu. Of course, do this only if you really want to delete the file. If you have to retrieve a file from Trash, double-click the Trash icon and then drag the file's icon back to the folder where you want to save it. You can retrieve a file from Trash until you empty the Trash.

✦ To rename a file or a directory, right-click the icon and choose Rename from the pop-up menu. Then you can type the new name or edit the name.

✦ To create a new folder, right-click in an empty area of the window on the right and choose New Folder from the pop-up menu. After the new folder icon appears, you can rename it by right-clicking and choosing Rename from the pop-up menu. If you don't have permission to create a folder, that menu item is grayed out.

Configuring GNOME

To configure GNOME (as well as other parts of Red Hat Linux), simply double-click on the map and compass Start Here icon (yes, the icons are hard to identify, but you can see the label). Figure 1-13 shows the resulting Nautilus window.

Figure 1-13:
You can configure the desktop and the system from the Start Here window.

This Nautilus window looks somewhat like the Control Panel in Microsoft Windows. As in the Windows Control Panel, you do many things from the Start Here window.

To configure the GNOME desktop from the window shown in Figure 1-13, do the following:

1. **Double-click the Preferences icon.**

Nautilus displays the Preferences window, shown in Figure 1-14, where you can configure many different items.

Figure 1-14: Indicate your preferences in this window.

2. **To select a background, double-click the Background icon.**

Nautilus launches the Background Preferences dialog box (Figure 1-15).

Figure 1-15: Select a background color or wallpaper from this dialog box.

In this dialog box, you can now select a background color or wallpaper (an image used as background) for the desktop:

a. **To pick wallpaper, click the Select Picture button in the upper-left corner of the window (refer to Figure 1-15) and go through the directories to select any JPEG file as the wallpaper.**

b. **Pick one of the images in the** /usr/share/wallpaper **directory, and then click OK; click Close to exit out of the dialog box.**

Figure 1-16 shows the GNOME desktop after I selected the alien-night.jpg file as the background.

3. **If you want to configure other aspects of the GNOME desktop or Red Hat Linux, simply double-click one of the icons in Figure 1-14 and give it a try. When you're done, click the X button in the upper-right corner of the Preferences window to exit.**

Figure 1-16:
The GNOME desktop looks more appealing with a new wallpaper.

Chapter 2: Exploring KDE

KDE (pronounced *kay-dee-ee*) is a GUI for Red Hat Linux. KDE is similar to Microsoft Windows, but it plays a different role: Unlike Microsoft Windows, which is also an operating system, KDE is just a GUI that runs on the Linux operating system. From your perspective, this means that if you don't like KDE, all you have to do is log out and then log back in with the other GUI — GNOME. (Try doing that with Microsoft Windows! On second thought, don't.)

The best way to get the feel for KDE is to explore it as a user. I give you a brief guided tour of KDE in this chapter. Then you can continue to explore and learn more as you continue to use KDE.

By the way, KDE is developed independent of Linux. In fact, KDE runs on other UNIX operating systems besides Linux. Visit the KDE home page at www.kde.org to keep up with KDE news.

Taking Stock of KDE

KDE is a complete desktop environment for users, but it is also a programming environment for developers. Here are some key facts about KDE:

✦ KDE is written in C++ and uses object-oriented development.

✦ KDE includes a GUI toolkit so that developers can write GUI applications using the toolkit.

✦ KDE supports an *object model* — software components that can interact with each other.

✦ KDE includes an office application suite. The office suite, KOffice, includes a spreadsheet (KSpread), a FrameMaker-like word processor (KWord), a presentation application (KPresenter), and a drawing program (KIllustrator). Red Hat has decided, however, to install and set up only the OpenOffice.org applications in KDE.

✦ KDE supports internationalization, and most KDE applications have been translated into over 25 languages.

Okay, you get the idea. KDE is not just a pretty face — there's some pretty powerful machinery underneath that polished exterior.

KDE desktop

If you have both GNOME and KDE installed on your system, you can select which GUI you want just before you log in. To select a KDE session, follow these steps:

1. **Click Session at the bottom of the graphical login screen (shown in Figure 2-1).**

A dialog box appears with a list of sessions.

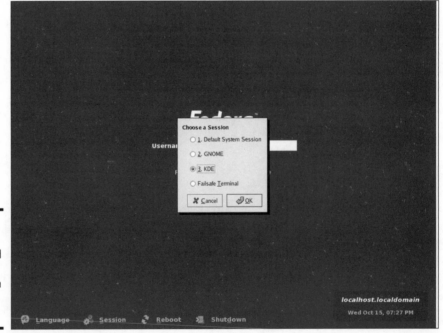

Figure 2-1:
Click
Session and
then click
KDE to get a
KDE
desktop.

2. **Click the KDE radio button in the dialog box, and then click OK to continue.**

3. **Type your user name and password to log in as usual.**

After that a screen (Figure 2-2) shows the progress as KDE starts up.

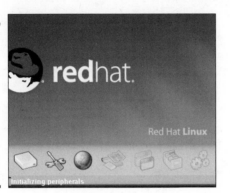

Figure 2-2:
This screen
shows
progress
as the
graphical
desktop
gets ready
for
business.

The initial KDE desktop (Figure 2-3) looks like any other popular GUI such as Microsoft Windows or Apple's Mac. More importantly, KDE desktop now looks surprisingly similar to the GNOME desktop (it didn't use to). This is no accident — Red Hat wanted to make it easier on us poor users by adopting a similar look and feel for both GNOME and KDE.

The KDE desktop shows icons for your folder, a trashcan for deleted files, and an icon for the floppy-disk drive. You also find a Start Here shortcut that you can use to configure the KDE desktop (and much more).

The other major feature of the KDE desktop is the bar along the bottom: the KDE panel, or simply, *the panel*. Similar to the Windows task bar, the panel has buttons for various applications, as well as a date-and-time display to the right. The middle part of the panel shows buttons for any applications you've started (or that were automatically started).

Figure 2-3:
The KDE
desktop
looks like
other
popular GUI
desktops.

Desktop pop-up menus

Right-click a clear area on the KDE desktop and a menu pops up (as in
Figure 2-4).

Figure 2-4:
Right-click
the KDE
desktop for
this pop-up
menu.

From this desktop menu, you can do a whole lot of things. You can create
items on the desktop — from directories and documents to icons for accessing the CD-ROM drive. You can also arrange the icons, lock the screen (if
you are stepping away from the PC for a while), or log out.

Desktop menu options with a right-pointing arrow have other menus that appear when you put the mouse pointer over the arrow. For example, Figure 2-4 shows the menu that appears when you mouse over Create New. You get to select what exactly you want to create on the desktop.

Table 2-1 explains what each menu option does. The menu items that don't apply are grayed out. Go ahead and click some of these menu options and see what happens. If you create some folders and other icons on the desktop now, you can always delete them later.

Table 2-1	KDE Desktop Menu Options
When You Select This Option	*It Does the Following*
Create New	Pops up another menu, from which you can select what you want to create — a directory, various types of documents, a shortcut to a device, or a Web site.
Bookmarks	Starts the bookmark editor.
Undo	Reverses a previous move, cut, or paste operation performed on a desktop item.
Paste	Pastes a previously cut or copied item.
Open Terminal	Opens a terminal window where you can type Linux commands.
Run Command	Prompts for a Linux command to run and then runs it (if you click Run).
Icons	Brings up another menu from which you can line up the desktop icons and arrange them in various ways.
Windows	Displays a menu from which you can *cascade* (put windows on top of each other with a slight offset between successive windows) or unclutter the windows currently appearing on the desktop.
Refresh Desktop	Redraws the desktop (gets rid of any glitches, such as a badly behaved program that leaves behind a mess on the desktop).
Configure Desktop	Starts the KDE Control Center, where you can customize the desktop (including which menu pops up when you click each of your mouse buttons).
Help	Opens the KDE Help Center window.
Lock Screen	Starts the screen saver and locks the screen (you have to type the password to get out of the screen-saver mode).
Logout	Lets you log out.

If your mouse has three buttons (or a wheel) and it's set up correctly in the X Window System, try using the middle mouse button to click an empty area of the KDE desktop (you can also scroll with the wheel in a wheel mouse, but only in windows that have something to scroll). You should see another menu. By default, such a *middle-click* brings up a menu with a list of currently open windows and the desktops. You can then click an item to switch to that window or desktop. If nothing happens when you middle-click, don't worry — you can still get to everything in KDE.

Icon pop-up menus

Right-clicking any desktop icon causes another menu to appear. Many items on this pop-up menu are the same no matter what icon you click — but right-clicking certain icons (for example, the Trash icon) will produce a somewhat different menu. Figure 2-5 shows the menu that appears when you right-click the Home folder icon.

Figure 2-5:
Right-click
an icon on
the KDE
desktop for
this type of
pop-up
menu.

Table 2-2 offers an overview of common menu options in the icon pop-up menus. As you'd expect, any menu option that does not apply is grayed out.

I bet you see a pattern here. It's the right-click. No matter where you are in KDE, *always right-click before you pick.* You're bound to find something useful when you right-click!

Note: If you simply rest the mouse pointer on a desktop icon, KDE displays a pop-up window with detailed information about that icon.

Table 2-2	KDE Icon Menu Options
When You Select This Option	*It Does the Following*
Open	Opens the file in a new Konqueror window. (Konqueror is the file manager-cum-Web browser in KDE.)
Undo	Reverses the last copy, cut, or paste operation, assuming you had just performed one of these operations.

When You Select This Option	It Does the Following
Cut	Cuts information about the icon and displays a menu with options such as e-mailing the item or editing its contents.
Copy	Copies information about the icon and displays a menu with options such as e-mailing the item or editing its contents.
Rename	Renames the icon (you have to enter the new name).
Move to Trash	Asks whether you want to move the icon to Trash (and does so if you say yes).
Delete	Asks whether you really want to delete the icon (and does so if you say yes).
Add to Bookmarks	Adds information about the icon to the bookmarks.
Open With...	Opens a dialog box where you can select an application in which to open the item that the icon represents.
Copy To	Displays another menu from which you can select the location where you want to copy the item that the icon represents.
Move To	Displays another menu from which you can select the location where you want to move the item that the icon represents.
Edit File Type	Brings up a file type editor where you can edit some information about the icon.
Properties	Displays the properties of the icon.

**Book II
Chapter 2**

Exploring KDE

Using the KDE Panel

The KDE panel is the long bar that stretches across the bottom of the KDE desktop. Figure 2-6 shows a typical view of the panel.

The panel has a lot of icons. Some of these icons start programs when you click them. Some show status information (such as which programs are currently running), as well other information such as date and time.

Starting at the left, the Red Hat icon is what KDE documentation calls the *K button* — it's like the Start button in Microsoft Windows. Then come a slew of icons that start various programs.

Figure 2-6:
This is a
typical view
of the KDE
panel.

When you mouse over an icon, a small help balloon pops up and gives you a helpful hint about the icon. For some icons, the balloon-help hint is quite useful. For others, it may be just the name of a KDE application (all of which usually start with a *K*). The name may or may not tell you something useful right off the bat. After you use KDE for a while, you recognize the names; in the meantime, balloon help provides gentle reminders of what each icon does.

To the right of these application icons, you see the Desktop Pager icon. That icon shows four small rectangles, numbered 1 through 4. Each rectangle represents a virtual desktop. Click a number to switch to that virtual desktop. This feature makes it seem like you have four separate desktops to work with. To be honest, I end up using only one desktop, but it's nice to know that the others are there if I ever need them. On the other hand, if you're writing code and preparing a user's guide for a new program, you could use one desktop for all the coding work and a second desktop for writing the user's guide. You can, of course, switch from one desktop to the other with a single mouse click.

The panel task bar appears to the right of the virtual Desktop Pager icon. The task bar displays a button for each running application in a rectangular area on the panel. You can click a button to reduce that application to an icon or to switch to that application.

The rightmost item on the panel is a digital clock that displays the current time. If you move the mouse over the time and then pause, the date appears in a small pop-up window. Right-clicking the clock brings up a menu from which you can adjust the date and time.

Now a little bit of technical detail about the panel and the icons. The panel itself is a KDE application called *the Kicker*. Each of its icons is either a button or an applet. The buttons start applications or perform special functions such as hiding all open windows. The applets are little applications (also called *plugins*). The applets run in the panel and do useful things (such as displaying the current date and time).

If you right-click any icon — or right-click anywhere on the panel — you get a pop-up menu where you can do something relevant to that icon (such as move it or remove it entirely). You can also set some preferences and add more buttons and applets to the panel.

The Main Menu

The leftmost icon on the KDE panel is what KDE documentation calls the K Menu button. (Now that Red Hat made both GNOME and KDE panels look about the same, I call this the Main Menu button). That's where you'll find everything you want to run in Red Hat Linux. In this section, I provide an overview of the Main Menu and point out some interesting items. You can then do further exploration yourself.

Click the Main Menu button to bring up the first level menu. Then mouse over any menu item with an arrow to bring the next level menu and so on. You can go through a menu hierarchy and make selections from the final menu.

A word about the way I refer to a menu selection. I use the notation Main Menu⇨Internet⇨Evolution Email to indicate the menu selection sequence that you'd use to select the mail reader (Figure 2-7). Similarly, I would say choose Main Menu⇨Internet⇨Mozilla Web Browser to start the Mozilla Web browser. You get the idea.

Figure 2-7: Click the Main Menu button and mouse over items to view the menu hierarchy.

In the first menu in the hierarchy, the first dozen or so items (from the top) give you access to all the applications and utilities in Red Hat Linux. Moving the mouse pointer over each of these brings up other menus, from which you can pick an application or utility to run. In the following list, I describe the menu categories you see in the first menu pane of the Main Menu. (Additional categories may appear if you install other software packages on your system.)

✦ **Accessories:** This menu has a host of utility programs, such as a scientific calculator, character selector, floppy formatter, dictionary, Palm Pilot or Handspring sync, and so on.

✦ **Games:** This menu brings up a menu of what else, games (and a whole lot of them at that).

✦ **Graphics:** This menu has programs such as the GIMP (an Adobe Photoshop–like program), a digital camera interface, a scanner interface, a screen capture program, and an Adobe Acrobat viewer.

✦ **Internet:** This menu (refer to Figure 2-7) is for Internet applications, such as the Web browser, e-mail reader, and Instant Messenger.

✦ **Office:** This menu brings up a menu of applications from the OpenOffice.org office suite (includes Writer word processor, Calc spreadsheet, Impress slide-presentation program, Draw drawing program, and much more).

✦ **Preferences:** This menu brings up another menu from which you can configure many aspects of the system. In particular, Preferences⇨ Desktop Settings Wizard gives you the option to customize the appearance and the behavior of the KDE desktop. You can also change your password from the Preferences⇨Password menu.

✦ **Programming:** This menu lets you run software development tools, such as the Emacs editor and the KDE development environment (KDevelop), provided you've installed these tools.

✦ **Sound & Video:** This menu has multimedia applications such as CD player, sound mixer, sound recorder, and volume control.

✦ **System Settings:** This menu lists over 15 tools for setting up your Red Hat Linux system. It includes tools for managing user accounts, configuring printers, and changing the `root` password. The **Server Settings** submenu provides access to tools for configuring the Web server, Domain Name System (DNS) server, and Network File System (NFS) server. You can also turn various services on or off from this menu.

✦ **System Tools:** This menu has a number of tools for performing tasks such as configuring the Internet connection, viewing the system logs, registering with the Red Hat Network, and opening a terminal window where you can type Linux commands.

The **More System Tools** submenu enables you to run many more tools, including a CD Writer, boot disk creator, Desktop Switching Tool, IBM 3278 terminal, and many more.

✦ **Control Center:** This item opens the KDE Control Center window from which you can configure the KDE desktop (in addition to what you can do from the Preferences menu).

✦ **Find Files:** This item brings up the Find Files tool from which you can search for files in your system.

✦ **Help:** This item starts the KDE Help Center — the online help in KDE.

✦ **Home:** This item displays the contents of your home folder in a Konqueror file-manager window.

✦ **Run Command:** This item displays a dialog box where you can enter the name of a program to run.

✦ **Lock Screen:** This item starts the screensaver and locks the screen so that you can leave your workstation temporarily. When you want to return to the desktop, KDE prompts you for your password (Figure 2-8).

✦ **Logout:** This item does just what it says — it logs you out (of course, only after you confirm that you *really want* to log out).

Figure 2-8:
KDE prompts for a password before opening a locked screen.

Enter Password
Naba Barkakati (naba)

Okay. That's all I'm telling you about KDE's Main Menu. You'll use the Main Menu a lot as you use Red Hat Linux. Even if it seems a bit much initially, you'll become very familiar with the menus as you spend more time using Red Hat Linux.

Applets

Applets are small programs that run inside the KDE panel. You can launch an applet by right-clicking an empty area of the KDE panel and choosing Add⇨Applet from the pop-up menu. Applets are really handy when you want to monitor some information, or just want a convenient way to run some applications.

One of the interesting applets is Dictionary. This applet displays a text-entry area on the panel. You can type a word and press Enter to look up its definition. Assuming that your Red Hat Linux PC has an Internet connection, this applet connects to the server `dict.org` and downloads a definition for the word you typed and displays it in a new window.

To add the Dictionary applet to the panel, right-click in an empty area of the KDE panel and choose Add⇨Applet⇨Dictionary. Figure 2-9 shows the menu hierarchy from which you select Dictionary.

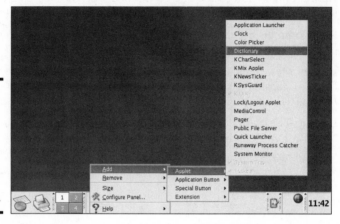

Figure 2-9: Here's where you can add applets to the panel from the Main Menu.

The Dictionary applet starts and displays a text-entry area (as in Figure 2-10) on the panel.

Figure 2-10: The Dictionary applet displays a text-entry area on the panel for looking up definitions of words.

To look up a word in the dictionary, click the text-entry area and type the word. Then press Enter. The Dictionary applet downloads the definition of the word from `dict.org` and displays the results in a new window. For example, Figure 2-11 displays the result of looking up the word *proffer*.

**Book II
Chapter 2**

Exploring KDE

Figure 2-11:
The
Dictionary
applet
displays the
definition
of words
in a new
window.

If you don't want the applet anymore, remove it: Right-click an empty area of the KDE panel and choose Remove⇨Applet⇨Dictionary.

KDE has many more applets (over 15, but who's counting?) that you can try. Their names show up in the Applet menu in Figure 2-9. (The grayed-out items are applets that are already running and can only be started once.) Table 2-3 gives you an overview of the applets in KDE.

If any applet listed in Table 2-3 strikes your fancy, try it. To find an applet, right-click an empty part of the KDE panel, choose Add⇨Applet, and then click the applet's name.

Table 2-3	KDE Applet Overview
Applet	*What It Does*
Application Launcher	Adds a small command line where you can type a Linux command and run it.
Clock	Displays the current time in a small digital clock and shows the date underneath.
Color Picker	Shows a dropper icon you can use to pick a color from anywhere on the desktop (you can then copy that color value to other configuration files).
Dictionary	Adds a small text-entry area where you can type a word and look it up in a dictionary (results appear in a new window).

(continued)

Table 2-3 *(continued)*

Applet	What It Does
KCharSelect	Shows accented versions of characters you can copy and paste into documents.
KMix Applet	Provides an interface for controlling sound volume and launching an audio-mixer application.
KNewsTicker	Displays the latest news from various sources (such as www.slashdot.org and dot.kde.org) in a scrolling ticker.
KSysGuard	Gathers and plots CPU and memory-usage information from one or more systems on a network (used to monitor servers).
Klipper	Provides a clipboard utility for cutting and pasting information.
Lock/Logout Applet	Provides two icons — a lock icon to lock the screen and an off switch to log out.
MediaControl	Displays a control panel for audio and video players.
Pager	Shows a view of the virtual desktops; use it to switch from one desktop to another (this applet is already running when you first log in).
Public File Server	Provides a public Web server (you can configure the directory that is being shared and the rate of data transfer).
Quick Launcher	Holds small icons for many applications (clicking an icon launches that application).
Runway Process Catcher	Shows a smiley face that turns angry when any process starts using too much CPU time or memory.
System Monitor	Graphically shows the amount of system resources (memory, CPU time) being used.
System Tray	Provides an area that can hold special applications such as Klipper.
Taskbar	Displays a button for each running application (this applet is already running when you first log in).

Using Konqueror

Konqueror is a file manager as well as a Web browser. It's intuitive to use — somewhat similar to the Windows Active Desktop. You can manage files and folders (and also view Web pages) with Konqueror.

Viewing files and folders

When you double-click a folder icon on the desktop, Konqueror starts automatically. For example, double-click the home icon in the upper-left corner of the KDE desktop. Konqueror runs and displays the contents of your home directory (think of a *directory* as a folder that can contain other files and folders). Figure 2-12 shows a typical user's home directory in Konqueror.

If you have used Windows Explorer, you can use Konqueror in a similar manner.

The Konqueror window is vertically divided into three parts:

✦ A narrow left window shows icons you can click to perform various tasks in Konqueror.

✦ The wider middle window shows a tree view of the current folder.

✦ The widest window (at the right) uses icons to show the files and folders in the current folder.

Konqueror uses different types of icons for different files and shows a preview of each file's contents. For image files, the preview is a thumbnail version of the image.

The Konqueror window's title bar shows the name of the currently selected directory. The Location text box (along the top of the window) shows the full name of the directory, using Konqueror terminology — in this case, Figure 2-12 shows the contents of the /home/naba directory.

Book II
Chapter 2

Exploring KDE

Figure 2-12:
You can
view
files and
folders in
Konqueror.

Between the left and right windows, the vertical row of buttons is for selecting other things to browse. When you click one of these buttons, the left window displays a tree menu of items you can browse. For example, to browse other parts of the file system, do the following:

1. **From the leftmost vertical column of icons in the Konqueror window (refer to Figure 2-12), click the Folder icon (the one that appears just above the star-shaped icon).**

   A tree menu of directories appears in the middle window.

2. **In the tree view, locate the folder you want to browse.**

   For example, to look at the etc folder, click the plus sign next to the etc folder. Konqueror displays the other folders in etc and changes the plus sign to a minus sign.

3. **To view the contents of the X11 subdirectory, scroll down and click X11.**

   The window on the right now shows the contents of the /etc/X11 directory, as shown in Figure 2-13.

Konqueror displays the contents of a folder using different types of icons. Each directory appears as a folder, with the name of the directory shown underneath the folder icon. Ordinary files, such as XF86Config, appear as a sheet of paper. The file named X is a shortcut to an executable file. The prefdm file is another executable file.

The Konqueror window has the usual menu bar and a toolbar. You can view the files and folders in other formats as well. For example, choose View⇨View Mode⇨Detailed List View to see the folder's contents using smaller icons in a list format (Figure 2-14), along with detailed information (such as the size of each file or directory, and at what time each was last modified).

Figure 2-13: Konqueror shows the contents of the /etc/X11 directory.

Figure 2-14: Konqueror shows a detailed list view of the /etc/X11 directory.

If you click any of the column headings — Name, Size, File Type, or Modified — along the top of the list view, Konqueror sorts the list according to that column. For example, click the Modified column heading, and Konqueror displays the list of files and folders sorted according to the time of last modification. Clicking the Name column heading sorts the files and directories alphabetically.

Not only can you move around different folders using Konqueror, you can also do things like move a file from one folder to another or delete a file. I won't outline each step because the steps are intuitive and similar to what you'd do in any GUI (such as Windows or the Mac interface). Here are some things you can do in Konqueror:

✦ **View a text file:** Click the filename and Konqueror runs the KWrite word processor, displaying the file in a new window.

✦ **Copy or move a file to a different folder:** Drag and drop the file's icon on the folder where you want the file to go. A menu pops up and asks you whether you want to copy, move, or simply link the file to that directory.

✦ **Delete a file or directory:** Right-click the icon, and choose Move to Trash from the pop-up menu. To permanently delete the file, right-click the Trashcan icon on the desktop, and choose Empty Trash from the pop-up menu. Of course, do this only if you really want to delete the file.

If you want to recover a file from the trash, double-click the Trashcan icon on the desktop and from that window drag and drop the file icon into the folder where you want to save the file. When asked whether you want to copy or move, select move. You can recover files from the trash until the moment you empty the trash.

✦ **Rename a file or a directory:** Right-click the icon, and choose Rename from the pop-up menu. Then you can type the new name or edit the old name.

✦ **Create a new folder:** Right-click in an empty area of the window on the right and choose Create New⇨Directory from the pop-up menu. Then type the name of the new directory and click OK. (If you don't have permission to create a directory, you get an error message.)

Viewing Web pages

Konqueror is much more than a file manager. With it, you can view a Web page as easily as you would view a folder. Just type a Web address in the Location box and see what happens. For example, Figure 2-15 shows the Konqueror window after I typed `www.irs.gov` in the Location text box on the toolbar and pressed Enter.

Figure 2-15: Konqueror can browse the Web as well.

Konqueror displays the Web site in the window on the right. The left window still shows whatever it was displaying earlier.

Configuring KDE

There are many ways to configure the KDE desktop, but I use the KDE Control Center for one-stop-shopping KDE configuration. Choose Main Menu⇨Control Center. The Control Center starts and shows summary information about the Red Hat Linux system in a window (Figure 2-16).

Book II
Chapter 2

Exploring KDE

Figure 2-16:
You can configure the KDE desktop from the KDE Control Center.

The Control Center window is vertically divided into two parts:

✦ The narrower left window shows a tree menu with 10 or so top-level categories of customization that you can perform.

✦ The wider right window is where you enter information.

To customize a specific category such as Appearance & Themes, click the plus sign (+) to the left of the label. The plus sign changes to a minus sign (–), and you get a list of all the items that you can specify. For example, to change the KDE desktop's background from the window shown in Figure 2-16, do the following:

1. **Click the plus sign next to Appearance & Themes; from the new items that appear, double-click Background.**

The Control Center displays the choices for desktop background, using the right window. You can select a background color or *wallpaper* (an image used as background) for your desktop here.

2. **To select wallpaper, click the Wallpaper tab (Figure 2-17) and then click the Browse button next to the name of the current wallpaper.**

   The Control Center brings up the Select Wallpaper dialog box (as in Figure 2-18).

Figure 2-17: Select a background color or wallpaper from this window.

Figure 2-18: Select a wallpaper image from this dialog box.

3. **Click the up arrow on the toolbar to go to the** root **directory.**

4. **In the** root **directory, navigate to** the /usr/share/wallpapers **directory.**

5. **Pick one of the JPEG image files from the list of files, and then click OK.**

6. **When you get back to the Control Center window, click Apply to put the new change into effect.**

   Figure 2-19 shows the KDE desktop after I selected the `alien-night.jpg` file as the wallpaper.

7. **If you want to configure other aspects of the KDE desktop, select another item in the Appearance & Themes list (refer to Figure 2-17) and give it a try.**

   Click Apply to try a new configuration; if you don't like the result, click Reset to revert to the old settings.

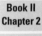

Figure 2-19:
The KDE desktop looks positively sci-fi with the right wallpaper.

Chapter 3: Learning the Shell

In This Chapter

✔ Opening terminal windows and virtual consoles

✔ Using the Bash shell

✔ Learning some Linux commands

✔ Writing shell scripts

Sometimes things just don't work. What do you do if the GUI desktop stops responding to your mouse clicks? What if the GUI won't start at all? You can still tell your Red Hat Linux system what to do, but you'll have to do it by typing commands into a text screen. In these situations, you'd be working with the *shell* — the Linux command interpreter. I introduce the Bash shell (the default shell in Red Hat Linux) in this chapter.

After you learn to work with the shell, you may even begin to like the simplicity and power of the Linux commands. And then, even if you're a GUI aficionado, someday soon you may find yourself firing up a terminal window and making the system sing and dance with two- or three-letter commands strung together by strange punctuation characters. (Hey, I can dream, can't I?)

Opening Terminal Windows and Virtual Consoles

First things first. If you're working in GNOME or KDE, where do you type commands for the shell? Good question.

The easiest way to get to the shell is to open a *terminal* (also called *console*) window. Both GNOME and KDE panels have an icon to open a terminal window. The icon looks like a monitor. Click that icon to get a terminal window. Now you can type commands to your heart's content.

If, for some reason, the GUI seems to be *hung* (you click and type but nothing happens), you can turn to the *virtual consoles*. (The *physical* console is the monitor-and-keyboard combination.) The idea of virtual consoles is to enable you to switch between several text consoles even though you have only one physical console. Whether you are running a GUI or not, you can then use different text consoles to type different commands.

To get to the first virtual console from the GNOME or KDE desktop, press Ctrl+Alt+F1. Press Ctrl+Alt+F2 for the second virtual console, and so on. Each of these virtual consoles is a text screen where you can log in and type Linux commands to perform various tasks. When you're done, type **exit** to log out.

You can use up to six virtual consoles. The seventh one is used for the GUI desktop. To get back to the GUI desktop, press Ctrl+Alt+F7.

Using the Bash Shell

If you've used MS-DOS, you may be familiar with COMMAND.COM, the DOS command interpreter. That program displays the infamous C:\> prompt. In Windows, you can see this prompt if you open a command window. (To open a command window in Microsoft Windows, choose Start⇨Run, type **command** in the text box, and then click OK.)

Red Hat Linux comes with a command interpreter that resembles COMMAND.COM in DOS, but can do a whole lot more. The Red Hat Linux command interpreter is called *shell*.

The default shell in Red Hat Linux is Bash. When you open a terminal window or log in at a text console, the Bash shell is what prompts you for commands. Then, when you type a command, the shell executes your command.

In addition to the standard Linux commands, Bash can execute any computer program. So you can type the name of an application (the name is usually more cryptic than what you see in GNOME or KDE menus) at the shell prompt, and the shell starts that application.

Learning the syntax of shell commands

Because a shell interprets what you type, it is important to know how the shell processes the text that you enter. All shell commands have this general format that starts with a command followed by options (some commands have no options):

```
command option1 option2 ... optionN
```

Such a single on-screen line of command is commonly referred to as a *command line*. On a command line, you enter a command, followed by zero or more options (or *arguments*). These strings of options — the *command-line options* (or command-line arguments) — modify the way the command works so that you can get it to do specific tasks.

The shell uses a blank space or tab to distinguish between the command and options. Naturally, you should help it by using a space or a tab to separate the command from the options and the options from one another.

An option can contain spaces — all you have to do is put that option inside quotation marks so that the spaces are included. For example, to search for my name in the password file, I enter the following `grep` command (`grep` is used for searching for text in files):

```
grep "Naba Barkakati" /etc/passwd
```

When `grep` prints the line with my name, it looks like this:

```
naba:x:500:500:Naba Barkakati:/home/naba:/bin/bash
```

If you created a user account with your user name, type the `grep` command with your user name as an argument.

In the output from the `grep` command, you can see the name of the shell (`/bin/bash`) following the last colon (`:`).

The number of command-line options and their format, of course, depends on the actual command. Typically, these options look like `-X`, where `X` is a single character. For example, the `ls` command lists the contents of a directory. You can use the `-l` option to see more details, like this:

```
[ashley@dhcppc4 ashley]$ ls -l
total 8
drwxrwxr-x   2 ashley    ashley     4096 Jun 29 13:35 Directory
drwx------   7 ashley    ashley     4096 Jun 29 11:44 Mail
```

The `[ashley@dhcppc4 ashley]$` part is the shell prompt for the user named `ashley`. On your system, the prompt depends on your user name. When showing examples, I omit the prompt.

If a command is too long to fit on a single line, you can press the backslash (\) key followed by Enter. Then, continue typing the command on the next line. For example, type the following command (press Enter after each line):

```
cat \
/etc/passwd
```

The cat command then displays the contents of the /etc/passwd file.

You can concatenate several shorter commands on a single line. Just separate the commands by semicolons (;). For example, the following command

```
cd; ls -l; pwd
```

changes the current directory to your home directory, lists the contents of that directory, and then shows the name of that directory.

Combining shell commands

You can combine simple shell commands to create a more sophisticated command. Suppose you want to find out whether a device file named sbpcd resides in your system's /dev directory because some documentation says you need that device file for a Sound Blaster Pro CD-ROM drive. You can use the command ls /dev to get a directory listing of the /dev directory and then browse through it to see whether that listing contains sbpcd.

Unfortunately, the /dev directory has a great many entries, so you find it hard to find any item that has sbpcd in its name. You can, however, combine the ls command with grep and come up with a command line that does exactly what you want. Here's that command line:

```
ls /dev | grep sbpcd
```

The shell sends the output of the ls command (the directory listing) to the grep command, which searches for the string sbpcd. That vertical bar (|) is known as a *pipe* because it acts as a conduit (think of a water pipe) between the two programs — the output of the first command is fed into the input of the second one.

Controlling command input and output

Most Linux commands have a common feature — they always read from the standard input (usually, the keyboard) and write to the standard output (usually, the screen). Error messages are sent to the standard error (usually to the screen as well). These three devices often are referred to as stdin, stdout, and stderr.

You can make a command get its input from a file and then send its output to another file. Just so you know, the highfalutin term for this feature is *input and output redirection* or *I/O redirection*.

Getting command input from a file

If you want a command to read from a file, you can redirect the standard input to come from that file instead of the keyboard. For example, type the following command:

```
sort < /etc/passwd
```

This command displays a sorted list of the lines in the /etc/passwd file. In this case, the less-than sign (<) redirects stdin so that the sort command reads its input from the /etc/passwd file.

Saving command output in a file

To save the output of a command in a file, redirect the standard output to a file. For example, type **cd** to change to your home directory and then type the following command:

```
grep typedef /usr/include/* > typedef.out
```

This command searches through all files in the /usr/include directory for the occurrence of the text typedef — and then saves the output in a file called typedef.out. The greater-than sign (>) redirects stdout to a file.

This command also illustrates another feature of Bash. When you use an asterisk (*), Bash replaces the asterisk with a list of all filenames in the specified directory. Thus, /usr/include/* means *all the files in the /usr/include directory.*

Saving error messages in a file

Sometimes you type a command and it generates a whole lot of error messages that scroll by so fast you can't tell what's going on. One way to see all the error messages is to save the error messages in a file so that you can see what happened. You can do that by redirecting stderr to a file.

For example, type the following command:

```
find / -name isapnp -print 2> finderr
```

This command looks throughout the file system for files named isapnp, but saves all the error messages in the file named finderr. The number 2 followed by the greater-than sign (2>) redirects stderr to a file.

If you want to simply discard the error messages instead of saving them in a file, use `/dev/null` as the filename, like this:

```
find / -name isapnp -print 2> /dev/null
```

That `/dev/null` is a special file — often called the *bit bucket* and sometimes glorified as the *Great Bit Bucket in the Sky* — that simply discards whatever it receives. So now you know what they mean when you hear phrases like, "Your mail probably ended up in the bit bucket."

Typing less with automatic command completion

Many commands take a filename as an argument. To view the contents of the text file named `/etc/modules.conf`, for example, type the following command:

```
cat /etc/modules.conf
```

That `cat` command displays the file `/etc/modules.conf`. For any command that takes a filename as an argument, you can use a Bash feature to avoid having to type the whole filename. All you have to type is the bare minimum (just the first few characters) to uniquely identify the file in its directory.

To see an example, type **cat /etc/mod** but don't press Enter; press Tab instead. Bash automatically completes the filename, so the command becomes `cat /etc/modules.conf`. Now press Enter to run the command.

Whenever you type a filename, press Tab after the first few characters of the filename. Bash probably can complete the filename so that you don't have to type the entire name. If you don't enter enough characters to uniquely identify the file, Bash beeps. Just type a few more characters and press Tab again.

Going wild with asterisks and question marks

There's another way to avoid typing long filenames. (After all, making less work for users is the idea of computers, isn't it?)

This particular trick involves using the asterisk (*) and question mark (?) and a few more tricks. These special characters are called *wildcards* because they match zero or more characters in a line of text.

If you know MS-DOS, you may have used commands such as `COPY *.* A:` to copy all files from the current directory to the A drive. Bash accepts similar wildcards in filenames. As you'd expect, Bash provides many more wildcard options than the MS-DOS command interpreter does.

You can use three types of wildcards in Bash:

✦ The **asterisk (*)** character matches zero or more characters in a file-name. That means * denotes all files in a directory.

✦ The **question mark (?)** matches any single character. So if you type `test?`, that matches any five-character text that begins with `test`.

✦ A **set of characters in brackets** matches any single character from that set. The string `[aB]*`, for example, matches any filename that starts with `a` or `B`.

Wildcards are handy when you want to do something to a whole lot of files. For example, to copy all the files from the `/mnt/cdrom` directory to the current directory, type the following:

```
cp /mnt/cdrom/* .
```

Bash replaces the wildcard character * with the names of all the files in the `/mnt/cdrom` directory. The period at the end of the command represents the current directory.

You can use the asterisk with other parts of a filename to select a more specific group of files. Suppose you want to use the `grep` command to search for the text `typedef struct` in all files of the `/usr/include` directory that meet the following criteria:

✦ The filename starts with `s`.

✦ The filename ends with `.h`.

The wildcard specification `s*.h` denotes all filenames that meet these criteria. Thus you can perform the search with the following command:

```
grep "typedef struct" /usr/include/s*.h
```

The string contains a space that you want the `grep` command to find, so you have to enclose that string in quotation marks. That way Bash does not try to interpret each word in that text as a separate command-line argument.

The question mark (?) matches a single character. Suppose that you have four files — `image1.pcx`, `image2.pcx`, `image3.pcx`, and `image4.pcx` — in the current directory. To copy these files to the `/mnt/floppy` directory, use the following command:

```
cp image?.pcx /mnt/floppy
```

Bash replaces the single question mark with any single character, and copies the four files to /mnt.

The third wildcard format — [...] — matches a single character from a specific set of characters enclosed in square brackets. You may want to combine this format with other wildcards to narrow down the matching filenames to a smaller set. To see a list of all filenames in the /etc/X11/xdm directory that start with x or X, type the following command:

```
ls /etc/X11/xdm/[xX]*
```

Repeating previously typed commands

To make it easy for you to repeat long commands, Bash stores up to 500 old commands. Bash keeps a *command history* (a list of old commands). To see the command history, type **history**. Bash displays a numbered list of the old commands, including those that you entered during previous logins.

If the command list is too long, you can limit the number of old commands you want to see. To see only the 10 most recent commands, type this command:

```
history 10
```

To repeat a command from the list that the history command shows, simply type an exclamation point (!), followed by that command's number. To repeat command number 3, type **!3**.

There is a way to repeat an old command without knowing its command number. Suppose you typed more /usr/lib/X11/xdm/xdm-config a few minutes ago, and now you want to look at that file again. To repeat the previous more command, type the following:

```
!more
```

Often, you may want to repeat the last command that you just typed, perhaps with a slight change. For example, you may have displayed the contents of the directory by using the ls -l command. To repeat that command, type two exclamation points as follows:

```
!!
```

Sometimes, you may want to repeat the previous command but add extra arguments to it. Suppose that ls -l shows too many files. Simply repeat that command, but pipe the output through the more command as follows:

```
!! | more
```

Bash replaces the two exclamation points with the previous command and then appends | `more` to that command.

 Here's the easiest way to recall previous commands. Just press the up-arrow key and Bash keeps going backward through the history of commands you previously typed. To move forward in the command history, press the down-arrow key.

Learning Linux Commands

You type Linux commands at the shell prompt. By *Linux commands*, I mean some of the commands that the Bash shell understands as well as the command-line utilities that come with Linux. In this section, I introduce you to a few major categories of Linux commands.

I can't possibly cover all the Linux commands in this chapter, but I want to give you a feel for the breadth of the commands by showing you a list of common Linux commands in Table 3-1. It lists common Linux commands by category. Before you start learning any Linux commands, you should browse this table.

Table 3-1	Overview of Common Linux Commands
Command Name	*Action*
Getting Online Help	
apropos	Finds online manual pages for a specified keyword.
info	Displays online help information about a specified command.
man	Displays online help information.
whatis	Similar to apropos, but searches for complete words only.
Making Commands Easier	
alias	Defines an abbreviation for a long command.
type	Shows the type and location of a command.
unalias	Deletes an abbreviation defined using alias.

(continued)

Table 3-1 *(continued)*

Command Name	Action
Managing Files and Directories	
cd	Changes the current directory.
chmod	Changes file permissions.
chown	Changes file owner and group.
cp	Copies files.
ln	Creates symbolic links to files and directories.
ls	Displays the contents of a directory.
mkdir	Creates a directory.
mv	Renames a file as well as moves a file from one directory to another.
rm	Deletes files.
rmdir	Deletes directories.
pwd	Displays the current directory.
touch	Updates a file's time stamp.
Finding Files	
find	Finds files based on specified criteria such as name, size, and so on.
locate	Finds files using a periodically updated database.
whereis	Finds files based in the typical directories where executable (also known as *binary*) files are located.
which	Finds files in the directories listed in the PATH environment variable.
Processing Files	
cat	Displays a file on standard output (can be used to concatenate several files into one big file).
cut	Extracts specified sections from each line of text in a file.
dd	Copies blocks of data from one file to another (used to copy data from devices).
diff	Compares two text files and finds any differences.

Command Name	Action
Processing Files	
expand	Converts all tabs into spaces.
file	Displays the type of data in a file.
fold	Wraps each line of text to fit a specified width.
grep	Searches for regular expressions within a text file.
less	Displays a text file, one page at a time (can go backward also).
lpr	Prints files.
more	Displays a text file, one page at a time (goes forward only).
nl	Numbers all nonblank lines in a text file and prints the lines to standard output.
paste	Concatenates corresponding lines from several files.
patch	Updates a text file using the differences between the original and revised copy of the file.
sed	Copies a file to standard output while applying specified editing commands.
sort	Sorts lines in a text file.
split	Breaks up a file into several smaller files with specified size.
tac	Reverses a file (last line first and so on).
tail	Displays the last few lines of a file.
tr	Substitutes one group of characters for another throughout a file.
uniq	Eliminates duplicate lines from a text file.
wc	Counts the number of lines, words, and characters in a text file.
zcat	Displays a compressed file (after decompressing).
zless	Displays a compressed file one page at a time (can go backward also).
zmore	Displays a compressed file one page at a time.

(continued)

Table 3-1 *(continued)*

Command Name	Action
Archiving and Compressing Files	
compress	Compresses files.
cpio	Copies files to and from an archive.
gunzip	Decompresses files compressed with GNU ZIP (gzip).
gzip	Compresses files using GNU ZIP.
tar	Creates an archive of files in one or more directories (originally meant for archiving on tape).
uncompress	Decompresses files compressed with compress.
Managing Processes	
bg	Runs an interrupted process in the background.
fg	Runs a process in the foreground.
free	Displays the amount of free and used memory in the system.
halt	Shuts down Linux and halts the computer.
kill	Sends a signal to a process (usually used to terminate a process).
ldd	Displays the shared libraries needed to run a program.
nice	Runs a process with lower priority (referred to as nice mode).
ps	Displays a list of currently running processes.
printenv	Displays the current environment variables.
pstree	Similar to ps, but shows parent-child relationships clearly.
reboot	Stops Linux and then restarts the computer.
shutdown	Shuts down Linux.
top	Displays a list of most processor- and memory-intensive processes.
uname	Displays information about the system and the Linux kernel.

Command Name	Action
Managing Users	
chsh	Changes the shell (command interpreter).
groups	Prints the list of groups that includes a specified user.
id	Displays the user and group ID for a specified user name.
passwd	Changes the password.
su	Starts a new shell as another user or root (when invoked without any argument).
Managing the File System	
df	Summarizes free and available space in all mounted storage devices.
du	Displays disk usage information.
fdformat	Formats a diskette.
fdisk	Partitions a hard disk.
fsck	Checks and repairs a file system.
mkfs	Creates a new file system.
mknod	Creates a device file.
mkswap	Creates a swap space for Linux in a file or a disk partition.
mount	Mounts a device (for example, the CD-ROM) on a directory in the file system.
swapoff	Deactivates a swap space.
swapon	Activates a swap space.
sync	Writes buffered (saved in memory) data to files.
tty	Displays the device name for the current terminal.
umount	Unmounts a device from the file system.
Working with Date and Time	
cal	Displays a calendar for a specified month or year.
date	Shows the current date and time or sets a new date and time.

Becoming root (superuser)

When you want to do anything that requires a high privilege level (for example, administering your system), you have to become root. Normally you log in as a regular user with your normal user name. When you need the privileges of the superuser, though, use the following command to become root:

```
su -
```

That's su followed by the minus sign (or hyphen). The shell then prompts you for the root password. Type the password and press Enter.

After you're done with whatever you wanted to do as root (and you have the privilege to do anything as root), type **exit** to return to your normal self.

Managing processes

Every time the shell executes a command that you type, it starts a process. The shell itself is a process. So are any scripts or programs that the shell runs.

Use the ps ax command to see a list of processes. When you type **ps ax**, Bash shows you the current set of processes. Here are a few lines of output from the ps ax command (I also included the —cols 132 option to ensure that you can see each command in its entirety):

```
ps ax --cols 132
  PID TTY         STAT    TIME COMMAND
    1 ?           S       0:04 init
    2 ?           SW      0:00 [keventd]
    3 ?           SW      0:00 [kapmd]
    4 ?           SWN     0:00 [ksoftirqd_CPU0]
    5 ?           SW      0:30 [kswapd]
... lines deleted ...
28550 pts/0       R       0:00 ps ax --cols 132
```

In this listing, the first column has the heading PID and shows a number for each process. PID stands for *process ID* (identification), which is a sequential number assigned by the Linux kernel. If you look through the output of the ps ax command, you see that the init command is the first process and that it has a PID or process number of 1. That's why init is referred to as the "mother of all processes."

The COMMAND column shows the command that created each process.

The process ID or process number is useful when you have to forcibly stop an errant process. Look at the output of the ps ax command and note the PID of the offending process. Then, use the kill command with that process number. To stop process number 28550, for example, type the following command:

```
kill -9 28550
```

Working with date and time

You can use the date command to display the current date and time or set a new date and time. Type the date command at the shell prompt and you get a result similar to the following:

```
date
Sat Jul 26 11:58:06 EDT 2003
```

As you can see, the date command alone displays the current date and time.

To set the date, log in as root and then type **date** followed by the date and time in the MMDDhhmmYYYY format where each character is a digit. For example, to set the date and time to December 31, 2003 and 9:30 p.m., you would type

```
date 123121302003
```

The MMDDhhmmYYYY date-and-time format is similar to the 24-hour military clock, and has the following meaning:

✦ MM is a two-digit number for the month (01 through 12).

✦ DD is a two-digit number for the day of the month (01 through 31).

✦ hh is a two-digit hour in 24-hour format (00 is midnight and 23 is 11:00 p.m.).

✦ mm is a two-digit number for the minutes (00 through 59).

✦ YYYY is the 4-digit year (such as 2003).

The other interesting date-related command is cal. If you type cal without any options, it prints a calendar for the current month. If you type cal followed by a number, cal treats the number as the year and prints the calendar for that year. To view the calendar for a specific month in a specific year, provide the month number (1 = January, 2 = February, and so on) followed by the year. Thus, to view the calendar for January 2004, type the following and you'll get the calendar for that month:

```
cal 1 2004
      January 2004
Su Mo Tu We Th Fr Sa
             1  2  3
 4  5  6  7  8  9 10
11 12 13 14 15 16 17
18 19 20 21 22 23 24
25 26 27 28 29 30 31
```

Processing files

You can search through a text file with `grep` and view a text file, a screen at a time, with `more`. For example, to search for my user name in the `/etc/passwd` file, I use

```
grep naba /etc/passwd
```

To view the `/etc/inittab` file a screenful at a time, I type

```
more /etc/inittab
```

As each screen pauses, I press the spacebar to go to the next page.

There are many more Linux commands that work on files — mostly on text files, but some commands also work on any file. I describe a few of the file-processing tools next.

Counting words and lines in a text file

I am always curious about the size of files. For text files, the number of characters is basically the size of the file in bytes (because each character takes up a byte of storage space). What about words and the number of lines, though?

The Linux `wc` command comes to the rescue. The `wc` command displays the total number of characters, words, and lines in a text file. For example, try the following command:

```
wc /etc/inittab
     53     229     1666 /etc/inittab
```

The second line shows the output. In this case, wc reports that there are 53 lines, 229 words, and 1,666 characters in the /etc/inittab file. If you simply want to see the number of lines in a file, use the -l option, like this:

```
wc -l /etc/inittab
     53 /etc/inittab
```

As you can see, in this case wc simply displays the line count.

If you don't specify a filename, the wc command expects input from the standard input. You can use the pipe feature of the shell to feed the output of another command to wc. This can be handy sometimes.

Suppose you want a rough count of the processes running on your system. You can get a list of all processes with the ps ax command, but instead of counting lines manually, just pipe the output of ps to wc and you get a rough count automatically:

```
ps ax | wc -l
      76
```

Here the ps command produced 76 lines of output. Because the first line simply shows the headings for the tabular columns, you can estimate that there are about 75 processes running on your system. (Of course, this count probably includes the processes used to run the ps and wc commands as well, but who's *really* counting?)

Sorting text files

You can sort the lines in a text file by using the sort command. To see how the sort command works, first type **more /etc/passwd** to see the current contents of the /etc/passwd file. Now type **sort /etc/passwd** to see the lines sorted alphabetically. If you want to sort a file and save the sorted version in another file, you have to use the Bash shell's output redirection feature like this:

```
sort /etc/passwd > ~/sorted.text
```

This command sorts the lines in the /etc/passwd file and saves the output in a file named sorted.text in your home directory.

Substituting or deleting characters from a file

Another interesting command is tr — it substitutes one group of characters for another (or deletes a selected character) throughout a file. Suppose that you occasionally have to use MS-DOS text files on your Red Hat Linux system. Although you may expect to use a text file on any system without any problems, there is one catch: DOS uses a carriage return followed by a line feed to mark the end of each line, whereas Red Hat Linux uses only a line feed.

On your Red Hat Linux system, you can get rid of the extra carriage returns in the DOS text file by using the `tr` command with the `-d` option. Essentially, to convert the DOS text file `filename.dos` to a Linux text file named `filename.linux`, type the following:

```
tr -d '\015' < filename.dos > filename.linux
```

In this command, `'\015'` denotes the code for the carriage-return character in octal notation.

Spilling a file into several smaller files

The `split` command is handy for those times when you want to copy a file to a floppy disk, but the file is too large to fit on a single floppy. You can then use the `split` command to break up the file into smaller files, each of which can fit on a floppy.

By default, `split` puts 1,000 lines into each file. The files are named by groups of letters like aa, ab, ac, and so on. You can specify a prefix for the filenames. For example, to split a large file called `hugefile.tar` into smaller files that fit into several high-density 3.5-inch floppy disks, use `split` as follows:

```
split -b 1440k hugefile.tar part.
```

This command splits the `hugefile.tar` file into 1440K chunks so each one can fit onto a floppy disk. The command creates files named `part.aa`, `part.ab`, `part.ac`, and so on.

To combine the split files back into a single file, use the `cat` command as follows:

```
cat part.?? > hugefile.tar
```

Writing Shell Scripts

If you have ever used MS-DOS, you may remember MS-DOS batch files. These are text files with MS-DOS commands. Similarly, shell scripts are also text files with a bunch of shell commands.

If you aren't a programmer, you may feel apprehensive about programming. But shell programming can be as simple as storing a few commands in a file. Right now you won't be able to write complex shell scripts, but you can certainly try out a simple shell script.

To try your hand at a little shell programming, type the following text at the shell prompt exactly as shown and then press Ctrl+D when you're done:

```
cd
cat > simple
#!/bin/sh
echo "This script's name is: $0"
echo Argument 1: $1
echo Argument 2: $2
```

The `cd` command changes the current directory to your home directory. Then the `cat` command displays whatever you type; in this case, I'm sending the output to a file named `simple`. After you press Ctrl+D, the `cat` command ends and you should again see the shell prompt. What you have done is created a file named `simple` that contains the following shell script:

```
#!/bin/sh
echo "This script's name is: $0"
echo Argument 1: $1
echo Argument 2: $2
```

The first line causes Linux to run the Bash shell program (its name is `/bin/bash`). The shell then reads the rest of the lines in the script.

Just as most Linux commands accept command-line options, a Bash script also accepts command-line options. Inside the script, you can refer to the options as $1, $2, and so on. The special name $0 refers to the name of the script itself.

To run this shell script, first you have to make the file executable (that is, turn it into a program) with the following command:

```
chmod +x simple
```

Now run the script with the following command:

```
./simple one two
This script's name is: ./simple
Argument 1: one
Argument 2: two
```

The `./` prefix to the script's name indicates that the `simple` file is in the current directory.

This script simply prints the script's name and the first two command-line options that the user types after the script's name.

Next, try running the script with a few arguments, as follows:

```
./simple "This is one argument" second-argument third
This script's name is: ./simple
Argument 1: This is one argument
Argument 2: second-argument
```

The shell treats the entire string within the double quotation marks as a single argument. Otherwise, the shell uses spaces as separators between arguments on the command line.

Most useful shell scripts are more complicated than this simple script, but this simple exercise gives you a rough idea of how to write shell scripts.

Place Linux commands in a file and use the `chmod` command to make the file executable. Voilà! You have created a shell script!

Chapter 4: Navigating the Red Hat Linux File System

In This Chapter

✔ Understanding the Red Hat Linux file system

✔ Navigating the file system with Linux commands

✔ Understanding file permissions

✔ Manipulating files and directories with Linux commands

To use files and directories well, you need to understand the concept of a hierarchical file system. Even if you use the GUI file managers to access files and folders (folders are another name for directories), you can benefit from a lay of the land of the file system.

In this chapter, I introduce you to the Linux file system. Then you learn to work with files and directories with several Linux commands.

Understanding the Red Hat Linux File System

Like any other operating system, Red Hat Linux organizes information in files and directories. Directories, in turn, hold the files. A *directory* is a special file that can contain other files and directories. Because a directory can contain other directories, this method of organizing files gives rise to a hierarchical structure. This hierarchical organization of files is called the *file system.*

The Red Hat Linux file system gives you a unified view of all storage in your PC. The file system has a single root directory, indicated by a forward slash (/). Then there is a hierarchy of files and directories. Parts of the file system can reside in different physical media, such as hard disk, floppy disk, and CD-ROM. Figure 4-1 illustrates the concept of the Red Hat Linux file system (which is the same in any Linux system) and how it spans multiple physical devices.

If you're familiar with MS-DOS or Windows, you may find something missing in the Red Hat Linux file system: There are no drive letters in Red Hat Linux. All disk drives and DVD/CD-ROM drives are part of a single file system.

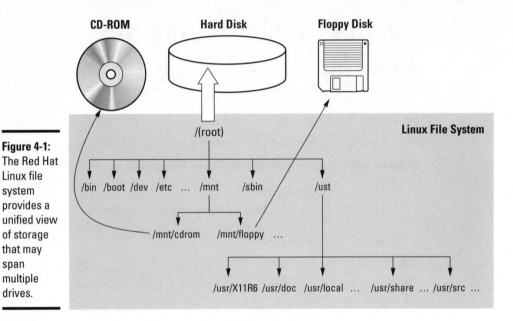

Figure 4-1: The Red Hat Linux file system provides a unified view of storage that may span multiple drives.

In Red Hat Linux, you can have long filenames (up to 256 characters), and filenames are case-sensitive. Often, these filenames have multiple extensions, such as `sample.tar.Z`. UNIX filenames can take many forms, such as the following: `index.html`, `Makefile`, `kernel-smp-2.4.18-3.i686.rpm`, `.bash_profile`, and `httpd_src.tar.gz`.

To locate a file, you need more than just the file's name. You also need information about the directory hierarchy. The extended filename, showing the full hierarchy of directories leading to the file, is called the *pathname*. As the name implies, it's the path to the file through the maze of the file system. Figure 4-2 shows a typical pathname for a file in Red Hat Linux.

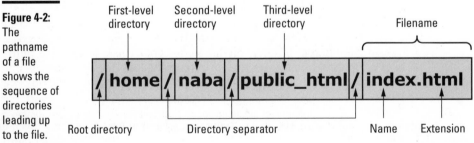

Figure 4-2: The pathname of a file shows the sequence of directories leading up to the file.

As Figure 4-2 shows, the pathname has the following parts:

✦ The `root` directory, indicated by a forward slash (/) character.

✦ The directory hierarchy, with each directory name separated from the previous one by a forward slash (/) character. A / appears after the last directory name.

✦ The filename, with a name and one or more optional extensions. (A period appears before each extension.)

The Red Hat Linux file system has a well-defined set of top-level directories, and some of these directories have specific purposes. You find it easier to find your way around the file system if you know the purpose of these directories. You'll also become adept at guessing where to look for specific types of files when you face a new situation. Table 4-1 briefly describes the top-level directories in the Red Hat Linux file system.

Book II
Chapter 4

Navigating the
Red Hat Linux
File System

Table 4-1	Top-Level Directories in the Red Hat Linux File System
Directory	*Description*
/	This is the `root` directory that forms the base of the file system. All files and directories are contained logically in the `root` directory, regardless of their physical locations.
/bin	Contains the executable programs that are part of the Linux operating system. Many Linux commands, such as `cat`, `cp`, `ls`, `more`, and `tar`, are located in `/bin`.
/boot	Contains the Linux kernel and other files that the LILO and GRUB boot managers need (the kernel and other files can be anywhere, but it's customary to place them in the `/boot` directory).
/dev	Contains special files that represent devices attached to the system.
/etc	Contains most system configuration files and the initialization scripts (in the `/etc/rc.d` subdirectory).
/home	Conventional location of the home directories of all users. User naba's home directory, for example, is `/home/naba`.
/lib	Contains library files for all programs stored in `/sbin` and `/bin` directories, including the loadable driver modules, needed to start Red Hat Linux.
/lost+found	Directory for lost files. Every disk partition has a `lost+found` directory.
/mnt	A directory for temporarily mounted file systems, such as CD-ROM drives, floppy disks, and Zip drives. Contains the `/mnt/floppy` directory for mounting floppy disks and the `/mnt/cdrom` directory for mounting the CD-ROM as well as DVD-ROM drive.

(continued)

Table 4-1 *(continued)*

Directory	Description
/opt	Provides a storage area for large application software packages.
/proc	A special directory that contains information about various aspects of the Red Hat Linux system.
/root	The home directory for the root user.
/sbin	Contains executable files representing commands typically used for system-administration tasks and used by the root user. Commands such as halt and shutdown reside in the /sbin directory.
/tmp	Temporary directory that any user can use as a *scratch* directory, meaning that the contents of this directory are considered unimportant and usually are deleted every time the system boots.
/usr	Contains the subdirectories for many important programs, such as the X Window System (in the /usr/X11R6 directory), and the online manual. Table 4-2 shows some of the standard subdirectories in /usr.
/var	Contains various system files (such as logs), as well as directories for holding other information, such as files for the Web server and anonymous FTP server.

The /usr and /var directories also contain a number of standard subdirectories. Table 4-2 lists the important subdirectories in /usr. Table 4-3 shows a similar breakdown for the /var directory.

Table 4-2   **Important /usr Subdirectories**

Subdirectory	Description
/usr/X11R6	Contains the XFree86 (X Window System) software.
/usr/bin	Contains executable files for many more Linux commands, including utility programs commonly available in Linux, but is not part of the core Linux operating system.
/usr/games	Contains some old Linux games.
/usr/include	Contains the header files (files with names ending in .h) for the C and C++ programming languages; also includes the X11 header files in the /usr/include/X11 directory and the Linux kernel header files in the /usr/include/linux directory.
/usr/lib	Contains the libraries for C and C++ programming languages; also contains many other libraries, such as database libraries, graphical toolkit libraries, and so on.
/usr/local	Contains local files. The /usr/local/bin directory, for example, is supposed to be the location for any executable program developed on your system.

Subdirectory	Description
/usr/sbin	Contains many administrative commands, such as commands for electronic mail and networking.
/usr/share	Contains shared data, such as default configuration files and images for many applications. For example, /usr/share/ gnome contains various shared files for the GNOME desktop; and /usr/share/doc has the documentation files for many Linux applications (such as the Bash shell, the Sawfish window manager, and The GIMP image-processing program).
/usr/share/man	Contains the online manual (which you can read by using the man command).
/usr/src	Contains the source code for the Linux kernel (the core operating system).

Table 4-3	Important /var Subdirectories
Subdirectory	Description
/var/cache	Storage area for cached data for applications.
/var/lib	Contains information relating to the current state of applications.
/var/lock	Contains lock files to ensure that a resource is used by one application only.
/var/log	Contains log files organized into subdirectories. The syslogd server stores its log files in /var/log, with the exact content of the files depending on the syslogd configuration file /etc/ syslog.conf. For example, /var/log/messages is the main system log file, /var/log/secure contains log messages from secure services (such as sshd and xinetd), and /var/ log/maillog contains the log of mail messages.
/var/mail	Contains user mailbox files.
/var/opt	Contains variable data for packages stored in the /opt directory.
/var/run	Contains data describing the system since it was booted.
/var/spool	Contains data that's waiting for some kind of processing.
/var/tmp	Contains temporary files preserved between system reboots.
/var/yp	Contains Network Information Service (NIS) database files.

Navigating the File System with Linux Commands

Although GUI file managers such as Nautilus (in GNOME) or Konqueror (in KDE) are easy to use, you can use them only if you have a working GUI desktop. Sometimes, you may not have a graphical environment to run a graphical file manager. For example, you may be logged in through a text terminal, or

X may not be working on your system. In those situations, you have to rely on Linux commands to work with files and directories. Of course, you can always use Linux commands, even in the graphical environment — all you have to do is open a terminal window and type the Linux commands.

In the sections that follow, I briefly show some Linux commands for moving around within the Red Hat Linux file system.

Command for directory navigation

In Red Hat Linux, when you log in as root, your home directory is /root. For other users, the home directory is usually in the /home directory. My home directory (when I log in as naba) is /home/naba. This information is stored in the /etc/passwd file. By default, only you have permission to save files in your home directory, and only you can create subdirectories in your home directory to further organize your files.

Linux supports the concept of a current directory, which is the directory on which all file and directory commands operate. After you log in, for example, your current directory is the home directory. To see the current directory, type the pwd command.

To change the current directory, use the cd command. To change the current directory to /usr/share/doc, type the following:

```
cd /usr/share/doc
```

Then, to change the directory to the bash-2.05b subdirectory in /usr/share/doc, type this command:

```
cd bash-2.05b
```

Now, if you use the pwd command, that command shows /usr/share/doc/bash-2.05b as the current directory.

These two examples show that you can refer to a directory's name in two ways:

✦ An *absolute pathname* (such as /usr/share/doc) that specifies the exact directory in the directory tree

✦ A *relative directory name* (such as bash-2.05b, which represents the bash-2.05b subdirectory of the current directory, whatever that may be)

If you type cd bash-2.05b in /usr/share/doc, the current directory changes to /usr/share/doc/bash-2.05b. However, if I type the same command in /home/naba, the shell tries to change the current directory to /home/naba/bash-2.05b.

Use the `cd` command without any arguments to change the current directory back to your home directory. No matter where you are, typing `cd` at the shell prompt brings you back home!

By the way, the tilde character (~) refers to your home directory. Thus the command `cd ~` also changes the current directory to your home directory. You can also refer to another user's home directory by appending that user's name to the tilde. Thus, `cd ~superman` changes the current directory to the home directory of `superman`.

Wait, there's more. A single dot (.) and two dots (..) — often referred to as *dot-dot* — also have special meanings. A single dot (.) indicates the current directory, whereas two dots (..) indicate the parent directory. For example, if the current directory is `/usr/share`, you go up one level to `/usr` by typing

Book II
Chapter 4

Navigating the Red Hat Linux File System

```
cd ..
```

Commands for directory listings and permissions

You can get a directory listing by using the `ls` command. By default, the `ls` command — without any options — displays the contents of the current directory in a compact, multicolumn format. For example, type the next two commands to see the contents of the `/etc/X11` directory:

```
cd /etc/X11
ls
```

The output looks like this (on the console you'd see some items in different colors):

```
applnk          prefdm       sysconfig   XftConfig.README-OBSOLETE  xserver
desktop-menus   proxymngr    twm         xinit                      xsm
fs              rstart       X           xkb
gdm             serverconfig xdm         Xmodmap
lbxproxy        starthere    XF86Config  Xresources
```

From this listing (without the colors), you cannot tell whether an entry is a file or a directory. To tell the directories and files apart, use the `-F` option with `ls` and you'll get more clues:

```
ls -F
applnk/          prefdm*       sysconfig/   XftConfig.README-OBSOLETE  xserver/
desktop-menus/   proxymngr/    twm/         xinit/                     xsm/
fs/              rstart/       X@           xkb@
gdm/             serverconfig/ xdm/         Xmodmap
lbxproxy/        starthere/    XF86Config   Xresources
```

The output from `ls -F` shows the directory names with a slash (/) appended to them. Plain filenames appear as is. The *at sign* (@) appended to the file named X indicates that this file is a link to another file (in other words, this filename simply refers to another file; it's a shortcut). An asterisk (*) is appended to executable files (see, for example, the prefdm file in the listing). The shell can run any executable file.

You can see even more detailed information about the files and directories with the -l option:

```
ls -l
```

For the /etc/X11 directory, a typical output from ls -l looks like the following:

```
total 80
drwxr-xr-x  4 root  root  4096 Sep 24 15:52 applnk
drwxr-xr-x  2 root  root  4096 Sep 24 14:59 desktop-menus
drwxr-xr-x  2 root  root  4096 Sep 24 16:12 fs
drwxr-xr-x  6 root  root  4096 Sep 24 15:37 gdm
drwxr-xr-x  2 root  root  4096 Sep 24 15:34 lbxproxy
-rwxr-xr-x  1 root  root  1298 Sep 4 13:23 prefdm
drwxr-xr-x  2 root  root  4096 Sep 24 15:34 proxymngr
drwxr-xr-x  4 root  root  4096 Sep 24 15:34 rstart
drwxr-xr-x  2 root  root  4096 Jul 10 2001 serverconfig
drwxr-xr-x  2 root  root  4096 Jul 10 2001 starthere
drwxr-xr-x  2 root  root  4096 Jul 10 2001 sysconfig
drwxr-xr-x  2 root  root  4096 Sep 24 15:36 twm
lrwxrwxrwx  1 root  root    27 Sep 24 16:28 X -> ../../usr/X11R6/bin/XFree86
drwxr-xr-x  3 root  root  4096 Sep 24 15:56 xdm
-rw-r--r--  1 root  root  3323 Sep 24 16:28 XF86Config
....< lines deleted >....
drwxr-xr-x  2 root  root  4096 Sep 24 15:34 xsm
```

This listing shows considerable information about every directory entry — each of which can be a file or another directory. Looking at a line from the right column to the left, you see that the rightmost column shows the name of the directory entry. The date and time before the name show when the last modifications to that file were made. To the left of the date and time is the size of the file, in bytes.

The file's group and owner appear to the left of the column that shows the file size. The next number to the left indicates the number of links to the file. (A *link* is like a shortcut in Windows.) Finally, the leftmost column shows the file's permission settings, which determine who can read, write, or execute the file.

The first letter of the leftmost column has a special meaning, as the following list shows:

✦ If the first letter is l, the file is a *symbolic link* (a shortcut) to another file.

✦ If the first letter is d, the file is a directory.

◆ If the first letter is a dash (-), the file is normal.

◆ If the first letter is b, the file represents a block device, such as a disk drive.

◆ If the first letter is c, the file represents a character device, such as a serial port or a terminal.

After that first letter, the leftmost column shows a sequence of nine characters. This appears as rwxrwxrwx when each letter is present. Each letter indicates a specific permission. A hyphen (-) in place of a letter indicates no permission for a specific operation on the file. Think of these nine letters as three groups of three letters (rwx), interpreted as follows:

◆ The leftmost group of rwx controls the *read*, *write*, and *execute* permission of the file's owner. In other words, if you see rwx in this position, the file's owner can read (r), write (w), and execute (x) the file. A hyphen in place of a letter indicates no permission. Thus the string rw- means the owner has read and write permission but no execute permission. Although executable programs (including shell programs) typically have execute permission, directories treat execute permission as equivalent to *use* permission — a user must have execute permission on a directory before he or she can open and read the contents of the directory.

◆ The middle three rwx letters control the read, write, and execute permission of any user belonging to that file's group.

◆ The rightmost group of rwx letters controls the read, write, and execute permission of all other users (collectively referred to as *the world*).

Book II
Chapter 4

Navigating the
Red Hat Linux
File System

Thus, a file with the permission setting rwx------ is accessible only to the file's owner, whereas the permission setting rwxr--r-- makes the file readable by the world.

An interesting feature of the ls command is that it does not list any file whose name begins with a period. To see these files, you must use the ls command with the -a option, as follows:

```
ls -a
```

Try this command in your home directory (and then compare the result with what you see when you don't use the -a option):

1. **Type cd to change to your home directory.**

2. **Type ls -F to see the files and directories in your home directory.**

3. **Type ls -aF to see everything, including the hidden files.**

Most Linux commands take single-character options, each with a minus sign (think of this sign as a hyphen) as a prefix. When you want to use several options, type a hyphen and *concatenate* (string together) the option letters, one after another. Thus, ls -al is equivalent to ls -a -l as well as ls -l -a.

Commands for changing permissions and ownerships

You may need to change a file's permission settings to protect it from others. Use the chmod command to change the permission settings of a file or a directory.

To use chmod effectively, you have to learn how to specify the permission settings. A good way is to concatenate letters from the columns of Table 4-4 in the order shown (Who/Action/Permission).

Note: You use only the single character from each column — the text in parentheses is for explanation only.

Table 4-4	Letter Codes for File Permissions	
Who	*Action*	*Permission*
u (user)	+ (add)	r (read)
g (group)	- (remove)	w (write)
o (others)	= (assign)	x (execute)
a (all)	s (set user ID)	

For example, to give everyone read access to all files in a directory, pick a (for *all*) from the first column, + (for *add*) from the second column, and r (for *read*) from the third column to come up with the permission setting a+r. Then use the whole set of options with chmod, like this:

```
chmod a+r *.
```

On the other hand, to permit everyone to execute one specific file, type

```
chmod a+x filename
```

Suppose you have a file named mystuff that you want to protect. You can make it accessible to no one but you if you type the following commands, in this order:

```
chmod a-rwx mystuff
chmod u+rw mystuff
```

The first command turns off all permissions for everyone, and the second command turns *on* the read and write permissions for the owner (you). Type `ls -l` to verify that the change took place (you should see a permission setting of `-rw-------`). Here's a sample output from `ls -l`:

```
-rw-------    1 naba      naba      3 Jun 30 18:45 mystuff
```

Note the third and fourth fields that show `naba naba`. These two fields show the file's user and group ownership. In this case, the name of the user is `naba` and the name of the group is `naba` as well (because Red Hat Linux creates a group for each user).

Sometimes you have to change a file's user or group ownership for everything to work correctly. For example, suppose you are instructed (by a manual, what else) to create a directory named `cups` and give it the ownership of user ID `lp` and group ID `sys`. How would you do it?

Well, you can log in as `root` and create the directory with the command `mkdir`:

```
mkdir cups
```

If you check the file's details with the `ls -l` command, you see that the user and group ownership is `root root`.

To change the owner, use the `chown` command. For example, to change the ownership of the cups directory to user ID `lp` and group ID `sys`, type

```
chown lp.sys cups
```

Commands for working with files

To copy files from one directory to another, use the `cp` command. For example, to copy the file `/usr/X11R6/lib/X11/xinit/Xclients` to the `Xclients.sample` file in the current directory (such as your home directory), type the following:

```
cp /usr/X11R6/lib/X11/xinit/Xclients Xclients.sample
```

If you want to copy a file to the current directory but retain the original name, use a period (`.`) as the second argument of the `cp` command. Thus, the following command copies the `XF86Config` file from the `/etc/X11` directory to the current directory (denoted by a single period):

```
cp /etc/X11/XF86Config .
```

Book II
Chapter 4

Navigating the
Red Hat Linux
File System

The cp command makes a new copy of a file and leaves the original intact.

If you want to copy the entire contents of a directory — including all subdirectories and their contents — to another directory, use the command cp -ar *sourcedir destdir* (this copies everything under *sourcedir* directory to *destdir*). For example, to copy all files from the /etc/X11 directory to the current directory, type the following command:

```
cp -ar /etc/X11 .
```

To move a file to a new location, use the mv command. The original copy is gone, and a new copy appears at the destination. You can use mv to rename a file. If you want to change the name of the today.list to old.list, use the mv command, as follows:

```
mv today.list old.list
```

On the other hand, if you want to move the today.list file to a subdirectory named saved, use this command:

```
mv today.list saved
```

An interesting feature of mv is that you can use it to move entire directories — with all their subdirectories and files — to a new location. If you have a directory named data that contains many files and subdirectories, you can move that entire directory structure to old_data by using the following command:

```
mv data old_data
```

To delete files, use the rm command. For example, to delete a file named old.list, type the following command:

```
rm old.list
```

Be careful with the rm command — especially when you log in as root. It's very easy to inadvertently delete important files with rm.

Commands for working with directories

To organize files in your home directory, you have to create new directories. Use the mkdir command to create a directory. For example, to create a directory named images in the current directory, type the following:

```
mkdir images
```

After you create the directory, you can use the `cd images` command to change to that directory.

You can create an entire directory tree by using the `-p` option with the `mkdir` command. For example, suppose your system has a `/usr/src` directory and you want to create the directory tree `/usr/src/book/java/examples/applets`. To create this directory hierarchy, type the following command:

```
mkdir -p /usr/src/book/java/examples/applets
```

When you no longer need a directory, use the `rmdir` command to delete it.

You can delete a directory only when the directory is empty.

To remove an empty directory tree, you can use the `-p` option, like this:

```
rmdir -p /usr/src/book/java/examples/applets
```

This command removes the empty parent directories of `applets`. The command stops when it encounters a directory that's not empty.

Commands for finding files

The `find` command is very useful for locating files (and directories) that meet your search criteria.

When I began using UNIX many years ago (Berkeley UNIX in the early 1980s), I was confounded by the `find` command. I stayed with one basic syntax of `find` for a long time before graduating to more complex forms. The basic syntax I learned first was for finding a file anywhere in the file system. Here's how it goes: Suppose you want to find any file or directory with a name that starts with `gnome`. Type the following `find` command to find these files:

```
find / -name "gnome*" -print
```

If you're not logged in as `root`, you may get a bunch of error messages. If these error messages annoy you, just modify the command as follows and the error messages are history (or, as UNIX aficionados say, *send 'em to the bit bucket*):

```
find / -name "gnome*" -print 2> /dev/null
```

Book II
Chapter 4

Navigating the
Red Hat Linux
File System

This command tells find to start looking at the root directory (/), to look for filenames that match gnome*, and to display the full pathname of any matching file. The last part (2> /dev/null) simply sends the error messages to a special file that's equivalent of simply ignoring them.

You can use variations of this simple form of find to locate a file in any directory (as well as any subdirectories contained in the directory). If you forget where in your home directory you have stored all files named report* (names that start with report), you can search for the files by using the following command:

```
find ~ -name "report*" -print
```

When you become comfortable with this syntax of find, you can use other options of find. For example, to find only specific types of files (such as directories), use the type option. The following command displays all top-level directory names in your Linux system:

```
find / -type d -maxdepth 1 -print
```

You probably don't have to use the complex forms of find in a typical Linux system — but if you ever need to, you can look up the rest of the find options by using the following command:

```
man find
```

Commands for mounting and unmounting

Suppose you want to access the files on this book's companion DVD when you are logged in at a text console (no GUI to help you). To do so, you have to first mount the DVD drive's file system on a specific directory in the Red Hat Linux file system.

Log in as root (or type su - to become root), insert the DVD in the DVD drive, and then type the following command:

```
mount /dev/cdrom /mnt/cdrom
```

This command mounts the file system on the device named /dev/cdrom (refers to the CD-ROM as well as the DVD-ROM drive) on the /mnt/cdrom directory (which is also called the *mount point*) in the Linux file system.

After the mount command successfully completes its task, you can access the files on the DVD by referring to the /mnt/cdrom directory as the top-level directory of the disc. In other words, to see the contents of the DVD, type

```
ls -F /mnt/cdrom
```

When you're done using the DVD — and before you eject it from the drive — you have to "unmount" the disc drive with the following umount command:

```
umount /dev/cdrom
```

It's customary to mount devices on directories in the /mnt directory. Red Hat Linux comes with the two predefined directories: /mnt/cdrom for mounting the DVD and /mnt/floppy for mounting the floppy drive.

Commands for checking disk-space usage

Book II
Chapter 4

I want to tell you about two commands — df and du — that you can use to check the disk-space usage on your system. These commands are simple to use. The df command shows you a summary of disk-space usage for all mounted devices, as shown in this example:

Navigating the
Red Hat Linux
File System

```
df
Filesystem           1K-blocks      Used Available Use%
    Mounted on
/dev/hda5            7392428     3583420   3433492  52% /
/dev/hda3             101107        9322     86564  10% /boot
none                  127376           0    127376   0%
    /dev/shm
/dev/cdrom            658144      658144         0 100%
    /mnt/cdrom
```

The output is a table that shows the device, the total kilobytes of storage, how much is in use, how much is available, the percentage being used, and the mount point.

To see the output of df in a more human-readable format, type df -h. Here is the output of the df -h command:

```
Filesystem           Size  Used Avail Use% Mounted on
/dev/hda5            7.1G  3.5G  3.3G  52% /
/dev/hda3             99M  9.2M   85M  10% /boot
none                 125M     0  125M   0% /dev/shm
/dev/cdrom           643M  643M     0 100% /mnt/cdrom
```

If you compare this output with the output of plain df (see previous listing), you see that df -h prints the sizes with terms like M for megabytes and G for gigabytes. These are clearly easier to understand than 1K-blocks.

The other command — du — is useful for finding out how much space a directory takes up. For example, type the following command to view the contents of all the directories in the /etc/rc.d directory (this directory contains system startup files):

```
du /etc/rc.d
288      /etc/rc.d/init.d
4        /etc/rc.d/rc0.d
4        /etc/rc.d/rc1.d
4        /etc/rc.d/rc2.d
4        /etc/rc.d/rc3.d
4        /etc/rc.d/rc4.d

4        /etc/rc.d/rc5.d
4        /etc/rc.d/rc6.d
352      /etc/rc.d
```

Each directory name is preceded by a number — which tells you the number of kilobytes of disk space used by that directory. Thus the /etc/rc.d directory, as a whole, uses 352K disk space whereas the /etc/rc.d/init.d subdirectory uses 288K. If you simply want the total disk space used by a directory (including all the files and subdirectories contained in that directory), use the -s option, as follows:

```
du -s /etc/rc.d
352      /etc/rc.d
```

The -s option causes du to print just the summary information for the /etc/rc.d directory.

Just as df -h prints the disk-space information in megabytes and gigabytes, you can use the du -h command to view the output of du in more human-readable form. For example, here's how I combine it with the -s option to see the space I'm using in my home directory (/home/naba):

```
du -sh /home/naba
29M      /home/naba
```

Chapter 5: Exploring Red Hat Linux Applications

In This Chapter

✓ Taking stock of Red Hat Linux applications

✓ Exploring office applications

✓ Setting up databases

✓ Playing with multimedia

✓ Working with images

Red Hat Linux comes with a whole lot of applications. All you have to do is look at the menus in GNOME or KDE and you'll see what I mean. Often, there is more than one application of each type. Both GNOME and KDE come with the OpenOffice.org office application suite with word processor and spreadsheet software. There are also many choices for CD players and multimedia players, not to mention the games and utility programs, as well as useful tools such as scanner and digital camera applications.

I give you an overview of some of these applications and briefly show you some interesting and useful applications. After you know about these applications, you can try them out when you need them.

Taking Stock of the Red Hat Linux Applications

Table 5-1 shows a sampling of major Red Hat Linux applications, organized by category. For the major applications, I also show a relevant Web site where you can get more information about that application. This list is by no means comprehensive. Red Hat Linux distribution comes with many more applications and utilities than the ones I show in this table.

If your system has both GNOME and KDE installed, then most of these applications should already be available from either GUI desktop.

I briefly introduce some of the applications from Table 5-1, selecting one or two from each category. I describe the Internet applications in Book V.

Table 5-1	A Sampling of Red Hat Linux Applications
Application	*Description*
Office Applications	
OpenOffice.org Writer	A free word processing program similar to Microsoft Word (`www.openoffice.org`)
OpenOffice.org Calc	A spreadsheet program similar to Microsoft Excel (`www.openoffice.org`)
OpenOffice.org Impress	A presentation application similar to Microsoft PowerPoint (`www.openoffice.org`)
OpenOffice.org Draw	A drawing program (`www.openoffice.org`)
OpenOffice.org Math	An equation editor for writing mathematical equations, which you can then include in OpenOffice.org Writer documents (`www.openoffice.org`)
Dia	A drawing program, designed to be like the Windows application called Visio (`www.gnome.org/gnome-office/dia.shtml`)
Office Tools	
GNOME Calculator	A simple calculator
KCalc	A calculator (part of KDE)
Aspell	A text-mode spell checker (`aspell.sourceforge.net`)
Dictionary	A graphical client for the `dict.org` dictionary server so you can look up words
Database	
PostgreSQL	A sophisticated object-relational database-management system that supports Structured Query Language (SQL) (`www.pgsql.com`)
MySQL	A popular relational database-management system that supports SQL (`www.mysql.com`)
Multimedia	
GNOME CD Player	An audio CD player (needs a working sound card)
KsCD	Audio CD player from KDE (needs a working sound card)
XMMS	X Multimedia System — a multimedia audio player that can play many different sound formats (`www.xmms.org`) — including MP3 files if you download a plug-in for the purpose
Cdrecord	A command-line application that can burn audio and data CD-R as well as DVD-R (`http://www.fokus.gmd.de/research/cc/glone/employees/joerg.schilling/private/cdrecord.html`)

Application	Description
Multimedia	
GnomeToaster	A GUI frontend for `cdrecord` and `cdrdao` that makes it easy to burn data and audio CDs (`gnometoaster.rulez.org`)
Grip	A GUI utility to extract tracks from audio CDs and save as Ogg Vorbis files that you can play (by using a media player) or burn onto an audio CD (`www.nostatic.org/grip`)
Gtkam	A digital camera application that works with over 150 digital cameras (`gphoto.sourceforge.net/proj/gtkam/`)
Graphics and Imaging	
The GIMP	The GNU Image Manipulation Program, an application suitable for tasks such as photo retouching, image composition, and image authoring (`www.gimp.org`)
GQView	A powerful image viewer (`gqview.sourceforge.net`)
Kview	A simple image viewer for KDE
Kghostview	A PostScript and PDF file viewer
Xsane	A graphical frontend for accessing scanners with the SANE (Scanner Access Now Easy) library (`www.xsane.org`)
Ksnapshot	A screen-capture program
Internet	
Ximian Evolution	A personal information management application that integrates e-mail, calendar, contact management, and online task lists (`www.ximian.com/products/ximian_evolution`)
GFTP	An FTP client for downloading files from the Internet
Gaim	An AOL Instant Messenger client (`gaim.sourceforge.net`)
Mozilla	A well-known open-source Web browser that started with source code from Netscape (`www.mozilla.org`)
KMail	An e-mail client for KDE (`kmail.kde.org`)

Book II
Chapter 5

Exploring Red Hat
Linux Applications

Office Applications and Tools

Word processor, spreadsheet, presentation software, calendar, calculator —
these are some of the staples of the office. Both GNOME and KDE come
with the OpenOffice.org (often shortened as *OO.o* or *Ooo*) suite of office
applications and tools. You can try out all of them one by one and see which

one takes your fancy. Each application is fairly intuitive to use. Even though some nuances of the user interface may be new to you, you can learn it after using it a few times. I briefly introduce a few of the following applications in this section:

- ✦ OpenOffice.org Writer — a Microsoft Word–like word processor
- ✦ OpenOffice.org Calc — a Microsoft Excel–like spreadsheet program
- ✦ OpenOffice.org Impress — a Microsoft PowerPoint–like presentation program
- ✦ OpenOffice.org Draw — a drawing and illustration application
- ✦ OpenOffice.org Math — a mathematical formula editor
- ✦ Calculators — GNOME calculator and KDE calculator
- ✦ aspell — a spelling checker
- ✦ Commercially available office applications for Linux

I cover the OpenOffice.org applications in separate chapters in Book III. Please turn to that book to learn more about Writer, Calc, Impress, Draw, and Math.

Calculators

You have a choice of the GNOME calculator or the KDE calculator. Both are scientific calculators, and you can do the typical scientific calculations, such as square root and inverse, as well as trigonometric functions, such as sine, cosine, and tangent.

To run the GNOME calculator, choose Main Menu⇨Accessories⇨Calculator from the GNOME desktop. Figure 5-1 shows the GNOME calculator.

Figure 5-1: Do your calculations on the GNOME calculator.

The KDE calculator has more features than the GNOME calculator. For example, it can perform calculations in hexadecimal, decimal, octal, and binary format. From the KDE desktop, you can start the KDE calculator by choosing Main Menu⇨Accessories⇨Scientific Calculator. Figure 5-2 shows the KDE calculator.

Figure 5-2: Square roots anyone? Compute it on the KDE calculator.

Commercially available office applications for Linux

Because office applications are important to many businesses as well as individuals, I want to briefly mention some of the commercial office applications available for Red Hat Linux. These commercial offerings include Anyware Office (formerly Applixware Office) and StarOffice. These products do cost some money, but the cost is usually less than that for Microsoft Office — the leading office application suite for Windows. (In case you don't know, Microsoft Office is a collection of several applications: Microsoft Word for word processing, Microsoft Excel for spreadsheets, Microsoft PowerPoint for presentation graphics, and Microsoft Access for databases.)

Another recent commercial product for Linux is CrossOver Office from CodeWeavers. With CrossOver Office, you can run your existing Microsoft Office applications such as Word, Excel, and PowerPoint under Linux and X Window System.

This book's companion DVD does not include any of these commercial office applications for Red Hat Linux, but I briefly describe them in the next few sections. You can visit each vendor's Web site for more about the products.

Anyware Office

Anyware Office, formerly known as Applixware Office, is another prominent office application suite for all Linux distributions, including Red Hat Linux.

In April 2000, Applix, Inc., formed a separate group — VistaSource, Inc. — that focuses solely on Linux applications.

Like other office suites, Anyware Office includes Words (for word processing), Spreadsheets (for spreadsheets), and Graphics and Presents (for presentation graphics). In addition, it also has Mail (an e-mail interface) and Data (an interactive relational database-browsing tool). Anyware Office can also read and write documents in Microsoft Office and Corel WordPerfect formats, as well as in several other file formats. Although trial versions are not offered, the entire Anyware Office suite is currently priced at less than $100 in the U.S.

You can learn more about Applixware at the VistaSource Web site (`www.vistasource.com/products`).

StarOffice

StarOffice is another commercial office applications suite; it was created by StarDivision of Hamburg, Germany, and recently purchased by Sun Microsystems. StarOffice is a cross-platform solution — it runs on Linux, Windows 95/98/Me/NT/2000/XP, Sun Solaris SPARC, and Sun Solaris x86. Also, StarOffice is available in several languages: English, French, German, Spanish, Italian, and Swedish.

StarOffice is unique in that it combines all of its components into a common desktop from which you can open new documents, drag and drop documents from one application to another, and access the Internet. Here's what StarOffice 6.0 includes:

✦ StarOffice Writer for word processing (Microsoft Word–compatible)

✦ StarOffice Calc for spreadsheets (Microsoft Excel–compatible)

✦ StarOffice Impress for presentations (Microsoft PowerPoint–compatible)

✦ StarOffice Draw for vector graphics drawing

✦ StarOffice Base for data management

You can buy a copy of StarOffice from `www.sun.com/staroffice`. You can also find the details of Sun's StarOffice licensing policy at the same URL.

In October 2000, Sun released the source code of StarOffice under opensource licenses. OpenOffice.org, an open-source project that Sun supports, released the OpenOffice.org 1.0 office productivity suite in May 2002. Red Hat Linux comes with OpenOffice.org 1.0.2. To learn more about OpenOffice.org, check out Book III but also visit `www.openoffice.org`.

CrossOver Office

Chances are better than good that you have Windows and Microsoft Office installed on your PC. When you decide to run Red Hat Linux on the PC, you can continue to run most Microsoft Office applications from the GNOME or KDE desktop. The convenience of running Microsoft Office in Linux comes from a commercial product called CrossOver Office.

CrossOver Office, from CodeWeavers, is a software package that enables you to install your Microsoft Office applications (only Office 97 or Office 2000, not Office XP) in Linux. You don't need Microsoft Windows to run the Office applications in CrossOver Office. You simply install CrossOver Office and then install Microsoft Office from the CD-ROM. After you install Microsoft Office, the Office applications will be available directly from GNOME or KDE desktop.

CrossOver Office uses Wine — an open-source implementation of the Windows Win32 and Win16 application programming interfaces (APIs) using the X Window System and designed to run in UNIX and Linux systems. Wine includes the Wine loader and WineLib. Wine loader can load and run Windows applications. WineLib is used for compiling and linking Windows applications in Linux. Wine is available free of charge from `www.winehq.com`.

CodeWeavers created CrossOver Office using a customized version of Wine so as to make sure that the Microsoft Office applications, especially Microsoft Word, Excel, and PowerPoint (from Office 97 or Office 2000) run properly on Wine. CodeWeavers charges a nominal amount for CrossOver Office — the list price is $54.95 for a single copy (with lower costs for multiple copies) — but all changes to Wine are returned to the Wine project. Thus, the Wine open-source project benefits from the sale of CrossOver Office.

You can learn more about CrossOver Office and purchase it at the CodeWeavers Web site (`www.codeweavers.com/products/office/`).

aspell spelling checker

The `aspell` utility is an interactive spelling checker. You can use it to check the spelling of words in a text file. To do so, simply type the following command in a terminal window:

```
aspell check filename
```

If you want to try out `aspell`, type some notes and save them in a text file named `notes.txt` (the filename can be anything, but I use this filename in the discussions). To run the spelling checker on that file, type the following command in a terminal window:

Book II
Chapter 5

Exploring Red Hat
Linux Applications

```
aspell check notes.txt
This note describes the *concensus* reached during the August
    16 meeting.
1) consensus              6) consensual
2) con census             7) consciences
3) con-census             8) incenses
4) condenses              9) consensus's
5) concerns               0) consensuses
i) Ignore                 I) Ignore all
r) Replace                R) Replace all
a) Add                    x) Exit
?
```

Everything from the second line on is what `aspell` displays. When `aspell` finds a misspelled word (any word that does not appear in its dictionary), it displays the sentence with the misspelled word (`concensus`) and highlights that word by enclosing it in a pair of asterisks. Below that sentence, `aspell` lists possible corrections, numbering them sequentially from 1. In this case, `aspell` lists `consensus` — the right choice — as the first correction for `concensus`.

At the end of the list of options, `aspell` displays a list of 16 other options — ten numbered 0 through 9, and six labeled with single letters i, r, a, I, R, and x — followed by a question mark prompt. You have to press one of the numbers or letters from the list shown in the output to indicate what you want `aspell` to do. The numbered options show ten possible replacement words for the misspelled word. Here are the meanings of the letter options:

✦ Space means accept the word this time.

✦ i means ignore the misspelled word.

✦ I means ignore all occurrences of the word.

✦ r means replace this occurrence (you have to type a replacement word).

✦ R means replace all occurrences (you have to type a replacement word).

✦ a means accept the word and add it to the your private dictionary.

✦ x means save the rest of the file and exit, ignoring misspellings.

These options are case sensitive. Make sure you don't have Caps Lock engaged.

Databases

Red Hat Linux comes with two relational databases — PostgreSQL and MySQL. I briefly show you how to use MySQL.

MySQL (pronounced *My Ess Que Ell*), is a popular *relational database* (the type of database that works as a collection of connected tables). You can use the Structured Query Language (SQL) to work with the database.

A Swedish company called MySQL AB develops MySQL (www.mysql.com). MySQL AB has released it as an open-source product.

To check whether MySQL is installed on your system, type rpm -q mysql. If a message informs you that the package is not installed, you can install it from the DVD using these steps:

1. **Log in as root and insert the DVD into the DVD drive.**

   If you are using GNOME or KDE, the DVD should mount automatically. If not, type the following command in a terminal window to mount the DVD:

   ```
   mount /mnt/cdrom
   ```

2. **Type the following commands to install MySQL:**

   ```
   cd /mnt/cdrom/RedHat/RPMS
   rpm -ivh mysql*
   ```

   This installs all the packages you need to use MySQL on your system.

To use MySQL, you have to first log in as root and start the database server with the following command:

```
/etc/init.d/mysqld start
```

The database server mysqld is a *daemon* (a background process that runs continuously) that accepts database queries from the MySQL monitor.

Now you have to design a database, create that database in MySQL, and load it with the data. To illustrate how to create and load a database, I set up a simple book catalog database.

Reviewing the steps to build the database

Follow this basic sequence of steps to build a database:

1. **Design the database.**

   This involves defining the tables and attributes that will be used to store the information.

2. **Create an empty database.**

   Before you can add tables, database systems require you to build an empty database.

3. **Create the tables in the database.**

   In this step, you define the tables using the `CREATE TABLE` statement of SQL.

4. **Load the tables with any fixed data.**

   For example, if you have a table of manufacturer names or publisher names (in the case of books), you want to load that table with information that's already known.

5. **Back up the initial database.**

   This step is necessary to ensure that you can create the database from scratch, if necessary.

6. **Load data into tables.**

   You may either load data from an earlier dump of the database or interactively through forms.

7. **Use the database.**

   Make queries, update records, or insert new records using SQL commands.

Designing the database

My simple example doesn't follow all the possible steps of database building. For the example, the database-design step is trivial because my book-catalog database includes only a single table. The attributes of that table are as follows:

+ Book's title with up to 50 characters

+ Name of first author with up to 20 characters

+ Name of second author (if any) with up to 20 characters

+ Name of publisher with up to 30 characters

+ Page count as a number

+ Year published as a number (such as 2002)

+ International Standard Book Number (ISBN), as a 10-character text (such as 0764542583)

I store the ISBN without the dashes embedded in a typical book's ISBN. I also use the ISBN as the primary key of the table because ISBN is a world-wide identification system for books. That means each book entry must have a unique ISBN, which we know to be true for books.

Creating an empty database

To create the empty database in MySQL, use the `mysqladmin` program. For example, to create an empty database named `books`, I type the following command:

```
mysqladmin create books
```

You have to log in as `root` to run the `mysqladmin` program. As the name suggests, `mysqladmin` is the database administration program for MySQL.

In addition to creating a database, you can use `mysqladmin` to remove a database and shut down the database server and check the MySQL version. For example, to see the version information, type the following command:

```
mysqladmin version
```

Using the MySQL monitor

After you create the empty database, all of your interactions with the database are through the `mysql` program — the MySQL monitor that acts as a client to the database server. You have to run `mysql` with the name of a database as an argument. The `mysql` program then prompts you for input. Here is an example:

```
mysql books
Reading table information for completion of table and column names
You can turn off this feature to get a quicker startup with -A

Welcome to the MySQL monitor. Commands end with ; or \g.
Your MySQL connection id is 10 to server version: 3.23.49

Type 'help;' or '\h' for help. Type '\c' to clear the buffer.

mysql>
```

When creating tables or loading data into tables, a typical approach is to place the SQL statements (along with `mysql` commands such as `\g`) in a file and then run `mysql` with the standard input directed from that file. For example, suppose a file named `sample.sql` contains some SQL commands that you want to try out on a database named `books`. Then, you should run `mysql` with the following command:

```
mysql books < sample.sql
```

I use `mysql` in this manner to create a database table.

Defining a table

To create a table named `books`, I edited a text file named `makedb.sql` and placed the following line in that file:

```
#
# Table structure for table 'books'
#
CREATE TABLE books (
    isbn CHAR(10) NOT NULL PRIMARY KEY,
    title CHAR(50),
    author1 CHAR(20),
    author2 CHAR(20),
    pubname CHAR(30),
    pubyear INT,
    pagecount INT
) \g
```

`CREATE TABLE books` is an SQL statement to create the table named `books`. The `\g` at the end of the statement is a `mysql` command. The attributes of the table appear in the lines enclosed in parentheses.

If a table contains fixed data, you can also include other SQL statements (such as `INSERT INTO`) to load the data into the table right after the table is created.

To execute the SQL statements in the `makedb.sql` file create the `books` table, I run `mysql` as follows:

```
mysql books < makedb.sql
```

Now the `books` database should have a table named `books`. (Okay, maybe I should have named them differently, but it seemed convenient to call them by the same name.) I can now begin loading data into the table.

Inserting records into a table

One way to load data into the table is to prepare SQL statements in another file and then run `mysql` with that file as input. For example, suppose I want to add the following book information into the `books` table:

```
isbn = '156884798X'
title = 'Linux SECRETS'
author1 = 'Naba Barkakati'
author2 = NULL
pubname = 'IDG Books Worldwide'
pubyear = 1996
pagecount = 900
```

Then, the following MySQL statement loads this information into the books table:

```
INSERT INTO books VALUES
( '156884798X', 'Linux SECRETS', 'Naba Barkakati', NULL,
'IDG Books Worldwide', 1996, 900) \g
```

On the other hand, suppose you have the various fields available in a different order (from the order in which the table's attributes are defined by the CREATE TABLE statement). In that case, you can use a different form of the INSERT INTO command to add the row, as shown in the following example:

```
INSERT INTO books (pubyear, author1, author2, title,
    pagecount, pubname, isbn) values
(1996, 'Naba Barkakati', NULL, 'Linux SECRETS', 900, 'IDG
    Books Worldwide', '156884798X')\g
```

Essentially, you have to specify the list of attributes as well as the values and make sure that the order of the attributes matches that of the values.

If I save all INSERT INTO commands in a file named additems.sql, then I can load the database from the mysql command line by using the source command like this (type **mysql books** to start the SQL client):

```
mysql> source additems.sql
```

Querying the database

You can query the database interactively through the mysql monitor. (Of course, you do have to know SQL to do this operation.) For example, to query the books database, I start the SQL client with the following command:

```
mysql books
```

Then I would type SQL commands at the mysql> prompt to look up items from the database. When done, I type **quit** to exit the mysql program. Here's an example (all of which I typed in a terminal window):

```
mysql> select title from books where pubyear < 2000 \g
+------------------------------------+
| title                              |
+------------------------------------+
| Linux SECRETS                      |
| Red Hat Linux SECRETS, 2nd Edition |
+------------------------------------+
2 rows in set (0.00 sec)
mysql> quit
Bye
```

To learn more about MySQL, consult Janet Valade's *PHP and MySQL For Dummies* by Wiley Publishing, Inc.

Multimedia Applications

Red Hat Linux includes quite a few multimedia applications — mostly multimedia audio players and CD players, but also applications for using digital cameras and burning CD-ROMs. To play some other multimedia files (such as MPEG video), you have to download and install additional software in your Red Hat Linux system. Here's a quick sketch of a few typical multimedia tasks and the applications you can use to perform these tasks:

✦ **Using digital cameras:** Use the Digital Camera tool to download photos from your digital camera in Red Hat Linux.

✦ **Playing audio CDs:** Use one of many audio CD players that come with Red Hat Linux.

✦ **Playing sound files:** Use XMMS, a multimedia audio player (you have to download some additional software to play MP3 files with XMMS). You can also download other players from the Internet.

✦ **Burning a CD:** Use X-CD-Roast to burn CDs.

Using digital cameras

Red Hat Linux comes with gtkam — a digital-camera application you can use to download pictures from digital cameras. gtkam is a GUI frontend to the gPhoto2 command-line application that works with many different makes and models of digital cameras. Depending on the model, the cameras can connect to the serial port or the Universal Serial Bus (USB) port. Visit the gPhoto Web site (`www.gphoto.org/gphoto2`) for the latest list of supported cameras.

To use gtkam with your digital camera, follow these steps:

1. **Connect your digital camera to the serial port or USB port (whichever interface the camera supports) and turn on the camera.**

2. **Choose Main Menu⇨Graphics⇨Digital Camera Tool to start gtkam.**

3. **From the gtkam menu, choose Camera⇨Add Camera.**

4. **In the dialog box that appears, click Detect.**

If your camera is supported, the camera should be detected. If not, you can try an alternate method that I describe in the steps that follow this list of steps.

gtkam displays a camera icon and the camera name on the left panel.

5. **Double-click the camera icon to download and view thumbnail pictures in the right panel.**

6. **Click the thumbnails to select the images you want to download; then choose File⊃Save or click the Save button on the toolbar.**

   gtkam then downloads the images and places each image in a separate file in your home directory. You can now edit the photos in The GIMP or your favorite photo editor.

Don't despair if gtkam does not recognize your digital camera. You can still access the digital camera's storage media (compact flash card, for example) as a USB mass storage device, provided your camera supports USB Mass Storage. To access the images on your digital camera, follow these steps:

1. **Read the camera manual and use the menu options of the camera to set the USB mode to Mass Storage.**

   If the camera does not support USB Mass Storage, then you cannot use this procedure to access the photos.

2. **Connect your digital camera to the USB port by using the cable that came with the camera and turn on the camera.**

   This causes Red Hat Linux to detect the camera, create the /mnt/camera directory, and add a line to the /etc/fstab file so that you can easily mount the camera's storage media on the /mnt/camera directory.

3. **To see whether the camera was detected, type the following command in a terminal window:**

   ```
   cat /proc/bus/usb/devices
   ```

   The output should show your camera as a mass storage device. For example, I get the following output when I connect my Nikon Coolpix 2500 as a USB mass storage device:

   ```
   T:  Bus=01 Lev=00 Prnt=00 Port=00 Cnt=00 Dev#=  1 Spd=12  MxCh= 2
   B:  Alloc=  0/900 us ( 0%), #Int=  0, #Iso=  0
   D:  Ver= 1.00 Cls=09(hub  ) Sub=00 Prot=00 MxPS= 8 #Cfgs=  1
   P:  Vendor=0000 ProdID=0000 Rev= 0.00
   S:  Product=USB UHCI Root Hub
   S:  SerialNumber=fcc0
   C:* #Ifs= 1 Cfg#= 1 Atr=40 MxPwr=   0mA
   I:  If#= 0 Alt= 0 #EPs= 1 Cls=09(hub  ) Sub=00 Prot=00 Driver=hub
   E:  Ad=81(I) Atr=03(Int.) MxPS=   8 Ivl=255ms
   T:  Bus=01 Lev=01 Prnt=01 Port=00 Cnt=01 Dev#=  2 Spd=12  MxCh= 0
   D:  Ver= 1.10 Cls=00(>ifc ) Sub=00 Prot=00 MxPS= 8 #Cfgs=  1
   P:  Vendor=04b0 ProdID=0108 Rev= 1.00
   S:  Manufacturer=NIKON
   S:  Product=Nikon Digital Camera E2500
   S:  SerialNumber=000003365943
   C:* #Ifs= 1 Cfg#= 1 Atr=c0 MxPwr=   0mA
   I:  If#= 0 Alt= 0 #EPs= 2 Cls=08(stor.) Sub=06 Prot=50 Driver=usb-storage
   E:  Ad=04(O) Atr=02(Bulk) MxPS=  64 Ivl=0ms
   E:  Ad=83(I) Atr=02(Bulk) MxPS=  64 Ivl=0ms
   ```

Book II
Chapter 5

Exploring Red Hat
Linux Applications

All the lines starting with the second T: line pertain to the Nikon Coolpix 2500 camera. You can see some of the details in the output, such as manufacturer name and camera model.

4. **Mount the camera's storage media by typing the following command:**

```
mount /mnt/camera
```

A camera icon appears on the GNOME desktop.

5. **Double-click the camera icon on the GNOME desktop.**

The camera's contents appear in a Nautilus file manager window. You can double-click the folders and find the one that contains the photos. Typically, these digital photos are JPEG files with cryptic filenames that carry the .jpg extension. In the default view, Nautilus displays thumbnails of the photos, so you don't have to worry about the cryptic filenames. Figure 5-3 shows the GNOME desktop with the camera icon and the Nautilus window showing the photos from my Nikon Coolpix 2500.

6. **Click to select photos and copy them to your hard disk.**

You can also type the cp command in a terminal window to copy all or selected images to a directory on your hard disk. For example, to copy all JPEG photos from the camera to the current directory, type:

```
cp /mnt/camera/*.jpg .
```

Figure 5-3: You can access the digital photos in your digital camera as a USB mass storage device.

7. **When you're done downloading the photos, right-click the camera icon on the GNOME desktop and choose Unmount Volume from the pop-up menu.**

    This causes Red Hat Linux to unmount the camera from the `/mnt/camera` directory, remove the `/mnt/camera` directory, and remove the line that was added to the `/etc/fstab` file.

8. **Power off the camera and disconnect the USB cable from the PC.**

Who needs gtkam when you can access the camera just like any other storage device!

Playing audio CDs

Both GNOME and KDE come with CD player applications. To play an audio CD, you need a sound card, and that sound card must be configured to work in Red Hat Linux.

If you are using the GNOME desktop, you can play audio CDs by using the GNOME CD Player application. Launch the GNOME CD Player by choosing Main Menu⇨Sound & Video⇨CD Player. Figure 5-4 shows this CD player playing a track from an audio CD.

Figure 5-4:
Play audio
CDs with
the GNOME
CD Player.

The GNOME CD Player displays the title of the CD and the name of the current track. The GNOME CD Player gets the song titles from the Compact Disc Database (CDDB) — a CD database on the Internet (`freedb.freedb.org`). This means you need an active Internet connection for the CD Player to download song information from the CD database. After the CD Player downloads information about a particular CD, it caches that information in a local database for future use. The CD player's user interface is intuitive, and you can learn it easily. One nice feature is that you can select a track by title, as shown in Figure 5-5.

If you use KDE as your desktop, you find a similar audio CD player in KDE. Start the KDE CD player by choosing Main Menu⇨Sound & Video⇨KsCD.

Figure 5-5:
In the
GNOME CD
Player, you
can select a
specific
audio track
to play.

Playing sound files

You can use the X Multimedia System (XMMS) to open and play a sound file. XMMS can play many types of sound files, including Ogg Vorbis and Windows WAV. You will find many WAV sound files — which usually have names that end with the `.wav` extension — in the `/usr/share/sounds` directory of your Red Hat Linux system.

You can also create WAV sound files from audio CD tracks by using the `cdda2wav` command-line application. For example, to convert the second track from an audio CD into a WAV file, type the following command:

```
cdda2wav -D /dev/cdrom -t2 -Owav
```

`cdda2wav` saves the track in a WAV file named `audio.wav`. You can then play the WAV file in XMMS. Watch out though — each track of an audio CD typically takes about 60MB of disk space in WAV format.

Red Hat has removed from XMMS the code needed to play MP3 files, so you have to translate MP3s into a supported format such as WAV before you can play them. Red Hat recommends that you use the Ogg Vorbis format for compressed audio files because Ogg Vorbis is a patent- and royalty-free format.

To start XMMS from the GNOME or KDE desktop, choose Main Menu⇨Sound & Video⇨Audio Player. XMMS has a simple user interface. To open a sound file, choose Window Menu⇨Play File, or press L to select a .wav or .ogg file from the Load File dialog box. Select a file and click OK. XMMS starts playing the sound file. Figure 5-6 shows a typical XMMS window when it's playing a sound file.

Figure 5-6:
You can play many different types of sound files in XMMS.

If you get an error message from XMMS, choose Window Menu⇨Options⇨ Preferences and then select the OSS Driver as the Output Plugin. If you want to adjust the volume or other attributes of the sound, start the audio mixer by choosing Main Menu⇨Sound & Video⇨Volume Control. The Volume Control window appears (Figure 5-7). Drag the sliders to adjust the volume, bass, treble, and other attributes of the sound.

Figure 5-7:
You can adjust the sound's volume and other attributes from this window.

Of course, many music files are in MP3 format and you end up with MP3 files when you rip a CD by using a utility such as grip. Wouldn't it be nice if you could get XMMS to play MP3 music? Well, you can do that easily. All you have to do is download and install the MPEG audio input plug-in for XMMS. That plug-in, in the form of an RPM file — `xmms-mpg123-1.2.7-21.i386.rpm` — is available from `havardk.xmms.org/dist/xmms-1.2.7-rh8-rh9-rpm/xmms-mpg123-1.2.7-21.i386.rpm` (for other versions of Red Hat Linux, look in an appropriate directory in `havardk.xmms.org/dist/`). After downloading the RPM file, log in as `root` and type **rpm -ivh xmms-mpg123*** to install the plug-in. The next time you run XMMS, you can play MP3 files in XMMS. Easy, isn't it?

Burning a CD

Red Hat Linux includes the GnomeToaster, a graphical CD burner application with a lot of features. It can create both data CDs and audio CDs. You can also *rip* (copy) music from audio CDs to files on the hard drive and then burn them onto a new audio CD. If you happen to download Red Hat Linux ISO images (a huge data file with the exact replica of a CD-ROM), you can use GnomeToaster to create a CD from that ISO image. In the next few sections, I briefly explain how to use GnomeToaster. If you want to learn more, visit `gnometoaster.rulez.org`.

GnomeToaster depends on many external programs to do its job. If these external programs do not exist, then some GnomeToaster features won't work. Although most programs used by GnomeToaster come with Red Hat Linux, a few are not part of the Red Hat Linux distribution. For example, GnomeToaster needs the `mpg123` program to convert MP3 audio files into a form suitable for recording on CD. Red Hat Linux does not come with the `mpg123` program, so you can't create audio CDs that include MP3 songs.

Before you can burn a CD, you need a CD-R or CD-RW drive (CD burner) connected to your PC. It can be an internal or an external CD burner. Internal CD burners are usually IDE (also known as ATAPI) devices connected to the same card that supports the PC's hard disk and any other CD-ROM drive.

If you have an external CD burner, it probably connects to your PC's USB port. When you connect such a burner to the USB port and power up the burner, Red Hat Linux should automatically recognize the device and load the appropriate USB driver. When you use GnomeToaster to burn a CD on a USB CD-R/RW drive, you do not have to do anything special — GnomeToaster automatically detects most CD-ROM and CD-R/RW drives on your system. You do, however, have to manually identify the ATAPI CD drives.

To start GnomeToaster, choose Main Menu⇨System Tools⇨More System Tools⇨CD Writer from the GNOME or KDE desktop. If you aren't logged in as `root`, you're prompted for the `root` password. The GnomeToaster main window appears, as shown in Figure 5-8. You can do everything — configure GnomeToaster and burn audio and data CDs — from the main window.

Identifying CD Drives

At startup, GnomeToaster tries to automatically detect CD burners and CD-ROM drives, but you have to help it identify ATAPI CD drives (most internal CD-ROM and CD-R/RW drives are of this type). I show you how.

To see whether GnomeToaster has detected all the CD drives, click Preferences on the toolbar at the top of the main window. GnomeToaster displays the Preferences dialog box (as in Figure 5-9) with seven tabs. Click the CDROM and Recorder Setup tab to see the list of CD drives it has detected.

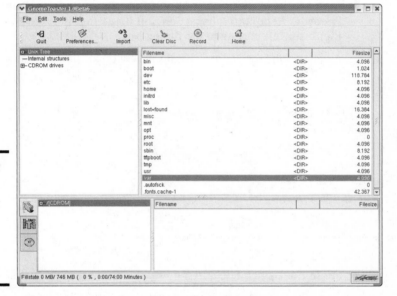

Figure 5-8: You can burn CDs from Gnome-Toaster's main window.

Figure 5-9: Configure Gnome-Toaster preferences from this dialog box.

Figure 5-9 shows the result of what GnomeToaster has detected on a system with an external CD burner and an internal ATAPI CD-ROM drive. In this case, GnomeToaster detected a CD burner (the dot to the left of the Drive Type column tells me that this is a CD burner). The list, however, does not show the ATAPI CD-ROM drive.

GnomeToaster can't detect ATAPI CD-ROM drives unless they are configured to be accessed through the ide-scsi driver. Because that's not the default setup in Red Hat Linux, you have to manually identify the ATAPI CD drives to GnomeToaster. To do so, follow these steps:

1. **In the GnomeToaster Preference dialog box, click the CDROM and Recorder Setup tab (Figure 5-9) and then click the Add button near the lower-left corner of the dialog box.**

A dialog box (see Figure 5-10) prompts you for information about the CD-ROM drive.

Figure 5-10: Tell Gnome-Toaster about any IDE/ATAPI CD drives on your system.

Please enter drive data	
Model (Model)	Manufacturer (Manufacturer)
Device File /dev/cdrom	Scsi ID 0,0
Mountpoint /mnt/cdrom	
☐ This Drive is a CD writer	
☐ Use SCSI Interface for DAE	
OK Cancel Prev	

2. **Fill in the Device File and Mountpoint fields and then click OK.**

Typically, you can enter /dev/cdrom (or /devhdc) in the device file-name and /mnt/cdrom in the Mountpoint field.

You can fill in the Model and Manufacturer for the CD drive, but these fields are not important.

Exploring the Preferences Dialog Box

In the GnomeToaster Preferences dialog box (shown in Figure 5-9), you can examine the other tabs and configure many more options. Typically, you'd leave everything else in their default settings, but here's an over-view of what you can do from the tabs in the GnomeToaster Preferences dialog box:

✦ **Common:** This tab enables you to specify the location of temporary files, whether to store data on your hard drive before writing to the CD, and the server with CD database where GnomeToaster can look up information about the CD. The default CD database server is `freedb.freedb.org`. (port 888). You can leave these options at their default settings.

✦ **ISO9660:** This tab is for setting options used when burning a data CD that uses the ISO 9660 file system (this is an internationally accepted standard method for storing files and directories on a CD-ROM so that you can read the same CD-ROM on any computer system, whether it's running Microsoft Windows, Macintosh, or Linux).

✦ **CD Digital Audio:** This tab specifies the settings that enable Gnome-Toaster to work with audio CDs. For example, the default setting causes GnomeToaster to run the `cdda2wav` program when it needs to extract a track from an audio CD. There are settings that specify how to extract information about an audio CD, including the disc title, disc artist, and information about each track.

✦ **Filetypes:** This tab contains information about file types and how to convert each type of file into a stream of data that can be recorded onto a CD. Each file type is indicated by the extension such as `.mp3` for MP3 files, `.wav` for WAV files, and `.ogg` for Ogg Vorbis audio files. For each file type, there is a command line that GnomeToaster runs to convert that file into data suitable for CD recording.

✦ **CDROM and Recorder Setup:** This tab displays information about the CD-ROM and CD-R/RW drives that GnomeToaster has detected. You can also manually add ATAPI CD drives to the list in this tab.

✦ **Audio System:** This tab shows the audio driver to be used to play sound.

✦ **Recorder:** This tab is for specifying how GnomeToaster records CDs. The most important options are the names of the recording clients — these are the programs that GnomeToaster runs to record CDs. By default, GnomeToaster uses `cdrecord` or `cdrdao` to record CDs. Both `cdrecord` and `cdrdao` come with Red Hat Linux.

Recording an Audio CD

With GnomeToaster, you can duplicate an audio CD or create a new audio CD by mixing and matching tracks you want. To make a new audio CD with all or some selected tracks from an existing audio CD, follow these steps:

1. **Place the original CD in the CD reader device (for example, the ATAPI CD-ROM drive that you identified in the CDROM and Recorder Setup tab of GnomeToaster Preferences).**

2. **Click the plus sign next to the CDROM drives in the top-left pane of the GnomeToaster window; then click the CD reader device name.**

   GnomeToaster displays the tracks in the top-right pane (see Figure 5-11) so that you can select the tracks to read.

Figure 5-11: Drag and drop audio tracks from a CD to create your own audio compilation.

3. **Click the Track Editor tab (the second tab from top) in the tabbed pane along the lower part of the GnomeToaster window.**

   GnomeToaster displays the track editor view where you prepare the tracks you want to burn onto a new audio CD.

4. **Drag a track from the track list onto the track editor pane.**

   GnomeToaster runs `cdda2wav` to convert the track into a format suitable for CD recording and saves the track to the hard drive. It can take a minute or two to read and save a typical track (of course, a long track takes longer to extract from the CD). GnomeToaster displays the progress in an information window. After copying the track to the editor, GnomeToaster shows the number of megabytes needed by the current tracks on the status bar at the bottom of GnomeToaster window (refer to Figure 5-11). That way you can keep track of how much room you have left on the CD, which can handle over 700MB of data.

5. **Repeat Step 4 to add other audio tracks to your new audio CD.**

6. **To delete a track from the track editor pane, select the track then right-click the track and choose Delete Track from the pop-up menu.**

7. **After your list is complete, insert a blank CD-R into the CD burner and then click the Record button on the GnomeToaster toolbar to start recording the CD.**

   GnomeToaster then begins to burn the CD and shows the progress in a window (shown in Figure 5-12). When the burn process is complete, GnomeToaster ejects the CD.

Figure 5-12:
Gnome-
Toaster
displays
progress
in burning
a new
audio CD.

8. **Play the CD in your Linux system — just quit GnomeToaster and plop the CD into the CD-ROM drive and it should play, assuming you have the sound card set up right.**

   You can also play the CD on a CD player.

By default, GnomeToaster burns the audio CD by using the Track-At-Once (TAO) mode that puts a two-second pause after each track. If you want to write the entire audio CD in a single step, you can do so by selecting the Disk-At-Once (DAO) mode. To select this mode, click the Recorder Settings tab (the last tab from the top in the lower tabbed pane) and then mark the Disc at Once check box — you can see this check box in the lower-left area in Figure 5-13. You can modify other recorder settings from this pane as well.

Incidentally, the Client output area in the right side of the lower pane in Figure 5-13 shows the output from the external command that GnomeToaster runs to record a CD. For example, when it used the cdrecord program to record the CD, the output from the cdrecord appears in this area. The current figure shows the cdrecord command's output after it recorded an audio CD with five tracks.

Figure 5-13:
Set various recorder settings, including recorder speed, from the lower pane.

Creating a Data CD

Saving files from your hard drive onto a CD is easy. To create a data CD, follow these steps:

1. **Click the plus sign next to the Unix Tree label on the top-left pane of the GnomeToaster window.**

   GnomeToaster displays the directory hierarchy in your system.

2. **Click a directory name.**

   GnomeToaster displays the contents of the directory in the top-right pane.

3. **Click the Folder tab (the topmost tab) in the tabbed pane along the lower part of GnomeToaster window.**

   GnomeToaster displays a virtual file system that represents the organization of the data CD you are preparing to burn.

4. **Drag files and directories from the top-right pane onto the virtual file system view in the lower-right pane.**

5. **Change to other directories as needed and continue until you have selected all the files and directories you want on the data CD.**

   GnomeToaster displays the current set of files, including the directory hierarchies, as shown in Figure 5-14.

Figure 5-14: Prepare the files and directories prior to burning a data CD using Gnome-Toaster.

6. **Insert a blank CD into the CD burner and then click the Record button on the toolbar.**

   GnomeToaster begins burning the data CD and ejects the disc when done.

Burning ISO Images

Linux distributions, including Red Hat Linux, are available for downloading from various Internet sites in the form of ISO images — an *ISO image* is an exact copy of an entire CD-ROM in a single, huge file. These files usually have the `.iso` extension. The *ISO* part of the name comes from the fact that the CD-ROM uses the ISO 9660 file system and *image* means the file is an exact replica of every bit of data on the CD-ROM.

You can use GnomeToaster to make a CD out of an ISO image. Just follow these steps:

1. **Click the plus sign next to the Unix Tree label on the top-left pane of the GnomeToaster window.**

   GnomeToaster displays the directory hierarchy in your system.

2. **Go to the directory that contains the ISO image file and click that directory's name.**

GnomeToaster displays the contents of the directory in the top-right pane. You should see the ISO image file listed.

3. **Click the Track Editor tab (the second tab from top) in the tabbed pane along the lower part of GnomeToaster window.**

   GnomeToaster displays the track editor view.

4. **Drag the ISO file from the top-right pane onto the track editor view in the lower-right pane.**

   GnomeToaster displays the ISO file's name in the track editor view and the amount of space it needs, as shown in Figure 5-15.

Figure 5-15: You can create a CD from an ISO image using Gnome-Toaster.

5. **Insert a blank CD into the CD burner and click the Record button on the toolbar.**

   GnomeToaster begins burning the ISO image onto the CD and ejects the disc when done.

Graphics and Imaging

You can use graphics and imaging applications to work with images and graphics (line drawings and shapes). I discuss two applications:

✦ **The GIMP** (*GNU Image Manipulation Program*) is a program for viewing and performing image-manipulation tasks, such as photo retouching, image composition, and image creation.

✦ **KGhostview** is a KDE application capable of displaying PostScript and PDF files.

The GIMP

The GIMP (GNU Image Manipulation Program) is an image-manipulation program written by Peter Mattis and Spencer Kimball and released under the GNU General Public License (GPL). It is installed if you select the Graphics Manipulation package when you install Red Hat Linux from this book's companion DVD. The GIMP is comparable to other image-manipulation programs, such as Adobe Photoshop and Corel Photopaint.

To try out the GIMP, choose Main Menu⇨Graphics⇨The GIMP from the GNOME or KDE desktop. The GIMP starts and displays a window with copyright and license information. Click the Continue button to proceed with the installation. The next screen shows the directories to be created when you proceed with a personal installation of The GIMP.

GIMP installation involves creating a directory called `.gimp-1.2` in your home directory and placing a number of files in that directory. This directory essentially holds information about any changes to user preferences you might make to The GIMP. Go ahead and click the Continue button at the bottom of the window. The GIMP creates the necessary directories, copies the necessary files to those directories, and guides you through a series of dialog boxes to complete the installation.

After the installation is done, click the Continue button. From now on, you won't see the installation window anymore; you have to deal with installation only when you run The GIMP for the first time.

The GIMP then loads any plug-ins — external modules that enhance its functionality. It displays a startup window that shows a message about each plug-in as it has loaded. After finishing the startup, The GIMP displays a tip of the day in a window. You can browse the tips and click the Close button to close the tip window. At the same time, The GIMP displays a number of windows (Figure 5-16).

These windows include a main toolbox window titled The GIMP; a Tool Options window; a Brush Selection window; and a Layers, Channels & Paths window. Of these, the main toolbox window is the most important — in fact, you can close the other windows and work by using the menus and buttons in the toolbox.

Book II
Chapter 5

Exploring Red Hat
Linux Applications

Figure 5-16:
Touch up
your photos
with The
GIMP.

The toolbox has three menus on the menu bar:

+ **The File menu** has options to create a new image, open an existing image, save and print an image, mail an image, and quit The GIMP.

+ **The Xtns menu** gives you access to numerous extensions to The GIMP. The exact content of the Xtns menu depends on which extensions are installed on your system.

+ **The Help menu** is where you can get help and view tips. For example, choose Help⇨Help to bring up The GIMP Help Browser with online information about The GIMP.

To open an image file in The GIMP, choose File⇨Open. This brings up the Load Image dialog box from which you can select an image file. You can change directories and select the image file you want to open. The GIMP can read all common image-file formats, such as GIF, JPEG, TIFF, PCX, BMP, PNG, and PostScript. After you select the file and click the OK button, The GIMP loads the image into a new window. Figure 5-16 shows an image The GIMP has opened, along with all the other GIMP windows.

The toolbox also has many buttons that represent the tools you use to edit the image and apply special effects. You can get pop-up help on each tool button by placing the mouse pointer on the button. You can select a tool by clicking the tool button, and you can apply that tool's effects to the image.

For your convenience, The GIMP displays a pop-up menu when you right-click your mouse on the image window. The pop-up menu has most of the options from the File and Xtns menus in the toolbox. You can then select specific actions from these menus.

You can do much more than just load and view images with the GIMP, but a complete discussion of all of its features is beyond the scope of this book. If you want to try the other features of The GIMP, consult The GIMP User Manual (GUM), available online at manual.gimp.org. You can also choose Xtns⇨Web Browser⇨GIMP.ORG⇨Documentation to access the online documentation for The GIMP (of course, you need an Internet connection for this to work).

Book II
Chapter 5

Exploring Red Hat
Linux Applications

Some documentation about The GIMP is installed in the /usr/share/doc directory. To go to that directory, type **cd /usr/share/doc/gimp*** (the actual directory name depends on the current version of The GIMP). The README file in that directory points you to other resources on the Web where you can learn more about The GIMP. In particular, visit The GIMP home page at www.gimp.org to learn the latest news about The GIMP and to find links to other resources.

KGhostview

KGhostview is a KDE application that's ideal for viewing and printing PostScript and PDF documents. For a long document, you can view and print selected pages. You can also view the document at various levels of magnification by zooming in or out.

To run KGhostview, choose Main Menu⇨Graphics⇨More Graphics Applications⇨PS/PDF Viewer from the GNOME or KDE desktop. This causes the KGhostview application window to appear. In addition to the menu bar and toolbar along the top edge, a vertical divide splits the main display area of the window into two parts.

To load and view a PostScript document in KGhostview, choose File⇨Open, or click the open folder icon on the toolbar. This action causes KGhostview to display a file-selection dialog box. Use this dialog box to navigate the file system and select a PostScript file. You can select one of the PostScript files that comes with Ghostscript. For example, open the file tiger.ps in the

`/usr/share/ghostscript/7.07/examples` directory. (If your system has a version of Ghostscript later than 7.07, you have to use the new version number in place of 7.07.)

To open the selected file, click the Open File button in the file selection dialog box. KGhostview opens the selected file, processes its contents, and displays the output in its window, as shown in Figure 5-17.

Figure 5-17:
KGhostview can display PostScript and PDF files.

KGhostview is useful for viewing various kinds of documentation that come in PostScript and PDF format (these files typically have the `.ps` or `.pdf` extension in their names).

Chapter 6: Using Text Editors

In This Chapter

✔ **Using GUI text editors**

✔ **Learning the** ed **text editor**

✔ **Learning the** vi **text editor**

*I*n Red Hat Linux, most system-configuration files are text files. If you write any shell scripts or other computer programs, they're text files too. Sometimes you have to edit these files using programs designed for that purpose: *text editors*. For example, you may need to edit files such as /etc/hosts, /etc/modules.conf, /etc/X11/XF86Config, /etc/ xinetd.d/telnet, and many more.

In this chapter, I introduce you to a few text editors — both the GUI editors and text-mode editors.

Using GUI Text Editors

Each of the GUI desktops — GNOME and KDE — comes with GUI text editors (these are text editors that have graphical user interfaces).

To use the GNOME text editor, choose Main Menu⇨Accessories⇨Text Editor from the GNOME desktop. You can open a file by clicking the Open button on the toolbar. This brings up the Open File dialog box. You can then change directories and select the file to edit by clicking the OK button.

The GNOME text editor then loads the file in its window. You can open more than one file and move among them as you edit the files. Figure 6-1 shows a typical editing session with the editor.

In this case, the editor has three files — fstab, hosts, and innittab (all from the /etc directory) — open for editing. The filenames appear as tabs below the toolbar of the editor's window. You can switch among the files by clicking the tabs.

Figure 6-1:
You can use
the GNOME
text editor
to edit
text files.

If you open a file for which you have only read permission, then the filename is preceded by the text RO- to indicate that the file is "read-only." In Figure 6-1, all the files are opened read-only because here I'm logged in as a normal user and I'm opening system files that only the root can modify.

The rest of the text-editing steps are intuitive. To enter new text, click to position the cursor and then begin typing. You can select text, copy, cut, and paste by using the buttons on the toolbar above the text-editing area.

From the KDE desktop, you can start the KDE text editor by choosing Main Menu⇨Accessories⇨Kate. To open a text file, choose File⇨Open from the menu. A dialog box appears. From this dialog box, you can go to the right directory, select the file to open, and click the OK button. The KDE text editor then opens the file and displays its contents in the window. You can then edit the file.

Text Editing with ed and vi

Red Hat Linux comes with two text-mode text editors:

✦ ed, a line-oriented text editor

✦ vi, a full-screen text editor that supports the command set of an earlier editor named ex

The ed and vi editors are cryptic compared to the graphical text editors. However, you should still learn the basic editing commands of ed and vi because sometimes these two may be the only editors available.

For example, if Red Hat Linux refuses to boot from the hard drive, you may have to boot from a floppy disk. In that case, you have to edit system files with the ed editor because that editor is small enough to fit on the floppy. I walk you through the basic text-editing commands of ed and vi. You'll see — they're not that hard.

Using ed

Typically, you have to use ed only when you boot a minimal version of Linux (for example, from a floppy you've set up as a boot disk), and the system doesn't support full-screen mode. In all other situations, you can use the vi editor that works in full-screen text mode.

Book II
Chapter 6

When you use ed, you work in either command mode or text-input mode:

Using Text Editors

+ **Command mode** is what you get by default. In this mode, anything that you type is interpreted as a command. The ed text editor has a simple command set where each command consists of one or more characters.

+ **Text-input mode** is for typing text. You can enter input mode with the commands a (append), c (change), or i (insert). After entering lines of text, you can leave input mode by entering a period (.) on a line by itself.

To practice editing a file, copy the /etc/fstab file to your home directory by issuing the following commands:

```
cd
cp /etc/fstab .
```

Now you should have a file named fstab in your home directory. Type the following command to begin editing a file in ed:

```
ed -p: fstab
621
:
```

This example uses the -p option to set the prompt to the colon character (:) and opens the fstab file (in the current directory, which should be your home directory) for editing. The ed editor opens the file, reports the number of characters in the file (621), displays the prompt (:), and waits for a command.

When you're editing with ed, it's helpful to make sure you always turn on a prompt character (use the -p option). Without the prompt, it's difficult to tell whether ed is in input mode or command mode.

After ed opens a file for editing, the current line is the last line of the file. To see the current line number (the current line is the line to which ed applies your command), use the . = command like this:

```
:.=
9
```

This output tells you that the fstab file has nine lines. (Your system's /etc/fstab file may have a different number of lines, in which case ed shows a different number.)

You can use the 1,$p command to see all lines in a file, as the following example shows:

```
:1,$p
LABEL=/                /                      ext3    defaults        1 1
LABEL=/boot            /boot                  ext3    defaults        1 2
none                   /dev/pts               devpts  gid=5,mode=620  0 0
none                   /proc                  proc    defaults        0 0
none                   /dev/shm               tmpfs   defaults        0 0
/dev/hda6              swap                   swap    defaults        0 0
/dev/cdrom             /mnt/cdrom             udf,iso9660
     noauto,owner,kudzu,ro 0 0
/dev/fd0               /mnt/floppy            auto    noauto,owner,kudzu 0 0
:
```

To go to a specific line, type the line number:

```
:6
/dev/hda6              swap           swap  defaults    0 0
:
```

The editor responds by displaying that line.

Suppose you want to delete the line that contains cdrom. To search for a string, type a slash (/) followed by the string that you want to locate:

```
:/cdrom
/dev/cdrom             /mnt/cdrom                 udf,iso9660
     noauto,owner,kudzu,ro 0 0
:
```

The editor locates the line that contains the string and then displays it. That line becomes the current line.

To delete the current line, use the d command as follows:

```
:d
:
```

To replace a string with another, use the s command. To replace cdrom with the string cd, for example, use this command:

```
:s/cdrom/cd/
:
```

To insert a line in front of the current line, use the i command:

```
:i
    (type the line you want to insert)
.   (type a single period to indicate you're done)
:
```

You can enter as many lines as you want. After the last line, enter a period (.) on a line by itself. That period marks the end of text-input mode, and the editor switches to command mode. In this case, you can tell that ed switched to command mode because you see the prompt (:).

When you're happy with the changes, you can write them to the file with the w command. If you want to save the changes and exit, type **wq** to perform both steps at the same time:

```
:wq
693
```

The ed editor saves the changes in the file, displays the number of saved characters, and exits. If you want to quit the editor without saving any changes, use the Q command.

These examples should give you an idea of how to use ed commands to perform the basic tasks of editing a text file. Table 6-1 lists some of the commonly used ed commands.

Table 6-1	Commonly Used ed Commands
Command	*Does the Following*
!command	Executes a shell command (for example, !pwd shows the current directory).
$	Goes to last line in the buffer.
%	Applies a command that follows to all lines in the buffer (for example, %p prints all lines).
+	Goes to next line.
+n	Goes to *n*th next line (where *n* is a number you designate).

(continued)

Table 6-1 *(continued)*

Command	Does the Following
,	Applies a command that follows to all lines in the buffer (for example, , p prints all lines); similar to %.
-	Goes to preceding line.
-n	Goes to *n*th previous line (where *n* is a number you designate).
.	Refers to the current line in the buffer.
/text/	Searches forward for the specified text.
;	Refers to a range of lines; current through last line in the buffer.
=	Prints line number.
?text?	Searches backward for the specified text.
^	Goes to the preceding line; also see the - command.
^n	Goes to *n*th previous line (where *n* is a number you designate); also see the -n command.
a	Appends after current line.
c	Changes specified lines.
d	Deletes specified lines.
i	Inserts text before current line.
n	Goes to line number *n*.
Press Enter	Displays next line and makes that line current.
q	Quits editor.
Q	Quits editor without saving changes.
r file	Reads and inserts contents of file after the current line.
s/old/new/	Replaces old string with new.
u	Undoes the last command.
W file	Appends contents of buffer to the end of the specified file.
w file	Saves buffer in the specified file (if no file is named, saves in the default file — the file whose contents ed is currently editing).

Using vi

The vi editor is a full-screen text editor, so you can view several lines at the same time. Most UNIX systems, including Red Hat Linux, come with vi. Therefore, if you learn the basic features of vi, you'll be able to edit text files on almost any UNIX system.

When vi edits a file, it reads the file into a *buffer* — a block of memory — so you can change the text in the buffer. The vi editor also uses temporary files during editing, but the original file isn't altered until you save the changes.

To start the editor, type **vi** and follow it with the name of the file you want to edit, like this:

```
vi /etc/fstab
```

The vi editor then loads the file into memory and displays the first few lines in a text screen and positions the cursor on the first line (Figure 6-2).

```
LABEL=/              /                    ext3    defaults        1 1
LABEL=/boot          /boot                ext3    defaults        1 2
none                 /dev/pts             devpts  gid=5,mode=620  0 0
none                 /proc                proc    defaults        0 0
none                 /dev/shm             tmpfs   defaults        0 0
/dev/hda6            swap                 swap    defaults        0 0
/dev/cdrom           /mnt/cdrom           udf,iso9660 noauto,owner,kudzu,r
o 0 0
/dev/fd0             /mnt/floppy          auto    noauto,owner,kudzu 0 0
~
~
~
~
~
~
~
~
~
~
~
~
~
~
~
"/etc/fstab" [readonly] 8L, 621C                     1,1           All
```

Figure 6-2: You can edit text files with the vi full-screen text editor.

The last line shows the pathname of the file as well as the number of lines (8) and the number of characters (621) in the file. In this case, the text [readonly] appears after the filename because I'm opening the /etc/fstab file while I am logged in as a normal user (which means I don't have permission to modify the file). Later, the last line in the vi display functions as a command-entry area. The rest of the lines display the file. If the file contains fewer lines than the screen, vi displays the empty lines with a tilde (~) in the first column.

The current line is marked by the cursor, which appears as a small black rectangle. The cursor appears on top of a character.

When using vi, you work in one of three modes:

✦ **Visual command mode** is what you get by default. In this mode, anything that you type is interpreted as a command that applies to the line containing the cursor. The vi commands are similar to the ed commands.

✦ **Colon command mode** is for reading or writing files, setting vi options, and quitting vi. All colon commands start with a colon (:). When you enter the colon, vi positions the cursor on the last line and waits for you to type a command. The command takes effect when you press Enter.

✦ **Text input mode** is for typing text. You can enter input mode with the command a (insert after cursor), A (append at end of line), or i (insert after cursor). After entering lines of text, you have to press Esc to leave input mode and re-enter visual command mode.

One problem with all these modes is that you cannot easily tell the current mode that vi is in. It can be frustrating to begin typing only to realize that vi is not in input mode.

If you want to make sure that vi is in command mode, just press Esc a few times. (Pressing Esc more than once doesn't hurt.)

To view online help in vi, type **:help** while in command mode. When you're done with help, type **:q** to exit the help screen and return to the file you're editing.

The vi editor initially positions the cursor on the first character of the first line — and one of the handiest things you can know is how to move the cursor around. To get a bit of practice, try the commands shown in Table 6-2.

Table 6-2	Cursor Movement Commands in vi
Keypress	*Does the Following*
Down arrow	Moves the cursor one line down.
Up arrow	Moves the cursor one line up.
Left arrow	Moves the cursor one character to the left.
Right arrow	Moves the cursor one character to the right.
W	Moves the cursor one word forward.
B	Moves the cursor one word backward.
Ctrl+D	Moves down half a screen.
Ctrl+U	Scrolls up half a screen.

You can go to a specific line number at any time. This is where a colon command comes in handy. To go to line 6, for example, type the following and then press Enter:

```
:6
```

When you type the colon, vi displays the colon on the last line of the screen. From then on, vi uses any text you type as a command. You have to press Enter to submit the command to vi. In colon-command mode, vi accepts all commands that the ed editor accepts — and then some.

To search for a string, first type a slash (/). The vi editor displays the slash on the last line of the screen. Type the search string and then press Enter. The vi editor locates the string and positions the cursor at the beginning of that string. Thus, to locate the string cdrom in the file /etc/fstab, type

```
/cdrom
```

To delete the line that contains the cursor, type **dd** (two lowercase *ds*). The vi editor deletes that line of text and makes the next line the current one.

To begin entering text in front of the cursor, type **i** (a lowercase *i* all by itself). The vi editor switches to text-input mode. Now you can enter text. When you finish entering text, press Esc to return to visual command mode.

After you finish editing the file, you can save the changes in the file with the :w command. To quit the editor without saving any changes, use the :q! command. If you want to save the changes and exit, you can type **:wq** to perform both steps at the same time. The vi editor saves the changes in the file and exits. You can also save the changes and exit the editor by pressing Shift+zz (hold the Shift key down and press the Z key twice).

In addition to these commands, vi accepts a large number of commands. Table 6-3 lists some commonly used vi commands, organized by task.

**Book II
Chapter 6**

Using Text Editors

Table 6-3	Commonly Used vi Commands
Command	*Does the Following*
Insert Text	
a	Inserts text after the cursor.
A	Inserts text at the end of the current line.
I	Inserts text at the beginning of the current line.
i	Inserts text before the cursor.

(continued)

Table 6-3 *(continued)*

Command	Does the Following
Delete Text	
D	Deletes up to the end of the current line.
dd	Deletes the current line.
dw	Deletes from the cursor to the end of the following word.
x	Deletes the character on which the cursor rests.
Change Text	
C	Changes up to the end of the current line.
cc	Changes the current line.
J	Joins the current line with the next one.
rx	Replaces the character under the cursor with x (where x is any character).
Move Cursor	
h or Left arrow	Moves one character to the left.
j or Down arrow	Moves one line down.
k or Up arrow	Moves one line up.
L	Moves cursor to the end of the screen.
l or Right arrow	Moves one character to the right.
w	Moves to the beginning of the following word.
Scroll Text	
Ctrl+D	Scrolls forward by half a screen.
Ctrl+U	Scrolls backward by half a screen.
Refresh Screen	
Ctrl+L	Redraws screen.
Cut and Paste Text	
P	Puts yanked line above the current line.
p	Puts yanked line below the current line.
yy	Yanks (copies) current line into an unnamed buffer.
Colon Commands	
:!*command*	Executes shell command.
:q	Quits editor.
:q!	Quits without saving changes.
:r *filename*	Reads file and inserts after current line.
:w *filename*	Writes buffer to file.
:wq	Saves changes and exits.

Command	Does the Following
Search Text	
/string	Searches forward for string.
?string	Searches backward for string.
Miscellaneous	
u	Undoes last command.
Esc	Ends input mode and enters visual command mode.
U	Undoes recent changes to current line.

Book III

OpenOffice.org

Contents at a Glance

Chapter 1: Writing with OpenOffice.org Writer

In This Chapter

✔ Getting documents from others

✔ Taking stock of OpenOffice.org Writer

✔ Getting started with Writer

✔ Preparing documents in Writer

*L*et's face it! The whole world, or so it seems, uses Microsoft Office, especially Microsoft Word, to write stuff. You have to work with the world to get your job done. Until recently, the lack of a freely available and good Microsoft Office–compatible office suite may have been holding you back from using Red Hat Linux as the primary desktop operating system. Well, your troubles are over. Red Hat Linux now comes with the OpenOffice.org office suite — a set of office productivity applications comparable to Microsoft Office and compatible with Microsoft Office as well. OpenOffice.org should already be installed on your system — all you have to do is select the *Office/Productivity* package group during Red Hat Linux installation. If you didn't install the *Office/Productivity* package group, follow the steps described in Book I, Chapter 3 to install that package group now.

OpenOffice.org Writer, or *Writer* for short, is at the heart of the OpenOffice.org office suite. Writer is a word processor that makes it easy for you to prepare many different types of documents on your Red Hat Linux system and, best of all, share files with others who use Microsoft Word.

Typically you might work with Microsoft Word files that your coworkers and friends (and maybe even family) send you. This chapter starts by explaining the many different ways in which you might receive a Microsoft Word file — and what to do when you receive such a file. The chapter then gives you an overview of how to open the document, work on it, track changes, and save it to a folder. Along the way, I provide tables that summarize how to perform common word processing tasks with Writer.

Before your expectations go sky-high, let me caution you that if you share files between Microsoft Word and Writer, you may run into some conversion problems; some Word features may not convert fully into equivalent Writer features. However, if you share only simple documents with Microsoft Word users (or if you simply want to prepare your own nicely formatted documents), Writer would work well for you.

By the way, if you're already a proficient Microsoft Word user, you should be able to start using Writer without much trouble because much of Writer works very much like Word.

Getting Documents from Others

If you're like me, you often work on documents that you share with your coworkers. One of you might prepare a draft and others would then edit and add to that draft. You typically receive the documents as e-mail attachments or on some storage medium (such as a floppy disk, Zip disk, or CD-ROM).

Before you start working on the document, you have to save it in a folder (directory) on your hard disk. Here are the different ways you can get the documents onto your hard disk:

✦ **E-mail:** Your e-mail reader (such as Mozilla Mail or Ximian Evolution) has an option to save attachments to a directory.

✦ **Floppy disk:** (I assume it's a DOS/Windows-format floppy disk you're using.) Insert the floppy into the A drive, open a terminal window (by choosing Main Menu⇨System Tools⇨Terminal), and type **mdir** to look at the contents of the floppy. Then type the following command to copy a specified file to the current directory:

```
mcopy a:filename.doc .
```

Here *filename.doc* is the Microsoft Word file you want to copy to the hard disk.

✦ **Zip disk:** Red Hat Linux should create an entry in the /etc/fstab file for the Zip drive so that you can mount it at the /mnt/zip directory. Insert the Zip disk into the drive and type **mount /mnt/zip** to mount it. You can now access the files on the Zip disk at the /mnt/zip directory. In other words, if there is a file at the top-level directory on the Zip disk, you can copy that file to the current directory on your hard disk with the following command:

```
cp /mnt/zip/filename.doc .
```

+ **CD-ROM:** If you're at the GNOME or KDE desktop, the contents of the CD-ROM should appear in a file manager window soon after you insert the CD-ROM into the CD-ROM drive. You can then drag and drop the file into a directory on your hard disk. If you aren't using a GUI desktop, type **mount /mnt/cdrom** to mount the CD-ROM, and then you can access the CD-ROM's contents at the /mnt/cdrom directory.

Now that you have a Microsoft Word file in your hands, all you need to do is open it in Writer and start working on it!

Taking Stock of OpenOffice.org Writer

Before you begin using Writer, I want to give you a quick overview of its major features. When you know what you can do with Writer, you can read the subsequent sections to find out how to perform specific tasks in Writer, such as formatting tables, printing documents, and tracking changes.

You can do the following with Writer:

+ Open and edit Microsoft Word files or convert Microsoft Word files to Writer format. One advantage of converting to Writer format is that Writer files are much smaller in size than corresponding Microsoft Word files.

+ Save documents in many different formats including Microsoft Word 97/2000/XP, Word 95, Word 6.0, Rich Text Format (RTF), StarWriter 5.0 (as well as 4.0 and 3.0), plain text, Adobe PDF, and Web page (HTML).

+ Insert graphics files of many different formats, including JPEG, GIF, ZSoft Paintbrush (PCX), TIFF, Windows BMP, Macintosh PICT, Encapsulated PostScript (EPS), Adobe Photoshop (PSD), AutoCAD DXF, and many more.

+ Create tables that can include calculations and add charts that update when the table contents change.

+ Perform complex page layouts with desktop publishing features such as text frames and floating frames.

+ Easily create and organize multiple files that make up a large project such as a book or a large report.

+ Create a *mail merge* where you write a single document with generic fields and have Writer automatically create many different customized documents by filling in the specific fields (such as name, address, and phone number) from a database.

Book III
Chapter 1

Writing with OpenOffice.org Writer

- ✦ Save versions of a document as you continue to change it, and revert to an older version if necessary.

- ✦ Compare changes and work collaboratively using the Versions system. Not only can you see what has changed and who changed it, but you can also accept or reject those changes individually (or in groups) according to certain criteria.

    A note of caution here: The versioning information doesn't export perfectly to some other formats — in particular, Microsoft Word.

- ✦ E-mail your documents directly from Writer.

- ✦ If you like, Writer can automatically complete the word you're typing by making a best guess — and you can accept the choice by pressing Enter. (If this feature drives you crazy, you can simply turn it off, just as you can configure many other features in Writer.)

Writer enables you to print a Writer document directly to an Adobe Portable Document Format (PDF) file. To electronically share a document in its final form, you can print the document to a PDF file and distribute that file. Anyone can easily view and print PDF files by using the free Adobe Reader (available at `www.adobe.com/products/acrobat/readstep2.html`).

Getting Started with Writer

The best way to learn to use Writer is to simply start using it. To start Writer, click the Writer icon on the panel (the icon showing some pieces of paper with a pen) or choose Main Menu➪Office➪OpenOffice.org Writer.

If this is your first time using Writer, the Address Data Source AutoPilot runs and prompts you for the source of address data already on your system. If you set this up, you can use the address data to create mail merge letters or documents that use the address information to fill in fields in a generic letter. If you have a Mozilla address book (for example) or other list of addresses, select that source and click Next to go through the AutoPilot's steps. Otherwise click Cancel to continue with Writer.

Writer might also display a dialog box offering you an opportunity to register as an OpenOffice.org user. Make an appropriate choice — whether you want to register now, be reminded later, never register, or indicate that you have already registered — and click OK.

Writer displays its main window (Figure 1-1) with an empty document and the Stylist — a window with a list of styles. In the following section, I describe this main window in some detail.

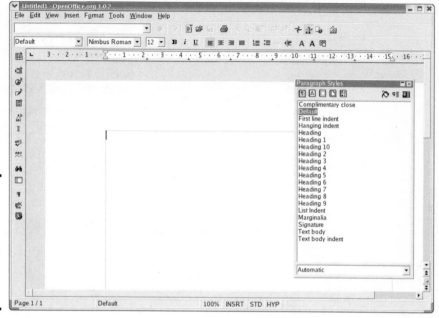

Figure 1-1:
You can start typing your document in Writer's main window.

If the Stylist window gets in the way, press F11 to toggle it on and off.

Using Writer is simple because it's so similar to other word processors that you've probably used, such as Microsoft Word. For example, you can type text into the blank document, format text, and save text when you're done. (I describe these tasks and more in a later section, "Preparing Documents in Writer.")

If you want to work on an existing document (for example, a Microsoft Word file) that you've saved on your hard disk, choose File⇨Open and then pick the document from the Open dialog. Then you can work on that document and save it in Word format, other word processing format, or in the default OpenOffice.org 1.0 Text Document format in a file with the .sxw extension.

Examining the Writer main window

To familiarize yourself with Writer, start by examining the user interface components packed into its main window, shown in Figure 1-2.

Object bar

Function bar

Menu bar

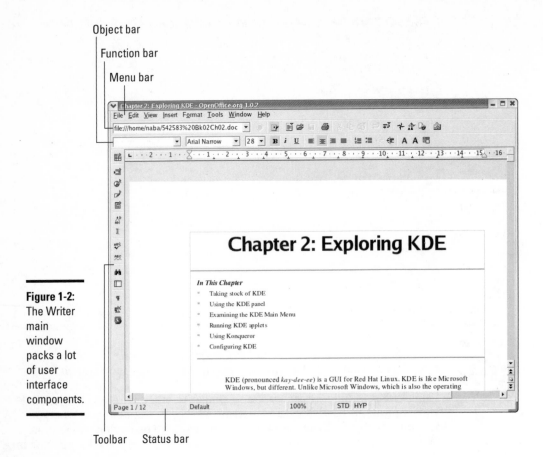

Figure 1-2:
The Writer
main
window
packs a lot
of user
interface
components.

Toolbar   Status bar

As Figure 1-2 shows, you can view the Writer window in terms of the follow-ing major parts:

✦ **Menu bar** provides the standard pull-down menus: File, Edit, Help, and so forth. Use these menus to perform all the tasks that Writer can do.

✦ **Function bar** shows the full pathname or the URL of the currently open file and also provides buttons for performing tasks, such as opening, saving, and printing a document. You can also click icons on the func-tion bar to open the Stylist (a list of paragraph, character, and page styles), the Navigator (a list of document parts such as headings, tables, and bookmarks), and the Gallery (a collection of predefined graphic objects such as 3D shapes, backgrounds, and bullets).

✦ **Object bar** enables you to format the document by applying styles, selecting fonts, or changing text attributes such as bold, italic, and underline. This bar changes depending on the type of object (such as plain text or graphics) that you've clicked.

✦ **Ruler** shows the page dimensions and the tab stops.

✦ **Toolbar,** located along the left side of the window, provides buttons that you can use to perform common document preparation tasks, such as insert tables, create forms, check spelling, and show the drawing functions.

✦ **Status bar** displays the usual information about the open document, including the current page number and the total page count. You can also click elements in the status bar to change certain settings, such as the text selection mode and the zoom factor for viewing the document.

In addition to these parts, the largest part of the Writer window is the work area where your document appears. That's where you focus most of your attention.

Use tooltips to get a clue about what a particular field or button does. Mouse over a field or a button and Writer displays a small tooltip window with a brief help message. If you want more information in the tooltips, turn on extended tooltips by choosing Help⇨Extended Tips. On the other hand, if you don't like these tooltips, toggle them off by choosing Help⇨Tips and Help⇨Extended Tips.

If you need it, help is available in Writer. Choose Help⇨Contents from the Writer menu. This brings up the OpenOffice.org Help window, shown in Figure 1-3, with help information about Writer. Click the links to view specific help information.

Setting up Writer

You don't really have to do any special setups to start using Writer. Even tasks such as printing should work right away provided you have set up a printer using the procedure described in Book I, Chapter 3. There are, however, some settings you may want to tinker with so that Writer works to your liking. For example, you might want to turn off AutoCorrect so that it doesn't suggest word completion, or you might want to hide some toolbars to get more workspace. You can set up most of these options from the View and Tools menus, which are located on the Menu bar (refer to Figure 1-2). In particular, you perform most of the setup tasks from the dialog box (Figure 1-4) that appears when you choose Tools⇨Options.

Book III
Chapter 1

Writing with
OpenOffice.org
Writer

Figure 1-3:
You can get
help about
Writer from
this window.

Figure 1-4:
Set up many
aspects
of Writer
from the
Tools⇨
Options
dialog box.

Table 1-1 summarizes the common setup tasks and how you can perform
them from Writer's menus.

Table 1-1	Common Setup Tasks in OpenOffice.org Writer
To Do This	*Use This Procedure*
Toggle various parts of Writer window on or off	Select the appropriate item such as Ruler, Status Bar, or Toolbars from the View menu and toggle that item on or off.
Customize toolbars	Choose View⇨Toolbars⇨Customize. You can also choose Tools⇨Configure and then click the tabs Status Bar and Toolbars to configure the appropriate toolbar. You can also right-click a toolbar and choose Configure from the pop-up menu.
Customize menus	Choose Tools⇨Configure and then click the Menu tab.
Change default locations of various files	Choose Tools⇨Options. Then choose OpenOffice.org⇨Paths and click the path you want to change. For example, click My Documents and specify the pathname for the default location of your documents.
Display font names in their font in the drop-down font list in the object bar	Choose Tools⇨Options. Then choose OpenOffice.org⇨View and turn on the check box marked Preview in Fonts Lists.
Show full menus including items that are not applicable	Choose Tools⇨Options. Then choose OpenOffice.org⇨View and turn on the check box labeled Inactive Menu Items.
Show or hide tooltips	Choose Help⇨Tips to toggle tooltips on or off and choose Help⇨Extended Tips to toggle extended tooltips on or off.
Always create a backup copy of the file	Choose Tools⇨Options. Then choose Load/Save⇨General and click the check box for Always Create Backup Copy.
Autosave every *XX* minutes	Choose Tools⇨Options. Then choose Load/Save⇨General and click the Autosave Every check box and select the number of minutes specifying how often to save the file.
Show nonprintable characters, such as paragraph marks, tabs, and so on	Choose Tools⇨Options. Then choose Text Document⇨Formatting Aids and turn on the check box of characters you want Writer to display.
Choose language and currency	Choose Tools⇨Options. Then choose Language Settings⇨Languages and select the Locale setting, Default currency, and the language for documents. If you use any Asian language, turn on the Enabled check box underneath the text `Asian languages support`.

(continued)

Table 1-1 *(continued)*

To Do This	Use This Procedure
Choose, create, or edit a custom dictionary	Choose Tools⇨Options. Then choose Language Settings⇨Writing Aids and add a new dictionary or edit words in an existing dictionary.
Change options for tracking changes	Choose Tools⇨Options. Then choose Text Document⇨Changes and select options for displaying changes to the document.
Change user information	Choose Tools⇨Options. Then choose OpenOffice.org⇨User Data and enter information about yourself.
Turn off Help Agent that pops up when you perform certain tasks for the first time	Choose Tools⇨Options. Then choose OpenOffice.org⇨General and turn off the Activate check box for the Help Agent.
Set up AutoCorrect and AutoFormat options	Choose Tools⇨AutoCorrect/AutoFormat and click the Options tab in the resulting dialog box. Turn on (or turn off) the AutoCorrect options to suit your needs and click OK. For example, to turn off automatic word completion, click the Word Completion tab and click the Complete Words check box to remove the check.

Preparing Documents in Writer

You'll have no problem preparing documents using Writer. Typically, you can simply click to position a cursor and then type your text. To format text, select a style for the paragraph or select text and then apply formatting such as boldface or italics. In the following sections, I provide some quick tips on how to perform specific document preparation tasks in Writer. I organize the tips into the following categories of tasks:

+ Editing and reviewing documents

+ Using styles and templates

+ Performing page layout

+ Creating and inserting graphics

+ Using fields

+ Working with large documents

Editing and reviewing documents

To edit a document, you have to open the file, move around within the document, insert and delete text, and save the file. You can perform most of these tasks intuitively because these steps are similar in most word processors. For that reason, I don't discuss in detail how to perform each of these tasks. Instead, in the following paragraphs, I highlight just a couple of features that you'll find particularly useful in your work. Then, in Table 1-2, I provide a list of commonly used tasks and how to perform them.

Typically, you review changes when you collaborate with others on a document and several of you make revisions to the document. To review changes, the changes have to be tracked. Writer has features to enable change tracking (or *redlining*, as it's commonly called). With Writer, you can examine the changes, accept or reject each change, and make more editing changes — even adding comments to explain why you made a change.

Writer has other features for easily editing a document. For example, you can search and replace text — even find all occurrences of text with a specific formatting style and change each occurrence.

Most of Writer's editing and change-tracking functions are in the Edit menu (shown in Figure 1-5). Some toolbar icons provide shortcuts to the menu.

**Book III
Chapter 1**

**Writing with
OpenOffice.org
Writer**

Figure 1-5:
Perform most editing and reviewing tasks from the Edit menu and its submenus.

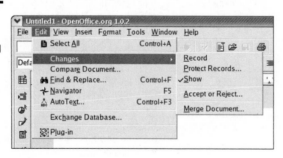

Table 1-2 summarizes some common editing and reviewing tasks and how to perform these tasks. The table does not mention the toolbar icons, but you can always mouse over each icon and read the tooltips to see which ones enable you to make specific editing and reviewing changes.

Table 1-2	Common Editing and Reviewing Tasks
To Do This	*Use These Steps*
Protect document for editing	Choose Edit⇨Changes⇨Protect Records and enter a password in the resulting dialog. To enable changes, choose Edit⇨Changes⇨Protect Records again and enter the password you entered earlier.
Jump quickly to different parts of a document	Choose Edit⇨Navigator or press F5. Open the appropriate category such as Headings, Tables, or Bookmarks and then double-click an item to jump to that location.
Find and replace text with specific formatting and style	Choose Edit⇨Find & Replace or press Ctrl+F. In the dialog box, enter the text to find, including any format, and enter the replacement text, if any. Then click Find or Replace depending on whether you simply want to find text or you want to find and replace with new text.
Select multiple blocks of text to copy, cut, or format as a group	Select the blocks of text while holding down the Ctrl key. Another way is to click STD on the status bar until it shows ADD and then select each block of text one by one.
Insert a special character	Position cursor and choose Insert⇨Special Character. Select font and character to insert.
Set some text in initial uppercase	Select the text. Choose Format⇨Character and click the Font Effects tab on the resulting dialog box. Choose Title from the Effects drop-down list.
Edit a hyperlink without activating the URL	Hold down the Alt key and click the hyperlink. Now you can edit the text in the hyperlink.
Move a paragraph up or down	Click paragraph and then press Ctrl+Up Arrow or Ctrl+Down Arrow to move the paragraph up or down.
Enable or disable change tracking	Choose Edit⇨Changes⇨Record to turn check mark on or off. When check mark is on, Writer tracks changes.
Show or hide changes on a document	Choose Edit⇨Changes⇨Show to turn check mark on or off. When check mark is on, Writer displays the changes with revision marks.
Insert comments to explain a change	Make the change, choose Edit⇨Changes⇨Comment, and then enter your comment in the dialog box that appears.
Insert notes — comments not associated with a change	Choose Insert⇨Note and type the note in the dialog box that appears.

To Do This	Use These Steps
Print the document to a PDF file	Choose File⇨Print. In the Print dialog box, click the list of printers and select PDF converter from the drop-down list. Click OK.
Save a version of the document	Choose File⇨Versions. From the resulting dialog box, select Save New Version. You can create new versions only after you have saved the document once.
Open an older version of a document	Choose File⇨Versions and select the version to open from the dialog box. Click Open.
Merge documents	Choose Edit⇨Changes⇨Merge Document. From the resulting Insert dialog box, select the document with which you want to merge the current document.
Accept or reject changes	Choose Edit⇨Changes⇨Accept or Reject and then accept and reject changes from the list that appears in a dialog box.
Create an AutoText entry	Choose Edit⇨AutoText or press CTRL+F3. Then enter the text and the shortcut.
Insert AutoText	Type the shortcut and press F3. For example, type BW and press F3 to enter the text "Best Wishes" (BW is a predefined shortcut for Best Wishes).
Count the number of words in the document	Choose File⇨Properties and click the Statistics tab in the resulting dialog box.
Look at the edit document properties	Choose File⇨Properties.
Check spelling	Choose Tools⇨Spellcheck⇨Check or press F7.
Exclude a word from spell check	Double-click to select the word. Right-click and select Character from the pop-up menu. Then click the Font tab and select [None] from the Language drop-down list.

Using styles and templates

In Writer, you can format pages, paragraphs, and blocks of text manually. For example, you can place the cursor on a paragraph, choose Format⇨ Paragraph, and then format various characteristics of the paragraph (such as indentation, spacing, and borders). This paragraph-by-paragraph formatting is okay for a short document, but it can be tedious and time-consuming if you have to format hundreds of paragraphs one by one. A better approach is to define a *style* — a collection of formatting characteristics stored under a particular, usually descriptive, name. Then you can simply apply that style to all paragraphs. If you need to change any aspect of the paragraphs, simply edit the style and voilà — all paragraphs with that style get the new formatting.

You may be familiar with paragraph and character styles in Microsoft Word, but Writer relies more on styles than Microsoft Word. Writer supports five types of styles: page, paragraph, character, numbering, and frame. Table 1-3 summarizes what each of these styles control.

Table 1-3	Five Types of Styles in Writer
This Style	*Controls This*
Page style	The page layout, including the margins, number of columns, headers, and footers.
Paragraph style	The look of a paragraph, such as the font, paragraph spacing, borders, bullets, numbering, and the style of the following paragraph.
Character style	The font style of selected text in a paragraph.
Numbering style	The number or bullet character and spacing that are used for numbered or bulleted lists.
Frame style	The size and position of the frame and the text-wrapping options.

In Writer, you can conveniently access and use all the document's styles in a floating window called the Stylist (Figure 1-6). Writer displays the Stylist by default, but you can show and hide it by pressing F11 (or choosing Format⇨Stylist).

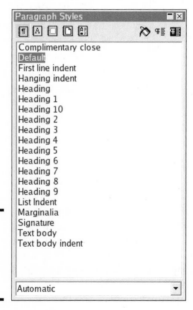

Figure 1-6:
Press F11
to toggle
Stylist on
and off.

The Stylist makes it very easy to organize and use the styles. The five icons along the top part of the Stylist refer to the five types of styles — paragraph, character, frame, page, and numbering — from leftmost to the right. You can click an icon to see all styles of that type. To apply a style, position the cursor where you want to apply the style and double-click the style from the Stylist. For character styles, select the text and then double-click the character style.

Writer also supports templates, just as Microsoft Word does. A *template* is a special document with a collection of styles for the kinds of layouts that the document needs. You can think of a template as a model for a specific type of document. For example, you might have templates for documents such as memos, letters, fax cover sheets, envelopes, and many more.

Writer does not come with any templates, but you can create or download templates from Web sites. A Writer template for writing manuscripts using the Modern Language Association (MLA) style (see `owl.english.purdue.edu/handouts/research/r_mla.html` for more information on the MLA style), for example, is available from `www.cc.mie-u.ac.jp/~lq20100/MLA-Template.stw`. You have to install the template file — `MLA-Template.stw` — before you can create documents using that template. Note that the `.stw` extension is used for OpenOffice.org template files.

To install a template file to use in Writer, follow these steps:

1. **Choose File⇨Template⇨Organize.**

The Template Management dialog box (shown in Figure 1-7) appears with the Default folder of templates on the left side and the current list of documents on the right.

Figure 1-7:
Import the template file into the Default template folder.

Book III
Chapter 1

**Writing with
OpenOffice.org
Writer**

2. **Right-click the Default folder icon and choose Import Template from the pop-up menu, as shown in Figure 1-7.**

   The Open dialog box appears.

3. **Navigate to the directory where you saved the template file, select the template file, and click Open.**

   The Open dialog box closes; the template now appears in the Default folder in the Template Management dialog box.

4. **Click Close to close the Template Management dialog box.**

To create a new document from a template you've installed, follow these steps:

1. **Choose File⇨New⇨Templates and Documents.**

   A dialog box appears with the templates. Double-click the Default folder to open it and view the templates.

2. **Select the template you want to use and click Open.**

   A new document appears, typically with some text illustrating the selected template's styles.

3. **Erase the text in the new document and start typing what you want.**

   To view the styles in that template, open the Stylist by pressing F11 and apply styles by double-clicking them in the Stylist.

Writer also enables you to perform many other tasks related to styles and templates. For example, you can create a style, apply a style to text, copy styles from one template to another, and so on. Table 1-4 summarizes how you can perform some common tasks involving styles and templates in Writer.

Table 1-4	Common Tasks Involving Styles and Templates
To Do This	*Follow These Steps*
Determine what template is associated with a document	Choose File⇨Properties and click the General tab in the resulting dialog box. Look for the template name in the Template field in the lower part of that tab.
Install a template file	Choose File⇨Template⇨Organize. Right-click the Default folder icon and choose Import Template from the pop-up menu. Select template from the Open dialog box and click Open.
Specify default template	Choose File⇨Templates⇨Organize. Double-click the Default folder on the left side of the dialog box to view the templates (you must have already installed templates). Select a template and click Commands on the right side of the dialog box. Then select Set As Default Template from the drop-down list.

To Do This	Follow These Steps
Create a new template	Create a document layout with styles you want in the template. Choose File⇨Templates⇨Save and assign a name to save the current file as a template.
Edit a template	Choose File⇨Templates⇨Edit. From the resulting Open dialog box, select the template file to edit.
Copy styles between templates	Choose File⇨Templates⇨Organize. Open the two templates. Select styles from one template and drag and drop them onto another template.
Create a new document from a template	Choose File⇨New⇨Templates and Documents. In the resulting dialog box, open a template folder, select a template, and click Open.
Apply a different template to a document	Start a new document based on the template you want to use. Then copy the contents of the old document into the new document.
Apply a style to text	Position cursor on text and Choose Format⇨Styles or press F11. Click the first button on the Stylist window's toolbar to view the paragraph styles. Then double-click a style to apply that style. After you apply a paragraph style once, the style appears in the drop-down list on the object bar.
Redefine a style	Choose style in the Stylist, right-click, choose Modify; or choose Format⇨Styles⇨Catalog, select style, click Modify.
Create a new style	Choose Format⇨Styles⇨Catalog, or press Ctrl+Y. Click New and define the style by filling in information in the resulting dialog box.
Use AutoPilot to create a document	Choose File⇨AutoPilot and then the document type you want to create. Fill in the information requested by the AutoPilot and click Create.

Performing page layout

In Writer, page styles control the page layout, and each page can have its own style. The usual approach is to define three page styles: First Page, Left Page, and Right Page. Define the First Page with whatever applies to the first page such as a special header and no page number. The Left Page is the style for the even (=) numbered pages and the Right Page style is for odd-numbered pages. For each page style, you can also define the page style that applies to the following page. The idea would be to define Left Page as the next page style for First Page and Right Page as the style of the page that follows the Left Page style. That way, the page styles will be correct for all the pages as long as you start with the First Page style. You may also want to define a Landscape page style so you can use it for pages that have to be in landscape orientation.

If you are familiar with Microsoft Word, you know that the page setup — paper size, orientation, margins, and so on — applies to all pages in the document. In Writer, a page style does not automatically apply to the entire document. Instead, each page has its own page style. Of course, you can choose to apply the same page style to all the pages. Essentially, you have more fine-grained control over page layouts in Writer.

A typical page layout task is to insert objects created in other OpenOffice.org applications, such as a Calc spreadsheet, an Impress slide, or a Draw drawing. You can insert such objects by choosing Insert⇨Object⇨OLE Object. Incidentally, OLE stands for Object Linking and Embedding, which is just a fancy term for the ability to create a document by adding components like charts and drawings that are created in different applications.

When you add components, keep this caveat in mind: You can edit a component directly in the document only by using the application that originally created the component.

A component that you can insert into a Writer document is a mathematical formula, and I mean serious formulas with integral signs and Greek letters like alpha and sigma. If you're writing a scientific paper with complex equations, you'll really appreciate this feature of OpenOffice.org. Here's a typical sequence of steps to insert a formula into a Writer document (this process is similar for inserting other components):

1. **Position the cursor and choose Insert⇨Object⇨Formula.**

   The user interface changes to that of OpenOffice.org Math — an application for writing mathematical formulas, and a small frame for the formula appears in the document. The formula is typeset in that frame.

2. **Select a formula type from the top two rows of the Selection window.**

   The lower rows in the Selection window show available formulas of that type. For example, the summation category (denoted by an uppercase Greek letter sigma) includes integral signs.

3. **Click a specific formula, such as an integral.**

   The Math command for this formula appears in the Commands window, and parts of the formula appear in the document.

4. **Fill in the arguments for the formula.**

   As you construct the formula with commands in the Commands window, the formatted formula appears in the document (Figure 1-8).

5. **To change the font size of the formula, choose Format⇨Font Size and specify the font size.**

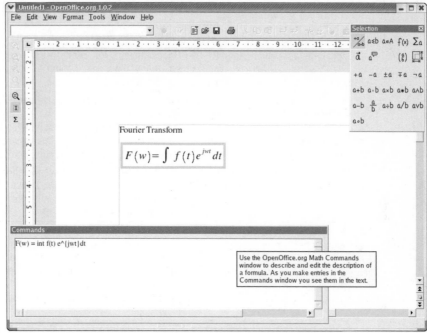

Book III
Chapter 1

Figure 1-8:
Insert a math formula into a Writer document by using the Math application.

Writing with OpenOffice.org Writer

6. **Click anywhere else in the Writer document to return to the Writer user interface.**

7. **Double-click the formula to edit it again.**

Of course, Writer has many page layout features. You can use tables, numbered and bulleted lists, and columns. Writer also supports *frames* — rectangular boxes in which you can place text, graphics, and even other frames. Using frames, you can place just about anything anywhere on the document. Table 1-5 summarizes how you can perform some common page layout tasks in Writer.

Table 1-5	Common Page Layout Tasks
To Do This	*Follow These Steps*
Insert a page break	Choose Insert➪Manual Break and then select Page break from the resulting dialog box.
Set page margins	Choose Format➪Page. Then click the Page tab and specify the margins.

(continued)

Table 1-5 *(continued)*

To Do This	*Follow These Steps*
Insert headers and footers	Choose Insert➪Header or Insert➪Footer and designate whether you want the header or footer on all pages or just the first page.
Insert header on only the first page	Put cursor on first page and choose Format➪Stylist (or press F5). Click the Page Styles icon (fourth icon from left) and double-click the First Page style. Choose Insert➪Header➪First Page, then type the text you want in the first page header.
Change page numbers from the automatic numbering sequence	Choose Insert➪Manual Break and then select Page Break and a style for the page. Then turn on the check box labeled Change Page Number and enter the page number you want.
Insert a landscape page in a portrait document	Press F11 to open the Stylist. Click the Page Styles icon (the fourth icon from left). Right-click Default style and select New. Name the new style Landscape and assign Default as next style, click the Page tab, select Landscape orientation, and click OK. Now choose Insert➪Manual Break, select Page Break, and style Landscape.
Lay out pages in columns	Choose Format➪Page and click the Columns tab in the resulting dialog box. Then select the number of columns and click OK.
Lay out selected text in columns	Select the text. Choose Insert➪Section and click the Columns tab in the resulting dialog box. Then select the number of columns and click Insert.
Use frames	Choose Insert➪Frame and select options from the tabs in the Frame dialog box. You can link frames so that text flows from one frame to the next.
Insert tables	Choose Insert➪Table or press Ctrl+F12. Format the table from the resulting dialog box.
Join two tables	Position the two tables one after the other, without any other text in between. Right-click either menu and select the Join Tables option (that option appears only when the tables are next to each other).
Insert objects created in other OpenOffice.org applications	Position cursor and choose Insert➪Object➪OLE Object. From the Insert OLE Object dialog box, select the type of object you want. If you are inserting an object from a file, select the Create from File radio button and click OK.

To Do This	Follow These Steps
Insert a math formula	Position cursor and choose Insert⇨Object⇨Formula. The user interface of the OpenOffice.org Math application appears. Use the formula selection and preparation windows to create the formula and adjust the font size. As you construct the formula, it appears in the document. Click anywhere else in the slide to return to Writer. Double-click the formula to edit it again.
Insert a chart	Position cursor and choose Insert⇨Chart to insert a chart with dummy data. Double-click the chart and the user interface of Impress appears. To edit the chart's dummy data, choose Edit⇨Chart Data. The dummy data appears in a mini-spreadsheet window. Edit data and click the green check mark. To change chart type, choose Format⇨Chart Type. Then pick the chart type from the resulting dialog box. Click elsewhere in the document to return to Writer.
Create an outline-style numbered list with items numbered 1, 1.1, 1.2, ... 2, 2.1, and so on	Type the list items, select them, and open the Stylist by pressing F11. Click the Numbering Styles icon (fifth icon from left) and double-click the Numbering 5 style. Click the list and note the right arrow on the object bar (the bar that shows the style name). Click the right arrow and the number list icons appear. Click each sub-numbered item and then click the right arrow icon.
Create a hanging indent	Press F11 to display the Stylist, if not already visible. Click the Paragraph Styles icon (the first icon from left). Place cursor on text and then double-click the Hanging indent style in the Stylist.
Preview page	Choose File⇨Page Preview. To return to editing, choose File⇨Page Preview again.
Show a vertical ruler	Choose Tools⇨Options. Then choose Text Document⇨View from the resulting dialog box. Turn on the check box labeled Vertical Ruler and click OK.

Creating and inserting graphics

Writer includes a drawing toolbar with tools that you can use to draw in the document. You can also insert into your document both line drawings and images from files in many different formats.

To create simple diagrams in your document, click the Show Drawing Functions icon (on the toolbar along the left side of the Writer window) and hold down the mouse button for a moment. The Draw Functions toolbar appears, as shown in Figure 1-9.

Figure 1-9:
The Draw
Functions
toolbar.

Click in the document where you want to add a diagram. Select a tool from the Draw Functions toolbar (Figure 1-9), and start drawing. To change the drawing tool, open the Draw Functions toolbar again and select another tool.

To keep the Draw Functions toolbar visible while you create a diagram, open the toolbar as usual, click the toolbar's top part, and then drag it away. The toolbar then turns into a *tearoff menu* (a small window that floats in the document window) from which you can easily select and use different drawing tools.

Writer also comes with a gallery of predefined graphics. To view the Gallery (shown in Figure 1-10), choose Tools⇨Gallery or click the Gallery icon (the rightmost icon on the Function bar). Select from the themes along the left side of the gallery. If you see a graphic you'd like to use, drag and drop it from the gallery to the location on the document where you want to insert it. Click the Gallery icon again to hide the graphics gallery.

Figure 1-10:
Drag and
drop
graphics
from the
gallery
onto your
document.

Table 1-6 summarizes how you might work in Writer to perform some common tasks involving graphics.

Table 1-6	Common Tasks Involving Graphics
To Do This	*Follow These Steps*
Create drawing objects	Click the Show Draw Functions icon on the left toolbar (mouse over and read tooltips to locate the icon). Select a drawing tool, and then draw on the document.
Insert graphics files	Choose Insert⇨Graphics⇨From File.
Anchor graphics	Right-click the graphics, select Anchor from pop-up menu and then an option to anchor graphics.
Wrap text around graphics	Right-click the graphics, select Wrap from the pop-up menu, and then one of several wrapping options.
Create captions for graphics	Right-click the graphics and select Caption from the pop-up menu.
Insert a watermark	Choose Format⇨Page and click the Background tab in the resulting dialog box. Choose Graphic from the As drop-down list, click the Browse button, and then select the graphics. Select other options such as whether you want the graphics to tile the page or just have a single copy at a specified position. You can also prepare a graphic with the drawing tools, right-click the graphic, and choose Arrange⇨To Background; right-click that graphic again and choose Anchor⇨To Page. The graphic should now appear as a watermark.
Insert a graphic (for example, a logo) on top of every page	Insert a header on each page by choosing Insert⇨Header⇨All. Click in the header, choose Insert⇨Graphics⇨From File, and then select the graphics file to insert.

Using fields

Think of *fields* as bits of information that might change, but you want to call them by a name and use them in your document. For example, you might want to insert today's date and the page numbers into the header of a document. You can do so by inserting fields that refer to the date and page numbers. Some of the predefined fields (such as date and page numbers) are easy to use. Simply choose Insert⇨Fields and then select the field you want to insert (Figure 1-11).

In addition to the fields you see in the Insert menu shown in Figure 1-11, you can pick from many more fields. Choose Insert⇨Fields⇨Other to open the Fields dialog box (Figure 1-12) where you can browse and pick other fields to use in your document. From the Fields dialog box, you can also change the format for a field. For example, you can select how the date field is shown in the document.

Book III
Chapter 1

Writing with OpenOffice.org Writer

Figure 1-11:
Choose
Insert⇨
Fields and
pick the
field to
insert.

Figure 1-12:
Use the
Fields dialog
box to pick
other fields
or select
formats.

Another type of useful field is a *reference* or a *bookmark*. The idea is to mark
a location in the document by a name and then refer to that location elsewhere by that assigned name. For example, you can insert a cross-reference
to the page where that location occurs.

Table 1-7 summarizes a few common tasks involving fields and how you can perform them in Writer.

Table 1-7	Common Tasks Involving Fields
To Do This	*Follow These Steps*
Insert a field	Choose Insert⇨Fields and select a predefined field (such as Page Numbers, Page Count, Date, File name) you want or select Other to pick fields from a dialog box.
Insert value of a formula in text	Position cursor and press F2. Enter formula on the object bar and click the green check mark. The value of the formula appears in the text as a field. To edit the formula again, select the field and press F2.
Insert a bookmark	Click the location you want to bookmark and then choose Insert⇨Bookmark. Enter the name for the bookmark and click OK.
Insert a cross-reference to a bookmark	Choose Insert⇨Cross-reference. Then select the bookmark you want to insert and the format in which the cross-reference appears in the text (for example, the page number or the name of the bookmark).
Set a reference	Click the text and then choose Insert⇨Cross-reference. Click Set Reference in the dialog box and assign a name to this reference.
Insert a cross-reference to a heading	Set a reference at the heading and position the cursor where you want to insert the cross-reference. Choose Insert⇨Cross-reference and click Insert Reference, select the reference, pick the format for the reference, and then click Insert.

Working with large documents

What's a large document? Well, I consider a large document any document over a hundred pages or so. Anything that might have a couple of chapters and need a table of contents and an index definitely qualifies as a large document — for example, a book. Writer includes features to do the "usual things" you'd want to do when working with these larger, more cumbersome documents, such as creating tables of content, inserting indexes, and adding entries to indexes.

Writer also enables you to tie together several Writer files into a single large document — what Writer refers to as a *master document*. Master documents are ideal for books, for example. You can keep the chapters in separate files and then organize these files into a book by using the master document feature. For a large project involving a master document, you have to plan a little and take care of the following key steps (refer to Table 1-8 for the specifics):

1. **Create a template with the styles you need as well as any fields you plan to use.**

   For more about styles and templates, see the appropriately named section "Using styles and templates," earlier in this chapter.

2. **Create the individual files and the master document by using the same template.**

3. **Insert the files into the master document — that's how you combine all the individual parts into the final product.**

4. **Add a table of contents and index and a bibliography, if needed.**

5. **Work on the component files.**

6. **Update table of contents and index.**

Table 1-8 summarizes some of the common tasks related to large documents and how you perform these tasks in Writer.

Table 1-8	Common Tasks Related to Large Documents
To Do This	*Follow These Steps*
Create a master document	Create a new file using a template you want. Then choose File⇨Send⇨Create Master Document. Assign a name, select a directory, and save the file. The Navigator window appears, from which you can select files to insert into the master document.
Insert a file into the master document	Use the Navigator to insert a file or choose Insert⇨File.
Insert index entries	Select the text you want to insert into the index. Then choose Insert⇨Indexes and Tables⇨Entry.
Create a table of contents, list of figures, or an index	Choose Insert⇨Indexes and Tables⇨Indexes and Tables. Click the Index/Table tab and select the type of table. For table of contents, select Table of Contents as the type. To select the paragraph styles that should be included in the table, click the Additional Styles check box and then click the adjacent button to designate styles to be included in the table.
Update table of contents or index	Right-click the table and then select Update Index/Table.
Insert footnotes and endnotes	Choose Insert⇨Footnote, select your options, and then click OK. Then type the footnote text.
Create a bibliographic database	Choose Tools⇨Bibliography Database. Then fill in the bibliography information in the Bibliography Database window.
Insert bibliographic references into text	Choose Insert⇨Indexes and Tables⇨Bibliographic Entry and pick the entry to insert.

Chapter 2: Preparing Spreadsheets with OpenOffice.org Calc

In This Chapter

✔ Taking stock of OpenOffice.org Calc

✔ Getting started with Calc

✔ Using Calc

Does the name VisiCalc mean anything to you? What about Lotus 1-2-3? I'm sure you have heard of Lotus 1-2-3, but maybe not VisiCalc — which was the first spreadsheet program that turned the IBM PC into a business tool. (Believe it or not, you can download and run VisiCalc even on today's PCs — for more information, visit Dan Bricklin's Web site at www.bricklin.com/history/vcexecutable.htm.)

Spreadsheet programs continue to be a staple of the office suite, and the OpenOffice.org suite is no exception. OpenOffice.org Calc, or just Calc for short, is the spreadsheet program in the OpenOffice.org suite.

All the spreadsheet programs that came after VisiCalc — from Lotus 1-2-3 to Microsoft Excel and Calc — still follow that visual model of a spreadsheet laid out in rows and columns. Of course, the newer spreadsheets (such as Excel and Calc) have many more bells and whistles, including fancy GUIs.

If you have used any other spreadsheet program such as Microsoft Excel, you'll be right at home when you start using Calc. Therefore, in this chapter, I don't try to give you detailed instructions on how to use Calc; instead, I provide a quick overview and some tables that summarize how to perform some common tasks in Calc.

Taking Stock of OpenOffice.org Calc

Before describing the types of tasks you can perform in Calc, I want to highlight the key features of Calc. Calc can do all the basic spreadsheet functions you expect in a spreadsheet program. Here are some things you can do with Calc:

✦ Open and edit Microsoft Excel files or convert Microsoft Excel files into Calc format. Calc uses an XML format and saves files with the .SXC extension.

✦ Save documents in many different formats including Microsoft Excel 97/ 2000/XP, Excel 95, Excel 5.0, dBASE, StarCalc 5.0 (as well as 4.0 and 3.0), SYLK (an old Microsoft format), comma-separated values (CSV), and Web page (HTML).

✦ Use charting tools to visualize data in 2D or 3D plots.

✦ Insert graphics files of many different formats, including JPEG, GIF, ZSoft Paintbrush (PCX), TIFF, Windows BMP, Macintosh PICT, Encapsulated PostScript (EPS), Adobe Photoshop (PSD), AutoCAD DXF, and many more.

✦ Save versions of a spreadsheet as you continue to change it, allowing you to revert to an older version if necessary.

✦ Use styles and templates to format your spreadsheet.

✦ Define cells to dynamically change format depending on the value in the cell.

✦ Easily exchange — import and export — data with existing databases by using the DataPilot.

✦ Set up cells to accept values from a set of specific values or ranges of valid values.

✦ Lock cells so that data can't be changed inadvertently.

✦ Perform scenario analysis by storing multiple values in the same block of cells — and define scenarios so that you can select a set of values for a specific scenario.

✦ Use the Goal Seek feature to determine the value of a cell that would give you a result you want from a formula.

Getting Started with Calc

The best way to learn to use Calc is to simply start using it. To start Calc, click the Calc icon — the icon showing a spreadsheet with a pie chart — on the panel or choose Main Menu⇨Office⇨OpenOffice.org Calc. The Calc window opens with a blank spreadsheet. You can then begin typing text and numbers into the cells and use formulas to calculate whatever you want.

Examining the Calc main window

To familiarize yourself with Calc, take a moment to examine the tools and icons packed into Calc's main window (shown in Figure 2-1).

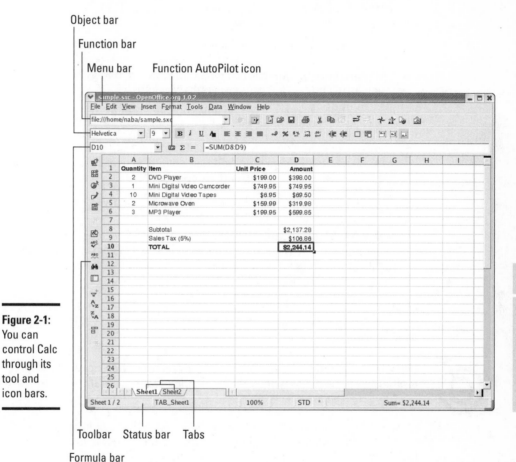

Object bar

Function bar

Menu bar   Function AutoPilot icon

Figure 2-1:
You can
control Calc
through its
tool and
icon bars.

Toolbar   Status bar   Tabs

Formula bar

Book III
Chapter 2

Preparing
Spreadsheets with
OpenOffice.org Calc

Notice the following major parts in the main Calc window (refer to Figure 2-1):

✦ **Menu bar** provides the standard pull-down menus: File, Edit, Help, and so forth. Use these menus to perform all the tasks that Calc can do.

✦ **Function bar** shows the full pathname or the URL of the currently open file and also provides buttons for performing routine tasks: opening, saving, and printing a document. You can also click icons on the Function bar to open the Stylist (a list of cell and page styles), the Navigator (a list of spreadsheet items such as sheets and graphics), and the Gallery (a collection of predefined graphic objects such as 3D shapes, backgrounds, and bullets).

✦ **Object bar** enables you to format the document by applying styles, selecting fonts, or changing text attributes (such as boldface, italics, and underlining). This bar changes depending on the type of object (such as plain text or graphics) you've clicked.

✦ **Formula bar** provides a field where you can enter formulas, create sums, and launch the Functions AutoPilot.

✦ **Toolbar,** located along the left side of the window, provides buttons that you can use to perform common tasks, such as inserting graphics, sorting cells, checking spelling, and grouping cells.

✦ **Tabs** along the bottom of the spreadsheet enable you to work with different sheets in the same file.

✦ **Status bar** displays information about the current sheet (the current sheet number, the page style, and so on). You can also click various elements in the status bar to change settings, such as the text selection mode and the zoom factor for viewing the spreadsheet.

In addition to these tool and icon bars, the largest part of the Calc window is the work area where your spreadsheet appears and where you focus most of your attention.

Use the tooltips to find out what an icon or menu option does. Mouse over a toolbar icon or a menu item and Calc displays a small tooltip window with a brief help message.

Note: Curious about that Function AutoPilot icon that's pointed out in Figure 2-1? Check out the section "Calculating and charting data," later in this chapter, where I show you how to use that handy little feature.

Setting up Calc

You can configure Calc through the Tools⇨Options dialog box. On the left side of the dialog box, click the plus sign (+) next to Spreadsheet. The plus sign turns to a minus sign (-) and a number of different categories of options appear (as in Figure 2-2). You can then click each category to configure various aspects of Calc.

Figure 2-2: Set up Calc from the Spreadsheet category in the Tools⇨ Options dialog box.

Using Calc

Preparing spreadsheets with Calc is a straightforward affair. Typically, you can enter text and numbers into the cells, resize the columns by dragging the vertical lines, and enter formulas to calculate the answers you need. To help you perform some common tasks in Calc, I provide some quick reference information organized into two broad categories of tasks:

✦ Entering and formatting data

✦ Calculating and charting data

Entering and formatting data

When entering and formatting data, use Calc in the same way that you use Microsoft Excel. You can type entries in cells, use formulas, and format the cells (such as specifying the type of value and the number of digits after the decimal point).

The Format menu (shown in Figure 2-3) contains many of the options for formatting the spreadsheet. Thanks to the tooltips, all you have to do is mouse over a menu item to get a hint about what that menu item does.

After you're done entering data into a spreadsheet, save it by choosing File⇨Save As. A dialog box appears, from which you can specify the file format, the directory location, and the name of the file. You've seen similar Save As dialog boxes a thousand times before. OpenOffice.org Calc can save the file in a number of formats, including Microsoft Excel 97/2000/XP, Microsoft Excel 95, Microsoft Excel 5.0, and text file with comma-separated values (CSV).

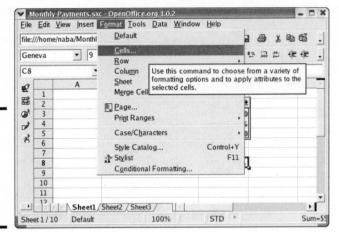

Figure 2-3:
Perform many formatting tasks from the Format menu.

If you want to exchange files with Microsoft Excel, save the spreadsheet in Microsoft Excel format (choose an appropriate version of Excel). Then you can transfer that file to a Windows system and open it in Microsoft Excel.

After you've saved the spreadsheet once, you can also save intermediate versions of a spreadsheet. To save a new version, choose File⇨Versions and then click Save New version in the next dialog box.

Table 2-1 summarizes some of the common data entry and formatting tasks in Calc. I also show the steps to print a spreadsheet to an Adobe Portable Document Format (PDF) file. To share a spreadsheet with people who don't use Calc or Excel, you can print the spreadsheet to a PDF file and then send that to others because anyone can easily view and print PDF files by using the free Adobe Reader (see www.adobe.com/products/acrobat/readstep2. html).

Table 2-1	Common Data Entry and Formatting Tasks
To Do This	*Follow These Steps*
Create a new spreadsheet	Choose File⇨New⇨Spreadsheet.
Create a spreadsheet from a template	Choose File⇨New⇨Templates and Documents. In the resulting dialog box, double-click a template folder, select a template, and click Open. Note that you won't see any templates here if you haven't added any templates yet.
Open an existing spreadsheet	Choose File⇨Open and select the file from the resulting Open dialog box.

To Do This	Follow These Steps
Add a sheet to the spreadsheet	Right-click the sheet tab where you want to add a new sheet. Choose Insert from the pop-up menu, fill in the options in the resulting dialog box, and click OK.
Entering data or formula into a cell	Click the cell and type the data. To type a formula, click the green check mark in the formula bar.
Wrap text	Right-click the cell and choose Format Cells from the pop-up menu. Click the Alignment tab in the dialog box and turn on Line break at the bottom of the dialog box.
Edit contents directly in cell	Double-click the cell and the cursor appears so that you can edit the contents.
Automatically fill cells	Fill the first cell with data (such as number, date, or cell reference) that you want to automatically increment as it fills in a range of cells. Select the cell and then drag the fill handle at the lower-right corner of the cell. As you move down (for instance), you'll see the cells getting automatically filled with numbers that get bigger as you go along.
Hide a row or a column	Right-click the row or column label and choose Hide from the pop-up menu.
Show hidden row or column	Select the rows or columns on both sides of the hidden row or column. Right-click row or column label and choose Show from the pop-up menu.
Autoformat a range of cells	Drag and select the cells. Choose Format⇨AutoFormat. From the resulting dialog box, select the format and options you want.
Bring in data from a data source	Choose Data⇨DataPilot⇨Start. Use the subsequent dialog boxes to select a source of data and to select the data you want to bring into the spreadsheet.
Move around the spreadsheet	Choose Edit⇨Navigator or press F5 to launch the Navigator window. Double-click an item such as a sheet to jump to that location.
Find and replace text in cells	Choose Edit⇨Find and Replace or press Ctrl+F. In the resulting dialog box, fill in the text to look for and the replacement text. Then click appropriate buttons (such as Find All, Find, Replace All, or Replace) to find and replace the text.
Create a non-scrolling region of rows or columns	Select the last row or column in the range that should not scroll. Choose Window⇨Freeze.
Apply style to cells	Press F11 or choose Format⇨Stylist to open the Stylist window. Click the cell to format and then double-click the style you want to apply.

(continued)

Table 2-1 *(continued)*

To Do This	Follow These Steps
Apply different styles depending on cell value	Select the cell that you want to format conditionally. Choose Format⇨Conditional Formatting. In the resulting dialog box, specify the conditions (such as whether cell value is greater than something) and the style you want to apply for each condition.
Insert graphics from a file	Click the cell where you want to insert graphics and then choose Insert⇨Graphics⇨From File. Select the graphics file from the Insert Graphics dialog box and then click Open.
Protect a sheet against any changes	Choose Tools⇨Protect⇨Sheet. Enter a password in the next dialog box.
Create a PDF version of the spreadsheet	Choose File⇨Print. In the Print dialog box, click the list of printers, and select PDF converter from the drop-down list. Click OK.
Save a spreadsheet	Choose File⇨Save As. In the dialog box, enter a file-name and select the format in which you want to save the file.
Save a version of the spreadsheet	Choose File⇨Versions. From the resulting dialog box, choose Save New Version. (You can create new versions only after you have saved the spreadsheet once.)
Open an older version of a spreadsheet	Choose File⇨Versions and select the version to open from the dialog box. Click Open.

Calculating and charting data

To perform calculations, use formulas you normally use in Microsoft Excel. For example, use the formula SUM(D2:D6) to add up the entries from cell D2 to D6. To set cell D2 as the product of the entries A2 and C2, type **=A2*C2** in cell D2.

To learn more about the functions available in OpenOffice.org Calc, choose Help⇨Contents from the menu. This opens the OpenOffice.org Help window from which you can browse the functions by category and click a function to read more about it.

One interesting feature of Calc is the support for scenarios. A *scenario* is simply a collection of values for one or more cells. Scenarios are useful when you compare the effect of some cells on other calculations in the spreadsheet. For example, the monthly payment on a loan would depend on the principal, the interest rate, and the duration of the loan. You can use Calc's scenario feature to compare the monthly payments for a number of different scenarios where each scenario has a certain combination of interest rate and loan duration in months. To use scenario for this comparison, follow these steps:

1. **Set up the spreadsheet cells with labels and values for the principal, annual interest rate in percentage, and loan duration in months. Calculate the monthly payment using this formula:**

   ```
   -PMT(MONTHLY_RATE,MONTHS,PRINCIPAL)
   ```

2. **Select the cells that you want to include in the scenario and choose Tools⇨Scenarios.**

   The Create Scenario dialog box appears.

3. **Fill in the scenario name, and then click OK.**

4. **Enter values into the cells — principal, interest rate, and months to repay loan.**

   The scenario name appears in a drop-down menu above the cells that constitute the scenario (as shown in Figure 2-4). The cell values define what that scenario means.

Book III
Chapter 2

Preparing
Spreadsheets with
OpenOffice.org Calc

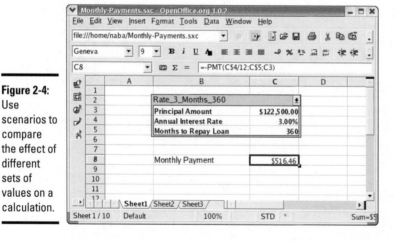

Figure 2-4:
Use scenarios to compare the effect of different sets of values on a calculation.

5. **Repeat Steps 2, 3, and 4 for other scenarios where each scenario has a combination of principal amount, rate, and loan duration in months.**

6. **Select a scenario from the drop-down list (refer to Figure 2-4) to see the monthly payment for that scenario.**

TIP

To figure out where a particular cell is being used in some calculation, click the cell and then choose Tools⇨Detective⇨Trace Dependents. Calc draws arrows to show where that cell is being used.

If you can't remember a function, use the Function AutoPilot to build the formula in a cell. To use the Function AutoPilot, follow these steps:

1. **Click the Function AutoPilot icon (refer to Figure 2-1) on the Formula bar.**

   The AutoPilot dialog box appears.

2. **Scroll down the list of functions and double-click the function you want.**

   Doing so causes the formula and its arguments to appear (Figure 2-5), waiting for you to specify the values to be used arguments.

3. **Click each argument and identify the cell that should be used as that argument.**

   When you specify all the arguments, the Result field (shown in Figure 2-5) shows the result of that formula.

Figure 2-5: Build formulas interactively by using the Function AutoPilot.

4. **Click OK.**

   The formula appears in the spreadsheet cell.

Table 2-2 summarizes some common computation and data-plotting tasks that you can perform in Calc.

Table 2-2	Common Calculation and Charting Tasks
To Do This	*Follow These Steps*
Add up rows or columns	Click the cell where you want the sum. Click the Sum icon (uppercase Greek letter "sigma") on the Formula bar. Calc inserts the sum of a logical range of cells. To change the range of cells, drag and highlight the cells you want to add. Then click the green check mark on the formula bar.
Build formulas with Function AutoPilot	Click the cell where you want the function. Click the Function AutoPilot icon on the Formula bar (the icon to the left of the Sum icon — uppercase Greek letter sigma). Click the Functions tab in the AutoPilot and select the function category and the specific function. Fill in other necessary information such as the range of cells used as argument to the function.
Insert a chart	Select the cells for the chart and choose Insert⇨Chart. Select options and type of chart from the resulting AutoFormat Chart dialog box. Click Create to insert the chart.
Edit a chart	Double-click the part of the chart you want to edit. Select options from the resulting dialog box. Use icons on the toolbar (which change when you double-click a chart) to do other tasks (such as turning parts of the chart on or off and changing the chart type).
Perform "goal seek"	Click the cell with the formula. Choose Tools⇨Goal Seek. In the Goal Seek dialog box, enter the target value for the formula. In the Variable cell field, enter the cell whose value should be adjusted to reach the goal. Click OK to complete goal seek.
Create scenarios	Select the cells whose values you plan to change for each scenario. Choose Tools⇨Scenarios. Assign a name to the scenario and click OK. Enter values in the cells. Repeat for each scenario you want to define.
Use scenarios	Define formulas that use the cells included in a scenario. You can then see the results for different scenarios by selecting each scenario from the drop-down list of scenarios.

Chapter 3: Making Presentations with OpenOffice.org Impress

In This Chapter

✔ Taking stock of OpenOffice.org Impress

✔ Getting started with Impress

✔ Using Impress

It seems the business world, or should I say the whole world, is full of PowerPoint rangers — those dedicated souls who live by their PowerPoint briefing packages (slide presentations). It's hard to imagine a meeting or a conference where someone isn't vigorously making points on-screen with PowerPoint. Let's face it: Such programs are here to stay. Making presentations is a fact of life; businesspeople have come to expect office-application suites to include some sort of presentation software.

Like Microsoft Office, the OpenOffice.org office application suite comes with its own PowerPoint-like presentation software — OpenOffice.org Impress (or Impress for short). If you have used Microsoft PowerPoint and you're already familiar with its nuts and bolts — the concept of a slide, how to add text and graphics to a slide, how to organize the slides, and how to run a slide show — then you'll find it easy to get started with Impress. Because some details of how you perform basic Impress tasks may differ from the way they're done in PowerPoint, I provide some quick reference tables to point you in the right direction. I start with an overview of Impress and then cover some categories of common tasks that you'll likely perform in Impress.

Taking Stock of OpenOffice.org Impress

You'll find that Impress can do all the usual things that presentation software such as Microsoft PowerPoint can do. For example, you can create professional-looking slide shows in Impress, using capabilities like these:

✦ Open and edit Microsoft PowerPoint files or convert Microsoft PowerPoint files to Impress format. One advantage of converting to Impress format is that Impress files are smaller in size than corresponding Microsoft PowerPoint files. Presentation files stored in Impress format are assigned filenames with the .sxi extension.

✦ Save documents in many different formats, including Microsoft PowerPoint 97/2000/XP, StarDraw 5.0 and 3.0, and StarImpress 5.0 and 4.0.

✦ Insert graphics and clip art from files of many different formats, including JPEG, GIF, ZSoft Paintbrush (PCX), TIFF, Windows BMP, Macintosh PICT, Encapsulated PostScript (EPS), Adobe Photoshop (PSD), AutoCAD DXF, and many more.

✦ Insert other OpenOffice.org documents (from programs such as Writer, Calc, and Draw) into a presentation.

✦ Use AutoPilot to quickly create a presentation.

✦ Use all the drawing tools from OpenOffice.org Draw to add drawings to the slides.

✦ Export a presentation to a Web page (HTML) with or without frames. You can also export the slides in any of the supported graphics file formats.

✦ Use layers to separate parts of the slide so that each part can be edited or viewed separately.

✦ Use special effects such as animated text and graphics, sound, and slide transition effects.

✦ Use FontWork (Format⇨FontWork) to create various text effects such as aligning text along a curve.

✦ Render text in 3D.

✦ Save versions of a presentation as you continue to change it and revert back to an older version, if necessary.

✦ Add speaker's notes to each slide and create handouts.

Getting Started with Impress

The best way to get comfortable using Impress is simply to start using it. To start Impress, click the Impress icon — the icon showing a bar chart with a slide — on the panel or choose Main Menu⇨Office⇨OpenOffice.org Impress.

The AutoPilot Presentation window (shown in Figure 3-1) appears and guides you through the steps of starting a new presentation.

As Figure 3-1 shows, you can create an empty presentation, create a presentation from a template, or open an existing presentation. If you select an empty presentation and click Next, the AutoPilot asks you to select the slide design and the slide-transition effect (that is, how Impress moves from one slide to the next). Then you can click Create to open the Impress window, where you can select the layout of your first slide. After you finish laying out a slide, you can proceed to insert new slides. For each slide, you can select the layout you want.

Figure 3-1:
This
AutoPilot
helps you
start a new
presentation
in Impress.

You can open and edit Microsoft PowerPoint files in Impress. To open an existing file, choose File➪Open and then select the file to open.

Before you start creating slides with Impress, take a moment to examine the Impress window (shown in Figure 3-2).

In Figure 3-2, note the major parts of the Impress window:

✦ **Menu bar** provides the standard pull-down menus such as File, Edit, and Help for performing all the tasks that Impress can do.

✦ **Function bar** shows the full pathname or the URL of the currently open file and also provides buttons for performing tasks such as opening, saving, and printing a document. You can also click icons on the function bar to open the Stylist, the Navigator, and the Gallery.

✦ **Object bar** enables you to format the document by applying styles, selecting fonts, or changing text attributes such as bold, italic, and underline. This bar changes according to the type of object you've clicked (for example, plain text or graphic image).

✦ **Toolbar** along the left side of the window provides buttons that you can use to perform common tasks, such as inserting graphics, sorting cells, checking spelling, and grouping cells.

✦ **Rulers** show the vertical and horizontal page dimensions.

✦ **Navigation bar** along the bottom of the slide enables you to change the views and select a slide to work with.

✦ **Status bar** displays information about the current slide such as the current slide number and the total count of slides. You can also click elements in the status bar and change settings such as the zoom factor for viewing the slide.

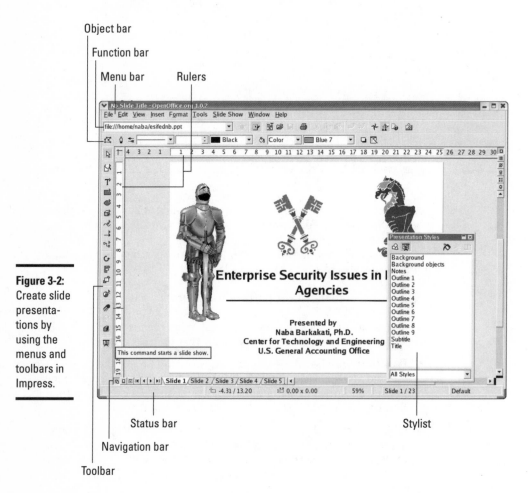

Figure 3-2: Create slide presentations by using the menus and toolbars in Impress.

Object bar

Function bar

Menu bar

Rulers

Status bar

Stylist

Navigation bar

Toolbar

In addition to these tool and icon bars, you can turn on two more toolbars (when visible, these toolbars appear at the bottom of the window, above the status bar):

✦ Choose View➪Toolbars➪Option Bar to turn on the option bar that appears below the navigation bar. The option bar displays icons through which you perform some drawing tasks such as edit curves, show grid lines, and indicate what happens when you click text and other objects.

✦ Choose View➪Toolbars➪Color Bar to turn on the color bar that appears at the bottom of the window, just above the status bar. The color bar displays colors that you can pick and use on objects. You can show or hide the color bar by clicking the downward-pointing arrow on the upper-left side of the color bar.

The largest part of the Impress window is the work area where you work on the current slide and where you focus most of your attention.

Use the tooltips to find out what an icon or menu option does (Figure 3-2 shows an example). Mouse over a toolbar icon or a menu item and Impress displays a small tooltip window with a brief help message.

You don't have to set up anything to start using Impress. However, if you ever need to configure some aspects of Impress, you can do so through the Tools➪Options and Tools➪Configure menus. In particular, the Presentation category (Figure 3-3) of the Tools➪Options window contains the options for Impress. You should go through each of the Presentation options to see what you can configure from this window.

**Book III
Chapter 3**

**OpenOffice.org
Impress**

Figure 3-3:
Set up
Impress
through
the options
in the
Presenta-
tion
category.

Options - Presentation

- OpenOffice.org
- Load/Save
- Language Settings
- Internet
- Text Document
- HTML Document
- Spreadsheet
- Presentation
  - General
  - View
  - Grid
  - Print
- Drawing
- Formula
- Chart
- Data Sources

Presentation

This is where you define the settings that apply to all newly saved presentations. Among other things, you decide which contents are displayed on the slides, which default unit of measure is used, if and how grid alignment is used, and if notes and handouts are always printed.

OK   Cancel   Help   Back

Using Impress

When you start Impress, the AutoPilot prompts you for the type of presentation you want. If Impress is already running, you get the AutoPilot when you choose File➪New➪Presentation. If you want a blank presentation, simply click Create in the first step of the AutoPilot. Impress displays the Modify Slide dialog box (as in Figure 3-4) with a gallery of slide layouts.

Figure 3-4:
Select the slide layout from this dialog box and click OK.

You can select a slide layout from the dialog box (refer to Figure 3-4) and click OK. Impress then displays an empty slide with the selected layout.

Typically a slide layout might have a title area and some text bullets. You can click and add the text to each of these areas. To insert any graphic image, choose Insert➪Graphics and pick the graphics file you want to insert. You can draw directly on the slide by using the drawing tools from the vertical toolbar along the left side of the Impress window. To see which tool does what, move the mouse over any icon and a tooltip gives you a hint.

After you finish working on a slide, you can insert another slide by selecting Insert➪Slide. Impress displays an Insert Slide dialog box (similar to the Modify Slide dialog box shown in Figure 3-4) where you can select the layout for the next slide.

To save a presentation, choose File➪Save from the menu. For new documents, you have to provide a filename and select the directory where to save the file.

That, in a nutshell, is how you create presentations in PowerPoint. In the following sections, I provide some quick reference tips for performing the following types of tasks with Impress:

✦ Preparing presentations

✦ Adding graphics and special effects

✦ Delivering presentations

Preparing presentations

Typically, you start with a blank slide with a specific layout. For example, the slide has a title area and a bulleted list for the points you want to make with the slide. You can click the title area, type the title, and then click the bulleted text area to start entering text. Then you add another slide and continue with the process until you finish the presentation.

If you're going to present information that's already in a Writer document (see Chapter 1 in this mini-book), you can use the outline of that Writer document to start a presentation. The Writer document does have to follow one rule — it must use the heading styles Heading 1, Heading 2, and so on for the major sections in the document.

To create a presentation from the outline of a Writer document that uses the heading styles, open the document in Writer and choose Send⇨Outline to Presentation from the Writer menu. You should see an Impress window open up with a new presentation that has slides based on the headings in the Writer document. Each Heading 1 style becomes a new slide and the Heading 2 and Heading 3 styles appear as bulleted text in the slides.

After working on the set of slides, you may want to rearrange the slides. To rearrange slides in a different order, choose View⇨Master View⇨Slides View. Impress displays an array of miniature-sized slides, arranged in a rectangular grid in the work area. Think of this as the slide sorter view because you can move the slides around and sort them in this view.

In the slide-sorter view shown in Figure 3-5, you can drag and drop slides into different positions and rearrange them in the order you want. To delete a slide in this view, click the slide to select it and press Delete (or choose Edit⇨Delete). When prompted to confirm the deletion, you can click Yes if you really want to delete the slide. Double-click a slide to return to the usual single-slide view.

Figure 3-5:
Arrange
slides in this
slide-sorter
view in
Impress.

As you work on the presentation, keep in mind these concepts:

✦ **Master slide:** You can think of the *master slide* as the background of
every slide. If you put text or other fields (such as date and page
number) on the master slide, those elements appear on every slide in
the presentation.

✦ **Layers:** You can have layers in both the master slide as well as each individual slide. Think of the layers as transparent sheets on which you place
some related text and graphics. The slide is then made up of these layers
superimposed on one another. You can use layers to group related information. For example, if you're drawing the plans for a house, you can put
all the dimensions on a separate layer. The nice part is that you can hide
or show layers easily. Just click the third icon from the left on the navigation bar (refer to Figure 3-2) or choose View⇨Layer.

✦ **Master notes and master handouts:** The idea is the same as that for
master slide. You can define some fields and text on the master notes or
master handout; these become part of the background for your notes
and handouts. The *notes* refer to any explanatory text you add to the
bottom of each slide. The *handouts* are printouts of the slides that can
be handed out to an audience at a briefing. Typically, several slides fit
on a page.

Well, I could go on and on, but you can learn best by simply starting to use Impress. If you need some help as you prepare presentations in Impress, consult Table 3-1 for information on how to perform some of the common tasks.

Table 3-1	Common Presentation Preparation Tasks
To Do This	*Follow These Steps*
Create a blank presentation	Choose File⇨New⇨Presentation and click Create in the AutoPilot window that appears. Select the slide layout from the Insert Slide dialog box.
Create a presentation from a Writer document	Choose Send⇨Outline to Presentation from the Writer menu. A new presentation appears in an Impress window with the Writer document's outline, built out of the heading styles Heading 1, Heading 2, and so on.
Open an existing presentation	Choose File⇨Open and then pick the file to open. If you are in the AutoPilot window, click Open existing presentation, select <Other position>, and click Create. Impress then displays the Open dialog box from which you can select a file to open.
Assign a title to the presentation	Choose File⇨Properties. Click the Description tab in the resulting dialog box and type in the Title field. This title appears in the Impress window's title bar.
Insert a slide	Choose Insert⇨Slide and select the slide layout from the Insert Slide dialog box.
Duplicate current slide	Choose Insert⇨Duplicate Slide.
Delete a slide	Right-click the slide tab and choose Delete Slide from the pop-up menu. Click Yes when asked to confirm.
Change layout of an existing slide	Choose Format⇨Modify Layout. Select a layout from the Insert Slide dialog box and click OK.
Creating a template	Prepare a presentation with slides representing all the styles you want. Choose File⇨Save As and save the file as an OpenOffice.org Presentation template.
Switch to slide view	Click the leftmost icon on the navigation bar along the bottom of the slide or choose View⇨Slide.
Edit master slide	Click the second icon from left on the navigation bar along the bottom of the slide (or choose View⇨Master⇨Slide). Edit the master slide (used as background for all slides).
Edit master notes	Choose View⇨Master⇨Notes. Edit the master notes page you want used as the background for all notes. You can insert fields such as page numbers and dates.
Add notes to a slide	Choose View⇨Master View⇨Notes View. Click in the notes area of slide and type the notes.

(continued)

Table 3-1 *(continued)*

To Do This	Follow These Steps
Work in outline view	Choose View⇨Master View⇨Outline View.
View slides in miniature format	Choose View⇨Master View⇨Slides View. You can rearrange the order of slides in this view.
Edit layers	Click the third icon from left on the navigation bar along the bottom of the slide (or choose View⇨Layer). Click a layer tab to edit that layer.
Insert layer	While editing the layer, right-click a layer tab and select Insert Layer from the pop-up menu.
Hide or show a layer	While editing the layer, right-click the layer tab and select Modify Layer from the pop-up menu. Deselect the Visible property and click OK. Turning the check mark on the Visible property makes the layer visible again.
Change zoom level	Right-click the zoom level on the status bar and select the new zoom level from the pop-up menu.
View slides in color, grayscale, or black and white	Choose View⇨Display Quality and then pick whether you want color, grayscale, or black and white.

Adding graphics and special effects

To jazz up your presentation, you might want to add graphics, charts, and other special effects to the slides. With Impress, you can do nearly everything you can think of — all you have to decide is how many bells and whistles your presentation needs. It's your call, but I recommend using these features judiciously lest they detract from your presentation's main message.

If you want to add some simple drawings to the slide, you can pick from the drawing tools on the vertical toolbar on the left side of the Impress window (refer to Figure 3-1) and start drawing on the slide. To insert an image into the slide, choose Insert⇨Graphics and then select the image file you want to insert.

You can also insert charts to graphically depict data. You start by inserting a chart with dummy data, and then you edit the data as well as other features of the chart. To add a chart and edit the data, follow these steps:

1. **Choose Insert⇨Chart.**

A chart with default chart type and dummy data appears.

2. **Resize the chart by dragging the handles around the border of the chart; then right-click the chart and choose Chart Data from the pop-up menu that appears (Figure 3-6).**

   A mini-spreadsheet appears with the dummy chart data.

3. **Edit the row and column labels and enter the data you want the chart to display.**

4. **When you're done editing the chart, click the green check mark (located to the right of the data entry area) to apply the changes and close the Chart Data window.**

5. **To change the chart type, right-click the chart and choose Chart Type from the pop-up menu that appears; choose a new type and click OK.**

You can do a lot more than just add graphics and charts to your slide presentations. You can insert spreadsheets and Writer documents into a slide, add text that runs along a curve, and add special effects to various elements in a slide. Table 3-2 summarizes some common graphics and special effects tasks, including information on how to perform each task.

Book III
Chapter 3

OpenOffice.org Impress

Figure 3-6:
Right-click the chart to modify the data and chart type.

Table 3-2	Common Graphics and Special Effects Tasks
To Do This	*Follow These Steps*
Draw on a slide	Select drawing tools from the vertical toolbar on the left side of the Impress window and draw on the slide using the mouse. You can also add text and text callouts (a text box with a line pointing to something you are trying to explain).
Apply text effects	Choose Format⇨FontWork. Select text and use FontWork tools to apply special effects to text such as place text along a curve and show a shadow.
Convert text or graphics to 3D	Right-click the text or graphic and choose Convert⇨To 3D. For text, make sure that you click the text frame, not the text itself.
Insert graphics from a file	Choose Insert⇨Graphics and then select the graphics file you want to insert.
Add a chart	Choose Insert⇨Chart to insert a dummy chart. Right-click the chart and select Chart Data from the pop-up menu. The dummy data appears in a mini-spreadsheet window. Edit data. To change chart type, right-click the chart and select Chart Type. Then pick a chart type from the resulting dialog box.
Adding graphics to a slide	Choose Insert⇨Graphics to select a graphics file to insert.
Insert a drawing prepared in Draw	Choose Insert⇨OLE Object. In the resulting dialog box, choose Create from File⇨Search. Select the drawing file from the Open dialog box and click Open. Click OK to insert the drawing from the file. Double-click the drawing to edit it later on.
Insert a formula	Choose Insert⇨Object⇨Formula. The OpenOffice.org Math application appears. Use the formula selection and preparation windows to create the formula and adjust the font size. As you construct the formula, it appears in the slide. Click anywhere else in the slide to return to Impress. Double-click the formula to edit it again.
Apply effects on objects in a slide	Choose Slide Show⇨Effects to open the Effects window. Choose View⇨Preview so that you can see the effects in a small preview window as you try them. Select the object to which you want to apply an effect, select the effect from the Effects window, and then click the green check mark. Observe the effect in the preview window. Stop when you like the effects. Apply effects to more objects if you want.

To Do This	Follow These Steps
Control how slides transition	Choose Slide Show➪Slide Transition to open the Slide Transition window. Choose View➪Preview so that you can see the effect of a transition in a small preview window as you apply each transition. Select a transition effect from the Slide Transition window, and click the green check mark. Observe the effect in the preview window. Stop when you like the effects. Apply transition effects to other slides as needed.

Delivering presentations

After you prepare a spectacular set of slides, you have to deliver it to your audience. This typically involves tasks such as preparing speaker's notes, running a slide show, converting the presentation into HTML for delivery via the Web, and printing handouts. Table 3-3 summarizes some common presentation delivery tasks.

You can also print an Impress presentation directly to an Adobe Portable Document Format (PDF) file. This makes it easy to electronically share a presentation with everyone because anyone can easily view and print PDF files by using the free Adobe Reader (available at www.adobe.com/products/acrobat/readstep2.html).

Table 3-3	Common Presentation Delivery Tasks
To Do This	*Follow These Steps*
Edit master handout	Choose View➪Master➪Handout. Edit the master handout that gets used as the background for all the handouts.
Prepare handouts	Choose View➪Master View➪Handout View. The view shows the handout page with a number of slides per page. To change layout, right-click handout and choose Slide➪Modify Slide from the pop-up menu. Select the layout (how many slides per page of handout) you want.
Print handouts	Choose View➪Master View➪Handout View. Choose File➪Print.
Run a slide show	Click the slide show icon (last one on the vertical toolbar) or choose Slide Show➪Slide Show or press Ctrl+F2. Click to advance through slides. Press Esc to stop slide show or at the last slide click to end show.

(continued)

Table 3-3 *(continued)*

To Do This	Follow These Steps
Creating a custom slide show	Choose Slide Show⇨Custom Slide Show. Click New in the Custom Slide Show window. Assign a name and then select the slides you want in the slide show, in the order you want them to appear. Drag the slides up or down to change that order. Click OK and then click Close.
Run a custom slide show	Choose Slide Show⇨Custom Slide Show. Select the custom slide show (you should see the name you used when creating slide show). Turn on the check box next to Use Custom Slide Show and then click Start.
Print the slides to a PDF file	Choose File⇨Print. In the Print dialog box, click the list of printers and select PDF converter from the drop-down list. Click OK.
Create an HTML version of the presentation	Choose File⇨Export. In the Export dialog box, enter a filename and select Web page as the format. Click Save. Go through the HTML Export steps, select the file type you want (for example, HTML with or without frames) as well as the format for the images (JPEG or GIF) used to represent each slide.

Chapter 4: Drawing with OpenOffice.org Draw

In This Chapter

✔ Taking stock of OpenOffice.org Draw

✔ Getting started with Draw

✔ Using Draw

Sometimes you need images, diagrams, and illustrations to make a point. Whether it's a quick sketch or a complex diagram, OpenOffice.org Draw, or Draw for short, provides you with the tools you need to prepare drawings.

Draw is a separate drawing program in the OpenOffice.org office application suite, but you can also access many of Draw's drawing tools from other OpenOffice.org applications, such as Writer and Impress. When you use Draw to prepare drawings, you save the drawing in a file. You can later insert the drawing as a Draw object into other OpenOffice.org documents, such as a Writer document or an Impress presentation. The nice part about inserting a Draw object into a Writer or Impress document is that you can always double-click and edit the drawing directly, even while it's in the Writer or Impress document.

In this chapter, I introduce you to the Draw application. I provide an overview and then provide quick references to help you perform some common drawing tasks in Draw.

Taking Stock of OpenOffice.org Draw

You'll find that Draw can do all the usual things that a typical drawing program can do. To give you a feel for Draw's features, here are some of things you can do with Draw:

✦ Use an array of standard drawing tools, such as polygons, circles, and Bézier curves.

✦ Use smart connector lines to draw flow charts, organization charts, and network diagrams.

+ Mix *vector graphics* (lines, geometric shapes, text) with *raster* images (JPEG, GIF, and other bitmapped formats).

+ Access Draw tools from other OpenOffice.org applications, such as Writer and Impress.

+ Use FontWork to apply special effects to text (such as laying out text along a curve and adding shadows).

+ Insert other OpenOffice.org objects (such as spreadsheets and slides) into your drawing.

+ Draw 3D shapes and intersect 3D objects.

+ Convert text and curves to 3D objects.

+ Crop images.

+ Control many aspects of image colors, such as brightness, contrast, and transparency.

+ Use layers to separate various parts of the drawing so that each part can be edited or viewed separately.

+ Export a drawing to a Web page (HTML) or other image-file formats such as EPS, JPEG, and GIF.

Getting Started with Draw

The best way to learn to use Draw is to simply start using it. To start Draw, choose Main Menu⇨Office⇨OpenOffice.org Draw. The Draw window appears with an empty drawing area. You can then select tools from the vertical tool-bar that appears on the left side of the Draw window and begin drawing. Figure 4-1 shows the Draw window with a not-so-typical drawing that includes text, 3D shapes, and an image.

Before you start using Draw, take some time to study the Draw window and the various tool and icon bars (as shown in Figure 4-1). Notice that the Draw window has the following major parts:

+ **Menu bar:** Provides the standard pull-down menus (such as File, Edit, and Help) for performing all the tasks that Draw can do.

+ **Function bar:** Shows the full pathname or the URL of the currently open file and also provides buttons for performing tasks such as opening, saving, and printing a document. You can also click icons on the function bar to open the Stylist (a list of graphics styles), the Navigator (a list of drawing items), and the Gallery (a collection of predefined graphic objects such as 3D shapes, backgrounds, and bullets).

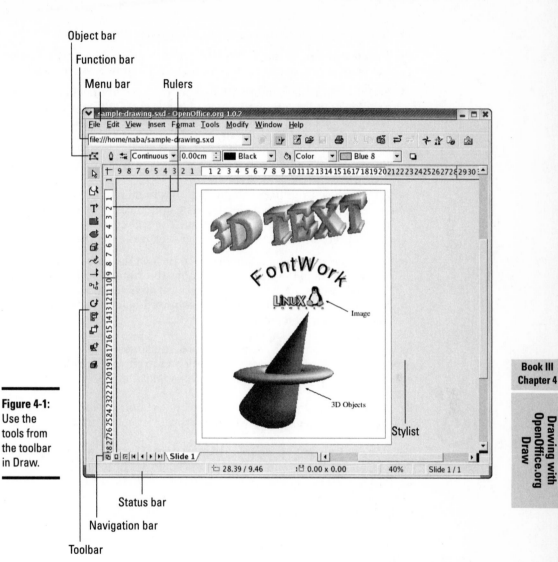

Object bar

Function bar

Menu bar   Rulers

Figure 4-1:
Use the
tools from
the toolbar
in Draw.

Stylist

Status bar

Navigation bar

Toolbar

Book III
Chapter 4

Drawing with
OpenOffice.org
Draw

✦ **Object bar:** Shows the common formatting and style attributes, including colors, that apply to the currently selected type of object such as
text, image, or vector graphics.

✦ **Toolbar:** Located along the left side of the window, the toolbar provides
icons that you can click to select tools for drawing or editing objects in
the drawing.

✦ **Rulers:** Show the vertical and horizontal page dimensions.

✦ **Navigation bar:** Located along the bottom of the slide, the navigation bar enables you to change views and select a drawing to work with.

✦ **Status bar:** Displays information about the current drawing, such as the location of the pointer and which object is currently selected. You can also click elements in the status bar and change settings, including the zoom factor for viewing the drawing.

In addition to these tool and icon bars, you can turn on two more toolbars:

✦ Choose View⇨Toolbars⇨Option Bar to turn on the option bar that appears below the navigation bar. The option bar displays icons through which you perform tasks, such as edit curves, show grid lines, and indicate what happens when you click text and other objects.

✦ Choose View⇨Toolbars⇨Color Bar to turn on the color bar that appears at the bottom of the window, just above the status bar. The color bar displays colors that you can pick and use on objects. You can show or hide the color bar by clicking the downward-pointing arrow on the upper-left side of the color bar.

As with other OpenOffice.org applications, the largest part of the Draw window is the work area where you work on the current drawing and where you spend most of your time in the application.

If you don't know what an icon or a menu does, mouse over that item and Draw displays a small tooltip window with a brief help message.

You don't have to set up anything to start using Draw. However, if you ever need to configure anything in Draw, you can do so through the Tools⇨ Options and Tools⇨Configure menus. In particular, the Drawing category of the Tools⇨Options window contains the options for Draw. Go through each of the Presentation options to see what you can configure from this window.

Using Draw

For the most part, you'll use the drawing tools located on the vertical tool-bar along the left side of the Draw window (refer to Figure 4-1). For some tasks, you'll use the menus and the color toolbar that you make visible by choosing View⇨Toolbars⇨Color Bar.

When using tools from the vertical toolbar, you have to learn to *long-click*. Don't worry, it's nothing complicated. You simply click an icon and hold down the mouse button until an additional toolbar flies out. That's a long click. After you try it and see it in action, you'll immediately get the hang of it.

Long-clicking works with any icon that has a small, right-pointing arrow. The icon shows the currently selected tool, but a long click brings out all the icons on a *flyout toolbar* — a toolbar that appears to slide out on-screen, showing other choices you can make. To use the flyout toolbars, follow these steps:

1. **Long-click (click and hold down the mouse) any icon with a right-pointing arrow until a toolbar flies out (Figure 4-2).**

   The toolbar shows icons representing the available tools (if a tool does not apply to the currently selected object, it's grayed out).

Figure 4-2:
A typical flyout toolbar.

Book III
Chapter 4

Drawing with
OpenOffice.org
Draw

2. **To have the tools available in a *tearoff menu* (a small window that floats in the Draw window), drag the flyout toolbar's top part and tear it off.**

   The tools now remain available in the tearoff menu (Figure 4-3), labeled for the name of the tool you've clicked on the toolbar. You can click and use any tool you want. When you don't need the tearoff menu anymore, click the X to close the menu.

Figure 4-3:
A tearoff
menu.

3. **To use tools directly from the flyout toolbar, click the tool you want.**

   The flyout toolbar disappears, and the cursor changes shape. You can use the selected tool to draw.

4. **To reuse the same tool, click normally on the icon on the vertical toolbar.**

   The cursor changes shape, and you can use the tool to draw.

When you know how to long-click and tear off a flyout toolbar, you might wonder how to remember what each icon on the toolbar does. My advice is don't try. Simply mouse over and read the tooltip. That's what the tooltips are for!

Try using the tools to prepare drawings. Consult Table 3-1 for hints on how to perform some common drawing tasks in Draw.

Table 3-1	Common Drawing Tasks
To Do This	*Follow These Steps*
Create a new drawing	Choose File⇨New⇨Drawing.
Open an existing drawing file	Choose File⇨Open and then select the file to open from the Open dialog box.
Apply styles	Press F11 to open the Stylist window, if it isn't already open. Select the object to which you want to apply a style. Double-click Style in Stylist.
Adding text and graphics objects to drawing	Select the icon for a drawing tool from the vertical toolbar on the left side of the Draw window. Use your mouse to draw by using the selected tool. Mouse over and use the tooltip to figure out what the different tools do.
Change an object's attributes	Right-click the object and select the attribute, such as line, area, position, and size that you want to change.
Duplicate an object	Select the object and choose Edit⇨Duplicate. In the Duplicate dialog box, make selections for placement and number of copies and click OK.

To Do This	*Follow These Steps*
Select multiple objects	Click objects while holding down the Shift key.
Group objects	Select the objects you want to group. Right-click selection and then select Group from the pop-up menu.
Ungroup objects	Right-click Group and select Ungroup from the pop-up menu.
Rotate objects	Select one or more objects. Click the Effects icon on the toolbar (use tooltip to find this icon) and select the rotate icon. Grab one of the handles that appears on the object and use it to rotate the object.
Align objects	Select the objects. Right-click the selection and select Alignment and the alignment type such as Left, Top, Center, and so on.
Distribute objects evenly	Select three or more objects. Right-click the selection and select Distribution. Use the Distribution dialog box to choose how you want the objects distributed on-screen.
Arrange order or objects	Select the objects. Right-click the selection and select Arrange and the placement order such as Bring to Front, Send Backward, and so on.
Add 3D objects to a drawing	Select a 3D object from the toolbar (the last icon from top in the vertical toolbar).
Convert text to 3D	Click to select the text frame. Then right-click the frame and choose Convert⇨To 3D. Click and rotate the 3D text to your liking.
Apply special effects to text	Choose Format⇨FontWork. Select the text frame to which you want to apply special effects. Select the effects you want from the FontWork window. (For example, you can place the text along a curve and show a shadow for the text.)
Add a background to text	Right-click the text frame and select Area. Select options for the text background from the resulting Area dialog box.
Apply font effects to text	Right-click the text frame and select Character from the pop-up menu. Click the Font Effects tab in the resulting Character dialog box. Select the effects (such as embossed or engraved characters) from the Font Effects tab.
Crop an image	Select the image and click the Crop icon (the rightmost icon on the object toolbar). Select the options you want from the Crop dialog box and click OK.

(continued)

**Book III
Chapter 4**

**Drawing with
OpenOffice.org
Draw**

Table 3-1 *(continued)*

To Do This	*Follow These Steps*
Changing an image's characteristics	Click an image and use the choices on the object bar to adjust the color, contrast, brightness, and transparency. You can change the red, green, and blue components in the image colors, and adjust an on-screen object's transparency from 0% (opaque) to 100% (fully transparent).
Merge two 3D objects into a single 3D object	Bring the two 3D objects near each other. Select the 3D object that should appear in the front and press Ctrl+X to cut it. Click the second object and press F3. Now press Ctrl+V to paste the front object onto the second object. The objects should now appear merged. Click and adjust the objects individually. Press Ctrl+F3 to end the process of merging the objects.
Export drawings to an image file	Choose File⇨Export. In the resulting Export dialog box, enter a filename and select the format you want. Supported formats include BMP (Windows Bitmap), EPS (Encapsulated PostScript), GIF, JPEG, PNG (Portable Network Graphics), PPM (Portable Pixmap), TIFF, and many more.

Book IV

Networking

The 5th Wave   By Rich Tennant

"I guess you could say this is the hub of our network."

Contents at a Glance

Chapter 1: Connecting to the Internet

In This Chapter

✔ **Understanding the Internet**

✔ **Deciding how to connect to the Internet**

✔ **Connecting to the Internet with DSL**

✔ **Connecting to the Internet with cable modem**

✔ **Setting up a dial-up PPP link**

The Internet is fast becoming a lifeline for most of us. Seems we can't get through a day without it (I know I could not write the book without it). Sometimes I wonder how we ever managed without the Internet — and it's a pretty safe bet that you want to connect your Red Hat Linux system to the Internet. In this chapter, I show you how to connect to the Internet in several different ways — depending on whether you have DSL, cable modem, or dial-up network connection.

Two of the options for connecting to the Internet — DSL and cable modem — involve connecting a special modem to an Ethernet card on your Red Hat Linux system. In these cases, you have to set up Ethernet networking on your Red Hat Linux system. (I explain this in Chapter 2 of this mini-book.) In this chapter, I show you in detail how to set up a DSL or a cable modem connection.

I also show you the other option — dial-up networking — that involves dialing up an Internet Service Provider (ISP) from your Red Hat Linux system.

Understanding the Internet

How you view the Internet depends on your perspective. Common folks like us see the Internet in terms of the services we use. For example, as users we think of the Internet as an information-exchange medium — with features such as

✦ **E-mail:** Send e-mail to any other user on the Internet, using addresses such as mom@home.net.

✦ **Web:** Download and view documents from millions of servers throughout the Internet.

✦ **Newsgroups:** Read newsgroups and post news items to newsgroups with names such as `comp.os.linux.networking` or `comp.os.linux.setup`.

✦ **Information sharing:** Download software, music files, videos, and so on. Reciprocally, you may provide files that users on other systems can download.

✦ **Remote access:** Log on to another computer on the Internet, assuming that you have access to that remote computer.

The techies among us would say the Internet is a worldwide *network of networks*. The term *internet* (without capitalization) is a short form of *internetworking* — the interconnection of networks. The Internet Protocol (IP) was designed with the idea of connecting many separate networks.

In terms of physical connections, the Internet is similar to a network of highways and roads. This similarity is what has prompted the popular press to dub the Internet "the Information Superhighway." Just as the network of highways and roads includes some interstate highways, many state roads, and many more residential streets, the Internet has some very high-capacity networks (for example, a 10-Gbps backbone can handle 10 billion bits per second) and a large number of lower-capacity networks ranging from 56 Kbps dial-up connections to 45 Mbps T3 links (*Kbps* is thousand-bits-per-second and *Mbps* is million-bits-per-second). The high-capacity network is the backbone of the Internet.

In terms of management, the Internet is not run by a single organization, nor is it managed by any central computer. You can view the physical Internet as a "network of networks" managed collectively by thousands of cooperating organizations. Yes, a collection of networks managed by *thousands* of organizations — sounds amazing, but it works!

Deciding How to Connect to the Internet

So you want to connect to the Internet, but don't know how? Let me count the ways. Nowadays you have three popular options for connecting homes and small offices to the Internet (of course, huge corporations and governments have many other ways to connect):

✦ **Digital Subscriber Line (DSL):** This is something your local telephone company, as well as other telecommunications companies, may offer. DSL provides a way to send high-speed digital data over a regular phone line. Typically, DSL offers data-transfer rates of between 128 Kbps and

1.5 Mbps. You can download from the Internet at much higher rates than when you send data from your PC to the Internet (*upload*). One caveat with DSL is that your home must be between 12,000 and 15,000 feet from your local central office (the phone-company facility where your phone lines end up). The distance limitation varies from provider to provider. In the U.S., you can check out the distance limits for many providers at `www.dslreports.com/distance`.

✦ **Cable modem:** If the cable television company in your area offers Internet access over cable, you can use that service to hook up your Red Hat Linux system to the Internet. Typically, cable modems offer higher data-transfer rates than DSL — for the same cost. Downloading data from the Internet via cable modem is much faster than sending data from your PC to the Internet. You can expect routine download speeds of 1.5 Mbps and upload speeds of around 128 Kbps, but sometimes you may get even higher speeds than these.

✦ **Dial-up networking:** This is what most of us were using before DSL and cable modems came along. You hook up your PC to a modem that's connected to the phone lines. Then dial up an ISP to connect to the Internet. That's why we call it *dial-up networking* — establishing a network connection between your Red Hat Linux PC and another network (the Internet) through a dial-up modem. In this case, the maximum data-transfer rate is 56 Kbps.

DSL and cable-modem service connect you to the Internet and also act as your Internet Service Provider (ISP); in addition to improved speed, what you're paying for is an IP address and your e-mail accounts. If you use a dial-up modem to connect to the Internet, first you have to connect to the phone line (for which you pay the phone company) and then select and pay a separate ISP — which gives you a phone number to dial and all the other necessary goodies (such as an IP address and e-mail accounts).

Table 1-1 summarizes all these options. You can consult that table and select the type of connection that's available to you and that best suits your needs.

Table 1-1	Comparison of Dial-Up, DSL, and Cable		
Feature	*Dial-up*	*DSL*	*Cable*
Equipment	Modem	DSL modem, Ethernet card	Cable modem, Ethernet card
Also requires	Phone service and an Internet Service Provider (ISP)	Phone service and location within 12,000 to 15,000 feet of central office	Cable TV connection
Connection type	Dial to connect	Always on, dedicated	Always on, shared

(continued)

Table 1-1 *(continued)*

Feature	Dial-up	DSL	Cable
Typical speed	56 Kbps maximum	640 Kbps download, 128 Kbps upload (higher speeds cost more)	1.5 Mbps download, 128 Kbps upload
One-time costs (estimate)	None	Install = $100–200; Equipment = $200–300 (may be leased and may require activation cost)	Install = $100–200; Equipment = $60–100 (may be leased)
Typical monthly cost (2003)	Phone charges = $20/month; ISP charges = $15–30/month	$50/month; may require monthly modem lease	$50/month; may require monthly modem lease

Note: Costs vary by region and provider. Costs shown are typical ones for U.S. metropolitan areas.

Connecting with DSL

DSL stands for *Digital Subscriber Line*. DSL uses your existing phone line to send digital data in addition to the normal analog voice signals (*analog* means continuously varying, whereas digital data is represented by 1s and 0). The phone line goes from your home to a central office, where the line connects to the phone company's network — by the way, the connection from your home to the central office is called the *local loop*. When you sign up for DSL service, the phone company has to hook up your phone line to some special equipment at the central office. That equipment can separate the digital data from voice. From then on, your phone line can carry digital data that can then be directly sent to an Internet connection at the central office.

How DSL works

A special box called a *DSL modem* takes care of sending digital data from your PC to the phone company's central office over your phone line. Your PC can connect to the Internet with the same phone line that you use for your normal telephone calls — you can make voice calls even as the line is being used for DSL. Figure 1-1 shows a typical DSL connection to the Internet.

Your PC talks to the DSL modem through an Ethernet connection, which means that you need an Ethernet card in your Red Hat Linux system.

Figure 1-1:
DSL
provides
high-speed
connection
to Internet
over a
regular
phone line.

Your PC sends digital data over the Ethernet connection to the DSL modem. The DSL modem sends the digital data at different frequencies than those used by the analog voice signals. The voice signals occupy a small portion of all the frequencies that the phone line can carry. DSL uses the higher frequencies to transfer digital data, so both voice and data can travel on the same phone line.

The distance between your home and the central office — the *loop length* — is a factor in DSL's performance. Unfortunately, the phone line can reliably carry the DSL signals over only a limited distance — typically three miles or less. This means that you can get DSL service only if your home (or office) is located within about three miles of your phone company's central office. Your phone company can tell you whether your location can get DSL or not. Often it has a Web site where you can type in your phone number and get a response about DSL availability. For example, try www.dslavailability.com for U.S locations.

DSL alphabet soup — ADSL, IDSL, SDSL

I have been using the term *DSL* as if there were only one kind of DSL. As you may imagine, nothing is ever that simple. There are, in fact, three variants of DSL, each with different features. Take a look:

+ **ADSL:** Asymmetric DSL, the most common form of DSL, has much higher download speeds (from the Internet to your PC) than upload speeds (from your PC to the Internet). ADSL can have download speeds of up to 8 Mbps and upload speeds of up to 1 Mbps. ADSL works best when your location is within about 2½ miles (12,000 feet) of your central office. ADSL service is priced according to the download and upload speeds you want. A popular form of ADSL, called G.lite, is specifically designed to work on the same line you use for voice calls. G.lite has a maximum download speed of 1.5 Mbps and maximum upload speed of 512 Kbps.

+ **IDSL:** ISDN DSL (ISDN is an older technology called *Integrated Services Digital Network*) is a special type of DSL that works at distances of up to five miles between your phone and the central office. The downside is that IDSL only offers downstream (from the Internet to your PC) and upstream (from your PC to the Internet) speeds of up to 144 Kbps.

+ **SDSL:** Symmetric DSL provides the equal download and upload speed of up to 1.5 Mbps. SDSL is priced according to the speed you want, with the higher speeds costing more. The closer your location is to the phone company central office, the faster the connection you can get.

DSL speeds are typically specified by two numbers separated by a slash, like this: 1500/384. The numbers refer to data-transfer speeds in kilobits per second (that is, thousands-of-bits per second, abbreviated Kbps). The first number is the download speed, the second the upload. Thus 1500/384 means you can expect to download from the Internet at a maximum rate of 1,500 Kbps (or 1.5 Mbps) and upload to the Internet at 384 Kbps. If your phone line's condition is not perfect, you may not get these maximum rates — both ADSL and SDSL adjust the speeds to suit existing line conditions.

The price of DSL service depends on which variant — ADSL, IDSL, or SDSL — you select. For most home users, the primary choice is ADSL (or, more accurately, the G.lite form of ADSL) with transfer speed ratings of 1500/128.

Typical DSL setup

To get DSL for your home or business, you have to contact a DSL provider. In addition to your phone company, there are many other DSL providers. No matter who provides the DSL service, some work has to be done at your central office — the place where your phone lines connect to the rest of the phone network. The work involves connecting your phone line to equipment that can work with the DSL modem at your home or office. The central office equipment and the DSL modem at your location can then do whatever magic is needed to send and receive digital data over your phone line.

Because of the need to set up your line at the central office, it takes some time after you place an order to get your line ready for DSL.

The first step for you is to check out the DSL providers that provide service and see if you can actually get the service. Because DSL can work only over certain distances — typically less than 2.5 miles — between your location and the central office, you have to check to see if you are within that distance limit. Contact your phone company to verify. You may be able to check this on the Web. Try typing into Google (`www.google.com`) the words **DSL**, **availability**, and your local phone company's name. You probably will get a Web site where you can type in your phone number and learn if DSL is available for your number.

If DSL is available, you can look for the types of service — ADSL versus SDSL — and the pricing. The price depends on the download and upload speeds you want. Sometimes phone companies offer a simple residential DSL (basically the G.lite form of ADSL) with a 1500/128 speed rating — meaning you can download at 1,500 Kbps and upload at 128 Kbps. Of course, these are the *maximums*, and your mileage may vary.

After selecting the type of DSL service and provider, you can place an order and have the provider install the necessary equipment at your home or office. Figure 1-2 shows a sample connection diagram for typical residential DSL service.

Figure 1-2:
You can connect a PC's Ethernet card directly to the DSL modem.

Wall plate   **DSL Modem**   Ethernet card in your PC

Microfilter   **Your PC**

Your phone

Here are some key points to note in Figure 1-2:

✦ Connect your DSL modem's data connection to the phone jack on a wall plate.

✦ Connect the DSL modem's Ethernet connection to the Ethernet card on your PC.

✦ When you connect other telephones or fax machines on the same phone line, install a *microfilter* between the wall plate and each of these devices.

Because the same phone line carries both voice signals and DSL data, you need the microfilters to protect the DSL data from possible interference. You can buy them at electronic stores or from the DSL provider.

When you connect your Red Hat Linux PC to the Internet using DSL, the connection is always on — and there is more potential for outsiders to break into the PC. You should make sure that the Red Hat Linux firewall setting is set at High Security. To configure the firewall settings, choose Main Menu⇨System Settings⇨Security Level from the GNOME desktop.

There is another way to protect your Red Hat Linux system from intruders and, as an added bonus, share the high-speed connection with other PCs in a local area network (LAN). To do this, you need a router that can perform Network Address Translation (NAT). Such a *NAT router* translates multiple private Internet Protocol (IP) addresses from an internal LAN into a single public IP address, which makes it possible for all the internal PCs to access the Internet.

If you also want to set up a local area network, you need an Ethernet hub to connect the other PCs to the network. Figure 1-3 shows a typical setup that connects a LAN to the Internet through a NAT router and a DSL modem.

Here are the points to note when setting up a connection like the one shown in Figure 1-3:

✦ You need a NAT router with two 10BaseT Ethernet ports (the 10BaseT port looks like a large phone jack, also known as an *RJ-45 jack*). Typically, one Ethernet port is labeled *Internet* (or *External* or *WAN* for *wide-area network*), and the other one is labeled *Local* or *LAN* (for *local area network*).

✦ You also need an Ethernet hub. For a small home network, you can buy a 4- or 8-port Ethernet hub. Basically, you want a hub with as many ports as the number of PCs you intend to connect to your local area network.

✦ Connect the Ethernet port of the DSL modem to the Internet port of the NAT router, using a 10BaseT Ethernet cable (these look like phone wires with bigger RJ-45 jacks and are often labeled *Category 5* or *Cat 5* wire).

✦ Connect the Local Ethernet port of the NAT router to one of the ports on the Ethernet hub, using a 10BaseT Ethernet cable.

✦ Now connect each of the PCs to the Ethernet hub. (Of course, to do so you must first have an Ethernet card installed and configured in each PC.)

You can also buy a NAT router with a built-in 4- or 8-port Ethernet hub. With such a combined router-hub, you need only one box to set up a LAN and connect it to the Internet via a DSL modem. These boxes are typically sold under the name Cable/DSL router because they work with both DSL and a cable modem.

Consult Chapter 2 of this mini-book for information on how to configure networking on the Red Hat Linux system so your system can access the Internet.

Figure 1-3:
A NAT router isolates your PC from the Internet and also lets you share the DSL connection with other PCs in a local area network.

Phone jack

Ethernet cables (10BaseT)

Ethernet hub

DSL modem

NAT router

Ethernet cables (10BaseT)

PCs in a local area network (LAN). Each PC must have a 10BaseT Ethernet card.

**Book IV
Chapter 1**

Connecting to the Internet

Connecting with Cable Modem

Cable TV companies also offer high-speed Internet access over the same coaxial cable that carries television signals to your home. After the cable company installs the necessary equipment at its facility to send and receive digital data over the coaxial cables, customers can sign up for cable Internet service. You can then get high-speed Internet access over the same cable that delivers cable TV signals to your home.

How cable modem works

A box called *cable modem* is at the heart of Internet access over the cable TV network (see Figure 1-4). The cable modem takes digital data from your PC's Ethernet card and puts in an unused block of frequency (think of it as another TV channel, but instead of pictures and sound, this channel carries digital data).

The cable modem places *upstream data* — data that's being sent from your PC to the Internet — in a different channel than the *downstream* data that's coming from the Internet to your PC. By design, the speed of downstream data transfers is much higher than that of upstream transfers. The assumption is that people download far more stuff from the Internet than they upload. (Probably true for most of us.)

Figure 1-4: Cable modems provide high-speed Internet access over the cable TV network.

The coaxial cable that carries all those hundreds of cable TV channels to your home is a very capable signal carrier. In particular, the coaxial cable can carry signals covering a huge range of frequencies — hundreds of mega-hertz (MHz). Each TV channel requires 6 MHz — and the coaxial cable can carry hundreds of such channels. The cable modem places the upstream data in a small frequency band and expects to receive the downstream data in a whole other frequency band.

At the other end of your cable connection to the Internet is the *Cable Modem Termination System* (CMTS) that your cable company installs at its central facility (refer to Figure 1-4). The CMTS connects the cable TV network to the Internet. It also extracts the upstream digital data sent by your cable modem (and by those of your neighbors as well) and sends all of it to the Internet. The CMTS also puts digital data into the upstream channels so your cable modem can extract that data and provide it to your PC via the Ethernet card.

Cable modems can receive downstream data at the rate of about 30 Mbps and send data upstream at around 3 Mbps. However, all the cable modems in a neighborhood share the same downstream capacity. Each cable modem filters out — separates — the data it needs from the stream of data that the CMTS sends out.

In practice, with a cable modem you can get downstream transfer rates of around 1.5 Mbps and upstream rates of 128 Kbps.

If you want to check your downstream transfer speed, go to `bandwidthplace.com/speedtest` and click the link to start the test. For my cable modem connection (for example), the tests reported a downstream transfer rate of about 1.4 Mbps.

Typical cable modem setup

To set up cable modem access, your cable TV provider must offer high-speed Internet access. If the service is available, you can call to sign up. The cable companies often have promotional offers such as no installation fee or a reduced rate for three months. Look for these offers. If you are lucky, they may have a promotion going on just when you want to sign up.

The installation is typically done by a technician, who splits your incoming cable into two — one side goes to the TV and the other to the cable modem. The technician provides information about the cable modem to the cable company's head end for setup at its end. When all that is done, you can plug in your PC's Ethernet card to the cable modem and you're all set to enjoy high-speed Internet access. Figure 1-5 shows a typical cable-modem hookup.

To cable
distribution box

10BaseT
Ethernet cable

Ethernet card
in your PC

2-way splitter

Coaxial
cables

Cable modem

Figure 1-5:
The cable
TV signal
is split
between
the TV and
the cable
modem.

Television set

Your PC

You need an Ethernet card in your PC because the cable modem connects to an Ethernet card. The cable company technician often provides an Ethernet card.

Here are some key points to note about the cable modem setup in Figure 1-5:

✦ Split the incoming cable TV signal into two parts by using a 2-way splitter (the cable company technician installs this). By the way, the 2-way splitter should be rated for 1 GHz; otherwise, it may not pass through the frequencies that contain the downstream data from the Internet.

✦ Connect one of the video outputs from the splitter to your cable modem's F-type video connector using a coaxial cable.

✦ Connect the cable modem's 10BaseT Ethernet connection to the Ethernet card on your PC.

✦ Connect your TV to the other video output from the two-way splitter.

When you use cable modem to connect your Red Hat Linux PC to the Internet, the connection is always on, so there is more chance that someone may try to break into the PC. You should set the firewall setting to High Security. To configure the firewall settings, choose Main Menu⇨System Settings⇨Security Level from the GNOME desktop.

You may want to add a NAT (Network Address Translation) router between your PC and the cable modem. As an added bonus, you can even share a cable modem connection with all the PCs in your own local area network (LAN) by adding an Ethernet hub. Better yet, buy a combination NAT-router-and-hub so you have only one box do the whole job. By the way, the NAT router/hubs are typically sold under the name *Cable/DSL router* because they work with both DSL and cable modem.

The NAT router translates private Internet Protocol (IP) addresses into a public IP address. When connected through a NAT router, any PC in the internal LAN can access the Internet as if it had its own unique IP address. Result: A single Internet connection can be shared among many PCs. (An ideal solution for an entire family of Net surfers!)

Figure 1-6 shows a typical setup with a cable modem connection being shared by a number of PCs in a LAN.

Here are the points to note when setting up a connection like the one shown in Figure 1-6:

✦ You need a Cable/DSL NAT router with two 10BaseT Ethernet ports (the 10BaseT port — also known as an RJ-45 jack — looks like a large phone jack). Typically, one Ethernet port is labeled *Internet* (or *External* or *WAN* for *wide area network*) and the other one is labeled *Local*.

✦ If you plan to set up a LAN, you also need an Ethernet hub. For a small home network, you can buy a 4- or 8-port Ethernet hub. Basically, you want a hub with as many ports as the number of PCs you intend to connect to your local area network.

✦ Consider buying a single box that acts as a NAT router and also a hub with a number of Ethernet ports.

✦ Connect the video cable to the video input port of the cable modem.

✦ Connect the Ethernet port of the cable modem to the Internet port of the NAT router using a 10BaseT Ethernet cable (these look like phone wires, except that the Ethernet cables have bigger RJ-45 jacks and are often labeled Category 5 or Cat 5 wire).

✦ Connect the Local Ethernet port of the NAT router to one of the ports on the Ethernet hub using a 10BaseT Ethernet cable.

✦ Now connect each of the PCs to the Ethernet hub. Of course, each PC must have an Ethernet card.

In Chapter 2 of this mini-book, I explain how to configure the PCs in such a LAN so that they can all access the Internet.

**Book IV
Chapter 1**

Connecting to
the Internet

Figure 1-6:
A NAT router isolates your PC from the Internet and also lets you share cable modem connection with other PCs in a local area network.

Setting Up Dial-Up Networking

Dial-up networking refers to connecting a PC to a remote network through a dial-up modem. If you are ancient enough to remember the days of dialing up with Procomm or some serial communications software, there is a significant difference between dial-up networking and the old days of serial communication. Both approaches use a modem to dial up a remote computer and to establish a communication path, but the serial-communication software makes your computer behave like a dumb terminal connected to the remote computer. The serial-communication software exclusively uses dial-up connection. You cannot run another copy of the communication software and use the same modem connection, for example.

In dial-up networking, both your PC and the remote system run network-protocol (called TCP/IP) software. When your PC dials up and sets up a communication path, the network protocols exchange data packets over that dial-up connection. The neat part is that any number of applications can use the same dial-up connection to send and receive data packets. So your PC becomes a part of the network to which the remote computer belongs. (If the remote computer is not on a network, dial-up networking creates a network that consists of the remote computer and your PC.)

In Chapter 2 of this mini-book, I describe TCP/IP protocol some more, but I have to use the term as well as a few other concepts — such as *Internet*

Protocol (IP) address and *Domain Name Service* (DNS) — when describing how to set up dial-up networking.

Setting up a TCP/IP network over a dial-up link involves specifying the protocol — the convention — for packaging a data packet over the communication link. *Point-to-Point Protocol* (PPP) is such a protocol for establishing a TCP/IP connection over any point-to-point link, including dial-up phone lines. Red Hat Linux supports PPP, and it comes with the configuration tools you can use to set up PPP so that your system can establish a PPP connection with your ISP.

Here's what you have to do to set up dial-up networking in Red Hat Linux:

1. Install an internal or external modem in your PC. If your PC did not already come with an internal modem, you can buy an external modem and connect it to the PC's serial or USB port.

2. Connect the modem to the phone line.

3. Get an account with an ISP. Every ISP provides you a phone number to dial, a user name, and a password. Additionally, the ISP should give you the full names of servers for e-mail and news. Typically, your system automatically gets an IP address.

4. Test your modem and make sure it's working. You can do this testing with a serial communication package called `minicom` that comes with Red Hat Linux.

5. Run the Internet Configuration Wizard to set up a PPP connection.

6. Activate the PPP connection to connect to the Internet.

I briefly go over these steps in the following sections.

Connecting the modem

Modem is a contraction of modulator/demodulator — a device that converts digital signals (string of 1s and 0s) into continuously varying analog signals that can be transmitted over telephone lines and radio waves. Thus, the modem is the intermediary between the digital world of the PC and the analog world of telephones. Figure 1-7 illustrates the concept of a modem.

Inside the PC, 1s and 0s are represented with voltage levels, but signals carried over telephone lines are usually tones of different frequencies. The modem sits between the PC and the telephone lines and makes data communication possible over the phone lines. The modem converts information back and forth between the voltage/no voltage representation of digital circuits and different frequency tones that are appropriate for transmission over phone lines.

Figure 1-7:
A modem bridges the digital world of PCs and the analog world of telephones.

Modem

Before you can dial out using an external modem, you have to make sure that the modem is properly connected to one of the serial or USB ports of your PC.

If you have an external modem, make sure that your modem is properly connected to the power supply and that the modem is connected to the telephone line. Buy the right type of cable to connect the modem to the PC. You need a straight-through serial cable to connect the modem to the PC. The connectors at the ends of the cable depend on the type of serial connector on your PC. The modem end of the cable needs a male 25-pin connector. The PC end of the cable often is a female 9-pin connector. You can buy modem cables at most computer stores. Often you can find 9-pin-female-to-25-pin-male modem cables sold under the label "AT Modem Cable." Connect USB modems by using a USB cable.

If your PC has an internal modem, all you have to do is connect the phone line to the phone jack that's at the back of the internal-modem card. If it's a winmodem, you still connect the phone line, but you also have to do a bit of research on the Internet and download a driver that makes the winmodem work in Red Hat Linux. After you install a working Linux driver for a winmodem, it works just like the older serialport modems.

Learning the serial-device names

The PC typically has two serial ports, called COM1 and COM2 in MS-DOS parlance. Many new PCs with *Universal Serial Bus* (USB) have only one serial port. The PC also can support two more serial ports: COM3 and COM4. Because of these port names, we often refer to the serial ports as *COM ports*.

Like other devices, the serial-port devices are represented by device files in the /dev directory. The serial ports also need *interrupt-request* (IRQ) numbers and I/O port addresses. Two IRQs — 3 and 4 — are shared among the four COM ports. Table 1-2 lists the serial-device names corresponding to the PC's COM ports, as well as the IRQs and I/O port addresses assigned to the four serial ports.

Winmodems: They *only* do Windows

A quick word of caution about the *winmodems* that come with many new PCs and laptops. These are software-based internal modems — totally different from the traditional hardware modems. Also known as *Windows modems* or *software modems,* they work only with special driver software (which in turn works only with Microsoft Windows). When it comes to winmodems and Linux, you're pretty much on your own — but you can find some useful guidance online at the Linux Winmodem Support homepage at www.linmodems.org. For example, I was able to find out that the winmodem in my laptop uses a Conexant chipset and that a Linux driver is available from www.linuxant.com/drivers/hsf/downloads-rh-i686.html. Then I downloaded an RPM file for my kernel version and installed it on the laptop, using the rpm command. After that, I could use my laptop's winmodem from Red Hat Linux applications.

Table 1-2	Device Names for Serial Ports		
COM port	*Device name*	*IRQ*	*I/O Address*
COM1	/dev/ttyS0	4	0x3f8
COM2	/dev/ttyS1	3	0x2f8
COM3	/dev/ttyS2	4	0x3e8
COM4	/dev/ttyS3	3	0x2e8

All of these devices should already be in your Red Hat Linux system. In a terminal window, type **ls -l /dev/ttyS*** to see a listing of these device files.

The device name will be different if your modem connects to a USB port or if you have a winmodem. For winmodems, you have to first download and install a driver. You should be able to locate Linux drivers for many winmodems by checking the www.linmodems.org Web site. In many cases, Linux winmodem drivers set up the modem device /dev/modem as a symbolic link to the actual device file. That way, you can refer to the modem device by the generic name /dev/modem instead of having to learn somewhat complicated device names.

Checking if the Linux kernel detected the serial port

To verify that the Linux kernel detected the serial port correctly, check the boot messages with the following command:

```
dmesg | grep ttyS
```

If you see a message such as the following, then Linux has detected a serial port in your PC:

```
ttyS0 at 0x03f8 (irq = 4) is a 16550A
```

In this case, the message indicates that the Linux kernel has detected the first serial port (COM1). It shows the I/O address (in hexadecimal), 0x3f8, and IRQ 4. The last part of the message — 16550A — refers to the identifying number of the *universal asynchronous receiver/transmitter* (UART) chip, which is at the heart of all serial communications hardware (the UART converts each byte to a stream of 1s and 0s, and vice versa when it receives such a stream).

You can also check for the serial ports with the setserial command. Type the following command to see detailed information about the serial ports:

```
setserial -g /dev/ttyS?
```

Any device that is listed in the output of this command with an unknown UART is either not installed or not detected by the Linux kernel.

Testing the modem

After you complete the physical installation of the modem and verify that the Linux kernel detected the serial port, you can try to dial out through the modem. The best approach is to use the Minicom serial communications program that comes with Red Hat Linux.

Minicom is similar to other communications software, such as Procomm or Crosstalk, that you may have used under MS-DOS or Windows.

To run Minicom, log in as root and type **minicom** at the shell prompt in the terminal window (or in a virtual console). Minicom runs and resets the modem. Figure 1-8 shows the result of running Minicom in a terminal window.

If you don't see the OK, it probably means that this particular serial-device name is not set correctly. To set the serial device, follow these steps:

1. **Press Ctrl+A and then Z.**

   Minicom displays its help screen.

2. **Press O.**

   Minicom displays its configuration menu.

3. **Use the arrow key to select Serial port setup and press Enter.**

   Minicom displays the serial port settings.

4. **Press A.**

Minicom puts the cursor in the line that shows the serial-device name. Edit the device name to match where your modem is connected. For example, if the modem is on the first serial port, make sure that the device name is /dev/ttyS0.

5. Press Enter twice.

Minicom returns to the configuration menu.

6. Select Save setup as dfl and press Enter.

Minicom saves the settings.

7. Select Exit and press Enter.

Minicom returns to online mode.

8. Press Ctrl+A and X.

Minicom prompts you to ask whether you really want to exit.

9. Press Enter to exit.

After setting the correct device name for the serial port where the modem is connected, make sure that your modem is powered on and connected to the phone line.

10. Start Minicom again (type minicom **in the terminal window).**

11. Press Ctrl+A to get the attention of the Minicom program.

After you press Ctrl+A, if you press Z, a help screen appears in the form of a text window. In the help screen, you can get information about other Minicom commands.

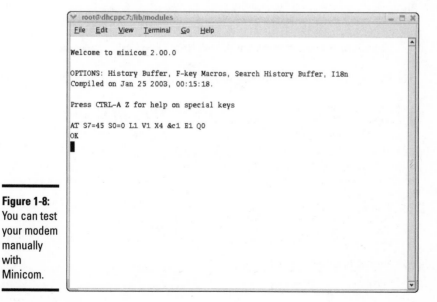

Figure 1-8:
You can test your modem manually with Minicom.

12. From the help screen, press Enter to go back to online mode.

In online mode, you can use the modem's AT commands to dial out. In particular, you can use the ATDT command to dial the phone number of another modem (for example, dial your ISP's number). When you get the login prompt, you know that the modem is working. Figure 1-9 shows the results of a typical dial-up using Minicom: only 38.4 Kbps with a 56 Kbps modem. (No wonder I needed DSL or cable modem!)

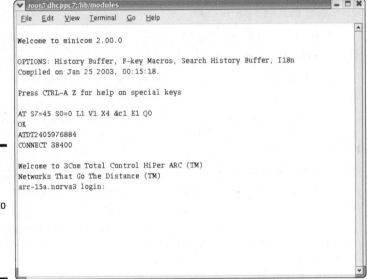

Figure 1-9:
Use the
ATDT
command to
manually
dial out
using
Minicom.

13. To exit Minicom, press Ctrl+A and then type X.

14. Press Enter again to close Minicom.

Setting up and activating a PPP connection

Most ISPs provide PPP dial-up access to the Internet through one or more systems that the ISP maintains. If you sign up for such a service, the ISP should provide you the information that you need to make a PPP connection to the ISP's system. Typically, this information includes the following:

✦ The phone number to dial to connect to the remote system

✦ The user name and password that you must use to log in to the remote system

✦ The names of the ISP's mail and news servers

✦ The IP address for your PPP connection. ISP does not provide this address if the IP address is assigned dynamically (this means the IP address may change every time your system establishes a connection).

✦ IP addresses of the ISP's *Domain Name Servers* (DNS). The ISP does not provide these addresses if it assigns the IP address dynamically.

Of this information, the first two items are what you need to set up a PPP connection.

Follow these steps to set up a PPP connection using Red Hat's Internet Configuration Wizard:

1. **Log in as** root **and choose Main Menu⟹System Tools⟹Internet Configuration Wizard from the GNOME desktop.**

If you are not logged in as root, type the root password when you're prompted for it.

The Select Device Type dialog box appears (as shown in Figure 1-10).

Figure 1-10: Configure the Modem connection from this dialog box.

2. **Select Modem connection from the Device Type list, and then click Forward.**

The Select Modem dialog box shows information about your modem.

3. **Click Forward to continue.**

The Select Provider dialog box appears.

4. **Fill in the connection information — the ISP's phone number, your login name, and password — in the text boxes (shown in Figure 1-11); click Forward to continue.**

**Book IV
Chapter 1**

Connecting to the Internet

Figure 1-11:
Fill in the connection information in this dialog box.

5. **Enter the IP settings — whether you want to automatically get an IP address or provide a static IP address — and then click Forward to continue.**

   Typically, you would select the option to automatically obtain an IP address and name server settings from the ISP.

6. **Click Apply to save the dial-up configuration information, and then close the Internet Configuration Wizard.**

   The Network Configuration dialog box appears with the name of the new dial-up connection in a list (Figure 1-12).

Figure 1-12:
Click Activate in the Network Configuration dialog box to establish the PPP connection.

7. **Select the connection name, and then click Activate.**

8. **When you're done, click Deactivate to turn the PPP connection off.**

Configuring CHAP and PAP authentication

The PPP server on your system has to authenticate itself to the ISP's PPP server before the PPP connection can get fully up and running. *Authentication* requires proving that you have a valid account with the ISP; essentially this involves providing a user name and a *secret* (that is, a password). PPP specifies two ways of exchanging the authentication information between the two ends of the connection:

+ **Challenge Handshake Authentication Protocol (CHAP)** requires the remote end to send a randomly generated challenge string along with the remote server's name. The local system looks up the secret, using the server's name; then it sends back a response that includes its name and a value that combines the secret and the challenge, using a one-way hash function. The remote system then checks that value against its own calculation of the expected hash value. If the values match, the authentication succeeds; otherwise, the remote system terminates the connection. In this case, the name and secret are stored in the /etc/ppp/chap-secrets file. Note that the remote system can repeat the CHAP authentication any time while the PPP link is up.

+ **Password Authentication Protocol (PAP)** is like the normal login process. When using PAP, the local system repeatedly sends a username (name) and password (secret) until the remote system acknowledges the authentication or ends the connection. The name and secret are stored in the /etc/ppp/pap-secrets file. Note that the user name and password are sent in the clear (that is, unencrypted).

The Linux PPP server supports both types of authentication. For both PAP and CHAP, the information that the PPP server needs is a name and a secret — a username-password pair. This authentication information is stored in the following configuration files:

+ /etc/ppp/chap-secrets stores the information for CHAP. Here's what a typical chap-secrets file looks like:

```
# Secrets for authentication using CHAP
# client      server      secret           IP addresses
  "naba"         *         "mypassword"
```

+ /etc/ppp/pap-secrets stores the information for PAP. Here's a typical pap-secrets file:

```
# Secrets for authentication using PAP
# client      server      secret           IP addresses
  "naba"         *         "mypassword"
```

**Book IV
Chapter 1**

**Connecting to
the Internet**

As you can see, the format of entries are the same for both `chap-secrets` and `pap-secrets`. There are four fields in each line, in the following order:

1. `client` — This field contains the name to be used during authentication. This is the username that you get from the ISP.

2. `server` — This field contains the name of the remote system to which you are authenticating the local system. If you don't know the server's name, put an asterisk to indicate any server.

3. `secret` — This field is the secret that your system's PPP server has to send to the remote system to authenticate itself. This is the password you received from the ISP.

4. `IP addresses` — This optional field can contain a list of the IP addresses that the local system may use when connecting to the specified server. Typically, this field is left blank because the local system usually gets a dynamic IP address from the server and (therefore) doesn't know what IP address it would use.

Chapter 2: Setting Up a Local Area Network

In This Chapter

✓ **Understanding TCP/IP networks**

✓ **Setting up an Ethernet LAN**

✓ **Configuring TCP/IP networking**

✓ **Connecting your LAN to the Internet**

Red Hat Linux comes with built-in support for TCP/IP (*Transmission Control Protocol/Internet Protocol*) networking, as do most modern operating systems from Windows to Mac OS. You can have TCP/IP networking over many different physical interfaces, such as Ethernet cards, serial ports, and parallel ports.

Typically, you use an Ethernet network for your local area network (LAN) — at your office or even your home (if you happen to have several systems at home). To connect to remote systems over a modem, you use TCP/IP networking over *Point-to-Point Protocol* (PPP).

This chapter describes how to set up an Ethernet network. Even if you have a single PC, you may need to set up an Ethernet network interface so you can connect your PC to high-speed Internet access that uses DSL or cable modem. (I cover DSL and cable modem in Chapter 1 of this mini-book.)

Understanding TCP/IP

You can understand TCP/IP networking best if you think in terms of a layered model with four layers. Think of each layer as responsible for performing a particular task. The layered model describes the flow of data between the physical connection to the network and the end-user application. Figure 2-1 shows the four-layer network model for TCP/IP.

In this four-layer model, information always moves from one layer to the next. For example, when an application sends data to another application, the data goes through the layers in this order: Application⇨Transport⇨Network⇨Physical. At the receiving end, the data goes up from Physical⇨Network⇨Transport⇨Application.

4	**Application**	Mail, file transfer, TELNET
3	**Transport**	TCP (Transmission Control Protocol) UDP (User Datagram Protocol)
2	**Network**	IP (Internet Protocol)
1	**Physical**	Ethernet

Figure 2-1:
You can understand TCP/IP using the four-layer network model.

Each layer has its own set of *protocols* — conventions — for handling and formatting the data. If you think of sending data as something akin to sending letters through the postal service, then a typical protocol would be a preferred sequence of actions for a task such as addressing an envelope (first the name, then the street address, and then city, state, and Zip or other postal code).

Here's what each of the four layers does, top to bottom:

✦ **Application layer:** Runs the applications that users use, such as e-mail readers, file transfers, and Web browsers. There are application-level protocols such as Simple Mail Transfer Protocol (SMTP) and Post Office Protocol (POP) for e-mail, Hyper Text Transfer Protocol (HTTP) for the Web, and File Transfer Protocol (FTP) for file transfers. Application-level protocols also have a *port number* that you can think of as an identifier for a specific application. For example, port 80 is associated with HTTP or the Web server.

✦ **Transport layer:** Sends data from one application to another. The two most important protocols in this layer are *Transmission Control Protocol* (TCP) and *User Datagram Protocol* (UDP). TCP guarantees delivery of data; UDP just sends the data without ensuring that it actually reaches the destination.

✦ **Network layer:** This layer is responsible for getting data packets from one *network* to another. If the networks are far apart, the data packets are routed from one network to the next until they reach their destination. The primary protocol in this layer is the Internet Protocol (IP).

+ **Physical layer:** Refers to the physical networking hardware (such as an Ethernet card or Token Ring card) that carries the data packets in a network.

The beauty of the layered model is that each layer only takes care of its specific task, leaving the rest to the other layers. The layers can mix and match — you can have a TCP/IP network over any type of physical network medium, from Ethernet to radio waves (in a wireless network). The software is modular as well because each layer can be implemented in different modules. For example, typically the Transport and Internet layers already exist as part of the operating system; any application can make use of these layers.

TCP/IP and the Internet

TCP/IP has become the protocol of choice on the Internet — the "network of networks" that evolved from ARPAnet. The U.S. Government's Advanced Research Projects Agency (ARPA) initiated research in the 1970s on a new way of sending information, using packets of data sent over a network. The result was ARPAnet: a national network of linked computers. Subsequently, ARPA acquired a Defense prefix and became DARPA. Under the auspices of DARPA, the TCP/IP protocols emerged as a popular collection of protocols for *internetworking* — communication among networks.

TCP/IP has flourished because the protocol is open. That means the technical descriptions of the protocol appear in public documents, so anyone can implement TCP/IP on specific hardware and software.

TCP/IP also made great inroads because stable, working software was available. Instead of a paper description of network architecture and protocols, the TCP/IP protocols *started out* as working software — and who can argue with what's already working? These days (as a result), TCP/IP rules the Internet.

IP addresses

When you have many computers on a network, you need a way to identify each one uniquely. In TCP/IP networking, the address of a computer is the IP address. Because TCP/IP deals with internetworking, the address is based on the concepts of a network address and a host address. You may think of the idea of a network address and a host address as having to provide two addresses to identify a computer uniquely:

+ Network address indicates the network on which the computer is located.

+ Host address indicates a specific computer on that network.

Next-generation IP (IPv6)

When the 4-byte IP address was created, the number of available addresses seemed adequate. Now, however, the 4-byte addresses are running out. The Internet Engineering Task Force (IETF) recognized the potential for running out of IP addresses in 1991 and began work on the next-generation IP addressing scheme. They called it IPng (for Internet Protocol Next Generation) and intended that it will eventually replace the old 4-byte addressing scheme (called IPv4, for IP Version 4).

Several alternative addressing schemes for IPng were proposed and debated. The final contender, with a 128-bit (16-byte) address, was dubbed IPv6 (for IP Version 6). On September 18, 1995, the IETF declared the core set of IPv6 addressing protocols to be an IETF Proposed Standard.

IPv6 is designed to be an evolutionary step from IPv4. The proposed standard provides direct interoperability between hosts using the older IPv4 addresses and any new IPv6 hosts. The idea is that users can upgrade their systems to use IPv6 when they want and that network operators are free to upgrade their network hardware to use IPv6 without affecting current users of IPv4. Sample implementations of IPv6 are being developed for many operating systems, including Linux. For more information about IPv6 in Linux, consult the Linux IPv6 FAQ/HOWTO at www.linuxhq.com/IPv6/.

The IPv6 128-bit addressing scheme allows for 170,141,183,460,469,232,000,000,000,000,000,000,000 unique hosts! That should last us for a while!

The network and host addresses together constitute an *IP address* and it's a 4-byte (32-bit) value. The convention is to write each byte as a decimal value and to put a dot (.) after each number. Thus you see network addresses such as 132.250.112.52. This way of writing IP addresses is known as *dotted-decimal* or *dotted-quad* notation.

In decimal notation, a byte (which has 8 bits) can have a value between 0 and 255. Thus a valid IP addresses can use only the numbers between 0 and 255 in the dotted-decimal notation.

Internet services and port numbers

The TCP/IP protocol suite has become the *lingua franca* of the Internet because many standard services are available on any system that supports TCP/IP. These services make the Internet tick by facilitating the transfer of mail, news, and Web pages. These services go by well-known names such as the following:

✦ **DHCP** (Dynamic Host Configuration Protocol) is for dynamically configuring TCP/IP network parameters on a computer. DHCP is primarily used to assign dynamic IP addresses and other networking information (such as name server, default gateway, and domain names) needed to configure TCP/IP networks. The DHCP server listens on port 67.

✦ **FTP** (File Transfer Protocol) is used to transfer files between computers on the Internet. FTP uses two ports — data is transferred on port 20, while control information is exchanged on port 21.

✦ **HTTP** (HyperText Transfer Protocol) is a protocol for sending documents from one system to another. HTTP is the underlying protocol of the Web. By default, the Web server and client communicate on port 80.

✦ **SMTP** (Simple Mail Transfer Protocol) is for exchanging e-mail messages between systems. SMTP uses port 25 for information exchange.

✦ **NNTP** (Network News Transfer Protocol) is for distribution of news articles in a store-and-forward fashion across the Internet. NNTP uses port 119.

✦ **TELNET** is used when a user on one system logs in to another system on the Internet (the user must provide a valid user ID and password to log in to the remote system). TELNET uses port 23 by default, but the TELNET client can connect to any port.

✦ **SNMP** (Simple Network Management Protocol) is for managing all types of network devices on the Internet. Like FTP, SNMP uses two ports: 161 and 162.

✦ **TFTP** (Trivial File Transfer Protocol) is for transferring files from one system to another (typically used by X terminals and diskless workstations to download boot files from another host on the network). TFTP data transfer takes place on port 69.

✦ **NFS** (Network File System) is for sharing files among computers. NFS uses Sun's Remote Procedure Call (RPC) facility, which exchanges information through port 111.

A well-known port is associated with each of these services. The TCP protocol uses each such port to locate a service on any system. (A *server process* — a special computer program running on a system — provides each service.)

Setting Up an Ethernet LAN

Ethernet is a standard way to move packets of data between two or more computers connected to a single cable. (You can create larger networks by connecting multiple Ethernet segments with gateways.) To set up an Ethernet local area network (LAN), you need an Ethernet card for each PC. Red Hat Linux supports a wide variety of Ethernet cards for the PC.

**Book IV
Chapter 2**

**Setting Up a Local
Area Network**

Ethernet is a good choice for the physical data-transport mechanism for the following reasons:

✦ Ethernet is a proven technology that has been in use since the early 1980s.

✦ Ethernet provides good data-transfer rates: typically 10 million bits per second (10 Mbps), although 100-Mbps Ethernet and Gigabit Ethernet (1,000 Mbps) are now available.

✦ Ethernet hardware is relatively low cost. (PC Ethernet cards cost about $20 U.S.)

✦ With wireless Ethernet, you can easily connect laptop PCs to your Ethernet LAN — without having to run wires all over the place. (Go to Chapter 3 of this mini-book for more information on wireless Ethernet.)

How Ethernet works

So what makes Ethernet tick? In essence, it's the same thing that makes playground recess work: taking turns.

In an Ethernet network, all systems in a segment are connected to the same wire. Because a single wire is used, a protocol has to be used for sending and receiving data because only one data packet can exist on the cable at any time. An Ethernet LAN uses a data-transmission protocol known as *Carrier-Sense Multiple Access/Collision Detection* (CSMA/CD) to share the single transmission cable among all the computers. Ethernet cards in the computers follow the CSMA/CD protocol to transmit and receive Ethernet packets.

The idea behind the CSMA/CD protocol is similar to the way in which you have a conversation at a party. You listen for a pause (that's sensing the carrier) and talk when no one else is speaking. If you and another person begin talking at the same time, both of you realize the problem (that's collision detection) and pause for a moment; then one of you starts speaking again. As you know from experience, everything works out.

In an Ethernet LAN, each Ethernet card checks the cable for signals — that's the carrier-sense part. If the signal level is low, the Ethernet card sends its packets on the cable; the packet contains information about the sender and the intended recipient. All Ethernet cards on the LAN listen to the signal, and the recipient receives the packet. If two cards send out a packet simultaneously, the signal level in the cable rises above a threshold, and the cards know a collision has occurred (two packets have been sent out at the same time). Both cards wait for a random amount of time before sending their packets again.

Ethernet was invented in the early 1970s at the Xerox Palo Alto Research Center (PARC) by Robert M. Metcalfe. In the 1980s, Ethernet was standardized by the cooperative effort of three companies: Digital Equipment Corporation (DEC), Intel, and Xerox. Using the first initials of the company names, that Ethernet standard became known as the DIX standard. Later, the DIX standard was included in the 802-series standards developed by the Institute of Electrical and Electronics Engineers (IEEE). The final Ethernet specification is formally known as IEEE 802.3 CSMA/CD, but people continue to call it *Ethernet*.

Ethernet sends data in *packets* (discrete chunks also known as *frames*). You don't have to hassle much with the innards of Ethernet packets, except to note the 6-byte source and destination addresses. Each Ethernet controller has a unique 6-byte (48-bit) address — at the Physical level, every packet must have one.

Ethernet cables

Any time you hear experts talking about Ethernet, you're also going to hear some bewildering terms used for the cables that carry the data. Here's a quick rundown.

The original Ethernet standard used a thick coaxial cable, nearly half an inch in diameter. This wiring is called *thickwire* or *thick Ethernet*, although the IEEE 802.3 standard calls it 10Base5. That designation means several things: The data-transmission rate is 10 megabits per second (10 Mbps); the transmission is baseband (which simply means that the cable's signal-carrying capacity is devoted to transmitting Ethernet packets only); and the total length of the cable can be no more than 500 meters. Thickwire was expensive, and the cable was rather unwieldy. Unless you're a technology history buff, you don't have to care one whit about 10Base5 cables.

Nowadays, two other forms of Ethernet cabling are more popular. The first alternative to thick Ethernet cable is *thinwire*, or 10Base2, which uses a thin, flexible coaxial cable. A thinwire Ethernet segment can be, at most, 185 meters long. The other, more recent, alternative is Ethernet over unshielded twisted-pair cable (UTP), known as 10BaseT.

To set up a 10BaseT Ethernet network, you need an Ethernet hub — a hardware box with RJ-45 jacks (these look like big telephone jacks). You build the network by running twisted-pair wires (usually, Category 5, or Cat5, cables) from each PC's Ethernet card to this hub. You can get a 4-port 10BaseT hub for about $50 U.S. Figure 2-2 shows a typical small 10BaseT Ethernet LAN that you might set up at a small office or your home.

Ethernet hub

Category 5
cables

Figure 2-2:
You can use
an Ethernet
hub to set
up a
10BaseT
Ethernet
LAN.

PCs with Ethernet card

When you install Red Hat Linux from this book's companion DVD-ROM on a
PC connected with an Ethernet card, the Red Hat installer should automatically detect the Ethernet card and install the appropriate drivers. The
installer should also let you set up TCP/IP networking.

When properly installed, the Linux kernel should load the driver for the
Ethernet card every time it boots. To verify that the Ethernet driver is
loaded, type the following command in a terminal window:

```
dmesg | grep 'grep eth0 /etc/modules.conf | cut -d ' ' -f 3'
```

This command searches the boot messages for any line that contains the
name of the first Ethernet card (the command in backquotes — `grep eth0
/etc/modules.conf | cut -d ' ' -f 3` — picks out the alias for the
eth0 device from the /etc/modules.conf file).

On my PC, I have an Intel Ethernet Pro 100 (e100) card installed, so I get the
following output when I type that command on my system:

```
e100: selftest OK.
e100: eth0: Intel(R) PRO/100 WfM PCI Adapter
```

You should see something similar, showing the name of your Ethernet card
and other relevant parameters.

Configuring TCP/IP Networking

When you set up TCP/IP networking during Red Hat Linux installation, the installation program prepares all appropriate configuration files using the information you provide. However, Red Hat Linux does come with the graphical network configuration tool that you can use to add a new network interface or alter information such as name servers and host names.

Use the Linux network configuration tool to set up networking if you're adding a new Ethernet card (or if your Ethernet card was not configured during installation).

To start the network configuration tool, log in as `root` and from the GNOME desktop, choose Main Menu⇨System Settings⇨Network. If you are not logged in as `root`, you're prompted for the `root` password.

The network configuration tool displays a tabbed dialog box, as shown in Figure 2-3.

Figure 2-3:
Configure
the Ethernet
network
with the
Red Hat
network
configur-
ation tool.

You can configure your network through the four tabs that appear along the top of the dialog box. Here's what each of the tabs does:

+ **Devices:** Here's where you find options for a new network interface (for example, an Ethernet card). You can set the IP address of the interface and then activate it. Information that you enter about a device is stored in various files in the `/etc/sysconfig` directory.

✦ **Hardware:** Here you add a new hardware device, such as an Ethernet card, modem, or an ISDN device. You can then provide information such as interrupt request (IRQ), I/O port numbers, and DMA channels for the device.

✦ **DNS:** Here you enter the host name for your system and enter the IP addresses of name servers. The name server addresses are stored in the /etc/resolv.conf file. The host name is stored in the HOSTNAME variable in the /etc/sysconfig/network file.

✦ **Hosts:** This tab shows you the local table of hosts and IP addresses from the /etc/hosts file and lets you add, remove, or edit entries.

To add and activate a new Ethernet network interface, do the following:

1. **In the Devices tab, click the New button.**

The Select Device Type dialog box appears.

2. **Select Ethernet connection and click Forward.**

The Select Ethernet Device dialog box appears.

3. **Select your Ethernet Card and click Forward.**

The Configure Network Settings dialog box appears (as in Figure 2-4).

Figure 2-4:
Configure
the network
settings in
this dialog
box.

4. **Select the way in which the Ethernet card gets its IP address:**

If it can automatically obtain an IP address (this is the case when the Ethernet card is connected to DSL or cable modem), select the

Automatically Obtain IP Address Settings with DHCP radio button. When you do so, also select the Automatically Obtain DNS Information from Provider check box.

Otherwise, select the Statically Set IP Addresses radio button, and then enter an IP address in the provided text box. For a home network, use a private IP address such as 192.168.0.2. (Anything that begins with *192.168.* would work.)

5. **Click Forward, and then Apply to complete the Ethernet setup.**

    You'll be back in the Network Configuration dialog box.

6. **Select the** eth0 **device, and then click Activate to turn the Ethernet network on.**

If you are running a private network, you may use IP addresses in the range 192.168.0.0 to 192.168.255.255. (There are other ranges of addresses reserved for private networks, but this range should suffice for most needs.)

Connecting Your LAN to the Internet

If you have a LAN with several PCs, you can connect the entire LAN to the Internet by using DSL or cable modem. Basically, you can share the high-speed DSL or cable modem connection with the all the PCs in the LAN.

In Chapter 1 of this mini-book, I explain how to set up DSL or cable modem. In this section, I briefly explain how to connect a LAN to the Internet so that all the PCs can access the Internet.

The most convenient way to connect a LAN to the Internet via DSL or cable modem is to buy a hardware device called DSL/Cable Modem NAT Router with a 4- or 8-port Ethernet hub. NAT stands for Network Address Translation; the NAT router can translate many private IP addresses into a single externally known IP address. The Ethernet hub part appears to you as a number of RJ-45 Ethernet ports where you can connect the PCs to set up a LAN. In other words, you need only one extra box besides the DSL or cable modem.

Figure 2-5 shows how you might connect your LAN to the Internet through a NAT router with a built-in Ethernet hub. Of course, you need a DSL or cable modem hookup for this to work (and you have to sign up with the phone company for DSL service or with the cable provider for cable Internet service).

When you connect a LAN to the Internet like this, the NAT router acts as a gateway for your LAN. The NAT router also dynamically provides IP addresses to the PCs in your LAN. Therefore, on each PC you should set up the networking options to indicate that the IP address is to be obtained dynamically.

Ethernet cables (10BaseT)

To Internet

NAT router and
Ethernet hub

Cable or DSL modem

Ethernet cables
(10BaseT)

Figure 2-5:
Connect
your LAN to
the Internet
through a
NAT Router
with a built-
in Ethernet
hub.

PCs in a local area network (LAN).
Each PC must have a 10BaseT
Ethernet card.

Your LAN can mix and match all kinds of computers — some may be
running Red Hat Linux and some may be running Microsoft Windows or
any other operating system that supports TCP/IP. On the Red Hat Linux PCs,
you can set up Ethernet networking using the network configuration tool
(choose Main Menu⇨System Settings⇨Network from the GNOME desktop).
When configuring the network settings (refer to Figure 2-4), remember
to select the Automatically Obtain IP Address Settings with DHCP radio
button. Also select the Automatically Obtain DNS Information from Provider
check box.

Chapter 3: Adding a Wireless Ethernet LAN

In This Chapter

✓ **Understanding wireless Ethernet networks**

✓ **Setting up the wireless hardware**

✓ **Configuring the wireless network**

*I*f you have laptop computers on your LAN — or if you don't want to run a rat's nest of wires to connect a PC to the LAN — you have the option of using a wireless Ethernet network. In a typical scenario, you have a cable modem or DSL connection to the Internet, and you want to connect one or more laptops with wireless network cards to access the Internet through the cable or DSL modem. This chapter shows you how to set up wireless networking for connecting to an Ethernet LAN and accessing the Internet.

Understanding Wireless Ethernet Networks

You've probably heard about Wi-Fi network. Wi-Fi stands for *Wireless Fidelity* network — a short-range wireless network similar to the wired Ethernet networks. A number of standards from an organization known as IEEE (the Institute of Electrical and Electronics Engineers) defines the technical details of how Wi-Fi networks work. Manufacturers use these standards to build the components that you can buy to set up a wireless network.

Until mid-2003, there were two popular IEEE standards — 802.11a and 802.11b — for wireless Ethernet networks. These two standards were finalized in 1999. A third standard — 802.11g — was finalized by the IEEE in the summer of 2003. All these standards specify how the wireless Ethernet network works at the physical level. You don't have to fret all the details of all those standards to set up a wireless network, but it's good to know some pertinent details so you can buy the right kind of equipment for your wireless network.

The three wireless Ethernet standards have the following key characteristics:

✦ **802.11b:** Operates in the 2.4GHz radio band (2.4GHz to 2.4835GHz) in up to three non-overlapping frequency bands or channels. Supports a maximum bit rate of 11Mbps per channel. One disadvantage of 802.11b is that the 2.4GHz frequency band is crowded — many devices (such as microwave ovens, cordless phones, medical and scientific equipment, as well as Bluetooth devices), all work within the 2.4GHz frequency band. Nevertheless, 802.11b is very popular in corporate and home networks.

✦ **802.11a:** Operates in the 5GHz radio band (5.725GHz to 5.850GHz) in up to eight non-overlapping channels. Supports a maximum bit rate of 54Mbps per channel. The 5GHz band is not as crowded as the 2.4GHz band, but the 5GHz band is not approved for use in Europe. Products conforming to 802.11a standard are available on the market, and there are wireless access points that are designed to handle both 802.11a and 802.11b connections.

✦ **802.11g:** Supports up to 54Mbps data rate in the 2.4GHz band (the same band that 802.11b uses). 802.11g achieves the higher bit rate by using a technology called OFDM (orthogonal frequency–division multiplexing), which is also used by 802.11a. Although 802.11g was only recently finalized, equipment that complies with it is already on the market. That's probably because 802.11.g has generated excitement by working in the same band as 802.11b but promising much higher data rates. Vendors are currently offering access points that can support both the 802.11b and 802.11g connection standards.

The maximum data throughput that a user sees is much less because all users of that radio channel share the capacity of the channel. Also, the data transfer rate decreases as the distance between the user's PC and the wireless access point increases.

To learn more about wireless Ethernet, visit `www.wi-fi.org`, the home page of the Wi-Fi Alliance — a nonprofit international association formed in 1999 to certify interoperability of wireless LAN products based on IEEE 802.11 standards.

Understanding infrastructure and ad hoc modes

The 802.11 standard defines two modes of operation for wireless Ethernet networks: infrastructure and ad hoc. *Ad-Hoc mode* is simply two or more wireless Ethernet cards communicating with each other without an access point.

Infrastructure mode refers to the approach in which all the wireless Ethernet cards communicate with each other and to the wired LAN through an access point. For the example considered in this book, your wireless Ethernet card should be set to infrastructure mode. In the configuration files, this mode is referred to as *managed mode*.

Is the WEP stream cipher good enough?

WEP uses the RC4 encryption algorithm, which is known as a *stream cipher*. Such an algorithm works by taking a short secret key and generating an infinite stream of *pseudorandom bits*. Before sending the data, the sending station performs an *exclusive-OR operation* between the pseudorandom bits and the bits representing the data packet, which results in a 1 when two bits are different and 0 if they are the same. The receiver has a copy of the same secret key, and generates an identical stream of pseudorandom bits — and performs an identical exclusive-OR operation between this pseudorandom stream and the received bits. Doing so regenerates the original, unencrypted data packet.

Such a method of stream cipher has a few problems. If a bit is flipped (from a 0 to 1 or vice versa) in the encrypted data stream, then the corresponding bit is flipped in the decrypted output — this can help an attacker derive the encryption key. Also, an eavesdropper who intercepts two encoded messages *that were encoded with the same stream* can generate the exclusive-OR of the original messages. That knowledge is enough to mount attacks that can eventually break the encryption.

To counter these weaknesses, WEP uses some defenses:

- ✔ Integrity Check (IC) Field — To make sure that data packets are not modified in transit, WEP uses an Integrity Check field in each packet.

- ✔ Initialization Vector (IV) — To avoid encrypting two messages with the same key stream, WEP uses a 24-bit initialization vector (IV) that augments the shared secret key to produce a different RC4 key for each packet. The IV itself is also included in the packet.

Experts say that both these defenses are poorly implemented, making WEP ineffective. IC and IV have two main problems:

- ✔ The Integrity Check field is implemented by using a checksum algorithm called 32-bit cyclic redundancy code (CRC-32); that checksum *is then included as part of the data packet*. Unfortunately, an attacker can flip arbitrary bits in an encrypted message and correctly adjust the checksum so the resulting message appears valid.

- ✔ The 24-bit IV is sent in the clear (unencrypted). This means that there are only 2^{24} possible initialization vectors (no big challenge for a fast machine), and they have to be reused after running through all of them. In other words, after sending 2^{24}, or 16,777,216 packets, the IV has to be repeated. The number might sound like a lot, but consider the case of a busy access point that sends 1,500-byte packets at a rate of 11 Mbps. Each packet has $8 \times 1{,}500 = 12{,}000$ bits. That means each second the access point sends $11{,}000{,}000/12{,}000 = 916$ packets. At that rate, the access point sends 16,777,216 packets in $16{,}777{,}216/916 = 18{,}315$ seconds or 5 hours. That means the IV is reused after 5 hours, and the time may be less than that because many messages are smaller than 1,500 bytes. Thus, an attacker has ample opportunities to collect two encrypted messages that are encrypted with the same key stream — and perform *statistical attacks* (which amount to trying the possible "combinations" really fast) to decrypt the message.

**Book IV
Chapter 3**

**Adding a Wireless
Ethernet LAN**

Understanding Wired Equivalent Privacy (WEP)

The 802.11 standard includes the Wired Equivalent Privacy (WEP) for protecting wireless communications from eavesdropping. WEP relies on a 40-bit or 104-bit secret key that is shared between a *mobile station* (such as a laptop with a wireless Ethernet card) and an *access point* (also called a *base station*). The secret key is used to encrypt data packets before they are transmitted, and an integrity check is performed to ensure that packets are not modified in transit. The 802.11 standard does not explain how the shared key is established. In practice, most wireless LANs use a single key that is shared between all mobile stations and access points. Such an approach, however, does not scale up very well to an environment such as a college campus because the keys are shared with all users — and you know how it is if you share a "secret" with hundreds of people. That's why WEP is typically not used on large wireless networks such as the ones at universities. In such wireless networks, you have to use other security approaches such as SSH (Secure Shell) to log in to remote systems. WEP, however, is good to use on your home wireless network.

WEP has its weaknesses, but it's better than nothing. You can use it in smaller wireless LANs where sharing the same key among all wireless stations is not an onerous task.

There is work underway to provide better security than WEP for wireless networks. The 802.11i standard, now under development, would use public-key encryption with digital certificates — along with an authentication, authorization, and accounting done on a RADIUS (Remote Authentication Dial-In User Service) server — to provide better security for wireless Ethernet networks.

While the 802.11i standard is in progress, the Wi-Fi Alliance — a multivendor consortium that supports Wi-Fi — is publishing an interim specification called Wi-Fi Protected Access (WPA) that's a precursor to 802.11i. WPA will replace the existing WEP standard and improve security by making some changes. For example, unlike WEP (which uses fixed keys), the WPA standard uses Temporal Key-Integrity Protocol (TKIP), which generates new keys for every 10K of data transmitted over the network. This makes WPA more difficult to break. You may want to consider WPA in the interim while work progresses on 802.11i.

Setting Up the Wireless Hardware

To set up the wireless connection, you need a wireless access point and a wireless network card in each PC. You can also set up an ad hoc wireless network among two or more PCs with wireless network cards, but that would be a standalone wireless LAN among those PCs only. In this section, I focus on the scenario where you want to set up a wireless connection to an established LAN that has a wired Internet connection through a cable modem or DSL.

In addition to the wireless access point, you would also need a cable modem or DSL connection to the Internet, along with a NAT router/hub, as described in the previous sections. Figure 3-1 shows a typical setup for wireless Internet access through an existing cable modem or DSL connection.

As Figure 3-1 shows, the LAN has both wired and wireless PCs. In this example, a cable or DSL modem connects the LAN to the Internet through a NAT router/hub. Laptops with wireless network cards connect the LAN through a wireless access point attached to one of the RJ-45 ports on the hub. To connect desktop PCs to this wireless network, you can use a USB wireless network card (which connects to a USB port).

If you have not yet purchased a NAT router/hub for your cable or DSL connection, consider buying a router/hub that has a built-in wireless access point.

To Internet

Ethernet cable (10BaseT)

NAT router and Ethernet hub

Cable or DSL modem

Wireless access point

Laptop PC with wireless Ethernet card

Ethernet cables (10BaseT)

Figure 3-1: Typical connection of a mixed wired-and-wireless Ethernet LAN to the Internet.

PCs in a local area network (LAN). Each PC must have a 10BaseT Ethernet card.

Configuring the Wireless Access Point

Configuring the wireless access point involves the following tasks:

✦ Setting a name for the wireless network (the technical term is ESSID).

✦ Setting the frequency or channel on which the wireless access point communicates with the wireless network cards. The access point and the cards must use the same channel.

✦ Deciding whether to use encryption.

✦ If encryption is to be used, setting the number of bits in the encryption key and the value of the encryption key. Twenty-four bits of the encryption key are internal to the access point; you specify only the remaining bits. Thus, for 64-bit encryption, you have to specify a 40-bit key, which comes to 10 hexadecimal digits (a *hexadecimal digit* is an integer from 0 through 9 or a letter from A through F). For a 124-bit encryption key, you specify 104 bits, or 26 hexadecimal digits.

✦ Setting the access method that wireless network cards must use when connecting to the access point. You can opt for either open access or shared key. The open-access method is typical (even when using encryption).

✦ Setting the wireless access point to operate in infrastructure (managed) mode (because that's the way you should connect wireless network cards to an existing Ethernet LAN).

The exact method of configuring a wireless access point depends on make and model; the vendor provides instructions to configure the wireless access point. You would typically work through a graphical client application on a Windows PC to do the configuration. If you enable encryption, make note of the encryption key; you have to specify that same key for each wireless network card.

Configuring Wireless Networking

On your Red Hat Linux laptop, the PCMCIA or PC Card manager should recognize the wireless network card and load the appropriate driver for the card. The wireless network card is treated like another Ethernet device — assign it a device name such as eth0 or eth1. If you already have an Ethernet card in the laptop, that card gets the eth0 device name, and the wireless PC card becomes the eth1 device.

You do have to configure certain parameters to enable the wireless network card to communicate with the wireless access point. For example, you have to specify the wireless network name assigned to the access point — and the encryption settings must match those on the access point. You can do everything from the graphical Network Configuration tool.

Follow these steps to configure and activate the wireless network connection on your Red Hat Linux system:

1. **Log in as** root **at the graphical login screen, and then choose Main Menu⇨System Settings⇨Network.**

The Network Configuration tool runs and its main window appears.

2. **Click New in the Network Configuration window's toolbar.**

The Add New Device Type window (shown in Figure 3-2) appears.

Figure 3-2:
Select
Wireless
connection
from this
window to
configure a
wireless
Ethernet
connection.

3. **Select Wireless connection from the window (Figure 3-2), and then click Forward.**

The Select Wireless Device window (as in Figure 3-3) appears.

4. **Select your wireless card from the list in the window (refer to Figure 3-3), and then click Forward.**

The Configure Wireless Connection window (shown in Figure 3-4) appears.

5. **Set the mode to Managed, specify the name of the wireless network (the one you want to connect to), and set the encryption key, if any. Then click Forward.**

The Configure Network Settings window (shown in Figure 3-5) appears.

Figure 3-3:
Select your
wireless
card from
the listed
devices.

Figure 3-4:
Set the
parameters
for the
wireless
connection
from this
window.

6. **Select the option for obtaining an IP address for the wireless network interface (refer to Figure 3-5); click Forward after making your selections.**

You can either specify a static IP address (meaning that the IP address does not change every time you boot) or let Red Hat Linux automatically get an IP address by using DHCP (a protocol for obtaining network configuration parameters, including IP addresses from a server on the network). Typically, you would select the option to automatically get an IP address.

Figure 3-5:
Configure
the network
settings of
the wireless
network
interface
from this
window.

The Create Wireless Device window (Figure 3-6) appears with a summary of the wireless network connection you're about to create.

Figure 3-6:
Check the
information
about the
wireless
connection
and click
Apply if the
information
is correct.

Book IV
Chapter 3

Adding a Wireless
Ethernet LAN

7. **Verify that the information shown in Figure 3-6 is correct, and then click Apply to create the wireless device.**

   The information shows the device name (in this case, `eth1`) that you're creating.

   The new device appears in the Network Configuration window (as shown in Figure 3-7).

Figure 3-7:
Activate
the new
wireless
device from
this window.

8. Select the new wireless device, and then click the Activate button on the toolbar (refer to Figure 3-7).

A dialog box informs you that the changes have to be saved before activating the wireless device and asks if you want to continue.

9. Click Yes and then OK when another dialog box prompts you to activate the network device.

If all goes well, the wireless network should be up and running after a few moments.

The Network Configuration tool saves your wireless network settings in a text file whose name depends on the wireless network device name. If the wireless network device name is eth0, the configuration is stored in the text file /etc/sysconfig/network-scripts/ifcfg-eth0. If the wireless device name is eth1, the file is /etc/sysconfig/network-scripts/ifcfg-eth1. This configuration file contains various settings for the wireless network card. Table 3-1 explains the meaning of the settings. Here is a slightly edited version of the /etc/sysconfig/network-scripts/ifcfg-eth1 file from my laptop PC:

```
USERCTL=no
PEERDNS=yes
TYPE=Wireless
DEVICE=eth0
HWADDR=00:02:2d:8c:f9:c4
BOOTPROTO=dhcp
ONBOOT=no
DHCP_HOSTNAME=
NAME=
```

```
ESSID='HOME'
CHANNEL=6
MODE=Managed
KEY=aecf-a00f-03
RATE=auto
```

If you ever manually edit the parameters in the configuration file, type the following command to reactivate the wireless network interface after editing the configuration file:

```
service pcmcia restart
```

Table 3-1	Settings in the Configuration File for a Wireless Ethernet Network Interface
This Parameter	*Means the Following*
BOOTPROTO	The name of the protocol to use to get the IP address for the interface. Should be either dhcp or bootp for Ethernet interface.
CHANNEL	Channel number (between 1 and 14 in U.S. and Canada). Must be the same as that set for the wireless access point. In managed mode, you don't need to specify the channel.
DEVICE	The device name for the wireless Ethernet network interface (eth0 for the first interface, eth1 for second, and so on).
ESSID	Extended Service Set (ESS) Identifier, also known as the wireless network name. It is case-sensitive and must be the same as the name specified for the wireless access point. Provide the name within single quotes (for example, 'HOME').
HWADDR	The hardware address (also called the MAC address) of the wireless network card (six pairs of colon-separated hexadecimal numbers; for example, 00:02:2d:8c:f9:c4). This address is automatically detected by the wireless card's device driver.
KEY	Encryption key; 10 hexadecimal digits for a 40-bit key (for example, 1fdf-3fde-fe) or 26 hexadecimal digits for a 104-bit key. (The keys are, in fact, 64-bit and 128-bit, but the encryption algorithm automatically generates 24 bits of the key, so you need to specify only the remaining bits.)
MODE	The mode of operation of the wireless network card. Set to Managed for a typical network that connects through a wireless access point.
NAME	A nickname for your wireless network. If you don't specify it, the host name is used as the nickname.
ONBOOT	Set to yes to activate the wireless interface at boot time; otherwise, set to no.

(continued)

Table 3-1 *(continued)*

This Parameter	Means the Following
PEERDNS	Set to yes to enable the interface to modify your system's /etc/resolv.conf file to use the DNS servers obtained from the DHCP server (this is the same server that provides the IP address for the interface). If you set this to no, the /etc/resolv.conf file is left unchanged.
RATE	Bit rate for the wireless connection (set to one of 1M, 2M, 5.5M, 11M, or auto). The M means Mbps or a million bits per second. Set to auto to use the maximum possible transmission rate.
TYPE	Set to Wireless for wireless network interface.
USERCTL	When set to yes, a non-root user can control the device. Set it to no so that only root can control the device.

To check the status of the wireless network interface, type the following command:

```
iwconfig
```

Here's a typical output from a Red Hat Linux laptop with a wireless Ethernet PC card:

```
lo        no wireless extensions.

eth0      no wireless extensions.

eth1      IEEE 802.11-DS  ESSID:"HOME"  Nickname:"localhost.localdomain"
          Mode:Managed  Frequency:2.437GHz  Access Point: 00:30:AB:06:2E:5D
          Bit Rate=11Mb/s   Tx-Power=15 dBm   Sensitivity:1/3
          Retry limit:4   RTS thr:off    Fragment thr:off
          Encryption key:AECF-A00F-03
          Power Management:off
          Link Quality:68/92  Signal level:-32 dBm  Noise level:-100 dBm
          Rx invalid nwid:0  Rx invalid crypt:0  Rx invalid frag:136
          Tx excessive retries:1  Invalid misc:0   Missed beacon:0
```

Here the eth1 interface refers to the wireless network card. I have edited the encryption key and some other parameters here, but the sample output shows what you would typically see when the wireless link is working.

Chapter 4: Managing the Network

In This Chapter

✔ Learning the TCP/IP configuration files

✔ Checking TCP/IP networks

✔ Configuring networks at boot time

*L*ike almost everything else in Red Hat Linux, TCP/IP setup is a matter of preparing numerous configuration files (text files you can edit with any text editor). Most of these configuration files are in the /etc directory. The Red Hat installer helps by hiding the details of the TCP/IP configuration files. Nevertheless, it's better if you know the names of the files and their purposes so that you can edit the files manually, if necessary.

Learning the TCP/IP Configuration Files

Running the Red Hat Network Configuration tool should be enough to get TCP/IP configured on your system. However, if you want to effectively manage the network, you should become familiar with the TCP/IP configuration files so you can edit the files, if necessary. (For example, if you want to check whether the name servers are specified correctly, you have to know about the /etc/resolv.conf file, which stores the IP addresses of name servers.)

Table 4-1 summarizes the basic TCP/IP configuration files. I describe these configuration files in the next few sections.

Table 4-1	Basic TCP/IP Network Configuration Files
This File	*Contains the Following*
/etc/hosts	IP addresses and host names for your local network as well as any other systems you access often
/etc/networks	Names and IP addresses of networks
/etc/host.conf	Instructions on how to translate host names into IP addresses
/etc/resolv.conf	IP addresses of name servers

(continued)

Table 4-1 *(continued)*

This File	Contains the Following
/etc/hosts.allow	Instructions on which systems can access Internet services on your system
/etc/hosts.deny	Instructions on which systems must be denied access to Internet services on your system
/etc/nsswitch.conf	Instructions on how to translate host names into IP addresses

/etc/hosts

The /etc/hosts text file contains a list of IP addresses and host names for your local network. In the absence of a name server, any network program on your system consults this file to determine the IP address that corresponds to a host name. Think of /etc/hosts as the local phone directory where you can look up the IP address (instead of a phone number) for a local host.

Here is the /etc/hosts file from a system, showing the IP addresses and names of other hosts on a typical LAN:

```
127.0.0.1        localhost        localhost.localdomain
# Other hosts on the LAN
192.168.0.100    lnbp933
192.168.0.50     lnbp600
192.168.0.200    lnbp200
192.168.0.233    lnbp233
192.168.0.40     lnbp400
```

As the example shows, each line in the file starts with an IP address, followed by the host name for that IP address. (You can have more than one host name for any given IP address.)

/etc/networks

/etc/networks is another text file that contains the names and IP addresses of networks. These network names are commonly used in the routing command (/sbin/route) to specify a network by name instead of by its IP address.

Don't be alarmed if your Linux PC does not have the /etc/networks file. Your TCP/IP network works fine without this file. In fact, the Red Hat Linux installer does not create a /etc/networks file.

/etc/host.conf

Red Hat Linux uses a special *library* (that is, a collection of computer code) called the *resolver library* to obtain the IP address that corresponds to a host name. The /etc/host.conf file specifies how names are resolved (that is, how the name gets converted to a numeric IP address). A typical /etc/host.conf file might contain the following lines:

```
order hosts, bind
multi on
```

The entries in the /etc/host.conf file tell the resolver library what services to use (and in which order) to resolve names.

The order option indicates the order of services. The sample entry tells the resolver library to first consult the /etc/hosts file, and then check the name server to resolve a name.

Use the multi option to indicate whether or not a host in the /etc/hosts file can have multiple IP addresses. Hosts that have more than one IP address are called *multihomed* because the presence of multiple IP addresses implies that the host has several network interfaces. (In effect, the host "lives" in several networks simultaneously.)

/etc/resolv.conf

The /etc/resolv.conf file is another text file used by the resolver — the library that determines the IP address for a host name. Here is a sample /etc/resolv.conf file:

```
search mtgmry1.md.home.com
nameserver 164.109.1.3
nameserver 164.109.10.23
```

The first line tells the resolver how to search for a host name. For example, when trying to locate a host name myhost, the search directive in the example would cause the resolver to try myhost.mtgmry1.md.home.com first, then myhost.md.home.com, and finally myhost.home.com.

The nameserver line provides the IP addresses of name servers for your domain. If you have multiple name servers, you should list them on separate lines. They are queried in the order in which they appear in the file.

If you do not have a name server for your network, you can safely ignore this file. TCP/IP should still work, even though you may not be able to refer to hosts by name (other than those listed in the /etc/hosts file).

/etc/hosts.allow

The `/etc/hosts.allow` file specifies which hosts are allowed to use the Internet services (such as TELNET and FTP) running on your system. This file is consulted before certain Internet services start. The services start only if the entries in the `hosts.allow` file imply that the requesting host is allowed to use the services.

The entries in `/etc/hosts.allow` are in the form of a *servername:IP address* format, where *server* refers to the name of the program providing a specific Internet service, and *IP address* identifies the host allowed to use that service. For example, if you want all hosts in your local network (which has the network address 192.168.0.0) to access the TELNET service (provided by the `in.telnetd` program), add the following line in the `/etc/hosts.allow` file:

```
in.telnetd:192.168.0.
```

If you want to let all local hosts have access to all Internet services, you can use the `ALL` keyword and rewrite the line as follows:

```
ALL:192.168.0.
```

Finally, to open all Internet services to all hosts, you can replace the IP address with `ALL`, as follows:

```
ALL:ALL
```

You can also use host names in place of IP addresses.

To learn the detailed syntax of the entries in the `/etc/hosts.allow` file, type **man hosts.allow** at the shell prompt in a terminal window.

/etc/hosts.deny

This file is just the opposite of `/etc/hosts.allow` — whereas `hosts.allow` specifies which hosts may access Internet services (such as TELNET and TFTP) on your system, the `hosts.deny` file identifies the hosts that must be denied services. The `/etc/hosts.deny` file is consulted if there are no rules in the `/etc/hosts.allow` file that apply to the requesting host. Service is denied if the `hosts.deny` file has a rule that applies to the host.

The entries in `/etc/hosts.deny` file have the same format as those in the `/etc/hosts.allow` file — they are in the form of a *server:IP address* format, where *server* refers to the name of the program providing a specific Internet service and *IP address* identifies the host that must not be allowed to use that service.

If you have already set up entries in the /etc/hosts.allow file to allow access to specific hosts, you can place the following line in the /etc/hosts.deny file to deny all other hosts access to any service on your system:

```
ALL:ALL
```

To learn the detailed syntax of the entries in the /etc/hosts.deny file, type **man hosts.deny** at the shell prompt in a terminal window.

/etc/nsswitch.conf

This file, known as the *name service switch* (NSS) file, specifies how services such as the name resolver library, NIS, NIS+, and local configuration files (such as /etc/hosts and /etc/shadow) interact.

NIS and NIS+ are *network information services* — another type of name-lookup service. Newer versions of the Linux kernel use the /etc/nsswitch.conf file to determine what takes precedence: a local configuration file, a service such as DNS (Domain Name Service), or NIS.

As an example, the following hosts entry in the /etc/nsswitch.conf file says that the resolver library should first try the /etc/hosts file, then try NIS+, and finally try DNS:

```
hosts:      files nisplus dns
```

You can learn more about the /etc/nsswitch.conf file by typing **info libc "Name Service Switch"** (including the quotes) in a terminal window.

Checking Out TCP/IP Networks

After you configure Ethernet and TCP/IP (whether during Red Hat Linux installation or by running the Network Configuration tool later on), you should be able to use various networking applications without any problem. If you do run into trouble, Red Hat Linux includes several tools to help you monitor and diagnose problems.

Checking the network interfaces

Use the /sbin/ifconfig command to view the currently configured network interfaces. The ifconfig command is used to configure a network interface (that is, to associate an IP address with a network device). If you run ifconfig without any command-line arguments, the command displays information about current network interfaces. The following is a typical invocation of ifconfig and the resulting output:

```
/sbin/ifconfig
eth0    Link encap:Ethernet HWaddr 02:60:8C:8E:C6:A9
        inet addr:192.168.0.5 Bcast:192.168.0.255 Mask:255.255.255.0
        UP BROADCAST NOTRAILERS RUNNING MULTICAST MTU:1500 Metric:1
        RX packets:8104 errors:0 dropped:0 overruns:0 frame:1
        TX packets:1273 errors:0 dropped:0 overruns:0 carrier:0
        collisions:4 txqueuelen:100
        RX bytes:869342 (848.9 Kb) TX bytes:232276 (226.8 Kb)
        Interrupt:5 Base address:0x300

lo      Link encap:Local Loopback
        inet addr:127.0.0.1 Mask:255.0.0.0
        UP LOOPBACK RUNNING MTU:16436 Metric:1
        RX packets:94 errors:0 dropped:0 overruns:0 frame:0
        TX packets:94 errors:0 dropped:0 overruns:0 carrier:0
        collisions:0 txqueuelen:0
        RX bytes:6184 (6.0 Kb) TX bytes:6184 (6.0 Kb)
```

This output shows that two network interfaces — the loopback interface (`lo`) and an Ethernet card (`eth0`) — are currently active on this system. For each interface, you can see the IP address, as well as statistics on packets delivered and sent. If the Red Hat Linux system had a dial-up PPP link up and running, you'd also see an item for the `ppp0` interface in the output.

Checking the IP routing table

The other network configuration command, `/sbin/route`, also provides status information when it is run without any command-line argument. If you're having trouble checking a connection to another host (that you've specified with an IP address), check the IP routing table to see whether a default gateway is specified. Then check the gateway's routing table to ensure that paths to an outside network appear in that routing table.

A typical output from the `/sbin/route` command looks like the following:

```
/sbin/route
Kernel IP routing table
Destination  Gateway       Genmask        Flags Metric Ref Use Iface
192.168.0.0  *             255.255.255.0  U     0      0   0   eth0
127.0.0.0    *             255.0.0.0      U     0      0   0   lo
default      192.168.0.1   0.0.0.0        UG    0      0   0   eth0
```

As this routing table shows, the local network uses the `eth0` Ethernet interface, and the default gateway is also that Ethernet interface. The default gateway is a routing device that handles packets addressed to any network other than the one in which the Red Hat Linux system resides. In this example, packets addressed to any network address other than those beginning with 192.168.0 are sent to the gateway — 192.168.0.1. The gateway forwards those packets to other networks (assuming, of course, that the gateway is connected to another network, preferably the Internet).

Checking connectivity to a host

To check for a network connection to a specific host, use the `ping` command. The `ping` command is a widely used TCP/IP tool that uses a series of Internet Control Message Protocol (ICMP, pronounced *eye-comp*) messages. ICMP provides for an Echo message to which every host responds. Using the ICMP messages and replies, `ping` can determine whether or not the other system is alive and can compute the round-trip delay in communicating with that system.

The following example shows how I run `ping` to see whether a system on my network is alive:

```
ping 192.168.0.1
```

Here is what this command displays on my home network:

```
PING 192.168.0.1 (192.168.0.1) from 192.168.0.7 : 56(84) bytes of data.
64 bytes from 192.168.0.1: icmp_seq=1 ttl=254 time=1.36 ms
64 bytes from 192.168.0.1: icmp_seq=2 ttl=254 time=1.33 ms
64 bytes from 192.168.0.1: icmp_seq=3 ttl=254 time=1.36 ms
64 bytes from 192.168.0.1: icmp_seq=4 ttl=254 time=1.34 ms

--- 192.168.0.1 ping statistics ---
4 packets transmitted, 4 received, 0% loss, time 3026ms
rtt min/avg/max/mdev = 1.338/1.352/1.366/0.038 ms
```

In Red Hat Linux, `ping` continues to run until you press Ctrl+C to stop it; then it displays summary statistics showing the typical time it takes to send a packet between the two systems. On some systems, `ping` simply reports that a remote host is alive. However, you can still get the timing information by using appropriate command-line arguments.

Checking network status

To check the status of the network, use the `netstat` command. This command displays the status of network connections of various types (such as TCP and UDP connections). You can view the status of the interfaces quickly with `netstat -i`, as follows:

```
netstat -i
Kernel Interface table
Iface  MTU   Met  RX-OK RX-ERR RX-DRP RX-OVR  TX-OK TX-ERR TX-DRP TX-OVR Flg
eth0   1500  0    1678  0      0      0       651   0      0      0      BMNRU
lo     16436 0    50    0      0      0       50    0      0      0      LRU
```

In this case, the output shows the current status of the loopback and Ethernet interfaces. Table 4-2 describes the meanings of the columns.

Table 4-2	Meaning of Columns in the Kernel Interface Table
Column	*Meaning*
Iface	Name of the interface
MTU	Maximum Transfer Unit — the maximum number of bytes that a packet can contain
RX-OK, TX-OK	Number of error-free packets received (RX) or transmitted (TX)
RX-ERR, TX-ERR	Number of packets with errors
RX-DRP, TX-DRP	Number of dropped packets
RX-OVR, TX-OVR	Number of packets lost due to overflow
Flg	A = receive multicast; B = broadcast allowed; D = debugging turned on; L = loopback interface (notice the flag on lo), M = all packets received, N = trailers avoided; O = no ARP on this interface; P = point-to-point interface; R = interface is running; and U = interface is up.

Another useful form of netstat option is -t, which shows all active TCP connections. Following is a typical result of netstat -t on one Red Hat Linux PC:

```
netstat -t
Active Internet connections (w/o servers)
Proto Recv-Q Send-Q Local Address        Foreign Address       State
tcp    0     0 dhcppc4:1031        www.redhat.com:http   ESTABLISHED
tcp    0   126 dhcppc4:telnet       192.168.0.6:1238      ESTABLISHED
tcp    0     0 dhcppc4:1032        www.redhat.com:https  ESTABLISHED
tcp    0     0 dhcppc4:1033        www.redhat.com:https  ESTABLISHED
tcp    0   138 dhcppc4:telnet       192.168.0.6:1238      ESTABLISHED
tcp    0     0 dhcppc4:ftp          192.168.0.6:1548      TIME_WAIT
```

In this case, the output columns show the protocol (Proto); the number of bytes in the receive and transmit queues (Recv-Q, Send-Q); the local TCP port in hostname:service format (Local Address); the remote port (Foreign Address); and the state of the connection.

Type **netstat -ta** to see all TCP connections — both active and the ones your Red Hat Linux system is listening to (with no connection established yet). For example, here's a typical output from the netstat -ta command:

```
Active Internet connections (servers and established)
Proto Recv-Q Send-Q Local Address        Foreign Address       State
tcp    0     0 *:1024         *:*           LISTEN
tcp    0     0 localhost.localdom:1025 *:*            LISTEN
tcp    0     0 *:sunrpc        *:*           LISTEN
tcp    0     0 *:x11          *:*           LISTEN
tcp    0     0 *:ftp          *:*           LISTEN
tcp    0     0 *:ssh          *:*           LISTEN
tcp    0     0 *:telnet        *:*           LISTEN
```

```
tcp    0    0 localhost.localdom:smtp *:*              LISTEN
tcp    0  138 dhcppc3:telnet       dhcppc4:1037       ESTABLISHED
tcp    0    0 dhcppc3:ftp          dhcppc4:1060      ESTABLISHED
```

Sniffing network packets

Sniffing network packets — sounds like something illegal, doesn't it? Nothing like that. *Sniffing* simply refers to viewing the TCP/IP network data packets. The concept is to capture all the network packets so you can examine them later.

If you feel like sniffing TCP/IP packets, you can use `tcpdump`, a command-line utility that comes with Red Hat Linux. As its name implies, it "dumps" (prints) the headers of TCP/IP network packets.

To use `tcpdump`, log in as `root` and type the `tcpdump` command in a terminal window. Typically, you would want to save the output in a file and examine that file later. Otherwise, `tcpdump` will start spewing out results that just flash by on the window. For example, to capture 1,000 packets in a file named `tdout` and attempt to convert the IP addresses to names, type the following command:

```
tcpdump -a -c 1000 > tdout
```

After capturing 1,000 packets, `tcpdump` quits. Then you can examine the output file, `tdout`. It's a text file, so you can simply open it in a text editor or type **more tdout** to view the captured packets.

Just to whet your curiosity, here are some lines from a typical output from `tcpdump`:

```
20:39:56.929241 dhcppc6.telnet > 192.168.0.6.4272: P 3225722544:3225722572(28)
    ack 1449612018 win 5840 (DF) [tos 0x10]
20:39:57.120308 192.168.0.6.4272 > dhcppc6.telnet: . ack 28 win 16199 (DF)
20:39:57.155930 arp who-has 192.168.0.1 tell dhcppc6
20:39:57.156915 arp reply 192.168.0.1 is-at 0:a0:c5:e1:ae:ae
20:39:57.156956 dhcppc6.1025 > 192.168.0.1.domain: 33598+ PTR? 6.0.168.192.in-
    addr.arpa. (42) (DF)
20:39:57.838984 192.168.0.1.domain > dhcppc6.1025: 33598 NXDomain* 0/1/0 (119)
    (DF)
20:39:57.840892 dhcppc6.1025 > 192.168.0.1.domain: 33599+ PTR? 1.0.168.192.in-
    addr.arpa. (42) (DF)
20:39:57.855757 192.168.0.1.domain > dhcppc6.1025: 33599 NXDomain 0/1/0 (119)
    (DF)
20:40:05.513863 192.168.0.1.router > 192.168.0.255.router: RIPv1-resp [items 2]:
    {0.0.0.0}(1) {68.49.48.0}(1) [ttl 1]
... lines deleted...
```

The output does offer some clues to what's going on — each line shows information about one network packet. Each line starts with a timestamp, followed by details of the packet, information such as where it originates and where it's going. I won't try to explain the details here, but you can type

**Book IV
Chapter 4**

**Managing the
Network**

man tcpdump to learn more about some of the details (and, more importantly, see what other ways you can use `tcpdump`).

Red Hat Linux comes with another packet sniffer called Ethereal. To learn more about Ethereal, visit `www.ethereal.com` and consult the documentation located in the `/usr/share/doc/ethereal*` directory (type **ls /usr/share/doc/ethereal*** to see the contents of that directory).

Configuring Networks at Boot Time

You want to start your network automatically every time you boot the system. For this to happen, various startup scripts must contain appropriate commands. You shouldn't have to do anything special other than configure your network (either during installation or by using the Red Hat Network Configuration tool at a later time). If the network balks at startup, however, you can troubleshoot by checking the files I mention in this section.

To initialize your network, the network activation script uses a set of text files in the `/etc/sysconfig` directory. For example, the script checks the variables defined in the `/etc/sysconfig/network` file to decide whether to activate the network. In `/etc/sysconfig/network`, you should see a line with the `NETWORKING` variable as follows:

```
NETWORKING=yes
```

The network is activated only if the `NETWORKING` variable is set to `yes`.

A number of scripts in the `/etc/sysconfig/network-scripts` directory activate specific network interfaces. For example, the configuration file for activating the Ethernet interface `eth0`, is the file `/etc/sysconfig/network-scripts/ifcfg-eth0`. Here is what a typical `/etc/sysconfig/network-scripts/ifcfg-eth0` file contains:

```
DEVICE=eth0
BOOTPROTO=dhcp
ONBOOT=yes
```

The `DEVICE` line provides the network device name. The `BOOTPROTO` variable is set to `dhcp`, indicating that the IP address is obtained dynamically by using the Dynamic Host Configuration Protocol (DHCP), a standard method. The `ONBOOT` variable says whether this network interface should be activated when Red Hat Linux boots. If your PC has an Ethernet card and you want to activate the `eth0` interface at boot time, `ONBOOT` must be set to `yes`.

Of course, the configuration file `ifcfg-eth0` in the `/etc/sysconfig/network-scripts` directory works only if your PC has an Ethernet card and the Linux kernel has detected and loaded the specific driver for that card.

Book V

Internet

The 5th Wave

By Rich Tennant

"I'm not saying I believe in anything. All I know is since it's been there our server is running 50% faster."

Contents at a Glance

Chapter 1: Exchanging Your E-Mail and Instant Messages

In This Chapter

✔ Understanding electronic mail

✔ Taking stock of mail readers and IM (Instant Messaging) clients

✔ Using Ximian Evolution

✔ Using Mozilla Mail

✔ Instant messaging with Gaim

*E*lectronic mail (e-mail) is a mainstay of the Internet. E-mail is great because you can exchange messages and documents with anyone on the Internet. One of the most common ways people use the Internet is to keep in touch with friends, acquaintances, loved ones, and strangers through e-mail. You can send a message to a friend thousands of miles away and get a reply within a couple of minutes. Essentially, you can send messages anywhere in the world from an Internet host, and that message typically makes its way to its destination within minutes — something you can't do with paper mail (also known as *snail mail*, and appropriately so).

I love e-mail because I can communicate without having to play the game of "phone tag," in which two people leave telephone messages for each other without successfully making contact. When I send an e-mail message, it waits in the recipient's mailbox to be read at the recipient's convenience. I guess I like the converse even better — when people send me e-mail, I can read and reply at *my* convenience.

Red Hat Linux comes with several mail clients that can download mail from your Internet service provider (ISP). You can also read e-mail and send e-mail using these mail clients. In this chapter, I mention most of the mail clients available in Red Hat Linux and describe a few of them. And when you know one, you can easily use any of the mail readers.

There is yet another type of "keeping in touch" that's more in line with today's teenagers. I'm talking about *IM* — instant messaging. IM is basically one-to-one chat, and Red Hat Linux includes IM clients for AOL Instant Messenger (or AIM). I briefly describe the AIM clients in this chapter.

Understanding Electronic Mail

E-mail messages are addressed to a user name at a host (*host* is just a fancy name for an online computer). That means if John Doe logs in with the *user name* jdoe, e-mail to him is addressed to jdoe. The only other piece of information needed to identify the recipient uniquely is the fully qualified *domain name* of the recipient's system. Thus, if John Doe's system is named someplace.com, his complete e-mail address becomes jdoe@someplace.com. Given that address, anyone on the Internet can send e-mail to John Doe.

How MUA and MTA work

There are two types of mail software:

+ **Mail-user agent (MUA)** is the fancy name for a mail reader — a client that you use to read your mail messages, write replies, and compose new messages. Typically, the mail-user agent retrieves messages from the mail server by using the POP3 or IMAP4 protocol. POP3 is the *Post Office Protocol Version 3*, and IMAP4 is the *Internet Message Access Protocol Version 4*. Red Hat Linux comes with mail-user agents such as Balsa, Mozilla Mail, KMail, and Ximian Evolution.

+ **Mail-transport agent (MTA)** is the fancy name for a mail server that actually sends and receives mail-message text. The exact method used for mail transport depends on the underlying network. In TCP/IP networks, the mail-transport agent delivers mail using the *Simple Mail-Transfer Protocol* (SMTP). Red Hat Linux includes sendmail, a powerful and popular mail-transport agent for TCP/IP networks.

Figure 1-1 shows how the MUAs and MTAs work with one another when Alice sends an e-mail message to Bob. (In case you didn't know, it's customary to use *Alice* and *Bob* to explain e-mail and cryptography — just pick up any book on cryptography and you'll see what I mean). And you may already know this, but the Internet is always diagrammed as a cloud — the boundaries of the Internet are so fuzzy that a cloud seems just right to represent it (or is it because no one knows where it starts and where it ends?).

The scenario in Figure 1-1 is typical of most people. Alice and Bob both connect to the Internet through an ISP and get and send their e-mail through their ISPs. When Alice types a message and sends it, her mail-user agent (MUA) sends the message to her ISP's mail-transfer agent (MTA) using the Simple Mail-Transfer Protocol (SMTP). The sending MTA then sends that message to the receiving MTA — Bob's ISP's MTA — using SMTP. When Bob connects to the Internet, his MUA downloads the message from his ISP's MTA using the POP3 (or IMAP4) protocol. That's the way mail moves around the Internet — from sending MUA to sending MTA to receiving MTA to receiving MUA.

Figure 1-1:
How Alice
sends
e-mail to
Bob (or all
about MUAs
and MTAs).

Mail message enhancements

Mail messages used to be plain text (and most still are), but many messages today have much more than text. Two typical new features of today's mail are

✦ **Attachments:** Many messages today include attached files, which can be anything from documents to images. The recipient can save the attachment on disk or open it directly from the mail reader. Unfortunately, this is one way hackers try to get viruses and worms into your PC. (If it's any consolation, most Windows-based viruses and worms do not work in Red Hat Linux.)

✦ **HTML messages:** Mail messages can be in *HTML* (HyperText Markup Language), the language used to lay out Web pages. When you read an HTML message on a capable mail reader, the message appears in its full glory with nice fonts and embedded graphics.

While HTML messages are nice, they don't appear right when you use a text-based mail reader. In a text mail reader, HTML messages appear as a bunch of gobbledygook (which is just the HTML code).

If you have an ISP account, all you need is a *mail client* (pardon me, a mail-user agent) to access your e-mail. In this case, your e-mail resides on your ISP's server and the mail reader downloads mail when you run it. You have to do some setup before you can start reading mail from your ISP's mail server. The setup essentially requires you to enter information that you get from your ISP — the mail server's name, server type (POP3, for example), your user name, and your password.

Taking Stock of Mail Readers and IM Clients in Red Hat Linux

Time was when most mail readers were text programs, but times have changed. Now mail readers are graphical applications capable of displaying HTML messages and handling attachments with ease. They are easy to use. If you know one, you can use any of the graphical mail readers. Red Hat Linux comes with several mail readers.

IM (instant messaging) is a more recent phenomenon, but Red Hat Linux tries to stay on top of things, so it comes with two AOL IM clients. Table 1-1 gives you an overview of the mail readers and IM clients in Red Hat Linux.

Table 1-1	Red Hat Linux Mail Readers and AIM Clients
Software	*Description*
KMail	The KDE e-mail client that supports both POP3 and IMAP
Mozilla Mail	A mail client and a news reader, part of the Mozilla open-source Web browser (open source incarnation of Netscape Communicator)
Ximian Evolution	A *personal information manager* (PIM) that includes e-mail, calendar, contact management, and an online task list
Gaim	An IM client for GNOME that supports a number of instant-messaging protocols, such as AOL IM, ICQ, Yahoo!, MSN, Gadu-Gadu, and Jabber
Kit	An AOL IM client for KDE

Using Ximian Evolution

I have heard so much about Ximian Evolution that I want to start with it. What better way than to jump right in!

Choose Main Menu⇨Internet⇨Evolution Email from the GNOME or KDE desktop. If this is your first time with Evolution, the Evolution Setup Assistant starts up (as in Figure 1-2).

Figure 1-2:
Evolution
Setup
Assistant
guides you
through the
initial setup.

Click Forward in the Welcome screen and the Setup Assistant guides you through the following steps:

1. **Enter your name and e-mail address in the Identity screen and click Forward.**

   For example, if your e-mail address is joe@someplace.com, that's what you enter. You can also specify a signature file — a text file whose contents get appended to every message you send out. Typically, you'd put your name and contact information in the signature file.

2. **Set up the options for receiving e-mail and click Forward.**

   Select the type of mail download protocol — POP or IMAP. Then provide the name of the mail server (for example, mail.comcast.net). You will be prompted for the password when Evolution connects to the mail server for the first time.

3. **Provide further information about receiving e-mail — how often to check for mail and whether to leave messages on the server — and then click Forward.**

   Typically, you would want to download the messages and delete them from the server (otherwise the ISP complains when your mail piles up).

4. **Set up the following options for sending e-mail and click Forward when you're done:**

   • Select the server type as SMTP.

- Enter the name of the server such as `smtp.comcast.net`.

- If the server requires you to log in, select the check box that says Server Requires Authentication.

- Enter your username — this is the same username you need to log in to your ISP's mail server. (Often you don't have to log in to send mail; you only log in when receiving — downloading — mail messages.)

5. **Indicate whether you want this e-mail account to be your default account, and, if you want, give this mail account a descriptive name; click Forward.**

6. **Set your time zone by clicking on a map; click Forward.**

7. **Click Apply to complete the Evolution setup.**

After you complete the setup, Evolution opens its main window (as in Figure 1-3).

Figure 1-3: Evolution takes care of mail, calendar, contact management, and to-do lists.

The main display area is vertically divided into two windows: a narrow Shortcuts window on the left (with a number of shortcut icons), and a bigger window where Evolution displays information relevant to the currently selected shortcut.

Initially, Evolution displays a summary view that shows information about your mail, appointments, and tasks, as well as other useful information such as weather. By default, Evolution initially displays the weather for Boston, Massachusetts, USA.

Some of the information that you see in the summary view comes from Web links. For example, the list of Red Hat Errata comes from the Red Hat Web site.

You can click the icons in the left window to switch to different views. Table 1-2 describes what happens when you click each of the five shortcut icons in the Evolution Shortcuts window.

Table 1-2	Shortcut Icons in Ximian Evolution	
What the Icon Looks Like	*Name of Icon*	*What It Does*
	Summary	Displays a summary view of all information — mail, calendar, tasks, and some other information.
	Inbox	Shows the contents of your inbox where you can read mail and send mail.
	Calendar	Opens your calendar where you can look up and add appointments
	Tasks	Shows your task ("to-do") list where you can add new tasks and check what's due when.
	Contacts	Opens your contact list where you can add new contacts or look up someone from your current list.

As the buttons in Table 1-2 show, Ximian Evolution has all the necessary components of a PIM — e-mail, calendar, task list, and contacts.

To access your e-mail in Evolution, click the Inbox icon. Evolution opens your inbox (as shown in Figure 1-4). If you had turned on the feature to automatically check for mail every so often, Evolution would have already prompted you for your mail password and downloaded your mail. The e-mail inbox looks very much like any other mail reader's inbox, such as the Outlook Express inbox.

To read a message, click the message in the upper window of the inbox and the message text appears in the lower window.

To reply to the current message, click the Reply button on the toolbar. A message composition window pops up (as shown in Figure 1-5). You can write your reply and then click the Send button on the toolbar to send the reply. Simple, isn't it?

Figure 1-4:
Read your
e-mail in the
Evolution
inbox.

To send a new e-mail, click the New Message button on the Evolution toolbar. A new message composition window appears where you can type your
message; then click Send.

Figure 1-5:
Compose
your reply in
this window,
and then
click the
Send
button.

Ximian Evolution comes with extensive online help. Choose Help⇨Table of Contents from the Evolution menu and *A User's Guide to Ximian Evolution* appears in a Mozilla window. You can then read the user's guide in the Mozilla Web browser.

Using Mozilla Mail

Mozilla Mail is the mail and news reader that comes with Mozilla — the open source successor to Netscape Communicator. Mozilla is a Web browser that also includes a mail and news reader.

To use Mozilla Mail, start by running the Mozilla Web browser. Click the Mozilla icon (the earth lassoed by the mouse cord) on the panel, and the Mozilla Web browser window appears. To access Mozilla Mail mail and news reader, choose Window⇨Mail and Newsgroups from the menu. Mozilla Mail runs, starts the Account Wizard (shown in Figure 1-6), and prompts you for information about your e-mail account.

Figure 1-6:
Provide your
e-mail
account
information
to Mozilla
Mail's
Account
Wizard.

Select the Email Account radio button and click Next. The Account Wizard then takes you through the following steps:

1. **Enter your identity information — your name and your full e-mail address such as** `joe@someplace.com` **— and then click Next.**

2. **Provide information about your ISP's mail server — the protocol type (POP or IMAP) as well as the incoming and outgoing server names — and click Next.**

The incoming server is the POP or IMAP server, whereas the outgoing server is the one through which you send mail out (it's the SMTP server).

3. **Enter the username that your ISP has given you; click Next.**

4. **Enter a name that you want to use to identify this account and click Next.**

   This is just for Mozilla Mail, so you can pick anything you want like "My home account."

   The Account Wizard then displays a summary of the information you entered.

5. **Verify the information; if it's correct, click Finish. Otherwise click Back and fix the errors.**

After you set up the e-mail account, the Mozilla Mail main window appears and shows you the contents of your inbox. Soon a dialog box pops up and asks you for your e-mail password. Mozilla Mail needs this to download your e-mail messages from your ISP. Enter your password and click OK.

Mozilla Mail downloads your messages and displays them in a familiar format. To read a message, click that message, and the full text appears in the lower window (as shown in Figure 1-7).

Figure 1-7:
You can read and send e-mail messages and a whole lot more from Mozilla Mail.

Mozilla Mail is intuitive to use. Most of the time you can click the toolbar buttons to do most anything you want to do with the e-mail messages. Here's what each toolbar button does:

✦ **Get Msgs:** Downloads messages from your e-mail accounts (you can set up as many as you want).

✦ **Compose:** Opens a window where you can compose and send a message.

✦ **Reply:** Opens a window where you can send back a reply to the person who sent you the message you are reading now.

✦ **Reply All:** Opens a window for sending a reply to everyone who was on the addressee list of the message you are reading now.

✦ **Forward:** Brings up the current message in a window so that you can forward it to someone else.

✦ **File:** Files selected messages in folders.

✦ **Next:** Shows the next unread message.

✦ **Delete:** Deletes the selected message.

✦ **Print:** Prints the message you are reading now.

✦ **Stop:** Stops the current message transfer.

If you use any GUI mail reader — from Microsoft Outlook Express to Novell GroupWise — you should find a similar set of toolbar buttons. In the following sections, I describe how to perform a few common e-mail-related tasks.

Managing your inbox

Mozilla Mail downloads your incoming mail and stores it in the inbox folder. You can see the folders organized along the narrow window on the left side (refer to Figure 1-7). There's a set of folders for each e-mail account you have set up. You have the following folders by default:

✦ **Inbox:** Holds all of your incoming messages for this e-mail account.

✦ **Drafts:** Contains the messages that you saved as drafts (click the Save button on the message composition window).

✦ **Templates:** Contains the messages you saved as templates.

✦ **Sent:** Holds all the messages you have sent.

✦ **Trash:** Contains the messages you have deleted (to empty the Trash folder, choose File⇨Empty Trash from the Mozilla Mail menu).

You can create other folders to better organize your mail. To create a folder, do the following:

1. **Choose File⇨New⇨Folder.**

The New Folder dialog box appears.

2. **Fill in the folder name and select where you want to put the folder (Figure 1-8); then click OK.**

The new folder appears in the left window of Mozilla Mail.

Figure 1-8:
You can create new folders to organize your mail messages in Mozilla Mail.

When you select a folder from the left window, Mozilla Mail displays the contents of that folder in the upper window on the right side. The list is normally sorted by date, with the latest messages shown at the end of the list. If you want to sort the list any other way — say, by sender or by subject — simply click that column heading and Mozilla Mail sorts the list according to that column.

Composing and sending messages

To send an e-mail message, you either write a new message or reply to a message you are reading. The general steps for sending an e-mail message are as follows:

1. **To reply to a message, click the Reply or Reply All button on the toolbar as you are reading the message. To write a new message, click the Compose button on the toolbar. To forward a message, click the Forward button.**

A message composition window appears (as shown in Figure 1-9).

2. **In the message composition window, type your message.**

The message can include links to Web sites and images. To insert any of these items, choose Insert⇨Link or Insert⇨Image from the menu.

3. **If it's a new message or a forwarded message, also type the e-mail addresses of the recipients.**

To select addressees from the Address Book, click the Address button on the toolbar. This opens up your Address Book, from which you can select the addressees.

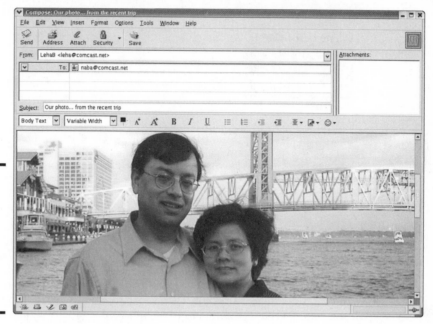

Figure 1-9:
Compose your message and then enter the addresses of the recipients.

4. **After preparing and addressing the message, click the Send button.**

   Mozilla Mail asks whether you want to send the message in HTML format or plain text or both.

5. **Select a format and then click Send to send the message.**

   If you've inserted images and Web links and you know the recipient can read HTML mail, be sure to select HTML format; otherwise, choose plain text.

If you want to complete a message later, click Save in the message composition window and then close the window. Mozilla Mail saves the message in the Drafts folder. When you're ready to work on that message again, go to the Drafts folder and then double-click the saved message to open it.

Instant Messaging with Gaim

You can use Gaim to keep in touch with all of your buddies on AOL Instant Messenger (or *AIM*, as it's commonly known). If you use AOL's AIM, you'll be right at home with Gaim, a client for the AOL AIM service.

Start Gaim by choosing Main Menu➪Internet➪Instant Messenger from the GNOME desktop. The initial Gaim window appears (Figure 1-10).

Figure 1-10:
Sign on to
AIM with
Gaim.

If you've used AIM before, you already have a screen name. Just type it in, enter the password, and then click Sign On. Gaim logs you in and opens the standard Buddy List window. The Buddy List is initially empty. To add buddies, choose Buddies➪Add a Buddy. In the Add Buddy window that appears, enter the screen name of the buddy and click Add. To create a new group, choose Buddies➪Add a Group. Type the name of the new group in the Add Group window that appears and then click Add.

If any of your buddies are online, their names show up in the Buddy List window. To send a message to a buddy, double-click the name and a message window pops up. And should someone send you a message, a message window pops up with the message and you can begin conversing in that window.

Well, if you know AIM, you know what to do: Have fun IM'ing with Gaim!

Chapter 2: Using the Web

In This Chapter

✔ Discovering the World Wide Web

✔ Understanding a URL

✔ Checking out Web servers and Web browsers

✔ Web browsing with Mozilla

✔ Creating Web pages with Mozilla Composer

I suspect you already know about the Web, but did you know that the Web, or more formally the World Wide Web, made the Internet what it is today? The Internet was around for quite a while, but it did not reach the masses until the Web came along in 1993.

Before the Web came along, you had to use arcane UNIX commands to download and use files — it was simply too complicated for most of us. With the Web, however, anyone could enjoy the benefits of the Internet by using a *Web browser* — a graphical application that downloads and displays Web documents. A click of the mouse is all it takes to go from reading a document from your company Web site to downloading a video clip from across the country.

In this chapter, I briefly describe the Web and introduce Mozilla — the primary Web browser (and, for that matter, a mail and news reader, too) in Red Hat Linux. I also briefly discuss how you can create your own Web pages.

Discovering the World Wide Web

If you have used a file server at work, you know the convenience of sharing files. You can use the word processor on your desktop to get to any document on the shared server.

Now imagine a word processor that enables you to open and view a document that resides on any computer on the Internet. You can view the document in its full glory, with formatted text and graphics. If the document makes a reference to another document (possibly residing on yet another computer), you can open that linked document by clicking the reference. That kind of easy access to distributed documents is essentially what the World Wide Web provides.

Of course, the documents have to be in a standard format so that any computer (with the appropriate Web browser software) can access and interpret the document. And a standard protocol is necessary for transferring Web documents from one system to another.

The standard Web document format is *HyperText Markup Language* (HTML), and the standard protocol for exchanging Web documents is *HyperText Transfer Protocol* (HTTP). HTML documents are text files and don't depend on any specific operating system, so they work on any system from Windows and Mac to any type of UNIX and Linux.

A *Web server* is software that provides HTML documents to any client that makes the appropriate HTTP requests. A *Web browser* is the client software that actually downloads an HTML document from a Web server and displays the contents graphically.

Like a giant spider's web

The World Wide Web is the combination of the Web servers and the HTML documents that the servers offer. When you look at it this way, the Web is like a giant book whose pages are scattered throughout the Internet. You use a Web browser running on your computer to view the pages — the pages are connected like a giant spider's web, with the documents everywhere (as in Figure 2-1).

Figure 2-1:
The Web is like billions of pages, scattered across the network, that you can read from your computer by using a Web browser.

Web pages

Web browser

If you can imagine that the Web pages — HTML documents — are linked by network connections that resemble a giant spider's web, you can see why the Web is called "the Web." The "World Wide" part comes from the fact that the Web pages are scattered around the world.

Links and URLs

Like the pages of real books, Web pages contain text and graphics. Unlike real books, however, Web pages can include multimedia, such as video clips, sound, and links to other Web pages that can actually take you to those Web pages.

The *links* in a Web page are references to other Web pages that you can follow to go from one page to another. The Web browser typically displays these links as underlined text (in a different color) or as images. Each link is like an instruction to you — something like, "For more information, please consult Chapter 4," that you might find in a real book. In a Web page, all you have to do is click the link; the Web browser brings up the referenced page, even though that document might actually reside on a far-away computer somewhere on the Internet.

The links in a Web page are referred to as *hypertext links* because when you click a link, the Web browser jumps to the Web page referenced by that link.

This arrangement brings up a question. In a real book, you might ask the reader to go to a specific chapter or page in the book. How does a hypertext link indicate the location of the referenced Web page? In the World Wide Web, each Web page has a special name, called a *Uniform Resource Locator* (URL). A URL uniquely specifies the location of a file on a computer. Figure 2-2 shows the parts of a URL.

Figure 2-2:
The parts of a Uniform Resource Locator (URL).

As Figure 2-2 shows, a URL has the following parts:

✦ **Protocol:** Name of the protocol that the Web browser uses to access the data from the file the URL specifies. In Figure 2-2, the protocol is `http://`, which means that the URL specifies the location of a Web page. Here are some of the common protocol types and their meanings:

- `file://` means the URL is pointing to a local file. You can use this URL to view HTML files without having to connect to the Internet. For example, `file:///var/www/html/index.html` opens the file `/var/www/html/index.html` from your Red Hat Linux system.

- `ftp://` means you can download a file using the File Transfer Protocol (FTP). For example, `ftp://ftp.purdue.edu/pub/uns/NASA/nasa.jpg` refers to the image file `nasa.jpg` from the `/pub/uns/NASA` directory of the FTP server `ftp.purdue.edu`. If you want to access a specific user account via FTP, use a URL in the following form:

  `ftp://username:password@ftp.somesite.com/`

  with the user name and password embedded in the URL (note that the password is in plain text and not secure).

- `http://` means the file should be downloaded by using the HyperText Transfer Protocol (HTTP). This is the well-known format of URL for all Web sites, such as `http://www.redhat.com` for Red Hat's home page. If the URL does not have a filename, the Web server sends a default HTML file named `index.html` (that's the default filename for the popular UNIX-based Apache Web servers; Microsoft Windows Web servers use a different default filename).

- `https://` specifies that the file is to be accessed through a Secure Sockets Layer (SSL) connection — a protocol designed by Netscape Communications for encrypted data transfers across the Internet. This form of URL is typically used when the Web browser sends sensitive information (such as credit card number, user name, and password) to a Web server. For example, a URL such as

  `https://some.site.com/secure/takeorder.html`

  might display an HTML form that requests credit card information and other personal information (such as name, address, and phone number).

- `mailto://` specifies an e-mail address you can use to send an e-mail message. For example, `mailto:webmaster@someplace.com` refers to the Webmaster at the host `someplace.com`.

- `news://` specifies a newsgroup you can read by means of the Network News Transfer Protocol (NNTP). For example,

  `news://news.md.comcast.giganews.com/comp.os.linux.setup`

accesses the `comp.os.linux.setup` newsgroup at the news server `news.md.comcast.giganews.com`. If you have a default news server configured for the Web browser, you can omit the news server's name and use the URL news: `comp.os.linux.setup` to access the newsgroup.

✦ **Domain name:** Contains the fully qualified domain name of the computer that has the file this URL specifies. You can also provide an IP address in this field. The domain name is not case sensitive.

✦ **Port:** Port number that is being used by the protocol listed in the first part of the URL. This part of the URL is optional; there are default ports for all protocols. The default port for HTTP, for example, is 80. If a site configures the Web server to listen to a different port, then the URL has to include the port number.

✦ **Directory path:** Directory path of the file being referred to in the URL. For Web pages, this field is the directory path of the HTML file. The directory path is case sensitive.

✦ **Filename:** Name of the file. For Web pages, the filename typically ends with `.htm` or `.html`. If you omit the filename, the Web server returns a default file (often named `index.html`). The filename is case sensitive.

✦ **HTML anchor:** Optional part of the URL that makes the Web browser jump to a specific location in the file. If this part starts with a question mark (?) instead of a hash mark (#), then the browser takes the text following the question mark to be a query. The Web server returns information based on such queries.

Web servers and Web browsers

The Web server serves up the Web pages, and the Web browser downloads them and displays them to the user. That's pretty much the story with these two cooperating software packages that make the Web work.

In a typical scenario, the user sits in front of a computer that's connected to the Internet and runs a Web browser. When the user clicks a link or types a URL into the Web browser, the browser connects to the Web server and requests a document from the server. The Web server sends the document (usually in HTML format) and ends the connection. The Web browser interprets and displays the HTML document with text and graphics. Figure 2-3 illustrates this typical scenario of a user browsing the Web.

The Web browser's connection to the Web server ends after the server sends the document. When the user browses through the downloaded document and clicks another hypertext link, the Web browser again connects to the Web server named in the hypertext link, downloads the document, ends the connection, and displays the new document. That's how the user can move from one document to another with ease.

Web Server

Web server sends back the requested Web page.

Internet

HTTP

Web Browser

Web browser connects to the server and requests a Web page.

User

Figure 2-3:
The Web browser requests documents and the Web server sends them.

A Web browser can do more than simply "talk" HTTP with the Web server — in fact, Web browsers can also download documents using FTP, and many have integrated mail and newsreaders as well.

Web Browsing in Red Hat Linux

Web browsing is fun because so many of today's Web pages are so full of graphics and multimedia. Then there's the element of surprise — you can click a link and end up at unexpected Web pages. Links are the most curious (and useful) aspect of the Web. You can start at a page that shows today's weather and a click later, you can be reading this week's issue of *Time* magazine.

To browse the Web, all you need is a Web browser and an Internet connection. I assume that you've already taken care of the Internet connection, so all you need to know are the Web browsers in Red Hat Linux.

Checking out the Web browsers in Red Hat Linux

Red Hat Linux comes with the Mozilla Web browser. Mozilla is an open-source version of Netscape Communicator, and it's replacing Netscape as the primary Web browser in Red Hat Linux.

Red Hat Linux includes several other Web browsers. I briefly mention the other browsers, but I focus on Mozilla in the rest of the discussions. Here are the major Web browsers that come with Red Hat Linux:

✦ **Mozilla:** The reincarnation of that old workhorse — Netscape Communicator — only better. Includes mail and a newsreader. The Web browser is called the Mozilla Navigator, or simply Navigator (just as it was in Netscape Communicator).

✦ **Epiphany:** The GNOME Web browser that uses parts of the Mozilla code to draw the Web pages, but has a simpler user interface than Mozilla. Epiphany is not installed by default, but it should be on the DVD included with this book. If you can't find Epiphany on the DVD, you can download it from `epiphany.mozdev.org`.

✦ **Konqueror:** The KDE Web browser that also doubles as a file manager and a universal viewer.

In addition to these three, many other applications are capable of downloading and displaying Web pages.

Starting Mozilla

From the GNOME desktop, you can start Mozilla in one of two ways:

✦ Click the Web Browser icon (the earth and mouse) on the GNOME or KDE panel.

✦ Choose Main Menu➪Internet➪Mozilla Web Browser from GNOME.

When Mozilla starts, it displays a browser window with a default home page (the main Web page on a Web server is known as the home page). You can configure Mozilla to use a different Web page as the default home page.

Learning Mozilla's user interface

Figure 2-4 shows a Web page from the Wiley Web site, as well as the main elements of the Mozilla browser window.

The Mozilla Web browser shows lots of features in its user interface, but you can master it easily. You can turn off some of the items that make it look busy. You can also start with just the basics to get going with Mozilla and then gradually expand to areas that you haven't yet explored.

Click to close the Sidebar

Figure 2-4:
The Mozilla
Web
browser in
action.

Mozilla toolbars

Starting from the top of the window, you see the standard menu bar, then a
Navigation toolbar, followed by a thinner Personal toolbar with icons such
as Home and Bookmarks. The area underneath the Personal toolbar is vertically split into two parts — a narrower, left side called the Sidebar and a
wider, right side where the current Web page appears.

Notice the X button on the Sidebar. If you click there, the Sidebar goes away.
(I usually like to get rid of the Sidebar, just so I can see more of the Web
page.) Go ahead and click the Sidebar X button to close it.

Without the Sidebar, the Mozilla window looks cleaner and simpler (Figure
2-5). Now you can see clearly the menu bar with the standard menus (File,
Edit, and so forth), followed by the two toolbars — Navigation toolbar and
Personal toolbar.

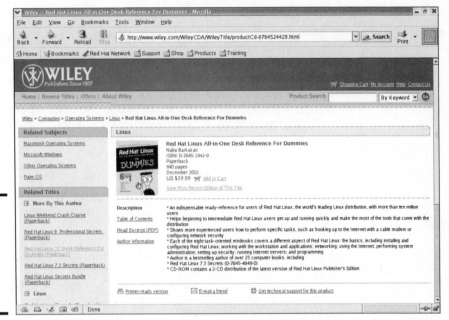

Figure 2-5:
Close the
Sidebar to
simplify
Mozilla's
user
interface.

Here's what you can do with the buttons on the Navigation toolbar that
appear just below the menu bar:

✦ **Back:** Move to the previous Web page.

✦ **Forward:** Move to the page from which you may have gone backward.

✦ **Reload:** Reload the current Web page.

✦ **Stop:** Stop loading the current page.

✦ **Location text box:** Show the URL of the current Web page. (Type a URL
in this box to view that Web page.)

✦ **Search:** Search the Netscape search site (`search.netscape.com`) with
the current Web page URL as a search string.

✦ **Print:** Print the current Web page (you can also preview how the page
will appear when printed).

✦ **Mozilla icon:** Go to the Mozilla.org Web site (`www.mozilla.org`).

Immediately below the Navigation toolbar comes the Personal toolbar with
the Home and Bookmarks buttons. These two buttons serve the following
purposes:

✦ **Home:** Takes you to the Home page.

✦ **Bookmarks:** Displays a menu from which you can bookmark the current page as well as manage your bookmarks.

There are two more links on the Personal toolbar. Clicking the Red Hat Network link takes you to the Red Hat Network site, where you can register to receive updates to Red Hat Linux. The rest of the links are organized into folders. Click a folder to view the drop-down list of links, and click the link you want to visit.

Status bar

You can think of the bar along the bottom edge of the Mozilla window as the status bar because the middle part of that area displays status information as Mozilla loads a Web page.

The left side of the status bar includes a number of icons. If you want a hint about what any of these icons do, simply mouse over the button, and Mozilla displays a small balloon help message. You can click these icons to open other Mozilla windows to perform various tasks. Table 2-1 explains what you can do with these icons.

Table 2-1	Icons on Mozilla's Status Bar
When You Click This Icon	*It Does the Following*
	Opens another Navigator (Web browser) window.
	Opens a Mozilla Mail window for reading mail and newsgroups.
	Opens an HTML composer window where you can prepare an HTML document.
	Opens the Address Book window for looking up addresses.
	Opens the ChatZilla window where you can join one or more Internet Relay Chat (IRC) channels and chat with others on those channels.

In the right corner of Mozilla's status bar, to the right of the status message, you see two icons. The icon on the left indicates that you're online; if you click it, Mozilla goes offline. The rightmost icon is a security padlock. Mozilla supports a secure version of HTTP that uses a protocol called *Secure Sockets*

Layer (SSL) to transfer encrypted data between the browser and the Web server. When Mozilla connects to a Web server that supports secure HTTP, the security padlock appears locked. Otherwise the security padlock is open, signifying an insecure connection. The URL for secure HTTP transfers begins with `https://` instead of the usual `http://` (note the extra `s` in `https`).

Mozilla displays status messages in the middle portion of the status bar. You can watch the messages in this area to see what's going on. When Mozilla is done downloading a Web page, it displays a message showing the number of seconds it took to download that page.

Mozilla menus

I haven't mentioned the Mozilla menus much. That's because you can usually get by without having to go to them. Nevertheless, it's worthwhile to take a quick look through the Mozilla menus so that you know what each one offers. Table 2-2 gives you an overview of the Mozilla menus.

Table 2-2	Mozilla Menus
This Menu	*Enables You to Do the Following*
File	Open a file or Web location, close the browser, send a Web page or link by mail, edit a Web page, print the current page, and quit Mozilla.
Edit	Copy and paste selections, find text in the current page, and edit your preferences.
View	Show or hide various toolbars, reload the current page, make the text larger or smaller, view the HTML code for the page, and view information about the page.
Go	Go backward and forward in the list of pages you have visited, or jump to other recently visited Web pages.
Bookmarks	Bookmark a page, manage the bookmarks, and add links to the Personal toolbar folder (these then appear in the Personal toolbar).
Tools	Search the Web and manage various aspects of the Web page, such as image loading, cookies, and stored passwords.
Window	Open other Mozilla windows (such as Mozilla Mail, Navigator, Address Book, and Composer).
Help	Get online help on Mozilla.

Changing your home page

Your *home page* is the page that Mozilla loads when you start it. By default, Mozilla loads a Web page from the Mozilla.org Web site. It's easy to change the home page.

First locate the page that you want to be the home page. You can get to that page any way you want. You can search on a search engine to find the page you want, you can type in the URL in the Location text box, or you may even accidentally end up on a page that you want to make your home page. It doesn't matter.

When you're viewing the Web page that you feel would be good as your home page, choose Edit⇨Preferences from the Mozilla menu. The Preferences window appears (as in Figure 2-6).

Figure 2-6: Click the Use Current Page button to make the current Web page your home page.

On the right side of Figure 2-6, notice that the Home Page radio button is on. This means Mozilla Navigator should display the home page when you start it up. Then there is a URL for the home page, and underneath there is a Use Current Page button. Click that button to make the current page your home page.

You can set a lot of other options using the Preferences window. Although I am not explaining all the options, you can click around to explore everything that you can do from this window. For example, you can click the Choose File button to select a file on your local system as the home page.

Changing Mozilla's appearance

Mozilla supports themes. A *theme* is basically the look and feel of Mozilla's user interface (which includes how the background and buttons look). The default theme is called the Classic theme, which gives you a look and feel that's similar to what Netscape used to have.

Mozilla comes with another theme called Modern, and you can download many other themes from the Net. Visit themes.mozdev.org to browse some of the available themes and download the ones you want to try. You can also get new themes by choosing View⇨Apply Theme⇨Get New Themes from the Mozilla menu.

Changing the theme is easy. If you want to see the theme that you're selecting before you select it, follow these steps:

1. **Choose Edit⇨Preferences from the Mozilla menu.**

The Preferences window appears.

2. **Click the plus sign next to Appearance on the left side of the window.**

The Appearance item opens up.

3. **Click the Themes item.**

The right side now shows the available themes.

4. **Click the theme you want.**

You see a preview of the buttons and the color in the area underneath the list of themes (Figure 2-7).

Figure 2-7:
Select a
theme to
change
Mozilla's
appearance.

5. **After you select a theme, click OK to close the Preferences window.**

A dialog box tells you that the new theme will take effect the next time you start Mozilla.

To see the full effect of a theme, close Mozilla and then start it again.

Surfing the Net with Mozilla

Where you go from the Mozilla home page depends on you. All you have to do is click and see where you end up. Move your mouse around. You know when you are on a link because the mouse pointer changes to a hand with an extended index finger. Click the link, and Mozilla downloads the Web page referenced by that link.

How you use the Web depends on what you want to do. When you first get started, you may explore a lot — browsing through Web sites and following links without any specific goal in mind. This is what you might call Web window shopping.

The other, more purposeful, use of the Web is to find specific information from the Net. For example, you might want to locate all the Web sites that contain documents with a specified keyword. For such searches, you can use one of many Web search tools that are available on the Net. For example, many people swear by Google (`www.google.com`). Mozilla's Search button takes you to the Netscape Search page (`search.netscape.com`).

A third type of use is a visit to a specific site with a known URL. For example, when reading about a specific topic in this book, you may come across a specific URL. In that case, you want to go directly to that Web page.

If you want to surf the Net with Mozilla, all you need is a starting Web page — then you can click whatever catches your fancy. For example, select the text in the Location text box in Mozilla's Navigation toolbar, type **search.netscape. com**, and then press Enter. You'll get to the Netscape Search page that shows Netscape's Web directory — organized by subject. There's your starting point. All you have to do is click and you're on your way!

Creating Web Pages

If you get your Internet access from an ISP, you probably get a free Web page as well. The only catch is you have to upload an HTML file for your Web page, which means you have to somehow prepare a Web page.

One way to prepare a Web page is to simply use a text editor and type HTML code. After all, a Web page is just a text file with HTML tags. Even though I won't put anyone through the agony of typing all those HTML tags, I want to show you a very basic HTML document, just so you know the structure.

Before I get into the HTML code, I want to give you a bit of good news. Mozilla comes with something called a Composer, which you can use to prepare HTML documents — Web pages — without having to learn HTML tags. Now that you know relief is on the way, I can quickly show you the innards of an HTML document.

Introducing HTML

Typically, when a client (a Web browser) connects to a Web server, the server sends back an HTML file named `index.html`. When you have your Web site, the `index.html` file is your home page. I introduce HTML by creating an `index.html` file and improving it through iterations. In the process, you see most of the important HTML features.

To begin, open any text editor and type the following lines of text:

```
<html>

<head>
<TITLE>
My Home Page
</TITLE>
</head>

<body>

<center>
<h1>
My Home Page
</h1>
</center>

<hr>
This page is under construction.
<hr>

Copyright &copy; 2003 Someone
<a href="mailto:webmaster@myplace.com">
<address>
webmaster@myplace.com
</address>
</a>

</body>
</html>
```

This is a bare-bones HTML file. Go ahead and save it with the filename `index.html`.

To see how it looks, choose File⇨Open File from the Mozilla menu. Browse through the directories and pick the `index.html` file from wherever you stored it. Click Open to open the file in Mozilla. Figure 2-8 shows how the Web page looks in Mozilla. By the way, the Mozilla window shown in Figure 2-8 has the Modern theme. That's why it looks different from the usual Mozilla window (see, for example, Figure 2-4).

Figure 2-8: View your HTML file in Mozilla to see how it looks.

Getting back to the Web page itself, it looks quite nice, doesn't it? No wonder we love Web pages.

At this point, you should correlate the Web page in Figure 2-8 with the HTML codes so that you can see the effect of each HTML tag. In particular, notice the following things:

✦ HTML tags are enclosed in angle brackets ⟨...⟩, and there is a pair of tags — a beginning tag and an ending tag — that goes like this ⟨/...⟩.

✦ HTML tags are not case sensitive. Thus, you can type the title tag as `<title>` or `<TITLE>`; both mean the same.

✦ The `<html>` ... `</html>` tag pair simply indicates that the document is an HTML document; that tag does not have any visual effect.

✦ The `<head>` ... `</head>` tags enclose the header information. In this case, the header defines the title of the page. That title appears in the title bar of the Mozilla window.

✦ The `<body>` ... `</body>` tag pair encloses the entire HTML document.

✦ The body of the Web page shows the text `My Home Page` in header level 1 (`<h1>` ... `</h1>`) and centered (`<center>` ... `</center>`).

✦ The `<hr>` tag causes the browser to display a horizontal rule.

✦ The HTML keyword `&copy;` displays a copyright symbol.

✦ The `<a href= ...>` ... `</a>` tag adds a hyperlink. All the lines between the start tag `<a href="mailto:webmaster@myplace.com">` and the end tag `</a>` are called the *anchor* (or `<a>`) *element.* The keyword `href` that appears in the start tag of the anchor element is called an attribute.

✦ The `<address>` ... `</address>` tags display the enclosed text as an address (in italics).

I won't go any further with the HTML tags; this much should give you a feel for the overall structure of a typical Web page.

If you're ever curious about the HTML code corresponding to any Web page, simply choose View⇨Page Source from the Mozilla menu to see the HTML code for the current page.

Composing Web pages with Mozilla Composer

Mozilla Composer is a graphical tool for creating Web pages without having to know much HTML. If you know HTML, you can certainly make use of that knowledge in Composer. One nice part is that you can create an attractive Web page even if you don't know any HTML.

A sample editing session in Composer

If you are creating a new Web page from scratch, choose Window⇨ Composer from the Mozilla menu.

If you want to edit an existing Web page and you've opened it in Mozilla, choose File⇨Edit Page. Mozilla opens a Composer window with the same HTML file.

You can start with the page shown in Figure 2-8 and begin editing it. In the Composer window, the Web page looks similar to that in Figure 2-8, but now it behaves like a word processor. You can start editing the text and changing the layout, just as you would in a word processor. To add text, simply click and type. To apply text-formatting effects such as boldface, italics, and underlining, use the text-formatting toolbar (which looks very much like similar toolbars in any word processor).

You can also insert images. Here's how:

1. **Gather the image files you want to use (in formats such as JPEG or GIF), and then save them somewhere on your Red Hat Linux PC.**

You can either prepare the images in a drawing and paint program or get the images from some other source (for example, from a Web site such as `thefreesite.com/Free_Graphics/Free_clipart/ index.html`).

2. **Position the cursor where you want an image; then choose Insert⇨Image from the Composer menu.**

   The Image Properties dialog box, shown in Figure 2-9, appears.

Figure 2-9:
You can add an image to a Web page from this dialog box.

3. **Click Choose File and select the image file from the Select Image File dialog box.**

4. **Enter alternate text for the image — this is the text that would appear in text-only browsers.**

   You can also enter a tooltip — the text that would appear as a user places the mouse over the image.

5. **After filling in all the information, click OK.**

   The image should appear where you positioned the cursor (Figure 2-10).

6. **Repeat Steps 2 through 5 for other images. After inserting all the images, choose File⇨Save to save the HTML file.**

   If you're creating a new Web page, Composer prompts you for a filename.

Figure 2-10 shows the Web page of Figure 2-8 after I added some text and inserted an image.

With this brief example, I have barely scratched the surface as far as what Composer can do. If you begin to try these features on sample Web pages, you'll figure out Composer's features in no time.

As you are working in Composer, if you ever wonder what any of the toolbar buttons do, simply mouse over the button and a small help balloon pops up with a helpful hint. Figure 2-11 shows an example of what happens when you mouse over the Link button.

Views in Composer

Notice that the Composer window has four tabs along the bottom. These tabs enable you to view the Web page in different forms. You typically edit the file in Normal view, but you can switch to the other views; for example, you can edit HTML directly if you so desire. To change to a different view, click on the tab.

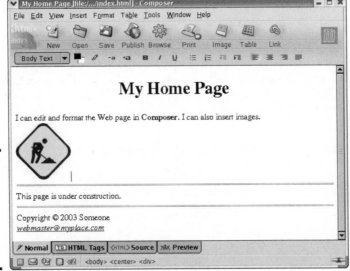

Figure 2-10: You can create or edit your Web pages in Composer.

The four tabs are as follows:

+ **Normal:** This view shows the Web page in nearly complete layout, but also lets you edit the page. You typically do most of your editing and formatting in this view.

+ **HTML Tags:** This view shows the Web page with the HTML tags as small icons. You can quickly check what HTML tags are affecting which parts of the document and, perhaps, fix any formatting problems.

Figure 2-11: Mouse over a button and Composer displays a balloon help.

✦ **<HTML> Source:** This view shows you the HTML text in its full glory. If you used WordPerfect, this is like WordPerfect's "Reveal Codes" option. If something weird happens to the Web page layout, you can go into this window, find the offending code, and fix it. Of course, you have to know some HTML, but don't worry — you'll start picking it up if you start working with Web pages. You can also use this view to write the Web page directly in HTML and go to Normal or Preview views to check up on the layout.

✦ **Preview:** This view essentially shows you what the Web page looks like in Mozilla Navigator. It's a quick way to check the final layout without having to open the file in a Navigator window. You cannot edit in this view.

The HTML Tags view can be handy when you want to quickly spot extraneous HTML tags. Figure 2-12 shows the HTML Tags view of the Web page shown in Figure 2-10.

Figure 2-12: HTML Tags view shows the HTML tags as icons.

Each tag appears in yellow, with a tag name such as CENTER (for centered text), BIG (for bigger font), H1 (for header level 1), IMG (for image), and so on. You can see whether any extraneous tags appear in the Web page — and remove them if you want (although they often don't do any harm — for example, when a blank line is centered).

Chapter 3: Reading Newsgroups

In This Chapter

✔ **Understanding newsgroups**

✔ **Reading newsgroups from your ISP**

✔ **Reading and searching newsgroups at some Web sites**

*I*nternet newsgroups are like the bulletin-board systems (BBSs) of the pre-Web age or the forums offered on online systems such as AOL and MSN. Essentially, newsgroups provide a distributed conferencing system that spans the globe. You can post articles — essentially e-mail messages to a whole group of people — and respond to articles others have posted.

Think of an Internet newsgroup as a gathering place — a virtual meeting place where you can ask questions and discuss various issues (and best of all, everything you discuss gets archived for posterity).

To participate in newsgroups, you need access to a news server — your Internet Service Provider (ISP) should give you this access. You also need a newsreader. Luckily, Red Hat Linux comes with software that you can use to read newsgroups: Pan and Mozilla Mail. In this chapter, I introduce you to newsgroups and show you how to read newsgroups with a few of the news-readers. I also briefly explain how you can read and search newsgroups for free from a few Web sites.

Understanding Newsgroups

Newsgroups originated in Usenet — a store-and-forward messaging network that was widely used for exchanging e-mail and news items. Usenet works like a telegraph in that news and mail are relayed from one system to another. In Usenet, the systems are not on any network; they simply dial up and use the UNIX-to-UNIX Copy Protocol (UUCP) to transfer text messages.

Although it's a very loosely connected collection of computers, Usenet has worked well and continues to be used because very little expense is involved in connecting to it. All you need is a modem and a site willing to store and forward your mail and news. You have to set up UUCP on your system, but you don't need a sustained network connection; just a few phone calls are all it takes to keep the e-mail and news flowing. The downside is that you cannot use TCP/IP services such as the Web, TELNET, or FTP.

From their Usenet origins, the newsgroups have now migrated to the Internet (even though the newsgroups are still called *Usenet newsgroups*). Instead of UUCP, the news is now transported by means of the Network News Transfer Protocol (NNTP).

Although (for most of the online world) the news-transport protocol has changed from UUCP to NNTP, the store-and-forward concept of news transfer remains. Thus, if you want to get news on your Red Hat Linux system, you have to find a news server from which your system can download news. Typically, this would be your ISP's news server.

Newsgroup hierarchy

The Internet newsgroups are organized in a hierarchy for ease of maintenance as well as ease of use. The newsgroup names show the hierarchy — written in Internet-speak — but easy to understand with a little bit of explanation.

A typical newsgroup name looks like this:

```
comp.os.linux.announce
```

This name says that `comp.os.linux.announce` is a newsgroup for announcements (`announce`) about the Linux operating system (`os.linux`) and that these subjects fall under the broad category of computers (`comp`).

As you can see, the format of a newsgroup name is a sequence of words separated by periods. These words denote the hierarchy of the newsgroup. Figure 3-1 illustrates the concept of hierarchical organization of newsgroups.

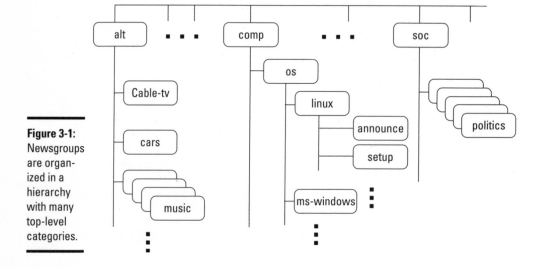

Figure 3-1:
Newsgroups are organized in a hierarchy with many top-level categories.

To understand the newsgroup hierarchy, compare the newsgroup name with the pathname of a file (for example, /usr/lib/X11/xinit/Xclients) in Linux. Just as a file's pathname shows the directory hierarchy of the file, the newsgroup name shows the newsgroup hierarchy. In filenames, a slash (/) separates the names of directories; in a newsgroup's name, a period (.) separates the different levels in the newsgroup hierarchy.

In a newsgroup name, the first word represents the newsgroup *category*. The comp.os.linux.announce newsgroup, for example, is in the comp category, whereas alt.books.technical is in the alt category.

Top-level newsgroup categories

Table 3-1 lists some of the major newsgroup categories. You'll find a wide variety of newsgroups covering subjects ranging from politics to computers. The Linux-related newsgroups are in the comp.os.linux hierarchy.

Table 3-1	Some Major Newsgroup Categories
Category	Subject
alt	"Alternative" newsgroups (not subject to any rules), which run the gamut from the mundane to the bizarre
bionet	Biology newsgroups
bit	Bitnet newsgroups
biz	Business newsgroups
clari	Clarinet news service (daily news)
comp	Computer hardware and software newsgroups (includes operating systems such as Linux and Microsoft Windows)
ieee	Newsgroups for the Institute of Electrical and Electronics Engineers (IEEE)
k12	Newsgroups devoted to elementary and secondary education
linux	Newsgroups devoted to Linux (includes a linux.redhat hierarchy)
misc	Miscellaneous newsgroups
news	Newsgroups about Internet news administration
rec	Recreational and art newsgroups
sci	Science and engineering newsgroups
soc	Newsgroups for discussing social issues and various cultures
talk	Discussions of current issues (think "talk radio")

This short list of categories is deceptive because it doesn't really tell you about the wide-ranging variety of newsgroups available in each category. The top-level categories alone number close to a thousand, but many top-level categories are distributed only in specific regions of the world. Because each newsgroup category contains several levels of subcategories, the overall count of newsgroups can be close to 60,000 or 70,000! The `comp` category alone has more than 500 newsgroups.

To browse newsgroup categories and get a feel for the breadth of topics covered by the newsgroups, visit the Free Usenet Newsgroup News Web site at `newsone.net`.

Linux-related newsgroups

Typically, you have to narrow your choice of newsgroups according to your interests. If you're interested in Linux, for example, you can pick one or more of these newsgroups:

✦ `comp.os.linux.admin` — Information about Linux system administration.

✦ `comp.os.linux.advocacy` — Discussions about promoting Linux.

✦ `comp.os.linux.announce` — Important announcements about Linux. This newsgroup is *moderated*, which means you must mail the article to a moderator, who then posts it to the newsgroup if the article is appropriate for the newsgroup (this keeps the riff-raff from clogging up the newsgroup with marketing pitches).

✦ `comp.os.linux.answers` — Questions and answers about Linux. All the Linux HOWTOs are posted in this moderated newsgroup.

✦ `comp.os.linux.development` — Current Linux development work.

✦ `comp.os.linux.development.apps` — Linux application development.

✦ `comp.os.linux.development.system` — Linux operating-system development.

✦ `comp.os.linux.hardware` — Discussions about Linux and various types of hardware.

✦ `comp.os.linux.help` — Help with various aspects of Linux.

✦ `comp.os.linux.misc` — Miscellaneous Linux-related topics.

✦ `comp.os.linux.networking` — Networking under Linux.

✦ `comp.os.linux.redhat` — Red Hat Linux-related topics.

✦ `comp.os.linux.setup` — Linux setup and installation.

✦ `comp.os.linux.x` — Discussions about setting up and running the X Window System under Linux.

✦ `linux.redhat` — Discussions about Red Hat Linux.

You have to be selective about what newsgroups you read because it's impossible to keep up with all the news, even in a specific area such as Linux. When you first install and set up Red Hat Linux, you might read newsgroups such as `comp.os.linux.redhat`, `comp.os.linux.setup`, `comp.os.linux.hardware`, and `comp.os.linux.x` (especially if you run X). After you have Linux up and running, you may want to find out about only new things happening in Linux. For such information, read the `comp.os.linux.announce` newsgroup.

Reading Newsgroups from Your ISP

If you have signed up with an ISP for Internet access, it should provide you with access to a news server. Such Internet news servers communicate by using the Network News Transfer Protocol (NNTP). Then you can use an NNTP-capable newsreader, such as Pan, to access the news server and read selected newsgroups. You can also read news by using the newsreader that comes with Mozilla (included with Red Hat Linux). This is the easiest way to access news from your Red Hat Linux Internet system.

My discussion of reading newsgroups assumes that you have obtained access to a news server from your ISP. The ISP provides you the name of the news server and any user name and password needed to set up your news account on the newsreader you use.

To read news, you need a *newsreader* — a program that enables you to select a newsgroup and view the items in that newsgroup. You also have to understand the newsgroup hierarchy and naming convention (described in the "Newsgroup hierarchy" section of this chapter). Now I show you how to read news from a news server.

If you don't have access to newsgroups through your ISP, you can try using one of the many public news servers that are out there. For a list of public news servers, visit NewzBot at `www.newzbot.com`. At this Web site, you can search for news servers that carry specific newsgroups.

Reading newsgroups with Mozilla Mail

You can browse newsgroups and post articles from Mozilla Mail, one of the components of Mozilla. When you're starting to read newsgroups for the first time, follow these steps to set up the news account:

1. **Click the Mozilla icon (the earth and mouse icon) or choose Main Menu⇨Internet⇨Mozilla Web Browser from the GNOME panel.**

   Mozilla starts.

2. **Choose Windows⇨Mail & Newsgroups from the Mozilla menu.**

   If you have not yet defined any mail or newsgroup account, the Account Wizard appears. Otherwise the Mozilla Mail and News (Mozilla Mail for short) window appears.

3. **Choose Edit⇨Mail & Newsgroups Account Settings from the Mozilla Mail menu.**

   A dialog box appears.

4. **Click Add Account.**

   The Account Wizard appears (as in Figure 3-2).

Figure 3-2:
Mozilla's
Account
Wizard
guides you
through the
newsgroup
account
setup.

5. **Select the Newsgroup Account radio button (Figure 3-2) and click Next.**

6. **Fill in your identity information — name and e-mail address — and click Next.**

7. **Enter your news server name and click Next.**

8. **Enter a descriptive name of the newsgroup account and click Next.**

9. **Click Finish to complete the newsgroup account setup.**

The new newsgroup account now appears in the list of accounts on the left side of the Mozilla Mail window. Click the newsgroup account name, and the right side of the window shows the options for the newsgroup account.

Click the Subscribe to newsgroups link. Mozilla Mail starts to download the list of newsgroups from the news server.

If your ISP's news server requires a user name and password, you're prompted for that information. After that, Mozilla Mail downloads the list of newsgroups and displays them in the Subscribe dialog box. (You can enter a search string in a text box to narrow the list.) When you find the newsgroups you want, mark the check box to subscribe to these newsgroups (as in Figure 3-3). Then click OK to close the dialog box.

Figure 3-3:
Indicate
which
newsgroups
you want to
subscribe to
in this dialog
box.

After you subscribe to newsgroups, these newsgroups appear under the newsgroup account name in the left side of the Mozilla Mail window. You can then read a newsgroup using these steps:

1. **Click a newsgroup name (for example,** comp.os.linux.announce**).**

 This brings up a dialog box that asks you how many message headers you want to download.

2. **Specify the number of headers (for example, 500) you want and then click OK to proceed.**

 Mozilla Mail downloads the headers from the newsgroup and displays a list in the upper-right area of the window.

3. **From the list of headers, click an item to read that article (as in Figure 3-4).**

To select other subscribed newsgroups, simply click the newsgroup's name in the left side of the window.

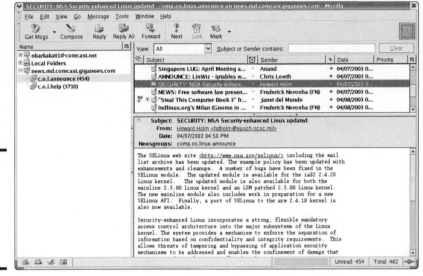

Figure 3-4:
Click an
article to
read it in
the lower
right hand
window.

Newsgroup subscriptions

Unlike magazines or newspapers, newsgroups don't require that you sub-scribe to them; you can read any newsgroup that is available on the news server. The news server's administrator may decide to exclude certain newsgroups. If they aren't included, however, you cannot read them.

The only thing that can be called "subscribing" is when you indicate the newsgroups you routinely want to read. The news server does not receive any of this subscription information — the information is used only by the newsreader to determine what to download from the news server.

How to post news

You can use any newsreader to post a news article (a new item or a reply to an old posting) to one or more newsgroups. The exact command for posting a news item depends on the newsreader. For example, in the Mozilla Mail newsreader, you follow these steps to post an article:

1. **Click Reply on the toolbar to post a follow-up to a news item you're reading. To post a new news article, click Compose.**

   A window appears where you can compose the message.

2. **Type the names of the newsgroups, just as you type the addresses of recipients when sending e-mail; then enter the subject and your message.**

   For this test posting, type `ignore` as the subject line and enter `misc.test` as the name of the newsgroup.

Otherwise, any site that receives your article replies by mail to tell you the article has reached the site; that's in keeping with the purpose of the `misc.test` newsgroup. Figure 3-5 shows the message being composed in Netscape Communicator.

Figure 3-5:
You can post follow-ups or new news articles from Mozilla Mail newsreader.

3. **After you finish composing the message, click Send on the toolbar (see Figure 3-5).**

Mozilla Mail sends the message to the news server, which in turn sends it to other news servers, and soon it's all over the world!

4. **To verify that the test message has reached the newsgroup, choose File⇨Subscribe; then subscribe to the `misc.test` newsgroup (that's where you've recently posted the new article). Look at the latest article (or one of the most recent ones) in `misc.test`, which should be the article you've recently posted.**

If you post an article and read the newsgroup immediately, you see the new article, but that does not mean the article has reached other sites on the Internet. After all, your posting shows up on your news server immediately because that's where you posted the article. Because of the store-and-forward model of news distribution, the news article gradually propagates from your news server to others around the world.

The `misc.test` newsgroup provides a way to see whether or not your news posting is really getting around. If you post to that newsgroup and don't include the word *ignore* in the subject, news servers acknowledge receipt of the article by sending an e-mail message to the address listed in the Reply To field of the article's header.

Reading and Searching Newsgroups at Web Sites

If you don't have access to newsgroups through your ISP, you can still read newsgroups and post articles to newsgroups at a number of Web sites. Some of them archive old news articles and provide good search capabilities, so you can search these for articles related to some question you may have.

The best part about reading newsgroups through a Web site is that you don't even need access to a news server and you can read news from your Web browser.

Table 3-2 lists Web sites that offer free access to Usenet newsgroups. There are some sites that offer Usenet newsgroup service for a fee. I don't list them here, but you can search for them in Google (`www.google.com`) — type the search words **usenet newsgroup access** and you should get a list of all Web sites that offer newsgroup access (including the ones that charge a fee).

Table 3-2	Web Sites with Free Access to Usenet Newsgroups
Web Site	*URL*
Google Groups	`groups.google.com`
NewsOne.Net	`newsone.net`
Mailgate	`www.mailgate.org`

One of the best places to read newsgroups, post articles, and search old newsgroup archives is Google Groups — the Google Usenet discussion forums — on the Web at `groups.google.com`. At that Web site, you can select a newsgroup to browse and you can post replies to articles posted on various newsgroups.

The best part of Google Groups is the search capability. You already know how good Google's Web search is; you get that same comprehensive search capability to locate newsgroup postings that relate to your search words. To search newsgroups, fill in the search form at `groups.google.com` and press Enter.

To browse newsgroups in Google Groups, ignore the search box and look at the list of high-level newsgroup categories such as `alt`, `comp`, and `soc`. Click the category, and you can gradually drill down to specific newsgroups. When viewing an article in Google Groups, you can click a link that enables you to post a follow-up to that article.

Chapter 4: Transferring Files with FTP

In This Chapter

✔ **Using the GNOME FTP client**

✔ **Using the Mozilla Web browser as FTP client**

✔ **Learning to use the FTP command**

*J*ust as the name implies, *File Transfer Protocol* (FTP) is used to transfer files between computers. For example, if your Internet service provider (ISP) gives you space for a personal Web page, you may have already used FTP to upload the Web page. Using an FTP client on your computer, you log in to your ISP account, provide your password, and then copy the files from your home system to the ISP's server.

You can also use FTP to download other files anonymously, such as open-source software from other computers on the Internet — in which case, you don't need an account on the remote system to download files. You can simply log in using the word anonymous as the user name and provide your e-mail address as the password (in fact, your Web browser can do this on your behalf, so you may not even know this is happening). This type of anonymous FTP is great for distributing files to anyone who wants them. For example, a hardware vendor might use anonymous FTP to provide updated device drivers to anyone who needs them.

Red Hat Linux comes with several FTP clients, both command-line ones and GUI ones. In this chapter, I introduce you to a few GUI FTP clients and, for the command-line FTP client, I describe the commands you use to work with remote directories.

Using Graphical FTP Clients

You can use one of the following GUI FTP clients in Red Hat Linux:

✦ gFTP — a graphical FTP client

✦ Mozilla Web browser for anonymous FTP downloads

For uploading files, you want to use gFTP because you typically have to provide a user name and password for such transfers. Web browsers work fine for anonymous downloads, which is how you typically download software from the Internet.

I briefly describe both GUI FTP clients in the next two sections.

Using gFTP

GNOME comes with gFTP, a graphical FTP client. To start gFTP, choose Main Menu⇨Internet⇨More Internet Applications⇨gFTP from the GNOME or KDE desktop. The gFTP window appears (as shown in Figure 4-1).

Figure 4-1: The gFTP window just before opening a connection to a remote FTP server.

The gFTP window has a menu bar with menus for performing various tasks. Just below the menu bar is a toolbar with a number of buttons and text fields. Here you can type the name or IP address of the remote host, the user name, and the password needed to log in to the remote host. Figure 4-1 shows the gFTP window after you have filled in this information.

To upload or download files using gFTP, follow these steps:

1. **Fill in the host name or the IP address of the remote system in the Host field.**

If you have used that host before, you can select it from the drop-down list that appears when you click the downward-pointing arrow next to the Host field.

2. **Provide the user name in the User field and the password in the Pass field, and then click the button with the icon showing two computers (to the left of the Host field).**

   This operation causes gFTP to connect to your chosen host and to log in with the user name and password you have provided. The lower part of the gFTP window shows the FTP protocol messages exchanged between the two systems.

3. **Observe this area for any indication of error messages.**

   The directory listing of the remote system appears in the right half of the gFTP window. The left half shows the current local directory.

4. **To upload one or more files from the current system to the remote system, select the files in the list on the left, and then click the right arrow button.**

5. **To download files from the remote system, select the filenames in the list on the right, and then click the left arrow button.**

6. **When you're done transferring files, choose FTP⇨Quit from the menu.**

As these steps show, transferring files with a GUI FTP client such as gFTP is a simple task.

Believe it or not, gFTP isn't for FTP transfers alone. It can also transfer files using the HTTP protocol and secure file transfers using the Secure Shell (SSH) protocol.

Using a Web browser as an FTP client

Any Web browser can act as an FTP client, but such programs are best for anonymous FTP downloads, where the Web browser can log in using the anonymous user name and any password.

In Red Hat Linux, you can use the Mozilla Web browser as an FTP client. All you have to know is how to write the URL so that the Web browser can tell that you want to download a file using FTP. The syntax of the FTP URL is like this:

```
ftp://hostname/pathname
```

The first part (`ftp://`) indicates that you want an FTP transfer. The `hostname` part should be the name of the FTP server (the name often starts with an `ftp` — for example, `ftp.netscape.com`). The *pathname* is the full directory path and filename of the file you want to download.

If you simply provide the hostname for the FTP server, the Web browser displays the contents of the anonymous FTP directory. If you want to try this on your Red Hat Linux system, start Mozilla (click the Mozilla icon on the GNOME panel) and then type the following line in the location text box:

```
ftp://localhost
```

Then press Enter. Mozilla shows the contents of the anonymous FTP directory on your Red Hat Linux system. Figure 4-2 shows a typical appearance of an anonymous FTP directory in Mozilla. You can click folders to see their contents and download any files.

Figure 4-2: You can use Mozilla to download files from anonymous FTP servers

When you use the `ftp://localhost` URL, you won't get a response from your system if you're not running an FTP server or if you have set up your firewall so that no FTP connections are allowed. On your system, log in as `root` and type **service vsftpd start** (in a terminal window) to start the FTP server.

The same approach of accessing anonymous FTP sites would work if you were to type the host name of some other anonymous FTP server. For example, try typing the following URL:

```
ftp://ftp.netscape.com
```

You should get the directory of the `ftp.netscape.com` server.

Using the Command-Line FTP Client

It's good to know how to use FTP from the command line — just in case. For example, your GUI desktop may not be working and what you have to do to fix the problem is to download some files. If you know how to use the command-line FTP client, you can download the files and take care of the problem. It's not that hard.

The best way to learn the command-line FTP client is to try it out. The command is called ftp, and you can try the ftp commands from your Red Hat Linux system. You don't even need any Internet connection because you can use the ftp command to connect to your own system — I show you how.

In the following sample FTP session, I use the command-line FTP client to log in using my user name (naba) and browse the directories on my system. When you try a similar operation, replace the name with your user name and provide your password. Here's the listing showing the commands (my comments appear in italics):

```
ftp localhost
Connected to localhost (127.0.0.1).
220 (vsFTPd 1.2.0)
Name (localhost:naba):    (I press Enter.)
331 Please specify the password.
Password:        (I type my password.)
230 Login successful. Have fun.
Remote system type is UNIX.
Using binary mode to transfer files.
ftp> help        (I type help to see a list of FTP commands.)
Commands may be abbreviated.  Commands are:

!           debug        mdir      sendport    site
$           dir          mget      put         size
account     disconnect   mkdir     pwd         status
append      exit         mls       quit        struct
ascii       form         mode      quote       system
bell        get          modtime   recv        sunique
binary      glob         mput      reget       tenex
bye         hash         newer     rstatus     tick
case        help         nmap      rhelp       trace
cd          idle         nlist     rename      type
cdup        image        ntrans    reset       user
chmod       lcd          open      restart     umask
close       ls           prompt    rmdir       verbose
cr          macdef       passive   runique     ?
delete      mdelete      proxy     send
ftp> help mget   (I can get help on a specific command.)
mget             get multiple files
ftp> cd /var/ftp (This changes directory to /var/ftp.)
250 Directory successfully changed.
ftp> ls    (This command lists the contents of the directory.)
227 Entering Passive Mode (127,0,0,1,248,180)
150 Here comes the directory listing.
drwxr-xr-x    2 0        0            4096 Jun 26 05:10 pub
226 Directory send OK.
ftp> bye         (This command ends the session.)
221 Goodbye.
```

As the listing shows, you can start the command-line FTP client by typing the command `ftp` *hostname*, where *hostname* is the name of the system you want to access. When the FTP client establishes a connection with the FTP server at the remote system, the FTP server prompts you for a user name and password. After you've supplied the information, the FTP client displays the `ftp>` prompt, and you can begin typing commands to perform specific tasks. If you can't remember a specific FTP command, type **help** to view a list of them. You can get additional help for a specific command by typing **help** *command*, where *command* is what you want help on.

Many FTP commands are similar to the Linux commands for navigating the file system. For example, `cd` changes directory, `pwd` prints the name of the current working directory, and `ls` lists the contents of the current directory. Two other common commands are `get` and `put` — `get` is what downloads a file from the remote system to your system, and `put` uploads (sends) a file from your system to the remote host.

Table 4-1 describes some commonly used FTP commands. You don't have to type the entire FTP command. For a long command, you have to type the first few characters only — enough to identify the command uniquely. For example, to delete a file, you can type **dele** and to change the file transfer mode to binary, you can type **bin**.

 When downloading files from the Internet, you almost always want to transfer the files in binary mode because the software is usually archived and compressed in a binary form (its files aren't plain text files). So always use the `binary` command to set the mode to binary. Then use the `get` command to download the files.

Table 4-1	Commonly Used FTP Commands
Command	*Description*
!	Executes a shell command on the local system. For example, `!ls` lists the contents of the current directory on the remote system.
?	Displays a list of commands (same as `help`).
append	Appends a local file to a remote file.
ascii	Sets the file-transfer type to ASCII (or plain text). This is the default file transfer type.
binary	Sets the file-transfer type to binary.
bye	Ends the FTP session with the remote FTP server and quits the FTP client.
cd	Changes the directory on the remote system. For example, `cd /pub/Linux` changes the remote directory to `/pub/Linux`.

Command	Description
chmod	Changes the permission settings of a remote file. For example, `chmod 644 index.html` changes the permission settings of the `index.html` file on the remote system.
close	Ends the FTP session with the FTP server and returns to the FTP client's prompt.
delete	Deletes a remote file. For example, `delete bigimage.jpg` deletes that file on the remote system.
dir	Lists the contents of the current directory on the remote system.
disconnect	Ends the FTP session and returns to the FTP client's prompt. (This is the same as `close`.)
get	Downloads a remote file. For example, `get junk.tar.gz junk.tgz` downloads the file `junk.tar.gz` from the remote system and saves it as the file `junk.tgz` on the local system.
hash	Turns on or off the hash-mark (#) printing that shows the progress of file transfer. When this feature is turned on, a hash mark is printed on-screen for every 1,024 bytes transferred from the remote system. (It's the command-line version of a progress bar.)
help	Displays a list of commands.
image	Same as `binary`.
lcd	Changes the current directory on the local system. For example, `lcd /var/ftp/pub` changes the current local directory to `/var/ftp/pub`.
ls	Lists the contents of the current remote directory.
mdelete	Deletes multiple files on a remote system. For example, `mdelete *.jpg` deletes all remote files with names ending in `.jpg` in the current directory.
mdir	Lists multiple remote files and saves the listing in a specified local file. For example, `mdir /usr/share/doc/w* wlist` saves the listing in the local file named `wlist`.
mget	Downloads multiple files. For example, `mget *.jpg` downloads all files with names ending in `.jpg`. If the prompt is turned on, the FTP client asks for confirmation before each file is downloaded.
mkdir	Creates a directory on the remote system. `mkdir images` creates a directory named `images` in the current directory on the remote system.
mls	Same as `mdir`.

(continued)

Table 4-1 *(continued)*

Command	Description
mput	Uploads multiple files. For example, mput *.jpg sends all files with names ending in .jpg to the remote system. If the prompt is turned on, the FTP client asks for confirmation before each file is sent.
open	Opens a connection to the FTP server on the specified host. For example, open ftp.netscape.com connects to the FTP server on the host ftp.netscape.com.
prompt	Turns the prompt on or off. When the prompt is on, the FTP client prompts you for confirmation before downloading or uploading each file during a multifile transfer.
put	Sends a file to the remote system. For example, put index.html sends the index.html file from the local system to the remote system.
pwd	Displays the full pathname of the current directory on the remote system. When you log in as a user, the initial current working directory is your home directory.
quit	Same as bye.
recv	Same as get.
rename	Renames a file on the remote system. For example, rename old.html new.html renames the file old.html to new.html on the remote system.
rmdir	Deletes a directory on the remote system. For example, rmdir images deletes the images directory in the current directory of the remote system.
send	Same as put.
size	Shows the size of a remote file. For example, size bigfile.tar.gz shows the size of that remote file.
status	Shows the current status of the FTP client.
user	Sends new user information to the FTP server. For example, user naba sends the username **naba**; the FTP server then prompts for the password for that user name.

Book VI

Administration

The 5th Wave   By Rich Tennant

"This part of the test tells us whether you're personally suited to the job of network administrator."

Contents at a Glance

Chapter 1: Performing Basic System Administration

In This Chapter

✔ **Becoming** `root`

✔ **Understanding the system startup process**

✔ **Taking stock of the system configuration files**

✔ **Viewing system information through the** `/proc` **file system**

✔ **Monitoring system performance**

✔ **Scheduling jobs**

*S*ystem administration refers to whatever has to be done to keep a computer system up and running; the *system administrator* is whoever is in charge of taking care of these tasks.

If you're running Red Hat Linux at home or in a small office, you're most likely the system administrator. Or maybe you're the system administrator for a whole LAN full of Red Hat Linux systems. No matter. In this chapter, I introduce you to basic system-administration procedures and show you how to perform some common tasks.

Red Hat Linux comes with quite a few graphical tools for performing specific system administration tasks. I describe some of these tools in this chapter, and the other chapters of this minibook.

Taking Stock of System Administration Tasks

So what *are* system administration tasks? My off-the-cuff reply is *anything you have to do to keep the system running well.* More accurately, though, a system administrator's duties include the following:

✦ **Adding and removing user accounts.** You have to add new user accounts and remove unnecessary user accounts. If a user forgets the password, you have to change the password.

✦ **Managing the printing system.** You have to turn the print queue on or off, check print-queue status, and delete print jobs if necessary.

✦ **Installing, configuring, and upgrading the operating system and various utilities.** You have to install or upgrade parts of the Linux operating system and other software packages.

✦ **Installing new software.** You have to install software that comes in Red Hat Package Manager (RPM) files. You also have to download and unpack software that comes in source-code form — and then build executable programs from the source code.

✦ **Managing hardware.** Sometimes you have to add new hardware and install drivers so the devices work properly.

✦ **Making backups.** You have to back up files, either in a Zip drive or on tape (if you have a tape drive).

✦ **Mounting and unmounting file systems.** When you want to access the files on a CD-ROM (for example), you have to mount that CD-ROM's file system on one of the directories in your Linux file system. You also have to mount floppy disks, in both Linux format and DOS format.

✦ **Automating tasks**. You have to schedule Linux tasks to take place automatically (at specific times) or jobs for people to perform periodically.

✦ **Monitoring the system's performance.** You may want to keep an eye on system performance to see where the processor is spending most of its time, and to see the amount of free and used memory in the system.

✦ **Starting and shutting down the system.** Although starting the system typically involves nothing more than powering up the PC, you do have to take some care when you want to shut down your Linux system. If your system is set up for a graphical login screen, you can perform the shutdown operation by selecting a menu item from the login screen. Otherwise you should use the `shutdown` command to stop all programs before turning off your PC's power switch.

✦ **Monitoring network status.** If you have a network presence (whether a LAN, a DSL line, or cable-modem connection), you may want to check the status of various network interfaces and make sure your network connection is up and running.

✦ **Setting up host and network security.** You have to make sure that system files are protected and protect your system against attacks over the network.

✦ **Monitoring security.** You have to keep an eye on any intrusions, usually by checking the log files.

That's a long list of tasks! I won't cover all of them in this chapter, but the rest of the mini-book describes most of these tasks. Here I focus on some of the basics, such as how to become `root` (the superuser), learning to set system-configuration files, monitoring system performance, and setting up periodic jobs.

How to become root

You have to be logged in as `root` to perform the system administration tasks. The `root` user is the superuser and the only account with all the privileges needed to do anything in the system.

Common wisdom says you should *not* normally log in as `root`. That's because when you're `root`, one misstep and you could easily delete all the files — especially when typing commands. Take, for example, the command `rm *.html` that you may type to delete all files that have the `.html` extension. What if you accidentally press the spacebar after the asterisk (*)? The shell takes the command to be `rm * .html` and — because * matches any filename — deletes everything in the current directory. Seems implausible until it happens to you!

Book VI Chapter 1

Performing Basic System Administration

Using the su - command

If you're logged in as a normal user, how do you do any system administration chores? Well, you become `root` for the time being. If you're working at a terminal window or console, type

```
su -
```

Then enter the `root` password in response to the prompt. From this point on, you're `root`. Do whatever you have to do. To return to your usual self, type

```
exit
```

That's it! It's that easy.

Becoming root for the GUI Utilities

If you use any of Red Hat's GUI utilities to perform a system administration chore, it's even easier. Typically, the utility pops up a dialog box that prompts you for the `root` password (as in Figure 1-1). Just type the password and press Enter. If you don't want to use the utility, click Close.

Figure 1-1:
Type the
root
password
and press
Enter to gain
root
privileges.

Recovering from a forgotten root password

To perform system administration tasks, you have to know the root pass-word. What happens if you forget the root password? Not to worry: Just reboot the PC and you can *reset* the root password by following these steps:

1. **Reboot the PC (select Reboot as you log out of the GUI screen) or power up as usual.**

Soon you see the graphical GRUB boot loader screen that shows the names of the operating systems you can boot.

2. **If you have more than one operating system installed, use the arrow key to select Red Hat Linux as your operating system. Then press *a* (just the letter "a").**

GRUB prompts you for commands to add to its default boot command.

3. **Press the spacebar, type the following, and then press Enter:**

```
nogui single
```

This causes Linux to start up as usual but to run in a single-user mode that does not require you to log in. The nogui command causes text boot messages to appear instead of a GUI screen as the system starts up. After Linux starts, you see the following command-line prompt:

```
sh-2.05b#
```

4. **Use the passwd command to change the root password as follows:**

```
sh-2.05b# passwd
Changing password for user root.
New password:
```

5. **Type the new root password that you want to use (it won't appear on-screen) and then press Enter.**

Linux asks for the password again, like this:

```
Retype new password:
```

6. **Type the password again, and press Enter.**

   If you enter the same password both times, the `passwd` command changes the password and displays the following message:

   ```
   passwd: all authentication tokens updated successfully.
   ```

7. **Now type** reboot **to reboot the PC.**

   After Linux starts, it displays the familiar login screen. Now you should be able to log in as `root` with the new password.

Make sure your Red Hat Linux PC is *physically* secure. As this procedure shows, anyone who can physically access your Red Hat Linux PC can simply reboot, set a new `root` password, and do whatever they want with the system. Another way to protect against resetting the password is to set a GRUB password, which causes GRUB to require a valid password before it boots Red Hat Linux. Of course, then you must remember and enter the GRUB password every time you boot your system!

Understanding How Red Hat Linux Boots

Knowing the sequence in which Red Hat Linux starts processes as it boots is important. You can use this knowledge to start and stop services, such as the Web server and Network File System (NFS). The next few sections provide you with an overview of how Red Hat Linux boots and starts the initial set of processes. These sections also familiarize you with the shell scripts that start various services on a Red Hat Linux system.

Understanding the init process

When Red Hat Linux boots, it loads and runs the core operating-system program from the hard drive. The core operating system is designed to run other programs. A process named `init` starts the initial set of processes on your Linux system.

```
ps ax | more
```

You get an output listing that starts off like this:

```
PID TTY     STAT   TIME COMMAND
  1 ?       S      0:03 init
```

The first column, with the heading `PID`, shows a number for each process. PID stands for *process ID* (identification) — a sequential number assigned by the Linux kernel. The first entry in the process list, with a PID of 1, is the `init` process. It's the first process, and it starts all other processes in your Red Hat Linux system. That's why init is sometimes referred to as the "mother of all processes."

What the init process starts depends on the following:

✦ The *run level*, an identifier that identifies a system configuration in which only a selected group of processes can exist

✦ The contents of the /etc/inittab file, a text file that specifies which processes to start at different run levels

✦ A number of shell scripts (located in the /etc/rc.d directory and its subdirectories) that are executed at specific run levels

There are seven run levels — 0 through 6 — and Table 1-1 shows their meanings.

Table 1-1	Run Levels in Red Hat Linux
Run Level	*Meaning*
0	Shut down the system
1	Run in single-user standalone mode (no one else can log in; you work at the text console)
2	Run in multiuser mode without the network services (in multiuser mode, other users can log in)
3	Run in full multiuser mode, but with a text-mode login
4	Unused in Red Hat Linux
5	All services running and graphical logon is enabled
6	Reboot the system

The current run level, together with the contents of the /etc/inittab file, controls which processes init starts. The initial default run level is 3 for text-mode login screens and 5 for the graphical login screen. You can change the default run level by editing a line in the /etc/inittab file.

To check the current run level, type the following command in a terminal window:

```
/sbin/runlevel
```

The runlevel command should print an output like this:

```
N 5
```

The first character of the output shows the previous run level (N means there is no previous run level), and the second character shows the current run level (5). In this case, the system was started at run level 5.

Examining the /etc/inittab file

The /etc/inittab file is the key to understanding the processes that init starts at various run levels. You can look at the contents of the file by using the more command, as follows:

```
more /etc/inittab
```

To see the contents of the /etc/inittab file with the more command, you don't have to log in as root.

To interpret the contents of the /etc/inittab file, follow these steps:

1. **Look for the line that looks like this:**

```
id:5:initdefault:
```

That line shows the default run level. In this case, it's 5.

2. **Find all the lines that specify what init should run at run level 5. Look for a line that has a 5 between the first two colons (:). Here are the two relevant lines:**

```
l5:5:wait:/etc/rc.d/rc 5
x:5:respawn:/etc/X11/prefdm -nodaemon
```

The first line specifies that init should execute the file /etc/rc.d/rc with 5 as an argument. The second line causes init to run /etc/X11/prefdm, a shell script that starts the graphical display manager. The display manager, in turn, displays the graphical login dialog box that enables you to log in to the system.

If you look at the file /etc/rc.d/rc, you find it's a shell script. You can study this file to see how it starts various processes for run levels 1 through 5.

Each entry in the /etc/inittab file tells init what to do at one or more run levels — you simply list all run levels at which the process should run. Each inittab entry has four fields — separated by colons — in the following format:

```
id:runlevels:action:process
```

Table 1-2 shows what each of these fields means.

Table 1-2	Meaning of the Fields in Each inittab Entry
Field	*Meaning*
id	A unique one- or two-character identifier. The init process uses this field internally. You can use any identifier you want, as long as you don't use the same identifier on more than one line.
runlevels	A sequence of zero or more characters, each denoting a run level. For example, if the runlevels field is 12345, that entry applies to each of the run levels 1 through 5. This field is ignored if the action field is set to sysinit, boot, or bootwait.
action	Tells the init process what to do with that entry. If this field is initdefault, for example, init interprets the runlevels field as the default run level. If this field is set to wait, init starts the program or script specified in the process field and waits until that process exits.
process	Name of the script or program that init has to start. Of course, some settings of the action field require no process field. For example, when action is initdefault, there is no need for a process field.

Trying a new run level with the init command

To try a new run level, you don't have to change the default run level in the /etc/inittab file. If you log in as root, you can change the run level (and, consequently, the processes that run in Red Hat Linux) by typing **init** followed by the run level (usually 1, 3, or 5).

For example, to put the system in single-user mode, type the following:

```
init 1
```

Thus, if you want to try run level 5 (assuming your system isn't set up for a graphical login screen yet) without changing the /etc/inittab file, enter the following command at the shell prompt:

```
init 5
```

The system should end all current processes and enter run level 5. By default, the init command waits 20 seconds before stopping all current processes and starting the new processes for run level 5.

To switch to run level 5 immediately, type the command **init -t0 5**. The number after the -t option indicates the number of seconds init waits before changing the run level.

You can also use the `telinit` command, which is simply a symbolic link (a shortcut) to `init`. If you make changes to the `/etc/inittab` file and want `init` to reload its configuration file, use the command `telinit q`.

Understanding the Red Hat Linux startup scripts

The `init` process runs a number of scripts at system startup. If you look at the `/etc/inittab` file, you find the following line near the beginning of the file:

```
# System initialization.
si::sysinit:/etc/rc.d/rc.sysinit
```

The first one is a comment line. The second line causes `init` to run the `/etc/rc.d/rc.sysinit` script — the first Red Hat Linux startup script that `init` runs. The `rc.sysinit` script performs many initialization tasks, such as mounting the file systems, setting the clock, configuring the keyboard layout, starting the network, and loading many other driver modules. The `rc.sysinit` script performs these initialization tasks by calling many other scripts and reading configuration files located in the `/etc/sysconfig` directory.

After executing the `/etc/rc.d/rc.sysinit` script, the `init` process runs the `/etc/rc.d/rc` script with the run level as argument. For example, for run level 5, the following line in `/etc/inittab` specifies what `init` has to execute:

```
l5:5:wait:/etc/rc.d/rc 5
```

This says that `init` should execute the command `/etc/rc.d/rc 5` and wait until that command completes.

The `/etc/rc.d/rc` script is somewhat complicated. Here's how it works:

✦ It changes to the directory corresponding to the run level. For example, to change to run level 5, the script changes to the `/etc/rc.d/rc5.d` directory.

✦ In the directory that corresponds with the run level, `/etc/rc.d/rc` looks for all files that begin with a `K` and executes each of them with the argument `stop`. This kills currently running processes. Then it locates all files that begin with an `S` and executes each file with an argument of `start`. This starts the processes needed for the specified run level.

To see what gets executed at run level 5, type the following command:

```
ls -l /etc/rc.d/rc5.d
```

In the resulting listing, the K scripts — the files whose names begin with K — stop ("kill") servers, whereas the S scripts start servers. The /etc/rc.d/rc script executes these files in exactly the order in which they appear in the directory listing.

A script with the name /etc/rc.d/rc.local is executed after all other scripts. So you can place in that script any command you want executed whenever your Red Hat Linux system boots.

Manually starting and stopping servers

Most server startup scripts reside in the /etc/init.d directory (the scripts are actually in /etc/rc.d/init.d, but /etc/init.d is a shortcut to /etc/rc.d/init.d). You can manually invoke scripts in this directory to start, stop, or restart specific processes — usually servers. For example, to stop the Web server (the server program is called httpd), type the following command:

```
/etc/rc.d/init.d/httpd stop
```

If httpd is already running and you want to restart it, type the following command:

```
/etc/init.d/httpd restart
```

You can enhance your system-administration skills by familiarizing yourself with the scripts in the /etc/init.d directory. To see its listing, type the following command:

```
ls /etc/init.d
```

For example, here is a typical list of scripts in my system:

```
aep1000       functions     keytable        nfslock       saslauthd    tux
anacron       gpm           killall         nscd          sendmail     vsftpd
apmd          halt          kudzu           ntpd          single       winbind
atd           httpd         lisa            pcmcia        smartd       xfs
autofs        innd          messagebus      portmap       smb          xinetd
bcm5820       iptables      microcode_ctl   postgresql    snmpd        ypbind
cpqarrayd     irda          named           pxe           snmptrapd    yppasswdd
crond         irqbalance    netfs           random        squid        ypserv
cups          isdn          network         rawdevices    sshd         ypxfrd
firstboot     kdcrotate     nfs             rhnsd         syslog
```

The script names give you some clue about which server the script can start and stop. For example, the nfs script starts and stops the processes required for NFS (Network File System) services. At your leisure, you may want to study some of these scripts to see what each one does. You don't

have to understand all the shell programming; the comments should help
you learn the purpose of each script.

Use the `service` command as a shortcut to run the scripts in `/etc/init.d`
that you use to start, stop, or restart servers. For example, to start the Web
server, you type this command:

```
service httpd stop
```

To restart that server, type the following command:

```
service httpd restart
```

Automatically starting servers at system startup

You want some servers to start automatically every time you boot the
system. For example, if you run a Web server, you want the `httpd` server
to start whenever the system starts. You can make that happen by using
the `chkconfig` command. For example, to set `httpd` to start whenever
the system boots into run level 3, 4, or 5, you type the following command
(while logged in as `root`):

```
chkconfig --level 345 httpd on
```

You can also use the `chkconfig` command to check which servers are turned
on or off. For example, to see the complete list of all servers for all run levels,
type the following command:

```
chkconfig --list
```

If you want to view the status of a single server, such as `httpd`, add that
server's name to the `chkconfig` command, like this:

```
chkconfig --list httpd
```

You should see an output similar to the following:

```
httpd      0:off  1:off  2:off  3:on  4:on  5:on  6:off
```

Taking Stock of Red Hat Linux
System Configuration Files

Red Hat Linux includes a host of configuration files. All of these files share
text files that you can edit with any text editor. To edit these configuration

files, you must log in as root. I don't discuss the files individually, but I show a selection of the configuration files in Table 1-3, along with a brief description of each. This listing gives you an idea of what types of configuration files a system administrator has to work with. In many cases, Red Hat Linux includes GUI utility programs to set up many of these configuration files.

Table 1-3	Red Hat Linux Configuration Files
Configuration File	*Description*
/boot/module-info	Module information for the Linux kernel
/boot/System.map	Map of the Linux kernel (maps kernel addresses into names of functions and variables)
/boot/vmlinuz	The Linux kernel (this is the operating system's core)
/etc/X11/XF86Config	Configuration file for XFree86 version 4.x
/etc/at.allow	Usernames of users allowed to use the at command to schedule jobs for later execution
/etc/at.deny	Usernames of users forbidden to use the at command
/etc/bashrc	Systemwide functions and aliases for the BASH shell
/etc/cups/cupsd.conf	Printer configuration file for the Common UNIX Printing System (CUPS) scheduler
/etc/fstab	Information about file systems available for mounting
/etc/group	Information about groups
/etc/grub.conf	The configuration for the Grand Unified Bootloader (GRUB) — the default boot loader in Red Hat Linux
/etc/hosts	List of IP numbers and their corresponding host names
/etc/hosts.allow	Hosts allowed to access Internet services on this system
/etc/hosts.deny	Hosts forbidden to access Internet services on this system
/etc/httpd/conf/httpd	Configuration file for the Apache Web server conf
/etc/init.d	Directory with scripts to start and stop many servers

Configuration File	Description
/etc/inittab	Configuration file used by the init process that starts all the other processes
/etc/issue	File containing message to be printed before displaying the text-mode login prompt (usually the Red Hat Linux version number)
/etc/lilo.conf	The configuration for the Linux Loader (LILO) — one of the boot loaders that can load the operating system from disk
/etc/login.defs	Default information for creating user accounts, used by the useradd command
/etc/modules.conf	Configuration file with directives for loading kernel modules (for example, Ethernet and sound drivers)
/etc/mtab	Information about currently mounted file systems
/etc/passwd	Information about all user accounts (actual passwords are stored in /etc/shadow)
/etc/profile	Systemwide environment and startup file for the BASH shell
/etc/rc.d	Directory that holds startup and shutdown scripts for the Red Hat Linux system
/etc/rc.d/rc.sysinit	Red Hat Linux initialization script
/etc/shadow	Secure file with encrypted passwords for all user accounts (can be read only by root)
/etc/shells	List of all the shells on the system that the user can use
/etc/skel	Directory that holds initial versions of files such as .bash_profile that are copied to new user's home directory
/etc/sysconfig	Red Hat Linux configuration files
/etc/termcap	Database of terminal capabilities and options
/etc/xinetd.conf	Configuration for the xinetd daemon that starts a number of Internet services on demand
/var/log/cron	Log file with messages from the cron process that runs scheduled jobs
/var/log/httpd/access_log	Web-server access log
/var/log/httpd/error_log	Web-server error log
/var/log/messages	System log

Book VI
Chapter 1

Performing
Basic System
Administration

Monitoring System Performance

When you're the system administrator, you must keep an eye on how well your Red Hat Linux system is performing. You can monitor the overall performance of your system by looking at information such as

✦ Central Processing Unit (CPU) usage

✦ Physical memory usage

✦ Virtual memory (swap space) usage

✦ Hard-drive usage

Red Hat Linux comes with a number of utilities you can use to monitor one or more of these performance parameters. Here I introduce a few of these utilities and show you how to understand the information presented by these utilities.

Using the top utility

To view the top CPU processes — the ones that are using most of the CPU time — you can use the text mode top utility. To start that utility, type **top** in a terminal window (or text console). The top utility then displays a text screen listing the current processes, arranged in the order of CPU usage, along with various other information, such as memory and swap space usage. Figure 1-2 shows a typical output from the top utility.

The top utility updates the display every 5 seconds. If you keep top running in a window, you can continually monitor the status of your Red Hat Linux system. To quit top, press Ctrl+C or close the terminal window.

```
  naba@dhcppc1:~                                                    _ □ ×
 File  Edit  View  Terminal  Go  Help
  17:27:26  up 12 days, 13:05,  3 users,  load average: 0.72, 0.69, 0.33
 73 processes: 72 sleeping, 1 running, 0 zombie, 0 stopped
 CPU states:   2.3% user   0.9% system   0.0% nice   0.0% iowait  96.6% idle
 Mem:    61420k av,   60044k used,    1376k free,      0k shrd,    2288k buff
                      41096k actv,    3404k in_d,    532k in_c
 Swap:  192772k av,   42836k used,  149936k free                  20136k cached

   PID USER     PRI  NI  SIZE  RSS SHARE STAT %CPU %MEM   TIME CPU COMMAND
  1919 root      15   0 18508 5584   576 S    1.1  9.0   0:08   0 X
 30924 naba      16   0  1168 1168   852 R    0.9  1.9   0:00   0 top
 30884 naba      15   0  6064 3028  1364 S    0.5  4.9   0:02   0 rhn-applet-gu
 30896 naba      15   0  7576 7568  5220 S    0.5 12.3   0:01   0 gnome-termina
     1 root      15   0   476  444   420 S    0.0  0.7   0:03   0 init
     2 root      15   0     0    0     0 SW   0.0  0.0   0:00   0 keventd
     3 root      15   0     0    0     0 SW   0.0  0.0   0:00   0 kapmd
     4 root      34  19     0    0     0 SWN  0.0  0.0   0:00   0 ksoftirqd_CPU
     9 root      15   0     0    0     0 SW   0.0  0.0   0:00   0 bdflush
     5 root      15   0     0    0     0 SW   0.0  0.0   0:05   0 kswapd
     6 root      15   0     0    0     0 SW   0.0  0.0   0:00   0 kscand/DMA
     7 root      15   0     0    0     0 SW   0.0  0.0   0:00   0 kscand/Normal
     8 root      15   0     0    0     0 SW   0.0  0.0   0:00   0 kscand/HighMe
    10 root      15   0     0    0     0 SW   0.0  0.0   0:00   0 kupdated
    11 root      25   0     0    0     0 SW   0.0  0.0   0:00   0 mdrecoveryd
    15 root      15   0     0    0     0 SW   0.0  0.0   0:01   0 kjournald
```

Figure 1-2:
You can see the top CPU processes by using the top utility.

The first six lines of the output screen (refer to Figure 1-2) provide summary information about the system. Here is what these six lines show:

+ The first line shows the current time, how long the system has been up, how many users are logged in, and three *load averages* — the average number of processes ready to run during the last 1, 5, and 15 minutes.

+ The second line lists the total number of processes and the status of these processes.

+ The third line shows CPU usage — what percentage of CPU time is used by user processes, what percentage by system (kernel) processes, and during what percentage of time the CPU is idle.

+ The fourth and fifth lines show how the physical memory is being used — the total amount, how much is used, how much is free, how much is shared, and how much is allocated to buffers (for reading from disk, for example).

+ The sixth line shows how the virtual memory (or swap space) is being used — the total amount of swap space, how much is used, how much is free, and how much is being cached.

The table that appears below the summary information (refer to Figure 1-2) lists information about the current processes, arranged in decreasing order by amount of CPU time used. Table 1-4 summarizes the meanings of the column headings in the table that top displays.

If the RSS field is drastically smaller than the SIZE field for a process, the process is using too little physical memory compared to what it needs. The result is a lot of swapping as the process runs. You can use the vmstat utility (which I discuss later in this section) to find out how much your system is swapping.

Table 1-4	**Meanings of Column Headings in top Utility's Output**
Heading	*Meaning*
PID	The process ID of the process
USER	Username under which the process is running
PRI	Priority of the process
NI	*Nice value* of the process — the value ranges from –20 (highest priority) to 19 (lowest priority) and the default is 0
SIZE	Total size of the process, in kilobytes
RSS	Total physical memory used by a task (typically shown in kilobytes, but an M suffix indicates megabytes)

(continued)

Book VI
Chapter 1

Performing
Basic System
Administration

Table 1-4 *(continued)*

Heading	Meaning
SHARE	Amount of shared memory used by process
STAT	State of the process (S for sleeping, D for uninterruptible sleep, R for running, Z for zombies — processes that should be dead, but are still running — or T for stopped; a trailing < means the process has negative nice value)
%CPU	Percentage of CPU time used since last screen update
%MEM	Percentage of physical memory used by the process
TIME	Total CPU time the process has used since it started
CPU	The processor where the process is running (this field is always zero if your system has only one processor)
COMMAND	Shortened form of the command that started the process

Using the GNOME system monitor

Like the text mode top utility, the GNOME System Monitor tool also enables you to view the system load in terms of the number of processes that are currently running, their memory usage, and the free disk space on your system. To run the tool, select Main Menu⇨System Tools⇨System Monitor. The tool starts and displays its output in a window, as shown in Figure 1-3.

The output is similar to the output you see when you type **top** in a text-mode console or a terminal window, except that with the System Monitor, you can decide which columns you want to see. Figure 1-3 shows the default view (the Process Listing tab) with the process name, user who is running the process, memory used, percentage of CPU time, and the process ID. The GNOME System Monitor keeps updating the display to reflect the current state of the system.

The GNOME System Monitor window has another tab labeled System Monitor. Click that tab to view a summary of CPU, memory, and disk usage. Figure 1-4 shows a typical view of the System Monitor tab.

The upper plot in Figure 1-4 shows the percentage of CPU usage with time. The next plot shows the history of memory use and swap space use. Disk-space use is summarized in a table at the bottom.

Using the uptime command

You can use the uptime command to get a summary of the system's state. Just type the command like this:

```
uptime
```

It displays output similar to the following:

```
15:03:21 up 32 days, 57 min, 3 users, load average: 0.13,
    0.23, 0.27
```

Figure 1-3: Use the GNOME System Monitor to view information about the current processes.

Figure 1-4: GNOME System Monitor displays summary CPU, memory, and disk usage information.

This output shows the current time, how long the system has been up, the number of users, and (finally) the three load averages — the average number of processes that were ready to run in the past 1, 5, and 15 minutes. Load averages greater than 1 imply that many processes are competing for CPU time simultaneously.

The load averages give you an indication of how busy the system is.

Using the vmstat utility

You can get summary information about the overall system usage with the vmstat utility. To view system usage information averaged over 5-second intervals, type the following command (the second argument indicates the total number of lines of output vmstat should display):

```
vmstat 5 8
```

You should see output similar to the following listing:

```
 procs                      memory      swap          io     system         cpu
 r  b  w   swpd   free   buff  cache   si   so    bi    bo   in    cs us sy id
 1  0  0      0  54652  10620 115648    0    0   123    25  123   212  3  1 96
 0  0  0      0  54644  10628 115648    0    0     0     7  108   239  2  0 98
 1  0  0      0  54628  10636 115656    0    0     2     3  149   359  5  1 94
 1  0  0      0  54244  10644 115956    0    0    60     4  173   547 13  3 84
 2  0  1      0  59748  10668 116280    0    0    65    27  154   652 18  2 80
 2  0  1      0  48536  10704 121488    0    0  1046    78  151   508 68  3 29
 0  1  0      0  46576  10740 123536    0    0   411   114  162   634 13  2 85
 2  0  0      0  45096  10752 123828    0    0    59    10  111   584 10  2 87
```

The first line of output shows the averages since the last reboot. After that, vmstat displays the 5-second average data seven more times, covering the next 35 seconds. The tabular output is grouped as six categories of information, indicated by the fields in the first line of output. The second line shows further details for each of the six major fields. You can interpret these fields using Table 1-5.

Table 1-5	Meaning of Fields in the vmstat Utility's Output
Field Name	*Description*
procs	Number of processes and their types: r = processes waiting to run; b = processes in uninterruptible sleep; w = processes swapped out, but ready to run
memory	Information about physical memory and swap-space usage (all numbers in kilobytes): swpd = virtual memory used; free = free physical memory; buff = memory used as buffers; cache = virtual memory that's cached
swap	Amount of swapping (the numbers are in kilobytes per second): si = amount of memory swapped in from disk; so = amount of memory swapped to disk

Field Name	Description
io	Information about input and output (the numbers are in blocks per second where the block size depends on the disk device): bi = rate of blocks sent to disk; bo = rate of blocks received from disk
system	Information about the system: in = number of interrupts per second (including clock interrupts); cs = number of context switches per second — how many times the kernel changed which process was running
cpu	Percentages of CPU time used: us = percentage of CPU time used by user processes; sy = percentage CPU time used by system processes; id = percentage of time CPU is idle

In the vmstat utility's output, high values in the si and so fields indicate too much swapping (*swapping* refers to the copying of information between physical memory and the virtual memory on the hard drive). High numbers in the bi and bo fields indicate too much disk activity.

Checking disk performance and disk usage

Red Hat Linux comes with the /sbin/hdparm program that you can use to control IDE or ATAPI hard drives that are common on most PCs. One feature of the hdparm program is that you can use the -t option to determine the rate at which data can be read from the disk into a buffer in memory. For example, here's the result of the command on my system:

```
/sbin/hdparm -t /dev/hda

/dev/hda:
 Timing buffered disk reads:  64 MB in  3.04 seconds = 21.05
   MB/sec
```

The command requires the IDE drive's device name (/dev/hda) as an argument. If you have an IDE hard drive, you can try this command to see how fast data can be read from your system's disk drive.

To display the space available in the currently mounted file systems, use the df command. If you want a more human-readable output from df, type the following command:

```
df -h
```

Here's a typical output from this command:

```
Filesystem           Size  Used Avail Use% Mounted on
/dev/hda5            7.1G  4.0G  2.8G  59% /
/dev/hda3             99M   14M   80M  15% /boot
none                 125M     0  125M   0% /dev/shm
```

As this example shows, the `-h` option causes the `df` command to show the sizes in gigabytes (G) and megabytes (M).

To check the disk space being used by a specific directory, use the `du` command — you can specify the `-h` option to view the output in kilobytes (k) and megabytes (M), as shown in the following example:

```
du -h /var/log
```

Here's a typical output of that command:

```
4.0K    /var/log/vbox
4.0K    /var/log/httpd
4.0K    /var/log/squid
4.0K    /var/log/samba
9.0M    /var/log/cups
480K    /var/log/gdm
4.0K    /var/log/news/OLD
8.0K    /var/log/news
11M     /var/log
```

The `du` command displays the disk space used by each directory and the last line shows the total disk space used by that directory. If you want to see only the total space used by a directory, use the `-s` option, like this:

```
du -sh /home
25M     /home
```

Viewing System Information via the /proc File System

Your Red Hat Linux system has a special file system called the `/proc` file system. You can find out many things about your system from this file system. In fact, you can even change kernel parameters through the `/proc` file system (just by writing to a file in that file system), thereby modifying the system's behavior.

The `/proc` file system isn't a real directory on the disk but a collection of data structures in memory, managed by the Linux kernel, that appears to you as a set of directories and files. The purpose of `/proc` (also called the *process file system*) is to give you access to information about the Linux kernel as well as to help you find out about all processes currently running on your system.

You can access the `/proc` file system just as you would access any other directory, but you have to know the meaning of various files to interpret the information. Typically, you can use the `cat` or `more` commands to view the contents of a file in `/proc`; the file's contents provide information about some aspect of the system.

As with any directory, start by looking at a detailed directory listing of
/proc. To do so, log in as root and type ls -l /proc in a terminal window.
In the output, the first set of directories (indicated by the letter d at the
beginning of the line) represents the processes that are currently running on
your system. Each directory that corresponds to a process has the process
ID (a number) as its name.

Notice also a very large file named /proc/kcore; that file represents the
entire physical memory of your system. Although /proc/kcore appears in
the listing as a huge file, no single physical file is occupying that much space
on your hard drive — so don't try to remove the file to reclaim disk space.

Several files and directories in /proc contain interesting information about
your Red Hat Linux PC. The /proc/cpuinfo file, for example, lists the key
characteristics of your system, such as processor type and floating-point
processor information. You can view the processor information by typing
cat /proc/cpuinfo. For example, here's what I get when I type **cat /proc/
cpuinfo** on my system:

```
processor       : 0
vendor_id       : GenuineIntel
cpu family      : 15
model           : 2
model name      : Mobile Intel(R) Celeron(R) CPU 1.50GHz
stepping        : 7
cpu MHz         : 1495.610
cache size      : 256 KB
fdiv_bug        : no
hlt_bug         : no
f00f_bug        : no
coma_bug        : no
fpu             : yes
fpu_exception   : yes
cpuid level     : 2
wp              : yes
flags           : fpu vme de pse tsc msr pae mce cx8 sep mtrr
    pge mca cmov pat pse36 clflush dts acpi mmx fxsr sse sse2
    ss ht tm
bogomips        : 2981.88
```

This output is from a 1.5 GHZ Celeron system. The listing shows many
interesting characteristics of the processor. Notice the line that starts with
fdiv_bug. Remember the infamous Pentium floating-point division bug?
The bug is in an instruction called fdiv (for *floating-point division*). Thus,
the fdiv_bug line indicates whether this particular Pentium has the bug
(fortunately, my PC's processor does not).

The last line in the /proc/cpuinfo file shows the BogoMips for the processor, as computed by the Linux kernel when it boots. BogoMips is something that Linux uses internally to time-delay loops.

Table 1-6 summarizes some of the files in the /proc file system that provide information about your Red Hat Linux system. You can view some of these files on your system to see what they contain, but note that not all files shown in Table 1-6 will be present on your system. The specific contents of the /proc file system depend on the kernel configuration and the driver modules that are loaded (which, in turn, depend on your PC's hardware configuration).

TIP

You can navigate the /proc file system just as you would work with any other directories and files in Red Hat Linux. Use the more or cat commands to view the contents of a file.

Table 1-6	Some Files and Directories in /proc
File Name	*Content*
/proc/apm	Information about advanced power management (APM)
/proc/bus	Directory with bus-specific information for each bus type such as PCI
/proc/cmdline	The command line used to start the Linux kernel (for example, ro root=LABEL=/)
/proc/cpuinfo	Information about the CPU (the microprocessor)
/proc/devices	Available block and character devices in your system
/proc/dma	Information about DMA (direct memory access) channels that are being used
/proc/driver/rtc	Information about the PC's real-time clock (RTC)
/proc/filesystems	List of supported file systems
/proc/ide	Directory containing information about IDE devices
/proc/interrupts	Information about interrupt request (IRQ) numbers and how they are being used
/proc/ioports	Information about input/output (I/O) port addresses and how they are being used
/proc/kcore	Image of the physical memory
/proc/kmsg	Kernel messages
/proc/ksyms	Kernel symbol table
/proc/loadavg	Load average (average number of processes waiting to run in the last 1, 5, and 15 minutes)
/proc/locks	Current kernel locks (used to ensure that multiple processes don't write to a file at the same time)

File Name	Content
/proc/meminfo	Information about physical memory and swap space usage
/proc/misc	Miscellaneous information
/proc/modules	List of loaded driver modules
/proc/mounts	List of mounted file systems
/proc/net	Directory with many subdirectories that contain information about networking
/proc/partitions	List of partitions known to the Linux kernel
/proc/pci	Information about PCI devices found on the system
/proc/scsi	Directory with information about SCSI devices found on the system (present only if you have a SCSI device)
/proc/stat	Overall statistics about the system
/proc/swaps	Information about the swap space and how much is used
/proc/sys	Directory with information about the system; you can change kernel parameters by writing to files in this directory (using this method to tune system performance requires expertise to do properly)
/proc/uptime	Information about how long the system has been up
/proc/version	Kernel version number

Scheduling Jobs in Red Hat Linux

As a system administrator, you may have to run some programs automatically at regular intervals or execute one or more commands at a specified time in the future. Your Red Hat Linux system includes the facilities to schedule jobs to run at any future date or time you want. You can also set up the system to perform a task periodically or just once. Here are some typical tasks you can perform by scheduling jobs on your Linux system:

+ Back up the files in the middle of the night.

+ Download large files in the early morning when the system isn't busy.

+ Send yourself messages as reminders of meetings.

+ Analyze system logs periodically and look for any abnormal activities.

You can set up these jobs by using the at command or the crontab facility of Red Hat Linux. In the next few sections, I introduce these job-scheduling features of Red Hat Linux.

Scheduling one-time jobs

If you want to run one or more commands at a later time, you can use the at command. The atd daemon — a program designed to process jobs submitted using at — runs your commands at the specified time and mails the output to you.

Before you try the at command, you need to know that the following configuration files control which users can schedule tasks using the at command:

✦ /etc/at.allow contains the names of the users who may submit jobs using the at command.

✦ /etc/at.deny contains the names of users not allowed to submit jobs using the at command.

If these files aren't present, or if there is an empty /etc/at.deny file, any user can submit jobs by using the at command. The default in Red Hat Linux is an empty /etc/at.deny file; with this default in place, anyone can use the at command. If you don't want some users to use at, simply list their usernames in the /etc/at.deny file.

To use at to schedule a one-time job for execution at a later time, follow these steps:

1. **Run the at command with the date or time when you want your commands executed.**

When you press Enter, the at> prompt appears, as follows:

```
at 21:30
at>
```

This is the simplest way to indicate the time when you want to execute one or more commands — simply specify the time in a 24-hour format. In this case, you want to execute the commands at 9:30 p.m. tonight (or tomorrow, if it's already past 9:30 p.m.). You can, however, specify the execution time in many different ways (see Table 1-7 for examples).

2. **At the at> prompt, type the commands you want to execute as if typing at the shell prompt; after each command, press Enter and continue with the next command. When you're finished entering the commands you want to execute, press Ctrl+D to indicate the end.**

Here is an example showing how to execute the ps command at a future time:

```
at> ps
at> <EOT>
job 1 at 2003-07-18 21:30
```

After you press Ctrl+D, the at command responds with a job number and the date and time when the job will execute.

Table 1-7	Formats for the Time of Execution with the at Command
Command	*When the Job Will Run*
at now	Immediately
at now + 15 minutes	15 minutes from the current time
at now + 4 hours	4 hours from the current time
at now + 7 days	7 days from the current time
at noon	At noontime today (or tomorrow, if already past noon)
at now next hour	Exactly 60 minutes from now
at now next day	At the same time tomorrow
at 17:00 tomorrow	At 5:00 p.m. tomorrow
at 4:45pm	At 4:45 p.m. today (or tomorrow, if it's already past 4:45 p.m.)
at 3:00 Aug 16, 2003	At 3:00 a.m. on August 16, 2003

After you enter one or more jobs, you can view the current list of scheduled jobs with the atq command:

```
atq
```

The output looks similar to the following:

```
4       2003-08-16 03:00 a root
5       2003-10-26 21:57 a root
6       2003-10-26 16:45 a root
```

The first field on each line shows the job number — the same number that the at command displays when you submit the job. The next field shows the year, month, day, and time of execution. The last field shows the jobs pending in the queue named a.

If you want to cancel a job, use the atrm command to remove that job from the queue. When removing a job with the atrm command, refer to the job by its number, as follows:

```
atrm 4
```

This deletes job 4 scheduled for 3:00 a.m. August 16, 2003.

When a job executes, the output is mailed to you. Type **mail** at a terminal window to read your mail and to view the output from your jobs.

Scheduling recurring jobs

Although at is good for running commands at a specific time, it's not useful for running a program automatically at repeated intervals. You have to use `crontab` to schedule such recurring jobs. You have to do this, for example, if you want to back up your files to tape at midnight every day.

You schedule recurring jobs by placing job information in a file with a specific format and submitting this file with the `crontab` command. The `cron` daemon — `crond` — checks the job information every minute and executes the recurring jobs at the specified times. Because the `cron` daemon processes recurring jobs, such jobs are also referred to as *cron jobs*.

Any output from a `cron` job is mailed to the user who submits the job. (In the submitted job-information file, you can specify a different recipient for the mailed output.)

Two configuration files control who can schedule `cron` jobs using `crontab`:

✦ `/etc/cron.allow` contains the names of the users who may submit jobs using the `crontab` command.

✦ `/etc/cron.deny` contains the names of users not allowed to submit jobs using the `crontab` command.

If the `/etc/cron.allow` file exists, only users listed in this file can schedule `cron` jobs. If only the `/etc/cron.deny` file exists, users listed in this file cannot schedule `cron` jobs. If neither file exists, the default Red Hat Linux setup enables any user to submit `cron` jobs.

To submit a `cron` job, follow these steps:

1. **Prepare a shell script (or an executable program in any programming language) that can perform the recurring task you want to perform.**

You can skip this step if you want to execute an existing program periodically.

2. **Prepare a text file with information about the times when you want the shell script or program (from Step 1) to execute, and then submit this file by using** `crontab`.

You can submit several recurring jobs with a single file. Each line with timing information about a job has a standard format with six fields — the first five specify when the job runs, and the sixth and subsequent fields constitute the actual command that runs. For example, here is a line that executes the `myjob` shell script in a user's home directory at five minutes past midnight each day:

```
5 0 * * * $HOME/myjob
```

Table 1-8 shows the meaning of the first five fields. Note that an asterisk (*) means all possible values for that field. Also, an entry in any of the first five fields can be a single number, a comma-separated list of numbers, a pair of numbers separated by a dash (indicating a range of numbers), or an asterisk.

3. **Suppose the text file** `jobinfo` **(in the current directory) contains the job information. Submit this information to** `crontab` **with the following command:**

```
crontab jobinfo
```

That's it! You should be set with the `cron` job. From now on, the `cron` job should run at regular intervals (as specified in the job information file), and you should receive mail messages with the output from the job.

To verify that the job is indeed scheduled, type the following command:

```
crontab -l
```

The output of the `crontab -l` command shows the `cron` jobs currently installed in your name. To remove your `cron` jobs, type **crontab -r**.

**Book VI
Chapter 1**

**Performing
Basic System
Administration**

Table 1-8	Format for the Time of Execution in crontab Files	
Field Number	*Meaning of Field*	*Acceptable Range of Values**
1	Minute	0–59
2	Hour of the day	0–23
3	Day of the month	0–31
4	Month	1–12 (1 means January, 2 means February, and so on) or the names of months using the first three letters (Jan, Feb, Mar, Apr, May, Jun, Jul, Aug, Sep, Oct, Nov, Dec)
5	Day of the week	0–6 (0 means Sunday, 1 means Monday, and so on) or three-letter abbreviations of weekdays (Sun, Mon, Tue, Wed, Thu, Fri, Sat)

* An asterisk in a field means all possible values for that field. For example, if an asterisk is in the third field, the job is executed every day.

If you log in as `root`, you can also set up, examine, and remove `cron` jobs for any user. To set up `cron` jobs for a user, use this command:

```
crontab -u username filename
```

Here, `username` is the user for whom you install the `cron` jobs, and `filename` is the file that contains information about the jobs.

Use the following form of `crontab` command to view the `cron` jobs for a user:

```
crontab -u username -l
```

To remove a user's `cron` jobs, use the following command:

```
crontab -u username -r
```

Note that the `cron` daemon also executes the cron jobs listed in the system-wide `cron`-job file `/etc/crontab`. Here's the default `/etc/crontab` file in Red Hat Linux (type **cat /etc/crontab** to view the file):

```
SHELL=/bin/bash
PATH=/sbin:/bin:/usr/sbin:/usr/bin
MAILTO=root
HOME=/

# run-parts
01 * * * * root run-parts /etc/cron.hourly
02 4 * * * root run-parts /etc/cron.daily
22 4 * * 0 root run-parts /etc/cron.weekly
42 4 1 * * root run-parts /etc/cron.monthly
```

The first four lines set up several environment variables for the jobs listed in this file. The `MAILTO` environment variable specifies the user who receives the mail message with the output from the `cron` jobs in this file.

The line that begins with a # is a comment line. The four lines following the `run-parts` comment execute the `run-parts` shell script (located in the `/usr/bin` directory) at various times with the name of a specific directory as argument. Each of the arguments to `run-parts` — `/etc/cron.hourly`, `/etc/cron.daily`, `/etc/cron.weekly`, and `/etc/cron.monthly` — are directories. Essentially, `run-parts` executes all scripts located in the directory that you provide as an argument.

Table 1-9 lists the directories where these scripts are located and when they are executed. You have to look at the scripts in these directories to know what gets executed at these periodic intervals.

Table 1-9	Script Directories for cron Jobs
Directory Name	*Contents*
`/etc/cron.hourly`	Scripts executed every hour
`/etc/cron.daily`	Scripts executed each day at 4:02 a.m.
`/etc/cron.weekly`	Scripts executed weekly on Sunday at 4:22 a.m.
`/etc/cron.monthly`	Scripts to be executed at 4:42 a.m. on the first day of each month

Chapter 2: Managing Users

Red Hat Linux is a multiuser system, so it has many user accounts. Even if you are the only user on your system, many servers require a unique username and group name. Take, for example, the Apache Web server. It runs under the username apache. There are a whole host of system users that are not for people, but just for running specific programs.

Also, users can belong to one or more groups. Typically, each username has a corresponding private group name. By default, each user belongs to that corresponding private group. However, you can define other groups for the purpose of providing access to specific files and directories based on group membership.

User and group ownerships of files are a way to make sure that only the right people (or the right process) can access the right files and directories. Managing the user and group accounts is a typical system administration job. It's not that hard to do this part of the job, given the tools that come with Red Hat Linux. I show you how.

Adding User Accounts

You get the chance to add user accounts when you boot your system for the first time after installing Red Hat Linux. The root account is the only one that you must set up during installation. If you didn't add other user accounts during the initial boot, you can do so later on, using the Red Hat User Manager or the useradd command to add new users on your system.

Creating other user accounts besides root is a good idea. Even if you're the only user of the system, logging in as a less-privileged user is good practice because that way you can't damage any important system files inadvertently. If necessary, you can type the su - command to log in as root and then perform any system administration tasks.

Using Red Hat User Manager to add user accounts

You can use the Red Hat User Manager to add user accounts. To start the Red Hat User Manager, log in as root at the graphical login screen and then choose Main Menu⇨System Settings⇨Users and Groups from the GNOME Panel. If you're not logged in as root, the Red Hat User Manager prompts you for the root password. If prompted, enter the password and click OK. Then the Red Hat User Manager window appears.

The window shows two tabs: Users and Groups (as in Figure 2-1). The Users tab displays the current list of users from the /etc/passwd file. The Groups tab lists the names of groups from the /etc/group. Initially, the Red Hat User Manager filters out any system users and groups. However, you can turn off the filter by choosing Preferences ⇨Filter system users and groups, so that the check mark next to that menu item disappears. Figure 2-1 shows the Red Hat User Manager window with a listing of all user accounts, including the system ones.

Figure 2-1:
You can manage user accounts and groups from the Red Hat User Manager window.

User Name	User ID	Primary Group	Full Name	Login Shell	Home Directory
root	0	root	root	/bin/bash	/root
bin	1	bin	bin	/sbin/nologin	/bin
daemon	2	daemon	daemon	/sbin/nologin	/sbin
adm	3	adm	adm	/sbin/nologin	/var/adm
lp	4	lp	lp	/sbin/nologin	/var/spool/lpd
sync	5	root	sync	/bin/sync	/sbin
shutdown	6	root	shutdown	/sbin/shutdown	/sbin
halt	7	root	halt	/sbin/halt	/sbin
mail	8	mail	mail	/sbin/nologin	/var/spool/mail
news	9	news	news	/bin/bash	/etc/news
uucp	10	uucp	uucp	/sbin/nologin	/var/spool/uucp
operator	11	root	operator	/sbin/nologin	/root
games	12	users	games	/sbin/nologin	/usr/games
gopher	13	gopher	gopher	/sbin/nologin	/var/gopher
ftp	14	ftp	FTP User	/sbin/nologin	/var/ftp
squid	23	squid		/sbin/nologin	/var/spool/squid
named	25	named	Named	/sbin/nologin	/var/named

You can add new users and groups or edit existing users and groups from the Red Hat User Manager window.

To edit the information for an existing user, follow these steps:

1. **Click the username in the list in the Users tab and then click the Properties button on the toolbar.**

That user's information appears in a User Properties dialog box (Figure 2-2).

Figure 2-2:
Edit an existing user's information in this dialog box.

Book VI
Chapter 2

Managing Users

2. **Edit the information and click OK to make the changes.**

To add a new user, follow these steps:

1. **Click the Add User button on the toolbar (refer to Figure 2-1).**

This action opens the Create New User dialog box (shown in Figure 2-3).

Figure 2-3:
Create a new user account by filling in the information in this dialog box.

2. **Fill in the requested information.**

   In particular, you must enter the username and the password. After filling in all the fields, click the OK button. The new user should now appear in the list on the Users tab in the Red Hat User Manager window.

Notice the Create a Private Group for the User check box. It's checked by default, and that means each new user is in a separate private user group. Sometimes you want a user to be in a specific group, however, so that the user can access the files owned by that group. Adding a user to another group is easy. For example, suppose I want to add the username naba to the group called wheel. I can do this simply by typing the following command in a terminal window:

```
usermod -G wheel naba
```

To remove a user account, click the username in the list on the Users tab that displays all user accounts (refer to Figure 2-1). Then click the Delete button on the toolbar.

Using commands to manage user accounts

If you're working from a text console, you can create a new user account by using the useradd command. Follow these steps to add an account for a new user:

1. **Log in as root.**

   If you're not already logged in as root, type su - to become root.

2. **Type the following useradd command with the -c option to create the account:**

   ```
   /usr/sbin/useradd -c "Ashley Barkakati" ashley
   ```

3. **Set Ashley's password by using the passwd command, as follows:**

   ```
   passwd ashley
   ```

   You're prompted for the password twice. If you type a password that someone can easily guess, the passwd program rejects it.

The useradd command consults the following configuration files to obtain default information about various parameters for the new user account:

✦ /etc/default/useradd — Specifies the default shell (/bin/bash) and the default home directory location (/home).

✦ /etc/login.defs — Provides systemwide defaults for automatic group and user IDs, as well as password-expiration parameters.

Examine these files with the `cat` or `more` commands to see what they contain.

You can delete a user account by using the `userdel` command. Simply type **/usr/sbin/userdel *username*** at the command prompt to delete a user's account. To wipe out that user's home directory as well, type **/usr/sbin/ userdel -r *username***.

To modify any information in a user account, use the `usermod` command. For example, if I want my username, `naba`, to have `root` as the primary group, I would type the following:

```
usermod -g root naba
```

To find out more about the `useradd`, `userdel`, and `usermod` commands, type **man useradd**, **man userdel**, or **man usermod** in a terminal window.

Understanding the /etc/passwd File

The `/etc/passwd` file is a list of all user accounts. It's a text file and any user can read it — no special privileges needed. Each line in `/etc/passwd` has seven fields, separated by colons (`:`).

Here is a typical entry from the `/etc/passwd` file:

```
naba:x:500:10:Naba Barkakati:/home/naba:/bin/bash
```

Figure 2-4 uses this typical entry to explain the meaning of the seven fields.

Figure 2-4:
This typical /etc/passwd entry illustrates the meaning of the various fields.

As the example shows, the format of each line in `/etc/passwd` looks like this:

```
username:password:UID:GID:GECOS:homedir:shell
```

Table 2-1 explains the meaning of the seven fields in each `/etc/passwd` entry.

Table 2-1	Meaning of the Fields in /etc/passwd File
This Field	*Contains*
username	An alphanumeric username, usually eight characters long and unique (Red Hat Linux allows usernames to be longer than eight characters, but some other operating systems do not)
password	When present, a 13-character encrypted password (an empty field means that no password is required to access the account; an x means the password is stored in the /etc/shadow file, which is more secure)
UID	A unique number that serves as the user identifier (root has a UID of 0 and usually the UIDs between 1 to 100 are reserved for non-human users such as servers; it's best to keep the UID less than 32,767)
GID	The default group ID of the group to which the user belongs (GID 0 is for group root; other groups are defined in /etc/group and users can be and usually are in more than one group at a time)
GECOS	Optional personal information about the user (the finger command uses this field and GECOS stands for General Electric Comprehensive Operating System, a long-forgotten operating system that's immortalized by the name of this field in /etc/passwd)
homedir	The name of the user's home directory
shell	The command interpreter (shell) such as Bash (/bin/bash) that's executed when this user logs in

Managing Groups

A group is a something to which users belong. A group has a name and an identification number (ID). After a group is defined, users can belong to one or more of these groups.

You can find all the existing groups listed in /etc/group. For example, here is the line that defines the group named wheel:

```
wheel:x:10:root,naba
```

As this example shows, each line in /etc/group has the following format, with four fields separated by colons:

groupname:password:GID:membership

Table 2-2 explains the meaning of the four fields in a group definition.

Table 2-2	Meaning of Fields in /etc/group File
Field Name	*Meaning*
groupname	The name of the group (for example, wheel)
password	The group password (an x means the password is stored in the /etc/shadow- file)
GID	The numerical group ID (for example, 10)
membership	A comma-separated list of usernames that belong to this group (for example, root,naba)

If you want to create a new group, you can simply click the Add Group button in the Red Hat User Manager (refer to Figure 2-1). An even quicker way is to use the groupadd command. For example, to add a new group called class with an automatically selected group ID, just type the following command in a terminal window (you have to be logged in as root):

```
groupadd class
```

Then you can add users to this group with the usermod command. For example, to add the users naba and ashley to the group named class, type the following commands:

```
usermod -G class naba
usermod -G class ashley
```

That's it. Now check /etc/group to find that it contains the following definition of class:

```
class:x:502:naba,ashley
```

It's that simple!

If you want to remove a group, use the `groupdel` command. For example, to remove group named `class`, type

```
groupdel class
```

Exploring the User Environment

When you log in as a user, you get a set of environment variables that control many aspects of what you see and do on your Red Hat Linux system. If you want to see your current environment, go ahead and type the following command in a terminal window:

```
env
```

(By the way, the `printenv` command also displays the environment, but `env` is shorter.)

The `env` command should print a long list of lines. That whole collection of lines is the current environment, and each line defines an environment variable. For example, here is a typical line displayed by the `env` command:

```
HOSTNAME=localhost.localdomain
```

This line defines the environment variable `HOSTNAME`, and it's defined as `localhost.localdomain`.

An *environment variable* is nothing more than a name associated with a string. For example, the environment variable named `PATH` is typically defined as follows:

```
PATH=/usr/local/bin:/bin:/usr/bin:/usr/X11R6/bin
```

The string to the right of the equal sign is the value of the `PATH` environment variable. By convention, the `PATH` environment variable is a sequence of directory names, each name separated from the preceding one by a colon (`:`).

Each environment variable has a specific purpose. For example, when the shell has to search for a file, it simply searches the directories listed in the `PATH` environment variable. The shell searches the directories in `PATH` in the order of their appearance. Therefore, if two programs have the same name, the shell executes the one it finds first.

In a fashion similar to the shell's use of the `PATH` environment variable, an editor such as `vi` uses the value of the `TERM` environment variable to figure out how to display the file you are editing with `vi`. To see the current setting of `TERM`, type the following command at the shell prompt:

```
echo $TERM
```

If you type this command in a terminal window, the output is as follows:

```
xterm
```

To define an environment variable in Bash, use the following syntax:

```
export NAME=Value
```

Here, `NAME` denotes the name of the environment variable, and `Value` is the string representing its value. Therefore, you set `TERM` to the value `xterm` by using the following command:

```
export TERM=xterm
```

After you define an environment variable, you can change its value by simply specifying the new value with the syntax `NAME=new-value`. For example, to change the definition of `TERM` to `vt100`, type **TERM=vt100** at the shell prompt.

With an environment variable such as `PATH`, you typically want to append a new directory name to the existing definition, rather than define the `PATH` from scratch. The following example shows how to accomplish this task:

```
export PATH="$PATH:/usr/games"
```

This command appends the string `:/usr/games` to the current definition of the `PATH` environment variable. The net effect is to add `/usr/games` to the list of directories in `PATH`.

Note that you also can write this `export` command as follows:

```
export PATH=${PATH}:/usr/games
```

After you type that command, you can access programs in the `/usr/games` directory such as `fortune`, a program that prints a terse and often witty (and sometimes confusing) saying. If you're curious, go ahead and type the following command:

```
fortune
```

What `fortune` prints is random, but it can be amusing. The result should be a terse, witty, and/or confusing saying.

PATH and TERM are only two of a handful of common environment variables. Table 2-3 lists some of the environment variables for a typical Red Hat Linux user.

Table 2-3	Typical Environment Variables in Red Hat Linux
Environment Variable	*Contents*
DISPLAY	The name of the display on which the X Window System displays output (typically set to :0.0)
HOME	Your home directory
HOSTNAME	The host name of your system
LOGNAME	Your login name
MAIL	The location of your mail directory
PATH	The list of directories in which the shell looks for programs
SHELL	Your shell (SHELL=/bin/bash for Bash)
TERM	The type of terminal

Changing User and Group Ownership of Files

In Red Hat Linux, each file or directory has two owners — a user and a group. The user and group ownerships can be used to control who can access a file or directory.

To view the owner of a file or directory, use the ls -l command to see the detailed listing of a directory. For example, here's a typical file's information:

```
-rw-rw-r-- 1 naba    naba    40909 07-14 20:37 composer.txt
```

In this example, the first set of characters shows the file's permission setting — who can read, write, or execute the file. The third and fourth fields (in this sample, naba naba) indicate the user and group owner of the file. Each user has a private group that has the same name as the username. So most files' user and group ownership appear to show the username twice.

As a system administrator, you may decide to change the group ownership of a file to a common group. For example, suppose you want to change the group ownership of the composer.txt file to the class group. To do that, log in as root and type the following command:

```
chgrp class composer.txt
```

This `chgrp` command changes the group ownership of `composer.txt` to `class`. After I tried this, I typed **ls -l** again to verify the ownership, and here's what I got:

```
-rw-rw-r--  1 naba    class   40909 07-14 20:37 composer.txt
```

You can use the `chown` command to change the user owner. The command has the following format:

```
chown username filename
```

For example, to change the user ownership of a file named `sample.jpg` to `naba`, type:

```
chown naba sample.jpg
```

In fact, `chown` can change both the user and group owner at the same time. For example, to change the user owner to `naba` and the group owner to `class`, type:

```
chown naba.class composer.txt
```

In other words, you simply append the group name to the username with a period in between, and use that as the name of the owner.

Chapter 3: Managing the File System

The *file system* refers to the organization of files and directories. As a system administrator, you have to perform certain operations to manage the file system. For example, you have to learn how to *mount* — add a file system on a storage medium by attaching it to the overall Red Hat Linux file system. You also have to back up important data and learn how to restore files from a backup. Other file system operations include sharing files with the *Network File System* (NFS) and accessing MS-DOS files. In this chapter, I show you how to perform all the file-system-management tasks.

Learning the Red Hat Linux File System

The files and directories in your PC store information in an organized manner just like paper filing systems. When you store information on paper, you typically put several pages in a folder and then save the folder in a file cabinet. If you have many folders, you probably have some sort of filing system. For example, you may label each folder's tab and then arrange them alphabetically in the file cabinet. You probably have several file cabinets, each with lots of drawers, which, in turn, contain folders full of pages.

Operating systems such as Red Hat Linux organize information in your computer in a manner similar to your paper filing system. Red Hat Linux uses a file system to organize all information in your computer. Of course, unlike a file cabinet, the storage medium isn't a metal cabinet and paper. Instead, Red Hat Linux stores information on devices such as hard drives, floppy-disk drives, and CD-ROM drives.

To draw an analogy between your computer's file system and a paper filing system, think of a disk drive as the file cabinet. The drawers in the file cabinet correspond to the directories in the file system. The folders in each drawer are also directories — because a directory in a computer file system can contain other directories. You can think of files as the pages inside the folder — and that's where the actual information is stored. Figure 3-1 illustrates the analogy between a file cabinet and the Red Hat Linux file system.

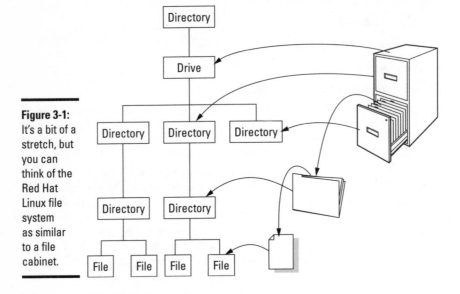

Figure 3-1: It's a bit of a stretch, but you can think of the Red Hat Linux file system as similar to a file cabinet.

The Red Hat Linux file system has a *hierarchical* structure — directories can contain other directories, which in turn contain individual files.

Everything in your Red Hat Linux system is organized in files and directories in the file system. To access and use documents and programs on your system, you have to be familiar with the file system.

Understanding the file system hierarchy

The Red Hat Linux file system is organized like a tree, with a *root directory* from which all other directories branch out. When you write a complete pathname, the root directory is represented by a single slash (/). Then there is a hierarchy of files and directories. Parts of the file system can be in different physical drives or different hard-drive partitions.

Red Hat Linux uses a standard directory hierarchy. Figure 3-2 shows the standard parts of the Red Hat Linux file system. Of course, you can create new directories anywhere in this structure.

Figure 3-2:
The Red Hat
Linux file
system
uses this
standard
directory
hierarchy.

Write the name of any file or directory by concatenating the names of directories that identify where that file or directory is and using the forward slash (/) as a separator. For example, in Figure 3-2 the usr directory at the top level is written as /usr because the root directory (/) contains usr. On the other hand, the X11R6 directory is inside the usr directory, which is inside the root directory (/). Therefore, the X11R6 directory is uniquely identified by the name /usr/X11R6. This type of full name is called *pathname* because the name identifies the path you take from the root directory to reach a file. Thus /usr/X11R6 is a pathname.

Each of the standard directories in the Red Hat Linux file system has a specific purpose. Table 3-1 summarizes these directories.

Table 3-1	Standard Directories in the Red Hat Linux File System
Directory	*Used to Store*
/bin	Executable files for user commands (for use by all users)
/boot	Files needed by the boot loader to load the Linux kernel
/dev	Device files
/etc	Host-specific system configuration files
/home	User home directories
/lib	Shared libraries and kernel modules
/mnt	Mount point for a temporarily mounted file system
/opt	Add-on application software packages
/root	Home directory for the root user
/sbin	Utilities for system administration
/tmp	Temporary files
The /usr Hierarchy	
/usr/X11R6	X Window System, Version 11 Release 6
/usr/bin	Most user commands

(continued)

Table 3-1 *(continued)*

Directory	Used to Store
/usr/include	Directory for standard include files used in developing Linux applications
/usr/lib	Libraries used by software packages and for programming
/usr/libexec	Libraries for applications
/usr/local	Any local software
/usr/sbin	Nonessential system administrator utilities
/usr/share	Shared data that does not depend on the system architecture (whether the system is a Intel PC or a Sun SPARC workstation)
/usr/src	Source code
The /var Hierarchy	
/var/cache	Cached data for applications
/var/lib	Information relating to the current state of applications
/var/lock	Lock files to ensure that a resource is used by one application only
/var/log	Log files organized into subdirectories
/var/mail	User mailbox files
/var/opt	Variable data for packages stored in /opt directory
/var/run	Data describing the system since it was booted
/var/spool	Data that's waiting for some kind of processing
/var/tmp	Temporary files preserved between system reboots
/var/yp	Network Information Service (NIS) database files

Mounting a device on the file system

The storage devices that you use in Red Hat Linux contain Linux file systems. Each device has its own local file system consisting of a hierarchy of directories. Before you can access the files on a device, you have to attach the device's directory hierarchy to the tree that represents the overall Red Hat Linux file system.

Mounting is the operation you perform to cause the file system on a physical storage device (a hard-drive partition or a CD-ROM) to appear as part of the Linux file system. Figure 3-3 illustrates the concept of mounting.

Figure 3-3 shows each device with a name that begins with /dev. For example, /dev/cdrom is the CD-ROM drive and /dev/fd0 is the floppy drive. These physical devices are mounted at specific mount points on the Red Hat Linux file system. For example, the CD-ROM drive, /dev/cdrom, is mounted on /mnt/cdrom in the file system. After mounting the CD-ROM in this way, the Red Hat directory on the CD-ROM appears as /mnt/cdrom/RedHat in the Red Hat Linux file system.

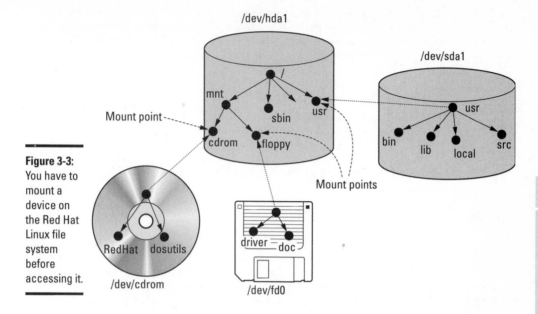

Managing the
File System

Figure 3-3:
You have to
mount a
device on
the Red Hat
Linux file
system
before
accessing it.

You can use the mount command to manually mount a device on the Red
Hat Linux file system at a specified directory. That directory is the *mount
point*. For example, to mount the CD-ROM drive at the /mnt/cdrom directory, you would type the following command (after logging in as root):

```
mount /dev/cdrom /mnt/cdrom
```

The mount command reports an error if the CD-ROM device is mounted
already or if no CD-ROM is in the drive. Otherwise, the mount operation succeeds, and you can access the CD-ROM's contents through the /mnt/cdrom
directory.

You can use any directory as the mount point. If you mount a device on a
nonempty directory, however, you cannot access the files in that directory
until you unmount the device by using the umount command. You should
always, therefore, use an empty directory as the mount point.

Red Hat Linux comes with the /mnt/cdrom directory for mounting CD-ROMs
and /mnt/floppy for mounting floppy drives.

To unmount a device when you no longer need it, use the umount command.
For example, to unmount the CD-ROM device, type

```
umount /dev/cdrom
```

The umount command succeeds as long as no one is using the CD-ROM. If you get an error when trying to unmount the CD-ROM, check to see whether the current working directory is on the CD-ROM. If you're currently working in one of the CD-ROM's directories, that also qualifies as a use of the CD-ROM.

Examining the /etc/fstab file

The mount command has the following general format:

```
mount device-name mount-point
```

However, you can mount the CD-ROM by typing one of the following commands:

```
mount /dev/cdrom
mount /mnt/cdrom
```

You can mount by specifying only the CD-ROM device name or the mount-point name because of what's in a file named /etc/fstab. There is a line in the /etc/fstab file for the /mnt/cdrom mount point. That entry specifies the CD-ROM device name and the file-system type. That's why you can mount the CD-ROM with a shorter mount command.

The /etc/fstab file is a *configuration file* — a text file containing information that the mount and umount commands use. Each line in the /etc/fstab file provides information about a device and its mount point in the Red Hat Linux file system. Essentially, the /etc/fstab file associates various mount points within the file system with specific devices, which enables the mount command to work from the command line with only the mount point or the device as argument.

Here is a /etc/fstab file from a typical Red Hat Linux system:

```
LABEL=/          /              ext3           defaults                        1 1
LABEL=/boot      /boot          ext3           defaults                        1 2
none             /dev/pts       devpts         gid=5,mode=620                  0 0
none             /proc          proc           defaults                        0 0
none             /dev/shm       tmpfs          defaults                        0 0
/dev/hda6        swap           swap           defaults                        0 0
/dev/cdrom       /mnt/cdrom     udf,iso9660    noauto,owner,kudzu,ro 0 0
/dev/fd0         /mnt/floppy     auto           noauto,owner,kudzu    0 0
```

The first field on each line shows a device name, such as a hard-drive partition (or it identifies a partition by a LABEL keyword). The second field is the mount point, and the third field indicates the type of file system on the device. You can ignore the last three fields for now.

This `/etc/fstab` file shows that the `/dev/hda6` device (the second logical partition on the first IDE hard drive) functions as a swap device for virtual memory, which is why both the mount point and the file-system type are set to `swap`.

The Linux operating system uses the contents of the `/etc/fstab` file to mount various file systems automatically. During Red Hat Linux startup, the `init` process executes a shell script that runs the `mount -a` command. That command reads the `/etc/fstab` file and mounts all listed file systems (except those with the `noauto` option). The third field on each line of `/etc/fstab` specifies the type of file system on that device, and the fourth field shows a comma-separated list of options that the `mount` command uses when mounting that device on the file system. Typically, you find the `defaults` option in this field. The `defaults` option implies — among other things — that the device mounts at boot time; that only the `root` user can mount the device; and that the device mounts for both reading and writing. If the options include `noauto`, then the device doesn't mount automatically as the system boots.

The `kudzu` option in the fourth field of `/etc/fstab` entries indicates that these lines were added to the `fstab` file by the `kudzu` hardware-detection utility — `kudzu` runs the `updfstab` command to add an entry in the `/etc/fstab` file for each removable drive it detects. You typically find that the entries for CD-ROM (`/dev/cdrom`) and floppy drive (`dev/fd0`) have the `kudzu` option in the fourth field. On a PC with an IDE Zip drive, for instance, the `/etc/fstab` file has another entry set up by `kudzu` that associates the `/mnt/zip` mount point with the Zip drive device (`/dev/hdd4`), as follows:

```
/dev/hdd4   /mnt/zip    auto noauto,owner,kudzu   0  0
```

Sharing Files with NFS

Sharing files through the Network File System (NFS) is simple and involves two basic steps:

✦ On the NFS server, export one or more directories by listing them in the `/etc/exports` file and by running the `/usr/sbin/exportfs` command. In addition, you must run the NFS server (you can do so by logging in as `root` and typing **service nfs start**).

✦ On each client system, use the `mount` command to mount the directories the server has exported.

The only problem in using NFS is that each client system must support it. Most PCs don't come with NFS — that means you have to buy NFS software separately if you want to share files by using NFS. If, however, all systems on your LAN run Linux (or other variants of UNIX with built-in NFS support), then it makes sense to use NFS.

Note that NFS has security vulnerabilities. Therefore, you should not set up NFS on systems directly connected to the Internet.

In the upcoming section, I walk you through an NFS setup, using an example of two Linux PCs on a LAN.

Exporting a file system with NFS

Start with the server system that *exports* — makes available to the client systems — the contents of a directory. On the server, you must run the NFS service and also designate one or more file systems that are to be exported, or made available to the client systems.

To export a file system, you have to add an appropriate entry to the /etc/exports file. For example, suppose you want to export the /home directory and you want to enable the host named LNBP75 to mount this file system for read-and-write operations (you can use a host's IP address in place of the host name). You can do so by adding the following entry to the /etc/exports file:

```
/home LNBP75(rw)
```

After adding the entry in the /etc/exports file, manually export the file system by typing **/usr/sbin/exportfs -a** in a terminal window. This command exports all file systems defined in the /etc/exports file.

Now start the NFS server — log in as root and type the following command in a terminal window:

```
service nfs start
```

To restart the NFS service, type **service nfs restart**.

When the NFS service is up, the server side of NFS is ready. Now you can try to mount the exported file system from a client system and access the exported file system.

If you ever make any changes to the exported file systems listed in the /etc/exports file, remember to restart the NFS service. To do so, type **service nfs restart** in a terminal window.

Mounting an NFS file system

To access an exported NFS file system on a client system, you have to mount that file system on a mount point — which is, in practical terms, nothing more than a local directory. For example, suppose you want to access the /home directory exported from the server named LNBP200 at the local directory /mnt/lnbp200 on the client system. To do so, follow these steps:

1. **Log in as** root, **and create the directory with the following command:**

```
mkdir /mnt/lnbp200
```

2. **Type the following command to perform the** mount **operation:**

```
mount lnbp200:/home/public /mnt/lnbp200
```

3. **Change the directory to /mnt/lnbp200 with the command** cd **/mnt/lnbp200.**

Now you can view and access exported files from this directory.

To confirm that the NFS file system is indeed mounted, log in as root on the client system and type **mount** in a terminal window. You should see a line similar to the following one about the NFS file system:

```
lnbp200:/home/public on /mnt/lnbp200 type nfs (rw,addr=192.168.1.200)
```

Book VI
Chapter 3

Managing the
File System

Backing Up and Restoring Files

Backing up and restoring files is a crucial system administration task. If something happens to your system's hard drive, you have to rely on the backups to recover important files. Here I present some backup strategies, describe several backup media, and explain how to back up and restore files by using the *tape archiver* (tar) program that comes with Red Hat Linux. Also, you find out how to perform incremental and automatic backups on tapes.

If you have a CD burner, you can also back up files by recording them on a CD-R. Consult Book II, Chapter 5 for information on how to burn a data CD.

Selecting a backup strategy and media

Your Red Hat Linux system's hard drive contains everything needed to keep the system running — as well as other files (such as documents and databases) that keep your business running. You have to back up these files so you can recover quickly and bring the system back to normal in case the hard drive crashes. Typically, you have to follow a strict regimen of regular backups because you can never tell when the hard drive may fail or the file system may get corrupted. To implement such a regimen, first decide which files you want to back up, how often, and what backup storage media to use. This process is what I mean by selecting a backup strategy and backup media.

Your choice of backup strategy and backup media depends on your assessment of the risk of business disruption due to hard-drive failure. Depending on how you use your Red Hat Linux system, a disk failure may or may not have much impact on you.

For example, if you use your Red Hat Linux system as a learning tool (to learn about Linux or programming), all you may need are backup copies of some system files required to configure Linux. In this case, your backup strategy can be to save important system-configuration files on one or more floppies every time you change any system configuration.

On the other hand, if you use your Red Hat Linux system as an office server that provides shared file storage for many users, the risk of business disruption due to disk failure is much higher. In this case, you have to back up all the files *every week* and back up any new or changed files *every day*. You should perform these backups in an automated manner (this is where you can use the job-scheduling features that I describe in Chapter 1 of this minibook). Also, you probably need a backup storage medium that can store large amounts (multiple gigabytes) of data on a single tape. In other words, for high-risk situations, your backup strategy is more elaborate and requires additional equipment (such as a tape drive).

Your choice of backup media depends on the amount of data you have to back up. For a small amount of data (such as system-configuration files), you can use floppy disks as the backup media. If your PC has a Zip drive, you can use Zip disks as backup media; these are good for backing up a single-user directory. To back up entire servers, use a tape drive, typically a 4mm or 8mm tape drive that connects to a SCSI controller. Such tape drives can store several gigabytes of data per tape, and you can use them to back up an entire file system on a single tape.

When backing up files to these media, you have to refer to the backup device by name. Table 3-2 lists device names for some common backup devices.

Table 3-2	Device Names for Common Backup Devices
Backup Device	*Linux Device Name*
Floppy disk	`/dev/fd0`
IDE Zip drive	`/dev/hdc4` or `/dev/hdd4`
SCSI Zip drive	`/dev/sda` (assuming it's the first SCSI drive; otherwise, the device name depends on the SCSI ID)
SCSI tape drive	`/dev/st0` or `/dev/nst0` (the n prefix means that the tape isn't rewound after files are copied to the tape)

Commercial backup utilities for Linux

In the next section, I explain how to back up and restore files using the tape archiver (`tar`) program that comes with Red Hat Linux. Although you can manage backups with `tar`, a number of commercial backup utilities come with graphical user interfaces and other features to simplify backups. Here are some well-known commercial backup utilities for Red Hat Linux:

✦ **BRU** — Backup and Restore Utility from The TOLIS Group, Inc. (`www.tolisgroup.com`)

✦ **LONE-TAR** — Tape-backup software package from Lone Star Software Corporation (`www.cactus.com`)

✦ **Arkeia** — Backup-and-recovery software for heterogeneous networks from Knox Software (`www.knox-software.com`)

✦ **CTAR** — Backup-and-recovery software for UNIX systems from UniTrends Software Corporation (`www.unitrends.com`)

✦ **BrightStor ARCserve Backup for Linux** — Data-protection technology for Linux systems from Computer Associates (`www3.ca.com/Solutions/Product.asp?ID=3370`)

Using the tape archiver — tar

You can use the `tar` command to archive files to a device such as a floppy disk or tape. The `tar` program creates an archive file that can contain other directories and files and (optionally) compress the archive for efficient storage. The archive is then written to a specified device or another file. In fact, many software packages are distributed in the form of a compressed `tar` file.

The command syntax of the `tar` program is as follows:

```
tar options destination source
```

Here, `options` are usually specified by a sequence of single letters, with each letter specifying what `tar` should do. The `destination` is the device name of the backup device. And `source` is a list of file or directory names denoting the files to back up.

Backing up and restoring a single-volume archive

For example, suppose you want to back up the contents of the `/etc/X11` directory on a floppy disk. Log in as `root`, place a disk in the floppy drive, and type the following command:

```
tar zcvf /dev/fd0 /etc/X11
```

The `tar` program displays a list of filenames as each file is copied to the compressed `tar` archive on the floppy disk. In this case, the options are `zcvf`, the destination is `/dev/fd0` (the floppy disk), and the source is the `/etc/X11` directory (which implies all its subdirectories and their contents). You can use a similar `tar` command to back up files to a tape — simply replace `/dev/fd0` with the tape device — such as `/dev/st0` for a SCSI tape drive.

Table 3-3 defines a few common `tar` options.

Table 3-3	Common tar Options
Option	*Does the Following*
c	Creates a new archive
f	Specifies the name of the archive file or device on the next field in the command line
M	Specifies a multivolume archive (the next section describes multivolume archives)
t	Lists the contents of the archive
v	Displays verbose messages
x	Extracts files from the archive
z	Compresses the `tar` archive using `gzip`

To view the contents of the `tar` archive you create on the floppy disk, type the following command:

```
tar ztf /dev/fd0
```

You should see a list of the filenames (each begins with `/etc/X11`) indicating what's in the backup. In this `tar` command, the `t` option lists the contents of the `tar` archive.

To extract the files from a `tar` backup, follow these steps while logged in as `root`:

1. Change the directory to `/tmp` by typing this command:

```
cd /tmp
```

This is where you can practice extracting the files from the `tar` backup. For a real backup, change the directory to an appropriate location (typically, you would type `cd /`).

2. Type the following command:

```
tar zxvf /dev/fd0
```

This `tar` command uses the `x` option to extract the files from the archive stored on `/dev/fd0` (the floppy disk).

Now if you check the contents of the /tmp directory, you notice that the tar command creates an etc/X11 directory tree in /tmp and restores all the files from the tar archive into that directory. The tar command strips off the leading / from the filenames in the archive and restores the files in the current directory. If you want to restore the /etc/X11 directory from the archive on the floppy, use this command:

```
tar zxvf /dev/fd0 -C /
```

The / at the end of the command denotes the directory where you want to restore the backup files.

You can use the tar command to create, view, and restore an archive. You can store the archive in a file or in any device you specify with a device name.

Backing up and restoring a multivolume archive

Sometimes the capacity of a single storage medium is less than the total storage space needed to store the archive. In this case, you can use the M option for a multivolume archive — meaning the archive can span multiple tapes or floppies. Note, however, that you cannot create a compressed, multivolume archive. That means you have to drop the z option. To see how multivolume archives work, log in as root, place one disk in the floppy drive, and type the following tar command:

```
tar cvfM /dev/fd0 /usr/share/doc/ghostscript*
```

Note the M option in the option letters; it tells tar to create a multivolume archive. The tar command prompts you for a second floppy when the first one is filled. Take out the first floppy, and insert another floppy when you see the following prompt:

```
Prepare volume #2 for `/dev/fd0' and hit return:
```

When you press Enter, the tar program continues with the second floppy. In this example, you need only two floppies to store the archive; for larger archives, the tar program continues to prompt for floppies in case more floppies are needed.

To restore from this multivolume archive, type **cd /tmp** to change the directory to /tmp. Then type

```
tar xvfM /dev/fd0
```

The tar program prompts you to feed the floppies as necessary.

Use the du -s command to determine the amount of storage you need for archiving a directory. For example, here's how you can get the total size of the /etc directory in kilobytes:

```
du -s /etc
11632   /etc
```

The resulting output shows that the /etc directory requires at least 11,632K of storage space to back up. If you plan to back up on multiple high-density floppies, you need about 11,632 kilobytes/1,400 kilobytes = 9 floppies.

Backing up on tapes

Although backing up on tapes is as simple as using the right device name in the tar command, you do have to know some nuances of the tape device to use it well. When you use tar to back up to the device named /dev/st0 (the first SCSI tape drive), the tape device automatically rewinds the tape after the tar program finishes copying the archive to the tape. The /dev/st0 device is called a rewinding tape device because it rewinds tapes by default.

If your tape can hold several gigabytes of data, you may want to write several tar archives — one after another — to the same tape (otherwise much of the tape may be left empty). If you plan to do so, your tape device shouldn't rewind the tape after the tar program finishes. To help you with scenarios like this, several Linux tape devices are nonrewinding. The nonrewinding SCSI tape device is called /dev/nst0. Use this device name if you want to write one archive after another on a tape.

After each archive, the nonrewinding tape device writes an *end-of-file* (EOF) marker to separate one archive from the next. Use the mt command to control the tape — you can move from one marker to the next or rewind the tape. For example, after you finish writing several archives to a tape using the /dev/nst0 device name, you can force the tape to rewind with the following command:

```
mt -f /dev/nst0 rewind
```

After rewinding the tape, you can use the following command to extract files from the first archive to the current disk directory:

```
tar xvf /dev/nst0
```

After that, you must move past the EOF marker to the next archive. To do so, use the following mt command:

```
mt -f /dev/nst0 fsf 1
```

This positions the tape at the beginning of the next archive. Now use the tar xvf command again to read this archive.

If you save multiple archives on a tape, you have to keep track of the archives yourself. This can be hard to remember, so you may be better off simply saving one archive per tape.

Performing incremental backups

Suppose you use `tar` to back up your system's hard drive on a tape. Because such a full backup can take quite some time, you don't want to repeat this task every night. (Besides, only a small number of files may have changed during the day.) To locate the files that need backing up, you can use the `find` command to list all files that have changed in the past 24 hours:

```
find / -mtime -1 -type f -print
```

Book VI
Chapter 3

This command prints a list of files that have changed within the last day. The `-mtime -1` option means you want the files that were last modified less than one day ago. You can now combine this `find` command with the `tar` command to back up only those files that have changed within the last day:

```
tar cvf /dev/st0 'find / -mtime -1 -type f -print'
```

When you place a command between single back quotes, the shell executes that command and places the output at that point in the command line. The net result is that the `tar` program saves only the changed files in the archive. What this process gives you is an *incremental backup* of only the files that have changed since the previous day.

Performing automated backups

In Chapter 1 of this mini-book, I show you how to use `crontab` to set up recurring jobs (called *cron jobs*). The Linux system performs these tasks at regular intervals. Backing up your system is a good use of the `crontab` facility. Suppose your backup strategy is as follows:

✦ Every Sunday at 1:15 a.m., your system backs up the entire disk on the tape.

✦ Monday through Saturday, your system performs an incremental backup at 3:10 a.m. by saving only those files that have changed during the past 24 hours.

To set up this automated backup schedule, log in as `root` and type the following lines in a file named `backups` (this example assumes that you use a SCSI tape drive):

```
15 1 * * 0 tar zcvf /dev/st0 /
10 3 * * 1-6 tar zcvf /dev/st0 'find / -mtime -1 -type f -print'
```

Next, submit this job schedule by using the following `crontab` command:

```
crontab backups
```

Now you should be set for an automated backup. All you need do is place a new tape in the tape drive everyday. You should also give each tape an appropriate label.

Accessing a DOS File System

If you have Microsoft Windows 95/98/Me installed on your hard drive, you've probably already mounted the DOS partition under Red Hat Linux. If not, you can easily mount DOS partitions in Red Hat Linux. Mounting makes the DOS directory hierarchy appear as part of the Linux file system. To identify the DOS partitions easily, you may want to mount the first DOS partition as `/dosc`, the second one as `/dosd`, and so on.

To determine whether your DOS hard drive partitions are set up to mount automatically, type the following `grep` command to look for the string `vfat` in the file `/etc/fstab`:

```
grep vfat /etc/fstab
```

If the output shows one or more lines that contain `vfat`, your Red Hat Linux system mounts DOS/Windows hard-drive partitions automatically.

If the `grep` command doesn't show any lines that contain the string `vfat` in `/etc/fstab`, then your system doesn't mount any DOS/Windows hard-drive partitions automatically. Of course, a very good reason for this situation may be that your hard drive doesn't *have* any DOS partitions.

Even if you don't have any DOS partitions on your hard drive, you should learn how to access a DOS file system from Red Hat Linux because you may have to access a DOS floppy disk on your Red Hat Linux system.

Mounting a DOS disk partition

To mount a DOS hard drive partition or floppy, use the `mount` command but include the option `-t vfat` to indicate the file system type as DOS. For example, if your DOS partition happens to be the first partition on your *IDE* (Integrated Drive Electronics) drive and you want to mount it on `/dosc`, use the following `mount` command:

```
mount -t vfat /dev/hda1 /dosc
```

The `-t vfat` part of the `mount` command specifies that the device you mount — `/dev/hda1` — has an MS-DOS file system. Figure 3-4 illustrates the effect of this `mount` command.

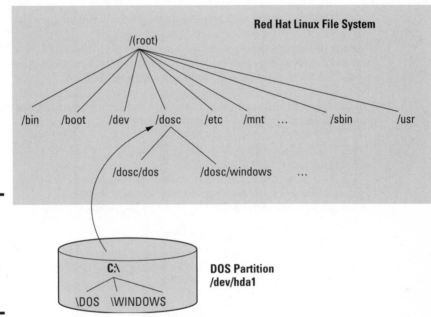

Figure 3-4:
Here's how you mount a DOS partition on the `/dosc` directory.

Figure 3-4 shows how directories in your DOS partition map to the Linux file system. What was the `C:\DOS` directory under DOS becomes `/dosc/dos` under Red Hat Linux. Similarly, `C:\WINDOWS` now is `/dosc/windows`. You probably can see the pattern. To convert a DOS filename to Linux (when you `mount` the DOS partition on `/dosc`), perform the following steps:

1. **Change the DOS names to lowercase.**

2. **Change `C:\` to `/dosc/`.**

3. **Change all backslashes (\) to slashes (/).**

Mounting DOS floppy disks

Just as you mount a DOS hard-drive partition on the Red Hat Linux file system, you can also mount a DOS floppy disk. You must log in as `root` to mount a floppy, but you can follow the steps shown in the latter part of this section to set up your system so that any user can mount a DOS floppy disk. You also have to know the device name for the floppy drive. By default, Linux defines the following two generic floppy-device names:

✦ `/dev/fd0` is the A drive (the first floppy drive)

✦ `/dev/fd1` is the B drive (the second floppy drive, if you have one)

As for the mount point, you can use any empty directory in the file system as the mount point, but the Red Hat Linux system comes with a directory, `/mnt/floppy`, specifically mounting a floppy disk.

To mount a DOS floppy disk on the `/mnt/floppy` directory, put the floppy in the drive and type the following command:

```
mount -t vfat /dev/fd0 /mnt/floppy
```

After you mount the floppy, you can copy files to and from the floppy by using the Linux copy command (`cp`). To copy the file `gnome1.pcx` from the current directory to the floppy, type the following:

```
cp gnome1.pcx /mnt/floppy
```

Similarly, to see the contents of the floppy disk, type the following:

```
ls /mnt/floppy
```

If you want to remove the floppy disk from the drive, first *unmount* the floppy drive. Unmounting removes the association between the floppy disk's file system and the mount point on the Red Hat Linux file system. Use the `umount` command to unmount the floppy disk like this:

```
umount /dev/fd0
```

You can set up your Red Hat Linux system so that any user can mount a DOS floppy. For example, to enable any user to mount a DOS floppy in the A drive on the `/a` directory, perform the following steps:

1. **Log in as** `root`.

2. **Create the** `/a` **directory (the mount point) by typing the following command in a terminal window:**

```
mkdir /a
```

3. **Edit the** `/etc/fstab` **file in a text editor (such as** `vi` **or Emacs), insert the following line, and then save the file and quit the editor:**

```
/dev/fd0    /a    vfat    noauto,user    0 0
```

The first field in that line is the device name of the floppy drive (/dev/ fd0); the second field is the mount directory (/a); and the third field shows the type of file system (vfat). The user option (which appears next to noauto) is what enables all users to mount DOS floppy disks.

4. **Log out and log in as a normal user.**

5. **To confirm that you can mount a DOS floppy as a normal user and not just as root, insert a DOS floppy in the A drive and type the following command:**

   ```
   mount /a
   ```

   The mount operation should succeed, and you should see a listing of the DOS floppy when you type the command **ls /a**.

6. **To unmount the DOS floppy, type** umount /a.

Using mtools

One way to access the MS-DOS file systems is to mount the DOS hard drive or floppy disk by using the mount command and then use regular Linux commands, such as ls and cp, to work with the mounted DOS file system. This approach of mounting a DOS file system is fine for hard drives. Linux can mount the DOS partition automatically at startup, and you can access the DOS directories on the hard drive at any time.

If you want a quick directory listing of a DOS floppy disk, however, mounting can soon become quite tedious. First, you have to mount the floppy drive. Then you must use the ls command. Finally, you must use the umount command before ejecting the floppy out of the drive.

This is where the mtools package comes to the rescue. The mtools package implements most common DOS commands; the commands use the same names as in DOS except that you add an m prefix to each command. Thus, the command for getting a directory listing is mdir, and mcopy copies files. The best part of mtools is the fact that you don't have to mount the floppy disk to use the mtools commands.

Because the mtools commands write to and read from the physical device (floppy disk), you must log in as root to perform these commands. If you want any user to access the mtools commands, you must alter the permission settings for the floppy drive devices. Use the following command to permit anyone to read from and write to the first floppy drive:

```
chmod o+rw /dev/fd0
```

Trying mtools

To try out mtools, follow these steps:

1. **Log in as** root **or type** su **- and then enter the** root **password.**

2. **Place an MS-DOS floppy disk in your system's A drive.**

3. **Type** mdir.

You should see the directory of the floppy disk (in the standard DOS directory-listing format).

Typically, you would use the mtools utilities to access the floppy disks. The default configuration file, /etc/mtools.conf, is set up to access the floppy drive as the A drive. Although you can edit that file to define C and D drives for your DOS hard-drive partitions, you can also access the hard drive partitions by using the Linux mount command to mount them. Because you can mount the hard-drive partitions automatically at startup, accessing them through the Linux commands is normally just as easy.

You also can access Iomega Zip drives through mtools. Simply specify a drive letter and the appropriate device's filename. For built-in IDE (ATAPI) Zip drives, try /dev/hdd4 as the device file and add the following line in the /etc/mtools.conf file:

```
drive e: file="/dev/hdd4"
```

After that you should be able to use mtools commands to access the Zip drive (refer to it as the E drive). For example, to see the directory listing, place a Zip disk in the Zip drive and type:

```
mdir e:
```

Learning the mtools commands

The mtools package is a collection of utilities. So far, I have been using mdir — the mtools counterpart of the DIR command in DOS. The other mtools commands are fairly easy to use.

If you know MS-DOS commands, using the mtools commands is easy. Type the DOS command in lowercase letters, and remember to add m in front of each command. Because the Linux commands and filenames are case-sensitive, you must use all lowercase letters as you type mtools commands.

Table 3-4 summarizes the commands available in mtools.

Table 3-4	The mtools Commands	
mtools Utility	*MS-DOS Command (If Any)*	*The mtools Utility Does the Following*
mattrib	ATTRIB	Changes MS-DOS file-attribute flags
mbadblocks		Tests a floppy disk and marks the bad blocks in the file allocation table (FAT)
mcd	CD	Changes an MS-DOS directory
mcopy	COPY	Copies files between MS-DOS and Linux
mdel	DEL or ERASE	Deletes an MS-DOS file
mdeltree	DELTREE	Recursively deletes an MS-DOS directory
mdir	DIR	Displays an MS-DOS directory listing
mdu		Lists space that a directory and its contents occupy
mformat	FORMAT	Places an MS-DOS file system on a low-level-formatted floppy disk. (Use fdformat to low-level-format a floppy in Red Hat Linux.)
minfo		Gets information about an MS-DOS file system
mkmanifest		Makes a list of short name equivalents
mlabel	LABEL	Initializes an MS-DOS volume label
mmd	MD or MKDIR	Creates an MS-DOS directory
mmove		Moves or renames an MS-DOS file or subdirectory
mmount		Mounts an MS-DOS disk
mpartition		Creates an MS-DOS file system as a partition
mrd	RD or RMDIR	Deletes an MS-DOS directory
mren	REN or RENAME	Renames an existing MS-DOS file
mshowfat		Shows FAT entries for an MS-DOS file
mtoolstest		Tests and displays the current mtools configuration
mtype	TYPE	Displays the contents of an MS-DOS file
mwrite	COPY	Copies a Linux file to MS-DOS
mzip		Performs certain operations on SCSI Zip disks

Book VI Chapter 3

Managing the File System

You can use the mtools commands just as you use the corresponding DOS commands. The mdir command, for example, works the same as the DIR command in DOS. The same goes for all the other mtools commands shown in Table 3-4.

You can use wildcard characters (such as *) with `mtools` commands, but you must remember that the Linux shell is the first program to see your command. If you don't want the shell to expand the wildcard character all over the place, *use quotation marks around filenames that contain any wildcard characters.* For example, to copy all *.txt files from the A drive to your current Red Hat Linux directory, use the following command:

```
mcopy "a:*.txt".
```

If you omit the quotation marks, the shell tries to expand the string a:*.txt with filenames from the current Linux directory. It also tries to copy those files (if any) from the DOS floppy disk.

On the other hand, if you want to copy files from the Linux directory to the DOS floppy disk, you do want the shell to expand any wildcard characters. To copy all *.jpg files from the current Linux directory to the DOS floppy disk, for example, use `mcopy` like this:

```
mcopy *.jpg a:
```

With the `mtools` utilities you can use the backslash character (\) as the directory separator, just as you would in DOS. However, when you type a filename that contains the backslash character, you must enclose the name in double quotation marks (" "). For example, here's a command that copies a file from a subdirectory on the A drive to the current Linux directory:

```
mcopy "a:\test\sample.dat".
```

Formatting a DOS floppy

Suppose you run Red Hat Linux on your home PC and MS-DOS is no longer on your system, but you want to copy some files onto an MS-DOS floppy disk and take the disk to your office. If you already have a formatted MS-DOS floppy, you can simply mount that floppy and copy the file to the floppy by using the Linux `cp` command. But what if you don't have a formatted DOS floppy? The `mtools` package again comes to the rescue.

The `mtools` package provides the `mformat` utility, which can format a floppy disk for use in MS-DOS. Unlike the DOS format command that formats a floppy in a single step, the `mformat` command requires you to follow a two-step process:

1. **Use the `fdformat` command to low-level-format a floppy disk.**

The `fdformat` command uses the floppy device name as the argument; the device name includes all parameters necessary for formatting the floppy disk.

Figure 3-5 illustrates the device-naming convention for the floppy-drive device. As shown in Figure 3-5, you use the following command to format a 3.5-inch, high-density floppy disk in your system's A drive:

```
fdformat /dev/fd0H1440
```

2. **Use the** `mformat` **command to put an MS-DOS file system on the low-level-formatted floppy disk.**

If the floppy is in drive A, type the following command to create a formatted DOS floppy:

```
mformat a:
```

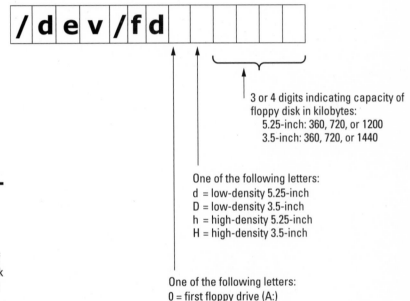

3 or 4 digits indicating capacity of
floppy disk in kilobytes:
   5.25-inch: 360, 720, or 1200
   3.5-inch: 360, 720, or 1440

One of the following letters:
d = low-density 5.25-inch
D = low-density 3.5-inch
h = high-density 5.25-inch
H = high-density 3.5-inch

One of the following letters:
0 = first floppy drive (A:)
1 = second floppy drive (B:)

Figure 3-5:
Here's how
you can
construct
the name of
a floppy disk
drive in Red
Hat Linux.

Chapter 4: Managing Applications

In This Chapter

✔ Learning RPMs

✔ Installing and removing software RPMs

✔ Building applications from source files

✔ Updating Red Hat Linux applications with Red Hat Network

*M*ost software packages for Red Hat Linux are distributed in special files called *Red Hat Package Manager* (RPM) files, which is why you should know how to install or remove software packages that come in the form of RPM files. In this chapter, I show you how to work with RPM files.

Many other open-source software packages come in source-code form, usually in compressed archives. You have to build and install the software to use it. I describe the steps you typically follow when downloading, building, and installing source-based software packages.

Finally, I briefly describe the Red Hat Network and how, after registering with it, you can use Red Hat's Update agent to update Red Hat Linux applications.

Working with Red Hat Package Manager

Red Hat Package Manager (RPM) is a system for packaging all the necessary files for a software product in a single file — called an *RPM file* or simply an *RPM*. In fact, the entire Red Hat Linux distribution is a whole lot of RPMs. The best way to work with RPMs is through the RPM commands. You have to type these commands at the shell prompt in a terminal window or a text console.

Using the RPM commands

When you install Red Hat Linux from the companion DVD, the Red Hat installer uses the `rpm` command to unpack the packages (RPM files) and to copy the contents to your hard drive.

You don't have to understand the internal structure of an RPM file, but you should know how to use the `rpm` command to work with RPM files. Here are some of the things you can do with the `rpm` command:

✦ Find out the version numbers and other information about the RPMs installed on your system.

✦ Install a new software package from an RPM. You may install a package you have skipped during the initial installation. For example, you have to install the source files for the Linux kernel before you can rebuild the kernel. You can do that with the `rpm` command.

✦ Remove (uninstall) unneeded software you have previously installed from an RPM. You may uninstall a package to reclaim the disk space, if you find that you rarely (or never) use the package.

✦ Upgrade an older version of an RPM with a new one. You may upgrade after you download a new version of a package from Red Hat's FTP server. Often you must upgrade an RPM to benefit from the fixes in the new version.

✦ Verify that an RPM is in working order. You can verify a package to check that all necessary files are in the correct locations.

As you can see, the `rpm` command is versatile — it can do a lot of different things depending on the options you use.

If you ever forget the `rpm` options, type the following command to see a list:

```
rpm --help | more
```

The number of `rpm` options will amaze you!

Understanding RPM filenames

An RPM contains a number of files, but it appears as a single file on your Red Hat Linux system. By convention, the RPM filenames have a specific format. To see the names of some of the RPM files on the companion DVD, follow these steps:

1. **Place the first DVD in the DVD drive. The DVD should be automatically mounted if you're using GNOME or KDE graphical desktops. Otherwise, mount it with the following command (you must be logged in as `root`):**

   ```
   mount /dev/cdrom
   ```

2. **Type the following command to go to the directory in which the RPMs are located:**

   ```
   cd /mnt/cdrom/RedHat/RPMS
   ```

3. **View the listing using the `ls` command. For example, to see RPMs with names that start with `cups`, type**

   ```
   ls cups*
   ```

You should see a listing that looks like this:

```
cups-1.1.19-5.i386.rpm
cups-libs-1.1.19-5.i386.rpm
```

As you may guess from the listing, the names of RPM files end with an .rpm extension. To understand the various parts of the filename, consider the following RPM:

```
cups-1.1.19-5.i386.rpm
```

This filename has the following parts, separated by dashes (-):

+ Package name — cups

+ Version number — 1.1.19

+ Release number — 5 (this is a Red-Hat-assigned release number)

+ Architecture — i386 (this package is for Intel 80386-compatible processors)

**Book VI
Chapter 4**

**Managing
Applications**

Usually, the package name is descriptive enough for you to guess what the RPM may contain. The version number is the same as that of the software package's current version number (even when it's distributed in some other form, such as a tar file). Red Hat assigns the release number to keep track of changes. The architecture should be i386 or noarch for the RPMs you want to install on a PC with an Intel x86-compatible processor.

Finding out about RPMs

As it installs packages, the rpm command builds a database of installed RPMs. You can use the rpm -q command to query this database to find out information about packages installed on your system.

For example, to find out the version number of the Linux kernel installed on your system, type the following rpm -q command:

```
rpm -q kernel
```

You should see a response similar to the following:

```
kernel-2.4.20-20.1.2013.nptl
```

The response is the name of the RPM for the kernel (this is the executable version of the kernel, not the source files). The name is the same as the RPM filename, except that the last part — .i386.rpm — isn't shown. In this case, the version part of the RPM tells you that the kernel is 2.4.20.

You can see a list of all installed RPMs by using the following command:

```
rpm -qa
```

You see a long list of RPMs scroll by your screen. To view the list one screen at a time, type

```
rpm -qa | more
```

If you want to search for a specific package, feed the output of `rpm -qa` to the `grep` command. For example, to see all packages with `kernel` in their names, type

```
rpm -qa | grep kernel
```

The result depends on what parts of the kernel RPMs are installed on a system. For example, on my system this command shows the following:

```
kernel-pcmcia-cs-3.1.31-13
kernel-source-2.4.20-20.1.2013.nptl
kernel-2.4.20-20.1.2013.nptl
```

You can query much more than a package's version number with the `rpm -q` command. By adding single-letter options, you can find out other useful information. For example, try the following command to see the files in the kernel package:

```
rpm -ql kernel
```

Here are a few lines from the output of this command:

```
/boot/System.map-2.4.20-20.1.2013.nptl
/boot/config-2.4.20-20.1.2013.nptl
/boot/vmlinux-2.4.20-20.1.2013.nptl
/boot/vmlinuz-2.4.20-20.1.2013.nptl
/dev/shm
/lib/modules
/lib/modules/2.4.20-20.1.2013.nptl/build
/lib/modules/2.4.20-20.1.2013.nptl/kernel
/lib/modules/2.4.20-20.1.2013.nptl/kernel/arch
/lib/modules/2.4.20-20.1.2013.nptl/kernel/arch/i386
/lib/modules/2.4.20-20.1.2013.nptl/kernel/arch/i386/kernel
/lib/modules/2.4.20-20.1.2013.nptl/kernel/arch/i386/kernel/cpuid.o
/lib/modules/2.4.20-20.1.2013.nptl/kernel/arch/i386/kernel/edd.o
/lib/modules/2.4.20-20.1.2013.nptl/kernel/arch/i386/kernel/microcode.o
/lib/modules/2.4.20-20.1.2013.nptl/kernel/arch/i386/kernel/msr.o
 (rest of the listing deleted)
```

Here are a few more useful forms of the rpm -q commands to query information about a package (to use any of these rpm -q commands, type the command, followed by the package name):

✦ rpm -qc — Lists all configuration files in a package.

✦ rpm -qd — Lists all documentation files in a package. These are usually the online manual pages (also known as *man pages*).

✦ rpm -qf — Displays the name of the package (if any) to which a specified file belongs.

✦ rpm -qi — Displays detailed information about a package, including version number, size, installation date, and a brief description.

✦ rpm -ql — Lists all the files in a package. For some packages, this can be a very long list.

✦ rpm -qs — Lists the state of all files in a package.

Book VI
Chapter 4

Managing
Applications

These rpm commands provide information about installed packages only. If you want to find information about an uninstalled RPM file, add the letter *p* to the command-line option of each command. For example, to view the list of files in the RPM file named rdist-6.1.5-27.1.i386.rpm, use the following command:

```
rpm -qpl rdist-*.rpm
```

Of course, this works only if the current directory *contains* that RPM file.

Installing an RPM

To install an RPM, use the rpm -i command. You have to provide the name of the RPM file as the argument. A typical example is installing an RPM from this book's companion DVD containing the Red Hat Linux RPMs. As usual, you have to mount the DVD and change to the directory in which the RPMs are located. Then use the rpm -i command to install the RPM. If you want to view the progress of the RPM installation, use rpm -ivh. A series of hash marks (#) is displayed as the package is unpacked.

For example, to install the kernel-source RPM (which contains the source files for the Linux operating system) from the companion DVD, I insert the DVD and after it's mounted, type the following commands:

```
cd /mnt/cdrom/RedHat/RPMS
rpm -ivh kernel-source*
```

You don't have to type the full RPM filename — you can use a few characters from the beginning of the name followed by an asterisk (*). Make sure you type enough of the name to identify the RPM file uniquely.

If you try to install an RPM that's already installed, the `rpm -i` command displays an error message. For example, here is what happens when I type the following command to install the `man` package on my system:

```
rpm -i man-1*
```

I get the following error message from the `rpm -i` command:

```
package man-1.5k-8 is already installed
```

To force the `rpm` command to install a package even if errors are present, just add `--force` to the `rpm -i` command, like this:

```
rpm -i --force man-1*
```

Removing an RPM

You may want to remove — uninstall — a package if you realize you don't really need the software. For example, if you have installed the X Window System development package but discover you're not interested in writing X applications, you can easily remove the package by using the `rpm -e` command.

You have to know the name of the package before you can remove it. One good way to find the name is to use `rpm -qa` in conjunction with `grep` to search for the appropriate RPM file. For example, to locate the X Window System development RPM, try the following command:

```
rpm -qa | grep XFree86
```

`XFree86-devel` happens to be the package name of the X Window System development RPM. To remove that package, type

```
rpm -e XFree86-devel
```

To remove an RPM, you don't need the full RPM filename; all you need is the package name — the first part of the filename up to the dash (-) before the version number.

The `rpm -e` command does not remove a package other packages need. For example, to remove the `vim-common` package, type the following command:

```
rpm -e vim-common
```

You get the following error message:

```
error: Failed dependencies:
        vim-common is needed by (installed) vim-minimal-6.2.14-1
        vim-common is needed by (installed) vim-enhanced-6.2.14-1
```

Upgrading an RPM

Use the `rpm -U` command to upgrade an RPM. You must provide the name of the RPM file that contains the new software. For example, if I have version 2.0.40 of Apache `httpd` (Web server) installed on my system but I want to upgrade to version 2.0.45, I download the RPM file `httpd-2.0.45-10.i386.rpm` from one of Red Hat update sites (listed at `www.redhat.com/mirrors.html`) and use the following command:

```
rpm -U httpd-2.0.45-10.i386.rpm
```

The `rpm` command performs the upgrade by removing the old version of the `httpd` package and installing the new RPM.

Whenever possible, you should upgrade rather than remove the old package and install a new one. Upgrading automatically saves your old configuration files, which saves you the hassle of reconfiguring the software after a fresh installation.

When you're upgrading the `kernel` packages that contain a ready-to-run Linux kernel, install it by using the `rpm -i` command (instead of the `rpm -U` command). That way you won't overwrite the current kernel.

Verifying an RPM

You may not do so often, but if you suspect that a software package isn't properly installed, use the `rpm -V` command to verify it. For example, to verify the kernel package, type the following:

```
rpm -V kernel
```

This causes `rpm` to compare the size and other attributes of each file in the package against those of the original files. If everything verifies correctly, the `rpm -V` command does not print anything. If there are any discrepancies, you see a report of them. For example, I have modified the configuration files for the Apache `httpd` Web server. Here is what I type to verify the `httpd` package:

```
rpm -V httpd
```

Here's the result I get:

```
S.5....T c /etc/httpd/conf/httpd.conf
```

In this case, the output from rpm -V tells me that a configuration file has changed. Each line of this command's output has three parts:

✦ The line starts with eight characters: Each character indicates the type of discrepancy found. For example, S means the size is different, and T means the time of last modification is different. Table 4-1 shows each character and its meaning. A period means that the specific attribute matches the original.

✦ For configuration files, a c appears next; otherwise, this field is blank. That's how you can tell whether or not a file is a configuration file. Typically, you shouldn't worry if a configuration file has changed; you probably made the changes yourself.

✦ The last part of the line is the full pathname of the file. From this part, you can tell exactly where the file is located.

Table 4-1	Characters Used in RPM Verification Reports
Character	*Meaning*
S	Size has changed.
M	Permissions and file type are different.
5	Checksum computed with the MD5 algorithm is different.
D	Device type is different.
L	Symbolic link is different.
U	File's user is different.
G	File's group is different.
T	File's modification time is different.

Building Software Packages from Source Files

Many open-source software packages are distributed in source-code form, without executable binaries. Before you can use such software, you have to build the executable binary files by compiling, and you have to follow some instructions to install the package. In this section, I show you how to build software packages from source files.

Downloading and unpacking the software

Open-source software source files are typically distributed in compressed tar archives. These archives are created by the tar program and compressed with the gzip program. The distribution is in the form of a single large file with the .tar.gz or .tar.Z extension — often referred to as a *compressed tarball*. If you want the software, you have to download the compressed tarball and unpack it.

Download the compressed `tar` file by using anonymous FTP or through your Web browser. Typically, this involves no effort on your part beyond clicking a link and saving the file in an appropriate directory on your system.

To try your hand at downloading and building a software package, you can practice on the X Multimedia System (XMMS) — a graphical X application for playing MP3 and other multimedia files. XMMS is bundled with Red Hat Linux and should already be installed on your system. However, there is no harm in downloading and rebuilding the XMMS package again.

Download the source files for XMMS from `www.xmms.org/download.php`. The files are packed in the form of a compressed `tar` archive. Click the `ftp` link for the source files and then save them in the `/usr/local/src` directory in your Red Hat Linux system. (Be sure to log in as `root`; otherwise, you cannot save in the `/usr/local/src` directory.)

Book VI
Chapter 4

Managing
Applications

After downloading the compressed `tar` file, examine the contents with the following `tar` command:

```
tar ztf xmms*.gz | more
```

You should see a listing similar to the following:

```
xmms-1.2.7/
xmms-1.2.7/Makefile.in
xmms-1.2.7/README
xmms-1.2.7/stamp-h1.in
xmms-1.2.7/ABOUT-NLS
xmms-1.2.7/AUTHORS
xmms-1.2.7/COPYING
xmms-1.2.7/ChangeLog
xmms-1.2.7/INSTALL
xmms-1.2.7/Makefile.am
xmms-1.2.7/NEWS
xmms-1.2.7/TODO
xmms-1.2.7/acconfig.h
xmms-1.2.7/acinclude.m4
xmms-1.2.7/aclocal.m4
xmms-1.2.7/config.guess
xmms-1.2.7/config.h.in
xmms-1.2.7/config.sub
xmms-1.2.7/configure
... rest of the output not shown ...
```

The output of this `tar` command shows you what's in the archive and gives you an idea of the directories that will be created after you unpack the archive. In this case, a directory named `xmms-1.2.7` will be created in the current directory, which, in my case, is `/usr/local/src`. From the listing, you'll also learn the programming language used to write the package. If you see .c and .h files, that means the source files are in the C programming language used to write many open-source software packages.

To extract the contents of the compressed tar archive, type the following tar command:

```
tar zxvf xmms*.gz
```

You'll again see the long list of files as they are extracted from the archive and copied to the appropriate directories on your hard drive.

Now you're ready to build the software.

Building the software from source files

After you unpack the compressed tar archive, all source files will be in a directory whose name is usually that of the software package with a version-number suffix. For example, the XMMS version 1.2.7 source files are extracted to the xmms-1.2.7 directory. To start building the software, change directories with the following command:

```
cd xmms*
```

You don't have to type the entire name — the shell can expand the directory name and change to the xmms-1.2.7 directory.

Nearly all software packages come with some sort of README or INSTALL file — a text file that tells you how to build and install the package. XMMS is no exception; it comes with a README file you can peruse by typing **more README**. There is also an INSTALL file that contains instructions for building and installing XMMS.

Most open-source software packages, including XMMS, also come with a file named COPYING. This file contains the full text of the *GNU General Public License* (GPL), which spells out the conditions under which you can use and redistribute the software. If you're not familiar with the GNU GPL, read this file and show the license to your legal counsel for a full interpretation and an assessment of applicability to your business.

To build the software package, follow the instructions in the README or INSTALL file. For the XMMS package, the README file lists some of the prerequisites (such as libraries) and tells you what commands to type to build and install the package. In the case of XMMS, the instructions tell you to use the following steps:

1. **Type** ./configure **to run a shell script that checks your system configuration and creates a file named** Makefile — **a file the** make **command uses to build and install the package. (You can type** ./configure —help **to see a list of options that configure accepts.)**

2. **Type** make **to build the software.**

   This step compiles the source files in all the subdirectories (compiling source code converts each source file into an object file — a file containing binary instructions that your PC's processor can understand).

3. **Type** make install **to install the software.**

   This step copies libraries and executable binary files to appropriate directories on your system.

**Book VI
Chapter 4**

**Managing
Applications**

Although these steps are specific to XMMS, most other packages follow these steps — configure, make, and install. The configure shell script guesses system-dependent variables and creates a Makefile with commands needed to build and install the software.

Usually, you don't have to do anything but type the commands to build the software, but you must install the software-development tools on your system. This means you must install the Software Development package when you install Red Hat Linux. To build and run XMMS, you must also install the X Software Development package because it's an X application.

To begin building XMMS, type the following command to run the configure script (you must be in the xmms-1.2.7 directory when you type this command):

```
./configure
```

The configure script starts running and prints lots of messages as it checks various features of your system — from the existence of the C compiler to various libraries needed to build XMMS. Finally, the configure script creates a Makefile you can use to build the software.

If the configure script displays error messages and fails, review the INSTALL and README files to find any clues to solving the problem. You may be able to circumvent it by providing some information to the configure script through command-line arguments.

After the configure script finishes, build the software by typing **make**. This command runs the GNU make utility, which reads the Makefile and starts compiling the source files according to information specified in the Makefile. The make command goes through all the source directories, compiles the source files, and creates the executable files and libraries needed to run XMMS. You'll see a lot of messages scroll by as each file is compiled. These messages show the commands used to compile and link the files.

The `make` command can take 10 to 15 minutes to complete. After `make` is done, you can install the XMMS software with the following command:

```
make install
```

This command also runs GNU `make`, but the `install` argument instructs GNU `make` to perform a specific set of commands from the `Makefile`. These instructions essentially go through all the subdirectories and copy various files to their final locations. For example, the binary executable files `xmms`, `gnomexmms`, `wmxmms`, and `xmms-config` are copied to the `/usr/bin` directory.

Now that you have installed XMMS, try running it from the GNOME or KDE desktop by typing **xmms** in a terminal window or by choosing Main Menu⇨Sound & Video⇨Audio Player. XMMS already comes with Red Hat Linux, but now you should get the new version of XMMS (the difference is that the newly built version can play MP3 files without any add-ons). From the XMMS window, press **L** to get the Load File dialog and select an MP3 file to play. Your PC must have a sound card, and the sound card must be configured correctly for XMMS to work. Figure 4-1 shows a typical view of XMMS playing an MP3 music clip.

Figure 4-1:
You can play MP3 music with the version of XMMS you built from source files.

Here's an overview of the steps you follow to download, unpack, build, and install a typical software package:

1. Use a Web browser to download the source code, usually in the form of a `.tar.gz` file, from the anonymous FTP site or Web site.

2. Unpack the file with a `tar zxvf` *filename* command.

3. Change the directory to the new subdirectory where the software is unpacked, with a command such as `cd` *software_dir*.

4. Read any `README` or `INSTALL` files to get a handle on any specific instructions you must follow to build and install the software.

5. The details of building the software may differ slightly from one software package to another, but typically you type the following commands to build and install the software:

    ```
    ./configure
    make
    make install
    ```

6. Read any other documentation that comes with the software to learn how to use the software and whether you must configure the software further before using it.

Installing SRPMS

You can install the source files and build various Red Hat Linux applications directly from the source files. Red Hat provides the source-code files in RPMs, just as with the executable binary files, and these source RPM files are generally known as SRPMS (for *source RPMs*).

To install a specific source RPM and build the application, follow these steps:

1. **Mount the DVD by typing** `mount /mnt/cdrom` **or waiting for GNOME desktop to mount the DVD.**

2. **Typically source RPMs would be in the SRPMS directory. Change to that directory by typing the following command:**

    ```
    cd /mnt/cdrom/SRPMS
    ```

3. **Install the source RPM file by using the** `rpm -i` **command. For example, to install the Web server (**`httpd`**) source, type**

    ```
    rpm -ivh httpd*.src.rpm
    ```

    The files would be installed in the `/usr/src/redhat/SOURCES` directory. A spec file with a `.spec` extension would be placed in the `/usr/src/redhat/SPECS` directory. The *spec file* describes the software and also contains information used to build and install the software.

4. **Use the** `rpmbuild` **command with the spec file to build the software. You perform different tasks from unpacking the source files to building and installing the binaries by using different options with the** `rpmbuild` **command. For example, to process the entire spec file, type:**

    ```
    rpmbuild -ba packagename.spec
    ```

    Here *packagename* is the name of the SRPM. This command should typically build the software and install the binary files.

Updating Red Hat Linux Applications with the Update Agent

Red Hat Linux comes with a service called Red Hat Network, designed to enable registered users to keep their Red Hat Linux system and applications current. The idea is that you register with the Red Hat Network and provide information about your system's hardware and the RPMs currently installed on your system. After you've done so, an Update Agent can download any new RPM files your system requires and install those files for you.

I briefly provide an overview of how to update your system by using the Update Agent and the Red Hat Network.

Registering with Red Hat Network

To take full advantage of the Red Hat Network's facilities, you must register with the Red Hat Network and provide information about your Red Hat Linux system. To register, follow these steps:

1. **Make sure your Internet connection is up; then choose Main Menu⇨System Tools⇨Red Hat Network.**

   A configuration dialog box appears, from which you can configure some options (such as what to do with downloaded packages, what packages to skip, and whether to verify authenticity of packages). Typically you can click OK to proceed. You also get a prompt that asks whether you want to install Red Hat's GPG key (used to verify that packages are securely signed by Red Hat). Click Yes to install the key.

2. **The Red Hat Update Agent runs and displays a message explaining the purpose of the program; click Forward to continue.**

   When you run the Red Hat Update Agent for the first time, it registers you with the Red Hat Network. It starts by displaying a privacy statement explaining the information to be collected and sent to Red Hat's server during registration. The information includes an inventory of RPM files on your system and an inventory of your system hardware.

3. **Read the privacy policy; if you want to continue, click Forward.**

   You're prompted for a username and password to establish a new user account with Red Hat.

4. **Fill in the requested information and click Forward to continue.**

   The next screen asks you to enter more information about yourself, including your name, address, and phone number.

5. **Again, fill in the requested information and then click Forward.**

The Red Hat Update Agent shows some information about your system and asks you to provide a name for the system profile (the collection of information about your system).

6. Enter a descriptive name and then click Forward.

The Red Hat Update Agent displays a list of RPMs (names of software packages) to be included in the profile information. When the Update Agent checks for updated software, it uses this list.

7. If you don't care about updating some of the packages, uncheck these names; then click Forward.

The Red Hat Update Agent informs you that it's about to send your system information to the Red Hat Network.

8. Click Forward to continue.

The Red Hat Update Agent sends your information (the information mentioned in the privacy statement) to the Red Hat Network. If all goes well, the upload begins and a progress bar shows the percentage sent so far. Otherwise, you may get a message from the server informing you that, because of high load, access to the Red Hat Network is limited to subscription customers only.

9. If you're denied access, you must try to register after waiting for some time.

After the Red Hat Update Agent successfully uploads your system profile to the Red Hat Network, the final window displays a message telling you to visit rhn.redhat.com to log in and to access Red Hat Network. That Web site is where you can also buy subscriptions to the Red Hat Network.

10. Click the Finish button to complete the registration process.

Updating Red Hat Linux packages

After you're registered with Red Hat Network, you can use the Red Hat Update Agent to update Red Hat Linux. Red Hat gives you a free subscription to Red Hat Network for one PC, but you have to pay for anything beyond that. If you want to buy a subscription, visit rhn.redhat.com, log in, and follow the directions.

To update software packages, follow these steps:

1. Log in as root, and choose Main Menu⇨System Tools⇨Red Hat Network.

The Red Hat Update Agent starts, and a dialog box prompts you to install Red Hat's public key in your GPG key ring. (*GPG* refers to GNU Privacy Guard or GnuPG, a program for encrypting, decrypting, and signing e-mail and other data using the OpenPGP Internet standard.) Red Hat's public GPG key is used to verify that Red Hat has securely signed the packages the Update Agent has downloaded.

2. **Click the Yes button to install Red Hat's key.**

3. **After the Red Hat Update Agent displays a window with a welcome message, click the Forward button to proceed.**

   The Update Agent retrieves a list of all available packages from the Red Hat Network. (This may take a few minutes.) Then the Update Agent downloads the headers for all available packages. For each download, a progress bar shows the percentage of data downloaded so far. The header download takes quite a bit of time over a slow connection to the Internet.

4. **After the Red Hat Update Agent downloads the headers, it displays a list of packages to be skipped. You can accept the list and click the Forward button to continue.**

   The Update Agent displays a list of all the packages available for update from Red Hat Network.

5. **Scroll through the list and pick the package updates you want to download; click the box to the left of a package's name to select it.**

   As you select packages, the Update Agent displays the total size of the packages you have selected so far.

6. **After selecting the packages, click the Forward button to proceed with the download.**

   The Update Agent then checks for any package dependencies and begins downloading the packages. Progress bars show the status of the download.

7. **After the download is finished, click the Forward button to proceed with the installation.**

8. **The Update Agent displays progress bars as it installs each package update. Click the Forward button when the installation is complete.**

   The Update Agent displays a message about the package(s) it has installed successfully.

9. **Click the Finish button to exit the Red Hat Update Agent.**

After you have registered with the Red Hat Network, you can use the Red Hat Update Agent to keep Red Hat Linux up-to-date.

Chapter 5: Managing Devices and Printers

In This Chapter

✔ **Understanding device drivers**

✔ **Managing loadable driver modules**

✔ **Managing USB devices**

✔ **Managing print queues**

*E*verything you use to work with your computer is a device. The keyboard and mouse you use to type and click around, the hard drive where you store everything, and the printer where you get your hard copies — these are all devices. And guess what — you have to manage them. It's not as hard as it sounds. All you have to do is load the device driver and (perhaps) configure the device a bit. This managing is easier to do if you understand device drivers a bit and get some practice using the tools Red Hat Linux includes to help you manage devices. In this chapter, I provide a brief overview of device drivers and explain how to manage driver modules. Because printers are a common type of device you have to manage, I also show you how to manage print queues.

Understanding Device Drivers

The Linux kernel treats all devices as files and uses a device just as it would use a file — opens it, writes data to it, reads data from it, and closes it when done. This ability to treat every device as a file comes through the use of device drivers. A *device driver* is a special program that controls a particular type of hardware. When the kernel writes data to the device, the device driver does whatever is appropriate for that device. For example, when the kernel writes data to the floppy drive, the floppy device driver puts that data onto the physical medium of the floppy disk. On the other hand, if the kernel writes data to the parallel port device, the parallel-port driver sends the data to the printer connected to the parallel port.

Thus, the device driver isolates the device-specific code from the rest of the kernel and makes a device look like a file. Any application can access a device by opening the file specific to that device. Figure 5-1 illustrates this concept of a Linux device driver.

Figure 5-1:
An applica-
tion can
access
a device
through a
special file
that, in turn,
uses a
device
driver.

Device files

As Figure 5-1 shows, applications can access a device as if it were a file. These files are special files called *device files*, and they appear in the /dev directory in the Red Hat Linux file system.

If you use the ls command to look at the list of files in the /dev directory, you'll see several thousand files. This does not mean that your system has several thousand devices. The /dev directory has files for all possible types of devices — that's why the number of device files is so large.

So how does the kernel know which device driver to use when an application opens a specific device file? The answer is in two numbers called the *major* and *minor device numbers*. Each device file is mapped to a specific device driver through these numbers.

To see an example of the major and minor device numbers, type the following command in a terminal window:

```
ls -l /dev/hda
```

You should see a line of output similar to the following:

```
brw-rw----  1 root    disk    3,  0 Jul 23 14:50 /dev/hda
```

In this line, the major and minor device numbers appear just before the date. In this case, the major device number is 3 and the minor device number is 0. The kernel selects the device driver for this device file by using the major device number.

You don't really have to know much about the device files and the device numbers, except to be aware of their existence.

Block devices

The first letter in the listing of a device file also provides an important clue. For the /dev/hda device, the first letter is a b, which indicates that /dev/hda is a *block device* — one that can accept or provide data in chunks (typically 512 bytes or 1KB). By the way, /dev/hda refers to the first IDE hard drive on your system (the C drive in Windows). Hard drives, floppy drives, and CD-ROM drives are all examples of block devices.

Character devices

If the first letter in the listing of a device file is a c, then the device is a *character device* — one that can receive and send data one character (one byte) at a time. For example, the serial ports and parallel port are character devices. To see the specific listing of a character device, type the following command in a terminal window:

```
ls -l /dev/ttyS0
```

The listing of this device should be similar to the following:

```
crw-rw----  1 root    uucp    4, 64 Jul 23 14:50 /dev/ttyS0
```

Notice that the very first letter is a c because /dev/ttyS0 — the first serial port — is a character device.

Network devices

Network devices that enable your system to interact with a network — for example, Ethernet and dial-up *point-to-point protocol* (PPP) connections — are somewhat special because they need no file to correspond to the device. Instead, the kernel uses a special name for the device. For example, the Ethernet devices are named eth0 for the first Ethernet card, eth1 for the second one, and so on. PPP connections are named ppp0, ppp1, and so on.

Because network devices aren't mapped to device files, there are no files corresponding to these devices in the /dev directory.

Managing Loadable Driver Modules

To use any device, the Linux kernel must contain the driver. If the driver code is linked into the kernel as a *monolithic* program (a program that's in the form of a single large file), then adding a new driver means rebuilding the kernel with the new driver code. Rebuilding the kernel means you have to reboot the PC with the new kernel before you can use the new device driver. Luckily, the Linux kernel uses a modular design that does away with rebooting hassles. Linux device drivers can be created in the form of modules that the kernel can load and unload without having to restart the PC.

Driver modules are one type of a broader category of software modules called Loadable Kernel Modules. Other types of kernel modules include code that can support new types of file systems, modules for network protocols, and modules that interpret different formats of executable files.

Loading and unloading modules

You can manage the loadable device driver modules by using a set of commands. You have to log in as `root` to use some of these commands. In Table 5-1, I summarize a few of the commonly used module commands.

Table 5-1	Commands to Manage Kernel Modules
This Command	*Does the Following*
insmod	Inserts a module into the kernel
rmmod	Removes a module from the kernel
depmod	Determines interdependencies between modules
ksyms	Displays a list of symbols along with the name of the module that defined the symbol
lsmod	Lists all currently loaded modules
modinfo	Displays information about a kernel module
modprobe	Inserts or removes a module or a set of modules intelligently (for example, if module A requires B, then modprobe automatically loads B when asked to load B)

If you have to use any of these commands, log in as `root` or type **su** - in a terminal window to become `root`.

To see what modules are currently loaded, type

```
lsmod
```

You should see a list of modules. For example, here is a list on one of my PCs:

```
Module            Size    Used by    Not tainted
nls_iso8859-1     3516    1    (autoclean)
nls_cp437         5148    1    (autoclean)
sd_mod            13516   2    (autoclean)
vfat              13036   1    (autoclean)
fat               38808   0    (autoclean) [vfat]
```

```
usb-storage         74560   1
scsi_mod           107576   2   [sd_mod usb-storage]
ide-cd              35712   0   (autoclean)
cdrom               33728   0   (autoclean) [ide-cd]
parport_pc          19076   1   (autoclean)
lp                   9060   0   (autoclean)
parport             37056   1   (autoclean) [parport_pc lp]
iptable_filter       2444   0   (autoclean) (unused)
ip_tables           15224   1   [iptable_filter]
autofs              13268   0   (autoclean) (unused)
orinoco_cs           5556   1
orinoco             39724   0   [orinoco_cs]
hermes               8100   0   [orinoco_cs orinoco]
ds                   8680   1   [orinoco_cs]
yenta_socket        13664   1
pcmcia_core         57248   0   [orinoco_cs ds
   yenta_socket]
3c59x               30736   0
floppy              56892   0   (autoclean)
keybdev              2976   0   (unused)
mousedev             5556   1
hid                 22276   0   (unused)
input                5888   0   [keybdev mousedev hid]
usb-uhci            26412   0   (unused)
usbcore             79136   1   [usb-storage hid usb-uhci]
ext3                73540   2
jbd                 52148   2   [ext3]
```

As you may expect, the list of modules depends on the types of devices installed on your system.

The first column lists the names of the modules in last-to-first order. Thus, the first module in the list is the last one to be loaded. The Size column shows the number of bytes that the module occupies in your PC's memory. The remaining columns show other information about each module, such as how many applications are currently using the module and the names of the modules that require the module.

The list displayed by lsmod includes all types of Linux kernel modules, not just device drivers. For example, the last two modules — jbd, and ext3 — are all part of the EXT3 file system (the latest file system for Linux).

Besides lsmod, one commonly used module command is modprobe. Use modprobe whenever you need to manually load or remove one or more modules. The best thing about modprobe is that you don't need to worry if a module requires other modules to work. The modprobe command automatically loads any other module that is needed by a module. On my system, for example, I can manually load the sound driver with the command

```
modprobe sound-slot-0
```

This command causes `modprobe` to load everything needed to make sound work. On one of my systems, the `modprobe sound-slot-0` command loads `soundcore`, `ac97_codec`, and `i810_audio` — in that order.

You can use `modprobe` with the `-r` option to remove modules. For example, to remove the sound modules, I use the following command:

```
modprobe -r sound-slot-0
```

This command gets rid of all the modules that the `modprobe sound-slot-0` command had loaded.

Using the /etc/modules.conf file

How does the `modprobe` command know that it should load the `opl3sa2` driver module when I use a module name `sound-slot-0`? The answer is in the `/etc/modules.conf` configuration file. That file contains a line that tells `modprobe` what it should load when it sees the module name `sound-slot-0`.

To view the contents of `/etc/modules.conf`, type

```
cat /etc/modules.conf
```

On one of my Red Hat Linux PCs, the file contains the following lines:

```
alias parport_lowlevel parport_pc
alias eth0 eepro100
alias usb-controller usb-uhci
alias sound-slot-0 opl3sa2
```

Each line that begins with the keyword `alias` defines a standard name for an actual driver module. For example, the second line defines `eepro100` as the actual driver name for the alias `eth0`, which stands for the first Ethernet card. Similarly, the fourth line defines `opl3sa2` as the module to load when I use the name `sound-slot-0`.

The `modprobe` command consults the `/etc/modules.conf` file to convert an alias to the real name of a driver module as well as for other tasks such as obtaining parameters for driver modules. For example, you can insert lines that begin with the `options` keyword to provide values of parameters that a driver may need.

For example, to set the interrupt request (IRQ) parameter for the sound card to 5, I would add the following line to the `/etc/modules.conf` file:

```
options opl3sa2 irq=5
```

This line specifies 5 as the value of the parameter named `irq` in the `opl3sa2` module.

If you want to know the names of the parameters that a module accepts, use the `modinfo` command. For example, to view information about the `opl3sa2` driver module, type

```
modinfo opl3sa2
```

From the resulting output, you can tell that `irq` is the name of the parameter for the Interrupt Request parameter.

Unfortunately, the information shown by the `modinfo` command can be somewhat cryptic. The only saving grace is that you may not have to do much more than use a graphical utility to configure the device, and the utility will take care of adding whatever is needed to configuration files such as `/etc/modules.conf`.

Managing USB Devices

Red Hat Linux comes with built-in support for the Universal Serial Bus (USB) — a serial bus that's gradually replacing the functionality of the PC's serial and parallel ports, as well as that of the keyboard and mouse ports. Nowadays, many PC peripherals — such as mouse, keyboard, printer, CD burner, scanner, modem, digital camera, memory card, and so on — are designed to connect to the PC through a USB port.

USB version 1.1 supports data-transfer rates as high as 12 Mbps — 12 million bits per second or 1.5 megabytes per second — compared with 115 Kbps or the 0.115 Mbps transfer rate of a standard serial port. You can daisy-chain up to 127 devices on a single USB bus. The bus also provides power to the devices, and you can attach or remove devices while the PC is running — a capability commonly referred to as *hot plug* or *hot swap*. USB version 2.0 (or USB 2.0 or USB2, for short) ups the ante by raising the data transfer rates to a whopping 480 Mbps, slightly faster than the competing IEEE 1394 (FireWire) bus. Nowadays many devices, such as CD burners and scanners, come with the high-speed USB2 interface. If your PC has older USB 1.1 ports, the USB2 devices can still work, albeit at lower data-transfer rates. Red Hat Linux supports both USB 1.1 and USB2 interfaces.

Using USB devices in Red Hat Linux is easy. You can hot-plug a device into a USB port, and the Linux kernel can detect and load the appropriate device drivers so applications can make use of the device. To be more precise, the `kudzu` hardware detection utility takes care of the chores necessary to make the USB device accessible to applications. For USB mass storage devices, such as CD drives or hard drivers, `kudzu` can also mount the device on the Linux file system. For examples of using USB mass-storage devices, see Book II, Chapter 5 where I discuss how Red Hat Linux detects a USB CD burner and how to access the photos in a digital camera through the USB interface.

To use a USB printer in Red Hat Linux, simply connect the printer to the USB port, power it up, and then follow the steps in Book I, Chapter 3 to configure a locally connected queue for the printer. The printer should show up with a device name such as `/dev/usb/lp0` (for the USB printer detected by `kudzu`), `/dev/usb/lp1` (for the second USB printer), and so on.

Using USB scanners in Red Hat Linux is as simple as using USB printers. Just plug the scanner into the USB port, power it up, and you should be able to access it by using the `xsane` — a graphical front-end for scanners that you can start by choosing Main Menu⇨Graphics⇨Scanning. Of course, the USB scanner make and model must be supported by `xsane`. To quickly check whether `kudzu` has detected your USB scanner, log in as `root` and type **sane-find-scanner** in a terminal window.

Even when `kudzu` does not automatically mount a USB mass storage device for easy access, you can manually mount the device. Consider, for example, the USB keychain storage device. Just as the name says, these are small memory cards, capable of storing anywhere from 32MB to 1GB. You can carry them around on a keychain — in effect, taking all your data with you wherever you go. Here's how you can use a USB keychain storage device that's already formatted for use in Microsoft Windows:

1. **Plug the keychain storage device into the PC's USB port.**

Sometimes the device plugs directly into the port, but for some devices you have to attach the keychain device to a USB cable and then plug the cable into the USB port.

Some USB keychain devices have a small switch on the side that controls whether the keychain is write-protected. If you plan to write to the device, first make sure it's not write-protected or locked.

2. **Create a mount point for the storage device. For example, I log in as** `root` **and create the following directory:**

```
mkdir /mnt/key
```

3. **If this is the only USB device plugged in, the device name is** /dev/sda1 **(USB storage devices appear as SCSI devices). Mount it with the following command:**

```
mount -o rw -t vfat /dev/sda1 /mnt/key
```

The `-t vfat` part of the command specifies that the file system on the keychain storage device is VFAT — the Windows file system that supports long filenames.

Now you can access the files on the keychain at the /mnt/key directory. To save a file to the USB keychain storage device, use a command of the following form:

```
cp filename /mnt/key
```

where *filename* is the name of the file you want to save.

When you're done using the device, unmount the USB keychain with this command:

```
umount /dev/sda1
```

That's it!

Managing Print Queues in Red Hat Linux

PCs typically come with one parallel port, typically used for connecting the printer to the PC. You can set up a printer fairly easily by using Red Hat's graphical printer-configuration utility, but you also have to learn how to manage the print queue.

Spooling and print jobs

Spooling refers to the capability to print in the background. When you print from a word processor in Windows, for example, the output first goes to a file on the disk. Then, while you continue working with the word processor, a background process sends that output to the printer. The Red Hat Linux printing environment also supports spooling.

Print job refers to what you print with a single print command. The printing environment queues print jobs by storing them in the spool directory. A background process periodically sends the print jobs from the spool directory to the printer.

Red Hat Linux —uses the Common UNIX Printing System (CUPS) for its printing environment. CUPS is a printing system based on the Internet Printing Protocol (IPP) — a protocol for distributed printing using Internet technologies. IPP assumes a client/server model with the client being an application and the server a "Printer" — an abstraction of an output device or a printing service provider. IPP supports a distributed printing environment with the clients and Printer servers communicating over the Internet. You could use an IPP client to print on a printer anywhere on the Internet. The client and Printer exchange data using the HTTP 1.1 protocol — the same protocol that Web servers use. The client application uses IPP to inquire about capabilities of a printer, submit print jobs, and inquire about — or cancel — print jobs.

TIP

If you have set up a CUPS print queue for a printer connected to your Red Hat Linux system (following the directions in Book I, Chapter 3), you can print on that printer from Windows XP and 2000 systems on your local area network. Windows 2000 and XP have built-in support for IPP — the protocol used by CUPS. To print on a CUPS print queue from a Windows XP system, add a network printer on the XP. In the Add Printer Wizard, select Connect to a Printer on the Internet or on a Home or Office Network and then enter the URL for the CUPS print queue. For example, for a CUPS print queue named `HPLaserjetRoom210` on a Red Hat Linux host whose IP address is 192.168.0.8, I enter the following URL for the print queue:

```
http://192.168.0.8:631/printers/HPLaserjetRoom210
```

As a Red Hat Linux user, you use a client program — `lp` or `lpr` — to send the files to be printed to a print scheduler called `cupsd` over a TCP/IP network connection. The `cupsd` scheduler then queues the files, processes them according to their file extensions (such as `.txt` or `.ps`), and sends them to the printer one by one. Thanks to various configuration files, the `cupsd` scheduler knows what to do to make sure that the file — be it a text file or an image file — gets printed properly.

Although you typically have only one printer connected to your PC, one advantage of the CUPS printing system is the capability to print on a printer connected to another system on a network. Printing to a remote printer is handled in the same fashion as printing to a local printer: The local `lp` or `lpr` program simply sends the files to the remote system's `cupsd` scheduler.

Printing with the lp command

You can print a file by using the `lp` or `lpr` command. For example, to print the file `/etc/inittab`, type the following in a terminal window:

```
lp /etc/inittab
```

The `lp` command queues a print job by sending the file and appropriate control information to the `cupsd` print scheduler. By default, the `cupsd` print scheduler accepts files to be printed, holds them in the print queue, and forwards them to the default printer (or to another system if the default printer is attached to a remote system on the network). The default printer is identified by the `<DefaultPrinter queuename>` entry in the CUPS configuration file `/etc/cups/cupsd.conf` (where *queuename* is the name of the print queue).

You can embellish the simple `lp` command with some options. If you have many different print queues defined, you can specify the destination of the print job with the `-d` option. For example, to send a print job to the Hewlett-Packard LaserJet print queue named `HPLaserjetRoom210` you would type the following command (the print queue name appears in the `/etc/cups/printers.conf` file):

```
lp -d HPLaserjetRoom210 testprint.ps
```

Checking the print queue using lpq

If you mistakenly print a large file and want to stop the print job before you waste too much paper, you can use the `lpq` command to look at the current print jobs and then cancel the large print job. Following is a typical listing of print jobs I get when I type **lpq** after submitting a file to the `HPLaserjetRoom210` print queue:

```
HPLaserjetRoom210 is ready and printing
Rank    Owner   Job     File(s)                 Total Size
active  root    2       testprint.ps            15360 bytes
```

The `lpq` command shows the job number (2) and the name of the file that I am printing (`testprint.ps`).

Canceling the print job using cancel

To remove a job from the print queue, use the `cancel` command. For example, to remove print job 2, type the following command:

```
cancel 2
```

You can get the same result with the following `lprm` command:

```
lprm 2
```

If you're in a hurry and want to cancel all print jobs you have submitted so far, use `cancel` with `-a` as the argument, as follows:

```
cancel -a
```

Checking the printer status using lpstat

To see the status of print jobs, use the `lpstat` command. Here is a typical output from the `lpstat` command:

```
lpstat
HPLaserjetRoom210-2     root        15360   Wed 25 Jan 2003 04:25:48 PM EST
```

The first field of the output shows the name of the queue with a job number appended to it (that number identifies the print job). You need that job number to cancel the print job.

Controlling the print queue

To see the names of printers connected to your system, use the `lpc status` command. On my system, the `lpc status` command shows the following:

```
lpc status
HPLaserjetRoom210:
        printer is on device 'parallel' speed -1
        queuing is enabled
        printing is enabled
        no entries
        daemon present
```

Notice that queuing and printing are both enabled for this printer. The last line tells you that the `cupsd` *daemon* (a server that runs all the time) is running and available to handle print jobs.

You can use the `accept` and `reject` commands to enable or disable queuing for a print queue. For example, to stop queuing further print jobs for the `HPLaserjetRoom210` printer, I type

```
reject HPLaserjetRoom210
```

This command disables queuing jobs for this printer. If anyone tries to send a print job using the `lp` command, the user receives an error message like this:

```
lp: unable to print file: server-error-not-accepting-jobs
```

If you want to allow queuing of print jobs, but want to start or stop the printing, use the `enable` and `disable` commands. When you disable printing, users can submit print jobs, but nothing gets printed until you enable printing again. For example, here is the command I use to disable printing on the `HPLaserjetRoom210` printer:

```
disable HPLaserjetRoom210
```

If you're trying to print, but nothing seems to be coming out of the printer, check the printer status with the `lpc status` command and make sure that the `cupsd` scheduler is present and that both queuing and printing are enabled. To allow the queuing of print jobs, use the `accept` command and to start printing, use the `enable` command.

Chapter 6: Upgrading and Customizing the Kernel

In This Chapter

✔ **Upgrading with a Red Hat kernel RPM**

✔ **Configuring the kernel**

✔ **Building a new kernel**

✔ **Building and installing the modules**

✔ **Installing the kernel and setting up GRUB**

*O*ne reason Linux is so exciting is that many programmers are constantly improving it. Some programmers, for example, write drivers that add support for new hardware, such as a new sound card or a new networking card. All these innovations come to you in the form of new versions of the Linux kernel.

Although you don't have to upgrade or modify the Linux operating system — the kernel — every time a new version is available, sometimes you have to upgrade simply because the new version corrects some problems or supports your hardware better. On the other hand, if an earlier kernel version has everything you need, there is no need to rush out and upgrade.

Sometimes you may want to rebuild the kernel even when there are no fixes or enhancements. The Linux kernel on the companion DVD is generic and uses modules to support all types of hardware. You may want to build a new kernel that links in the drivers for only the devices installed on your system. In particular, if you have a SCSI hard drive, you may want to create a kernel that supports your SCSI adapter. Depending on your needs, you may also want to change some of the kernel configuration options, such as creating a kernel that's specific for your processor (instead of a generic Intel 386 processor).

In this chapter, I explain how to upgrade a kernel using a kernel RPM as well as how to rebuild and install a new Linux kernel.

Upgrading with a Red Hat Kernel RPM

Red Hat distributes all software updates, including new versions of kernels, in the form of RPM files. To download and install the kernel RPMs, follow these steps:

1. **Use a Web server to download the kernel RPM files from Red Hat's FTP server (I explain the details in the next section).**

   If you want to rebuild the kernel, you have to download the `kernel-source` RPM corresponding to the new version of the kernel.

2. **Install the RPMs by using the** `rpm -i` **command.**

3. **Create a new, initial RAM disk by running the** `/sbin/mkinitrd` **command.**

4. **Reconfigure GRUB to boot the new kernel.**

5. **Try out the new kernel by rebooting the system.**

I further describe these steps in the next few sections.

Downloading new kernel RPMs

Red Hat makes software updates available in the form of RPMs — packages — at its FTP server or one of the mirror sites listed at `www.redhat.com/download/mirror.html`. The updates are organized in directories according to Red Hat Linux version numbers. For example, any updates for Red Hat Linux 9 for Intel x86 systems reside in the `9/en/os/i386` directory. Use a Web browser (for example, Mozilla) to visit the FTP site and download any kernel RPMs available at that site.

Installing the kernel RPMs

To install the kernel and the modules, follow these steps:

1. **Log in as** `root`.

2. **Use the** `cd` **command to change the directory to where the RPM files (the ones you have downloaded from Red Hat's FTP server) are located.**

3. **Type the following command to install the kernel RPM:**

   ```
   rpm -ivh kernel*.rpm
   ```

You have to install the `kernel-source` RPM only if you want to build a new kernel.

When you install a new kernel RPM, the installation process creates a new initial RAM disk image — a file that the kernel can copy into a block of memory and use as a memory-resident disk. That file's name begins with `initrd` (`initrd` is shorthand for *initial RAM disk*) and has the kernel version number in the filename. The kernel RPM installation also adds a description of the kernel to the GRUB configuration file — `/etc/grub.conf`. For example, here is a typical GRUB configuration file after I installed a new kernel RPM:

```
title Red Hat Linux (2.4.20-8)
        root (hd0,2)
        kernel /vmlinuz-2.4.20-8 ro root=LABEL=/
        initrd /initrd-2.4.20-8.img
title Red Hat Linux (2.4.20-6)
        root (hd0,2)
        kernel /vmlinuz-2.4.20-6 ro root=LABEL=/
        initrd /initrd-2.4.20-6.img
```

Next time you reboot the system, these two kernels would appear as choices in the GRUB boot screen. From that screen you can select which kernel you want to boot.

Trying out the new kernel

After installing the new kernel RPM, creating the initial RAM disk file, and reconfiguring GRUB, it's time to try the new kernel. To restart the system, log in as `root` and type the following command from the Linux prompt:

```
reboot
```

You may also reboot the system from the graphical login screen. Select Reboot from the Options menu on the login dialog box.

When the system reboots and you see the GRUB screen, press the arrow key to select the new kernel's name.

After Red Hat Linux starts, you should see the usual graphical login screen. Log in as a user, open a terminal window, and type the `uname -sr` command to see the version number. The response should show that your system is running the new version of the kernel.

Rebuilding the Kernel

Rebuilding the kernel refers to creating a new binary file for the core Linux operating system. This binary file is the one that runs when Red Hat Linux boots. You may wonder why you would ever want to rebuild the kernel. Well, here are a few reasons:

✦ After you initially install Linux, you may want to create a new kernel that includes support for only the hardware installed on your system. In particular, if you have a SCSI adapter, you may want to create a kernel that links in the SCSI driver. The kernel in the companion DVD includes the SCSI driver as an external module you load at startup.

✦ If you have a system with hardware for which only experimental support is available, you have to rebuild the kernel to include that support into the operating system.

✦ You may want to recompile the kernel and generate code that works well on your specific Pentium processor (instead of the generic 386 processor code that comes in the standard Red Hat Linux distribution).

Never rebuild and install a new kernel without first making sure you have an emergency boot floppy. If you do have an emergency boot floppy, use the `mkbootdisk` command to create the boot floppy. Type **man mkbootdisk** to learn the syntax of that command. The exact command line to build the emergency boot floppy depends on the kernel version number. For example, to create a boot floppy for version 2.4.20-8, log in as `root` and type the following command in a terminal window (you have to insert a blank floppy disk when prompted):

```
mkbootdisk -device /dev/fd0 2.4.20-8
```

Replace 2.4.20-8 with the version number of your Linux kernel (type the `uname -r` command to see the version number).

To rebuild the Linux kernel, you need the kernel source files. The kernel source files are not normally installed. Use the following steps to install the kernel source files on your system:

1. **Log in as `root` and insert the Red Hat Linux DVD–ROM into the DVD drive.**

2. **If the DVD drive does not mount automatically, type the following command to mount the DVD drive:**

```
mount /mnt/cdrom
```

If you're using GNOME or KDE, the DVD is automatically mounted, and you should not have to perform this step manually.

3. **Change the directory to the `RedHat/RPMS` directory on the DVD, and use the `rpm` command to install the kernel source files. Type the following commands:**

```
cd /mnt/cdrom/RedHat/RPMS
rpm -ivh kernel-source*
```

After the rpm command finishes installing the kernel source package, the source files appear in the `/usr/src/linux-2.4` directory.

If you cannot find the `kernel-source` RPM on this book's DVD, you have to download that file from one of the mirror sites listed at `www.redhat.com/download/mirror.html`. Click the Distribution link next to one of the listed FTP sites and then look in the directory corresponding to the Red Hat Linux version number. For example, the RPM files for Red Hat Linux 9 should be in the `9/en/os/i386/RedHat/RPMS` directory. Use a Web browser to download the `kernel-source` RPM file and install it by following the previous steps.

Building the kernel involves the following phases:

✦ Configuring the kernel

✦ Building the kernel

✦ Building and installing the modules (if any)

✦ Installing the kernel and setting up GRUB

I explain these phases in the next few sections, but first you should know the difference between linking in a driver vs. building a driver as a loadable module.

**Book VI
Chapter 6**

Upgrading and
Customizing the
Kernel

Creating a monolithic vs. a modular kernel

You have two options for the device drivers needed to support various hardware devices in Linux:

✦ **Link in support:** You can link the drivers for all hardware on your system into the kernel. The size of the kernel grows as device driver code is incorporated into the kernel. A kernel that links in all necessary code is called a *monolithic kernel* because it's one big file.

✦ **Use modules:** You can create the device drivers in the form of loadable modules. A *module* is a block of code the kernel can load after it starts running. A typical use of modules is to add support for a device without having to rebuild the kernel for each new device. Modules don't have to be device drivers; they can also add new functionality to the kernel. A kernel that uses modules is called a *modular kernel*.

You don't have to create a fully monolithic or fully modular kernel. In fact, it's common practice to link some support directly into the kernel but build infrequently used device drivers in the form of modules. For a company such as Red Hat, it makes sense to distribute a modular kernel. Red Hat provides a generic kernel, along with a large number of modules that can support many different types of hardware. Then the Red Hat installer configures the system to load only modules that are needed to support the hardware installed in a user's system.

When you create a custom kernel for your hardware configuration, you may want to link all required device drivers into the kernel. You can keep the size of such a monolithic kernel under control because you link in device drivers only for the hardware installed on your system.

Configuring the kernel

The first phase in rebuilding a kernel is to configure it. To configure the kernel, log in as `root`. Then change the kernel source directory by using the `cd` command as follows:

```
cd /usr/src/linux*
```

To configure the kernel, you have to indicate which features and device drivers you want to include in your Linux kernel. In essence, you build your very own version of the Linux kernel with just the features you want.

Red Hat Linux provides several ways for you to configure the kernel:

✦ Type **make menuconfig** to enter the kernel-configuration parameters through a text-based interface similar to the one the Red Hat installation program uses.

✦ Type **make xconfig** to use an X Window System-based configuration program to configure the kernel. You have to run X to use this configuration program with a graphical interface.

✦ Type **make config** to use a shell script that prompts you for each configuration option one by one. You can use this configuration program from the Linux command prompt. When you use this option, you undergo a long question-and-answer process to specify the configuration parameters. For each question, respond with a *y* to link support into the kernel, *m* to build a module, and *n* to skip the support for that specific device.

The `make menuconfig`, `make xconfig`, and `make config` commands achieve the same end result — each stores your choices in a text file named `.config` located in the `/usr/src/linux*` directory. Because the filename starts with a period, you don't see it when you use the `ls` command alone to list the directory. Instead, type **ls -a** to see the `.config` file in the directory listing.

The kernel configuration step merely captures your choices in the `.config` file. (In fact, the `.config` file does not exist until you configure the kernel once.) The kernel file does not change until you compile the kernel with the `make` command. That means you can go through the kernel configuration option as many times as you want. If you want to start over with default settings, type the following command before you start configuring the kernel:

```
make mrproper
```

Running the kernel configuration tool

You can use any of the configuration tools — `make xconfig`, `make menuconfig`, or `make config` — to configure the kernel, but the easiest way is to log in as `root` and type the following command in a terminal window:

```
make xconfig
```

This command builds an X Window System-based configuration tool and runs it. The initial Linux Kernel Configuration window displays a set of buttons, each representing a category of kernel configuration options, as shown in Figure 6-1.

Figure 6-1:
You can
configure
groups of
kernel
options
through the
buttons in
this window.

Linux Kernel Configuration		_ □ ✕
Code maturity level options	Fusion MPT device support	Console drivers
Loadable module support	IEEE 1394 (FireWire) support (EXPERIMENTAL)	Sound
Processor type and features	I2O device support	USB support
General setup	Network device support	Additional device driver support
Memory Technology Devices (MTD)	Amateur Radio support	Bluetooth support
Parallel port support	IrDA (infrared) support	Kernel hacking
Plug and Play configuration	ISDN subsystem	Cryptographic options
Block devices	Old CD-ROM drivers (not SCSI, not IDE)	Library routines
Multi-device support (RAID and LVM)	Input core support	
Networking options	Character devices	Save and Exit
Telephony Support	Multimedia devices	Quit Without Saving
ATA/IDE/MFM/RLL support	Crypto Hardware support	Load Configuration from File
SCSI support	File systems	Store Configuration to File

Through the four buttons, grouped together in the lower-right corner of the window, you can perform tasks such as saving the configurations and exit.

To change a category of configuration options, click the relevant button. For example, if you click the Processor Type and Features button in the upper-left corner, the configuration program displays another window with all the options you can set. From the new window you can then set specific options. For example, Figure 6-2 shows a drop-down menu from which you can pick the specific processor type (in this case, Pentium III/Celeron).

Notice the Help buttons along the right edge of the window. Whenever you have a question about a configuration option, click the corresponding Help button to view help information for that option. Figure 6-3 shows the result of clicking the Help button next to the Processor Type option. Click OK to close the Help window after you finish reading the information.

Figure 6-2: Select a processor type from the drop-down menu.

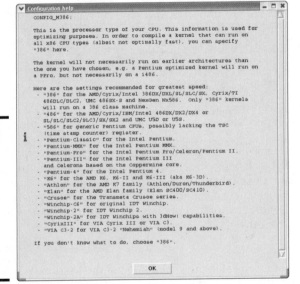

Figure 6-3: Context-sensitive help is available in the xconfig kernel configuration tool.

You can follow these steps to specify options for each category of options:

1. **In the main window (refer to Figure 6-1), click the option category.**

The configuration program displays another window with the options for that category (refer to Figure 6-2).

2. **Set the options you want. Click the appropriate radio box (*y* for yes and *n* for no) to indicate your choice. If you need help on an option, click the Help button next to that option.**

3. **After completing that category of options, click Main Menu to return to the window of Figure 6-1 or click Next to move on to the next category of options.**

I describe some of the important and interesting categories of options. The section headings match the labels on the buttons in Figure 6-1, so you can easily locate a section that interests you.

A final word of caution before you start configuring the kernel options. Many kernel options depend on one another. For example, if the parallel port option isn't set to Yes, then the configuration program grays out all options related to parallel port devices. The best way to logically proceed through the configuration steps is to start with the button at the upper-left corner — Code Maturity Level Options — and then click Next on each successive window. That way, you always set the options in the correct order.

Code maturity level options

The very first group of options has only one item — you're asked if you want to use experimental device drivers or not. If you want to try some experimental drivers such as the ones that support IEEE 1394 (FireWire), then set this option to Yes.

Loadable module support

This group of options (see Figure 6-4) asks you about support for loadable modules. You want to include support for modules, so set the first option to Yes. The next option is about including version information in each module. If modules have version information, the module is checked for compatibility with the current kernel version. Because it's easy to unload a module that does not work, I tend to set this option to No. However, you may safely accept the default and press Enter. The third question asks whether or not you want the kernel to be capable of loading required modules. You should set this option to Yes.

Figure 6-4:
Enable loadable module support from this configuration window.

Processor type and features

This set of options (Figure 6-5) is for setting the processor type and support for specific processor-related features. The first option of this set queries you about your system's processor type. If you answer 386, the compiled kernel can run on any other processor (such as a 486 or any type of Pentium). However, if you're creating a kernel specifically for your system, select your processor type from the drop-down list that appears when you click on the processor family. You can also enable symmetric multiprocessing (SMP) support from this window, but you should do so only if your system's motherboard has two or more processors.

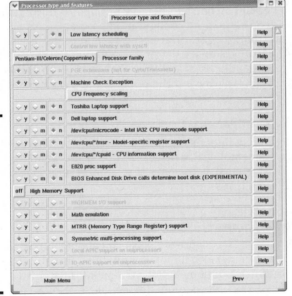

Figure 6-5:
Set the processor type and other processor-related features in this configuration window.

General setup

This is a set of general options (Figure 6-6) that deals with networking, PCI bus, MCA bus, parallel port, and advanced power management (APM) BIOS support. You can simply accept the default settings for these options. If you don't understand what an option means, click the Help button next to an option to get help on that option.

Parallel port support

These options (Figure 6-7) are important if you use any devices such as printers or parallel-port Zip drives connected to the parallel port of your PC. Set the *Parallel port support* and *PC-style hardware* options to Module so the drivers are built as modules.

Figure 6-6:
You can set many general features from this configuration window.

Figure 6-7:
Specify options for the parallel port support from this configuration window.

Plug-and-Play configuration

These options (Figure 6-8) ask if you want to enable Plug-and-Play (PnP) support in the kernel. If you enable PnP support, the kernel automatically configures PnP devices (just as Windows does). Accept the default settings of Yes for these two options.

Figure 6-8:
Turn on plug-and-play support through these options.

Block devices

Block devices (such as disk drives) transfer data in chunks (as opposed to keyboards, which transfer data one character at a time). This set of options (shown in Figure 6-9) involves the floppy and IDE (Integrated Drive Electronics) devices connected to the PC's parallel port as well as other block devices.

Figure 6-9:
Set options for block devices from this configuration window.

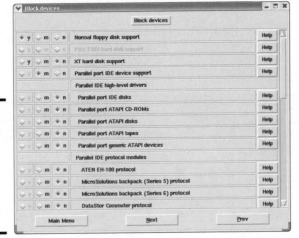

The first option asks whether you want floppy-drive support. Because most PCs do have a floppy drive, your answer generally is Yes. Select the Module for the Parallel Port IDE Device Support option if you have external CD-ROM or disk devices that connect through your PC's parallel port.

If you scroll down the list of options in Figure 6-9, you find more options for block devices. Setting the Loopback Device Support option to Yes or Module lets the Linux kernel manipulate an entire file system inside a single large file. This is useful if you want to check a CD image before burning the CD.

The RAM Disk Support option allows the kernel to use a portion of your system's memory as a disk capable of storing a file system. Typically, a RAM disk functions only during system startup when the hard drive may not be available yet. The RAM disk is essential if you're booting a SCSI disk and you haven't compiled the SCSI drivers into the kernel.

Networking options

This set of options (shown in Figure 6-10) deals with networking. How you set these options depends on how you want to use your Red Hat Linux system in a network. Always enable the TCP/IP Networking option because the X Window System uses TCP/IP networking (even if your PC isn't on any network).

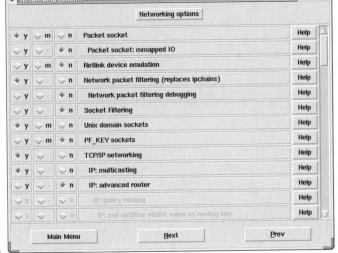

Figure 6-10:
Configure the net-working options from this configuration window.

Set the Network Packet Filtering (Replaces ipchains) option to Yes if you want to use your Red Hat Linux system as a *firewall* — an intermediary system that controls information flowing between a local area network (LAN) and the Internet.

Telephony support

With the right hardware and software, the telephony support options enable you to use the Red Hat Linux system for making phone calls over the Internet (also known as *voiceover IP* or *VoIP*). You can choose to build driver modules for telephony support if you have a telephony card, such as the Internet

PhoneJACK or Internet LineJACK manufactured by Quicknet Technologies, Inc. If you have no Quicknet telephony cards, you can safely set these options to No.

ATA/IDE/MFM/RLL support

When you're configuring an operating system, you have to expect a fair share of acronyms — this one has four acronyms: ATA, IDE, MFM, and RLL. All of these relate to hard drives or the interface that links disk drives to the PC. Here's what they mean:

✦ **ATA** stands for *AT Attachment* and refers to the PC-AT style interface used to connect hard drives and DVD/CD-ROM drives to the PC's motherboard.

✦ **IDE** stands for *Integrated Drive Electronics* and refers to the original PC hard drives that integrate the disk controller onto the hard drive itself. The IDE interface is more accurately described as *AT Attachment Packet Interface* or ATAPI. You typically see the terms IDE, ATA, and ATAPI used interchangeably.

✦ **MFM** stands for *Modified Frequency Modulation,* the way data was encoded on older hard drives. These hard drives can work over an IDE interface.

✦ **RLL** stands for *Run Length Limited,* an old technique for storing data on hard drive from the early days of the PC. RLL disks can work over an IDE interface.

You should leave the *ATA/IDE/MFM/RLL support* set to Yes. When you press Next from this window, you get another configuration window (Figure 6-11) with many more options involving IDE devices, such as hard drives and ATAPI CD-ROM and DVD-ROM drives.

The first option is for enhanced IDE support, which refers to full-featured IDE controllers that can control up to 10 IDE interfaces. Because each IDE interface can have a master and a slave device, Linux can access a total of up to 20 IDE devices (such as disks or DVD/CD-ROM drives). You should leave this option set to Yes.

The second button in Figure 6-11 is a comment that refers you to the file `Documentation/ide.txt` for help with IDE devices. To read these help files (these are all text files), type the following command to change the directory:

```
cd /usr/src/linux*/Documentation
```

Now you can browse the directory for text files relating to specific devices. You can also use GNOME or KDE file managers to browse the documentation.

Note that `IDE/ATAPI FLOPPY` refers to IDE floppy drives, such as Iomega Zip drive or Imation Superdisk LS-120 drive. If you have a IDE ZIP drive, set this option to Module or Yes.

IDE, ATA and ATAPI Block devices

Figure 6-11:
Set options
for IDE
devices
from this
configura-
tion
window.

SCSI support

SCSI stands for *Small Computer Systems Interface* — a type of interface through which you can connect multiple devices (such as hard drives and scanners) to the PC. This set of options (shown in Figure 6-12) has to do with SCSI devices. If your system has a SCSI adapter, start by setting the SCSI Support option to Yes. After that, you can set the options relating to the types of devices (disk, tape, CD-ROM) connected to the SCSI adapter. Finally, you must enable support for the specific SCSI adapter model on your system.

If your system has a SCSI adapter, always select y for all the needed SCSI options. In particular, select y for the SCSI low-level driver for your specific brand of SCSI adapter.

IEEE 1394 (FireWire) support (Experimental)

IEEE 1394 is a high-speed serial bus for connecting peripherals to PCs. Apple calls this bus FireWire; Sony calls it i.Link. IEEE 1394 is similar to USB, but it can transfer data at rates up to 400Mbps, which is more than 30 times the data rate of the older USB version 1.1 (note that USB 2.0 is even faster; it can transfer data at rates of up to 480Mbps). Because of its high data-transfer rates, IEEE 1394 is ideal for connecting high-speed peripherals such as digital audio and video devices and external hard drives to the PC.

The Linux kernel includes experimental support for the IEEE 1394 bus. Currently, Linux supports IEEE 1394 chipsets that are compatible with Texas Instruments PCILynx/PCILynx2 and OHCI chipsets. If your PC has an IEEE 1394 adapter, you can build the necessary drivers through these options (as shown in Figure 6-13).

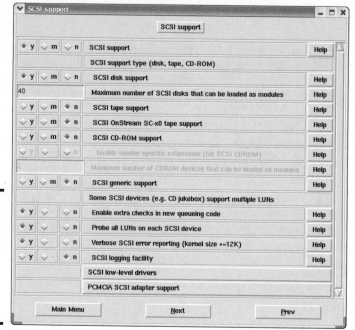

Figure 6-12:
Enable
support for
various
SCSI
devices
from this
window.

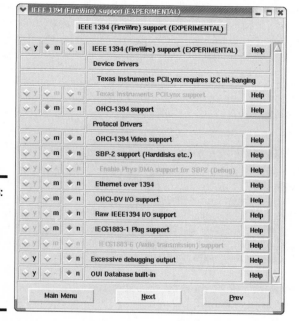

Figure 6-13:
Configure
support for
IEEE 1394
(FireWire)
devices
from this
window.

Because the IEEE 1394 drivers are experimental, you can set these options only if you have said Yes to experimental drivers in the code maturity level options.

To learn more about using IEEE 1394 peripherals in Linux, visit the Web site of the IEEE 1394 for Linux project at www.linux1394.org.

I2O device support

Pronounced *eye-two-oh*, I2O refers to Intelligent Input/Output — a new device driver architecture independent of the operating system and the controlled device. The basic concept of I2O is to separate the part responsible for managing the device from the part that contains operating system-specific details (it's called the I2O Split Driver model). The two parts of an I2O driver are the OS Services Module (OSM), which works with the operating system, and the Hardware Device Module (HDM) that interfaces with the particular device the driver manages. The OSM and HDM communicate by passing messages to each other. To learn more about I2O, visit the Intelligent-IO.com Web site at www.intelligent-io.com. Linux comes with some I2O drivers for SCSI and PCI devices. You can configure these drivers from this category of options.

**Book VI
Chapter 6**

**Upgrading and
Customizing the
Kernel**

Network device support

This category of options involves the drivers for network interface cards. It includes the configuration of network devices such as Ethernet, Token Ring, ARCnet, and AppleTalk network adapters. If you have an Ethernet card installed on your PC, remember to build the driver for your Ethernet card by selecting Yes or Module for that card.

You can also enable dial-up and wide area network (WAN) support by using SLIP and PPP through options in this category.

ISDN subsystem

This set of options enables you to include support for *ISDN* (Integrated Services Digital Network) — a digital telephone line you can use to connect the Linux system to the Internet. These ISDN-related options include the configuration of specific ISDN adapters.

You should build the ISDN driver only if your PC has an ISDN card. If you anticipate adding an ISDN card and purchasing ISDN service from the phone company, you can build the driver as a module. Read the file /usr/src/ linux*/Documentation/isdn/README for more information on how to set up and use the ISDN driver in Linux.

Character devices

These options deal with configuring character devices, which include devices connected to the serial and parallel ports. These options also include configuration of multiport serial interface cards that enable you to connect multiple terminals or other devices to your Red Hat Linux system. Answer No if you don't have any such devices on your system.

This list of options includes the Parallel Printer Support option. If you plan to connect a printer to the parallel port, set this option to Yes.

A subcategory of the character device options refers to I2C support. I2C — pronounced *eye-squared-see* — is a protocol Philips has developed for communication over a pair of wires at rates between 10 and 100kHz. System Management Bus (SMBus) is a subset of the I2C protocol. Many modern motherboards have an SMBus meant for connecting devices such as EEPROM (electrically erasable programmable read-only memory) and chips for hardware monitoring. Linux supports the I2C and SMBus protocols. You need this support for Video for Linux. If you have any hardware sensors or video equipment that needs I2C support, set the I2C support option to *m* (for module) and answer *m* to the specific driver for your hardware. To learn more about the I2C, read the documentation in the `/usr/src/linux*/Documentation/i2c` directory. In particular, the `summary` file briefly describes the I2C and SMBus protocols.

Other subcategories of character devices include

+ **Mice:** You can specify the type of mouse on your PC (what's important is how the mouse is connected to the PC, not the make and model of the mouse). You have choices such as bus mouse, PS/2 mouse, and specialized devices such as digitizer pad and touch screen.

+ **Joysticks:** You can set the options for any joysticks or special game controllers (steering wheel, game pad, and so on) on your PC.

+ **Watchdog cards:** You can enable support for special watchdog cards that can monitor the PC's status (including the temperature, for instance) and reboot the PC when necessary. This can be helpful if you want to have a networked PC automatically reboot after it hangs up for whatever reason.

+ `Ftape` **or the floppy-tape device driver:** If you have a tape drive connected to your floppy controller, you can configure it through this category of options.

+ **PCMCIA character devices:** These options are for configuring PC card modems and serial ports that are meant for laptop or notebook PCs.

Multimedia devices

This category of options configures support for multimedia devices such as video cameras, television tuners, and FM radio cards. For more information

on these devices, consult the documentation in the `/usr/src/linux*/`
`Documentation/video4linux` directory.

File systems

Through this category of options (shown in Figure 6-14), you can turn on support for specific types of file systems. You'd be amazed by the many different file systems that the Linux kernel can support. Table 6-1 lists some of the file systems that Linux can support. You would typically build a kernel with support for the core Linux file systems (ext2 and ext3), CD-ROM file system (ISO 9660 and Joliet), and DOS/Windows file systems (MSDOS, FAT, and VFAT).

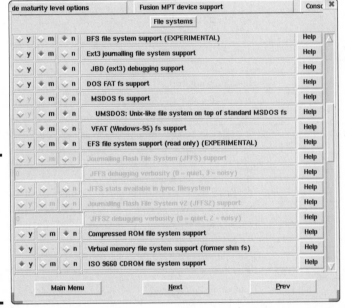

Figure 6-14:
Turn on
support for
specific file
systems
from this
configura-
tion
window.

Table 6-1	Some File Systems Supported by Linux Kernel
File System	**Description**
Apple Macintosh	The Macintosh HFS file system (Linux can read and write Macintosh-formatted floppy disks and hard drives).
Coda	An advanced network file system that is similar to NFS but that better supports disconnected operation (for example, laptops) and is a better security model.
Ext2	The second extended file system — the current standard file system for Linux.

(continued)

Table 6-1 *(continued)*

File System	Description
Ext3	Ext2 file system with support for journaling — a facility that allows quick recovery of the disk after a crash.
FAT	Refers to any File Allocation Table (FAT)-based file system (including MS-DOS and Windows 95 VFAT file systems).
HPFS	The OS/2 HPFS file system (Linux can only read HPFS files).
ISO 9660	The standard ISO 9660 file system used on CD-ROMs (this is also known as the High Sierra File System and is referred to as `hsfs` on some UNIX workstations).
Joliet	Microsoft's Joliet extension for the ISO 9660 CD-ROM file system, which allows for long filenames in Unicode format. (Unicode is the new 16-bit character code that can encode the characters of almost all languages of the world.)
MSDOS	The MS-DOS file system.
NFS	Network File System for sharing files and directories from other systems on a network.
NTFS	NT file system (NTFS) — the file system used by Microsoft Windows NT (Linux can only read NTFS disks).
`/proc`	A virtual file system through which you can get information about the kernel. The `/proc` file system does not exist on the disk; files are created when you access them.
ROM	A very small, read-only, memory-resident file system used in the initial RAM disk (`initrd`) during Red Hat Linux installation.
SMB	File system that uses Server Message Block (SMB) protocol to access shared directories from networked PCs running Windows 95/98/NT/2000.
System V	File system used by SCO, Xenix, and Coherent variants of UNIX for Intel PCs.
UDF	A new file system used on some CD-ROMs and DVDs. (For example, UDF file system is used on rewritable CDs written in packet mode or written by UDF utilities such as DirectCD.)
UFS	File system used by the BSD (Berkeley Software Distribution) variants of UNIX (such as SunOS, FreeBSD, NetBSD, and NeXTstep).
VFAT	Windows 95/98/NT/2000 file systems with long filenames.

Sound

Use this set of options to configure sound card support. If you have a sound card installed, start by answering *y* or *m* to the Sound Card Support option. After that, you have to enable a number of options for the sound card installed in your PC. You can always select *m* to build the sound support in the form of modules that you can load when needed.

USB support

Use this category of options (Figure 6-15) to configure support for the Universal Serial Bus (USB) — a serial bus that comes built into most new PCs. USB version 1.1 supports data-transfer rates as high as 12Mbps — 12 million bits per second or 1.5 megabytes per second — compared with 115Kbps or the 0.115Mbps transfer rate of a standard serial port (such as COM1). You can daisy-chain up to 127 devices on a USB bus. The bus also provides power to the devices, and you can attach or remove devices while the PC is running — a capability commonly referred to as *hot swapping*. USB version 2.0 (or USB 2.0 or USB2, for short) ups the data-transfer ante to 480Mbps, slightly faster than the competing IEEE 1394 (FireWire) bus.

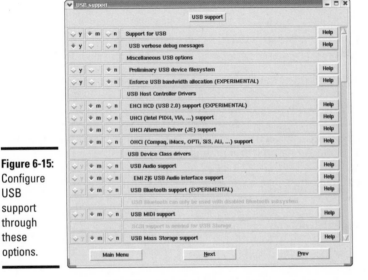

Figure 6-15:
Configure
USB
support
through
these
options.

USB can replace the functionality of the PC's serial and parallel ports, as well as the keyboard and mouse ports. Nowadays, many PC peripherals — such as mouse, keyboard, printer, scanner, modem, digital camera, and so on — are designed to connect to the PC through a USB port.

If your PC has a USB Port, set the USB support option to *y* or *m*. Then you have to answer *m* to the UHCI or OHCI option, depending on the type of USB interface — UHCI (Intel) or OHCI (Compaq and others) — your PC has. To determine the type of USB interface, type **lspci** and look for the USB controller's make and model in the output. If the controller is by Intel, use the UHCI driver.

For USB 2.0 support, you can set the EHCI HCD (that's host controller device) option to *y* or *m*.

After you select the UHCI or OHCI interface support, you have to build the driver modules for specific USB devices on your system. For more information on USB devices, consult the documentation in the `/usr/src/linux*/Documentation/usb` directory — especially the links in the `usb-help.txt` file.

Kernel hacking

This set of options enables you to use the SysRq key (equivalent to pressing Alt+PrintScreen on your keyboard) to get important status information right after a system crash. This information is useful if you're a Linux developer who expects to debug the kernel. Most users set these options to No (because most users run a stable version of the kernel and don't expect to fix kernel errors).

Building the Kernel

After configuring the kernel options, click the Save and Exit button in the main configuration window (refer to Figure 6-1). Now you have to build the kernel. This involves typing three commands to perform three tasks.

Initiate the next three tasks by using a single command line (you can enter multiple semicolon-separated commands on the same line) so you can type the line; then press Enter, and take a break. This part takes a while. Depending on your system, making a new kernel can take anywhere from a few minutes to over an hour.

Type the following on a single line to initiate the process:

```
make dep; make clean; make zImage
```

The `make dep` command determines which files have changed and what must be compiled again. The `make clean` command deletes old, unneeded files (such as old copies of the kernel). Finally, `make zImage` creates the new kernel in a compressed file named `zImage` and places it in a certain directory.

If you link too many features into the kernel (by answering Yes to many configuration options), the kernel file size may be too big to fit in the 640K of memory a PC can use as it boots up. This 640K limit exists because Intel x86 processors start in real mode and can only access 1MB of memory, of which 640K is available for programs. This limit is a leftover from the old MS-DOS days, and it applies only as the Linux kernel is initially loaded as the PC starts. In this case, the `make` command displays an error message such as the following:

```
System is too big. Try using bzImage or modules.
```

If you get a "System is too big" error, type **make bzImage** to use a different type of compressed kernel that may fit within the memory limits. Otherwise, go through the `make config step` again and eliminate unnecessary features by selecting No for those configuration questions. For other features you really need or may want to try out, select *m* to create modules. Although the kernel size is limited at startup, the kernel can load as many modules as it needs once the boot process is complete.

As the kernel is built, you see a lot of messages on-screen. When it's all over, there is a new kernel in the form of a compressed file named `zImage` in the `/usr/src/linux*/arch/i386/boot` directory.

To use the new kernel, you have to copy the kernel to the `/boot` directory under a specific name and edit the `/etc/grub.conf` file to set up GRUB — the boot loader. Before you proceed with the kernel installation, however, you have to build and install the modules.

Building and Installing the Modules

If you select any modules during the kernel configuration, you have to build the modules and install them. Perform these tasks with the following steps:

1. **Type the following commands to build the modules:**

   ```
   cd /usr/src/linux*
   make modules
   ```

   The current set of modules in a directory is named after the version of the Linux kernel your system is running. For example, if your system runs kernel version 2.4.20-20.1.2013.nptl, the modules are in the following directory:

   ```
   /lib/modules/2.4.20-20.1.2013.nptl
   ```

2. **Move the module directory to a new location as follows:**

   ```
   mv /lib/modules/2.4.20-20.1.2013.nptl
      /lib/modules/2.4.20-20.1.2013.nptl-old
   ```

3. **Install the new modules with the following command:**

   ```
   make modules_install
   ```

Now you can install the kernel and make it available for GRUB to boot.

Installing the New Kernel and Setting Up GRUB

Red Hat Linux uses GRUB to load the Linux kernel from the disk. The configuration file `/etc/grub.conf` lists the kernel binary file that GRUB runs. You can examine the contents of the GRUB configuration file by typing the following command:

```
cat /etc/grub.conf
```

Here is what I see when I try this command on one of my systems:

```
# grub.conf generated by anaconda
#
# Note that you do not have to rerun grub after making changes to this file
# NOTICE:  You have a /boot partition.  This means that
#          all kernel and initrd paths are relative to /boot/, eg.
#          root (hd0,2)
#          kernel /vmlinuz-version ro root=/dev/hda5
#          initrd /initrd-version.img
#boot=/dev/hda
default=0
timeout=10
splashimage=(hd0,2)/grub/splash.xpm.gz
title Red Hat Linux (2.4.20-20.1.2013.nptl)
        root (hd0,2)
        kernel /vmlinuz-2.4.20-20.1.2013.nptl ro root=LABEL=/
        initrd /initrd-2.4.20-20.1.2013.nptl.img
title Windows XP
        rootnoverify (hd0,1)
        chainloader +1
```

Here's what the lines in /etc/grub.conf file mean (the lines that begin with # are comments):

✦ default=0 — Specifies the first boot entry as the default one that GRUB should boot. If this were set to 1, GRUB would boot the second boot.

✦ timeout=10 — Causes GRUB to boot the default entry automatically after waiting for 10 seconds. If other boot entries are in the file, the user may select another one from a boot menu GRUB displays.

• The four lines starting with title Red Hat Linux (2.4.20-20.1.2013.nptl) constitute the first boot entry — and this entry defines a specific kernel file GRUB can boot. You can make GRUB boot another kernel by adding a similar section to the configuration file. Here's the meaning of the lines in this boot entry:

• root (hd0,2) — Sets the root device to the third partition of the first hard drive. This is where Red Hat Linux is installed on this particular system.

• kernel /vmlinuz-2.4.20-20.1.2013.nptl ro root=LABEL=/ — Identifies the kernel GRUB loads. In this case, the kernel file is vmlinuz-2.4.20-20.1.2013.nptl, which is located in the root device. In my system, that partition is mounted on the /boot directory. In other words, GRUB loads the kernel file /boot/vmlinuz-2.4.20-20.1.2013.nptl.

- `initrd /initrd-2.4.20-20.1.2013.nptl.img` line specifies a
  file that contains an initial RAM disk (`initrd` stands for initial RAM
  disk) image that serves as a file system before the disks are available.
  The Linux kernel uses the RAM disk — a block of memory used as a
  disk — to get started; then it loads other driver modules and begins
  using the hard drive.

✦ The three lines starting with `title Windows XP` are the second boot
  entry and refer to the Windows XP operating system that happens to be
  on this system. The text next to the title line appears in the GRUB menu.

On systems that have a Windows partition, the GRUB configuration file typically includes another section with details for the operating system (perhaps
Windows XP or Windows 2000) on that partition.

To configure GRUB to boot the new Linux kernel (the one you just built),
follow these steps:

1. **Copy the new kernel binary to the** `/boot` **directory.**

The new, compressed kernel file is in the `/usr/src/linux*/arch/`
`i386/boot` directory. If you have typed the command `make zImage`,
the kernel filename is `zImage`; if you have built the kernel with the `make`
`bzImage` command, the filename is `bzImage`. I simply copy that file to
the `/boot` directory with the same name:

```
cp /usr/src/linux*/arch/i386/boot/zImage /boot
```

If the kernel filename is `bzImage`, make sure you use `bzImage` instead
of `zImage`. You can use any other filename you want, as long as you use
the same filename when referring to the kernel in the `/etc/grub.conf`
file in Step 3.

2. **Save the old** `System.map` **file in the** `/boot` **directory, and copy the**
new map file.

I assume you have rebuilt kernel version 2.4.20-20.1.2013.nptl after
changing some configuration options:

```
mv /boot/System.map-2.4.20-20.1.2013.nptl /boot/System.map-
   2.4.20-20.1.2013.nptl-old
cp /usr/src/linux*/System.map /boot/System.map-2.4.20-20.1.2013.nptl
cd /boot
ln -s System.map-2.4.20-20.1.2013.nptl System.map
```

3. **Use your favorite text editor to edit the** `/etc/grub.conf` **file to add**
the following lines just after the `timeout` **line in the file:**

```
title Red Hat Linux (2.4.20-20.1.2013.nptl NEW)
        root (hd0,2)
        kernel /zImage ro root=LABEL=/
```

On your system, you should make sure the `root` line is correct — instead of (`hd0,2`), you should list the correct disk partition where the Linux `root` directory (`/`) is located. Also, use the correct filename for the kernel image file (for example, `/bzImage` if the kernel file is so named).

Note that I don't show the `initrd` line anymore because I assume you're no longer using a modular SCSI driver, even if your system has a SCSI adapter.

4. **Save the** `grub.conf` **file, and exit the editor.**

Now you're ready to reboot the system and try out the new kernel.

Rebooting the System

After you finish configuring GRUB, you can restart the system. While you're still logged in as `root`, type the following command to reboot the system:

```
reboot
```

When you see the GRUB screen, select the name you have assigned to the new kernel in the `/etc/grub.conf` file.

After the system reboots, you should see the familiar graphical login screen. To see proof that you're indeed running the new kernel, log in as a user, open a terminal window, and type **uname -srv**. This command shows you the kernel version, as well as the date and time when this kernel was built. If you have upgraded the kernel source, you should see the version number for the new kernel. If you have simply rebuilt the kernel for the same old kernel version, the date and time should match the time when you rebuilt the kernel. That's your proof that the system is running the new kernel.

If the system hangs (nothing seems to happen — there is no output on the screen and no disk activity), you may have skipped a step during the kernel rebuild. You can power the PC off and on to reboot. This time, select the name of the old working kernel at the GRUB screen.

If you cannot boot the older version of Red Hat Linux either, use the emergency boot disk (containing an earlier, but working, version of Linux) to start the system. Then you can repeat the kernel rebuild and installation process, making sure you follow all the steps correctly.

Book VII

Security

The 5th Wave
By Rich Tennant

"Room service? Please send someone up to refresh the mini bar, make up the room and defrag the harddrive."

Contents at a Glance

Chapter 1: Understanding Network and Host Security

In This Chapter

✔ **Establishing a security policy and framework**

✔ **Understanding host-security issues**

✔ **Understanding network-security issues**

✔ **Translating computer-security terminology**

✔ **Keeping up with security news and updates**

*I*n this chapter, I explain why you should worry about security and then give you a high-level view of how to get a handle on security. I explain the idea of an overall security framework and explain the two key aspects of security — host security and network security. I end this chapter by introducing you to the terminology used in discussing computer security.

Why Worry About Security?

In today's networked world, you have to worry about your Red Hat Linux system's security. For a standalone system, or a system used in an isolated local area network (LAN), you have to focus on protecting the system from the users and the users from one another. In other words, you don't want a user to modify or delete system files, whether intentionally or unintentionally. Also, you don't want a user destroying another user's files.

If your Red Hat Linux system is connected to the Internet, you have to secure the system from unwanted accesses over the Internet. These intruders — or *crackers*, as they are commonly known — typically impersonate a user, steal or destroy information, and even deny you access to your own system (this is known as a *Denial of Service* or *DoS* attack).

By its very nature, an Internet connection makes your system accessible to any other system on the Internet. After all, the Internet connects a huge number of networks across the globe. In fact, the client/server architecture of Internet services, such as HTTP (Web) and FTP, rely on the wide-open network access the Internet provides. Unfortunately, the easy accessibility to Internet services running on your system also means anyone on the Net can easily access your system.

If you operate an Internet host that provides information to others, you certainly want everyone to access your system's Internet services, such as FTP and Web servers. However, these servers often have vulnerabilities that crackers may exploit in order to cause harm to your system. You need to know about the potential security risks of Internet services — and the precautions you can take to minimize the risk of someone exploiting the weaknesses of your FTP or Web server.

You also want to protect your company's internal network from outsiders, even though your goal is to provide information to the outside world through a Web or FTP server. You can protect your internal network by setting up an Internet *firewall* — a controlled access point to the internal network — and placing the Web and FTP servers on a host outside the firewall.

Establishing a Security Framework

The first step in securing your Red Hat Linux system is to set up a *security policy* — a set of guidelines that state what you enable users (as well as visitors over the Internet) to do on your Red Hat Linux system. The level of security you establish depends on how you use the Red Hat Linux system — and on how much is at risk if someone gains unauthorized access to your system.

If you're a system administrator for one or more Red Hat Linux systems at an organization, you probably want to involve company management, as well as the users, in setting up the security policy. Obviously, you cannot create a draconian policy that blocks all access (that would prevent anyone from effectively working on the system). On the other hand, if the users are creating or using data valuable to the organization, you have to set up a policy that protects the data from disclosure to outsiders. In other words, the security policy should strike a balance between the users' needs and the need to protect the system.

For a standalone Red Hat Linux system, or a home system that you occasionally connect to the Internet, the security policy can be just a listing of the Internet services you want to run on the system and the user accounts you plan to set up on the system. For any larger organization, you probably have one or more Red Hat Linux systems on a LAN connected to the Internet — preferably through a firewall (to reiterate, a firewall is a device that controls the flow of Internet Protocol — IP — packets between the LAN and the Internet). In such cases, it's best to think of computer security across the entire organization systematically. Figure 1-1 shows the key elements of an organization-wide framework for computer security.

The security framework outlined in Figure 1-1 starts with the development of a security policy based on business requirements and risk analysis.

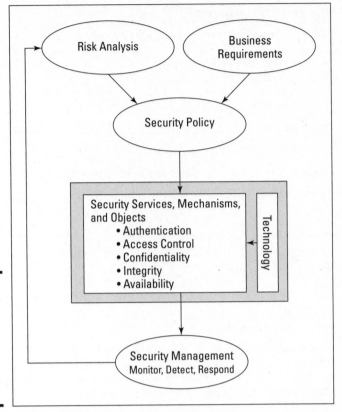

Figure 1-1:
Start with a compre-
hensive framework
for computer
security.

Determine business requirements for security

The business requirements identify the security needs of the business —
the computer resources and information you have to protect (including any
requirements imposed by applicable laws, such as the requirement to protect the privacy of some types of data). Typical security requirements may
include items such as the following:

✦ Enable access to information by authorized users

✦ Implement business rules that specify who has access to what
information

✦ Employ a strong user-authentication system

✦ Deny malicious or destructive actions on data

✦ Protect data from end to end as it moves across networks

✦ Implement all security and privacy requirements that applicable laws
impose

Perform risk analysis

Risk analysis is all about identifying and assessing risks — potential events that can harm your Red Hat Linux system. The analysis involves determining the following and performing some analysis to determine the priority of handling the risks:

✦ **Threats:** What you're protecting against

✦ **Vulnerabilities:** Weaknesses that may be exploited (these are the risks)

✦ **Probability:** The likelihood that vulnerability will be exploited

✦ **Impact:** The effect of exploiting a specific vulnerability

✦ **Mitigation:** What to do to reduce vulnerabilities

Typical threats

Before I further describe risk analysis, here are some typical threats to your Red Hat Linux system:

✦ **Denial of Service:** The computer and network are tied up so legitimate users cannot make use of the systems. For businesses, Denial of Service can mean loss of revenue.

✦ **Unauthorized access:** Use of the computer and network by someone who isn't an authorized user. The unauthorized user can steal information or maliciously corrupt or destroy data. Some businesses may be hurt by the negative publicity from the mere act of an unauthorized user gaining access to the system, even if there is no explicit damage to any data.

✦ **Disclosure of information to the public:** The unauthorized release of information to the public. For example, the disclosure of a password file enables potential attackers to figure out username and password combinations for accessing a system. Exposure of other sensitive information, such as financial and medical data, may be a potential liability for a business.

Typical vulnerabilities

The threats to your system and network come from exploitation of vulnerabilities in your organization's resources — both computer and people. Some common vulnerabilities are the following:

✦ People's foibles (divulging passwords, losing security cards, and so on)

✦ Internal network connections (routers, switches)

✦ Interconnection points (gateways — routers and firewalls — between the Internet and the internal network)

+ Third-party network providers (ISPs, long-distance carriers) with looser security

+ Operating system security holes (potential holes in Internet servers, such as those associated with `sendmail`, `named`, `bind`, and so on)

+ Application security holes (known security holes in specific applications)

The 1-2-3 of risk analysis (probability and impact)

To perform risk analysis, assign a numeric value to the probability and impact of each potential vulnerability. To develop a workable risk analysis, do the following for each vulnerability or risk:

1. Assign subjective ratings of Low, Medium, and High for the probability. As the ratings suggest, Low probability means a lesser chance that the vulnerability will be exploited; High probability means a greater chance.

2. Assign similar ratings to impact. What you consider impact is up to you. If the exploitation of a vulnerability will affect your business greatly, assign it a High impact.

3. Assign a numeric value to the three levels — Low = 1, Medium = 2, and High = 3 — for both probability and impact.

4. Multiply the probability by the impact — you can think of this product as the *risk level*. Then make a decision to develop protections for vulnerabilities that exceed a specific threshold for the product of probability and impact. For example, you may choose to handle all vulnerabilities with a probability-times-impact greater than 6.

If you want to characterize the probability and impact with finer gradations, pick a scale of 1 through 5 (for example) instead of 1 through 3, and follow the same steps as before.

Establish security policy

Using risk analysis and any business requirements you may have to address (regardless of risk level) as a foundation, you can craft a security policy for the organization. The security policy typically addresses the following areas:

+ **Authentication:** What method will be used to ensure that a user is the real user? Who gets access to the system? What is the minimum length and complexity of passwords? How often do users change passwords? How long can a user be idle before that user is logged out automatically?

+ **Authorization:** What can different classes of users do on the system? Who can have the `root` password?

✦ **Data protection:** What data must be protected? Who has access to the data? Is encryption necessary for some data?

✦ **Internet access:** What are the restrictions on users (from the LAN) accessing the Internet? What Internet services (such as Web, Internet Relay Chat, and so on) can users access? Are incoming e-mails and attachments scanned for viruses? Is there a network firewall? Are virtual private networks (VPNs) used to connect private networks across the Internet?

✦ **Internet services:** What Internet services are allowed on each Linux system? Are there any file servers? Mail servers? Web servers? What services run on each type of server? What services, if any, run on Linux systems used as desktop workstations?

✦ **Security audits:** Who tests whether the security is adequate? How often is the security tested? How are problems handled when found during security testing?

✦ **Incident handling:** What are the procedures for handling any computer security incidents? Who must be informed? What information must be gathered to help with the investigation of incidents?

✦ **Responsibilities:** Who is responsible for maintaining security? Who monitors log files and audit trails for signs of unauthorized access? Who maintains the database of security policy?

Implement security solutions (mitigation)

After you analyze the risks — vulnerabilities — and develop a security policy, you have to select the mitigation approach: how to protect against specific vulnerabilities. This is where you develop an overall security solution based on security policy, business requirements, and available technology — a solution that consists of the following:

✦ Services (authentication, access control, encryption)

✦ Mechanisms (username/password, firewalls)

✦ Objects (hardware, software)

Manage security

In addition to implementing security solutions, you have to install security management that continually monitors, detects, and responds to any security incidents.

The combination of the risk analysis, security policy, security solutions, and security management provides the overall security framework. Such a framework helps establish a common level of understanding of security concerns — and a common basis for the design and implementation of security solutions.

Securing Red Hat Linux

After you have defined a security policy, you can proceed to secure the system according to the policy. The exact steps depend on what you want to do with the system — whether it's a server or a workstation and how many users must access the system.

To secure the Red Hat Linux system, you have to handle two broad categories of security issues:

✦ **Host security issues** that relate to securing the operating system and the files and directories on the system

✦ **Network security issues** that refer to the threat of attacks over the network connection

Understanding the host security issues

Here are some high-level guidelines to address host security (I cover some of these topics in detail in Chapter 2 of this mini-book):

✦ When installing Red Hat Linux, select only the package groups you need for your system. Don't install unnecessary software. For example, if your system is used as a workstation, you don't have to install most of the servers (Web server, news server, and so on).

✦ Create initial user accounts and make sure all passwords are strong enough that password-cracking programs can't "guess" them. Red Hat Linux includes tools to enforce strong passwords.

✦ Set file ownerships and permissions to protect important files and directories. Use the new access control lists (ACLs) to manage who gets to use which files and directories.

✦ Use the GNU Privacy Guard (GnuPG) to encrypt or decrypt files with sensitive information and to authenticate files that you download from Red Hat. GnuPG comes with Red Hat Linux, and you can use the gpg command to perform the tasks such as encrypt or decrypt a file and digitally sign a file.

✦ Use file integrity checking tools, such as Tripwire, to monitor any changes to crucial system files and directories.

✦ Periodically check various log files for signs of any break-ins or attempted break-ins. These log files are in the /var/log directory of your system.

✦ Install security updates from Red Hat, as soon as they become available. These security updates fix known vulnerabilities in Red Hat Linux.

Understanding network security issues

The issue of security comes up as soon as you connect your organization's internal network to the Internet. This is true even if you connect a single computer to the Internet, but security concerns are more pressing when an entire internal network is opened to the world.

If you're an experienced system administrator, you already know that it's not the cost of managing an Internet presence that worries corporate management; their main concern is security. To get your management's backing for the Web site, you have to lay out a plan to keep the corporate network secure from intruders.

You may think that you can avoid jeopardizing the internal network by connecting only the external servers, such as Web and FTP servers, to the Internet. However, employing this simplistic approach isn't wise. It's like deciding not to drive because you may have an accident. Not having a network connection between your Web server and your internal network also has the following drawbacks:

✦ You cannot use network file transfers, such as FTP, to copy documents and data from your internal network to the Web server.

✦ Users on the internal network cannot access the corporate Web server.

✦ Users on the internal network don't have access to Web servers on the Internet. Such a restriction makes a valuable resource — the Web — inaccessible to the users in your organization.

A practical solution to this problem is to set up an Internet firewall and to put the Web server on a highly secured host outside the firewall.

In addition to using a firewall, here are some of the other steps you should take to address network security (I explain these further in Chapter 3 of this mini-book):

✦ Enable only those Internet services you need on a system. In particular, don't enable services that are not properly configured.

✦ Use Secure Shell (`ssh`) for remote logins. Don't use the "r" commands, such as `rlogin` and `rsh`.

✦ Secure any Internet services such as FTP or TELNET that you want to run on your system. You can use the TCP wrapper access control files — `/etc/hosts.allow` and `/etc/hosts.deny` — to secure some of these services.

✦ Promptly fix any known vulnerabilities of Internet services that you choose to run. Typically you do this by downloading and installing the latest server RPM file from Red Hat.

Learning Computer Security Terminology

Computer books, magazine articles, and experts on computer security use a number of terms with unique meanings. You need to know these terms to understand discussions about computer security (and to communicate effectively with security vendors). Table 1-1 describes some of the commonly used computer security terms.

Table 1-1	Commonly Used Computer Security Terminology
Term	*Description*
Application gateway	A proxy service that acts as a gateway for application-level protocols, such as FTP, TELNET, and HTTP.
Authentication	The process of confirming that a user is indeed who he or she claims to be. The typical authentication method is a challenge-response method wherein the user enters a username and secret password to confirm his or her identity.
Backdoor	A security weakness a cracker places on a host in order to bypass security features.
Bastion host	A highly secured computer that serves as an organization's main point of presence on the Internet. A bastion host typically resides on the perimeter network, but a dual-homed host (with one network interface connected to the Internet and the other to the internal network) is also a bastion host.
Buffer overflow	A security flaw in a program that enables a cracker to send an excessive amount of data to that program and to overwrite parts of the running program with code in the data being sent. The result is that the cracker can execute arbitrary code on the system and possibly gain access to the system as a privileged user. The new `exec-shield` feature of the Linux kernel protects against buffer overflows.
Certificate	An electronic document that identifies an entity (such as an individual, an organization, or a computer) and associates a public key with that identity. A certificate contains the certificate holder's name, a serial number, expiration date, a copy of the certificate holder's public key, and the digital signature of the Certificate Authority so a recipient can verify that the certificate is real.
Certificate Authority (CA)	An organization that validates identities and issues certificates.
Cracker	A person who breaks into (or attempts to break into) a host, often with malicious intent.
Confidentiality of data	A state of being accessible to no one but you (usually achieved by encryption).
Decryption	The process of transforming encrypted information into its original, intelligible form.

(continued)

Table 1-1 *(continued)*

Term	Description
Denial of Service (DoS)	An attack that uses so many of the resources on your computer and network that legitimate users cannot access and use the system.
Digital signature	A one-way MD5 or SHA-1 hash of a message encrypted with the private key of the message originator, used to verify the integrity of a message and ensure nonrepudiation.
DMZ	Another name for the perimeter network. (DMZ originally stood for *demilitarized zone*, the buffer zone separating the warring North and South in Korea and Vietnam.)
Dual-homed host	A computer with two network interfaces (think of each network as a home).
Encryption	The process of transforming information so it's unintelligible to anyone but the intended recipient. The transformation is done by a mathematical operation between a key and the information.
Firewall	A controlled-access gateway between an organization's internal network and the Internet. A dual-homed host can be configured as a firewall.
Hash	The result when a mathematical function converts a message into a fixed-size numeric value known as a *message digest* (or *hash*). The MD5 algorithm, for example, produces a 128-bit message digest; the Secure Hash Algorithm-1 (SHA-1) generates a 160-bit message digest. The hash of a message is encrypted with the private key of the sender to produce the digital signature.
Host	A computer on a network that is configured to offer services to other computers on the network.
Integrity	Of received data, a state of being the same as originally sent (that is, unaltered in transit).
IPSec (IP Security Protocol)	A security protocol for the Network layer of the OSI Networking Model, designed to provide cryptographic security services for IP packets. IPSec provides encryption-based authentication, integrity, access control, and confidentiality (visit `www.ietf.org/html.charters/ipsec-charter.html` for the list of RFCs related to IPSec).
IP spoofing	An attack in which a cracker figures out the IP address of a trusted host and then sends packets that appear to come from the trusted host. The attacker can send packets but cannot see responses. However, the attacker can predict the sequence of packets and essentially send commands that set up a backdoor for future break-ins.
Nonrepudiation	A security feature that prevents the sender of data from being able to deny ever having sent the data.

Term	Description
Packet	A collection of bytes, assembled according to a specific protocol, that serves as the basic unit of communication on a network. On TCP/IP networks, for example, the packet may be referred to as an *IP packet* or a *TCP/IP packet*.
Packet filtering	Selective blocking of packets according to type of packet (as specified by the source and destination IP address or port).
Perimeter network	A network between the Internet and the protected internal network. The perimeter network (also known as DMZ) is where the bastion host resides.
Port scanning	A method of discovering which ports are open (in other words, which Internet services are enabled) on a system. Performed by sending connection requests to the ports, one by one. This procedure is usually a precursor to further attacks.
Proxy server	A server on the bastion host that enables internal clients to access external servers (and enables external clients to access servers inside the protected network). There are proxy servers for various Internet services, such as FTP and HTTP.
Public key cryptography	An encryption method that uses a pair of keys — a private key and a public key — to encrypt and decrypt the information. Anything encrypted with the public key can be decrypted only with the corresponding private key, and vice versa.
Public Key Infrastructure (PKI)	A set of standards and services that enables the use of public key cryptography and certificates in a networked environment. PKI facilitates tasks, such as issuing, renewing, and revoking certificates, and generating and distributing public and private key pairs.
Screening router	An Internet router that filters packets.
Setuid program	A program that runs with the permissions of the owner regardless of who runs the program. For example, if a setuid program is owned by `root`, that program has `root` privileges regardless of who has started the program. Crackers often exploit vulnerabilities in setuid programs to gain privileged access to a system.
Symmetric key encryption	An encryption method wherein the same key is used to encrypt and decrypt the information.
Threat	An event or activity, deliberate or unintentional, with the potential for causing harm to a system or network.
Trojan Horse	A program that masquerades as a benign program, but, in fact, is a backdoor used for attacking a system. Attackers often install a collection of Trojan Horse programs that enable the attacker to freely access the system with `root` privileges, yet hide that fact from the system administrator. Such collections of Trojan Horse programs are called *rootkits*.

(continued)

Table 1-1 *(continued)*

Term	Description
Virus	A self-replicating program that spreads from one computer to another by attaching itself to other programs.
Vulnerability	A flaw or weakness that may cause harm to a system or network.
Worm	A self-replicating program that copies itself from one computer to another over a network.

Keeping Up with Security News and Updates

To keep up with the latest security alerts, you may want to visit one or more of the following sites on a daily basis:

- ✦ CERT Coordination Center at `www.cert.org`
- ✦ Computer Incident Advisory Capability (CIAC) at `www.ciac.org/ciac/`
- ✦ National Infrastructure Protection Center at `www.nipc.gov`

If you have access to Internet newsgroups, you can periodically browse the following:

- ✦ `comp.security.announce` — A moderated newsgroup that includes announcements from CERT about security.
- ✦ `comp.security.unix` — A newsgroup that includes discussions of UNIX security issues, including items related to Red Hat Linux.

If you prefer to receive regular security updates through e-mail, you can also sign up for (subscribe to) various mailing lists:

- ✦ `redhat-watch-list` — Follow the directions in `www.redhat.com/mailing-lists/` to subscribe to this mailing list.
- ✦ `linux-security` — Follow the directions in `www.redhat.com/mailing-lists/` to subscribe to this mailing list.
- ✦ FOCUS-LINUX — Fill out the form in `www.securityfocus.com/cgi-bin/subscribe.pl` to subscribe to this mailing list focused on Linux security issues.
- ✦ Cert Advisory mailing list — Follow the directions in `www.cert.org/contact_cert/certmaillist.html` to subscribe to this mailing list.

Finally, you should check the Red Hat Web site at `www.redhat.com/apps/support/errata/index.html` for updates that may fix any known security problems with Red Hat Linux.

Chapter 2: Securing the Host

In This Chapter

✓ **Securing passwords**

✓ **Protecting files and directories**

✓ **Encrypting and signing files with GnuPG**

✓ **Monitoring system security**

*H*ost is the techie term for your Red Hat Linux system — especially when you use it to provide services on a network. But the term makes sense even when you think of the computer by itself; it's the host for everything that runs on it — the operating system and all the applications. A key aspect of computer security is to secure the host.

In this chapter, I take you through a few key steps you should follow in securing your Red Hat Linux host. These steps include installing operating system updates, protecting passwords, protecting the files and directories, using encryption if necessary, and monitoring the security of the system. You can monitor host security by examining log files for any suspicious activities and by using the Tripwire tool to see whether anyone has messed with important files on your system.

Installing Operating System Updates

Red Hat Linux and related application updates come in RPM files. To manually download and install the updates, follow these steps:

1. **Log in as** `root` **and create a directory for the updates:**

   ```
   mkdir /usr/local/updates
   cd /usr/local/updates
   ```

2. **Use the** `wget` **command to download the updates from Red Hat's FTP site.**

   For example, to download the updates for the i386 version of Red Hat Linux version 9, type

   ```
   wget ftp://updates.redhat.com/9/en/os/i386/\*.rpm
   wget ftp://updates.redhat.com/9/en/os/noarch/\*.rpm
   ```

3. **Install all updates with the following command:**

```
rpm -F *
```

4. **Delete the update files with the command:**

```
rm -fr /usr/local/updates
```

Securing Passwords

Historically, UNIX passwords are stored in the /etc/passwd file, which any user can read. For example, a typical old-style /etc/passwd file entry for the root user looks like this:

```
root:t6Z7NWDK1K8sU:0:0:root:/root:/bin/bash
```

The fields are separated by colons (:), and the second field contains the password in encrypted form. To check whether a password is valid, the login program encrypts the plain-text password the user enters and compares the password with the contents of the /etc/passwd file. If there is a match, the user is allowed to log in.

Password-cracking programs work just like the login program, except that these programs pick one word at a time from a dictionary, encrypt the word, and compare the encrypted word with the encrypted passwords in the /etc/passwd file for a match. To crack the passwords, the intruder needs the /etc/passwd file. Often, crackers use weaknesses of various Internet servers (such as mail and FTP) to get a copy of the /etc/passwd file.

Recently, several improvements have made passwords more secure in Red Hat Linux. These include shadow passwords and pluggable authentication modules, and you can install these easily as you install Red Hat Linux. During Red Hat Linux installation, one step involves making selections in an Authentication Configuration screen. If you accept the default selections — Enable MD5 passwords and Enable shadow passwords — you automatically enable more secure passwords in Red Hat Linux.

Shadow passwords

Obviously, leaving passwords lying around where anyone can get at them — even if they're encrypted — is bad security. So instead of storing passwords in the /etc/passwd file (which any user can read), Red Hat Linux now stores them in a shadow password file, /etc/shadow. Only the superuser (root) can read this file. For example, here is the entry for root in the new-style /etc/passwd file:

```
root:x:0:0:root:/root:/bin/bash
```

In this case, note that the second field contains an x instead of an encrypted password. The x is the *shadow password*; the actual encrypted password is now stored in the /etc/shadow file where the entry for root is like this:

```
root:$1$AAAni/yN$uESHbzUpy9Cgfoo1Bf0tSO:11077:0:99999:7:-1:-1:134540356
```

The format of the /etc/shadow entries with colon-separated fields resembles the entries in the /etc/passwd file, but the meanings of most fields differ. The first field is still the username, and the second one is the encrypted password.

The remaining fields in each /etc/shadow entry control when the password expires. You don't have to interpret or change these entries in the /etc/shadow file. Instead, use the chage command to change the password-expiration information. For starters, you can check a user's password-expiration information by using the chage command with the -l option, as follows (in this case, you have to be logged in as root):

```
chage -l root
```

This command displays expiration information, including how long the password lasts and how often you can change the password.

If you want to ensure that the user is forced to change a password every 90 days, you can use the -M option to set the maximum number of days that a password stays valid. For example, to make sure that user naba is prompted to change the password in 90 days, I log in as root and type the following command:

```
chage -M 90 naba
```

You can do this for each user account to ensure that all passwords expire when appropriate, and that all users must pick new passwords.

Pluggable authentication modules (PAMs)

In addition to improving the password file's security by using shadow passwords, Red Hat Linux also improves the actual encryption of the passwords stored in the /etc/shadow file, using the MD5 message-digest algorithm described in RFC 1321 (www.faqs.org/rfcs/rfc1321.html or www.cis. ohio-state.edu/cgi-bin/rfc/rfc1321.html). MD5 reduces a message of any length to a 128-bit message digest (or *fingerprint*) of a document so you can digitally sign it by encrypting it with your private key. MD5 works quite well for password encryption, too.

Another advantage of MD5 over older-style password encryption is that the older passwords were limited to a maximum of eight characters; new passwords (encrypted with MD5) can be much longer. Longer passwords are harder to guess, even if the /etc/shadow file falls into the wrong hands.

You can tell that MD5 encryption is in effect in the /etc/shadow file; the encrypted passwords are longer, and they all sport the 1 prefix, as in the second field of the following sample entry:

```
root:$1$AAAni/yN$uESHbzUpy9Cgfoo1Bf0tSO:11077:0:99999:7:-1:-1:134540356
```

An add-in program module called a *pluggable authentication module* (PAM) performs the actual MD5 encryption. Red Hat Linux PAMs provide a flexible method for authenticating users. By setting the PAMs' configuration files, you can change your authentication method on the fly, without having to actually modify vital programs (such as login and passwd) that verify a user's identity.

Red Hat Linux uses PAM capabilities extensively. The PAMs reside in many different modules (more about this momentarily); their configuration files are in the /etc/pam.d directory of your system. Check out the contents of this directory on your system by typing the following command:

```
ls /etc/pam.d
```

Each configuration file in this directory specifies how users are authenticated for a specific utility. For example, there is a file for login, passwd, and su. Here's what I see when I type **cat /etc/pam.d/passwd** file on my system:

```
#%PAM-1.0
auth        required      pam_stack.so service=system-auth
account     required      pam_stack.so service=system-auth
password    required      pam_stack.so service=system-auth
```

These lines indicate that authentication, account management, and password checking should all be done by using the pam_stack module (/lib/security/pam_stack.so) with the argument service=system-auth. Essentially, the pam_stack module refers to another configuration file in the /etc/pam.d directory. In this case, the configuration file is /etc/pam.d/system-auth. Here's the content of the /etc/pam.d/ system-auth file on my Red Hat Linux PC:

```
#%PAM-1.0
# This file is auto-generated.
# User changes will be destroyed the next time authconfig is run.
```

```
auth   required /lib/security/$ISA/pam_env.so
auth   sufficient /lib/security/$ISA/pam_unix.so likeauth nullok
auth   required /lib/security/$ISA/pam_deny.so
account required /lib/security/$ISA/pam_unix.so
password required /lib/security/$ISA/pam_cracklib.so retry=3 type=
password sufficient /lib/security/$ISA/pam_unix.so nullok use_authtok
md5 shadow
password required /lib/security/$ISA/pam_deny.so
session required /lib/security/$ISA/pam_limits.so
session required /lib/security/$ISA/pam_unix.so
```

Here's a brief explanation of what some of these lines in the configuration file do:

✦ The first `auth` line loads the PAM module `/lib/security/pam_env.so`. This module can set or unset environment variables (the `$ISA` in `/lib/security/$ISA/pam_env.so` refers to an environment variable that's typically not defined, so the effective pathname for the PAM module is `/lib/security/pam_env.so`).

✦ The second `auth` line specifies an authentication module that checks the user's identity by using the PAM module `/lib/security/pam_unix.so` with the argument string `likeauth nullok`. The options in the argument string have the following meanings:

  • `likeauth` — Returns the same value whether the module is used to set new credentials or authenticate an existing username.

  • `nullok` — Allows a blank password.

✦ The third `auth` line in the `/etc/pam.d/system-auth` file denies access to the system if the `pam_unix.so` module's authentication is unsuccessful.

✦ The `account` line in the `/etc/pam.d/system-auth` file checks to make sure that the user account has not expired, that the user is allowed to log in at a given time of day, and so on.

✦ The next two `password` lines in the `/etc/pam.d/system-auth` file specify how passwords are set:

  • The first password line uses the `/lib/security/pam_cracklib.so` module to try to crack the new password (that's what the `cracklib` in the module's name indicates).

- The `retry=3` part indicates that the user can try to enter a new password three times at most. The second `password` line indicates that the MD5 encryption is used to store the password in the `/etc/shadow` file.

When you're done setting the `/etc/pam.d/passwd` configuration file, your choices apply when you use the `passwd` command to change passwords. Here's an example where I am trying to change my password (my comments are shown in italics):

```
passwd
Changing password for user naba.
Changing password for naba
(current) UNIX password:  I type my current password
New password: I type "xyzz"
BAD PASSWORD: it is too short
New password:  I type "transport" as password
BAD PASSWORD: it is based on a dictionary word
New password:  I type "naba12" as the new password
BAD PASSWORD: it is based on your username
passwd: Authentication token manipulation error
```

In this case, the `passwd` program is using the PAM module to check my identity (when I first type my current password) and make sure that each of the new passwords I try are strong. Finally, the PAM modules abort the `passwd` program after I fail to select a good password in three tries.

Protecting Files and Directories

One important aspect of securing the host is to protect important system files — and the directories that contain these files. You can protect the files through the file ownership and through the permission settings that control who can read, write, or (in the case of executable programs) execute the file.

The default Red Hat Linux file security is controlled through the following settings for each file or directory:

- User ownership
- Group ownership
- Read, Write, Execute permissions for owner
- Read, Write, Execute permissions for group
- Read, Write, Execute permissions for others (everyone else)

Viewing ownerships and permissions

You can see these settings for a file when you look at the detailed listing with the `ls -l` command. For example, type the following command to see the detailed listing of the `/etc/inittab` file:

```
ls -l /etc/inittab
```

The resulting listing should look something like this:

```
-rw-r--r--  1 root    root      1756 Aug 1 17:00 /etc/inittab
```

The first set of characters describes the file permissions for user, group, and others. The third and fourth fields show the user and group that own this file. In this case, both user and group names are the same: `root`.

Changing file ownerships

You can set the user and group ownerships with the `chown` command. For example if the file `/dev/hda` should be owned by the user `root` and the group `disk`, then you would type the following command as `root` to set up this ownership:

```
chown root.disk /dev/hda
```

To change the group ownership alone, use the `chgrp` command. For example, here's how you can change the group ownership of a file to the group named `accounting`:

```
chgrp accounting ledger.out
```

Changing file permissions

Use the `chmod` command to set the file permissions. To use `chmod` effectively, you have to learn how to specify the permission settings. One way is to concatenate one or more letters from each of the following tables, in the order shown (Who/Action/Permission) in Table 2-1:

Table 2-1	File Permission Codes	
Who	*Action*	*Permission*
u user	+ add	r read
g group	- remove	w write
o others	= assign	x execute
a all	s set user ID	

To give everyone read and write access to all files in a directory, type **chmod a+rw ***. On the other hand, to permit everyone to execute a specific file, type **chmod a+x** *filename*.

Another way to specify a permission setting is to use a three-digit sequence of numbers. In a detailed listing, the read, write, and execute permission settings for the user, group, and others appear as the sequence

```
rwxrwxrwx
```

with dashes in place of letters for disallowed operations. Think of rwxr-wxrwx as three occurrences of the string rwx. Now assign the values r=4, w=2, and x=1. To get the value of the sequence rwx, simply add the values of r, w, and x. Thus, rwx = 7. Using this formula, you can assign a three-digit value to any permission setting. For example, if the user can read and write the file but everyone else can only read the file, the permission setting is rw-r--r-- (that's how it appears in the listing), and the value is 644. Thus, if you want all files in a directory to be readable by everyone but writable only by the user, use the following command:

```
chmod 644 *
```

Setting default permission

What permission setting does a file get when you (or a program) creates a new file? The answer is in what is known as the user file-creation mask that you can see and set using the umask command.

Type **umask**, and it prints out a number showing the current file-creation mask. The default setting is different for the root user and other normal users. For the root user the mask is set to 022, whereas the mask for normal users is 002. To see the effect of this file-creation mask and to interpret the meaning of the mask, follow these steps:

1. **Log in as** root **and type the following command:**

   ```
   touch junkfile
   ```

   This creates a file named junkfile with nothing in it.

2. **Type** ls -l junkfile **to that file's permissions.**

   You should see a line similar to the following:

   ```
   -rw-r--r--  1 root    root       0 Aug 24 10:56 junkfile
   ```

   Interpret the numerical value of the permission setting by converting each three-letter permission in the first field (excluding the very first letter) into a number between 0 and 7. For each letter that's present, the first letter gets a value of 4, second letter is 2, and the third is 1. For example, rw- translates to 4+2+0 (because the third letter is missing) or 6. Similarly, r-- is 4+0+0 = 4. Thus the permission string -rw-r--r-- becomes 644.

3. **Subtract the numerical permission setting from 666 and what you get is the** umask **setting.**

   In this case, 666 - 644 gives us a umask of 022.

Thus, a umask of 022 results in a default permission setting of 666-022 = 644. When you rewrite 644 in terms of a permission string, it becomes rw-r--r--.

To set a new umask, type **umask** followed by the numerical value of the mask. Here is how you should go about it:

1. **Figure out what permission settings you want for new files.**

   For example, if you want new files that can be read and written only by the owner and by nobody else, then the permission setting would look like this:

   ```
   rw-------
   ```

2. **Convert the permissions into a numerical value by using the conversion method that assigns 4 to the first field, 2 to the second, and 1 to the third.**

   Thus, for files that are readable and writable only by their owner, the permission setting is 600.

3. **Subtract the desired permission setting from 666 to get the value of the mask.**

   For a permission setting of 600, the mask then becomes 666 - 600 = 066.

4. **Use the** umask **command to set the file-creation mask:**

   ```
   umask 066
   ```

A default umask of 022 is good for system security because it translates to files that have read and write permission for the owner and read permissions for everyone else. The bottom line is that you don't want a default umask that results in files that are writable by the whole wide world.

Checking for set user ID permission

There is another permission setting that can be a security hazard. This permission setting, called the set user ID (or setuid for short), applies to executable files. When the setuid permission is enabled, the file is executed under the user ID of the file's owner. In other words, if an executable program is owned by `root` and the `setuid` permission is set, then no matter who executes that program, it runs as if being executed by `root`. This means that that program can do a lot more (for example, read all files, create new files, and delete files) than what a normal user program could do. Another risk is that if a `setuid` program file has some security hole, crackers can do a lot more damage through such programs than through other vulnerabilities.

You can find all `setuid` programs with a simple find command:

```
find / -type f -perm +4000 -print
```

You should see a list of files such as the following:

```
/usr/bin/chage
/usr/bin/gpasswd
/usr/bin/chfn
/usr/bin/chsh
/usr/bin/newgrp
/usr/bin/passwd
/usr/bin/at
/usr/bin/rcp
/usr/bin/rlogin
/usr/bin/rsh
/usr/bin/sudo
/usr/bin/crontab
... lines deleted ...
```

Many of the programs have the `setuid` permission because they need it, but check the complete list and make sure that there are no strange `setuid` programs (for example, `setuid` programs in a user's home directory).

If you want to see how these permissions are listed by the `ls` command, type **ls -l /usr/bin/passwd** and you should see the permission settings:

```
-r-s--x--x   1 root    root        16128 Jun  5 23:03 /usr/bin/passwd
```

The s in the owner's permission setting (`r-s`) tells you that the `setuid` permission is set.

Using exec-shield

Buffer overflow is (if you'll pardon the expression) the root cause of many Linux security holes. When buffer overflow occurs, a cracker can overwrite data storage areas of memory with instructions designed to execute nasty commands. But what if the Linux kernel refused to execute instructions from any data area? Poof! — no more buffer overflows! That's exactly what the latest Linux kernel does: It protects against the common buffer overflow type of vulnerabilities by making many parts of a program's memory (including the stack where temporary variables are stored) not executable. This feature of the Linux kernel is called `exec-shield`.

The best part about `exec-shield` is that you don't have to fix the applications that have the buffer overflow problem. All you have to do is turn on the feature. To make the process even easier, Red Hat Linux enables `exec-shield` by default.

Some programs may have trouble working correctly when `exec-shield` is enabled. If you have to turn off `exec-shield`, log in as `root` and type the following command from a terminal window:

```
echo 0 > /proc/sys/kernel/exec-shield
```

That command sets the `exec-shield` kernel option to 0. The `exec-shield` option can take one of three values — 0, 1, and 2. Think of these values as four different levels of security. Table 2-2 summarizes the meaning of the four values of `exec-shield`. Red Hat Linux sets `exec-shield` to 1 by default.

Table 2-2	Four Levels of Security Using Exec Shield
This Value of exec-shield	*Has This Meaning*
0	exec-shield is always disabled.
1	exec-shield is enabled for programs compiled with the newest version of gcc compiler.
2	exec-shield is always enabled.

To set `exec-shield` to its default value, type:

```
echo 1 > /proc/sys/kernel/exec-shield
```

Encrypting and Signing Files with GnuPG

Red Hat Linux comes with the *GNU Privacy Guard* (GnuPG or, simply GPG) encryption and authentication utility. With GPG, you can create your public and private key pair, encrypt files using your key, and also digitally sign a message to authenticate that it's really from you. If you send a digitally signed message to someone who has your public key, the recipient can verify that it was you who signed the message.

Understanding public key encryption

The basic idea behind public key encryption is to use a pair of keys — one private and the other public — that are related but can't be used to guess one from the other. Anything encrypted with the private key can be decrypted only with the corresponding public key, and vice versa. The public key is for distribution to other people while you keep the private key in a safe place.

You can use public key encryption to communicate securely with others; Figure 2-1 illustrates the basic idea. Suppose Alice wants to send secure messages to Bob. Each of them would generate public and private key pairs, after which they'd exchange their public keys. Then, when Alice wants to send a message to Bob, she simply encrypts the message using Bob's public key and sends the encrypted message to him. Now the message is secure from any eavesdropping because only Bob's private key can decrypt the message — and only Bob has that key. When Bob receives the message, he uses his private key to decrypt the message and read it.

Figure 2-1:
Bob and Alice can commu-nicate securely with public key encryption.

Bob's public key

Bob's private key

Alice

Alice encrypts the message using Bob's public key.

Bob

Bob decypts the message using his private key.

At this point, you should stop and think and say "Wait a minute!" How does Bob know the message really came from Alice? What if someone else uses Bob's public key and sends a message as if it came from Alice? This is where digital signature comes in.

Understanding digital signatures

The purpose of digital or electronic signatures is the same as pen-and-ink signatures, but how you sign digitally is completely different. Unlike pen-and-ink signatures, your digital signature depends on the message you're signing. The first step in creating a digital signature is to apply a mathematical function on the message and reduce it to a fixed-size message digest (also called *hash* or a *fingerprint*). No matter how big your message is, the message digest is always around 128 or 160 bits, depending on the hashing function.

The next step is to apply public key encryption. Simply encrypt the message digest with your private key, and you get the digital signature for the message. Typically, the digital signature is appended to the end of the message, and voilà! — you get an electronically signed message.

What good does the digital signature do? Well, anyone who wants to verify that the message is indeed signed by you takes your public key and decrypts the digital signature. What they get is the message digest (the encrypted hash) of the message. Then they apply the same hash function to the message and compare the computed hash with the decrypted value. If the two match, then no one has tampered with the message. Because your public key was used to verify the signature, the message must have been signed with the private key known only to you. So the message must be from you!

In the theoretical scenario of Alice sending private messages to Bob, Alice can digitally sign her message to make sure that Bob can tell that the message is really from her. Figure 2-2 illustrates the use of digital signature along with normal public key encryption.

Here's how Alice sends her private message to Bob with the assurance that Bob can really tell it's from her:

1. Alice uses software to compute the message digest of the message and then encrypts the digest using her private key. This is her digital signature for the message.

2. Alice encrypts the message, (again, using some convenient software *and* Bob's public key.

3. She sends both the encrypted message and the digital signature to Bob.

4. Bob decrypts the message using his private key.

5. Bob decrypts the digital signature using Alice's public key. This gives him the message digest.

**Book VII
Chapter 2**

Securing the Host

Figure 2-2:
Alice can
digitally
sign her
message so
that Bob
can tell it's
really from
her.

6. Bob computes the message digest of the message and compares it with what he got by decrypting the digital signature.

7. If the two message digests match, Bob can be sure that the message really came from Alice.

Using GPG

GPG includes the tools you need to use public key encryption and digital signatures. What you use is the gpg command. You can learn to use GPG gradually as you begin using encryption. I show you some of the typical tasks you may perform with GPG.

Generating the key pair

The first thing you have to do is generate your own private-public key pair. Type the following command in a terminal window to generate the key pair:

```
gpg --gen-key
```

If this is your first time with gpg, it creates a .gnupg directory in your home directory and a file named options in that directory. Then gpg exits with a message that asks you to run gpg again. Now you can rerun the command. The steps for generating the key pairs go like this:

1. **Type the** gpg --gen-key **command again.**

   You should see a message like this:

   ```
   Please select what kind of key you want:
       (1) DSA and ElGamal (default)
       (2) DSA (sign only)
       (5) RSA (sign only)
   Your selection?
   ```

2. **Press Enter for the default choice because it's good enough.**

   GPG then prompts you for the key size (the number of bits).

3. **Again, press Enter to accept the default value of 1024 bits.**

   GPG asks you when the keys should expire. The default is to never expire.

4. **If the default is what you want (and why not?), press Enter.**

5. **When GPG asks if you really want the keys to never expire, press y to confirm.**

   GPG prompts you for your name, then your e-mail address, and finally a comment so that the key pair can be associated with your name.

6. **Type each piece of requested information and press Enter.**

7. **When GPG gives you a chance to change the information or confirm it as is, confirm by typing o and then pressing Enter.**

   GPG next prompts you for a passphrase that will be used to protect your private key.

8. **Type a long phrase that includes lower- and uppercase letters, numbers, and punctuation marks — the longer the better — and then press Enter.**

   Careful though; pick a passphrase that you can easily remember.

   GPG generates the keys. It may ask you to perform some work on the PC so that the random number generator can generate enough random numbers for the key-generation process.

Exchanging keys

To communicate with others, you have to give them your public key. You also have to get public keys from those who may send you a message (or someone who might sign a file and you want to verify the signature). GPG keeps the public keys in your key ring. To list the keys in your key ring, type

```
gpg --list-keys
```

To send your public key to someone or place it on a Web site, you have to export the key to a file. The best way is to put the key in what GPG documentation calls an *ASCII-armored* format with a command like this:

```
gpg --armor --export naba@comcast.net > nabakey.asc
```

This command saves my public key in an ASCII-armored format (it basically looks like garbled text) in a file named `nabakey.asc`. Of course, you should replace the e-mail address with your e-mail address (the one you used when you created the key) and the output file name to something different.

After you export the public key to a file, you can mail that file to others or place it in a Web site for use by others.

When you import a key from someone else, you typically get it in an ASCII-armored format as well. For example, if I have Red Hat's GPG public key in a file named `redhatkey.asc`, I would import it into my key ring with the following command:

```
gpg --import redhatkey.asc
```

Use the `gpg --list-keys` to verify that the key is in your key ring. For example, here's what I see when I type **gpg--list-keys** on my system:

```
gpg: please see http://www.gnupg.org/faq.html for more information
/home/naba/.gnupg/pubring.gpg
--------------------------------
pub  1024D/CF492215 2002-08-23 Naba Barkakati (Author) <naba@comcast.net>
sub  1024g/47FED643 2002-08-23

pub  1024D/DB42A60E 1999-09-23 Red Hat, Inc <security@redhat.com>
sub  2048g/961630A2 1999-09-23
```

The next step is to check the fingerprint of the new key. I type the following command to get the fingerprint of the Red Hat key:

```
gpg --fingerprint security@redhat.com
```

This causes GPG to print the fingerprint:

```
pub  1024D/DB42A60E 1999-09-23 Red Hat, Inc <security@redhat.com>
    Key fingerprint = CA20 8686 2BD6 9DFC 65F6 ECC4 2191 80CD DB42 A60E
sub  2048g/961630A2 1999-09-23
```

At this point, you should verify the key fingerprint with someone at Red Hat. For a company like Red Hat, you can verify the fingerprint from a Web page (`www.redhat.com/solutions/security/news/publickey.html`). If you think the key fingerprint is good, you can sign the key and validate it. Here's the command you use to sign the key:

```
gpg --sign-key security@redhat.com
```

GPG displays a message and prompts you on the level of key verification you have performed:

```
gpg: Warning: using insecure memory!
gpg: please see http://www.gnupg.org/faq.html for more information

gpg: checking the trustdb
gpg: checking at depth 0 signed=0 ot(-/q/n/m/f/u)=0/0/0/0/0/1
pub 1024D/DB42A60E created: 1999-09-23 expires: never    trust: -/-
sub 2048g/961630A2 created: 1999-09-23 expires: never
(1). Red Hat, Inc <security@redhat.com>


pub 1024D/DB42A60E created: 1999-09-23 expires: never    trust: -/-
        Fingerprint: CA20 8686 2BD6 9DFC 65F6 ECC4 2191 80CD DB42 A60E

   Red Hat, Inc <security@redhat.com>

How carefully have you verified the key you are about to sign actually belongs
to the person named above? If you don't know what to answer, enter "0".

   (0) I will not answer. (default)
   (1) I have not checked at all.
   (2) I have done casual checking.
   (3) I have done very careful checking.

Your selection?
```

After you answer and press Enter, GPG asks for confirmation and then prompts you for your passphrase. After that GPG signs the key.

Because the key verification and signing is a potential weak link in GPG, be careful about what keys you sign. By signing a key, you basically say that you trust the key to be from that person or organization.

Signing a file

You find it useful to sign files if you send out a file to someone and want to assure the recipient that no one has tampered with the file and that it was you who sent the file. GPG makes it very easy to sign a file. You can compress and sign a file named message with the following command:

```
gpg -o message.sig -s message
```

To verify the signature, type

```
gpg --verify message.sig
```

To get back the original document, simply type

```
gpg -o message --decrypt message.sig
```

Sometimes you don't care about keeping a message secret, but simply want to sign it to indicate that the message is from you. In such a case, you can generate and append a clear text signature with the following command:

```
gpg -o message.asc --clearsign message
```

This command basically appends a clear text signature to the text message. Here's a typical clear text signature block:

```
-----BEGIN PGP SIGNATURE-----
Version: GnuPG v1.0.7 (GNU/Linux)

iD8DBQE9ZYUtjre6e89JIhURAmUzAKDAK8tdQMRrA2qSpaG8rKpYO5dZuACeI9kT
26EaLE5s/zHDiapiW+geXdo=
=U26+
-----END PGP SIGNATURE-----
```

When a message has a clear text signature appended, you can use GPG to verify the signature with the following command:

```
gpg --verify message.asc
```

The last line of the output should say that it's a good signature.

Encrypting and decrypting documents

To encrypt a message meant for a recipient, you can use the `--encrypt` (or `-e`) GPG command. Here's how you might encrypt a message for me if you had my public GPG key:

```
gpg -o message.gpg -e -r naba@comcast.net message
```

The message would be encrypted using my public key (without any signature, but you can add the signature with an `-s` command).

When I receive the `message.gpg` file, I have to decrypt it using my private key. Here's the command I would use:

```
gpg -o message --decrypt message.gpg
```

GPG then prompts me for the passphrase to unlock my private key and then decrypts the message and saves the output in the file named `message`.

If you simply want to encrypt a file and no one else has to decrypt the file, you can use GPG to perform what is called *symmetric encryption*. In this case, you provide a passphrase to encrypt the file with the following GPG command:

```
gpg -o secret.gpg -c somefile
```

GPG prompts you for the passphrase and asks you to repeat the passphrase (to make sure that you didn't mistype anything). Then GPG encrypts the file using a key generated from the passphrase.

To decrypt a file encrypted with a symmetric key, type

```
gpg -o myfile --decrypt secret.gpg
```

GPG prompts you for the passphrase. If you enter the correct passphrase, GPG decrypts the file and saves the output (in this example) in the file named myfile.

Monitoring System Security

Even if you have secured your system, you have to monitor the log files periodically for signs of intrusion. You may want to install the Tripwire software to monitor the integrity of critical system files and directories. Red Hat Linux does not come with the Tripwire package. To use Tripwire, first you have to download it from www.tripwire.org/downloads/index.php. You should download the source *tarball* (a compressed archive of source files) and then build Tripwire. (Book VI, Chapter 4 provides more information on how to build software packages from source files.) After you build and install Tripwire, you can configure it to monitor any changes to specified system files and directories on your system.

You should periodically examine the log files. Many Red Hat Linux applications, including some servers, write log information using the logging capabilities of syslogd. On Red Hat Linux systems, the log files written by syslogd reside in the /var/log directory. Make sure that only the root user can read and write these files.

The syslogd configuration file is /etc/syslog.conf. The default configuration of syslogd should generate the necessary log files; however, if you want to examine and understand the configuration file, type **man syslog.conf** for more information.

You should routinely monitor the following log files:

✦ /var/log/messages contains a wide variety of logging messages, from user logins to messages from services started by the TCP wrapper.

✦ /var/log/secure contains reports from services, such as in.telnetd and in.ftpd, which xinetd starts through the TCP wrapper.

✦ /var/log/maillog contains reports from sendmail.

✦ /var/log/xferlog contains a log of all FTP file transfers.

Red Hat Linux comes with a graphical log-file viewer utility. To use this tool, select Main Menu⇨System Tools⇨System Logs from the GNOME panel. Figure 2-3 shows the System Logs utility.

Figure 2-3: Use the Red Hat System Logs utility to view log files.

The System Logs utility is simple to use. Click the log filename in the left window and view the contents in the scrolling text window to the right.

Because many potential intruders use port-scanning tools in an attempt to establish TCP/IP connections to well-known ports on your system, you should look for messages that indicate attempted connections from unknown hosts (as indicated by names or IP addresses). To do this type of checking, click Security Log in the left window and then browse the log messages that appear in the right window. You'll see lines such as the following:

```
Jun 22 19:30:37 dhcppc1 xinetd[1691]: START: telnet pid=15174 from=192.168.0.4
Jun 22 20:23:00 dhcppc1 xinetd[1691]: START: sgi_fam pid=15356 from=<no address>
```

These lines show you the type of connection (telnet, sgi_fam, and so on) and the IP addresses from where the connections originated. If you want to browse through these messages using a text editor, you can find them in the /var/log/secure file.

Chapter 3: Securing the Network

*T*o secure your Red Hat Linux system, you have to pay attention to both host security and network security. The distinction between the two types of security is somewhat arbitrary because securing the network involves fixing up things on the host that relate to what Internet services your system offers. In this chapter, I explain how you can secure the Internet services (mostly by not offering unnecessary services), how you can use a firewall to stop unwanted network packets from reaching your network, and how to use Secure Shell for secure remote logins.

Securing Internet Services

For an Internet-connected Red Hat Linux system (or even one on a TCP/IP LAN that's not connected to the Internet), a significant threat is the possibility that someone could use one of many Internet services to gain access to your system. Each service — such as mail, Web, or FTP — requires running a server program that responds to client requests arriving over the TCP/IP network. Some of these server programs have weaknesses that can allow an outsider to log in to your system — maybe with `root` privileges. Luckily, Red Hat Linux comes with some facilities you can use to make the Internet services more secure.

Potential intruders can employ a port-scanning tool — a program that attempts to establish a TCP/IP connection at a port and to look for a response — to check which Internet servers are running on your system. Then, to gain access to your system, the intruders can potentially exploit any known weaknesses of one or more services.

Using chkconfig to disable standalone services

To provide Internet services such as Web, mail, and FTP, your Red Hat Linux system has to run server programs that listen to incoming TCP/IP network requests. Some of these servers are started when your system boots, and they run all the time. We call such servers *standalone servers*. The Web server and mail server are examples of standalone servers. The other servers are started on demand by another server called `xinetd`.

You can turn the standalone servers on or off by using the `chkconfig` command. Here's how you should use `chkconfig` to stop unneeded services:

✦ Log in as `root` and type **chkconfig --list** to view all the services set to start automatically at run levels 0 through 6 (see Book VI, Chapter 1 for more on run levels).

✦ The services for run levels 3 and 5 matter most because your Red Hat Linux system is usually at run level 3 (text mode) or 5 (graphical login). Type **runlevel** to see the current run level.

✦ Decide which services you don't need. What you need or don't need depends on how you use your Red Hat Linux system. For example, if it's just a personal workstation, you don't have to run most services.

✦ To stop a service, use the following form of the `chkconfig` command:

```
chkconfig --level 345 service_name off
```

where *service_name* is the name of the service you want to turn off. For example, to prevent the `ypserv` service from automatically starting at run levels 3, 4, and 5, type the following command:

```
chkconfig --level 345 ypserv off
```

Using this approach, you can use `chkconfig` to stop all unneeded services from starting at boot time.

To stop a service immediately, use the `service` command like this:

```
service service_name stop
```

where *service_name* is the name of the service to stop. For example, if the mail server (`sendmail`) is already running, you can stop it with the following command:

```
service sendmail stop
```

Configuring the xinetd server to disable services

In addition to standalone servers such as Web server (`httpd`), mail (`sendmail`), and domain name server (`named`), you have to configure another server separately. That other server, `xinetd` (the Internet super server), starts a host of other Internet services, such as FTP, TELNET, and so on whenever a client makes a request over the network. The `xinetd` server includes some security features that you can use to disable the services that it can start on demand.

The xinetd server reads a configuration file named /etc/xinetd.conf at startup. This file, in turn, refers to configuration files stored in the /etc/xinetd.d directory. The configuration files in /etc/xinetd.d tell xinetd which ports to listen to and which server to start for each port. Type **ls /etc/xinetd.d** to see a list of the files in the /etc/xinetd.d directory on your system. On my system, here's what the ls /etc/xinetd.d command lists:

```
chargen       daytime-udp  imap   ktalk   rlogin   services  time
chargen-udp   echo         imaps  ntalk   rsh      sgi_fam   time-udp
cups-lpd      echo-udp     ipop2  pop3s   rsync    talk
daytime       finger       ipop3  rexec   servers  telnet
```

This list shows all the services xinetd can start. However, the configuration file for a service can also turn off a service simply by having a disable = yes line in the file. For example, here's the telnet file's content:

```
# default: on
# description: The telnet server serves telnet sessions;
#      it uses unencrypted username/password pairs for
#      authentication.
service telnet
{
        flags            = REUSE
        socket_type      = stream
        wait             = no
        user             = root
        server           = /usr/sbin/in.telnetd
        log_on_failure   += USERID
        disable          = yes
}
```

Notice the last line in the configuration file — that line disables the TELNET service.

I won't explain the format of the xinetd configuration files, except to reiterate that you can turn off a service simply by adding the following line in the configuration file somewhere between the two curly braces {...}:

```
        disable          = yes
```

You can also use the chkconfig command to turn on or off the services controlled by xinetd. For example, to allow the TELNET service, type the following command:

```
chkconfig telnet on
```

Depending on how you use your system, you may be able to disable many of the services. If you don't want anyone to log in remotely or download files from your system, simply disable the TELNET and FTP services.

**Book VII
Chapter 3**

**Securing the
Network**

After you make any changes to the `xinetd` configuration files, you must restart the `xinetd` server; otherwise, the changes won't take effect. To restart the `xinetd` server, type the following command:

```
service xinetd restart
```

This stops the `xinetd` server and then starts it again. When it restarts, it'll read the configuration files, and the changes will take effect.

Another security feature of `xinetd` is its use of the TCP wrapper to start various services. The *TCP wrapper* is a block of code that provides an access-control facility for Internet services, acting like a protective package for your message. The TCP wrapper can start other services, such as FTP and TELNET; but before starting a service, it consults the `/etc/hosts.allow` file to see whether the host requesting service is allowed that service. If nothing appears in `/etc/hosts.allow` about that host, TCP wrapper checks the `/etc/hosts.deny` file to see if it should deny the service. If both files are empty, TCP wrapper provides access to the requested service.

Here are the steps to follow to tighten the access to the services that `xinetd` is configured to start:

1. **Use a text editor to edit the `/etc/hosts.deny` file, adding the following line into that file:**

```
ALL:ALL
```

This setting denies all hosts access to any Internet services on your system.

2. **Edit the `/etc/hosts.allow` file and add to it the names of hosts that can access services on your system.**

For example, to enable only hosts from the 192.168.1.0 network and the `localhost` (IP address 127.0.0.1) to access the services on your system, place the following line in the `/etc/hosts.allow` file:

```
ALL: 192.168.1.0/255.255.255.0 127.0.0.1
```

3. **If you want to permit access to a specific Internet service to a specific remote host, you can do so by using the following syntax for a line in `/etc/hosts.allow`:**

```
server_program_name: hosts
```

Here *server_program_name* is the name of the server program (for example, `in.telnetd` for TELNET), and *hosts* is a comma-separated list of hosts that can access the service. You may also write *hosts* as a network address or an entire domain name, such as `.mycompany.com`. For example, here's how you can give TELNET access to all systems in the `mycompany.com` domain:

```
in.telnetd: .mycompany.com
```

 Edit configuration files in the `/etc/xinetd.d` directory to turn off unneeded services; use the `/etc/hosts.deny` and `/etc/hosts.allow` files to control access to the services that are allowed to run on your system. After you edit the files in the `/etc/xinetd.d` directory, remember to type **service xinetd restart** to restart the `xinetd` server.

Using Secure Shell (SSH) for Remote Logins

Red Hat Linux comes with the *Open Secure Shell* (OpenSSH) software, a suite of programs that provides a secure replacement for the Berkeley `r` commands: `rlogin` (remote login), `rsh` (remote shell), and `rcp` (remote copy). OpenSSH uses public key cryptography to authenticate users and to encrypt the communication between two hosts, so users can securely log in from remote systems and copy files securely.

In this section, I briefly describe how to use the OpenSSH software in Red Hat Linux. To learn more about OpenSSH and read the latest news about it, visit `www.openssh.com` or `www.openssh.org`.

The OpenSSH software is installed during Red Hat Linux installation. Table 3-1 lists the main components of the OpenSSH software.

Book VII Chapter 3

Securing the Network

Table 3-1	Components of the OpenSSH Software
Component	*Description*
`/usr/sbin/sshd`	This is the Secure Shell daemon that must run on a host if you want users on remote systems to use the `ssh` client to log in securely. When a connection from an `ssh` client arrives, `sshd` performs authentication using public-key cryptography and establishes an encrypted communication link with the `ssh` client.
`/usr/bin/ssh`	This is the Secure Shell client that users can run to log in to a host that is running `sshd`. Users can also use `ssh` to execute a command on another host.
`/usr/bin/slogin`	A symbolic link to `/usr/bin/ssh`.
`/usr/bin/scp`	The secure copy program that works like `rcp`, but securely. The `scp` program uses `ssh` for data transfer and provides the same authentication and security as `ssh`.

(continued)

Table 3-1 *(continued)*

Component	Description
/usr/bin/ ssh-keygen	You use this program to generate the public and private key pairs you need for the public key cryptography used in OpenSSH. The ssh-keygen program can generate key pairs for both RSA and DSA (Digital Signature Algorithm) authentication.
/etc/ssh/ sshd_config	This configuration file for the sshd server specifies many parameters for sshd — including the port to listen to, the protocol to use (there are two versions of SSH protocols, SSH1 and SSH2, both supported by OpenSSH), and the location of other files.
/etc/ssh/ ssh_config	This is the configuration file for the ssh client. Each user can also have a ssh configuration file named config in the .ssh subdirectory of the user's home directory.

OpenSSH uses public key encryption where the sender and receiver both have a pair of keys — a public key and a private key. The public keys are freely distributed, and each party knows the other's public key. The sender encrypts data by using the recipient's public key. Only the recipient's private key can then decrypt the data.

To use OpenSSH, do both of the following:

✦ If you want to support SSH-based remote logins on a host, start the sshd server on your system. Type **ps ax | grep sshd** to see if the server is already running. If not, log in as root, and type the following command at the shell prompt to ensure that the sshd server starts at system reboot:

```
chkconfig --level 35 sshd on
```

To start the sshd server immediately, type the following command:

```
service sshd start
```

✦ Generate the host keys with the following command:

```
ssh-keygen -d -f /etc/ssh/ssh_host_key -N ''
```

The -d flag causes the ssh-keygen program to generate DSA keys, which the SSH2 protocol uses. If you see a message saying that the file /etc/ssh/ssh_host_key already exists, that means that the key pairs were generated during Red Hat Linux installation. You can then use the existing file without having to regenerate the keys.

A user who wants to log in using `ssh` must also generate the public and private key pair. For example, here is what I do so I can log in from another system on my Red Hat Linux system using SSH:

1. I type the following command to generate the DSA keys for use with SSH2:

   ```
   ssh-keygen -d
   ```

   I am prompted for a passphrase, and the last message informs me that my public key is saved in `/home/naba/.ssh/id_dsa.pub`.

2. I copy my public key — the `/home/naba/.ssh/id_dsa.pub` file — to the remote system and save it as the `~/.ssh/authorized_keys2` file (this refers to the `authorized_keys2` file in the `.ssh` subdirectory of the other system, assuming that the remote system is also another Red Hat Linux system). Note that the 2 in the name of the `authorized_keys2` file refers to the SSH2 protocol.

3. To log in to my account on my Red Hat Linux system (with host name `lnbp200`), I type the following command on the remote system:

   ```
   ssh lnbp200 -l naba
   ```

4. When prompted for my password on the `lnbp200` host, I enter the password. I can also log in to this account with the following equivalent command:

   ```
   ssh naba@lnbp200
   ```

If I simply want to copy a file securely from the `lnbp200` system, I can use `scp` like this:

```
scp lnbp200:/etc/ssh/ssh_config .
```

This command securely copies the `/etc/ssh/ssh_config` file from the `lnbp200` host to the system from which I type the command.

Setting Up Simple Firewalls

An Internet *firewall* is an intermediary between your internal network and the Internet. The firewall controls access to and from the protected internal network.

If you connect an internal network directly to the Internet, you have to make sure that every system on the internal network is properly secured — which can be nearly impossible because it takes only one careless user to render the entire internal network vulnerable. A firewall is a single point of connection to the Internet: You can direct all your efforts toward making that firewall system a daunting barrier to unauthorized external users.

To be useful, a firewall should have the following general characteristics:

✦ It must control the flow of packets between the Internet and the internal network.

✦ It must *not* provide dynamic routing because dynamic routing tables are subject to route *spoofing* — use of fake routes by intruders. Instead, the firewall should use static routing tables (which you can set up with the `route` command on Red Hat Linux systems).

✦ It must not allow any external user to log in as `root`. That way, even if the firewall system is compromised, the intruder is blocked from using `root` privileges from a remote login.

✦ It must be kept in a physically secure location.

✦ It must distinguish between packets that come from the Internet and packets that come from the internal protected network. This feature allows the firewall to reject packets that come from the Internet, but have the IP address of a trusted system on the internal network.

✦ It should act as the SMTP mail gateway for the internal network. The sendmail software should be set up so that all outgoing mail appears to come from the firewall system.

✦ It should not have any user accounts. However, the firewall system may have to have a few user accounts for those internal users who need access to external systems. External users who need access to the internal network should use SSH for remote login (see discussion of SSH earlier in this chapter).

✦ It should keep a log of all system activities, such as successful and unsuccessful login attempts.

✦ It should provide DNS name-lookup service to the outside world to resolve any host names that should be known to the outside world.

✦ It should provide good performance so it doesn't hinder the internal users' access to specific Internet services (such as HTTP and FTP).

A firewall can take many different forms. Here are three common forms of a firewall:

✦ **Screening router with packet filtering:** This simple firewall uses a router capable of filtering (blocking) packets according to their IP addresses.

✦ **Dual-homed host with proxy services:** In this case, a host with two network interfaces — one on the Internet and the other on the internal network — runs proxy services that act as a gateway for services, such as FTP and HTTP.

✦ **Perimeter network with bastion host:** This firewall configuration includes a perimeter network between the Internet and the protected internal network. A secure bastion host resides on the perimeter network and provides various services.

In a large organization, you may also have to isolate smaller internal networks from the corporate network. You can set up such internal firewalls the same way you set up Internet firewalls.

In the next few sections, I describe the common forms of a firewall: screening router with packet filtering, dual-homed host, perimeter network with bastion host, and application gateway.

Screening the router with packet filtering

If you were to directly connect your organization's internal network to the Internet, you would have to use a router to ensure proper exchange of packets between the internal network and the Internet. Most routers can block a packet according to its source or its destination IP address (as well as the port number it seeks to use). The router's packet-filtering capability can serve as a simple firewall. Figure 3-1 illustrates the basic concept of packet filtering.

**Book VII
Chapter 3**

**Securing the
Network**

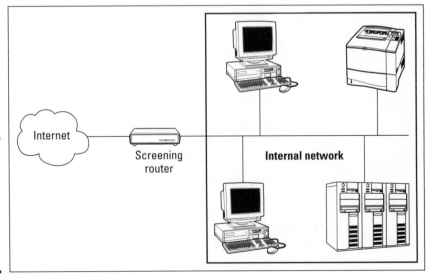

Figure 3-1:
Packet
filtering with
a screening
router
provides
a simple
firewall.

Many router vendors, such as Cisco and 3Com, offer routers that can be programmed to perform packet filtering. The exact details of filtering depend on the router vendor, but all routers operate according to rules that refer to the basic attributes of an Internet packet:

✦ Source IP address

✦ Destination IP address

✦ Protocol (TCP, UDP, or ICMP)

✦ Source port number (if protocol is TCP or UDP)

✦ Destination port number (if protocol is TCP or UDP)

✦ ICMP message type

In addition, the router knows the physical interface on which the packet arrived and the interface on which the packet will go out (if it's not blocked by the filtering rules).

Most packet filters operate in the following sequence:

1. You define the rules for allowing or blocking specific types of packets based on IP addresses and port numbers. These packet-filtering rules are stored in the router.

2. The screening router examines the header of each packet that arrives for the information (such as IP addresses and port numbers) to which your rules apply.

3. The screening router applies the rules in the order in which they are stored.

4. If a rule allows the packet to be forwarded, the router sends the packet to its destination.

5. If a rule blocks the packet, the router drops the packet (stops processing it).

6. If none of the rules applies, the packet is blocked. This rule epitomizes the security philosophy that one should "deny unless expressly permitted."

Although packet filtering with a screening router is better than no security, packet filtering suffers from the following drawbacks:

✦ It's easy for the network administrator to introduce errors inadvertently into the filtering rules.

✦ Packets are filtered on the basis of IP addresses, which represent specific hosts. Essentially, packet filtering either blocks or routes all packets from a specific host. That means that anyone who breaks into a trusted host can immediately gain access to your protected network.

✦ Because it's based on IP addresses, packet filtering can be defeated by a technique known as *IP spoofing*, whereby a cracker sends packets with the IP address of a trusted host (by appropriating the IP address of a trusted host and setting up an appropriate route); packets with these fake IP addresses can then gain access to your system.

✦ Packet filtering is susceptible to routing-attack programs that can create a bogus route, allowing an intruder to receive all packets meant for the protected internal network.

✦ The screening routers that implement packet filtering don't keep logs of activities. That makes it hard for you to determine if anyone is attempting to break into the protected network. As you see in the next section, a dual-homed host can provide logging.

✦ A screening router does not hide the host names and IP addresses of the internal network. Outsiders can access and use this exposed information to mount attacks against the protected network.

A more sophisticated approach is to use an application gateway that controls network traffic, based on specific applications instead of on a per-packet basis. You can implement an application gateway with a dual-homed host, known also as a *bastion host*.

Dual-homed host

A *dual-homed host* is a system with two network interfaces — one connected to the Internet and the other on an internal network that needs protection. The term "dual-homed" refers to the fact that the host "lives" in two networks.

In fact, if your operating system supports IP routing — the ability to forward network packets from one interface to another — the dual-homed host can serve as a router. However, you must turn off the IP forwarding feature to use the dual-homed host as a firewall system.

The Linux kernel supports the IP forwarding feature. If you plan to use a dual-homed host as a firewall, you have to use the `sysctl` command to disable IP forwarding.

With IP forwarding turned off, systems on both networks — the internal network as well as the Internet — can reach the dual-homed host, but no one from the Internet can access the internal network (nor can anyone from the internal network access the Internet). In this configuration, the dual-homed host completely isolates the two networks. Figure 3-2 shows the basic architecture of a dual-homed host.

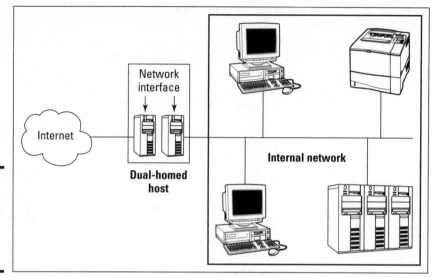

Figure 3-2:
A dual-
homed host
can act as
an Internet
firewall.

The dual-homed host is turned into a firewall by running application gateways — proxy services — on the dual-homed host. These proxy services allow specific applications, such as FTP and HTTP, to work across the dual-homed host. That means that you can configure the firewall so that internal clients (on the internal network) are able to access Web and FTP servers on the Internet.

Your public Web site can also run on the dual-homed host and be accessible to everyone on the Internet.

Don't allow user logins on the dual-homed host. Anyone logged in to the host can have access to both the internal network *and* the Internet. Because the dual-homed host is your only barrier between the Internet and the internal network, it's best not to increase the chances of a break-in by allowing users to log in to the firewall system. Putting user accounts there increases the chance of an intruder gaining access to the firewall by cracking a user's password.

Perimeter network with bastion host

An Internet firewall is often more complicated than a single dual-homed host that connects to both the Internet and the protected internal network. In particular, if you provide a number of Internet services, you may need more than one system to host them. Imagine that you have two systems: one to run the Web and FTP servers and the other to provide mail (SMTP) and domain name system (DNS) lookups. In this case, you place these two systems on a network that sits between the Internet and the internal network. Figure 3-3 illustrates this concept of an Internet firewall.

Figure 3-3:
A more
complete
Internet
firewall
includes a
perimeter
network and
bastion
hosts.

In this case, the firewall includes a perimeter network that connects to
the Internet through an exterior router. The perimeter network, in turn,
connects to the internal network through an interior router. The perimeter
network has one or more hosts that run Internet services, including proxy
servers (about which more in a moment) that allow internal hosts to access
Web servers on the Internet.

The term *bastion host* refers to any system on the perimeter network because
such a system is on the Internet and has to be well fortified. The dual-homed
host is also a bastion host because the dual-homed host is also accessible
from the Internet and has to be protected.

In the firewall configuration shown in Figure 3-3, the perimeter network is
known as a DMZ (demilitarized zone) network because that network acts
as a buffer between the Internet and the internal network (just as a real-life
DMZ is a buffer between North and South Korea).

Usually, you would combine a packet-filtering router with a bastion host.
Your Internet Service Provider typically provides the external router, which
means you don't have much control over that router's configuration. But
you provide the internal router, which means you can choose a screening
router and employ some packet-filtering rules. For example, you might
employ the following packet-filtering rules:

✦ From the internal network, allow only packets addressed to the bastion
host.

✦ From the DMZ, allow only packets originating from the bastion host.

✦ Block all other packets.

This ensures that the internal network communicates with only the bastion host (or hosts).

Like the dual-homed host, the bastion host also runs an application gateway that provides proxy services for various Internet services, such as TELNET, FTP, SMTP, and HTTP.

Application gateway

The bastion host or the dual-homed host is the system that acts as the intermediary between the Internet and the protected internal network. As such, that system serves as the internal network's gateway to the Internet. Toward this end, the system runs software to forward and filter TCP/IP packets for various services, such as TELNET, FTP, and HTTP. The software for forwarding and filtering TCP/IP packets for specific applications are known as *proxy servers*. Figure 3-4 illustrates a proxy server's role in a firewall.

Figure 3-4:
A proxy server lets internal hosts access Internet servers.

A *proxy server* accepts a connection for a specific protocol, such as FTP, and forwards the request to another server. In other words, the proxy server acts as a proxy for an actual server. Because it acts as a gateway for a specific application (such as HTTP or FTP), a proxy server is also known as an *application gateway*.

Unlike a screening router, which blocks packets only on the basis of information in the packet header (such as source and destination IP addresses), a proxy server uses the packet's data to decide what to do. For example, a proxy server does not blindly forward packets to an Internet service. The proxy server can enforce a site's security policy and disallow certain operations, depending on the specific application. For example, an FTP proxy server may prevent users from internal networks from using the FTP `put` command to send files to the Internet.

Accessing an Internet service through a proxy server can be a bit more involved than accessing that service directly. For example, a user on the internal network establishes a TELNET session with an Internet host with the following steps:

1. The user establishes a TELNET session with the firewall host — the system that runs the TELNET proxy. To do this, the user has to enter a username and password so that the firewall host can verify that the user has permission to connect to the Internet.

2. The user enters a command (which the TELNET proxy accepts) to connect to the Internet host. The TELNET proxy, in turn, establishes a TELNET connection between itself and the Internet host.

3. The TELNET proxy on the firewall begins passing packets back and forth between the Internet host and the user's system (until the user ends the TELNET session with the Internet host).

Besides acting as a gateway, the TELNET proxy also logs the user's session with the Internet host. The logging is part of an application gateway's security feature because the log file keeps track of all firewall accesses (as well as attempted accesses that may fail because of a wrong username or password).

Although the TELNET session involves two steps — first TELNET to the firewall host and then connect to the Internet host — the process of accessing services through a proxy need not be too cumbersome. The exact steps you take to access services through a firewall depend on the proxy software and the client program you use to access a service. With the right client program, proxies can be transparent to the user. For example, many Web browsers make it easy to access a Web site through an HTTP proxy. All you have to do is indicate through a menu choice the HTTP proxy you want to use.

**Book VII
Chapter 3**

**Securing the
Network**

Enabling Packet Filtering on Your Red Hat Linux System

Your Red Hat Linux system comes with built-in packet filtering software in the form of something called `netfilter` that's in the Linux kernel. All you have to do is use the `iptables` command to set up the rules for what happens to the packets based on the IP addresses in their headers and the network connection type.

The built-in packet filtering capability is handy when you don't have a dedicated firewall between your Red Hat Linux system and the Internet. This is the case, for example, when you connect your Red Hat system to the Internet through a DSL or cable modem. You can essentially have a packet filtering firewall inside your Red Hat Linux system, sitting between the kernel and the applications.

Using the security level configuration tool

You can turn on different levels of packet filtering through the graphical Security Level Configuration tool. To run the tool, log in as `root` and select Main Menu ➪ System Settings ➪ Security Level. The Security Level Configuration window appears (Figure 3-5).

Figure 3-5: You can set up predefined levels of packet filtering with this tool.

You can select two predefined levels of simple firewalling (more precisely, packet filtering) with the Security Level Configuration tool:

✦ **Disable firewall:** Does not perform any filtering, and all connections are allowed (you can still turn off Internet services by not running the servers or disabling them in the `xinetd` configuration files). This security level is fine if your Red Hat Linux system is inside a protected local area network or if you have a separate firewall device.

✦ **Enable firewall:** Turns on packet filtering. You can then select the services you want to allow and the network devices that you trust.

You can allow incoming packets meant for specific Internet services such as SSH, TELNET, and FTP. If you select a network interface such as `eth0` (the first Ethernet card) as trusted, then all network traffic over that interface will be allowed without any filtering.

Using the iptables command

It's somewhat complex to use the `iptables` command. `iptables` uses the concept of a chain, which is a sequence of rules. Each rule says what to do with a packet if the header contains certain information (such as the source or destination IP address). If a rule does not apply, `iptables` consults the next rule in the chain. By default, there are three chains:

- ✦ **INPUT** chain: The first set of rules against which packets are tested. The packets continue to the next chain only if the input chain does not specify `DROP` or `REJECT`.

- ✦ **FORWARD** chain: Contains the rules that apply to packets attempting to pass through this system to another system (for example, when you use a Red Hat Linux system as a router between your LAN and the Internet).

- ✦ **OUTPUT** chain: Includes the rules applied to packets before they are sent out (either to another network or to an application).

You can add rules to these chains or create new chains of rules by using the `iptables` command. You can also view the current chains and save them to a file. For example, if you have done nothing else, the `iptables -L` command should show the following:

```
Chain INPUT (policy ACCEPT)
target     prot opt source                destination

Chain FORWARD (policy ACCEPT)
target     prot opt source                destination

Chain OUTPUT (policy ACCEPT)
target     prot opt source                destination
```

In this case, all three chains — `INPUT`, `FORWARD`, and `OUTPUT` — show the same `ACCEPT` policy, which means everything is wide open.

If you're setting up a packet filter, the first thing you do is specify the packets that you want to accept. For example, to accept packets from the 192.168.0.0 network, add the following rule to the input chain:

```
iptables -A INPUT -s 192.168.0.0/24 -j ACCEPT
```

Now add a rule to drop everything except local loopback (the lo network interface) traffic and stop all forwarding with the following commands:

```
iptables -A INPUT -i ! lo -j REJECT
iptables -A FORWARD -j REJECT
```

The first iptables command, for example, appends to the input chain (-A INPUT) the rule that if the packet does not come from the lo interface (-i ! lo), iptables should reject the packet (-j REJECT).

Before rejecting all other packets, you may also add more rules to each of the INPUT chains to allow specific packets in. You can select packets to accept or reject based on many different parameters such as IP addresses, protocol types (TCP, UDP), network interface, or port numbers.

Don't type iptables commands from a remote login session. A rule that begins denying packets from all addresses can also stop what you type from reaching the system; after that happens, you may have no way of accessing the system over the network. To avoid unpleasant surprises, always type iptables rules at the *console* — the keyboard and monitor that are connected directly to your Red Hat Linux PC that is running the packet filter. If you want to delete all filtering rules in a hurry, you can flush them by typing the following command:

```
iptables -F
```

I won't provide all the details of the iptables commands in this section. Suffice to say that you type **man iptables** to read a summary of the commands. You can also read about netfilter and iptables at www. iptables.org.

After you define the rules by using the iptables command, they are in the memory and will be gone when you reboot the system. To save them, use the iptables-save command to store the rules in a file. For example, you can save the rules in a file named iptables.rules by using the following commands:

```
iptables-save > iptables.rules
```

Here's a listing of the iptables.rules file, generated on a Red Hat Linux system:

```
# Generated by iptables-save v1.2.7a on Sun Jun 22 18:12:40 2003
*filter
:INPUT ACCEPT [976:61298]
:FORWARD ACCEPT [0:0]
:OUTPUT ACCEPT [938:131584]
```

```
-A INPUT -s 192.168.0.0/255.255.255.0 -j ACCEPT
-A INPUT -i ! lo -j REJECT --reject-with icmp-port-unreachable
-A FORWARD -j REJECT --reject-with icmp-port-unreachable
COMMIT
# Completed on Sun Jun 22 18:12:40 2003
```

In case you're curious, these rules correspond to the following `iptables` commands I used to configure the filter:

```
iptables -A INPUT -s 192.168.0.0/24 -j ACCEPT
iptables -A INPUT -i ! lo -j REJECT
iptables -A FORWARD -j REJECT
```

If you want to load these saved rules into `iptables`, use the following command:

```
iptables-restore < iptables.rules
```

On a Red Hat Linux system, the process of saving and restoring firewall rules is automated by saving the `iptables` rules in the file `/etc/sysconfig/iptables` and by enabling `iptables` with the following command:

```
chkconfig iptables on
```

That should ensure that the `/etc/init.d/iptables start` command is executed at system startup. The `/etc/init.d/iptables` script then runs the `/sbin/iptables-restore` command to restore the `iptables` rules from the `/etc/sysconfig/iptables` file.

Chapter 4: Performing Security Audits

In This Chapter

✔ **Understanding computer security audits**

✔ **Learning a security test methodology**

✔ **Reviewing host and network security**

✔ **Exploring security testing tools**

Y ou see the term "audit" and you think tax audit, right? Well, there are many different types of audits, and one of them is a *computer security audit*. The purpose of a computer security audit is to basically test your system and network security. For larger organizations, the security audit may be done by an independent auditor (much like the auditing of financial statements). If you have only a few Red Hat Linux systems or a small network, you can do the security audit as a self-assessment, just to figure out if you're doing everything okay or not.

In this chapter, I explain how to perform computer security audits and show you a number of free tools and resources to help you test your system's security.

Understanding Security Audits

An *audit* is simply an independent assessment of whatever it is you're auditing. So a computer security audit is an independent assessment of computer security. If someone is conducting a computer security audit of your organization, he or she typically focuses on two areas:

✦ Independent verification of whether your organization is complying with its existing policies and procedures for computer security. This is the nontechnical part of the security audit.

✦ Independent testing of how effective your security controls (any hardware and software mechanisms you use to secure the system) are. This is the technical part of the security audit.

Why do we need security audits? We need them for the same reason we need financial audits — mainly to verify that everything is being done the way it's supposed to be done. For public as well as private organizations, management may want independent security audits to assure themselves that their security is A-OK. Irrespective of your organization's size, you can always perform security audits on your own, either to prepare for independent security audits or simply to know that you're doing everything right.

No matter whether you have independent security audits or a self-assessment, here are some of the benefits you get from security audits:

+ Periodic risk assessments that consider internal and external threats to systems and data.

+ Periodic testing of the effectiveness of security policies, security controls, and techniques.

+ Identification of any significant deficiencies in your system's security (so you know what to fix).

+ In the case of self-assessments, preparation for any annual independent security testing that your organization might have to face.

Nontechnical aspects of security audits

The nontechnical side of computer security audits focuses on your organizationwide security framework. The audit examines how well the organization has set up and implemented the policies, plans, and procedures for computer security. Some of the items to be verified include

+ Risks are periodically assessed.

+ There is an entitywide security program plan.

+ A security program-management structure is put in place.

+ Computer security responsibilities are clearly assigned.

+ Effective security-related personnel policies are in place.

+ The security program's effectiveness is monitored and changes are made when needed.

As you may expect, the nontechnical aspects of the security audit involve reviewing documents and interviewing appropriate individuals to learn how the organization manages computer security. Of course, for a small organization or a home PC, it's ridiculous to expect plans and procedures in documents. In those cases, you just need to make sure that you have some technical controls in place to secure your system and your network connection.

Technical aspects of security audits

The technical side of computer security audits focuses on testing the technical controls that secure your hosts and network. The testing involves determining

+ **How well the host is secured.** Are all operating system patches applied? Are the file permissions set correctly? Are user accounts protected? Are file changes monitored? Are log files monitored? And so on.

+ **How well the network is secured.** Are unnecessary Internet services turned off? Is a firewall installed? Are remote logins secured with tools such as SSH? Are TCP wrapper-access controls used? And so on.

Typically, security experts use automated tools to perform these two security reviews — host and network.

Learning a Security Test Methodology

A key element of a computer security audit is the security test that checks the technical mechanisms used to secure a host and the network. The security test methodology follows these high-level steps:

1. Take stock of the organization's networks, hosts, network devices (routers, switches, firewalls, and so on), and how the network is connected to the Internet.

2. If there are many hosts and network connections, determine what are the important hosts and network devices that should be tested. The importance of a host depends on the kind of applications it runs.

3. Test the hosts individually. Typically, this involves logging in as a system administrator and then checking various aspects of host security, from passwords to system log files.

4. Test the network. This is usually done by attempting to break through the network defenses from another system on the Internet. If there is a firewall, the testing checks that the firewall is indeed configured correctly.

5. Analyze the test results of both host and network tests to determine the vulnerabilities and risks.

Each of the two types of testing — host and network — focuses on three areas that comprise overall computer security:

+ **Prevention:** Includes the mechanisms (nontechnical and technical) that help prevent attacks on the system and the network.

✦ **Detection:** Refers to techniques such as monitoring log files, checking file integrity, and intrusion detection systems that can detect when someone is about to or has already broken into your system.

✦ **Response:** Includes the steps such as reporting an incident to authorities and restoring important files from backup that you perform when a computer security incident has occurred.

For host and network security, each of these areas has some overlaps. For example, prevention mechanisms for host security such as good passwords or file permissions can also provide network security. Nevertheless, it helps to think in terms of the three areas — prevention, detection, and response.

Before you can think of prevention, however, you have to know the types of problems you're trying to prevent. In other words, what are the common security vulnerabilities? The prevention and detection steps typically depend on what these vulnerabilities are.

Some common computer vulnerabilities

The specific tests of the host and network security depend on the common vulnerabilities. Basically, the idea is to check if a host or a network has the vulnerabilities that crackers are most likely to exploit.

Online resources on computer vulnerabilities

There are several online resources that identify and categorize computer security vulnerabilities:

✦ **SANS Institute** publishes a list of the Top 20 most critical Internet security vulnerabilities at `www.sans.org/top20/`.

✦ **CVE** (Common Vulnerabilities and Exposures) is a list of standardized names of vulnerabilities. For more information on CVE, see `cve.mitre.org` (the list has over 2,500 names of vulnerabilities). It's common practice to use the CVE name to describe vulnerabilities.

✦ **ICAT Metabase** is a searchable index of information on computer vulnerabilities, published by National Institute of Standards and Technology (NIST), a United States government agency. The ICAT vulnerability index is online at `icat.nist.gov`. ICAT lists over 5,800 vulnerabilities, and it provides links to vulnerability advisory and patch information for each vulnerability. ICAT also publishes a Top 10 List that lists the vulnerabilities that were most queried during the past year.

Typical Top 20 computer vulnerabilities

The SANS Top 20 vulnerabilities list includes three types of vulnerabilities: general ones that affect all systems, Windows, and UNIX. Of these, the general and UNIX vulnerabilities are relevant to Red Hat Linux. Table 4-1 summarizes the general and UNIX vulnerabilities that apply to Red Hat Linux. You can read the complete details about these vulnerabilities at `www.sans.org/top20.htm`.

Table 4-1	Some Common Computer Vulnerability Types
Vulnerability Type	*Description*
General Vulnerabilities	
Default install options	These are the vulnerabilities introduced due to default install options that often install unneeded software or configure software less securely.
Weak or no password	Many user accounts have weak passwords that can be easily cracked by password-cracking programs. Also, some software packages may add user accounts with no password or a standard password that everyone knows.
Incomplete or no backups	If a security incident occurs, the files may have to be restored from backups. However, it's a common mistake to either not do backups regularly or not test the backups for completeness.
Large number of open ports	The open ports refer to Internet services that are enabled on a system. Sometimes there are many unnecessary Internet services running on a system.
Incorrect or no filtering of packets	An IP address–based packet filter can cut back on attacks, but many systems don't have any packet filtering enabled. With `iptables`, it's easy to turn on packet filtering in Red Hat Linux.
Incomplete or no logging	The system logs are the only way to figure out the sequence of events that led to someone breaking into your system. Unfortunately, sometimes the logging isn't set up correctly.
Vulnerable CGI programs	This vulnerability refers to the common gateway interface (CGI) that's used on Web servers to process interactive Web pages (for example, forms that request input from users). A CGI program with vulnerability (such as buffer flow) can provide attackers a way to do bad things to your system.
UNIX Vulnerabilities	
RPC buffer overflows (NFS, NIS)	Services such as Network File System (NFS) and Network Information System (NIS) use remote procedure calls (RPC) and there are some known vulnerabilities in RPC.

(continued)

Table 4-1 *(continued)*

Vulnerability Type	Description
Sendmail vulnerabilities	Sendmail is a complex program used to transport mail messages from one system to another, and some versions of Sendmail have vulnerabilities.
BIND (DNS) weaknesses	Berkeley Internet Name Domain (BIND) is a package that implements Domain Name System (DNS), the Internet's name service that translates a name to an IP address. Some versions of BIND have vulnerabilities.
R command (rlogin, rsh, rcp)	The so-called R commands allow an attacker to exploit vulnerabilities, providing easy access to any system that has an implicit trust relationship with others (the R commands assume a trust relationship).
LPD (remote printing) vulnerabilities	LPD is the print server process and it listens on port 515 for remote printing requests. Unfortunately, the remote printing capability has a buffer-overflow vulnerability.
Default SNMP strings	Simple Network Management Protocol (SNMP) is used to remotely monitor and administer various network-connected systems that range from routers to computers. SNMP lacks good access control; if SNMP is running on your system, an attacker may be able to reconfigure or shut down your system.

Host security review

When reviewing host security, focus on assessing the security mechanisms in each of the following areas:

+ **Prevention:** Install operating system updates, use secure passwords, improve file permissions, set up a password for a boot loader, and use encryption.

+ **Detection:** Capture log messages and check file integrity with Tripwire.

+ **Response:** Make routine backups and develop incident response procedures.

Next I review a few of these host security mechanisms.

Operating system updates

Red Hat issues Red Hat Linux updates as soon it learns of any security vulnerabilities, but it's up to you or a system administrator to download and install the updates. One way to keep up with the Red Hat Linux security patches is to sign up for the Red Hat Network service (it's free for a single machine, but charges a subscription for more than one machine).

You can install the patches by using the `rpm` command. If you place all current updates in a single directory, you can use the following command to install them:

```
rpm -F *.rpm
```

For larger organizations, an authorized system administrator should install the operating system updates.

To assess whether the operating system updates are current, an auditor gets a current list of updates for key Red Hat Linux components and then uses the `rpm` command to check if they are installed. For example, if a list shows that `glibc` version 2.3.2 is what the system should have, the auditor types the following command to view the current `glibc` version number:

```
rpm -q glibc
```

If the version number is less than 2.3.2, the conclusion is that operating system updates are not being installed.

File permissions

Key system files should be protected with appropriate file ownerships and file permissions. The key procedures in assigning file system ownerships and permissions are as follows:

+ Figure out which files contain sensitive information and why. Some files may contain sensitive data related to your work or business, whereas many other files are sensitive because they control the Red Hat Linux system configuration.

+ Maintain a current list of authorized users and what they are authorized to do on the system.

+ Set up passwords, groups, file ownerships, and file permissions to allow only authorized users to access the files.

Table 4-2 lists some important system files in Red Hat Linux, showing the numeric permission setting for each file.

Table 4-2	Important System Files and Their Permissions	
File Pathname	*Permission*	*Description*
`/boot/grub/grub.conf`	600	GRUB bootloader configuration file
`/etc/cron.allow`	400	List of users permitted to use `cron` to submit periodic jobs

(continued)

Table 4-2 *(continued)*

File Pathname	Permission	Description
/etc/cron.deny	400	List of users who cannot use `cron` to submit periodic jobs
/etc/crontab	644	Systemwide periodic jobs
/etc/hosts.allow	644	List of hosts allowed to use Internet services that are started using TCP wrappers
/etc/hosts.deny	644	List of hosts denied access to Internet services that are started using TCP wrappers
/etc/logrotate.conf	644	File that controls how log files are rotated
/etc/pam.d	755	Directory with configuration files for pluggable authentication modules (PAMs)
/etc/passwd	644	Old-style password file with user-account information but not the passwords
/etc/rc.d	755	Directory with system-startup scripts
/etc/securetty	600	TTY interfaces (terminals) from which `root` can log in
/etc/security	755	Policy files that control system access
/etc/shadow	400	File with encrypted passwords and password-expiration information
/etc/shutdown.allow	400	Users who can shut down or reboot by pressing Ctrl+Alt+Delete
/etc/ssh	755	Directory with configuration files for the Secure Shell (SSH)
/etc/sysconfig	755	System configuration files
/etc/sysctl.conf	644	Kernel configuration parameters
/etc/syslog.conf	644	Configuration file for the `syslogd` server that logs messages
/etc/vsftpd	600	Configuration file for the very secure FTP server
/etc/vsftpd.ftpusers	600	List of users who cannot use FTP to transfer files
/etc/xinetd.conf	644	Configuration file for the `xinetd` server
/etc/xinetd.d	755	Directory containing configuration files for specific services that the `xinetd` server can start

File Pathname	Permission	Description
/var/log	755	Directory with all log files
/var/log/lastlog	644	Information about all previous logins
/var/log/messages	644	Main system message log file
/var/log/secure	400	Security-related log file
/var/log/wtmp	664	Information about current logins

Another important check is to look for executable program files that have the setuid permission. If a program has setuid permission and it's owned by root, then the program runs with root privileges, no matter who is actually running the program. You can find all setuid programs with the following find command:

```
find / -perm +4000 -print
```

You may want to save the output in a file (just append > *filename* to the command) and then examine the file for any unusual setuid programs. For example, a setuid program in a user's home directory would be unusual.

Password security

Verify that the password, group, and shadow password files are protected. In particular, the shadow password file should be write-protected and readable only by root. The filenames and their recommended permissions are shown in Table 4-3:

Table 4-3	Ownership and Permission of Password Files	
File Pathname	Ownership	Permission
/etc/group	root.root	644
/etc/passwd	root.root	644
/etc/shadow	root.root	400

Incident response

Incident response is the policy that answers the question of what to do if something unusual does happen to the system — it tells you how to proceed if someone has broken into your system.

Your response to an incident depends on how you use your system and how important it is to you or your business. For a comprehensive incident response, here are some key points to remember:

✦ Figure out how critical and important your computer and network are and identify who or what resources can help you protect your system.

✦ Take steps to prevent and minimize potential damage and interruption.

✦ Develop and document a comprehensive contingency plan.

✦ Periodically test the contingency plan and revise the procedures as appropriate.

Network security review

Network security review focuses on assessing the security mechanisms in each of the following areas:

✦ **Prevention:** Set up a firewall, enable packet filtering, disable unnecessary xinetd services, turn off unneeded Internet services, use TCP wrappers for access control, and use SSH for secure remote logins.

✦ **Detection:** Use network intrusion detection and capture system logs.

✦ **Response:** Develop incident response procedures.

I briefly describe some key steps in assessing the network security.

Services started by xinetd

Many Internet services such as TELNET and sgi_fam (sgi_fam monitors changes to files) are started by the xinetd server. The decision to turn on some of these services depends on factors such as how the system is connected to the Internet and how the system is being used. You can usually turn off most xinetd services.

Check which xinetd services are turned on by using one of the following ways:

✦ Check the configuration files in the /etc/xinetd.d directory for all the services that xinetd can start. If a service is turned off, the configuration file has a line like this:

```
disable = yes
```

Remember that the disable = yes line doesn't count if it's commented out by placing a # at the beginning of the line.

✦ Type the following command to disable a service that xinetd can start:

```
chkconfig servicename off
```

where *servicename* is the name of the service (such as telnet or sgi_fam). To check the names of the services that xinetd can start, type the following command:

```
chkconfig --list | more
```

In the output, look for the lines that follow:

```
xinetd based services:
```

These lines list all the services that `xinetd` can start and whether they are on or off. For example, here are a few lines showing the status of `xinetd` services on a system:

```
chargen-udp:    off
rsync:  off
chargen:        off
daytime-udp:    off
daytime:        off
echo-udp:       off
echo:   off
services:       off
servers:        off
time-udp:       off
time:   off
cups-lpd:       off
sgi_fam:        on
ktalk:  off
imap:   off
... lines deleted ...
```

In this case, the `sgi_fam` (a server that reports changes to any file) service is on, but everything else is off.

Also check the following files for any access controls used with the `xinetd` services:

✦ `/etc/hosts.allow` lists hosts allowed to access specific services.

✦ `/etc/hosts.deny` lists hosts that should be denied access to services.

Standalone services

Many services such as the `httpd` (Web server) and `sendmail` (mail server) start automatically at boot time, assuming they are configured to start that way. You can use the `chkconfig` command to check which of these stand-alone servers are set to start at various run levels (see Book VI, Chapter 1 for more about run levels). Typically, your Red Hat Linux system starts up at run level 3 (for text login) or 5 (for graphical login). Therefore, what matters is the setting for the servers in levels 3 and 5. To view the list of servers, type the following command:

```
chkconfig --list | more
```

Here's a partial listing of what you might see:

```
gpm            0:off   1:off   2:on    3:on    4:on    5:on    6:off
kudzu          0:off   1:off   2:off   3:on    4:on    5:on    6:off
syslog         0:off   1:off   2:on    3:on    4:on    5:on    6:off
rawdevices     0:off   1:off   2:off   3:on    4:on    5:on    6:off
netfs          0:off   1:off   2:off   3:on    4:on    5:on    6:off
network        0:off   1:off   2:on    3:on    4:on    5:on    6:off
random         0:off   1:off   2:on    3:on    4:on    5:on    6:off
saslauthd      0:off   1:off   2:off   3:off   4:off   5:off   6:off
pcmcia         0:off   1:off   2:on    3:on    4:on    5:on    6:off
keytable       0:off   1:on    2:on    3:on    4:on    5:on    6:off
apmd           0:off   1:off   2:on    3:on    4:on    5:on    6:off
atd            0:off   1:off   2:off   3:on    4:on    5:on    6:off
autofs         0:off   1:off   2:off   3:on    4:on    5:on    6:off
iptables       0:off   1:off   2:on    3:on    4:on    5:on    6:off
irda           0:off   1:off   2:off   3:off   4:off   5:off   6:off
isdn           0:off   1:off   2:on    3:on    4:on    5:on    6:off
sshd           0:off   1:off   2:on    3:on    4:on    5:on    6:off
portmap        0:off   1:off   2:off   3:on    4:on    5:on    6:off
nfs            0:off   1:off   2:off   3:off   4:off   5:off   6:off
nfslock        0:off   1:off   2:off   3:on    4:on    5:on    6:off
sendmail       0:off   1:off   2:on    3:on    4:on    5:on    6:off
rhnsd          0:off   1:off   2:off   3:on    4:on    5:on    6:off
crond          0:off   1:off   2:on    3:on    4:on    5:on    6:off
...lines deleted...
```

The first column shows the names of the servers. Look at the column of entries that begin with 3: and the ones that begin with 5:. These are the ones that show the status of the server for run levels 3 and 5. The ones that appear as on are automatically started when your Red Hat Linux system starts.

If you're doing a self-assessment of your network security and you find that some servers should not be running, you can turn them off for run levels 3 and 5 with the chkconfig command like this:

```
chkconfig --level 35 servicename off
```

Replace *servicename* with the name of the server you want to turn off.

If you're auditing network security, make a note of all the servers that are turned on — and then try to determine whether they should really *be* on, according to what you know about the system. The decision to turn a particular service on depends on how your system is used (for example, as a Web server or as a desktop system) and how it's connected to the Internet (say, through a firewall or directly).

Penetration test

A penetration test is the best way to tell what services are really running on a Red Hat Linux system. *Penetration testing* involves trying to get access to your system from an attacker's perspective. Typically, you perform this test from a system on the Internet and try to see if you can break in or, at a minimum, get access to services running on your Red Hat Linux system.

One aspect of penetration testing is to see what ports are open on your Red Hat Linux system. The port number is simply a number that identifies specific TCP/IP network connections to the system. The attempt to connect to a port succeeds only if a server is running on that port (or put another way, if a server is "listening on that port"). A port is considered to be open if a server responds when a connection request for that port arrives.

The first step in penetration testing is to perform a port scan. The term *port scan* is used to describe the automated process of trying to connect to each port number to see if a valid response comes back. Many available automated tools can perform port scanning — Red Hat Linux comes with a popular port-scanning tool called nmap (which I describe later in this chapter).

After performing a port scan, you know the potential vulnerabilities that could be exploited. Not all servers have security problems, but many servers have well-known vulnerabilities, and an open port provides a cracker a way to attack your system through one of the servers. In fact, you can use automated tools called *vulnerability scanners* to identify vulnerabilities that exist in your system. (I describe some vulnerability scanners next.) Whether your Red Hat Linux system is connected to the Internet directly (through DSL or cable modem) or through a firewall, use the port-scanning and vulnerability-scanning tools to figure out if you have any holes in your defenses. Better you than them!

Exploring Security Testing Tools

Many automated tools are available to perform security testing. Some of these tools are meant for finding the open ports on every system in a range of IP addresses. Others look for the vulnerabilities associated with open ports. Yet other tools can capture (or *sniff*) those weaknesses and help you analyze them so you can glean useful information about what's going on in your network.

You can browse a list of the top 50 security tools (based on an informal poll of nmap users) at www.insecure.org/tools.html. Table 4-4 lists a number of these tools by category. I describe a few of the freely available vulnerability scanners in the next few sections.

Table 4-4	Some Popular Computer Security Tools
Type	*Names of Tools*
Port scanners	nmap, Strobe
Vulnerability scanners	Nessus Security Scanner, SAINT, SARA, Whisker (CGI scanner), ISS Internet Scanner, CyberCop Scanner, Vetescan, Retina Network Security Scanner

(continued)

Table 4-4 *(continued)*

Type	*Names of Tools*
Network utilities	Netcat, `hping2`, Firewalk, Cheops, `ntop`, `ping`
Host security tools	Tripwire, lsof
Packet sniffers	`tcpdump`, Ethereal, `dsniff`, `sniffit`
Intrusion-detection systems (IDSs)	Snort, Abacus `portsentry`, `scanlogd`, NFR, LIDS
Password-checking tools	John the Ripper, LC4
Log-analysis and monitoring tools	`logcolorise`, `tcpdstats`, `nlog`, `logcheck`, Swatch

nmap

nmap (short for *network mapper*) is a port-scanning tool. It can rapidly scan large networks and determine what hosts are available on the network, what services they are offering, what operating system (and the operating system version) they are running, what type of packet filters or firewalls are in use, and dozens of other characteristics. Red Hat Linux comes with nmap. You can read more about nmap at www.insecure.org/nmap.

If you want to try out nmap to scan your local area network, just type a command similar to the following (replace the IP address range with addresses appropriate for your network):

```
nmap -O -sS 192.168.0.2-10
```

Here's a typical output listing from that command:

```
Starting nmap 3.27 ( www.insecure.org/nmap/ ) at 2003-06-22 18:41 EDT
Interesting ports on 192.168.0.2:
(The 1618 ports scanned but not shown below are in state: closed)
Port       State       Service
135/tcp    open        loc-srv
139/tcp    open        netbios-ssn
445/tcp    open        microsoft-ds
1025/tcp   open        NFS-or-IIS
5000/tcp   open        UPnP
Remote operating system guess: Windows Millennium Edition (Me), Win 2000, or Win
XP

Interesting ports on 192.168.0.3:
(The 1618 ports scanned but not shown below are in state: closed)
Port       State       Service
21/tcp     open        ftp
22/tcp     open        ssh
23/tcp     open        telnet
```

```
111/tcp    open       sunrpc
6000/tcp   open       X11
Remote operating system guess: Linux Kernel 2.4.0 - 2.5.20
<<Lines deleted...>>
Nmap run completed -- 9 IP addresses (3 hosts up) scanned in 95.420 seconds
```

As you can see, nmap displays the names of the open ports and hazards a guess at the operating system name and version number.

Nessus

The Nessus Security Scanner is a modular security auditing tool that uses plug-ins written in Nessus scripting language to test for a wide variety of network vulnerabilities. Nessus uses a client-server software architecture with a server called nessusd and a client called nessus.

Before you try to install Nessus, you must install the sharutils RPM. That package includes the uudecode utility that the Nessus installation script needs. The sharutils package isn't installed with any of the standard package groups, so you have to install it yourself.

To install sharutils, follow these steps:

1. **Mount the companion CDs one by one and locate the package whose name starts with** sharutils.

   To find the correct CD, try the following sequence of commands after mounting the CD on /mnt/cdrom:

   ```
   cd /mnt/cdrom/RedHat/RPMS
   ls sharutils*
   ```

2. **After you find the** sharutils **package, install it with the following command:**

   ```
   rpm -ivh sharutils*.rpm
   ```

To download and install Nessus, follow these steps:

1. **Read the instructions at** www.nessus.org/download.html. **Then click a link to the package you want to download. Follow the instructions and download the files** nessus-installer.sh **and** MD5.

2. **Type the following command to install Nessus (you must have the development tools, including the GIMP Toolkit, installed):**

   ```
   sh nessus-installer.sh
   ```

Respond to the prompts from the installer script to finish the installation. You can usually press Enter to accept the default choices.

After the installation is complete, follow these steps to use Nessus:

1. **Log in as** `root` **and type the following command to create the Nessus SSL certificate used for secure communication between the Nessus client and the Nessus server:**

   ```
   nessus-mkcert
   ```

2. **Provide the requested information to complete the certificate-generation process.**

3. **Create a** `nessusd` **account with the following command:**

   ```
   nessus-adduser
   ```

4. **When prompted, enter user name, password, and any rules (press Ctrl+D if you don't know what rules to enter). Then press y.**

5. **If you want to, you can configure** `nessusd` **by editing the configuration file** `/usr/local/etc/nessus/nessusd.conf`**.**

   If you want to try out Nessus, you can proceed with the default configuration file.

6. **Start the Nessus server with this command:**

   ```
   nessusd -D
   ```

7. **Run the Nessus client by typing the following command in a terminal window:**

   ```
   nessus
   ```

   The Nessus Setup window appears (Figure 4-1).

8. **Type a** `nessusd` **username and password and then click Log In.**

9. **When Nessus displays the certificate used to establish the secure connection and asks if you accept it, click Yes.**

   After the client connects to the server, the Log in button changes to Log out, and a Connected label appears at its left.

10. **On the Target selection tab, enter a range of IP addresses to scan all hosts in a network.**

    For example, to scan the first eight hosts in a private network 192.168.0.0, I enter the address as:

    ```
    192.168.0.0/29
    ```

11. **Click Start the Scan.**

    Nessus starts scanning the IP addresses and checks for many different vulnerabilities. Progress bars show the status of the scan (Figure 4-2).

Figure 4-1:
The Nessus client screen looks like this after a user logs in.

Book VII Chapter 4

Performing Security Audits

Figure 4-2:
Nessus shows the status of the scan through progress bars.

After Nessus completes the vulnerability scan of the hosts, it displays the result in a nice combination of graphical and text formats (Figure 4-3). The report is interactive: You can click a host address to view the report on that host, and you can drill down on a specific vulnerability (including the CVE number that identifies the vulnerability).

Figure 4-3:
Nessus displays results of scanning in an interactive report.

SAINT

Security Administrator's Integrated Network Tool (SAINT) scans hosts for a variety of security vulnerabilities. For the vulnerabilities it finds, SAINT shows the Common Vulnerabilities and Exposures (CVE) identifier. Older versions of SAINT are free, but the latest version is available only to those who purchase SAINTWriter or SAINTexpress.

You can download a restricted (limited to scanning two hosts only) 15-day trial version of SAINT from www.saintcorporation.com/products/ download.html and see what it can do. You can decide whether to buy the full version or not.

I won't describe the steps for downloading and installing the trial version. You will find the instructions on the page from which you download the free trial version of SAINT.

SARA

Security Auditor's Research Assistant (SARA) is a vulnerability-scanning tool based on SAINT. SARA scans for known vulnerabilities, including those in the CVE list and the SANS Top 20 List (www.sans.org/top20/).

To try out SARA, download the latest version of SARA from www.arc.com/sara/downloads/. After downloading the compressed `tar` file, build and install the software using these steps:

1. **Unpack `tar` file with the command**

   ```
   tar zxvf sara*
   ```

2. **To configure SARA, type the following commands:**

   ```
   cd sara*
   ./configure
   ```

3. **To build the software, type**

   ```
   make
   ```

After SARA is built, run it with the following command:

```
./sara
```

SARA starts a Web browser and displays its user interface in the Web browser.

You can perform various tasks by clicking the links along the left side of the Web browser. For example, to perform a vulnerability scan, click the Target Selection link. SARA brings up a form where you can provide information about hosts and networks to scan. You can also specify the scanning level — anywhere from light to extreme.

After filling in the information, click the Start the Scan button at the bottom of the form. SARA starts to perform the vulnerability scan. During the scan, SARA displays a data-collection page that indicates progress of the scan.

After the scan is complete, you can proceed to data analysis and view the vulnerability information.

Book VIII

Internet Servers

The 5th Wave   By Rich Tennant

Now maybe these folks have a decent disaster recovery plan and maybe they don't...

DANGER WILD RHINOCEROS

Contents at a Glance

Chapter 1: Managing the Servers

The Internet is a world of clients and servers. Clients make requests to servers, and servers respond to the requests. For example, your Web browser is a client that downloads information from Web servers and displays it to you. Of course, the clients and servers are computer programs that run on a wide variety of computers. A Red Hat Linux system is an ideal system to run a wide variety of servers from a Web server to a Windows file and print server. In this chapter, I provide an overview of typical Internet service, its client/server architecture, and how to manage the servers in Red Hat Linux. You can use the information in this chapter to manage any server running on your Red Hat Linux system.

Understanding Internet Services

Internet services are network applications designed to deliver information from one system to another. By design, each Internet service is implemented in two parts — a *server* that provides information, and one or more *clients* that request information.

Such *client/server* architecture is the most common way to build distributed information systems. The clients and servers are computer programs that run on these computers and communicate through the network. The neat part is that you can be running a client at your desktop computer and access information from a server running on a computer anywhere in the world (as long as it's on the Internet).

The Web itself, e-mail, and FTP (File Transfer Protocol) are examples of Internet services that use the client/server model. For example, when you use the Web, you use the Web-browser client to download and view Web pages from the Web server.

Client/server architecture requires clients to communicate with the servers. That's where the *Transmission Control Protocol/Internet Protocol* — TCP/IP — comes in. TCP/IP provides a standard way for clients and servers to exchange packets of data. In the next few sections, I explain how TCP/IP-based services communicate.

TCP/IP and sockets

Client/server applications, such as Web and FTP, use TCP/IP for data transfers between client and server. These Internet applications typically use TCP/IP communications by using the *Berkeley Sockets interface* (so named because the socket interface was introduced in Berkeley UNIX around 1982). The sockets interface is nothing physical — it's simply some computer code that a computer programmer can use to create applications that can communicate with other applications on the Internet.

Even if you don't write network applications using sockets, you may have to use or set up many network applications. Knowledge of sockets can help you understand how network-based applications work, which in turn helps you find and correct any problems with these applications.

Socket definition

Network applications use sockets to communicate over a TCP/IP network. A *socket* represents one end-point of a connection. Because a socket is bidirectional, data can be sent as well as received through it. A socket has three attributes:

✦ The *network address* (the IP address) of the system

✦ The *port number,* identifying the process (a process is a computer program running on a computer) that exchanges data through the socket

✦ The *type of socket,* identifying the protocol for data exchange

Essentially, the IP address identifies a computer (host) on the network; the port number identifies a process (server) on the node; and the socket type determines the manner in which data is exchanged — through a connection-oriented (stream) or connectionless (datagram) protocol.

Connection-oriented protocols

The socket type indicates the protocol being used to communicate through the socket. A connection-oriented protocol works like a normal phone conversation. When you want to talk to your friend, you have to dial your friend's phone number and establish a connection before you can have a conversation. In the same way, connection-oriented data exchange requires both the sending and receiving processes to establish a connection before data exchange can begin.

In the TCP/IP protocol suite, TCP — *Transmission Control Protocol* — supports a connection-oriented data transfer between two processes running on two computers on the Internet. TCP provides reliable two-way data exchange between processes.

As the name TCP/IP suggests, TCP relies on IP — *Internet Protocol* — for delivery of packets. IP does not guarantee delivery of packets; nor does it deliver packets in any particular sequence. IP does, however, efficiently move packets from one network to another. TCP is responsible for arranging the packets in the proper sequence, detecting whether or not errors have occurred, and requesting retransmission of packets in case of an error.

TCP is useful for applications intended to exchange large amounts of data at a time. In addition, applications that need reliable data exchange use TCP. (For example, FTP uses TCP to transfer files.)

In the sockets model, a socket that uses TCP is referred to as a *stream socket*.

Connectionless protocols

A *connectionless* data-exchange protocol does not require the sender and receiver to explicitly establish a connection. It's like shouting to your friend in a crowded room — you can't be sure that your friend hears you.

In the TCP/IP protocol suite, the *User Datagram Protocol* (UDP) provides connectionless service for sending and receiving packets known as *datagrams*. Unlike TCP, UDP does not guarantee that datagrams ever reach their intended destination. Nor does UDP ensure that datagrams are delivered in the order they have been sent.

UDP is used by applications that exchange small amounts of data at a time, or by applications that don't need the reliability and sequencing of data delivery. For example, SNMP (*Simple Network Management Protocol*) uses UDP to transfer data.

In the sockets model, a socket that uses UDP is referred to as a *datagram socket*.

Sockets and the client/server model

It takes two sockets to complete a communication path. When two processes communicate, they use the client/server model to establish the connection. Figure 1-1 illustrates the concept. The server application listens on a specific port on the system — the server is completely identified by the IP address of the system where it runs and the port number where it listens

**Book VIII
Chapter 1**

**Managing the
Servers**

for connections. The client initiates connection from any available port and tries to connect to the server (identified by the IP address and port number). When the connection is established, the client and the server can exchange data according to their own protocol.

Figure 1-1: Client and server processes use two sockets to communicate.

The sequence of events in socket-based data exchanges depends on whether the transfer is connection-oriented (TCP) or connectionless (UDP).

For a connection-oriented data transfer using sockets, the server "listens" on a specific port, waiting for clients to request connection. Data transfer begins only after a connection is established.

For connectionless data transfers, the server waits for a datagram to arrive at a specified port. The client does not wait to establish a connection; it simply sends a datagram to the server.

Regardless of whether it's a server or a client, each application first creates a socket. Then it *associates* (binds) the socket with the local computer's IP address and a port number. The IP address identifies the machine (where the application is running), and the port number identifies the application using the socket.

Servers typically listen to a well-known port number so that clients can connect to that port to access the server. For a client application, the process of binding a socket to the IP address and port is the same as that for a server, but the client can use 0 as the port number; the sockets library automatically uses an unused port number for the client.

For a connection-oriented stream socket, the communicating client and server applications have to establish a connection. The exact steps for establishing a connection depend on whether the application is a server or a client.

In the client/server model, the server has to be up and running before the client can run. After creating a socket and binding the socket to a port, the server application sets up a queue of connections, which determines how many clients can connect to the server. Typically, a server listens to anywhere from one to five connections. However, the size of the listen queue is one of the parameters you can adjust (especially for a Web server) to ensure that the server responds to as many clients as possible. After setting up the listen queue, the server waits for a connection from a client.

Establishing the connection from the client side is somewhat simpler. After creating a socket and binding the socket to an IP address, the client establishes connection with the server. To make the connection, the client must know the host name or IP address of the server, as well as the port on which the server accepts connection. All Internet services have well-known standard port numbers.

After a client establishes connection to a server via a connection-oriented stream socket, the client and server can exchange data by calling the appropriate sockets' API functions. Like a conversation between two persons, the server and client alternately send and receive data — the meaning of the data depends on the message protocol that the server and clients use. Usually, a server is designed for a specific task; inherent in that design is a message protocol that the server and clients use to exchange necessary data. For example, the Web server and the Web browser (client) communicate by using the HTTP (HyperText Transfer Protocol).

Internet services and port numbers

The TCP/IP protocol suite is the *lingua franca* of the Internet because the Internet services "speak" TCP/IP. These services make the Internet tick by making possible the transfer of mail, news, and Web pages. Each Internet service has its own protocol that relies on TCP/IP for the actual transfer of the information. Each service also has one or more assigned port numbers that it uses to do whatever it's designed to do. Here are some well-known Internet services and their associated protocols:

+ **DHCP (Dynamic Host Configuration Protocol)** is for dynamically configuring TCP/IP network parameters on a computer. DHCP is primarily used to assign dynamic IP addresses and other networking information such as name server, default gateway, and domain names that are needed to configure TCP/IP networks. The DHCP server listens on port 67.

+ **FTP (File Transfer Protocol)** is used to transfer files between computers on the Internet. FTP uses two ports: Data is transferred on port 20, and control information is exchanged on port 21.

+ **HTTP (HyperText Transfer Protocol)** is for sending documents from one system to another. HTTP is the underlying protocol of the Web. By default, the Web server and client communicate on port 80.

**Book VIII
Chapter 1**

**Managing the
Servers**

✦ **SMTP (Simple Mail Transfer Protocol)** is for exchanging e-mail messages between systems. SMTP uses port 25 for information exchange.

✦ **NNTP (Network News Transfer Protocol)** is for distribution of news articles in a store-and-forward fashion across the Internet. NNTP uses port 119.

✦ **TELNET** enables a user on one system to log in to another system on the Internet (the user must provide a valid user ID and password to log in to the remote system). TELNET uses port 23 by default. However, the TELNET client can connect to any specified port.

✦ **NFS (Network File System)** is for sharing files among computers. NFS uses Sun's Remote Procedure Call (RPC) facility, which exchanges information through port 111.

✦ **NTP (Network Time Protocol)** is used by client computers to synchronize the system time with that on a server (one with a more accurate clock). NTP uses port 123.

✦ **SNMP (Simple Network Management Protocol)** is for managing all types of network devices on the Internet. Like FTP, SNMP uses two ports: 161 and 162.

✦ **TFTP (Trivial File Transfer Protocol)** is for transferring files from one system to another (typically used by X terminals and diskless workstations to download boot files from another host on the network). TFTP data transfer takes place on port 69.

Each service is provided by a *server process* — a computer program that runs on a system awaiting client requests that arrive at the well-known port associated with its service. Thus, the Web server expects client requests at port 80, the standard port for HTTP service.

The /etc/services text file on your Red Hat Linux system stores the association between a service name and a port number (as well as a protocol). Here is a small subset of entries in the /etc/services file from a Red Hat Linux system:

```
ftp-data     20/tcp
ftp          21/tcp
ssh          22/tcp              # SSH Remote Login Protocol
ssh          22/udp              # SSH Remote Login Protocol
telnet       23/tcp
smtp         25/tcp      mail
time         37/tcp      timserver
time         37/udp      timserver
rlp          39/udp      resource     # resource location
nameserver   42/udp      name         # IEN 116
whois        43/tcp      nicname
```

A quick look through the entries in the /etc/services file shows the breadth of networking services available under TCP/IP.

Note that port number 80 is designated for Web service. In other words, if you set up a Web server on your system, that server listens to port 80. By the way, IANA — the Internet Assigned Numbers Authority (www.iana.org) — is the organization responsible for coordinating the assignment of port numbers below 1,024.

Using the xinetd Super Server

The client/server architecture of Internet services requires that the server be up and running before a client makes a request for service. A simplistic idea would be to run all the servers all the time — impractical because each server process would use up system resources in the form of memory and processor time. Besides, you don't really need *all* the services up and ready at all times. A smart solution to this problem is to run a single server, xinetd, that listens to all the ports and then starts the appropriate server when a client request comes in. (The xinetd server is a replacement for an older server named inetd, offering improved access control and logging. The name xinetd stands for *extended inetd*.)

For example, when a client tries to connect to the TELNET port, xinetd starts the TELNET server and lets it communicate directly with the client (and the TELNET server exits when the client disconnects).

Because it starts various servers on demand, xinetd is known as the Internet super server. Typically, a UNIX system starts xinetd when the system boots. The xinetd server reads a configuration file named /etc/xinetd.conf at startup. This file tells xinetd which ports to listen to and what server to start for each port. The file can contain instructions that include other configuration files. In Red Hat Linux, the /etc/xinetd.conf file looks like the following:

```
# Simple configuration file for xinetd
#
# Some defaults, and include /etc/xinetd.d/

defaults
{
        instances               = 60
        log_type                = SYSLOG authpriv
        log_on_success          = HOST PID
        log_on_failure          = HOST
        cps                     = 25 30
}
includedir /etc/xinetd.d
```

Comment lines begin with the pound sign (#). The `defaults` block of attributes, enclosed in curly braces (`{...}`), specifies default values for some attributes. These default values apply to all other services in the configuration file. The `instances` attribute is set to 60, which means there can be, at most, 60 servers simultaneously active for any service.

The last line in the `/etc/xinetd.conf` file uses the `includedir` directive to include all files inside the `/etc/xinetd.d` directory, excluding files that begin with a period (`.`). The idea is that the `/etc/xinetd.d` directory would contain all service configuration files — one file for each type of service the `xinetd` server is expected to manage.

Here is the listing of files that appears when I type the `ls /etc/xinetd.d` command on a typical Red Hat Linux system:

```
chargen       daytime-udp  imap    ktalk    rlogin    services  time
chargen-udp   echo         imaps   ntalk    rsh       sgi_fam   time-udp
cups-lpd      echo-udp     ipop2   pop3s    rsync     talk
daytime       finger       ipop3   rexec    servers   telnet
```

Each of these files specifies the attributes for one service. For example, the following listing shows the contents of the `/etc/xinetd.d/telnet` file, which specifies the `xinetd` configuration for the TELNET service:

```
# description: The Telnet server serves Telnet sessions; it uses
#       unencrypted username/password pairs for authentication.
service telnet
{
        flags           = REUSE
        socket_type     = stream
        wait            = no
        user            = root
        server          = /usr/sbin/in.telnetd
        log_on_failure  += USERID
        disable         = yes
}
```

The filename (in this case, `telnet`) can be anything; what matters is the service name that appears next to the `service` keyword in the file. In this case, the line `service telnet` tells `xinetd` the name of the service. `xinetd` uses this name to look up the port number from the `/etc/services` file. To look for `telnet` in the `/etc/services` file, type the following command:

```
grep "^telnet" /etc/services
```

The command displays the following lines:

```
telnet          23/tcp
telnet          23/udp
telnets         992/tcp
telnets         992/udp
```

The first two lines of the listing that begin with `telnet` show that the port number of the TELNET service is 23. This tells `xinetd` that any connection requests arriving at port 23 are meant for TELNET service. The configuration file `/etc/xinetd.d/telnet` then tells `xinetd` what to do to take care of these service requests.

The attributes in `/etc/xinetd.d/telnet`, enclosed in curly braces, have the following meanings:

+ The `flags` attribute provides specific instructions about how to run the servers that `xinetd` starts. The `REUSE` flag means that the service is left running even if `xinetd` is restarted. Note that the `REUSE` flag is now implicitly assumed to be set for all services.

+ The `socket_type` attribute is set to `stream`, which tells `xinetd` that the TELNET service uses a connection-oriented TCP socket to communicate with the client. For services that use the connectionless UDP sockets, this attribute would be set to `dgram`.

+ The `wait` attribute is set to `no`, which tells `xinetd` to start a new server for each request. If this attribute is set to `yes`, `xinetd` waits until the server exits before starting the server again.

+ The `user` attribute provides the user ID that `xinetd` uses to run the server. In this case, the server runs the TELNET server as `root`.

+ The `server` attribute specifies the program to run for this service. In this case, `xinetd` runs the `/usr/sbin/in.telnetd` program to provide TELNET service.

+ The `disable` attribute turns off the service if it's set to `yes`. By default the `disable` attribute is set to `yes` and TELNET is turned off.

Browse through the files in the `/etc/xinetd.d` directory on your Red Hat Linux system to find out the kinds of services `xinetd` is set up to start. Some of these services, such as `finger`, provide information that intruders may use to break into your system. If they are not already disabled, you may want to turn off these services by placing the following line inside the curly braces that enclose all attributes:

```
disable        = yes
```

On the other hand, if you can't seem to connect to your Red Hat Linux system by using `telnet`, check the appropriate file in the `/etc/xinetd.d` directory and make sure the `disable` attribute is set to `no`, or that line is *commented out* (changed from a line of code to a nonrunning comment by placing # at the beginning of the line).

**Book VIII
Chapter 1**

**Managing the
Servers**

When you make such a change to the `xinetd` configuration files, you must restart the `xinetd` server by typing the following command:

```
/etc/init.d/xinetd restart
```

If you want to type a little less, use the following command that does the exact same thing:

```
service xinetd restart
```

You can also use the `chkconfig` command to disable and enable services started by `xinetd`. For example, to enable the TELNET service, log in as `root` and type the following command:

```
chkconfig telnet on
```

To turn TELNET off again, type **chkconfig telnet off**.

Running Standalone Servers

Starting servers through `xinetd` is a smart approach, but it's not efficient if a service has to be started very often. If the Web server were controlled by `xinetd`, you'd have a situation where that server is started often because every time a user clicks a link on a Web page, a request arrives for the Web service. For such high-demand services, it's best to start the server in a standalone manner, to run as a *daemon* — a process that runs continuously and never dies. That means the server listens on the assigned port and whenever a request arrives, the server handles it by making a copy of itself. In this way, the server keeps running as long as the machine is running — in theory, forever. A more efficient strategy, used for Web servers, is to run multiple copies of the server and let each copy handle some of the incoming requests.

You can easily configure your Red Hat Linux system to start various stand-alone servers automatically. I show you how in this section.

Starting and stopping servers manually

To start a service that's not running, use the server command. For example, if the Web server (`httpd`) isn't running, you can start it by running a special shell script with the following command:

```
/etc/init.d/httpd start
```

That command runs the /etc/init.d/httpd script with start as the argument. If the httpd server is already running and you want to stop it, run the same command with stop as the argument, like this:

```
/etc/init.d/httpd stop
```

To stop and start a server again, just use restart as the argument:

```
/etc/init.d/httpd restart
```

Red Hat Linux includes another script called service that does the same job, but is a bit easier to remember. Basically, you can strip off the /etc/init.d and replace it with service followed by a space. Thus, to start httpd, you would type this:

```
service httpd start
```

What are all the services that you can start and stop? Well, the answer is in the files in the /etc/init.d directory. To get a look at it, type the following command:

```
ls /etc/init.d
```

All the files you see listed in response to this command are the services installed on your Red Hat Linux system — and you can start and stop them as needed. For example, here's a typical list of services on a Red Hat Linux system:

```
aep1000     functions    keytable        nfslock      saslauthd    tux
anacron     gpm          killall         nscd         sendmail     vsftpd
apmd        halt         kudzu           ntpd         single       winbind
atd         httpd        lisa            pcmcia       smartd       xfs
autofs      innd         messagebus      portmap      smb          xinetd
bcm5820     iptables     microcode_ctl   postgresql   snmpd        ypbind
cpqarrayd   irda         named           pxe          snmptrapd    yppasswdd
crond       irqbalance   netfs           random       squid        ypserv
cups        isdn         network         rawdevices   sshd         ypxfrd
firstboot   kdcrotate    nfs             rhnsd        syslog
```

That's over 50 services!

Starting servers automatically at boot time

You can start, stop, and restart servers manually by using the scripts in the /etc/init.d directory, but you would want some of the services to start as soon as you boot the Red Hat Linux system. You can configure servers to start automatically at boot time by using the chkconfig command or a graphical server configuration utility.

Using the chkconfig command

The chkconfig program is a command-line utility for checking and updating the current setting of servers in Red Hat Linux. Various combinations of servers are set up to start automatically at different run levels. Each *run level* represents a system configuration in which a selected set of processes runs. You're usually concerned about run levels 3 and 5 because run level 3 is for text-mode login and run level 5 is for logging in through a graphical interface.

The chkconfig command is simple to use. For example, suppose you want to automatically start the named server at run levels 3 and 5. All you have to do is log in as root and type the following command at the shell prompt:

```
chkconfig --level 35 named on
```

To see the status of the named server, type the following command:

```
chkconfig --list named
```

You should see a line of output similar to the following:

```
named    0:off  1:off  2:off  3:on   4:off  5:on   6:off
```

The output shows you the status of the named server at run levels 0 through 6. As you can see, named is set to run at run levels 3 and 5.

If you want to turn off named, you can do so with this command:

```
chkconfig --level 35 named off
```

You can use chkconfig to see the status of all services, including the ones started through xinetd. For example, you can view the status of all services by typing the following command:

```
chkconfig --list | more
```

Here's a typical output:

```
gpm            0:off  1:off  2:on   3:on   4:on   5:on   6:off
kudzu          0:off  1:off  2:off  3:on   4:on   5:on   6:off
syslog         0:off  1:off  2:on   3:on   4:on   5:on   6:off
rawdevices     0:off  1:off  2:off  3:on   4:on   5:on   6:off
netfs          0:off  1:off  2:off  3:on   4:on   5:on   6:off
network        0:off  1:off  2:on   3:on   4:on   5:on   6:off
random         0:off  1:off  2:on   3:on   4:on   5:on   6:off
saslauthd      0:off  1:off  2:off  3:off  4:off  5:off  6:off
microcode_ctl  0:off  1:off  2:on   3:on   4:on   5:on   6:off
keytable       0:off  1:on   2:on   3:on   4:on   5:on   6:off
```

```
anacron      0:off  1:off  2:on   3:on   4:on   5:on   6:off
atd          0:off  1:off  2:off  3:on   4:on   5:on   6:off
irda         0:off  1:off  2:off  3:off  4:off  5:off  6:off
snmpd        0:off  1:off  2:off  3:off  4:off  5:off  6:off
... many lines of output deleted ...
```

The output shows the status of each service for each of the run levels from
0 through 6. For each run level, the service is either on or off. At the very
end of the listing, `chkconfig` displays a list of the services that `xinetd`
controls. Each `xinetd`-based service is also marked on or off, depending
on whether or not `xinetd` is configured to start the service.

Note that services can typically be configured to run under `xinetd` or on a
standalone basis. For example, prior to version 8.1, Red Hat Linux used to
start the FTP service under control of `xinetd`. Starting with version 8.1,
however, the Very Secure FTP server (`vsftpd`) is set up as a standalone
server. Nowadays, if you have to start the FTP service, type **service vsftpd
start**. To start the FTP service automatically at boot time, type **chkconfig
vsftpd on**.

Using the Red Hat service configuration utility

If you don't like typing the `chkconfig` commands, you can use a graphical
service configuration utility program to configure the services. To run the
service configuration utility, log in as `root` and choose Main Menu⇨System
Settings⇨Server Settings⇨Services from the GNOME or KDE desktop. You
can then turn services on or off from the Service Configuration window (as
in Figure 1-2).

Figure 1-2:
From the
Service
Configur-
ation
window,
you can set
services to
start
automat-
ically at
boot time.

The service configuration utility shows the names of services in a scrolling list. Each line in the list shows the name of a service with a box in front of the name. A check mark in the box indicates that the service is already selected to start at boot time for the current run level. When the dialog box first appears, many services are already selected.

You can scroll up and down the list and click the box to select or deselect a service. If you click the box, the check mark alternately turns on and off. To learn more about a service, click the service name and a brief description appears in the right side of the window. For example, Figure 1-2 shows the help text for the atd service. Additionally, the utility also shows you whether the selected service is currently running or not.

After you select all the servers you want to start when the system boots, click Save on the toolbar to save the changes. Then choose File⇨Quit to exit.

By default, the service configuration utility configures the selected services for the current run level. That means if you're doing this from the graphical desktop, the system is in run level 5 and the services you configure are set to start at run level 5. If you want to set up the services for a different level, select that run level from the Edit Runlevel menu.

Table 1-1 shows a list of the services, along with a brief description of each one. The first column shows the name of the service, which is the same as the name of the program that has to run to provide the service. You may not see all of these services listed when you run the service configuration utility on your system because the exact list of services depends on what is installed on your Red Hat Linux system.

Table 1-1	Some Common Services in Red Hat Linux
Service Name	*Description*
aep1000	Loads and unloads the driver for the Accelerated Encryption Processing card called the AEP1000, which can do encryption fast (use this only if you have the card installed in your system).
anacron	Executes commands that are scheduled to run periodically.
apmd	Monitors the Advanced Power Management (APM) BIOS and logs the status of electric power (AC or battery backup).
atd	Runs commands scheduled by the at and cron commands.
autofs	Automatically mounts file systems (for example, when you insert a CD-ROM in the CD-ROM drive).

Service Name	Description
bcm5820	Loads and unloads the driver for Broadcom's BCM5820 Cryptonet SSL (secure sockets layer) accelerator chip (use this service only if you have the hardware installed).
crond	Runs user-specified programs according to a periodic schedule set by the crontab command.
cups	Runs the Common UNIX Printing System (CUPS) daemon (cupsd).
cups-lpd	Enables applications to use the legacy LPD (line printer daemon) protocol to communicate with CUPS.
finger	Answers finger protocol requests (for user information, such as login name and last login time). You have to enable xinetd for this service to run.
firstboot	Runs the first time you boot Red Hat Linux and enables you to set the date and time, create user accounts, register with Red Hat Network, and install other CD-ROMs.
gpm	Enables use of mouse in text-mode screens.
httpd	This is the Apache World Wide Web (WWW) server.
imap	Allows remote IMAP (Internet Message Access Protocol) clients to download mail messages. You have to enable xinetd for this service to run.
imaps	Allows remote IMAP (Internet Message Access Protocol) clients with secure sockets layer (SSL) support to securely download mail messages. You have to enable xinetd for this service to run.
innd	This is the InterNetNews daemon—the Internet news server you can use to support local newsgroups on your system.
ipop3	Allows remote POP3 (Post Office Protocol version 3) clients to download mail messages. You have to enable xinetd for this service to run.
iptables	Automates a packet-filtering firewall with iptables.
irda	Supports communications with IrDA-compliant infrared devices in Linux. (IrDA is a standard for infrared wireless communication at speeds ranging from 2400bps to 4Mbps.)
irqbalance	Distributes interrupts to the processors in a multiprocessor system to balance the load among the processors.
isdn	Starts and stops ISDN (Integrated Services Digital Network) services — a digital communication service over regular phone lines (enable only if you have ISDN service).
keytable	Loads the selected keyboard map as specified in the file /etc/sysconfig/keyboard. You should leave this service running on your system.
kudzu	Probes for new hardware and configures changed hardware.

(continued)

Book VIII
Chapter 1

Managing the
Servers

Table 1-1 *(continued)*

Service Name	Description
lisa	Starts and stops the LAN Information Server (LISa) daemon that can display information about hosts in the local area network (LAN) by broadcasting on TCP port 7741. To learn more about LISa, visit `lisa-home.sourceforge.net`.
messagebus	Runs the D-BUS daemon that enables applications to receive notification of system events such as the addition of a new hardware device. To learn more about D-BUS, see `www.freedesktop.org/software/dbus/`.
named	This is a server for the Domain Name System (DNS) that translates host names into IP addresses. You can run a copy on your system if you want.
netfs	Enables you to mount and unmount all network file systems (NFS, Samba, and Netware).
network	Enables you to activate or deactivate all network interfaces configured to start at system boot time.
nfs	Enables sharing of file systems specified in the `/etc/exports` file using the Network File System (NFS) protocol.
nfslock	Provides file-locking capability for file systems exported using the Network File System (NFS) protocol, so other systems (running NFS) can share files from your system.
ntalk	Provides support for chatting with users on different systems.
ntpd	This is the server for Network Time Protocol version 4 (NTPv4) that is used for synchronizing clocks on computers in a network.
pcmcia	Provides support for PCMCIA devices.
pop3s	Allows remote POP3 (Post Office Protocol version 3) clients that support SSL to securely download mail messages. You have to enable `xinetd` for this service to run.
portmap	Server used by any software that relies on Remote Procedure Calls (RPC). For example, NFS requires the `portmap` service.
postgresql	Starts or stops the PostgreSQL server that handles database requests. (PostgreSQL is a free database that comes with Red Hat Linux.)
pxe	Server for preboot execution environment (PXE) that's used to boot other systems over the network.
random	Server needed to generate high-quality random numbers on the Red Hat Linux system.
rawdevices	Assigns raw devices to block devices (needed for applications such as Oracle).
rexec	Supports remote execution with authentication based on username and password. You have to enable `xinetd` for this service to run.

Service Name	Description
rhnsd	Periodically connects to the Red Hat Network Services servers to check for updates and notifications.
rlogin	Server that supports remote login. You have to enable xinetd for this service to run.
rsh	Server that supports remote execution of commands. You have to enable xinetd for this service to run.
rsync	Server that supports remote copying of files. You have to enable xinetd for this service to run.
saslauthd	Supports authentication using the Cyrus-SASL (Simple Authentication and Security Layer) software.
sendmail	Moves mail messages from one machine to another. Start this service if you want to send mail from your Red Hat Linux system. If you don't plan to use your Red Hat Linux system as a mail server, don't start the sendmail server because it can slow down the booting process and consume unnecessary resources.
sgi_fam	Implements a file alternation monitor (FAM) that can be used to get reports when files change.
smb	Starts and stops the Samba smbd and nmbd services that support LAN Manager services on a Red Hat Linux system.
snmpd	Simple Network Management Protocol (SNMP) service used for network management functions.
squid	A caching server for Internet objects — anything that can be accessed through HTTP and FTP.
sshd	Server for the OpenSSH (Secure Shell) secure remote login facility.
syslog	Service used by many other programs (including other services) to log various error and status messages in a log file (usually, the /var/log/messages file). You should always run this service.
talk	Server that supports chatting with users on other systems. You have to enable xinetd for this service to run.
telnet	Server that supports TELNET remote login sessions. You have to enable xinetd for this service to run.
tux	This is the kernel-based HTTP server.
vsftpd	Very Secure FTP daemon for file transfers using the File Transfer Protocol (FTP).
winbind	Starts and stops the Samba winbindd server that provides a name-switch capability similar to that provided by the /etc/nsswitch.conf file.
xfs	Server that starts and stops the X Font Server.

Book VIII Chapter 1

Managing the Servers

(continued)

Table 1-1 *(continued)*

Service Name	Description
xinetd	This is the Internet super server, a replacement for the older inetd. It starts other Internet services, such as TELNET and FTP, whenever they are needed.
yppasswdd	Service needed for password changes in Network Information System (NIS). You don't have to start yppasswdd unless you're using NIS.
ypserv	The server for Network Information System (NIS). You don't have to start ypserv unless you're using NIS.
ypxfrd	A server that helps ypserv. Start this service only if you're using Network Information System (NIS).

Chapter 2: Running the Apache Web Server

The World Wide Web (*WWW* or the *Web*) has catapulted the Internet into the mainstream because Web browsers make it easy for users to browse documents stored on various Internet hosts. Whether you run a small business or manage computer systems and networks for a large company, chances are good that you have to set up and maintain a Web server. Because it has built-in networking support, a Red Hat Linux PC makes an affordable Web server. This chapter describes how to configure the Apache Web server on a Red Hat Linux PC.

Exploring HTTP

Web servers provide information using HTTP. Web servers are also known as *HTTP daemons* (because continuously running server processes are called daemons in UNIX) or *HTTPD* for short. The Web server program (such as the Apache Web server that comes with Red Hat Linux) is usually named httpd.

HTTP stands for *HyperText Transfer Protocol*. The *HyperText* part refers to the fact that Web pages include hypertext links. The *Transfer Protocol* part refers to the standard conventions for transferring a Web page across the network from one computer to another. Although you really don't have to understand HTTP to set up a Web server or use a Web browser, taking a look at its workings does help you understand how the Web works.

You can get a firsthand experience with HTTP by using the TELNET program to connect to the port where a Web server listens. On most systems, the Web server listens to port 80 and responds to any HTTP requests sent to that port. Therefore you can use the TELNET program to connect to port 80 of a system (if it has a Web server) and try some HTTP commands.

Is HTTP an Internet Standard?

Despite its widespread use in the Web since 1990, HTTP was not an Internet standard until recently. All Internet standards are first distributed as a *Request for Comment* (RFC). The first HTTP-related RFC was RFC 1945, "HyperText Transfer Protocol — HTTP/1.0" (T. Berners-Lee, R. Fielding, and H. Frystyk, May 1996). However, RFC 1945 is considered an informational document, not a standard.

RFC 2616, "HyperText Transfer Protocol — HTTP/1.1" (R. Fielding, J. Gettys, J. Mogul, H. Frystyk, L. Masinter, P. Leach, T. Berners-Lee, June 1999) is the Draft Internet standard for HTTP.

To read these RFCs, point your Web browser to either `www.rfc-editor.org/rfc.html` or `www.cis.ohio-state.edu/htbin/rfc/rfc-index.html`.

To learn more about HTTP/1.1 and other Web-related standards, use a Web browser to access `www.w3.org/pub/WWW/Protocols/`.

To see an example of HTTP at work, follow these steps:

1. **Make sure your Linux PC's connection to the Internet is up and running.**

   If you use SLIP or PPP, for example, make sure you have established a connection.

2. **Type the following command:**

   ```
   telnet www.gao.gov 80
   ```

3. **After you see the** `Connected...` **message, type the following HTTP command and then press Enter twice:**

   ```
   GET / HTTP/1.0
   ```

   In response to this HTTP command, the Web server returns some useful information, followed by the contents of the default HTML file (usually called `index.html`).

The following is what I get when I try the `GET` command on the U. S. General Accounting Office's Web site:

```
Trying 161.203.16.2...
Connected to www.gao.gov.
Escape character is '^]'.
Date: Sun, 13 Jul 2003 17:49:23 GMT
Server: Apache
Connection: close
Content-Type: text/html

<!DOCTYPE HTML PUBLIC "-//W3C//DTD HTML 4.0 Transitional//EN"
        "http://www.w3.org
```

```
/TR/REC-html40/loose.dtd">

<HTML>
<HEAD>
<TITLE>The United States General Accounting Office</TITLE>
...... (lines deleted)
</HEAD>

...... (lines deleted)

</BODY>
</html>
Connection closed by foreign host.
```

When you try this example with TELNET, you see exactly what the Web server sends back to the Web browser. The first few lines are administrative information for the browser. The server returns this information:

✦ A line that shows that the server uses HTTP protocol version 1.1 and a status code of 200 indicating success:

```
HTTP/1.1 200 OK
```

✦ The current date and time. A sample date and time string looks like this:

```
Date: Sun, 13 Jul 2003 17:49:23 GMT
```

✦ The name of the Web-server software. For example, for a site running the Apache Web server, the server returns the following string:

```
Server: Apache
```

The server suppresses the version number and other details so crackers cannot easily exploit known security holes in specific versions of Apache Web server.

✦ The type of document the Web server returns. For HTML documents, the content type is reported as follows:

```
Content-type: text/html
```

The document itself follows the administrative information. An HTML document has the following general layout:

```
<title>Document's title goes here</title>
<html>
<body optional attributes go here >
... The rest of the document goes here
</body>
</html>
```

You can identify this layout by looking through the listing that shows what the Web server returns in response to the GET command. Because the example uses a telnet command to get the document, you see the HTML content as lines of text. If you were to access the same Web site (`www.gao.gov`) with a Web browser (such as Mozilla), you would see the page in its graphical form (as in Figure 2-1).

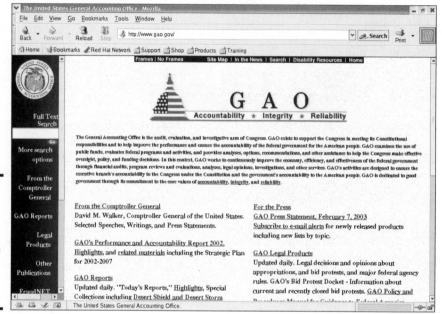

Figure 2-1: The www. gao.gov Web site viewed with the Mozilla Web browser.

The example of HTTP commands shows the result of the `GET` command. `GET` is the most common HTTP command; it causes the server to return a specified HTML document.

The other two HTTP commands are `HEAD` and `POST`. The `HEAD` command is almost like `GET`: It causes the server to return everything in the document except the body. The `POST` command sends information to the server; it's up to the server to decide how to act on the information.

Exploring the Apache Web Server

You probably already know how it feels to use the Web, but you may not know how to set up a Web server so you, too, can provide information to the world through Web pages. To become an information provider on the Web, you have to run a Web server on your Red Hat Linux PC on the Internet. You also have to prepare the Web pages for your Web site — a task that may be more demanding than the Web server setup.

Among the available Web servers, the Apache Web server is the most popular, and it comes with Red Hat Linux. The Apache Web server started out as an improved version of the NCSA HTTPD server but soon grew into a separate development effort. Like NCSA HTTPD, the Apache server is developed and maintained by a team of collaborators. Apache is freely available over the Internet.

Installing the Apache Web server

Depending on the Red Hat Linux installation options, the Apache Web server may be already installed in your system. To find out whether it's installed, type the following command:

```
rpm -q httpd
```

If the Web server is installed, you should see an output like this:

```
httpd-2.0.45-14
```

If you get a message that `httpd` is not installed, then you can install it easily from this book's companion DVD using these steps:

1. **Log in as** `root` **and insert the DVD into the DVD drive.**

   If you're in the GNOME or KDE graphical desktop, the DVD should be automatically mounted. If not, type the command **mount /dev/cdrom** to mount the DVD.

2. **Type the following commands to install the Apache Web server:**

   ```
   cd /mnt/cdrom/RedHat/RPMS
   rpm -ivh httpd*
   ```

That's it! You can now run the Apache Web server.

Starting the Apache Web server

Even if the Apache Web server is installed, it may not be set up to start at boot time. If you want to try it out, you have to start the server. To do so, log in as `root` and type the following command:

```
service httpd start
```

To see whether the `httpd` process (`httpd` is the name of the Apache Web server program) is running, type the following command:

```
ps ax | grep httpd
```

**Book VIII
Chapter 2**

Running the Apache Web Server

Why is it called Apache?

According to the information about the Apache Web server project on www.apache.org/foundation/faq.html, the Apache group was formed in March 1995 by a number of people who provided patch files that had been written to fix bugs in NCSA HTTPD 1.3. The result after applying the patches to NCSA HTTPD was what they called *a patchy server* (that's how the name Apache came about). The Apache Group has now evolved into The Apache Software Foundation (ASF), a nonprofit corporation that was incorporated in Delaware, U.S.A., in June 1999. ASF has a number of other ongoing projects. You can read about these projects at www.apache.org. In particular, visit httpd.apache.org for more information about the Apache Web server project.

According to the July 2003 Netcraft Web Server Survey at news.netcraft.com/archives/web_server_survey.html, the Apache Web server is the most popular — 63.72 percent of the 42,298,371 sites reported using the Apache server. Microsoft Internet Information Server (IIS) is a distant second, with 25.95 percent of the sites.

The output should show a number of httpd processes. It's a common approach to run several Web server processes — one parent and several child processes — so several HTTP requests can be handled efficiently by assigning each request to an httpd process.

If there is no httpd process, errors may be lurking in the Apache configuration file. If this is the case, some error messages should appear and give you a clue about the cause of the error. You have to fix the problem in the configuration file and start the server again.

If the httpd processes are up and running, you can use the TELNET program to see whether it works, but first you have to add a default home page in the /var/www/html directory. If you don't have time to prepare one, copy the Web page that's supposed to be sent out in case of errors. Here's the command you type (while logged in as root) to get it:

```
cp /var/www/error/noindex.html /var/www/html/index.html
```

Now you have a default home page and you can type the following command in a terminal window to check whether the Web server is working:

```
telnet localhost 80
```

After you get the Connected message, type

```
HEAD / HTTP/1.0
```

Then press Enter twice. You should get a response that looks similar to the following (with different dates and numbers, of course):

```
Trying 127.0.0.1...
Connected to localhost.
Escape character is '^]'.
HTTP/1.1 200 OK
Date: Sun, 13 Jul 2003 18:11:11 GMT
Server: Apache/2.0.45 (Red Hat Linux)
Last-Modified: Sun, 13 Jul 2003 18:10:15 GMT
ETag: "bdf93-b52-b7b3efc0"
Accept-Ranges: bytes
Content-Length: 2898
Connection: close
Content-Type: text/html; charset=UTF-8

Connection closed by foreign host.
```

The response shows some information about the Web server and the default home page. You can also check out the Web server by using a Web browser such as Mozilla running on your Red Hat Linux system. For example, if your system's IP address is 192.168.0.5, use the URL http://192.168.0.5/ and see what happens. You should see a Web page with the title "Test Page for the Apache Web Server on Red Hat Linux."

If you want to start the Apache Web server automatically at boot time, type the following command to set it up:

```
chkconfig --levels 35 httpd on
```

Configuring the Apache Web Server

Red Hat Linux configures the Apache Web server software to use these directories:

+ The Web server program — httpd — is installed in the /usr/sbin directory.

+ The Apache Web server configuration file — httpd.conf — is located in the /etc/httpd/conf directory. The configuration file is a text file with directives that specify various aspects of the Web server. The /etc/httpd/conf directory also contains information about the Secure Sockets Layer (SSL) implementation needs. (The SSL implementation comes as part of the Apache Web server.)

+ The Apache Web server is set up to serve the HTML documents from the /var/www/html directory. Therefore you should place your Web pages in this directory.

✦ If you have any Common Gateway Interface (CGI) programs — programs the Web server can invoke to access other files and databases — you should place these in the `/var/www/cgi-bin/` directory.

✦ The `/var/log/httpd` directory is meant for Web server log files (access logs and error logs).

✦ The `/etc/init.d/httpd` script starts the `httpd` process as your Red Hat Linux system boots, provided you have enabled it by using the `chkconfig` command.

Using Apache configuration tools

Red Hat Linux comes with a graphical configuration tool that you can use to configure the Apache Web server. To run this configuration tool, log in as `root` and choose Main Menu⇨System Settings⇨Server Settings⇨HTTP Server from the GNOME desktop. The Apache Configuration dialog box appears (as in Figure 2-2).

Figure 2-2:
You can configure the Apache HTTP server from this configuration window.

The Apache Configuration dialog box is organized into four tabs. You can set various options from each of these tabs:

✦ **Main:** From this tab you can specify the IP addresses and port number where Apache should expect requests for Web service. You can also set the e-mail address of the Webmaster.

✦ **Virtual Hosts:** Here you can set up virtual hosts. I discuss the options for virtual hosts later in this chapter. You can also edit the default settings that apply to all virtual hosts. Clicking the Edit Default Settings button in the Virtual Hosts tab brings up another dialog box (as in Figure 2-3) from which you can set a number of different options.

Figure 2-3:
You can configure the virtual host properties from this configuration window.

+ **Server:** This tab has settings for the server such as the user and group names under which the HTTP server should run and the locations of the file where the process ID is stored.

+ **Performance Tuning:** On this tab you can set some parameters that control overall performance. You can set the maximum number of connections allowed, the timeout period for connections, and the maximum number of requests per connection.

Initially the configuration window displays the default values from the configuration file `/etc/httpd/conf/httpd.conf`. After you make any changes, click the OK button. The configuration tool prompts you to ask whether you really want to save the changes and exit. If you do, click Yes and you should be done.

When you configure the Apache HTTP server from this configuration tool, all you're doing is changing options and attributes stored in the `/etc/httpd/conf/httpd.conf` file. You can just as easily make the changes by editing the configuration file, which is a plain text file. In the next sections, I introduce you to some common configuration directives in the Apache configuration file.

Apache configuration files

The Apache server's operation is controlled by the `httpd.conf` configuration file located in the `/etc/httpd/conf` directory. This file controls how the server runs, what documents it serves, and who can access these documents.

In the next few sections, I summarize key information about the `httpd.conf` configuration file. Typically, you don't have to change anything in the configuration files to run the Apache Web server. However, it's useful to know the format of the configuration files and the meaning of the various keywords used in them.

As you study the configuration files in the /etc/httpd/conf directory, keep these syntax rules in mind:

✦ Each configuration file is a text file that you can edit with your favorite text editor and view with the more command.

✦ All comment lines begin with a #.

✦ Each line can have only one directive.

✦ Extra spaces and blank lines are ignored.

✦ All entries, except pathnames and URLs, are case insensitive.

The httpd.conf configuration file

The /etc/httpd/conf/httpd.conf file is the main HTTP-daemon configuration file — it includes directives that control how the Apache Web server runs. For example, the httpd.conf file specifies the port number the server uses, the name of the Web site, and the e-mail address to which mail is sent in case of any problems with the server. In addition, httpd.conf also includes information on where the Web pages are located and who can access what directories.

In the following sections, I present the Apache directives grouped in three separate categories: general HTTPD directives, resource configuration directives, and access control directives. Finally, I explain how virtual hosts can be set up in Apache Web server so that a single Web server can handle Web requests sent to several IP addresses or host names.

General HTTPD directives

Some interesting items from the httpd.conf file are

✦ ServerName specifies the host name of your Web site (of the form www.your.domain) and the port number where the Web server accepts connections. ServerName is used only when redirecting a Web page to another Web page. The name should be a registered domain name other users can locate through their name servers. Here is an example:

    ServerName   www.myhost.com:80

If you don't have a registered domain name, use the IP address of your Red Hat Linux system.

✦ ServerAdmin is the e-mail address that the Web server provides to clients in case any errors occur. The default value for ServerAdmin is root@localhost. You should set this to a valid e-mail address that anyone on the Internet can use to report errors your Web site contains.

Many more directives control the way that the Apache Web server works. The following list summarizes some of the directives you can use in the `httpd.conf` file. You can leave most of these directives in their default settings, but it's important to know about them if you're maintaining a Web server.

♦ `Listen` *IP-Address:Port* — Forces the Web server to listen to a specific IP address and port number. By default, the Web server responds to all IP addresses associated with the host.

♦ `User` *name [#id]* — Specifies the user name (or ID) the HTTP daemon uses. You can leave this directive at the default setting (`apache`). If you specify a user ID, use a hash (#) prefix for the numeric ID.

♦ `Group` *name [#id]* — Specifies the group name (or ID) of the HTTP daemon when running in standalone mode. The default group name is `apache`.

♦ `ServerRoot` *pathname* — Specifies the directory where the Web server is located. By default, the configuration and log files are expected to reside in subdirectories of this directory. In Red Hat Linux, `ServerRoot` is set to `/etc/httpd`.

♦ `ServerName` *www.company.com*:80 — Sets the server's host name to *www.company.com* and the port number to 80. `ServerName` is used only when redirecting a Web page to another.

♦ `StartServers` *num* — Sets the number of child processes that start as soon as the Apache Web server runs. The default value is 8.

♦ `MaxSpareServers` *num* — Sets the desired maximum number of idle child-server processes (a child process is considered idle if it's not handling an HTTP request). The default value is 20.

♦ `MinSpareServers` *num* — Sets the desired minimum number of idle child server processes (a child process is considered idle if it's not handling an HTTP request). A new spare process is created every second if the number falls below this threshold. The default value is 5.

♦ `Timeout` *numsec* — Sets the number of seconds that the server waits for a client to send a query after the client establishes connection. The default timeout is 300 seconds (five minutes).

♦ `ErrorLog` *filename* — Sets the file where `httpd` logs the errors it encounters. If the filename does not begin with a slash (/), the name is taken to be relative to `ServerRoot`. The default `ErrorLog` is `/etc/httpd/logs/error_log`, but `/etc/httpd/logs` is a symbolic link to the `/var/log/httpd` directory. Therefore the log files are in the `/var/log/.httpd` directory. Typical error-log entries include events such as server restarts and any warning messages, such as the following:

```
[Sun Jul 13 14:10:34 2003] [notice] Apache/2.0.45 (Red Hat Linux)
    configured -- resuming normal operations
[Sun Jul 13 15:47:03 2003] [error] [client 192.168.0.2] File does not
    exist: /var/www/html/sample.html
```

✦ TransferLog *filename* — Sets the file where httpd records all client accesses (including failed accesses). The default TransferLog is /var/log/httpd/access_log. The following example shows how a typical access is recorded in this log file:

```
192.168.0.2 - - [13/Jul/2003:15:46:56 -0400] "GET / HTTP/1.1" 200 2898
    "-" "Mozilla/4.0 (compatible; MSIE 6.0; Windows NT 5.1)"
192.168.0.2 - - [13/Jul/2003:15:46:56 -0400] "GET /icons/apache_pb.gif
    HTTP/1.1"
 200 2326 "http://192.168.0.6/" "Mozilla/4.0 (compatible; MSIE 6.0;
    Windows NT 5.1)"
192.168.0.2 - - [13/Jul/2003:15:46:56 -0400] "GET /icons/powered_by.gif
    HTTP/1.1" 200 581 "http://192.168.0.6/" "Mozilla/4.0 (compatible;
    MSIE 6.0; Windows NT 5.1)"
```

✦ LogFormat *formatstring formatname* — Specifies the format of log-file entries for the TransferLog. This format is also used by the CustomLog directive to produce logs in a specific format.

✦ CustomLog *filename formatname* — Sets the name of the custom log file where httpd records all client accesses (including failed accesses) in a format specified by *formatname* (which you define using a LogFormat directive).

✦ PidFile *filename* — Sets the file where HTTPD stores its process ID. The default PidFile is /var/run/httpd.pid. You can use this information to kill or restart the HTTP daemon. The following example shows how to restart httpd:

```
kill -HUP 'cat /var/run/httpd.pid'
```

✦ MaxClients *num* — Sets the limit on the number of clients that can simultaneously connect to the server. The default value is 150. The value of MaxClients cannot be more than 256.

✦ LoadModule *module* modules/modfile.so — Loads a module that was built as a Dynamic Shared Object (DSO). You have to specify the module name and the module's object file. Because the order in which modules are loaded is important, you should leave these directives as they appear in the default configuration file. Note that the mod_ssl module provides support for encryption using the Secure Sockets Layer (SSL) protocol.

Resource configuration directives

The resource configuration directives specify the location of the Web pages, as well as how to specify the data types of various files. To get started, you can leave the directives at their default settings. These are some of the resource configuration directives for the Apache Web server:

✦ DocumentRoot *pathname* — Specifies the directory where the HTTP server finds the Web pages. In Red Hat Linux, the default DocumentRoot is /var/www/html. If you place your HTML documents in another directory, set DocumentRoot to that directory.

✦ UserDir *dirname* — Specifies the subdirectory below a user's home directory where the HTTP server looks for Web pages when a username appears in the URL (in an URL such as http://www.psn.net/~naba, for example, which includes a username with a tilde prefix). By default, the UserDir feature is turned off by setting *dirname* to disable. If you want it enabled, you can set it to public_html, which means that a user's Web pages are in the public_html subdirectory of that user's home directory.

✦ DirectoryIndex *filename1 filename2* ... — Indicates the default file or files to be returned by the server when the client does not specify a document. The default DirectoryIndex is index.html. If httpd does not find this file, it returns an index (basically, a nice-looking listing of the files) of that directory provided indexing is allowed for that directory.

✦ AccessFileName *filename* — Specifies the name of the file that may appear in each directory that contains documents and that indicates who has permission to access the contents of that directory. The default AccessFileName is .htaccess. The syntax of this file is the same as that of Apache access-control directives, which I discuss in the next section.

✦ AddType *type/subtype extension* — Associates a file extension with a MIME data type (of the form *type/subtype*, such as text/plain or image/gif). Thus, to have the server treat files with the .lst extension as plain text files, specify the following:

```
AddType text/plain .lst
```

The default MIME types and extensions are listed in the /etc/mime.types file.

✦ AddEncoding *type extension* — Associates an encoding type with a file extension. To have the server mark files ending with .gz or .tgz as encoded with the x-gzip encoding method (the standard name for the GZIP encoding), specify the following:

```
AddEncoding x-gzip gz tgz
```

✦ DefaultType *type/subtype* — Specifies the MIME type that the server should use if it cannot determine the type from the file extension. If you don't specify DefaultType, HTTPD assumes the MIME type to be text/html. In the default httpd.conf file, DefaultType is specified as text/plain.

✦ Redirect *requested-file actual-URL* — Specifies that any requests for *requested-file* are to be redirected to *actual-URL*.

✦ Alias *requested-dir actual-dir* — Specifies that the server use *actual-dir* to locate files in the *requested-dir* directory (in other words, *requested-dir* is an alias for *actual-dir*). To have requests for the /icons directory go to /var/www/icons, specify the following:

```
Alias /icons/ /var/www/icons/
```

✦ `ScriptAlias` *requested-dir actual-dir* — Specifies the real name of the directory where scripts for the Common Gateway Interface (CGI) are located. The default configuration file contains this directive:

```
ScriptAlias /cgi-bin/ "/var/www/cgi-bin/"
```

This directive means that when a Web browser requests a script, such as `/cgi-bin/test-cgi`, the HTTP server runs the script `/var/www/cgi-bin/test-cgi`.

✦ `DefaultIcon` *iconfile* — Specifies the location of the default icon that the server should use for files that have no icon information. By default, `DefaultIcon` is `/icons/unknown.gif`.

✦ `ReadmeName` *filename* — Specifies the name of a `README` file whose contents are added to the end of an automatically generated directory listing. The default `ReadmeName` is `README`.

✦ `HeaderName` *filename* — Specifies the name of a header file whose contents are prepended to an automatically generated directory listing. The default `HeaderName` is `HEADER`.

✦ `AddDescription` *"file description" filename* — Specifies that the *file description* string be displayed next to the specified filename in the directory listing. You can use a wildcard, such as `*.html`, as the filename. For example, the following directive describes files ending with `.tgz` as GZIP compressed tar archives:

```
AddDescription "GZIP compressed tar archive" .tgz
```

✦ `AddIcon` *iconfile extension1 extension2 ...* — Associates an icon with one or more file extensions. The following directive associates the icon file `/icons/text.gif` with the file extension `.txt`:

```
AddIcon /icons/text.gif .txt
```

✦ `AddIconByType` *iconfile MIME-types* — Associates an icon with a group of file types specified as a wildcard form of MIME types (such as `text/*` or `image/*`). To associate an icon file of `/icons/text.gif` with all `text` types, specify the following:

```
AddIconByType (TXT,/icons/text.gif) text/*
```

This directive also tells the server to use TXT in place of the icon for clients that cannot accept images. (Browsers tell the server what types of data they can accept.)

✦ `AddIconByEncoding` *iconfile encoding1 encoding2 ...* — Specifies an icon to be displayed for one or more encoding types (such as `x-compress` or `x-gzip`).

✦ `IndexIgnore` *filename1 filename2 ...* — Instructs the server to ignore the specified filenames (they typically contain wildcards) when preparing a directory listing. To leave out README, HEADER, and all files with names that begin with a period (.), a trailing tilde (~), or a trailing hash mark (#), specify the following:

```
IndexIgnore .??* *~ *# HEADER* README* RCS CVS *.v *.t
```

✦ IndexOptions *option1 option2* ... — Indicates the options you want in the directory listing prepared by the server. Options can include one or more of the following:

- FancyIndexing turns on the fancy directory listing that includes filenames and icons representing the files' types, sizes, and last-modified dates.

- IconHeight=N specifies that icons are N pixels tall.

- IconWidth=N specifies that icons are N pixels wide.

- NameWidth=N makes the filename column N characters wide.

- IconsAreLinks makes the icons act like links.

- ScanHTMLTitles shows a description of HTML files.

- SuppressHTMLPreamble does not add a standard HTML preamble to the header file (specified by the HeaderName directive).

- SuppressLastModified stops display of the last date of modification.

- SuppressSize stops display of the file size.

- SuppressDescription stops display of any file description.

- SuppressColumnSorting stops the column headings from being links that enable sorting the columns.

✦ ErrorDocument *errortype filename* — Specifies a file the server should send when an error of a specific type occurs. You can also provide a text message for an error. Here are some examples:

```
ErrorDocument 403 "Sorry, no access to this directory"
ErrorDocument 403 /error/noindex.html
ErrorDocument 404 /cgi-bin/bad_link.pl
ErrorDocument 401 /new_subscriber.html
```

If you don't have the ErrorDocument directive, the server sends a built-in error message. The *errortype* can be one of the following HTTP/1.1 error conditions (see RFC 2616 at www.ietf.org/rfc/rfc2616.txt or www.cis.ohio-state.edu/htbin/rfc/rfc2616.html for more information):

- 400 — Bad Request

- 401 — Unauthorized

- 402 — Payment Required
- 403 — Forbidden
- 404 — Not Found
- 405 — Method Not Allowed
- 406 — Not Acceptable
- 407 — Proxy Authentication Required
- 408 — Request Timeout
- 409 — Conflict
- 410 — Gone
- 411 — Length Required
- 412 — Precondition Failed
- 413 — Request Entity Too Large
- 414 — Request URI Too Long
- 415 — Unsupported Media Type
- 416 — Requested Range Not Satisfiable
- 417 — Expectation Failed
- 500 — Internal Server Error
- 501 — Not Implemented
- 502 — Bad Gateway
- 503 — Service Unavailable
- 504 — Gateway Timeout
- 505 — HTTP Version Not Supported

✦ `TypesConfig` *filename* — Specifies the file that contains the mapping of file extensions to MIME data types. (MIME stands for Multipurpose Internet Mail Extensions, a way to package attachments in a single message file.) The server reports these MIME types to clients. If you don't specify a `TypesConfig` directive, HTTPD assumes that the `TypesConfig` file is `/etc/mime.types`. The following are a few selected lines from the default `/etc/mime.types` file:

```
application/msword              doc
application/pdf                 pdf
application/postscript          ai eps ps
application/x-tcl               tcl
audio/mpeg                      mpga mp2 mp3
audio/x-pn-realaudio            ram rm
audio/x-wav                     wav
```

```
image/gif                      gif
image/jpeg                     jpeg jpg jpe
image/png                      png
text/html                      html htm
text/plain                     asc txt
video/mpeg                     mpeg mpg mpe
```

Each line shows the MIME type (such as `text/html`), followed by the file extensions for that type (`html` or `htm`).

Access control directives

Access control directives enable you to control who can access different directories in the system. These are the global access configuration directives. You can also have another access configuration file that uses a name specified by the `AccessFileName` directive in every directory from which the Apache Web server can serve documents. (That *per-directory* access configuration file is named `.htaccess` by default.)

Stripped of most of its comment lines, the access control directive has this format:

```
# First, we configure the "default" to be a
# very restrictive set of permissions.
<Directory />
    Options FollowSymLinks
    AllowOverride None
</Directory>

# The following directory name should
# match DocumentRoot in httpd.conf
<Directory /var/www/html>
    Options Indexes FollowSymLinks
    AllowOverride None
    order allow,deny
    allow from all
</Directory>

# The directory name should match the
# location of the cgi-bin directory
<Directory "/var/www/cgi-bin">
    AllowOverride None
    Options None
    Order allow,deny
    Allow from all
</Directory>
```

Access control directives use a different syntax from the other Apache directives. The syntax is like that of HTML. Various access control directives are enclosed within pairs of tags, such as `<Directory>` ... `</Directory>`.

The following list describes some of the access control directives. In particular, notice the `AuthUserFile` directive; you can have password-based access control for specific directories.

✦ `Options` *opt1 opt2* ... — Specifies the access control options for the directory section in which this directive appears. The options can be one or more of the following:

- `None` disables all access control features.

- `All` turns on all features for the directory.

- `FollowSymLinks` enables the server to follow symbolic links.

- `SymLinksIfOwnerMatch` follows symbolic links, only if the same user of the directory owns the linked directory.

- `ExecCGI` enables execution of CGI scripts in the directory.

- `Includes` enables server-side `include` files in this directory (the term *server-side include* refers to directives, placed in an HTML file, that the Web server processes before returning the results to the Web browser).

- `Indexes` enables clients to request indexes (directory listings) for the directory.

- `IncludesNOEXEC` disables the #exec command in server-side `includes`.

✦ `AllowOverride` *directive1 directive2* ... — Specifies which access control directives can be overridden on a per-directory basis. The directive list can contain one or more of the following:

- `None` stops any directive from being overridden.

- `All` enables overriding of any directive on a per-directory basis.

- `Options` enables the use of the `Options` directive in the directory-level file.

- `FileInfo` enables the use of directives controlling document type, such as `AddType` and `AddEncoding`.

- `AuthConfig` enables the use of authorization directives, such as `AuthName`, `AuthType`, `AuthUserFile`, and `AuthGroupFile`.

- `Limit` enables the use of `Limit` directives (`allow`, `deny`, and `order`) in a directory's access-configuration file.

✦ `AuthName` *name* — Specifies the authorization name for a directory.

✦ `AuthType` *type* — Specifies the type of authorization to be used. The only supported authorization type is Basic.

✦ `AuthUserFile` *filename* — Specifies the file in which usernames and passwords are stored for authorization. For example, the following directive sets the authorization file to `/etc/httpd/conf/passwd`:

```
AuthUserFile /etc/httpd/conf/passwd
```

You have to create the authorization file with the `/usr/bin/htpasswd` support program. To create the authorization file and add the password for a user named `jdoe`, specify the following:

```
/usr/bin/htpasswd -c /etc/httpd/conf/passwd jdoe
```

When prompted for the password, enter the password and then confirm it by typing it again.

✦ `AuthGroupFile` *filename* — Specifies the file to consult for a list of user groups for authentication.

✦ `order` *ord* — Specifies the order in which two other directives — `allow` and `deny` — are evaluated. The order is one of the following:

    • `deny,allow` causes the Web server to evaluate the `deny` directive before `allow`.

    • `allow,deny` causes the Web server to evaluate the `allow` directive before `deny`.

    • `mutual-failure` enables only hosts in the `allow` list.

✦ `deny from` *host1 host2...* — Specifies the hosts denied access.

✦ `allow from` *host1 host2...* — Specifies the hosts allowed access. To enable all hosts in a specific domain to access the Web documents in a directory, specify the following:

```
order deny,allow
allow from .nws.noaa.gov
```

✦ `require` *entity en1 en2...* — This directive specifies which users can access a directory. *entity* is one of the following:

    • `user` enables only a list of named users.

    • `group` enables only a list of named groups.

    • `valid-user` enables all users listed in the `AuthUserFile` access to the directory (provided they enter the correct password).

Virtual host setup

A useful feature of the Apache HTTP server is that it can handle virtual Web servers. *Virtual hosting* simply means that a single Web server can respond to many different IP addresses and serve Web pages from different directories, depending on the IP address. That means you can set up a single Web

**Book VIII
Chapter 2**

**Running the Apache
Web Server**

server to respond to both `www.big.org` and `www.tiny.com` and serve a unique home page for each host name. A server with this capability is known as a *multi-homed* Web server, a *virtual* Web server, or a server with *virtual host support*.

As you might guess, Internet service providers (ISPs) use the virtual host feature of Apache Web server to offer virtual Web sites to their customers. You need the following to support virtual hosts:

+ The Web server must be able to respond to multiple IP addresses (each with a unique domain name) and must enable you to specify document directories, log files, and other configuration items for each IP address.

+ The host system must be able to associate multiple IP addresses with a single physical network interface. Red Hat Linux can do so.

+ Each domain name associated with the IP address must be a unique, registered domain name with proper DNS entries.

For the latest information on how to set up virtual hosts in an Apache HTTP server, consult the following URL:

`http://httpd.apache.org/docs-2.0/vhosts`

The Apache HTTP server can respond to different host names with different home pages. You have two options when supporting virtual hosts:

+ **Run multiple copies of the** `httpd` **program, one for each IP address.** In this case, you create a separate copy of the `httpd.conf` configuration file for each host and use the `Listen` directive to make the server respond to a specific IP address.

+ **Run a single copy of the** `httpd` **program with a single** `httpd.conf` **file.** In the configuration file, set `Listen` to a port number only (so the server responds to any IP address associated with the host), and use the `VirtualHost` directive to configure the server for each virtual host.

Run multiple HTTP daemons only if you don't expect heavy traffic on your system; the system may not able to respond well because of the overhead associated with running multiple daemons. However, you may need multiple HTTP daemons if each virtual host has a unique configuration need for the following directives:

+ `UserId` and `GroupId` (the user and group ID for the HTTP daemon)

+ `ServerRoot` (the `root` directory of the server)

+ `TypesConfig` (the MIME type configuration file)

For a site with heavy traffic, configure the Web server so that a single HTTP daemon can serve multiple virtual hosts. Of course, this recommendation implies that there is only one configuration file. In that configuration file, use the `VirtualHost` directive to configure each virtual host.

Most ISPs use the `VirtualHost` capability of Apache HTTP server to provide virtual Web sites to their customers. Unless you pay for a dedicated Web host, you typically get a virtual site where you have your own domain name but share the server and the actual host with many other customers.

The syntax of the `VirtualHost` directive is as follows:

```
<VirtualHost hostaddr>
    ... directives that apply to this host
    ...
</VirtualHost>
```

With this syntax, you use `<VirtualHost>` and `</VirtualHost>` to enclose a group of directives that applies only to the particular virtual host identified by the *hostaddr* parameter. The *hostaddr* can be an IP address or the fully qualified domain name of the virtual host.

You can place almost any Apache directives within the `<VirtualHost>` block. At a minimum, Webmasters include the following directives in the `<VirtualHost>` block:

+ `DocumentRoot`, which specifies where this virtual host's documents reside

+ `Servername`, which identifies the server to the outside world (this should be a registered domain name DNS supports)

+ `ServerAdmin`, the e-mail address of this virtual host's Webmaster

+ Redirect, which specifies any URLs to be redirected to other URLs

+ `ErrorLog`, which specifies the file where errors related to this virtual host are to be logged

+ `CustomLog`, which specifies the file where accesses to this virtual host are logged

When the server receives a request for a document in a particular virtual host's `DocumentRoot` directory, it uses the configuration parameters within that server's `<VirtualHost>` block to handle that request.

Here is a typical example of a `<VirtualHost>` directive that sets up the virtual host `www.lnbsoft.com`:

```
<VirtualHost www.lnbsoft.com>
    DocumentRoot    /home/naba/httpd/htdocs
    ServerName   www.lnbsoft.com
    ServerAdmin   webmaster@lnbsoft.com
    ScriptAlias   /cgi-bin/   /home/naba/httpd/cgi-bin/
    ErrorLog   /home/naba/httpd/logs/error_log
    CustomLog   /home/naba/httpd/logs/access_log common
</VirtualHost>
```

Here the name `common` in the `CustomLog` directive refers to the name of a format defined earlier in the `httpd.conf` file by the `LogFormat` directive, as follows:

```
LogFormat "%h %l %u %t \"%r\" %>s %b" common
```

This format string for the log produces lines in the log file looks like this:

```
dial236.dc.psn.net - - [13/Jul/2003:18:09:00 -0500] "GET /
    HTTP/1.0" 200 1243
```

The format string contains two letter tokens that start with a percent sign (%). The meaning of these tokens is shown in Table 2-1.

Table 2-1	LogFormat Tokens
Token	**Meaning**
%b	The number of bytes sent to the client, excluding header information
%h	The host name of the client machine
%l	The identity of the user, if available
%r	The HTTP request from the client (for example, `GET / HTTP/1.0`)
%s	The server response code from the Web server
%t	The current local date and time
%u	The user name the user supplies (only when access control rules require user name/password authentication)

Chapter 3: Setting Up the FTP Server

In This Chapter

✓ Installing the FTP server

✓ Configuring the FTP server

✓ Setting up anonymous FTP

*F*ile Transfer Protocol (FTP) is a popular Internet service for transferring files from one system to another. *Anonymous FTP* is another popular Internet service for distributing files. The neat thing about anonymous FTP is that if a remote system supports anonymous FTP, anyone can use FTP with the `anonymous` user ID and can download files from that system. Although anonymous FTP is useful for distributing data, it poses a security risk if it's not set up properly.

Red Hat Linux comes with several FTP clients and the "very secure" FTP daemon (`vsftpd`), written by Chris Evans. Red Hat Linux also includes an RPM called `anonftp` that sets up the files you need to support anonymous FTP. In this chapter, I show you how to configure the FTP server through text configuration files and how to control access to the FTP server. I also describe anonymous FTP — how it's set up and how to ensure that it's secure.

Installing the FTP Server

During Red Hat Linux installation, you have the option to install the FTP Server software. To check whether the FTP server is already installed, type the following command:

```
rpm -q vsftpd
```

If the software is indeed installed, you should see an output similar to the following:

```
vsftpd-1.2.0-2.1
```

If you get a message saying that the package isn't installed, you can easily install it from the companion DVD. To install the RPM files for FTP, log in as root and place the DVD in the DVD drive. If you're using the GNOME or KDE desktop, the DVD should mount automatically. If not, type the following command to mount the DVD:

```
mount /mnt/cdrom
```

Then type the following command to change the directory:

```
cd /mnt/cdrom/RedHat/RPMS
```

This is where you find the RPM files for FTP. You can install both the FTP server and the anonymous FTP package with the following RPM commands:

```
rpm -ivh vsftpd*
rpm -ivh anonftp*
```

Configuring the FTP Server

Red Hat Linux comes with the very secure FTP daemon (vsftpd), written by Chris Evans. The executable file for vsftpd is /usr/sbin/vsftpd, and it uses a number of configuration files in the /etc and /etc/vsftpd directories. By default, the vsftpd server is disabled; if you want to use the FTP server, first you have to enable it. In this section, I show you how.

In previous versions of Red Hat Linux, the vsftpd server was set up to run under xinetd — the Internet super server. This required editing a configuration file in /etc/xinetd.d directory to enable the vsftpd server. However, starting in Red Hat Linux 8.1, the vsftpd server is configured to run standalone, and there is an initialization script (or *initscript*) — /etc/init.d/vsftpd — to start and stop the server. To start the vsftpd server, log in as root and type the following command:

```
service vsftpd start
```

You can also type the following command as root to turn on vsftpd so that it starts at system startup:

```
chkconfig --level 35 vsftpd on
```

After you start the vsftpd server, the default settings should be all you need to begin using the server. That's because other FTP clients can now connect and request files from your FTP server. However, you should learn about the configuration files in case you have to customize them some other time.

vsftpd configuration files

The `vsftpd` server consults a number of configuration files located in the `/etc` and `/etc/vsftpd` directories. These directories control many aspects of the FTP server such as whether it runs standalone, who can download files, and whether to allow anonymous FTP. The key configuration files for `vsftpd` are the following:

✦ `/etc/vsftpd.conf` controls how the `vsftpd` server works (for example, whether it should allow anonymous logins, allow file uploads, and so on).

✦ `/etc/vsftpd.ftpusers` lists names of users who cannot access the FTP server.

✦ `/etc/vsftpd.user_list` lists names of users who are denied access (not even prompted for password). However, if the `userlist_deny` option is set to NO in `/etc/vsftpd.conf`, then these users are allowed to access the FTP server.

You can usually leave most of these configuration files with their default settings. However, just in case you have to change something to make `vsftpd` suit your needs, I explain the configuration files briefly in the next few sections.

/etc/vsftpd.conf file

To find out what you can have in the `/etc/vsftpd.conf` file and how these lines affect the `vsftpd` server's operation, start by looking at the `/etc/vsftpd.conf` file that's installed by default in Red Hat Linux. The comments in this file tell you what each option does.

By default, `vsftpd` allows almost nothing. The options in `/etc/vsftpd.conf` loosen the restrictions so that users can use FTP. It's up to you to decide how loose the settings should be. Note that most options are set to YES. That's because most of the default settings are NO. To reverse the intent of an option, just comment out that option by placing a # at the beginning of its line.

Here are some of the options you can set in `/etc/vsftpd.conf`:

✦ `anon_mkdir_write_enable=YES` enables anonymous FTP users to create new directories. This is another risky option, and you may want to set this to NO, even if you allow anonymous users to upload files.

✦ `anon_upload_enable=YES` means anonymous FTP users can upload files. This option takes effect only if `write_enable` is already set to YES and the directory has write permissions for everyone. Remember that allowing anonymous users to write on your system can be very risky because someone could fill up the disk or use your disk for their personal storage.

✦ `anonymous_enable=YES` enables *anonymous FTP* (users can log in with the user name `anonymous` and provide their e-mail address as a password). Comment out this line if you don't want anonymous FTP.

✦ `ascii_download_enable=YES` enables file downloads in ASCII mode. Unfortunately, a malicious remote user can issue the `SIZE` command with the name of a huge file and essentially cause the FTP server to waste huge amounts of resources opening that file and determining its size. This is a typical technique used in a Denial of Service attack (which I mention later in this section).

✦ `ascii_upload_enable=YES` enables file uploads in ASCII mode (for text files).

✦ `async_abor_enable=YES` causes `vsftpd` to recognize `ABOR` (abort) requests that arrive at any time. You may have to enable it to allow older FTP clients to work with `vsftpd`.

✦ `banned_email_file=/etc/vsftpd.banned_emails` specifies the file with the list of banned e-mail addresses (used only if `deny_email_enable` is set to `YES`).

✦ `chown_uploads=YES` causes uploaded anonymous files to be owned by a different user specified by the `chown_username` option. Don't enable this option unless absolutely necessary, and don't specify `root` as the `chown_username` (that's a disaster just waiting to happen).

✦ `chown_username=name` specifies the user name that would own files uploaded by anonymous FTP users.

✦ `chroot_list_enable=YES` causes `vsftpd` to confine all users except those on a list specified by the `chroot_list_file` to their home directories when they log in for FTP service. This prevents these users from getting to any other files besides what's in their home directories.

✦ `chroot_list_file=/etc/vsftpd.chroot_list` is the list of users who are either confined to their home directories or not, depending on the setting of `chroot_local_user`.

✦ `connect_from_port_20=YES` causes `vsftpd` to make sure that data transfers occur through port 20 (the FTP data port).

✦ `data_connection_timeout=120` is the time in seconds after which an inactive data connection is timed out.

✦ `deny_email_enable=YES` causes `vsftpd` to check a list of banned e-mail addresses and deny access to anyone who tries to log in anonymously with a banned e-mail address as password.

✦ `dirmessage_enable=YES` causes `vsftpd` to display messages when FTP users change to certain directories.

✦ `ftpd_banner=Welcome to my FTP service.` sets the banner that `vsftpd` displays when a user logs in. You can change the message to anything you want.

✦ `idle_session_timeout=600` is the time (in seconds) after which an idle session (refers to the situation where someone connects and does not do anything) times out and `vsftpd` logs the user out.

✦ `listen=YES` causes `vsftpd` to listen for connection requests and, consequently, run in standalone mode. Set this to `NO` if you want to run `vsftpd` under `xinetd`.

✦ `local_enable=YES` causes `vsftpd` to grant local users access to FTP.

✦ `local_umask=022` means whatever files FTP writes will have a permission of 644 (read access for everyone, but write access for owner only). You can set it to any file permission mask setting you want. For example, if you want no permissions for anyone but the owner, change this to 077.

✦ `ls_recurse_enable=YES` enables FTP users to recursively traverse directories by using the `ls -R` command.

✦ `nopriv_user=ftp` identifies a unprivileged user account that the FTP server can use.

✦ `pam_service_name=vsftpd` is the name of the Pluggable Authentication Module (PAM) configuration file that is used when `vsftpd` must authenticate a user. By default the PAM configuration files are in `/etc/pam.d` directory. That means the `vsftpd` PAM configuration file is `/etc/pam.d/vsftpd`.

✦ `tcp_wrappers=YES` enables support for access control through TCP wrapper that consults the files `/etc/hosts.allow` and `/etc/hosts.deny` (for more information about TCP wrapper, see Book VII, Chapter 3).

✦ `userlist_deny=YES` causes `vsftpd` to deny access to the users listed in the `/etc/vsftpd.user_list` file. These users are not even prompted for a password.

✦ `write_enable=YES` causes `vsftpd` to allow file uploads to the host.

✦ `xferlog_enable=YES` turns on the logging of file downloads and uploads (always a good idea, but takes disk space).

✦ `xferlog_file=/var/log/vsftpd.log` specifies the full pathname of the `vsftpd` log file. The default is `/var/log/vsftpd.log`.

✦ `xferlog_std_format=YES` causes `vsftpd` to generate log files in a standard format used by other FTP daemons.

**Book VIII
Chapter 3**

**Setting Up the
FTP Server**

/etc/vsftpd.ftpusers file

The vsftpd server uses the *Pluggable Authentication Module* (PAM) to authenticate users when they try to log in (just as the normal login process uses PAM to do the job). The PAM configuration file for vsftpd is /etc/pam.d/vsftpd. That PAM configuration file refers to /etc/vsftpd.ftpusers like this:

```
auth    required    /lib/security/pam_listfile.so item=user sense=deny
        file=/etc/vsftpd.ftpusers onerr=succeed
```

This basically says that anyone listed in the /etc/vsftpd.ftpusers should be denied login. The default /etc/vsftpd.ftpusers file contains the following list of users:

```
root
bin
daemon
adm
lp
sync
shutdown
halt
mail
news
uucp
operator
games
nobody
```

/etc/vsftpd.user_list file

If the userlist_deny option is set to YES, vsftpd does not allow users listed in the /etc/vsftpd.user_list file any access to FTP services. It does not even prompt them for a password. However, if userlist_deny is NO, the meaning is reversed and these users are the only ones allowed access (but the PAM configuration still denies anyone on the /etc/vsftpd.ftpusers list).

Setting Up Secure Anonymous FTP

Anonymous FTP refers to the use of the user name anonymous, which anyone can use with FTP to transfer files from a system. Anonymous FTP is a common way to share files on the Internet.

If you have used anonymous FTP to download files from Internet sites, you already know the convenience of that service. Anonymous FTP makes information available to anyone on the Internet. If you have a new Red Hat Linux application that you want to share with the world, set up anonymous

FTP on your Linux PC and place the software in an appropriate directory. After that, all you have to do is announce to the world (probably through a posting in the `comp.os.linux.announce` newsgroup) that you have a new program available. Now anyone can get the software from your system at his or her convenience.

Even if you run a for-profit business, you can use anonymous FTP to support your customers. If you sell a hardware or software product, you may want to provide technical information or software "fixes" through anonymous FTP.

Unfortunately, the convenience of anonymous FTP comes at a price. If you don't configure the anonymous FTP service properly, intruders and pranksters may gain access to your system. Some intruders may simply use your system's disk as a temporary holding place for various files; others may fill your disk with junk files, effectively making your system inoperable (this sort of attack is called a *Denial of Service* attack). At the other extreme, an intruder may gain user-level (or, worse, `root`-level) access to your system and do much more damage. The default anonymous FTP setup in Red Hat Linux employs the necessary security precautions.

Trying anonymous FTP

To see anonymous FTP in action, try accessing your system by using an FTP client. For example, in the following sample session, I have accessed the FTP server from a terminal window on the same system (my input appears in boldface):

```
ftp localhost
Connected to localhost (127.0.0.1).
220 (vsFTPd 1.1.3)
Name (localhost:naba): anonymous
331 Please specify the password.
Password:          <-- I can type anything as password
230 Login successful. Have fun.
Remote system type is UNIX.
Using binary mode to transfer files.
ftp> ls -l
227 Entering Passive Mode (127,0,0,1,169,190)
150 Here comes the directory listing.
drwxr-xr-x    2 0        0            4096 Jun 06 04:36 pub
226 Directory send OK.
ftp> bye
221 Goodbye.
```

When you successfully log in for anonymous FTP, you access the home directory of the user named `ftp` (the default directory is `/var/ftp`). Place the publicly accessible files — the ones you want to enable others to download from your system — in the `/var/ftp/pub` directory.

Key features of anonymous FTP

The key features of an anonymous FTP setup are as follows:

✦ There is a user named `ftp` whose home directory is `/var/ftp`. The user does not have a shell assigned. Here is what you get when you search for `ftp` in the `/etc/passwd` file:

```
grep ftp /etc/passwd
```

The output should be something like this:

```
ftp:x:14:50:FTP User:/var/ftp:/sbin/nologin
```

The `x` in the second field means that no one can log in with the user name `ftp`.

✦ Here is the full permission setting and owner information for the `/var/ftp` directory:

```
drwxr-xr-x    3 root     root      4096 Jun 22 12:10 ftp
```

As this line shows, the `/var/ftp` directory is owned by `root`, and the permission is set to 755 (only `root` can read, write and execute; everyone else can only read and execute).

✦ You can view the contents of the `/var/ftp` directory with the `ls -la` command. The result is as follows:

```
total 12
drwxr-xr-x    3 root     root      4096 Jun 22 12:10 .
drwxr-xr-x   21 root     root      4096 Jun 22 12:10 ..
drwxr-xr-x    2 root     root      4096 Jun  6 00:36 pub
```

✦ The `pub` directory is where you place any files that you want to enable others to download from your system through anonymous FTP.

Chapter 4: Serving Up
Mail and News

In This Chapter

✔ **Installing and using** `sendmail`

✔ **Testing mail delivery manually**

✔ **Configuring** `sendmail`

✔ **Installing the InterNetNews (INN) server**

✔ **Configuring and starting INN**

✔ **Setting up local newsgroups**

*E*lectronic mail (e-mail) is one of the popular services available on Internet hosts. E-mail software comes in two parts: a mail-transport agent (MTA), which physically sends and receives mail messages; and a mail-user agent (MUA), which reads messages and prepares new messages. In this chapter, I describe the e-mail service and show you how to configure the `sendmail` server on a Red Hat Linux PC.

Internet newsgroups provide another convenient way, besides e-mail, to discuss various topics and to share your knowledge with others. Red Hat Linux comes with the software you need to read newsgroups and to set up your own system as a news server. In this chapter, I describe how to configure and run the InterNetNews server, a popular news server. I also show you how to set up local newsgroups for your corporate intranet (or even your home network).

Installing the Mail Server

If you install the mail server software during Red Hat Linux installation, you don't have to do much more to begin using the mail service. To see whether the mail server is already installed, type the following command:

```
rpm -q sendmail
```

You're all set if the response looks like this:

```
sendmail-8.12.9-7
```

This output says that `sendmail` version 8.12.9 is installed on the system.

If the output message tells you that `sendmail` isn't installed, you can use the Red Hat Package Manager (RPM) to install the individual packages needed for running and configuring `sendmail`. To install the RPM files for `sendmail`, log in as `root` and insert the second CD-ROM in the CD-ROM drive. If you're using GNOME or KDE, the CD-ROM should be automatically mounted. Otherwise, type the following command to mount the CD-ROM:

```
mount /mnt/cdrom
```

Then type the following commands to install the `sendmail` files:

```
cd /mnt/cdrom/RedHat/RPMS
rpm -ivh sendmail*
```

This should install two packages:

✦ `sendmail` — A complex mail transport agent (MTA)

✦ `sendmail-cf` — Configuration files for `sendmail`

Using sendmail

To set up your system as a mail server, you must configure the `sendmail` mail-transport agent properly. `sendmail` has the reputation of being a complex but complete mail-delivery system. Just one look at `sendmail`'s configuration file, `/etc/mail/sendmail.cf`, should convince you that `sendmail` is indeed complex. Luckily, you don't have to be an expert on the `sendmail` configuration file. All you need is one of the predefined configuration files — like the one that's installed on your system — to use `sendmail`.

Your system should already have a working `sendmail` configuration file — `/etc/mail/sendmail.cf`. The default file assumes you have an Internet connection and a name server. Provided you have an Internet connection, you should be able to send and receive e-mail from your Red Hat Linux PC.

To ensure that mail delivery works correctly, your system's name must match the system name your ISP has assigned to you. Although you can give your system any host name you want, other systems can successfully deliver mail to your system only if your system's name is in the ISP's name server.

A mail-delivery test

To try out the `sendmail` mail-transfer agent, you can use the `mail` command to compose and send a mail message to yourself at a different address. For example, here's how I send myself a message using the `mail` command:

```
mail naba@comcast.net
Subject: Testing e-mail
This is from my Red Hat Linux system.
.
Cc: Press Ctrl+D
```

The `mail` command is a simple mail-user agent. In the preceding example, I specify the addressee — `naba@comcast.net` — in the command line. The `mail` program prompts for a subject line. Following the subject, I enter my message and end it with a line that contains only a period. When prompted for a Cc:, I press Ctrl+D. After I end the message, the mail-user agent passes the message to `sendmail` — the mail-transport agent — for delivery to the specified address. Because my system is already connected to the Internet, `sendmail` delivers the mail message immediately.

To verify the delivery of mail, I check my mail from my ISP and see that the message has arrived. I can also send a reply back, provided my system has an official DNS host name and is in the ISP's DNS database.

Thus, the initial `sendmail` configuration file that comes with Red Hat Linux should be adequate for sending and receiving e-mail, provided that your Red Hat Linux system has an Internet connection and a registered domain name.

The mail-delivery mechanism

On an Internet host, the `sendmail` mail-transport agent delivers mail using the Simple Mail Transfer Protocol (SMTP). SMTP-based mail-transport agents listen to the TCP port 25 and use a small set of text commands to exchange information with other mail-transport agents. In fact, SMTP commands are simple enough that you can use them manually from a terminal to send a mail message. The following example shows how I use SMTP commands to send a mail message to my account on the Red Hat Linux PC from a `telnet` session running on the same system:

```
telnet localhost 25
Trying 127.0.0.1...
Connected to localhost.
Escape character is '^]'.
220 localhost.localdomain ESMTP Sendmail 8.12.9/8.12.9; Tue, 15 Jul 2003
    19:22:24 -0400
help
214-2.0.0 This is sendmail version 8.12.9
214-2.0.0 Topics:
214-2.0.0      HELO     EHLO     MAIL     RCPT     DATA
214-2.0.0      RSET     NOOP     QUIT     HELP     VRFY
214-2.0.0      EXPN     VERB     ETRN     DSN      AUTH
214-2.0.0      STARTTLS
214-2.0.0 For more info use "HELP <topic>".
214-2.0.0 To report bugs in the implementation send email to
214-2.0.0      sendmail-bugs@sendmail.org.
214-2.0.0 For local information send email to Postmaster at your site.
214 2.0.0 End of HELP info
```

Book VIII
Chapter 4

Serving Up
Mail and News

```
HELP DATA
214-2.0.0 DATA
214-2.0.0        Following text is collected as the message.
214-2.0.0        End with a single dot.
214 2.0.0 End of HELP info
HELO localhost
250 localhost.localdomain Hello localhost.localdomain [127.0.0.1], pleased to
    meet you
MAIL FROM: naba
553 5.5.4 naba... Domain name required for sender address naba
MAIL FROM: naba@localhost
250 2.1.0 naba@localhost... Sender ok
RCPT TO: naba
250 2.1.5 naba... Recipient ok
DATA
354 Enter mail, end with "." on a line by itself
Testing... 1 2 3
Sending mail by telnet to port 25
.
250 2.0.0 h6FNMOLw002082 Message accepted for delivery
quit
221 2.0.0 localhost.localdomain closing connection
Connection closed by foreign host.
```

The `telnet` command opens a TELNET session to port 25 — the port on
which `sendmail` expects SMTP commands. The `sendmail` process on the
Red Hat Linux system immediately replies with an announcement.

I type `HELP` to view a list of SMTP commands. To get help on a specific command, I can type `HELP commandname`. The listing shows the help information `sendmail` prints when I type `HELP DATA`.

I type `HELO localhost` to initiate a session with the host. The `sendmail`
process replies with a greeting. To send the mail message, I start with the
`MAIL FROM:` command that specifies the sender of the message (I enter the
user name on the system from which I am sending the message). `sendmail`
requires a domain name along with the user name.

Next, I use the `RCPT TO:` command to specify the recipient of the message.
If I want to send the message to several recipients, all I have to do is provide
each recipient's address with the `RCPT TO:` command.

To enter the mail message, I use the `DATA` command. In response to the
`DATA` command, `sendmail` displays an instruction that I should end the
message with a period on a line by itself. I enter the message and end it
with a single period on a separate line. The `sendmail` process displays a
message indicating that the message has been accepted for delivery.
Finally, I quit the `sendmail` session with the `QUIT` command.

Afterward, I log in to my Red Hat Linux system and check mail with the `mail`
command. The following is the session with the `mail` command when I display the mail message I've sent through the sample SMTP session with
`sendmail`:

```
mail
Mail version 8.1 6/6/93.  Type ? for help.
"/var/spool/mail/naba": 1 message 1 new
>N  1 naba@localhost.local  Tue Jul 15 19:25  12/479
& 1
Message 1:
From naba@localhost.localdomain  Tue Jul 15 19:25:20 2003
Date: Tue, 15 Jul 2003 19:22:24 -0400
From: Naba Barkakati <naba@localhost.localdomain>

Testing... 1 2 3
Sending mail by telnet to port 25

& q
Saved 1 message in mbox
```

As this example shows, the SMTP commands are simple enough to understand. This example should help you understand how a mail-transfer agent uses SMTP to transfer mail on the Internet. Of course, e-mail programs usually automate this whole process — and so does the `sendmail` program (through settings in the `sendmail` configuration file `/etc/mail/sendmail.cf`).

The sendmail configuration file

You don't have to understand everything in the `sendmail` configuration file, `/etc/mail/sendmail.cf`, but you should know how that file is created. That way, you can make minor changes if necessary and regenerate the `/etc/mail/sendmail.cf` file.

Before you can regenerate the `sendmail.cf` file, you have to install the `sendmail-cf` package. To check whether the `sendmail-cf` package is installed, type

```
rpm -q sendmail-cf
```

If the command doesn't print the name of the `sendmail-cf` package, you have to install the package. This RPM file is in the second CD-ROM bundled with this book. To install that package, log in as `root` and insert the second CD-ROM into the CD-ROM drive. In GNOME or KDE, the CD-ROM should mount automatically. Otherwise, you can mount the CD-ROM with the following command:

```
mount /mnt/cdrom
```

Then install the package by typing the following commands:

```
cd /mnt/cdrom/RedHat/RPMS
rpm -ivh sendmail-cf*
```

The `sendmail-cf` package installs in the `/usr/share/sendmail-cf` directory all the files needed to generate a new `sendmail.cf` configuration file. As I explain in the next few sections, the `sendmail.cf` file is generated from a number of m4 *macro files* (text files in which each line eventually expands to multiple lines that mean something to some program). These macro files are organized into a number of subdirectories under `/usr/share/sendmail-cf`. You can read the `README` file in `/usr/share/sendmail-cf` to learn more about the creation of `sendmail` configuration files.

Now that you've taken care of the prerequisites, you can learn how to regenerate the `sendmail.cf` file.

m4 macro processor

The m4 macro processor is used to generate the `sendmail.cf` configuration file, which comes with the `sendmail` package in Red Hat Linux. The main macro file, `sendmail.mc`, is included with the `sendmail` package, but that file needs other m4 macro files that are in the `sendmail-cf` package.

So what's a macro? A *macro* is basically a symbolic name for code that handles some action, usually in a shorthand form that substitutes for a long string of characters. A *macro processor* such as m4 usually reads its input file and copies it to the output, processing the macros along the way. The processing of a macro generally involves performing some action and generating some output. Because a macro generates a lot more text in the output than merely the macro's name, the processing of macros is referred to as *macro expansion*.

The m4 macro processor is *stream-based*. That means it copies the input characters to the output while it's busy expanding any macros. The m4 macro processor does not have any concept of lines, so it copies newline characters (that mark the end of a line) to the output. That's why you see the word `dnl` in most m4 macro files; `dnl` is an m4 macro that stands for "delete through newline." The `dnl` macro deletes all characters starting at the `dnl` up to and including the next newline character. The newline characters in the output don't cause any harm; they merely create unnecessary blank lines. The `sendmail` macro package uses `dnl` to avoid such blank lines in the output configuration file. Because `dnl` basically means delete everything up to the end of the line, m4 macro files also use `dnl` as the prefix for comment lines.

To see a very simple use of m4, consider the following m4 macro file that defines two macros — `hello` and `bye` — and uses them in a form letter:

```
dnl  #########################################################
dnl  #  File: ex.m4
dnl  #  A simple exmapls of m4 macros
dnl  #########################################################
define('hello', 'Dear Sir/Madam')dnl
```

```
define('bye',
'Sincerely,


Customer Service')dnl
dnl Now type the letter and use the macros
hello,

This is to inform you that we received your recent inquiry.
We will respond to your question soon.

bye
```

Type this text (using your favorite text editor) and save it in a file named
ex.m4. You can name a macro file anything you like, but it's customary to
use the .m4 extension for m4 macro files.

Before you process the macro file by using m4, note the following key points
about the example:

✦ Use the dnl macro to start all the comment lines (for example, the first
   four lines in the example).

✦ End each macro definition with the dnl macro. Otherwise, when m4
   processes the macro file, it produces a blank line for each macro
   definition.

✦ Use the built-in m4 command define to define a new macro. The macro
   name and the value are both enclosed between a pair of left and right
   quotes (' . . . '). Note that you cannot use the plain single quote to
   enclose the macro name and definition.

Now process the macro file ex.m4 by typing the following command:

```
m4 ex.m4
```

m4 processes the macros and displays the following output:

```
Dear Sir/Madam,

This is to inform you that we received your recent inquiry.
We will respond to your question soon.

Sincerely,


Customer Service
```

Sounds just like a typical customer service form letter, doesn't it?

If you compare the output with the ex.m4 file, you'd see that m4 prints the form letter on standard output, expanding the macros hello and bye into their defined values. If you want to save the form letter in a file called letter, use the shell's output redirection feature, like this:

```
m4 ex.m4 > letter
```

What if you want to use the word hello or bye in the letter without expanding them? You can do so by enclosing these macros in a pair of quotes ('...'). You have to do so for other predefined m4 macros, such as define. To use define as a plain word, not as a macro to expand, type **'define'**.

sendmail.mc file

The simple example in the preceding section should give you an idea of how m4 macros are defined and used to create configuration files such as the sendmail.cf file. You find many complex macros stored in files in the /usr/share/sendmail-cf directory. A top-level macro file, sendmail.mc, described later in this section, brings in these macro files with the include macro (used to copy a file into the input stream).

By defining its own set of high-level macros in files located in the /usr/share/sendmail-cf directory, sendmail essentially creates its own macro language. The sendmail macro files use the .mc extension. The primary sendmail macro file you should configure is sendmail.mc, located in the /etc/mail directory.

Unlike the /etc/mail/sendmail.cf file, the /etc/mail/sendmail.mc file is short and should be easier to work with. Here is the full listing of the /etc/mail/sendmail.mc file that comes with Red Hat Linux:

```
divert(-1)dnl
dnl #
dnl # This is the sendmail macro config file for m4. If you make changes to
dnl # /etc/mail/sendmail.mc, you will need to regenerate the
dnl # /etc/mail/sendmail.cf file by confirming that the sendmail-cf package is
dnl # installed and then performing a
dnl #
dnl #     make -C /etc/mail
dnl #
include('/usr/share/sendmail-cf/m4/cf.m4')dnl
VERSIONID('setup for Red Hat Linux')dnl
OSTYPE('linux')dnl
dnl #
dnl # Uncomment and edit the following line if your outgoing mail needs to
dnl # be sent out through an external mail server:
dnl #
dnl define('SMART_HOST','smtp.your.provider')
dnl #
define('confDEF_USER_ID',''8:12'')dnl
define('confTRUSTED_USER', 'smmsp')dnl
dnl define('confAUTO_REBUILD')dnl
define('confTO_CONNECT', '1m')dnl
define('confTRY_NULL_MX_LIST',true)dnl
```

```
define('confDONT_PROBE_INTERFACES',true)dnl
define('PROCMAIL_MAILER_PATH','/usr/bin/procmail')dnl
define('ALIAS_FILE', '/etc/aliases')dnl
dnl define('STATUS_FILE', '/etc/mail/statistics')dnl
define('UUCP_MAILER_MAX', '2000000')dnl
define('confUSERDB_SPEC', '/etc/mail/userdb.db')dnl
define('confPRIVACY_FLAGS', 'authwarnings,novrfy,noexpn,restrictqrun')dnl
define('confAUTH_OPTIONS', 'A')dnl
dnl #
dnl # The following allows relaying if the user authenticates, and disallows
dnl # plaintext authentication (PLAIN/LOGIN) on non-TLS links
dnl #
dnl define('confAUTH_OPTIONS', 'A p')dnl
dnl #
dnl # PLAIN is the preferred plaintext authentication method and used by
dnl # Mozilla Mail and Evolution, though Outlook Express and other MUAs do
dnl # use LOGIN. Other mechanisms should be used if the connection is not
dnl # guaranteed secure.
dnl #
dnl TRUST_AUTH_MECH('EXTERNAL DIGEST-MD5 CRAM-MD5 LOGIN PLAIN')dnl
dnl define('confAUTH_MECHANISMS', 'EXTERNAL GSSAPI DIGEST-MD5 CRAM-MD5 LOGIN PLA
IN')dnl
dnl #
dnl # Rudimentary information on creating certificates for sendmail TLS:
dnl #      make -C /usr/share/ssl/certs usage
dnl #
dnl define('confCACERT_PATH','/usr/share/ssl/certs')
dnl define('confCACERT','/usr/share/ssl/certs/ca-bundle.crt')
dnl define('confSERVER_CERT','/usr/share/ssl/certs/sendmail.pem')
dnl define('confSERVER_KEY','/usr/share/ssl/certs/sendmail.pem')
dnl #
dnl # This allows sendmail to use a keyfile that is shared with OpenLDAP's
dnl # slapd, which requires the file to be readble by group ldap
dnl #
dnl define('confDONT_BLAME_SENDMAIL','groupreadablekeyfile')dnl
dnl #
dnl define('confTO_QUEUEWARN', '4h')dnl
dnl define('confTO_QUEUERETURN', '5d')dnl
dnl define('confQUEUE_LA', '12')dnl
dnl define('confREFUSE_LA', '18')dnl
define('confTO_IDENT', '0')dnl
dnl FEATURE(delay_checks)dnl
FEATURE('no_default_msa','dnl')dnl
FEATURE('smrsh','/usr/sbin/smrsh')dnl
FEATURE('mailertable','hash -o /etc/mail/mailertable.db')dnl
FEATURE('virtusertable','hash -o /etc/mail/virtusertable.db')dnl
FEATURE(redirect)dnl
FEATURE(always_add_domain)dnl
FEATURE(use_cw_file)dnl
FEATURE(use_ct_file)dnl
dnl #
dnl # The -t option will retry delivery if e.g. the user runs over his quota.
dnl #
FEATURE(local_procmail,'','procmail -t -Y -a $h -d $u')dnl
FEATURE('access_db','hash -T<TMPF> -o /etc/mail/access.db')dnl
FEATURE('blacklist_recipients')dnl
EXPOSED_USER('root')dnl
dnl # The following causes sendmail to only listen on the IPv4 loopback address
dnl # 127.0.0.1 and not on any other network devices. Remove the loopback
dnl # address restriction to accept email from the internet or intranet.
dnl #
```

Book VIII
Chapter 4

Serving Up
Mail and News

```
DAEMON_OPTIONS('Port=smtp,Addr=127.0.0.1, Name=MTA')dnl
dnl #
dnl # The following causes sendmail to additionally listen to port 587 for
dnl # mail from MUAs that authenticate. Roaming users who can't reach their
dnl # preferred sendmail daemon due to port 25 being blocked or redirected find
dnl # this useful.
dnl #
dnl DAEMON_OPTIONS('Port=submission, Name=MSA, M=Ea')dnl
dnl #
dnl # The following causes sendmail to additionally listen to port 465, but
dnl # starting immediately in TLS mode upon connecting. Port 25 or 587 followed
dnl # by STARTTLS is preferred, but roaming clients using Outlook Express can't
dnl # do STARTTLS on ports other than 25. Mozilla Mail can ONLY use STARTTLS
dnl # and doesn't support the deprecated smtps; Evolution <1.1.1 uses smtps
dnl # when SSL is enabled-- STARTTLS support is available in version 1.1.1.
dnl #
dnl # For this to work your OpenSSL certificates must be configured.
dnl #
dnl DAEMON_OPTIONS('Port=smtps, Name=TLSMTA, M=s')dnl
dnl #
dnl # The following causes sendmail to additionally listen on the IPv6 loopback
dnl # device. Remove the loopback address restriction listen to the network.
dnl #
dnl # NOTE: binding both IPv4 and IPv6 daemon to the same port requires
dnl #        a kernel patch
dnl #
dnl DAEMON_OPTIONS('port=smtp,Addr=::1, Name=MTA-v6, Family=inet6')dnl
dnl #
dnl # We strongly recommend not accepting unresolvable domains if you want to
dnl # protect yourself from spam. However, the laptop and users on computers
dnl # that do not have 24x7 DNS do need this.
dnl #
FEATURE('accept_unresolvable_domains')dnl
dnl #
dnl FEATURE('relay_based_on_MX')dnl
dnl #
dnl # Also accept email sent to "localhost.localdomain" as local email.
dnl #
LOCAL_DOMAIN('localhost.localdomain')dnl
dnl #
dnl # The following example makes mail from this host and any additional
dnl # specified domains appear to be sent from mydomain.com
dnl #
dnl MASQUERADE_AS('mydomain.com')dnl
dnl #
dnl # masquerade not just the headers, but the envelope as well
dnl #
dnl FEATURE(masquerade_envelope)dnl
dnl #
dnl # masquerade not just @mydomainalias.com, but @*.mydomainalias.com as well
dnl #
dnl FEATURE(masquerade_entire_domain)dnl
dnl #
dnl MASQUERADE_DOMAIN(localhost)dnl
dnl MASQUERADE_DOMAIN(localhost.localdomain)dnl
dnl MASQUERADE_DOMAIN(mydomainalias.com)dnl
dnl MASQUERADE_DOMAIN(mydomain.lan)dnl
MAILER(smtp)dnl
MAILER(procmail)dnl
```

If you make changes to the /etc/mail/sendmail.mc file, you must generate the /etc/mail/sendmail.cf file by running the sendmail.mc file through the m4 macro processor with the following command (you have to log in as root):

```
m4 /etc/mail/sendmail.mc > /etc/mail/sendmail.cf
```

The comments also tell you that you need the sendmail-cf package to process this file.

From the previous section's description of m4 macros, you can see that the sendmail.mc file uses define to create new macros. You can also see the liberal use of dnl to avoid inserting too many blank lines into the output.

The other uppercase words (such as OSTYPE, FEATURE, and MAILER) are sendmail macros. These are defined in the .m4 files located in the subdirectories of the /usr/share/sendmail-cf directory and are incorporated into the sendmail.mc file with the following include macro:

```
include('/usr/share/sendmail-cf/m4/cf.m4')dnl
```

The /usr/share/sendmail-cf/m4/cf.m4 file, in turn, includes the cfhead.m4 file, which includes other m4 files, and so on. The net effect is that, as the m4 macro processor processes the sendmail.mc file, the macro processor incorporates many m4 files from various subdirectories of /usr/share/sendmail-cf.

Here are some key points to note about the /etc/mail/sendmail.mc file:

+ VERSIONID('setup for Red Hat Linux') macro inserts the version information enclosed in quotes into the output.

+ OSTYPE('linux') specifies Linux as the operating system. You have to specify this early to ensure proper configuration.

  It's customary to place this macro right after the VERSIONID macro.

+ MAILER(smtp) describes the mailer. According to instructions in the /usr/share/sendmail-cf/README file, MAILER declarations should always be placed at the end of the sendmail.mc file, and MAILER(smtp) should always precede MAILER(procmail). The mailer smtp refers to the SMTP mailer.

+ FEATURE macros request various special features. For example, FEATURE('blacklist_recipients') turns on the capability to block incoming mail for certain user names, hosts, or addresses. The specification for what mail to allow or refuse is placed in the access database (/etc/mail/access.db file). You also need the FEATURE('access_db') macro to turn on the access database.

✦ MASQUERADE_AS('mydomain.com') causes sendmail to label outgoing mail as having come from the host mydomain.com (replace this with your domain name). The idea is for a large organization to set up a single sendmail server that handles the mail for many subdomains and makes everything appear to come from a single domain (for example, mail from many departments in a University would appear to come from the University's main domain name).

✦ MASQUERADE_DOMAIN(subdomain.mydomain.com) instructs sendmail to send mail from an address such as user@subdomain.mydomain.com as having originated from the same username at the domain specified by the MASQUERADE_AS macro.

The sendmail macros such as FEATURE and MAILER are described in the /usr/share/sendmail-cf/README file. Consult that file to learn more about the sendmail macros before you make changes to the sendmail.mc file.

Typically, you have to add your system's host name in the last line of the /etc/mail/sendmail.mc file. Follow these steps to add the host name:

1. **If the host name is** mycompany.com, **edit the** Cw **line in** /etc/mail/sendmail.mc **as follows:**

```
Cwlocalhost.localdomain mycompany.com mycompany
```

2. **Rebuild the** /etc/mail/sendmail.cf **file with the command:**

```
m4 /etc/mail/sendmail.mc > /etc/mail/sendmail.cf
```

3. **Restart** sendmail **with the following command:**

```
service sendmail restart
```

sendmail.cf file syntax

The sendmail.cf file's syntax is designed to be easy to parse by the sendmail program because sendmail reads this file whenever it starts. Human readability was not a primary consideration when the file's syntax was designed. Still, with a little explanation, you can understand the meaning of the control lines in sendmail.cf.

Each sendmail control line begins with a single-letter operator that defines the meaning of the rest of the line. A line that begins with a space or a tab is considered a continuation of the previous line. Blank lines and lines beginning with a pound sign (#) are comments.

Often, there is no space between the single-letter operator and the arguments that follow the operator. This makes the lines even harder to understand. For example, sendmail.cf uses the concept of a *class* — essentially a collection of phrases. You can define a class named P and add the phrase REDIRECT to that class with the following control line:

```
CPREDIRECT
```

Because everything is jumbled together, it's hard to decipher. On the other hand, to define a class named Accept and set it to the values OK and RELAY, write the following:

```
C{Accept}OK RELAY
```

This may be slightly easier to understand because the delimiters (such as the class name, Accept) are enclosed in curly braces.

Other — more recent — control lines are even easier to understand. For example, the line

```
O HelpFile=/etc/mail/helpfile
```

defines the option HelpFile as the filename /etc/mail/helpfile. That file contains help information sendmail uses when it receives a HELP command.

Table 4-1 summarizes the one-letter control operators used in sendmail.cf. Each entry also shows an example of that operator. This table should help you understand some of the lines in sendmail.cf.

Table 4-1	Control Operators Used in sendmail.cf
Operator	**Description**
C	Defines a class; a variable (think of it as a set) that can contain several values. For example, Cwlocalhost adds the name localhost to the class w.
D	Defines a macro, a name associated with a single value. For example, DnMAILER-DAEMON defines the macro n as MAILER-DAEMON.
F	Defines a class that's been read from a file. For example, Fw/etc/mail/local-host-names reads the names of hosts from the file /etc/mail/local-host-names and adds them to the class w.
H	Defines the format of header lines that sendmail inserts into a message. For example, H?P?Return-Path: <$g> defines the Return-Path: field of the header.
K	Defines a map (a key-value pair database). For example, Karith arith defines the map named arith as the compiled-in map of the same name.
M	Specifies a mailer. The following lines define the procmail mailer: Mprocmail,P=/usr/bin/procmail,F=DFMSPhnu9, S=EnvFromSMTP/HdrFromSMTP,R=EnvToSMTP/HdrFromSMTP, T=DNS/RFC822/X-Unix,A=procmail -Y -m $h $f $u

(continued)

Table 4-1 *(continued)*

Operator	Description
O	Assigns a value to an option. For example, `O AliasFile=/etc/aliases` defines the `AliasFile` option to `/etc/aliases`, which is the name of the `sendmail` alias file.
P	Defines values for the precedence field. For example, `Pjunk=-100` sets to `-100` the precedence of messages marked with the header field `Precedence: junk`.
R	Defines a rule (a rule has a left-hand side and a right-hand side; if input matches the left-hand side, it's replaced with the right-hand side — this is called *rewriting*). For example, the rewriting rule `R$* ; $1` strips trailing semicolons.
S	Labels a ruleset you can start defining with subsequent R control lines. For example, `Scanonify=3` labels the next ruleset as `canonify` or ruleset 3.
T	Adds a user name to the trusted class (class `t`). For example, `Troot` adds `root` to the class of trusted users.
V	Defines the major version number of the configuration file. For example, `V10/Berkeley` defines the version number as 10.

Other sendmail files

The `/etc/mail` directory contains other files that `sendmail` uses. These files are referenced in the `sendmail` configuration file, `/etc/mail/sendmail.cf`. For example, here's how you can search for the `/etc/mail` string in the `/etc/mail/sendmail.cf` file:

```
grep "\/etc\/mail" /etc/mail/sendmail.cf
```

Here's what the `grep` command displays as a result of the search on my Red Hat Linux system:

```
Fw/etc/mail/local-host-names
FR-o /etc/mail/relay-domains
Kmailertable hash -o /etc/mail/mailertable.db
Kvirtuser hash -o /etc/mail/virtusertable.db
Kaccess hash -T<TMPF> -o /etc/mail/access.db
#O ErrorHeader=/etc/mail/error-header
O HelpFile=/etc/mail/helpfile
O StatusFile=/etc/mail/statistics
O UserDatabaseSpec=/etc/mail/userdb.db
#O ServiceSwitchFile=/etc/mail/service.switch
#O DefaultAuthInfo=/etc/mail/default-auth-info
Ft/etc/mail/trusted-users
```

You can ignore the lines that begin with a hash mark or number sign (#) because `sendmail` treats those lines as comments. The other lines are `sendmail` control lines that refer to other files in the `/etc/mail` directory.

Here's what some of these `sendmail` files are supposed to contain (note that not all of these files have to be present in your `/etc/mail` directory, and even when present, some files may be empty):

✦ `/etc/mail/access` — Names and/or IP addresses of hosts allowed to send mail (useful in stopping *spam* — unwanted mail)

✦ `/etc/mail/access.db` — Access database generated from `/etc/mail/access` file

✦ `/etc/mail/helpfile` — Help information for SMTP commands

✦ `/etc/mail/local-host-names` — Names by which this host is known

✦ `/etc/mail/mailertable` — Mailer table used to override how mail is routed

✦ `/etc/mail/relay-domains` — Hosts that permit relaying

✦ `/etc/mail/trusted-users` — List of users allowed to send mail using other user's names without a warning

✦ `/etc/mail/userdb.db` — User database file containing information about each user's login name and real name

✦ `/etc/mail/virtusertable` — Database of users with virtual-domain addresses hosted on this system

The .forward file

Users can redirect their own mail by placing a `.forward` file in their home directory. The `.forward` file is a plain-text file with a comma-separated list of mail addresses. Any mail sent to the user is then forwarded to these addresses. If the `.forward` file contains a single address, all e-mail for that user is redirected to that single e-mail address. For example, suppose a `.forward` file containing the following line is placed in the home directory of a user named `emily`:

```
ashley
```

This causes `sendmail` to automatically send all e-mail addressed to `emily` to the user name `ashley` on the same system. User `emily` does not receive mail at all.

You can also forward mail to a user name on another system by listing a complete e-mail address. For example, I have added a `.forward` file with the following line to send my messages (addressed to my username, `naba`) to the mail address `naba@comcast.net`:

```
naba@comcast.net
```

Now suppose I want to keep a copy of the message on this system, in addition to forwarding to the address `naba@comcast.net`. I can do so by adding the following line to the `.forward` file:

```
naba@comcast.net, naba\
```

I simply append my user name and end the line with a backslash. The backslash (\) at the end of the line stops `sendmail` from repeatedly forwarding the message (because when a copy is sent to my user name on the system, `sendmail` processes my `.forward` file again — the backslash tells `sendmail` not to forward the message repeatedly).

Invoking procmail in the .forward file

An interesting use of the `.forward` file is to run `procmail` to handle some mail messages automatically. For example, suppose you want to delete any e-mail message that comes from an address containing the string `mailing_list`. Here's what you do to achieve that:

1. **Create a `.forward` file in your home directory and place the following line in it:**

   ```
   "| /usr/bin/procmail"
   ```

   This line causes `sendmail` to run the external program `/usr/bin/procmail` and to send the e-mail messages to the input stream of that program.

2. **Create a text file named `.procmailrc` in your home directory and place the following lines in that file:**

   ```
   # Delete mail from an address that contains
       mailing_list
   :0
   * ^From:.*mailing_list
   /dev/null
   ```

3. **Log in as `root` and set up a symbolic link in `/etc/smrsh` to the `/usr/bin/procmail` program with the following command:**

   ```
   ln -s /usr/bin/procmail /etc/smrsh/procmail
   ```

   This step is necessary because `sendmail` uses the SendMail Restricted Shell — `smrsh` — to run external programs. Instead of running `/usr/bin/procmail`, `smrsh` runs `/etc/smrsh/procmail`. That's why you need the symbolic link. This is a security feature of `sendmail` that controls what external programs it can run.

That's it! Now, if you receive any messages from an address containing `mailing_list`, the message will be deleted.

With `procmail`, you can perform other chores, such as automatically storing messages in a file or forwarding messages to others. All you have to do is create an appropriate `.procmailrc` file in your home directory. To learn more about `procmail`, type **man procmail**. To see examples of `.procmailrc`, type **man procmailex**.

The sendmail alias file

In addition to the `sendmail.cf` file, `sendmail` also consults an alias file named `/etc/aliases` to convert a name into an address. The location of the alias file appears in the `sendmail` configuration file.

Each *alias* is typically a shorter name for an e-mail address. The system administrator uses the `sendmail` alias file to forward mail, to create mailing lists (a single alias that identifies several users), or to refer to a user by several different names. For example, here are some typical aliases:

```
barkakati: naba
naba: naba@lnbsoft
all: naba, leha, ivy, emily, ashley
```

The first line says that mail addressed to `barkakati` should be delivered to the user named `naba` on the local system. The second line indicates that mail for `naba` should really be sent to the username `naba` on the `lnbsoft` system. The last line defines `all` as the alias for the five users `naba`, `leha`, `ivy`, `emily`, and `ashley`. That means mail sent to `all` would go to these five users.

After defining any new aliases in the `/etc/aliases` file, you must log in as `root` and make the new alias active by typing the following command:

```
sendmail -bi
```

Installing the News Server

If you install the news server during Red Hat Linux installation, you don't have to do much more to begin using the news services. Otherwise, you can use the Red Hat Package Manager (RPM) to install the InterNetNews (INN) — a TCP/IP-based news server.

To check whether INN is already installed, type the following command:

```
rpm -q inn
```

If INN is installed, you should see a line similar to this:

```
inn-2.3.5-4
```

If you get a message saying the package isn't installed, you can install it manually from the companion CD-ROM. Log in as `root` and insert the first CD-ROM into the CD-ROM drive. If you're using GNOME or KDE desktop, the CD-ROM should mount automatically. Otherwise, type the following command to mount it:

```
mount /mnt/cdrom
```

Then type the following commands to install INN:

```
cd /mnt/cdrom/RedHat/RPMS
rpm -ivh inn-*
```

Configuring and Starting the INN Server

Much of the *InterNetNews* (INN) software, bundled with Red Hat Linux, is ready to go as soon as you install the RPM. All you need is to brush up a bit on the various components of INN, edit the configuration files, and start `innd` — the INN server. By the way, sometimes I refer to the INN server as the *news server*.

If you want to support a selection of Internet newsgroups, you also have to arrange for a *news feed* — this is the source from which your news server gets the newsgroup articles. Typically, you can get a news feed from an ISP, but the ISP charges an additional monthly fee to cover the cost of resources required to provide the feed. You need the name of the upstream server that provides the news feed, and you have to provide that server with your server's name and the newsgroups you want to receive.

Depending on the newsgroups you want to receive and the number of days you want to retain articles, you have to set aside appropriate disk space to hold the articles. The newsgroups are stored in a directory hierarchy (based on the newsgroup names) in the `/var/spool/news` directory of your system. If you're setting up a news server, you may want to devote a large disk partition to the `/var/spool/news` directory.

In your news server's configuration files, enter the name of the server providing the news feed. At the same time, add to the configuration files the names of any downstream news servers (if any) that receive news feeds from your server. Then you can start the news server and wait for news to arrive. Monitor the log files to ensure that the news articles are being sorted and stored properly in the `/var/spool/news` directory on your system.

When you have news up and running, you must run news maintenance and cleanup scripts. These are run using the `cron` jobs. On Red Hat Linux, a `cron` job is already set up to run the `/usr/bin/news.daily` script to perform the news maintenance tasks.

In the following sections, I introduce you to INN setup, but you can learn more about INN from the Internet Software Consortium (ISC), a nonprofit corporation dedicated to developing and maintaining open source Internet software, such as BIND (an implementation of Domain Name System), DHCP (Dynamic Host Configuration Protocol), and INN. Rich Salz originally wrote INN; ISC took over the development of INN in 1996. You can learn more about INN and can access other resources at ISC's INN Web page at `www.isc.org/products/INN`.

InterNetNews components

INN includes several programs that deliver and manage newsgroups. It also includes a number of files that control how the INN programs work. The most important INN programs are the following:

✦ `innd` — The news server. It runs as *a daemon* — a background process that keeps itself running to provide a specific service — and listens on the NNTP port (TCP port 119). The `innd` server accepts connections from other feed sites, as well as from local newsreader clients, but it hands off local connections to the `nnrpd`.

✦ `nnrpd` — A special server invoked by `innd` to handle requests from local newsreader clients.

✦ `expire` — Removes old articles based on the specifications in the text file `/etc/news/expire.ctl`.

✦ `nntpsend` — Invokes the `innxmit` program to send news articles to a remote site by using NNTP. The configuration file `/etc/news/nntpsend.ctl` controls the `nntpsend` program.

✦ `ctlinnd` — Enables you to control the `innd` server interactively. The `ctlinnd` program can send messages to the control channel of the `innd` server.

The other vital components of INN are the control files. Most of these files are in the `/etc/news` directory of your Red Hat Linux system, though a few are in the `/var/lib/news` directory. Between those two directories, you have over 30 INN control files. Some important files include the following:

✦ `/etc/news/inn.conf` — Specifies configuration data for the `innd` server. (To view online help for this file, type **man inn.conf**.)

✦ `/etc/news/newsfeeds` — Specifies what articles to feed downstream to other news servers. (The file is complicated, but you can get help by typing **man newsfeeds**.)

✦ `/etc/news/incoming.conf` — Lists the names and addresses of hosts that provide news feeds to this server. (To view online help for this file, type **man incoming.conf**.)

✦ `/etc/news/storage.conf` — Specifies the storage methods to be used when storing news articles. (To view online help for this file, type **man storage.conf**.)

✦ `/etc/news/expire.ctl` — Controls expiration of articles, on a per-newsgroup level, if desired. (To view online help for this file, type **man expire.ctl**.)

✦ `/var/lib/news/active` — Lists all active newsgroups, showing the oldest and newest article number for each, and each newsgroup's posting status. (To view online help for this file, type **man active**.)

✦ `/var/lib/news/newsgroups` — Lists newsgroups, with a brief description of each.

✦ `/etc/news/readers.conf` — Specifies hosts and users that are permitted to read news from this news server and post news to newsgroups. The default file allows only the `localhost` to read news; you have to edit it if you want to allow other hosts in your local area network to read news. (To view online help for this file, type **man readers.conf**.)

In the next few sections, I describe how to set up some of the important control files.

The inn.conf file

This file holds configuration data for all INN programs — which makes it the most important file. Each line of the file has the value of a parameter in the following format:

```
parameter:      value
```

Depending on the parameter, the value is a string, a number, or `true` or `false`. As in many other configuration files, comment lines begin with a number or pound sign (#).

Most of the parameters in the default `inn.conf` file in the `/etc/news` directory should not require changes. You may want to edit one or more of the parameters shown in Table 4-2.

Table 4-2	Configuration Parameters in /etc/news/inn.conf
Parameter Name	*Description*
`mta`	Set this to the mail transfer agent that will be used by `innd` to transfer messages. The default is to use `sendmail`.
`organization`	Set this to the name of your organization in the way you want it to appear in the `Organization:` header of all news articles posted from your system. Users may override this by defining the `ORGANIZATION` environment variable.

Parameter Name	Description
ovmethod	Sets the type of overview storage method (the *overview* is an index of news articles in the newsgroup). The default method is tradindexed, which is fast for reading news, but slow for storing news items.
pathhost	Set this to the name of your news server as you want it to appear in the Path header of all postings that go through your server. If pathhost isn't defined, the fully qualified domain name of your system is used.
pathnews	Set this to the full pathname of the directory that contains INN binaries and libraries. In Red Hat Linux, pathnews is set to /usr/lib/news.
domain	Set this to the domain name for your server.
allownewnews	Set this to true if you want INN to support the NEWNEWS command from newsreaders. Because this command can drastically reduce your server's performance, INN documentation recommends that you set this to false.
storageapi	Set this to true if you want articles to be stored using the Storage Manager API (application programming interface). The default setting of false causes INN to use the traditional article-storage method of storing one article per file. If you set this to true, you have to choose between the storage methods timehash and cnfs, and you have to create new spool and database files (type **man storage.conf** to read more about cnfs and timehash storage methods). For a small number of newsgroups, you can leave this option at its default value of false.
hiscachesize	Set this to the size in kilobytes that you want INN to use for caching recently used history file entries. The default setting of 0 disables history caching. Because history caching can greatly increase the number of articles your server can process per second, you may want to set a value of 16384 (for 16MB).
innflags	Set this to any flags you want to pass to the INN server process when it starts up.

The newsfeeds file

The newsfeeds file specifies how incoming news articles are redistributed to other servers and to INN processes. If you provide news feeds to other servers, you have to list these news feeds in this file. (You also must have an entry labeled ME, which serves a special purpose that I explain later in this section.)

Book VIII
Chapter 4

Serving Up Mail and News

The `newsfeeds` file contains a series of entries, one for each feed. Each feed entry has the following format:

```
site[/exclude,exclude...]\
    :pattern,pattern...[/distrib,distrib...]\
    :flag,flag...\
    :param
```

Each entry has four fields separated by colons (`:`). Usually, the entries span multiple lines, and a backslash (\) at the end of the line is used to continue a line to the next. Here's what the four fields mean:

✦ The first field, `site`, is the name of the feed. Each name must be unique, and for feeds to other news servers, the name is set to the host name of the remote server. Following the name is an optional slash and an `exclude` list (`/exclude,exclude...`) consisting of a list of names. If any of the names in this list appear in the Path line of an article, that article won't be forwarded to the feed. You can use an `exclude` list if you don't want to receive articles from a specific source.

✦ The second field consists of a comma-separated list of newsgroup patterns, such as `*,@alt.binaries.warez.*,!control*,!local*`, followed by an optional distribution list. The distribution list is a list of comma-separated keywords, with each keyword specifying a specific set of sites to which the articles are distributed. The newsgroup patterns essentially define a subscription list of sites that receive this news feed. An asterisk matches all newsgroups. A pattern beginning with an @ causes newsgroups matching that pattern to be dropped. A pattern that begins with an exclamation mark (!) means the matching newsgroups are not sent. By the way, the simple pattern-matching syntax used in INN configuration files is referred to as a *wildmat* pattern.

✦ The third field is a comma-separated list of *flags* — fields that determine the feed-entry type and set certain parameters for the entry. There are numerous flags; type **man newsfeeds** and read the man page for more information about the flags.

✦ The fourth field is for parameters whose values depend on the settings in the third field. Typically, this field contains names of files or external programs that the INN server uses. You can learn more about this field from the `newsfeeds` man page.

Now that you know the layout of the `/etc/news/newsfeeds` file, you can study that file as an example. The default file contains many sample feed entries, but only two are commented out:

✦ `ME` is a special feed entry that's always required. It serves two purposes. First, the newsgroup patterns listed in this entry are preprended to all newsgroup patterns in all other entries. Second, the ME entry's distribution list determines what distributions your server accepts from remote sites.

✦ The controlchan feed entry is used to set up INN so an external program is used to handle control messages (these messages are used to create new newsgroups and remove groups). For example, the following controlchan entry specifies the external program /usr/lib/news/bin/controlchan to handle all control messages, except cancel messages (meant for canceling an article):

```
controlchan!\
        :!*,control,control.*,!control.cancel\
        :Tc,Wnsm:/usr/lib/news/bin/controlchan
```

In addition to these feed entries, you add entries for any actual sites to which your news server provides news feeds. Such entries have the format

```
feedme.domain.com\
                :!junk,!control/!foo\
                :Tm:innfeed!
```

where *feedme.domain.com* is the fully qualified domain name of the site to which your system sends news articles.

The incoming.conf file

The incoming.conf file describes which hosts are allowed to connect to your host to feed articles. For a single feed, you can add an entry like

```
peer mybuddy {
    hostname: a-feed-site.domain.com
}
```

where *mybuddy* is a label for the peer and *a-feed-site.domain.com* identifies the site that feeds your site.

Keep in mind that simply adding a site's name in the incoming.conf file does not cause that remote site to start feeding your site news — it simply enables your server to accept news articles from the remote site. At the remote site, your buddy has to configure his or her server to send articles to your site.

The readers.conf file

This file specifies the host names or IP addresses from which newsreader clients (such as Mozilla) can retrieve newsgroups from your server. For example, the following `readers.conf` file allows *read access* and *post access* (meaning you can submit articles) from `localhost` and from any host in the network 192.168.0.0:

```
auth "localhost" {
    hosts: "localhost, 127.0.0.1, stdin"
    default: "<localhost>"
}
access "localhost" {
    users: "<localhost>"
    newsgroups: "*"
    access: RPA
}
auth "localnet" {
    hosts: 192.168.0.0/24
    default: "<localnet>"
}
access "localnet" {
    users: "<localnet>"
    newsgroups: "*"
    access: RPA
}
```

InterNetNews startup

In addition to the configuration files, you also have to initiate `cron` jobs that perform periodic maintenance of the news server. In Red Hat Linux, these `cron` jobs are already set up. Therefore, you're now ready to start the INN server — `innd`.

Before you start `innd`, you must run `makehistory` and `makedbz` to initialize and rebuild the INN history database. Type **man makehistory** and **man makedbz** to learn more about these commands. Type the following commands to create an initial history database, associated indexes, and set the ownerships and permissions of some files:

```
/usr/lib/news/bin/makehistory -b -f history -O -l 30000 -I
cd /var/lib/news
/usr/lib/news/bin/makedbz -s 'wc -l < history' -f history
chown news.news *
chown news.news /var/spool/news/overview/group.index
chmod 664 /var/spool/news/overview/group.index
```

As with any other servers in Red Hat Linux, to start `innd`, log in as `root` and type the following command:

```
service innd start
```

To ensure that `innd` starts at boot time, type the following command:

```
chkconfig --level 35 innd on
```

If you change any configuration file (such as `inn.conf` or `newsfeeds`), restart the `innd` server with the following command:

```
service innd restart
```

Type **ps ax** to see whether the `innd` process is up and running. If all goes well, you should see two processes such as the following listed in the output of the `ps ax` command:

```
23789 ?     S   0:00 /usr/lib/news/bin/innd -p4
23794 ?     S   0:00 /usr/bin/perl /usr/lib/news/bin/controlchan
```

The `/var/log/spooler` file contains all status and error messages from `innd`. Type the following command to see the last few messages in that file:

```
tail /var/log/spooler
```

Setting Up Local Newsgroups

If you want to use newsgroups as a way to share information within your company, you can set up a hierarchy of local newsgroups. Then you can use these newsgroups to create virtual communities within your company, where people with shared interests can informally discuss issues and exchange knowledge.

Defining a newsgroup hierarchy

The first task is to define a hierarchy of newsgroups and decide what each newsgroup will discuss. For example, if your company name is XYZ Corporation, here's a partial hierarchy of newsgroups you might define:

+ `xyz.general` — General items about XYZ Corporation

+ `xyz.weekly.news` — Weekly news

+ `xyz.weekly.menu` — The weekly cafeteria menu and any discussions about it

+ `xyz.forsale` — A listing of items offered for sale by employees

+ `xyz.jobs` — Job openings at XYZ Corporation

✦ `xyz.wanted` — Wanted (help, items to buy, and so on) postings by employees

✦ `xyz.technical.hardware` — Technical discussions about hardware

✦ `xyz.technical.software` — Technical discussions about software

Updating configuration files

Here are the steps you follow to update the configuration files for your local newsgroups and then restart the news server:

1. **Add descriptive entries for each of these newsgroups to the** `/var/lib/news/newsgroups` **file.**

Here are the entries from the default `/var/lib/news/newsgroups` file:

```
control          Various control messages (no posting).
control.cancel     Cancel messages (no posting).
control.checkgroups   Hierarchy check control messages (no posting).
control.newgroup    Newsgroup creation control messages (no posting).
control.rmgroup    Newsgroup removal control messages (no posting).
junk           Unfiled articles (no posting).
```

Add to this file a line for each local newsgroup — type its name, followed by a brief description. For example, here's what you might add for the `xyz.general` newsgroup:

```
xyz.general        General items about XYZ Corporation
```

2. **Edit the** `ME` **entry in the** `/etc/news/newsfeeds` **file and add the phrase** `!xyz.*` **to the comma-separated list of newsgroup patterns.**

This ensures that your local newsgroups are not distributed outside your site.

3. **Add a storage method to be used for the local newsgroups.**

For example, you can add the following lines in `/etc/news/storage.conf` to define the storage method for the new `xyz` hierarchy of newsgroups (change `xyz` to whatever you name your local newsgroups):

```
method tradspool {
    class: 1
    newsgroups: xyz.*
}
```

4. **To make these changes effective, restart the news server with the command:**

```
service innd restart
```

Adding the newsgroups

The final step is to add the newsgroups. After you have configuration files updated and `innd` running, it's very easy to add a local newsgroup. Log in as `root` and use `ctlinnd` to perform this task. For example, here's how you add a newsgroup named `xyz.general`:

```
/usr/lib/news/bin/ctlinnd newgroup xyz.general
```

That's it! That command adds the `xyz.general` newsgroup to your site. If you use the traditional storage method, the `innd` server creates the directory `/var/spool/news/articles/xyz/general` and stores articles for that newsgroup in that directory (this happens the first time someone posts a news article to that newsgroup).

After you've created all the local newsgroups, users from your intranet should be able to post news articles and read articles in the local newsgroups. If they have problems accessing the newsgroups, make sure that the `/etc/news/readers.conf` file contains the IP addresses or names of the hosts that should be able to access the `innd` server.

Testing your newsgroups

For example, I add a newsgroup named `local.news` on an INN server running on my Red Hat Linux system by using the instructions explained in the previous sections. Then I start Mozilla on another Red Hat Linux system on the LAN and set up a new news account with the news server set to my INN server. Next, I access the `local.news` newsgroup by typing **news:local.news** as the URL. Try it! I bet you'll like it.

Chapter 5: Setting Up
DNS and NIS

In This Chapter

✔ Understanding DNS

✔ Learning about BIND

✔ Configuring DNS

✔ Setting up a caching name server

✔ Configuring a primary name server

✔ Understanding NIS

✔ Configuring NIS servers and clients

✔ Trying out NIS

*D*omain Name System (DNS) is an Internet service that converts a fully qualified domain name, such as www.redhat.com, into its corresponding IP address such as 216.148.218.195. You can think of DNS as the directory of Internet hosts — DNS is the reason why you can use easy-to-remember host names even though TCP/IP requires numeric IP addresses for data transfers. DNS is basically a hierarchy of distributed DNS servers. In this chapter, I provide an overview of DNS and show you how to set up a caching DNS server on your Red Hat Linux system.

Network Information System (NIS) is another client/server service designed to manage information shared among several host computers on a network. Typically, NIS maintains a common set of user accounts and other system files on a UNIX or Linux system for a group of hosts on a local area network (LAN). This service, among others, enables a user to log in on all hosts with the same username and password. This chapter briefly describes the NIS client and server software, and I show you how to use them on a Red Hat Linux system.

Understanding Domain Name System (DNS)

In TCP/IP networks, each network interface (for example, an Ethernet card or a dial-up modem connection) is identified by an IP address. Because IP addresses are hard to remember, an easy-to-remember name is assigned to the IP address — much like the way a name goes with a telephone number. For example, instead of having to remember that the IP address of Red Hat's Web server is 216.148.218.195, you can simply refer to that host by its name, `www.redhat.com`. When you type `www.redhat.com` as the URL in a Web browser, the name `www.redhat.com` has to be translated into its corresponding IP address. This is where the concept of DNS comes in.

What is DNS?

Domain Name System is a distributed, hierarchical database that holds information about computers on the Internet. That information includes host name, IP address, and mail-routing specifications. Because this information resides in many DNS hosts on the Internet, DNS is called a *distributed* database. The primary job of DNS is to associate host names to IP addresses and vice versa.

In ARPANET — the precursor to today's Internet — the list of host names and corresponding IP addresses was maintained in a text file named `HOSTS.TXT`, which was managed centrally and periodically distributed to every host on the network. As the number of hosts grew, this static host table quickly became unreasonable to maintain. DNS was proposed by Paul Mockapetris to alleviate the problems of a static host table. As formally documented in Request for Comment (RFC) 882 and 883 (published in November 1983, see `www.faqs.org/rfcs/rfc882.html` and `www.faqs.org/rfcs/rfc883.html`), the original DNS introduced two key concepts:

✦ Use of hierarchical domain names, such as `www.ee.umd.edu` and `www.redhat.com`

✦ Distributed responsibility for managing the host database by using DNS servers throughout the Internet

DNS as we know it today is an Internet standard documented in RFCs 1034 and 1035. The standard has been updated and extended by several other RFCs — 1101, 1183, 1348, 1876, 1982, 1996, 2065, 2181, 2136, 2137, 2308, 2535, 2845, and 2931. The earlier updates define data encoding, whereas later ones focus on improving DNS security. To read these and other RFCs online, visit Ohio State University's Internet RFC page at this Web address:

`www.cis.ohio-state.edu/hypertext/information/rfc.html`

DNS defines the following:

✦ A hierarchical domain-naming system for hosts.

✦ A distributed database that associates every domain name with an IP address.

✦ Library routines (resolvers) that network applications can use to query the distributed DNS database. (This library is called the *resolver library.*)

✦ A protocol for DNS clients and servers to exchange information about names and IP addresses.

Nowadays, all hosts on the Internet rely on DNS to access various Internet services on remote hosts. As you may know from personal experience, when you obtain Internet access from an Internet service provider (ISP), your ISP provides you with the IP addresses of *name servers* — the DNS servers your system accesses whenever host names have to be mapped to IP addresses.

If you have a small LAN, you may decide to run a DNS server on one of the hosts or to use the name servers provided by the ISP. For medium-sized networks with several subnets, you can run a DNS server on each subnet to provide efficient DNS lookups. On a large corporate network, the corporate domain (such as `microsoft.com`) is further subdivided into a hierarchy of subdomains; several DNS servers may be used in each subdomain.

In the following sections, I provide an overview of the hierarchical domain-naming convention and describe BIND — the DNS software used on most UNIX systems, including Red Hat Linux.

Learning hierarchical domain names

DNS uses a hierarchical tree of domains to organize the *namespace* — the entire set of names. Each higher-level domain has authority over its lower-level subdomains. Each domain represents a distinct block of the namespace and is managed by a single administrative authority. Figure 5-1 illustrates the hierarchical organization of the DNS namespace.

Figure 5-1: The DNS namespace is organized in a hierarchy.

The root of the tree is called the *root domain* and is represented by a single dot (.). The top-level, or root-level, domains come next. The top-level domains are further divided into second-level domains, which, in turn, can be broken into further subdomains.

The top-level domains are relatively fixed and include well-known domains such as COM, NET, ORG, EDU, GOV, and MIL. These are the commonly used top-level domains in the United States. These top-level domains came about as the Internet came to widespread use in the early the 1990s.

There is another set of top-level domain names for the countries. These domain names use the two-letter country codes assigned by the International Organization for Standardization (abbreviated as ISO; see www.iso.ch). For example, the top-level country code domain for the United States is US. In the United States, many local governments and organizations use the US domain. For example, mcps.k12.md.us is the domain name of the Montgomery County Public Schools in the state of Maryland, USA.

The *fully qualified domain name* (FQDN) is constructed by stringing together the subdomain names, from lower- to higher-level, using dots (.) as separators. For example, REDHAT.COM is a fully qualified domain name; so is EE.UMD.EDU. Note that each of these may also refer to a specific host computer. Figure 5-2 illustrates the components of a fully qualified domain name.

Figure 5-2: A fully qualified domain name has a hierarchy of components.

ee.umd.edu

Top level domain
Second level domain
Subdomain or host name

Domain names are case-insensitive. Therefore, as far as DNS is concerned, the domains UMD.EDU and umd.edu both represent University of Maryland's domain. The norm, however, is to type domain names in all lowercase.

Exploring Berkeley Internet Domain Name (BIND)

Most UNIX systems, including Red Hat Linux, come with the BIND system — a well-known implementation of DNS. The BIND software is installed during Red Hat Linux installation, as long as you select the DNS Name Server package group when selecting the packages for installation.

To see which version of BIND is installed on your Red Hat Linux system, type the following command:

```
rpm -q bind
```

If BIND is installed, this command should display a line similar to the following with the version number of the RPM file:

```
bind-9.2.2-19
```

As this output shows, BIND Version 9.2.2 is installed on my system.

BIND includes three major components:

✦ The `named` daemon — the name server — that responds to queries about host names and IP addresses

✦ A resolver library that applications can use to resolve host names into IP addresses (and vice versa)

✦ Command line DNS utility programs (DNS clients), such as `dig` (Domain Internet Groper) and `host` that users can use to query DNS

I describe these components of BIND in the next few sections. In later sections, I explain how to configure the resolver and the name server.

named — the BIND name server

The `named` daemon is the name server that responds to queries about host names and IP addresses. Based on the configuration files and the local DNS database, `named` either provides answers to queries or asks other servers and caches their responses. The `named` server also performs a function referred to as *zone transfer*, which involves copying data among the name servers in a domain.

The name server operates in one of three modes:

✦ **Primary or Master** — In this case, the name server keeps the master copy of the domain's data on disk. There is one primary server for each domain or subdomain.

✦ **Secondary or Slave** — A secondary name server copies its domain's data from the primary server using a zone transfer operation. You can have one or more secondary name servers for a domain.

✦ **Caching** — A *caching name server* loads the addresses of a few authoritative servers for the root domain and gets all domain data by caching responses to queries it has resolved by contacting other name servers. Primary and secondary servers also cache responses.

A name server can be authoritative or not, depending on what information it's providing. As the term implies, the response from an authoritative name server is supposed to be accurate. The primary and secondary name servers are authoritative for their own domains, but they are not authoritative for responses provided from cached information.

Caching name servers are never authoritative because all their responses come from cached information.

To run a name server on your Red Hat Linux system, you have to run `named` with the appropriate configuration files. Later in this chapter, you learn about the configuration files and data files that control how the name server operates.

Resolver library

Finding an IP address for a host name is referred to as *resolving the host name*. Network-aware applications, such as a Web browser or an FTP client, use a *resolver library* to perform the conversion from the name to an IP address. Depending on the settings in the `/etc/host.conf` file, the resolver library consults the `/etc/hosts` file or makes a DNS query to resolve a host name to its IP address. The resolver library queries the name servers listed in the `/etc/resolv.conf` file.

You don't have to learn much about the resolver library unless you're writing network-aware applications. To run Internet services properly, all you have to know is how to configure the resolver. Later in this chapter, I show you how to configure this and other aspects of DNS.

DNS utility programs

You can use the DNS utility programs — `dig` and `host` — to try out DNS from the shell prompt interactively. These utility programs are DNS clients. You can use them to query the DNS database and debug any name server you may set up on your system. By default, these programs query the name server listed in your system's `/etc/resolv.conf` file.

You can use `dig`, the Domain Internet Groper program, to look up IP addresses for a domain name or vice versa. For example, to look up the IP address of `ftp.redhat.com`, type

```
dig ftp.redhat.com
```

`dig` prints the results of the DNS query with a great amount of detail. Look in the part of the output labeled `ANSWER SECTION:` for the result. For example, here's what that section looks like for this sample query:

```
;; ANSWER SECTION:
ftp.redhat.com.          300     IN     A       66.187.232.30
```

Reverse lookups (finding host names for IP addresses) are also easy with `dig`. For example, to find the host name corresponding to the IP address 66.187.232.30, type the following:

```
dig -x 66.187.232.30
```

Again, the answer appears in the `ANSWER SECTION:` of the output, which, for this example, looks like this:

```
;; ANSWER SECTION:
30.232.187.66.in-addr.arpa. 539 IN      PTR     ftp.redhat.com.
```

In this case, the host name corresponding to the IP address 66.187.232.30 happens to be `ftp.redhat.com`.

You can also query DNS by using the `host` program. The `host` program produces output in a compact format. For example, here's a typical use of `host` to look up an IP address for a host name:

```
host www.gao.gov
```

This generates the following one-liner:

```
www.gao.gov has address 161.203.16.2
```

By default, `host` prints the IP address and any *MX record* (these records list the names of mail handlers for the host).

For a reverse lookup, use the `-t ptr` option, along with the IP address as an argument, like this:

```
host -t ptr 161.203.16.2
```

Here's the relay from `host`:

```
2.16.203.161.in-addr.arpa. domain name pointer www.gao.gov.
```

In this case, host prints the PTR record (from the DNS database) that shows the host name corresponding to the IP address.

You can also try other types of records, such as `CNAME` (for canonical name), as follows:

```
host -t cname www.ee.umd.edu
```

The response from `host` says

```
www.ee.umd.edu is an alias for edison.eng.umd.edu.
```

This indicates that the *canonical name* (or alias) for `www.ee.umd.edu` is `edison.eng.umd.edu`.

Configuring DNS

You configure DNS by using a number of configuration files. The exact set of files depends on whether you're running a name server and, if so, the type of name server — caching or primary. Some configuration files are needed whether you run a name server or not.

Configuring the resolver

You don't need a name server running on your system to use the DNS clients (`dig` and `host`). You can use them to query your domain's name server. Typically, your ISP provides you with this information. You have to list the IP addresses of these name servers in the `/etc/resolv.conf` file — the resolver library reads this file to determine how to resolve host names. The format of this file is

```
domain your-domain.com
search your-domain.com
nameserver A.B.C.D
nameserver X.Y.Z.W
```

where `A.B.C.D` and `X.Y.Z.W` are the IP addresses (dot-separated numeric addresses, such as 192.168.0.1) of the primary and secondary name servers your ISP provides you.

The `domain` line lists the local domain name. The `search` line specifies the domains on which a host name is searched first (usually, you put your own domain in the search line). The domain listed on the `search` line is appended to any host name before the resolver library tries to resolve it. For example, if you look for a host named `mailhost`, the resolver library first tries `mailhost.your-domain.com`; if that fails, it tries `mailhost`. The `search` line applies to any host name you try to access. For example, if you're trying to access `www.redhat.com`, the resolver first tries `www.redhat.com.your-domain.com` and then `www.redhat.com`.

Another important configuration file is `/etc/host.conf` — this file tells the resolver what to do when attempting to resolve a host name. A typical `/etc/host/conf` file contains the following line:

```
order hosts,bind
```

This tells the resolver to consult the `/etc/hosts` file first and, if that fails, to query the name server listed in the `/etc/resolv.conf` file. The `/etc/hosts` file usually lists any local host names and their IP addresses. Here's a typical line from the /etc/hosts file:

```
127.0.0.1    lnbp200  localhost.localdomain  localhost
```

This line says that the IP address 127.0.0.1 is assigned to the host names lnbp200, localhost.localdomain, and localhost.

In the latest version of Linux kernel that uses GNU C Library version 2 (glibc 2) or later, the name service switch (NSS) file, /etc/nsswitch.conf, controls how services such as the resolver library, NIS, NIS+, and local files such as /etc/hosts and /etc/shadow interact. For example, the following hosts entry in the /etc/nsswitch.conf file specifies that the resolver library should first try the /etc/hosts file, then try NIS+, and finally try DNS:

```
hosts:      files nisplus dns
```

To learn more about the /etc/nsswitch.conf file and what it does, type **info libc "Name Service Switch"** in a terminal window.

Configuring a caching name server

A simple, but useful, name server is one that finds answers to host-name queries by using other name servers and then remembers the answer (by saving it in a cache) the next time you need it. This caching name server can shorten the time it takes to access hosts you have accessed recently; the answer is already in the cache.

When you install the DNS Name Server package group during Red Hat Linux installation, the configuration files for a caching name server are also installed. That means you can start running the caching name server without much work on your part. This section describes the configuration files and what you have to do to start the caching name server.

the /etc/named.conf file

The first configuration file you need is /etc/named.conf. The named server reads this configuration file when it starts. You already have this file if you have installed the DNS Name Server during Red Hat Linux installation. Here's what the default /etc/named/conf file contains:

```
// generated by named-bootconf.pl

options {
    directory "/var/named";
    /*
     * If there is a firewall between you and nameservers you want
     * to talk to, you might need to uncomment the query-source
```

```
    * directive below. Previous versions of BIND always asked
    * questions using port 53, but BIND 8.1 uses an unprivileged
    * port by default.
    */
    // query-source address * port 53;
};

//
// a caching only nameserver config
//
controls {
    inet 127.0.0.1 allow { localhost; } keys { rndckey; };
};
zone "." IN {
    type hint;
    file "named.ca";
};

zone "localhost" IN {
    type master;
    file "localhost.zone";
    allow-update { none; };
};

zone "0.0.127.in-addr.arpa" IN {
    type master;
    file "named.local";
    allow-update { none; };
};

include "/etc/rndc.key";
```

Comments are C-style (/* ... */) or C++-style (starts with //). The file contains block statements enclosed in curly braces ({...}) and terminated by a semicolon (;). A block statement, in turn, contains other statements, each ending with a semicolon.

This /etc/named.conf file begins with an options block statement with a number of option statements. The directory option statement tells named where to look for all other files that appear on file lines in the configuration file. In this case, named looks for the files in the /var/named directory.

The controls statement in /etc/named.conf contains security information so the rndc command can connect to the named service at port 953 and interact with named. In this case, the controls statement contains the following line:

```
inet 127.0.0.1 allow { localhost; } keys { rndckey; };
```

This says the rndc can connect from localhost with the key named rndc (the file /etc/rndc.key defines the key and the encryption algorithm to be used).

The rndc (remote name daemon control) utility is a successor to the older ndc (for *name daemon controller*) utility used to control the named server by sending it messages over a special control channel, a TCP port where named listens for messages. The rndc utility uses a cryptographic key to authenticate itself to the named server. The named server has the same cryptographic key so it can decode the authentication information sent by rndc.

After the options statement, the /etc/named.conf file contains several zone statements, each enclosed in curly braces and terminated by a semicolon. Each zone statement defines a zone. The first zone is named "." (root zone); it's a hint zone that specifies the root name servers.

The next two zone statements in /etc/named.conf are master zones. The syntax for a *master zone statement* for an Internet class zone (indicated by the IN keyword) is as follows:

```
zone "zone-name" IN {
        type master;
        file "zone-file";
        [...other optional statements...]
};
```

The zone-name is the name of the zone, and zone-file is the zone file that contains the resource records (RR) — the database entries — for that zone. I describe zone file formats and resource record formats in the next two sections.

Zone file formats

The zone file typically starts with a number of directives, each of which begins with a dollar sign ($) followed by a keyword. Two commonly used directives are $TTL and $ORIGIN.

For example, the line

```
$TTL    86400
```

uses the $TTL directive to set the default Time To Live (TTL) for subsequent records with undefined TTLs. The value is in seconds, and the valid TTLs are in the range 0 to 2147483647 seconds. In this case, the directive sets the default TTL as 86400 seconds (or one day).

The $ORIGIN directive sets the domain name that will be appended to any unqualified records. For example, the following $ORIGIN directive sets the domain name to localhost:

```
$ORIGIN localhost.
```

If there is no $ORIGIN directive, the initial $ORIGIN is the same as the zone name that comes after the zone keyword in the /etc/named.conf file.

After the directives, the zone file contains one or more resource records. These records follow a specific format, which is outlined in the next section.

Resource record (RR) formats

You have to understand the format of the resource records before you can understand and intelligently work with zone files. Each resource record has the following format (the optional fields are shown in square brackets):

```
[domain] [ttl] [class] type data [;comment]
```

The fields are separated by tabs or spaces and may contain some special characters, such as an @ symbol for the domain and a semicolon (;) to indicate the start of a comment.

The first field, which must begin at the first character of the line, identifies the domain. You can use the @ symbol to use the current $ORIGIN for the domain name for this record. If you have multiple records for the same domain name, leave the first field blank.

The optional ttl field specifies the Time To Live — the duration for which the data can be cached and considered valid. You can specify the duration in one of the following formats:

✦ N, where N is a number meaning N seconds

✦ NW, where N is a number meaning N weeks

✦ ND, where N is a number meaning N days

✦ NH, where N is a number meaning N hours

✦ NM, where N is a number meaning N minutes

✦ NS, where N is a number meaning N seconds

The letters W, D, H, M, and S can also be in lowercase. Thus, you can write 86400 or 1D (or 1d) to indicate a duration of one day. You can also combine these to specify more precise durations, such as 5w6d16h to indicate 5 weeks, 6 days, and 16 hours.

The class field specifies the network type. The most commonly used value for this field is IN for Internet.

Next in the resource record is the type field, which denotes the type of record (such as SOA, NS, A, or PTR). Table 5-1 lists the DNS resource record types. The data field comes next, and it depends on the type field.

Table 5-1		DNS Resource Record Types
Type	*Name*	*Description*
SOA	Start of Authority	Indicates that all subsequent records are authoritative for this zone.
NS	Name Server	Identifies authoritative name servers for a zone.
A	Address	Specifies the IP address corresponding to a host name.
PTR	Pointer	Specifies the name corresponding to an address (used for reverse mapping — converting an IP address to a host name).
MX	Mail Exchanger	Identifies the host that accepts mail meant for a domain (used to route e-mail).
CNAME	Canonical Name	Defines the nickname or alias for a host name.
KEY	Public Key	Stores a public key associated with a DNS name.
CERT	Digital Certificate	Holds a digital certificate.
HINFO	Host Info	Identifies the hardware and operating system for a host.
RP	Responsible Person	Provides the name of a technical contact for a domain.
SRV	Services	Lists well-known network services provided by the domain.
TXT	Text	Used to include comments and other information in the DNS database.

You should learn to read the resource records, at least the ones of type SOA, NS, A, PTR, and MX, which are some of the most commonly used. Next, I briefly describe these records, illustrating each record type through an example.

A typical SOA record has the following format:

```
@       1D IN SOA        @ root (
                         42                 ; serial
                         3H                 ; refresh -- 3 hours
                         15M                ; retry -- 15 minutes
                         1W                 ; expiry -- 1 week
                         1D )               ; minimum -- 1 day
```

The first field specifies the domain as an @, which means the current domain (by default, the zone name, as shown in the /etc/named.conf file). The next field specifies a TTL of one day for this record. The class field is set to IN, which means the record is for Internet. The type field specifies the record type as SOA. The rest of the fields constitute the data for the SOA record. The data includes the name of the primary name server (in this case, @, or the current domain), the e-mail address of the technical contact, and five different times enclosed in parentheses.

The NS record specifies the authoritative name servers for a zone. A typical NS record looks like the following:

```
.           3600000  IN  NS     A.ROOT-SERVERS.NET.
```

In this case, the NS record lists the authoritative name server for the root zone (notice that the name of the first field is a single dot). The Time-To-Live field specifies the record to be valid for 1,000 hours (3,600,000 seconds). The class is IN, for Internet; and the record type is NS. The final field lists the name of the name server (A.ROOT-SERVERS.NET.), which ends with a dot.

An A record specifies the address corresponding to a name. For example, the following A record shows the address of A.ROOT-SERVERS.NET. as 198.41.0.4:

```
A.ROOT-SERVERS.NET.     3600000     A     198.41.0.4
```

In this case, the network class isn't specified because the field is optional, and the default is IN.

PTR records are used for reverse mapping — converting an address to a name. Consider the following example:

```
1       IN     PTR     localhost.
```

This record comes from a file for a zone named 0.0.127.in-addr.arpa. Therefore, this record says that the name associated with the address 127.0.0.1 is localhost.

An MX record specifies the name of a host that accepts mail on behalf of a specific domain. For example, here's a typical MX record:

```
naba    IN    MX    10    mailhub.lnbsoft.com.
```

This says that mail addressed to the host named naba in the current domain should be sent to mailhub.lnbsoft.com (this host is called a mail exchanger). The number 10 is the preference value. For a list of multiple MX records with different preference values, the ones with lower preference values are tried first.

Armed with this bit of information about resource records, you can go through the zone files for the caching name server.

the /var/named/named.ca file

Information about the root name servers is in the file `/var/named/`
`named.ca`, as specified in the zone statement for the root zone in the
`/etc/named.conf` file. The following listing shows the `/var/named/`
`named.ca` file from a Red Hat Linux system:

```
;       This file holds the information on root name servers needed to
;       initialize cache of Internet domain name servers
;       (e.g. reference this file in the "cache  .  <file>"
;       configuration file of BIND domain name servers).
;
;       This file is made available by InterNIC
;       under anonymous FTP as
;           file                /domain/named.cache
;           on server           FTP.INTERNIC.NET
;
;       last update:   Nov 5, 2002
;       related version of root zone:   2002110501
;
;
; formerly NS.INTERNIC.NET
;
.                       3600000  IN  NS   A.ROOT-SERVERS.NET.
A.ROOT-SERVERS.NET.     3600000      A    198.41.0.4
;
; formerly NS1.ISI.EDU
;
.                       3600000      NS   B.ROOT-SERVERS.NET.
B.ROOT-SERVERS.NET.     3600000      A    128.9.0.107
;
; formerly C.PSI.NET
;
.                       3600000      NS   C.ROOT-SERVERS.NET.
C.ROOT-SERVERS.NET.     3600000      A    192.33.4.12
;
; formerly TERP.UMD.EDU
;
.                       3600000      NS   D.ROOT-SERVERS.NET.
D.ROOT-SERVERS.NET.     3600000      A    128.8.10.90
;
; formerly NS.NASA.GOV
;
.                       3600000      NS   E.ROOT-SERVERS.NET.
E.ROOT-SERVERS.NET.     3600000      A    192.203.230.10
;
; formerly NS.ISC.ORG
;
.                       3600000      NS   F.ROOT-SERVERS.NET.
F.ROOT-SERVERS.NET.     3600000      A    192.5.5.241
;
; formerly NS.NIC.DDN.MIL
;
.                       3600000      NS   G.ROOT-SERVERS.NET.
G.ROOT-SERVERS.NET.     3600000      A    192.112.36.4
;
; formerly AOS.ARL.ARMY.MIL
;
.                       3600000      NS   H.ROOT-SERVERS.NET.
H.ROOT-SERVERS.NET.     3600000      A    128.63.2.53
```

```
;
; formerly NIC.NORDU.NET
;
.                                 3600000       NS     I.ROOT-SERVERS.NET.
I.ROOT-SERVERS.NET.               3600000       A      192.36.148.17
;
; operated by VeriSign, Inc.
;
.                                 3600000       NS     J.ROOT-SERVERS.NET.
J.ROOT-SERVERS.NET.               3600000       A      192.58.128.30
;
; housed in LINX, operated by RIPE NCC
;
.                                 3600000       NS     K.ROOT-SERVERS.NET.
K.ROOT-SERVERS.NET.               3600000       A      193.0.14.129
;
; operated by IANA
;
.                                 3600000       NS     L.ROOT-SERVERS.NET.
L.ROOT-SERVERS.NET.               3600000       A      198.32.64.12
;
; housed in Japan, operated by WIDE
;
.                                 3600000       NS     M.ROOT-SERVERS.NET.
M.ROOT-SERVERS.NET.               3600000       A      202.12.27.33
; End of File
```

This file contains NS and A resource records that specify the names of authoritative name servers and their addresses for the root zone (indicated by the " . " in the first field of each NS record).

The comment lines in the file begin with a semicolon. These comments give you hints about the location of the root name servers. There are 13 root name servers for the Internet; most root servers are located in the United States. This file is a necessity for any name server because the name server has to be able to reach at least one root name server.

the /var/named/localhost.zone file

The /etc/named.conf file includes a zone statement for the localhost zone that specifies the zone file as localhost.zone. That file is located in the /var/named directory of your Red Hat Linux system. Here's a listing of what the /var/named/localhost.zone file contains:

```
$TTL    86400
$ORIGIN localhost.
@              1D IN SOA       @ root (
                              42              ; serial (d. adams)
                              3H              ; refresh
                              15M             ; retry
                              1W              ; expiry
                              1D )            ; minimum

           1D IN NS        @
           1D IN A         127.0.0.1
```

This zone file starts with a $TTL directive that sets the default TTL to one day (86,400 seconds) for subsequent records with undefined TTLs. Next, a $ORIGIN directive sets the domain name to localhost.

After these two directives, the /var/named/localhost.zone file contains three resource records (RRs): an SOA record, an NS record, and an A record. The SOA and the NS record specify the localhost as the primary authoritative name server for the zone. The A record specifies the address of localhost as 127.0.0.1.

the /var/named/named.local file

The third zone statement in the /etc/named.conf file specifies a reverse-mapping zone named 0.0.127.in-addr.arpa. For this zone, the zone file is /var/named/named.local, which contains the following:

```
$TTL      86400
@         IN    SOA    localhost. root.localhost.  (
                                  1997022700 ; Serial
                                  28800      ; Refresh
                                  14400      ; Retry
                                  3600000    ; Expire
                                  86400 )    ; Minimum
          IN    NS     localhost.

1         IN    PTR    localhost.
```

The SOA and NS records specify localhost as the primary name server.

The SOA record also shows root.localhost. as the e-mail address of the technical contact for the domain. Note that the DNS zone files use a user.host. (notice the ending period) format for the e-mail address. When sending any e-mail to the contact, you have to replace the first dot with an @ and remove the final dot.

Caching name server: startup and test

Now that you have studied the configuration files for the caching name server, you can start the name server and see it in operation. To start the name server, log in as root and type the following command in a terminal window:

```
service named start
```

This command starts named — the name-server daemon.

To ensure that the named server starts every time you reboot the system, type the following command while logged in as root:

```
chkconfig --level 35 named on
```

The `named` server writes diagnostic log messages in the `/var/log/messages` file. After you start `named`, you can check the log messages by opening `/var/log/messages` in a text editor. If there are no error messages from `named`, you can proceed to test the name server.

Before you try the caching name server, you have to specify that name server as your primary one. To do so, make sure that the first line in the `/etc/resolv.conf` file is the following:

```
nameserver 127.0.0.1
```

Now you can use `host` to test the name server. For example, to look up the IP address of `www.gao.gov` by using the caching name server on `localhost`, type the following command:

```
host www.gao.gov localhost
```

Here's the resulting output from the `host` command:

```
Using domain server:
Name: localhost
Address: 127.0.0.1#53
Aliases:
www.gao.gov. has address 161.203.16.2
```

As the output shows, the `host` command uses `localhost` as the DNS server and returns the IP address of `www.gao.gov`. If you get an output similar to this, the caching name server is up and running.

Configuring a primary name server

The best way to configure a primary name server is to start by configuring a caching name server (as explained in the previous sections). Then, add master zones for the domains for which you want this to be the primary name server. For example, suppose I want to define a primary name server for the `naba.net` domain. Here are the steps I go through to configure that primary name server (after I log in as `root`):

1. **Add the following zone statements to** `/etc/named.conf` **file:**

```
zone "naba.net" IN {
    type master;
    file "naba.zone";
};
zone "0.168.192.in-addr.arpa" IN {
    type master;
    file "0.168.192.zone";
};
```

2. **Create the zone file** `/var/named/naba.zone` **with the following lines in it:**

```
$TTL    86400
$ORIGIN naba.net.
@            1D IN SOA        @ root.naba.net (
                             100           ; serial
                             3H            ; refresh
                             15M           ; retry
                             1W            ; expiry
                             1D )          ; minimum

             1D IN NS         @
             1D IN A          192.168.0.7

  wxp    IN    A    192.168.0.2
```

3. **Create the zone file** `/var/named/0.168.192.zone` **with the following lines in it:**

```
$TTL    86400
; Remember zone name is: 0.168.192.in-addr.arpa
@        IN     SOA      naba.net. root.naba.net  (
                                  1       ; Serial
                                  28800   ; Refresh
                                  14400   ; Retry
                                  3600000 ; Expire
                                  86400 ) ; Minimum
         IN     NS       naba.net.

7        IN     PTR      naba.net.
2        IN     PTR      wxp.naba.net.
```

4. **To test the new configuration, restart the** `named` **server with the following command:**

```
service named restart
```

5. **Use** `dig` **or** `host` **to query the DNS server.**

For example, here's how I use `host` to check the address of the host `wxp.naba.net` at the DNS server running on `localhost`:

```
host wxp.naba.net localhost
```

This command results in the following output:

```
Using domain server:
Name: localhost
Address: 127.0.0.1#53
Aliases:

wxp.naba.net has address 192.168.0.2
```

If you want to use `dig` to check the DNS server, type the following command:

```
dig @localhost wxp.naba.net
```

That `@localhost` part specifies the DNS server that `dig` should contact.

When you have successfully used `dig` to contact a DNS server, you can get a bit fancier with what you ask that server to do. Here, for example, is the command I type to try a reverse lookup with the IP address 192.168.0.2:

```
host 192.168.0.2 localhost
```

This command displays the following output:

```
Using domain server:
Name: localhost
Address: 127.0.0.1#53
Aliases:

2.0.168.192.in-addr.arpa domain name pointer wxp.naba.net
```

Understanding Network Information Service (NIS)

Network Information Service (NIS) was developed by Sun Microsystems as a way to share information among all computers in a local area network. The types of information NIS most commonly uses include the following:

+ User names and passwords from files such as `/etc/passwd` and `/etc/shadow`

+ Group information from the `/etc/group` file

Normally, each system has its own copy of information in respective files, and any changes require updating the files on each system individually. Using NIS, you can maintain a single set of configuration files for a collection of computers in an NIS server. All other computers running NIS clients can then access the files. For example, if your user name and password are in the NIS password database, you will be able to log in on all computers on the network running NIS client programs.

NIS was originally called Sun Yellow Pages (YP), but the name *Yellow Pages* is a registered trademark of British Telecom in the United Kingdom, so Sun Microsystems had to change the name. To this day, however, many NIS commands — and the NIS package names — begin with the letters `yp`.

How NIS works

If you want to use NIS in a network, you must set up at least one computer as an NIS server. You can have multiple NIS servers in a network, each serving a different collection of computers. You can also have a master NIS server and one or more slave NIS servers that receive a copy of the master's database. The group of computers a master NIS server supports is called an NIS domain or YP domain.

The master NIS server runs the `ypserv` daemon (this is the NIS server daemon) that maintains the shared information in DBM databases. (DBM refers to Data Base Management, a library of functions that maintains key-value pairs in a database.) The NIS databases are called *maps*. You can create these NIS maps directly from the text-configuration files — such as `/etc/passwd` and `/etc/group` — by using the `/usr/lib/yp/makedbm` program that comes with the NIS server software. More accurately, the `ypserv` daemon uses the `Makefile` in the `/var/yp` directory to create the maps for all shared configuration files.

The master NIS server provides the maps to all NIS client computers. The clients run the `ypbind` daemon through which various client programs access the master NIS server. In addition to a master server, one or more NIS slave servers may be set up to provide the NIS maps in case the master is unavailable or down. The NIS slave servers periodically copy the NIS maps from the master server (using the `/usr/lib/yp/ypxfr` command) and can provide these maps to clients when the master is down.

You can think of NIS as a way of distributing the same set of configuration files among all computers in an NIS domain. You get the benefits of sharing the same files (such as the same user name and password for all machines), yet you can still edit and maintain just one set of files — the files on the master NIS server.

In the next few sections, I explain how to set up your Red Hat Linux system as an NIS client and as an NIS server.

Setting up NIS client

If your network uses NIS centrally to administer users and passwords, you can set up your Red Hat Linux PC as an NIS client. In fact, when you install Red Hat Linux from this book's companion CD-ROMs, you can enable NIS from the Authentication Configuration screen in the GUI installer.

During Red Hat Linux installation, the Authentication Configuration screen shows you a number of different options for authenticating users — the default being shadow passwords and the MD5 password. One of these options is a button labeled Enable NIS. You can click this button to set up your Red Hat Linux PC as an NIS client. Of course, you should do so only if your network is set up with an NIS server.

If you do select the Enable NIS option, you have to provide the following information:

✦ Specify the NIS domain name. The domain name refers to the group of computers the NIS server serves.

✦ Specify the name of the NIS server.

✦ Indicate whether or not you want your PC to use IP broadcast to find NIS servers in the local network.

If you did not configure your system as an NIS client during Red Hat Linux installation, you can do so by performing these general procedures:

1. Define your NIS domain name.

2. Set up the NIS configuration file (`/etc/yp.conf`).

In this file, you specify the master NIS and slave servers that provide NIS maps to your Red Hat Linux PC.

3. Configure the NIS client daemon — `ypbind` — to start when your system boots.

I show you how to perform the specific steps to accomplish these tasks in the next three sections.

NIS domain-name setup

The NIS domain name identifies the group of computers that a particular NIS server supports. You can set the NIS domain name of your system by using the `domainname` command. For example, to set your NIS domain name to `admin`, log in as `root` and type the following command in a terminal window:

```
domainname admin
```

If you type `domainname` without any arguments, the command prints the current NIS domain name.

To ensure that the NIS domain name is set as soon as your system boots, the command should be run from one of the startup scripts. You can do so by adding the following line to the `/etc/sysconfig/network` file on your Red Hat Linux system:

```
NISDOMAIN="admin"
```

Of course, you should use the NIS domain name appropriate to your network.

The NIS domain is different from the DNS domain names discussed earlier in this chapter. Pick an NIS domain name that's not related to the DNS domain name. Doing so makes it harder for crackers to guess your NIS domain name (if they know the NIS domain name, there is a risk that they can get the NIS password database).

NIS configuration-file setup

The `ypbind` daemon, described in the next section, needs information about the NIS domains and NIS servers to do its job. It finds this information in the `/etc/yp.conf` configuration file. The `ypbind` daemon reads the `/etc/yp.conf` file when it starts up or when it receives the `SIGHUP` signal (as it does, for example, when you restart `ypbind` with the `kill -HUP` command).

To specify one or more NIS servers for the local domain (which you have already set with the `domainname` command), all you need in `/etc/yp.conf` are lines such as the following:

```
ypserver nisadmin
ypserver 192.168.0.4
```

You can use a name such as `nisadmin` if that name is listed in the `/etc/hosts` file (that way, `ypbind` can resolve the name into an IP address without having to use NIS). Otherwise, you should specify the NIS server's IP address.

In `/etc/yp.conf`, you can also specify specific NIS servers for specific NIS domains, like this:

```
domain sales server nissales
domain admin server nisadmin
```

A third type of entry in the `/etc/yp.conf` file specifies that `ypbind` should use IP broadcast in the local network to find an NIS server for a specified domain. To do so, add a line such as the following to `/etc/yp.conf`:

```
domain admin broadcast
```

NIS client-daemon setup

Every computer in an NIS domain, including the server, runs the `ypbind` daemon. Various NIS client applications, such as `ypwhich`, `ypcat`, and `yppoll`, need the `ypbind` daemon to obtain information from the master NIS server. More precisely, the C library contacts the `ypbind` daemon to locate the NIS server for the domain. Then the C library contacts the server directly to obtain administrative information. The client applications get the information through functions in the C library.

To interactively start `ypbind`, log in as `root` and type the following command:

```
service ypbind start
```

If you want `ypbind` to start when the system boots, type the following commands:

```
chkconfig --add ypbind
chkconfig --level 35 ypbind on
```

Setting up an NIS server

To set up your Red Hat Linux system as an NIS server, first set it up as an NIS client — set the NIS domain name, configure the `/etc/yp.conf` file, and configure the `ypbind` daemon. (Note that the `ypbind` daemon won't work until you have an NIS server up and running.) After the client configuration, you can configure the NIS server. This requires that you perform the following tasks:

✦ Create the NIS maps using `ypinit`.

✦ Configure the master NIS server — `ypserv`.

✦ Optionally, configure one or more slave NIS servers.

I explain these steps in the next two sections.

NIS map creation

Creating NIS maps involves converting the text files, such as `/etc/passwd` and `/etc/group` into DBM files using `makedbm`. The map creation is controlled by `/var/yp/Makefile`, a file that can be used by the `make` command to perform specific tasks.

You can configure what you want the NIS server to share with the clients in the NIS domain. You do so by editing the `Makefile` in the `/var/yp` directory. Open `/var/yp/Makefile` in a text editor and locate the line that begins with `all:`. Here is a typical excerpt from the `Makefile`, showing the comments before the `all:` line:

```
# If you don't want some of these maps built, feel free to comment
# them out from this list.

all: passwd group hosts rpc services netid protocols mail \
    # netgrp shadow publickey networks ethers bootparams printcap \
    # amd.home auto.master auto.home auto.local passwd.adjunct \
    # timezone locale netmasks
```

As the comment lines (the ones that begin with #) indicate, you can comment out any maps you don't want to build. In the preceding example, the maps listed in the last three lines won't be built.

Next, edit the `/var/yp/securenets` file (or create a new file if it does not exist) to specify the IP addresses of client computers that can access the NIS maps. For example, to allow connections from the `localhost` and hosts in the `192.168.0.0` network, use the following as the content of the `/var/yp/securenets` file:

```
# Always allow access for localhost
host      127.0.0.1
# allow connections from any host
# on the 192.168.0.0 network
255.255.255.0   192.168.0.0
```

The last line allows only those computers on the local network with IP addresses in the range `192.168.0.1` through `192.168.0.254` to access the NIS maps.

Next, you should generate the NIS map database by running the `/usr/lib/yp/ypinit` program with the `-m` option. Here is a sample session with that program:

```
/usr/lib/yp/ypinit -m
```

The program asks you for names of hosts that will run NIS servers. It automatically selects your host as an NIS server and prompts for the names of any other NIS servers. You can add the server names one at a time and press Ctrl+D when you're done. Then you have to verify that the list of NIS servers is correct (type **y**). After that, the program generates the NIS maps as specified by the `all:` line in the `Makefile`. The map files are stored in a subdirectory of `/var/yp` that has the same name as the NIS domain name you have previously set for your system. For example, for the NIS domain `admin`, the map files are in the `/var/yp/admin` directory.

Master NIS server configuration

To configure the NIS server daemon, `ypserv`, you have to prepare the configuration file `/etc/ypserv.conf`. You can learn about the syntax of this file by typing the command **man ypserv.conf**.

You can add lines in `/etc/ypserv.conf` that specify access rules — which hosts can access which maps. The format of the access rules is as follows:

```
Host : Map : Security : mangle [: field_to_mangle]
```

The `field_to_mangle` is optional; it indicates which field in the map file should be mangled (the default is the second field because the password is in the second field of most files, such as `/etc/passwd`). To *mangle a field* is to replace it with an `x` if the request comes from an unprivileged host. The rest of the fields have the following meanings:

✦ Host — IP address or a wildcard (*) indicating to whom the rule applies.

✦ Map — Name of the map to which the rule applies. (The names of the maps are the same as those of the map files in the /var/yp/domainname directory, where domainname is your NIS domain name.)

✦ Security — One of the following: none (to allow access always); port (to access from a port less than 1024); deny (to deny access to the map); or des (to require DES authentication).

✦ mangle — One of the following: yes (the field specified by field_to_mangle should be replaced by an x if the request is from unauthorized host) or no (do not mangle).

For example, the following lines in the /etc/ypserv.conf file restrict access to the password map to systems in the 192.168.0 network:

```
192.168.0    :    passwd.byname    : port    : yes
192.168.0    :    passwd.byuid     : port    : yes
```

If you don't specify any access rules, ypserv allows all computers to access all maps.

After you have set up the /etc/ypserv.conf file, you can start the NIS server with the following command:

```
service ypserv start
```

To ensure that ypserv starts whenever you reboot the system, type the following command to enable it:

```
chkconfig --level 35 ypserv on
```

To handle password changes from clients, you must also run the rpc.yppasswdd server on the master NIS server for the domain. The rpc.yppasswdd server enables users on client systems to type the yppasswd command and change their password in the NIS database. If you don't have the rpc.yppasswdd server running on the master NIS server, users will get the following error message when they type the yppasswd command:

```
yppasswd: yppasswdd not running on NIS master host
```

To correct this problem, log in as root, and type

```
service yppasswdd start
```

To start rpc.yppasswdd automatically at system startup, type

```
chkconfig --level 35 yppasswdd on
```

After you have the master NIS server up and running, you can test it by using various NIS client programs, such as `ypwhich`, `yppoll`, `ypcat`, and `ypmatch`.

Configuring a slave NIS server

To set up a system as a slave NIS server, first set it up as an NIS client and verify that the client works. In particular, type **ypwhich -m** and look for a list of NIS maps and the name of the master NIS server for each map. (In the next section, I show you how the `ypwhich -m` command works.)

After you confirm that the system is configured as an NIS client, type the following command to set up the system as a slave NIS server:

```
/usr/lib/yp/ypinit -s nismaster
```

where `nismaster` is the name of the master NIS server for the domain.

Trying out NIS

After you have a master NIS server in your network and you have the `ypbind` client running, you can try out various NIS client programs and other utilities to see if everything is working correctly.

NIS servers and clients use Remote Procedure Call (RPC) to exchange information. RPC requires the `portmap` service, which maps RPC services to TCP and UDP ports. When a server that supports RPC starts up, it registers itself with `portmap` and lists both the services it supports and the ports it uses. Your Red Hat Linux system should already have `portmap` up and running. You can check for it with the following command:

```
ps ax | grep portmap
```

In the output you should see a line showing the `portmap` process. For example, here's a output of this command on a Red Hat Linux system:

```
  525 ?        S     0:00 portmap
26222 pts/2    S     0:00 grep portmap
```

To see if the `ypserv` and `ypbind` processes are running on the master NIS server, type the following command:

```
rpcinfo -p
```

The output should show `ypserv` and `ypbind` in the last column.

To figure out which NIS server your system is using, try the `ypwhich` command. Here is a typical example:

```
ypwhich
```

The output should be the name of the host that runs the NIS master server.

You can also use the ypwhich command to view the master NIS server for all available maps, by typing this command:

```
ypwhich -m
```

The output shows a list of the available NIS maps — and, for each map, the name of its master NIS server.

To view the name of the master NIS server and information about a specific NIS map, use the yppoll command. For example, here is a yppoll query for the passwd.byname map:

```
yppoll passwd.byname
```

The output shows the NIS domain name and the name of the master server.

Use the ypcat command to print the values of the keys in an NIS map. For example, here is a ypcat query for the NIS map group.byname:

```
ypcat group.byname
```

The output is a list of group names and group IDs. Here's a typical output:

```
ivy:!:503:
ashley:!:502:
emily:!:501:
naba:!:500:
```

You can use ypmatch to look at the entries in an NIS map that match a specific key. For example, here is a ypmatch command line that looks for entries that match the key naba in the group.byname map:

```
ypmatch naba group.byname
```

Here's the output that matches the key naba:

```
naba:!:500:
```

If you compare this with the output from ypcat that shows all the group names, you can see that ypmatch shows the line corresponding to the group name naba.

Chapter 6: Running Samba and NFS

In This Chapter

✔ **Sharing files with NFS**

✔ **Using the Red Hat NFS Server Configuration tool**

✔ **Installing and configuring Samba**

✔ **Setting up a Windows server using Samba**

*I*f your local area network is like many others, it needs the capability to share files between systems that run Linux and other systems that don't. Thus, Red Hat Linux includes two prominent file-sharing services:

✦ **Network File System (NFS)** is for sharing files with other UNIX systems (or PCs with NFS client software)

✦ **Samba** is for file sharing and print sharing with Windows systems.

In this chapter, I describe how to share files using both NFS and Samba.

Sharing Files through NFS

Sharing files through NFS is simple and involves two basic steps:

✦ On the Red Hat Linux system that runs the NFS server, you export (share) one or more directories by listing them in the /etc/exports file and by running the exportfs command. In addition, you must run the NFS server by logging in as root and typing the command **service nfs start**.

✦ On each client system, you use the mount command to mount the directories that your server has exported.

The only problem in using NFS is that each client system must support it. Microsoft Windows doesn't come with NFS. That means you have to buy NFS software separately if you want to share files by using NFS. However, it makes sense to use NFS if all systems on your LAN run Linux (or other variants of UNIX with built-in NFS support).

Note that NFS has security vulnerabilities. You should not set up NFS on systems directly connected to the Internet.

In the next few sections, I walk you through NFS setup, using an example of two Red Hat Linux PCs on a LAN.

Exporting a file system with NFS

Start with the server system that exports — makes available to the client systems — the contents of a directory. On the server, you must run the NFS service and also designate one or more file systems that are to be exported — made available to the client systems.

To export a file system, you have to add an appropriate entry to the /etc/exports file. For example, suppose you want to export the /home directory and you want to enable the host named LNBP75 to mount this file system for read and write operations. You can do so by adding the following entry to the /etc/exports file:

```
/home LNBP75(rw,sync)
```

If you want to give access to all hosts on a LAN such as 192.168.0.0, you could change this line to:

```
/home 192.168.0.0/24(rw,sync)
```

Every line in the /etc/exports file has this general format:

```
directory     host1(options)   host2(options)   ...
```

The first field is the directory being shared via NFS, followed by one or more fields that specify which hosts can mount that directory remotely and a number of options within parentheses. You can specify the hosts with names or IP addresses, including ranges of addresses.

The options within parentheses denote the kind of access each host is granted and how user and group IDs from the server are mapped to ID the client. (For example, if a file is owned by root on the server, what owner should that be on the client?) Within the parentheses, commas separate the options. For example, if a host is allowed both read and write access — and all IDs are to be mapped to the anonymous user (by default this is the user named nobody) — then the options would look like this:

```
(rw,all_squash)
```

Table 6-1 shows the options you can use in the /etc/exports file. There are two types of options — general options and user ID mapping options.

Table 6-1	Options in /etc/exports
This Option	*Does the Following*
General Options	
secure	Allows connections only from ports 1024 or lower (default).
insecure	Allows connections from 1024 or higher.
ro	Allows read-only access (default).
rw	Allows both read and write access.
sync	Performs write operations (this means writing information to the disk) when requested (by default).
async	Performs write operations when the server is ready.
no_wdelay	Performs write operations immediately.
wdelay	Waits a bit to see whether related write requests arrive, and then performs them together (by default).
hide	Hides an exported directory that's a subdirectory of another exported directory (by default).
no_hide	Behaves exactly the opposite of hide.
subtree_check	Performs subtree checking, which involves checking parent directories of an exported subdirectory whenever a file is accessed (by default).
no_subtree_check	Turns off subtree checking (opposite of subtree_check).
insecure_locks	Allows insecure file locking.
User ID Mapping Options	
all_squash	Maps all user IDs and group IDs to the anonymous user on the client.
no_all_squash	Maps remote user and group IDs to similar IDs on the client (by default).
root_squash	Maps remote root user to the anonymous user on the client (by default).
no_root_squash	Maps remote root user to the local root user.
anonuid=UID	Sets the user ID of the anonymous user to be used for the all_squash and root_squash options.
anongid=GID	Sets the group ID of the anonymous user to be used for the all_squash and root_squash options.

After adding the entry in the /etc/exports file, manually export the file system by typing the following command in a terminal window:

```
exportfs -a
```

This command exports all file systems defined in the /etc/exports file.

Now you can start the NFS server processes. To do so, log in as `root` and type the following command in a terminal window:

```
service nfs start
```

If you want the NFS server to start when the system boots, type the following command to turn it on:

```
chkconfig --level 35 nfs on
```

When the NFS service is up, the server side of NFS is ready. Now you can try to mount the exported file system from a client system, and access the exported file system as needed.

If you ever make any changes to the exported file systems listed in the `/etc/exports` file, remember to restart the NFS service. To do so, log in as `root` and type the following command in a terminal window:

```
service nfs restart
```

Mounting an NFS file system

To access an exported NFS file system on a client system, you have to mount that file system on a mount point. The *mount point* is nothing more than a local directory. For example, suppose you want to access the `/home` directory exported from the server named LNBP200 at the local directory `/mnt/lnbp200` on the client system. To do so, follow these steps:

1. **Log in as** `root` **and create the directory with the command**

    ```
    mkdir /mnt/lnbp200
    ```

2. **Type the following command to mount the directory from the remote system (**LNBP200**) on the local directory** `/mnt/lnbp200`**:**

    ```
    mount lnbp200:/home /mnt/lnbp200
    ```

After these steps, you can view and access exported files from the local directory `/mnt/lnbp200`.

To confirm that the NFS file system is indeed mounted, log in as `root` on the client system and type **mount** in a terminal window. You should see a line similar to the following about the NFS file system:

```
lnbp200:/home/public on /mnt/lnbp200 type nfs (rw,addr=192.168.0.4)
```

Using the Red Hat NFS Server Configuration tool

Red Hat Linux comes with a graphical NFS Server Configuration tool that makes it easy to configure and start the NFS server. To configure the NFS server using this tool, follow these steps:

1. Log in as `root` **and choose Main Menu⇨System Settings⇨Server Settings⇨NFS Server from the GNOME or KDE desktop.**

The NFS Server Configuration window appears.

2. Click Add on the toolbar.

The Add NFS Share dialog box appears.

3. Use the dialog box to add directories you want to share via NFS.

Start by specifying the directory, who has access to it (the hosts or IP addresses), and what type of access (read-only or read-write). Figure 6-1 shows the settings for `/home` directory being shared read-write with all hosts in the 192.168.0.0 network.

Figure 6-1:
Specify
the share
directory
and basic
permissions
from this
dialog box.

4. Click the General Options tab in the Add NFS Share dialog box and set the options you want (as shown in Figure 6-2).

These options correspond to the options listed in the General Options section of Table 6-1.

Figure 6-2:
Specify the
general
options for a
NFS share
from this
dialog box.

5. **Click the User Access tab in the Add NFS Share dialog box and set the options you want (Figure 6-3).**

   These options correspond to the options listed in the User ID Mapping Options section of Table 6-1.

Figure 6-3:
Specify the
user access
options for a
NFS share
from this
dialog box.

6. **Click OK in the Add NFS Share dialog box.**

   The NFS Configuration tool saves the settings in the /etc/exports file and starts the NFS server.

7. **Choose File⇨Quit to exit the NFS Configuration tool.**

After completing these steps, you can mount the NFS shares on other hosts in your network.

Setting Up a Windows Server Using Samba

If you rely on Windows for file sharing and print sharing, then you probably use Windows in your servers and clients. If so, you can still move to a Red Hat Linux PC as your server without losing Windows file- and print-sharing capabilities; Red Hat Linux can be set up as a Windows server. When you install Red Hat Linux from this book's companion CD-ROMs, you also get a chance to install the Samba software package, which performs that setup. All you have to do is select the Windows File Server package group during installation.

After you install and configure Samba on your Linux PC, your client PCs —
even if they're running the old Windows for Workgroups operating system
or the more recent Windows 95/98/NT/2000/XP versions — can access
shared disks and printers on the Red Hat Linux PC. To do so, they use the
Server Message Block (SMB) protocol, the underlying protocol in Windows
file and print sharing.

With the Samba package installed, you can make your Red Hat Linux PC a
Windows client, which means that the Red Hat Linux PC can access the
disks and printers that a Windows server manages.

The Samba software package has these major components:

✦ `/etc/samba/smb.conf`: This is the Samba configuration file the SMB
server uses.

✦ `/etc/samba/smbusers`: This Samba configuration file shows the Samba
user names corresponding to user names on the local Red Hat Linux PC.

✦ `nmbd`: This is the NetBIOS name server, which clients use to look up
servers. (NetBIOS stands for Network Basic Input/Output System —
an interface that applications use to communicate with network
transports, such as TCP/IP.)

✦ `nmblookup`: This command returns the IP address of a Windows PC
identified by its NetBIOS name.

✦ `smbadduser`: This program adds users to the SMB password file.

✦ `smbcacls`: This program manipulates Windows NT access control lists
(ACLs) on shared files.

✦ `smbclient`: This is the Windows client, which runs on Linux and allows
Linux to access the files and printer on any Windows server.

✦ `smbcontrol`: This program sends messages to the `smbd`, `nmbd`, or
`winbindd` processes.

✦ `smbd`: The SMB server, which accepts connections from Windows clients
and provides file- and print-sharing services.

✦ `smbmount`: This program mounts a Samba share directory on a Red Hat
Linux PC.

✦ `smbpasswd`: This program changes the password for an SMB user.

✦ `smbprint`: This script enables printing on a printer on a SMB server.

✦ `smbstatus`: This command lists the current SMB connections for the
local host.

✦ `smbtar`: This program backs up SMB shares directly to tape drives on
the Red Hat Linux system.

**Book VIII
Chapter 6**

**Running Samba
and NFS**

✦ `smbumount`: This program unmounts a currently mounted Samba share directory.

✦ `testparm`: This program ensures that the Samba configuration file is correct.

✦ `winbindd`: This server resolves names from Windows NT servers.

In the following sections, I describe how to install Samba from the companion CD-ROM and how to print from the Red Hat Linux PC to a shared printer on a Windows PC.

Checking whether Samba is installed

Check whether Samba is installed by typing the following command in a terminal window:

```
rpm -q samba
```

If you see an output similar to the following, Samba is already installed on your system:

```
samba-3.0.0-5rc1
```

If you get a message saying that the package isn't installed, follow these steps to install Samba from this book's companion CD-ROM:

1. **Log in as** `root` **and insert the first DVD into the drive. If you're using GNOME or KDE, the DVD should automatically be mounted. If not, type the following command to mount the DVD:**

    ```
    mount /mnt/cdrom
    ```

2. **Change the directory to the DVD — specifically to the directory where the Red Hat Package Manager (RPM) packages are located — with the following command:**

    ```
    cd /mnt/cdrom/RedHat/RPMS
    ```

3. **Use the following rpm command to install Samba:**

    ```
    rpm -ivh samba*
    ```

    If Samba is already installed, this command returns an error message. Otherwise, the rpm command installs Samba on your system by copying various files to their appropriate locations.

After installing the Samba software you have to configure Samba before you can use it.

Configuring Samba

To set up the Windows file-sharing and print-sharing services, use the graphical Samba Server Configuration tool following these steps:

1. **Choose Main Menu⇨System Settings⇨Server Settings⇨Samba.**

   If you aren't logged in as root, enter the root password when prompted. Then the Samba Server Configuration window appears.

2. **Click the Add button.**

   The Create Samba Share dialog box appears.

3. **Enter the name of the directory to share or click Browse and select a directory (the directory must already exist). Also select the permission — either read-only or both read and write (see Figure 6-4).**

   Figure 6-4 shows a typical example that shares the /home/public directory. If the directory does not exist, you can create the directory by logging in as root and typing **mkdir /home/public** in a terminal window.

4. **On the Access tab of the Create Samba Share dialog box, type in the users who should have access to the shared directory or select the Allow Access to Everyone radio button, and then click OK.**

Figure 6-4: Enter information about the directory you want to share.

The Samba Server Configuration tool creates the Samba share by adding entries in the configuration file /etc/samba/smb.conf.

5. **To set the Samba server's workgroup name, choose Preferences⇨ Server Settings in the Samba Server Configuration tool. Then enter the same workgroup name as your Windows network in the Basic tab of the Server Settings dialog box (see Figure 6-5).**

Figure 6-5:
Enter the name of your workgroup and a description.

6. **On the Security tab of the Server Settings dialog box, select the name of guest user (if you want one) and select the authentication mode.**

   If you set the authentication mode as User, users can log in with a username and password to access the Samba share.

7. **To add users who can access the Samba share, choose Preferences⇨ Samba Users in the Samba Server Configuration tool; in the Samba Users dialog box, click Add User and fill in the requested information — user name and password — in the Create New Samba User dialog box.**

   Start by identifying the Unix username and then set a Samba username and Samba password for that user (see Figure 6-6).

Figure 6-6:
Add information about users who can access the Samba share.

8. **When you're done adding users, click OK to close the Samba Users dialog box.**

This creates the appropriate Samba configuration files in the /etc/samba directory and starts the Samba service. In particular, the file /etc/samba/smb.conf contains the configuration details for the Samba share you just created.

After adding a Samba share, type the following command to verify that the Samba configuration file is okay:

```
testparm
```

If the command says that it loaded the files okay, you're all set to go. The testparm command also displays the contents of the Samba configuration file.

To start the SMB services automatically when the system reboots, type the following command:

```
chkconfig --level 35 smb on
```

Trying out Samba

You can now try to access the Samba server on the Red Hat Linux system from one of the Windows systems on the LAN. Double-click the Network Neighborhood icon on the Windows 95/98/Me desktop. On Windows XP, choose Start⇨My Network Places and then click View Workgroup Computers. This should show all the computers on the same workgroup.

As you can see from the label (Figure 6-6), Lnblp1 is actually a Red Hat Linux system running Samba.

Figure 6-7:
You can view the Fedora Samba server from Windows XP.

**Book VIII
Chapter 6**

Running Samba and NFS

When you see the Samba server, you can open it by double-clicking the icon. You're prompted for your Samba username and the Samba password, and, after you enter that information correctly, you can access the folders and printers (if any) on the Samba share. For example, Figure 6-8 shows the shared resources on my Samba server running on Fedora. As you can see, there are two shared folders — one is my home directory and the other is the `public` share that I've created with the Samba Server Configuration tool. You can then open these folders to further explore the contents of the directories.

Figure 6-8:
Shared
resources
on a Fedora
Samba
server, as
viewed from
Windows
XP.

Book IX

Programming

The 5th Wave — By Rich Tennant

@RICHTENNANT

My job consists of working with the kernel all day.

Contents at a Glance

Chapter 1: Red Hat Linux Programming Essentials

In This Chapter

✔ Learning programming

✔ Exploring the software development tools in Red Hat Linux

✔ Compiling and linking programs with GCC

✔ Learning to use make

✔ Debugging programs with gdb

✔ Understanding the implications of GNU GPL and LGPL

Your Red Hat Linux system comes loaded with all the tools you need to develop software. In particular, it has all the GNU software development tools, such as GCC (C and C++ compiler), GNU make, and the GNU debugger. In this chapter, I introduce you to programming, describe these software development tools, and show you how to use them. Although I use examples in the C and C++ programming languages, the focus is not on showing how to program in those languages, but to show how to use various software development tools (such as compilers, make, and debugger).

I also briefly explain how the Free Software Foundation's GNU Public License (GPL) may affect any plans you might have to develop Linux software. You need to know this because you use GNU tools and GNU libraries to develop software in Linux.

Learning Programming

If you've written computer programs in any programming language, you can start writing programs on your Red Hat Linux system very quickly. If you've never written a computer program, however, you need two basic resources before you get into it: a look at the basics of programming, and a quick review of computers and the major parts that make them up. In this section, I give you an overview of computer programming — just enough to get you going.

A simplified view of a computer

Before you get a feel for computer programming, you need to understand where computer programs fit into the rest of your computer. Figure 1-1 shows a simplified view of a computer, highlighting the major parts that are important to a programmer.

Figure 1-1:
A simplified view of a computer and how it runs programs.

At the heart of a computer is the *central processing unit* (CPU) that performs the instructions contained in a computer program. The specific piece of hardware that does the job (which its makers call a *microprocessor* and the rest of us call a *chip*) varies by system: In a Pentium PC, it's a Pentium; in a Sun SPARC workstation, it's a SPARC chip; in an HP UNIX workstation, it's a PA-RISC chip. These microprocessors have different capabilities but the same mission: Tell the computer what to do.

Random Access Memory (RAM), or just *memory*, serves as the storage for computer programs while they're being executed by the CPU. If a program works on some data, that data is also stored in the memory. The contents of the memory are not permanent; they go away (never to return) when the computer is shut down or when a program is no longer running.

The *hard disk*, or *disk*, serves as the permanent storage space for computer programs and data. The disk is organized into files, which are in turn organized in hierarchical directories and subdirectories (somewhat like organizing paper folders into the drawers in a file cabinet). Each file is essentially a block of storage capable of holding a variety of information. For example, a file may be a human-readable text file — or it may be a collection of computer instructions that makes sense only to the CPU. When you create computer programs, you work a lot with files.

For a programmer, the other two important items are the *input* and *output* — the way a program gets input from the user and displays output to the user. The user provides input through the keyboard and output appears on the monitor. However, a program may also accept input from a file and send output to a file.

Role of the operating system

The operating system is a special collection of computer programs whose primary purpose is to load and run other programs. All operating systems include one or more command processors (called *shells* in Red Hat Linux) that allow users to type commands and perform tasks such as running a program or printing a file. Most operating systems also include a graphical user interface (such as GNOME and KDE in Red Hat Linux) that allows the user to perform most tasks by clicking on-screen icons. Red Hat Linux, Windows (whether the NT, 2000, or XP version), and various versions of UNIX are examples of operating systems.

It's the operating system that gives a computer its personality. For example, you can run Windows 2000 or Windows XP on a PC. On that same PC, you can also install and run Red Hat Linux. That means, depending on the operating system installed on it, the selfsame PC could be a Windows 2000, Windows XP, or a Red Hat Linux system.

Computer programs are built "on top of" the operating system. That means a computer program must make use of the capabilities that the operating system includes. For example, computer programs read and write files by using built-in capabilities of the operating system. (And if the operating system can't make coffee, then no program can tell it to and still expect positive results.)

Although the details vary, most operating systems support a number of similar concepts. As a programmer, you need to be familiar with the following handful of concepts:

✦ A *process* is a computer program that is currently running in the computer. Most operating systems allow multiple processes to run simultaneously.

✦ A *command processor*, or *shell*, is a special program that allows the user to type commands and perform various tasks, such as run any program, look at a host of files, or print a file. In Windows 2000 or Windows XP, you can type commands in a Command Prompt window.

✦ The term *command line* refers to the commands that a user types to the command processor. Usually a command line contains a command and one or more *options* — the command is the first word in the line and the rest are the options (specific behaviors demanded of the computer).

✦ *Environment variables* are essentially text strings with a name. For example, the PATH environment variable refers to a string that contains the names of directories. Operating systems use environment variables to provide useful information to processes. To see a list of environment variables in a Windows 2000 or Windows XP system, type **SET** in the Command Prompt window. In Red Hat Linux, you can use the printenv command to see the environment variables.

Basics of computer programming

A *computer program* is a sequence of instructions for performing a specific task like adding two numbers or searching for some text in a file. Consequently, computer programming involves *creating* that list of instructions, telling the computer how to complete a specific task. The exact instructions depend on the programming language that you use. For most programming languages, you have to go through the following steps to create a computer program:

1. Use a text editor to type in the sequence of commands from the programming language.

This is the sequence of commands that accomplishes your task. This human-readable version of the program is called the *source file* or *source code*. You can create the source file using any application (such as a word processor) that can save a document in plain text form.

Always save your source code as plain text (the filename depends on the type of programming language). Word processors can sometimes put extra instructions in their documents that tell the computer to display the text in a particular font or other format. Trust me, your program is much better off without such stuff.

2. Use a *compiler* program to convert that text file — the source code — from human-readable form into machine-readable *object code*.

Typically, this step also combines several object code files into a single machine-readable computer program, something that the computer can actually run.

3. Use a special program called *debugger* to track down any errors and find which lines in the source file might have caused the errors.

4. Go back to Step 1 and use the text editor to fix the errors and repeat the rest of the steps.

The first three steps are referred to as the *Edit-Compile-Debug cycle* of programming because most programmers have to repeat this sequence several times before a program works correctly.

In addition to learning the basic programming steps, you also need to be familiar with the following terms and concepts:

✦ *Variables* are used to store different types of data. You can think of each variable as being a placeholder for data — kind of like a mailbox, with a name and room to store data. The content of the variable is its value.

✦ *Expressions* combine variables by using operators. An expression may add several variables; another may extract a part of a string.

✦ *Statements* perform some action, such as assigning a value to a variable or printing a string.

✦ *Flow-control statements* allow statements to be executed in various orders, depending on the value of some expression. Typically, flow-control statements include `for`, `do-while`, `while`, and `if-then-else` statements.

✦ *Functions* (also called *subroutines* or *routines*) allow you to group several statements and give them a name. This feature allows you to execute the same set of statements by invoking the function that represents those statements. Typically, a programming language provides many predefined functions to perform tasks such as opening (and reading from) a file.

Exploring the Software Development Tools in Red Hat Linux

Red Hat Linux includes these traditional UNIX software development tools:

✦ Text editors such as `vi` and `emacs` for editing the source code. (To learn more about `vi`, see Book II, Chapter 6.)

✦ A C compiler for compiling and linking programs written in C — the programming language of choice for writing UNIX applications (though nowadays many programmers are turning to C++ and Java). Red Hat Linux includes the GNU C and C++ compilers. Originally, the GNU C Compiler was known as GCC — which now stands for *GNU Compiler Collection* (see description in `gcc.gnu.org`).

✦ The GNU `make` utility for automating the software *build process* — the process of combining object modules into an executable or a library.

✦ A debugger for debugging programs. Red Hat Linux includes the GNU debugger `gdb`.

✦ A version-control system to keep track of various revisions of a source file. Linux comes with RCS (Revision Control System) and CVS (Concurrent Versions System). Nowadays most open-source projects use CVS as their version-control system.

These tools are installed automatically if you select the Development Tools when you install Red Hat Linux from this book's companion DVD. In the next few sections, I briefly describe how to use these software development tools to write applications for Red Hat Linux.

GNU C and C++ compilers

The most important software development tool in Red Hat Linux is GCC — the GNU C and C++ compiler. In fact, GCC can compile three languages: C, C++, and Objective-C (a language that adds object-oriented programming capabilities to C). You use the same gcc command to compile and link both C and C++ source files. The GCC compiler supports ANSI standard C, making it easy to port any ANSI C program to Linux. In addition, if you've ever used a C compiler on other UNIX systems, you're right at home with GCC.

Using GCC

Use the gcc command to invoke GCC. By default, when you use the gcc command on a source file, GCC preprocesses, compiles, and links to create an executable file. However, you can use GCC options to stop this process at an intermediate stage. For example, you might invoke gcc by using the -c option to compile a source file and to generate an object file, but not to perform the link step.

Using GCC to compile and link a few C source files is very simple. Suppose you want to compile and link a simple program made up of two source files. I use the following program source for this task; it's stored in the file area.c, and it's the main program that computes the area of a circle whose radius is specified through the command line:

```
#include <stdio.h>
#include <stdlib.h>

/* Function prototype */
double area_of_circle(double r);

int main(int argc, char **argv)
{
   if(argc < 2)
   {
     printf("Usage: %s radius\n", argv[0]);
     exit(1);
   }
   else
   {
     double radius = atof(argv[1]);
```

```
      double area = area_of_circle(radius);
      printf("Area of circle with radius %f = %f\n",
         radius, area);
   }
   return 0;
}
```

We need another file that actually computes the area of a circle. Here's the listing for the file circle.c, where I define a function that computes the area of a circle:

```
#include <math.h>

#define SQUARE(x) ((x)*(x))

double area_of_circle(double r)
{
   return 4.0 * M_PI * SQUARE(r);
}
```

For such a simple program, of course, I could have placed everything in a single file, but I needed this contrived example to show you how to handle multiple files.

To compile these two files and to create an executable file named area, you use this command:

```
gcc -o area area.c circle.c
```

This invocation of GCC uses the -o option to specify the name of the executable file. (If you don't specify the name of an output file with the -o option, GCC saves the executable code in a file named a.out.)

If you have too many source files to compile and link, you can compile the files individually and generate *object files* (that have the .o extension). That way, when you change a source file, you need to compile only that file — then you just link the compiled file to all the object files. The following commands show how to separate the compile and link steps for the sample program:

```
gcc -c area.c
gcc -c circle.c
gcc -o area area.o circle.o
```

The first two commands run gcc with the -c option compiling the source files. The third gcc command links the object files into an executable named area.

In case you are curious, here's how you run the `area` program (to compute the area of a circle with a radius of 1):

```
./area 1
```

The program generates the following output:

```
Area of circle with radius 1.000000 = 12.566371
```

Incidentally, you have to add the `./` prefix to the program's name (`area`) only if the current directory is not in the `PATH` environment variable. There is no harm in adding the prefix, even if your `PATH` contains the current directory.

Compiling C++ programs

GNU CC is a combined C and C++ compiler, so the `gcc` command also can compile C++ source files. GCC uses the file extension to determine whether a file is C or C++. C files have a lowercase `.c` extension, whereas C++ files end with `.C` or `.cpp`.

Although the `gcc` command can compile a C++ file, that command does not automatically link with various class libraries that C++ programs typically require. That's why it's easier to compile and link a C++ program by using the `g++` command, which, in turn, runs `gcc` with appropriate options.

Suppose you want to compile the following simple C++ program stored in a file named `hello.C` (it's customary to use an uppercase C extension for C++ source files):

```
#include <iostream>

int main()
{
   using namespace std;
   cout << "Hello from Red Hat Linux!" << endl;
}
```

To compile and link this program into an executable program named `hello`, use this command:

```
g++ -o hello hello.C
```

The command creates the `hello` executable, which you can run as follows:

```
./hello
```

The program displays the following output:

```
Hello from Red Hat Linux!
```

A host of GCC options controls various aspects of compiling C and C++ programs.

Exploring GCC options

Here is the basic syntax of the `gcc` command:

```
gcc options filenames
```

Each option starts with a hyphen (`-`) and usually has a long name, such as `-funsigned-char` or `-finline-functions`. Many commonly used options are short, however, such as `-c`, to compile only, and `-g`, to generate debugging information (needed to debug the program by using the GNU debugger, `gdb`).

You can view a summary of all GCC options by typing the following command in a terminal window:

```
man gcc
```

Then you can browse through the commonly used GCC options. Usually, you do not have to provide GCC options explicitly because the default settings are fine for most applications. Table 1-1 lists some of the GCC options you may use.

Table 1-1	Commonly Used GCC Options
Option	*Meaning*
`-ansi`	Support ANSI standard C (ISO C89) syntax only. (This option disables some GNU C-specific features, such as the `asm` and `typeof` keywords.)
`-c`	Compile and generate object file only.
`-DMACRO`	Define the macro with the string "1" as its value.
`-DMACRO=DEFN`	Define the macro as `DEFN` where `DEFN` is some text string.
`-E`	Run only the C preprocessor.
`-fallow-single-precision`	Perform all math operations in single precision.
`-fpcc-struct-return`	Return all `struct` and `union` values in memory, rather than return in registers. (Returning values this way is less efficient, but at least it's compatible with other compilers.)
`-fPIC`	Generate position-independent code (PIC) suitable for use in a shared library.
`-freg-struct-return`	When possible, return `struct` and `union` values in registers.

(continued)

Table 1-1 *(continued)*

Option	Meaning
-g	Generate debugging information. (The GNU debugger can use this information.)
-I *DIRECTORY*	Search the specified directory for files you include by using the #include preprocessor directive.
-L *DIRECTORY*	Search the specified directory for libraries.
-l *LIBRARY*	Search the specified library when linking.
-mcpu=*cputype*	Optimize code for a specific processor (*cputype* can take many different values — some common ones are i386, i486, i586, and i686).
-o *FILE*	Generate the specified output file (used to designate the name of an executable file).
-O0	Do not optimize.
-O or -O1	Optimize the generated code.
-O2	Optimize even more.
-O3	Perform optimizations beyond those done for -O2.
-Os	Optimize for size (to reduce the total amount of code).
-pedantic	Generate errors if any non-ANSI standard extensions are used.
-pg	Add extra code to the program so that, when run, it generates information the gprof program can use to display timing details for various parts of the program.
-shared	Generate a shared object file (typically used to create a shared library).
-U*MACRO*	Undefine the specified macro.
-v	Display the version number of GCC.
-w	Don't generate any warning messages.
-Wl,*OPTION*	Pass the *OPTION* string (containing multiple comma-separated options) to the linker. To create a shared library named libXXX.so.1, for example, use the following flag: -Wl,-soname,libXXX.so.1.

The GNU make utility

When an application is made up of more than a few source files, compiling and linking the files by manually typing the gcc command can get very tiresome. Also, you do not want to compile every file whenever you change something in a single source file. This is where the GNU make utility comes to your rescue.

The `make` utility works by reading and interpreting a *makefile* — a text file that describes which files are required to build a particular program, as well as how to compile and link the files to build the program. Whenever you change one or more files, `make` determines which files should be recompiled — and issues the appropriate commands for compiling those files and rebuilding the program.

Makefile names

By default, GNU `make` looks for a makefile that has one of the following names, in the order shown:

✦ `GNUmakefile`

✦ `makefile`

✦ `Makefile`

In UNIX systems, using `Makefile` as the name of the makefile is customary because it appears near the beginning of directory listings where the upper-case names appear before the lowercase names.

When you download software from the Internet, you usually find a `Makefile`, together with the source files. To build the software, you have only to type `make` at the shell prompt and `make` takes care of all the steps necessary to build the software.

If your makefile does not have a standard name (such as `Makefile`), you have to use the `-f` option with `make` to specify the makefile's name. If your makefile is called `myprogram.mak`, for example, you have to run `make` using the following command line:

```
make -f myprogram.mak
```

The makefile

For a program that's made up of several source and header files, the makefile specifies the following:

✦ The items that `make` will create — usually the object files and the executable. It's common to use the term *target* to refer to any item that `make` has to create.

✦ The files or other actions required to create the target.

✦ Which commands should be executed to create each target.

Suppose you have a C++ source file named `form.C` that contains the following preprocessor directive:

```
#include "form.h"  // Include header file
```

The object file `form.o` clearly depends on the source file `form.C` and the header file `form.h`. In addition to these dependencies, you must specify how `make` should convert the `form.C` file to the object file `form.o`. Suppose you want `make` to invoke g++ (because the source file is in C++) with these options:

✦ `-c` (compile only)

✦ `-g` (generate debugging information)

✦ `-O2` (optimize some)

In the makefile, you can express this with the following rule:

```
# This a comment in the makefile
# The following lines indicate how form.o depends
# form.C and form.h and how to create form.o.

form.o: form.C form.h
        g++ -c -g -O2 form.C
```

In this example, the first noncomment line shows `form.o` as the target and `form.C` and `form.h` as the dependent files.

The line following the dependency indicates how to build the target from its dependents. This line must start with a tab.

The benefit of using `make` is that it prevents unnecessary compilations. After all, you can run g++ (or `gcc`) from a shell script to compile and link all the files that make up your application, but the shell script compiles everything, even if the compilations are unnecessary. GNU `make`, on the other hand, builds a target, only if one or more of its dependents have changed since the last time the target was built. `make` verifies this change by examining the time of the last modification of the target and the dependents.

`make` treats the target as the name of a goal to be achieved; the target does not have to be a file. You can have a rule such as this one:

```
clean:
        rm -f *.o
```

This rule specifies an abstract target named `clean` that does not depend on anything. This dependency statement says that to create the target `clean`, GNU `make` should invoke the command `rm -f *.o`, which deletes all files that have the `.o` extension (namely the object files). Thus, the net effect of creating the target named `clean` is to delete the object files.

Variables (or macros)

In addition to the basic capability of building targets from dependents, GNU `make` includes many nice features that make it easy for you to express the dependencies and rules for building a target from its dependents. If you need to compile a large number of C++ files by using GCC with the same options, for example, typing the options for each file is tedious. You can avoid this repetitive task by defining a variable or macro in `make` as follows:

```
# Define macros for name of compiler
CXX= g++

# Define a macro for the GCC flags
CXXFLAGS= -O2 -g -mcpu=i686

# A rule for building an object file
form.o: form.C form.h
        $(CXX) -c $(CXXFLAGS) form.C
```

In this example, `CXX` and `CXXFLAGS` are `make` variables. (GNU `make` prefers to call them *variables*, but most UNIX `make` utilities call them *macros*.)

To use a variable anywhere in the makefile, start with a dollar sign ($) followed by the variable within parentheses. GNU `make` replaces all occurrences of a variable with its definition; thus it replaces all occurrences of `$(CXXFLAGS)` with the string `-O2 -g -mcpu=i686`.

GNU `make` has several predefined variables that have special meanings. Table 1-2 lists these variables. In addition to the variables listed in Table 1-2, GNU `make` considers all environment variables (such as `PATH` and `HOME`) to be predefined variables as well.

Table 1-2	Some Predefined Variables in GNU make
Variable	*Meaning*
`$%`	Member name for targets that are archives. If the target is `libDisp.a(image.o)`, for example, `$%` is `image.o`, and `$@` is `libDisp.a`.
`$*`	Name of the target file without the extension.
`$+`	Names of all dependent files with duplicate dependencies, listed in their order of occurrence.
`$<`	The name of the first dependent file.
`$?`	Names of all dependent files (with spaces between the names) that are newer than the target.
`$@`	Complete name of the target.

(continued)

Table 1-2 *(continued)*

Variable	Meaning
$^	Names of all dependent files, with spaces between the names. Duplicates are removed from the dependent filenames.
AR	Name of the archive-maintaining program (Default value: ar).
ARFLAGS	Flags for the archive-maintaining program (Default value: rv).
AS	Name of the assembler program that converts the assembly language to object code (Default value: as).
ASFLAGS	Flags for the assembler.
CC	Name of the C compiler: (Default value: cc).
CFLAGS	Flags to be passed to the C compiler.
CO	Name of the program that extracts a file from RCS (Default value: co).
COFLAGS	Flags for the RCS co program.
CPP	Name of the C preprocessor (Default value: $(CC) -E).
CPPFLAGS	Flags for the C preprocessor.
CXX	Name of the C++ compiler (Default value: g++).
CXXFLAGS	Flags to be passed to the C++ compiler.
FC	Name of the FORTRAN compiler (Default value: f77).
FFLAGS	Flags for the FORTRAN compiler.
LDFLAGS	Flags for the compiler when it is supposed to invoke the linker ld.
RM	Name of the command to delete a file (Default value: rm -f).

A sample makefile

You can write a makefile easily if you use the predefined variables of GNU make and its built-in rules. Consider, for example, a makefile that creates the executable xdraw from three C source files (xdraw.c, xviewobj.c, and shapes.c) and two header files (xdraw.h and shapes.h). Assume that each source file includes one of the header files. Given these facts, here is what a sample makefile might look like:

```
##############################################################
# Sample makefile
# Comments start with '#'
#
##############################################################

# Use standard variables to define compile and link flags

CFLAGS= -g -O2
# Define the target "all"
```

```
all: xdraw

OBJS=xdraw.o xviewobj.o shapes.o

xdraw: $(OBJS)

# Object files
xdraw.o: Makefile xdraw.c xdraw.h

xviewobj.o: Makefile xviewobj.c xdraw.h

shapes.o: Makefile shapes.c shapes.h
```

This makefile relies on the GNU `make` implicit rules. The conversion of `.c` files to `.o` files uses the built-in rule. Defining the variable `CFLAGS` passes the flags to the C compiler.

The target named `all` is defined as the first target for a reason — if you run GNU `make` without specifying any targets in the command line (see the `make` syntax described in the following section), then the command builds the first target it finds in the makefile. By defining the first target `all` as `xdraw`, you can ensure that `make` builds this executable file, even if you do not explicitly specify it as a target. UNIX programmers traditionally use `all` as the name of the first target, but the target's name is immaterial; what matters is that it is the first target in the makefile.

How to run make

Typically, you run `make` by simply typing the following command at the shell prompt:

```
make
```

When run this way, GNU `make` looks for a file named `GNUmakefile`, `makefile`, or `Makefile` — in that order. If `make` finds one of these makefiles, it builds the first target specified in that `makefile`. However, if `make` does not find an appropriate makefile, it displays the following error message and then exits:

```
make: *** No targets specified and no makefile found.  Stop.
```

If your makefile happens to have a different name from the default names, you have to use the `-f` option to specify the makefile. The syntax of the `make` command with this option looks like this:

```
make -f filename
```

where *filename* is the name of the makefile.

Even when you have a makefile with a default name such as `Makefile`, you may want to build a specific target out of several targets defined in the makefile. In that case, you have to use the following syntax when you run `make`:

```
make target
```

For example, if the makefile contains the target named `clean`, you can build that target with this command:

```
make clean
```

Another special syntax overrides the value of a `make` variable. For example, GNU `make` uses the `CFLAGS` variable to hold the flags used when compiling C files. You can override the value of this variable when you invoke `make`. Here is an example of how you can define `CFLAGS` to be the option `-g -02`:

```
make CFLAGS="-g -02"
```

In addition to these options, GNU `make` accepts several other command-line options. Table 1-3 lists the GNU `make` options.

Table 1-3	Options for GNU make
Option	*Meaning*
-b	Ignore but accept for compatibility with other versions of `make`.
-C DIR	Change to the specified directory before reading the makefile.
-d	Print debugging information.
-e	Allow environment variables to override definitions of similarly named variables in the makefile.
-f FILE	Read *FILE* as the makefile.
-h	Display the list of `make` options.
-i	Ignore all errors in commands executed when building a target.
-I DIR	Search specified directory for included makefiles (the capability to include a file in a makefile is unique to GNU `make`).
-j NUM	Specify the number of commands that `make` can run simultaneously.
-k	Continue to build unrelated targets, even if an error occurs when building one of the targets.
-l LOAD	Don't start a new job if load average is at least *LOAD* (a floating-point number).
-m	Ignore but accept for compatibility with other versions of `make`.
-n	Print the commands to be executed, but do not execute them.

Option	Meaning
-o *FILE*	Do not rebuild the file named *FILE*, even if it is older than its dependents.
-p	Display the make database of variables and implicit rules.
-q	Do not run anything, but return zero if all targets are up-to-date; return 1 if anything needs updating and 2 if an error occurs.
-r	Get rid of all built-in rules.
-R	Get rid of all built-in variables and rules.
-s	Work silently (without displaying the commands as they are executed).
-t	Change the timestamp of the files.
-v	Display the version number of make and a copyright notice.
-w	Display the name of the working directory before and after processing the makefile.
-W FILE	Assume that the specified file has been modified (used with -n to see what happens if you modify that file).

The GNU debugger

Although make automates the process of building a program, that part of programming is the least of your worries when a program does not work correctly or when a program suddenly quits with an error message. You need a debugger to find the cause of program errors. Red Hat Linux includes gdb — the versatile GNU debugger with a command-line interface.

Like any debugger, gdb lets you perform typical debugging tasks, such as the following:

+ Set the breakpoint so that the program stops at a specified line.

+ Watch the values of variables in the program.

+ Step through the program one line at a time.

+ Change variables in an attempt to fix errors.

The gdb debugger can debug C and C++ programs.

Preparing to debug a program

If you want to debug a program by using gdb, you have to ensure that the compiler generates and places debugging information in the executable. The debugging information contains the names of variables in your program and the mapping of addresses in the executable file to lines of code in the source file. gdb needs this information to perform its functions, such as stopping after executing a specified line of source code.

To ensure that the executable is properly prepared for debugging, use the -g option with GCC. You can do this by defining the variable CFLAGS in the makefile as

```
CFLAGS= -g
```

Running gdb

The most common way to debug a program is to run gdb by using the following command:

```
gdb progname
```

progname is the name of the program's executable file. After it runs, gdb displays the following message and prompts you for a command:

```
GNU gdb Red Hat Linux (5.3post-1.20021129.37rh)
Copyright 2003 Free Software Foundation, Inc.
GDB is free software, covered by the GNU General Public License, and you are
welcome to change it and/or distribute copies of it under certain conditions.
Type "show copying" to see the conditions.
There is absolutely no warranty for GDB. Type "show warranty" for details.
This GDB was configured as "i386-redhat-linux-gnu".
(gdb)
```

You can type gdb commands at the (gdb) prompt. One useful command is help — it displays a list of commands as the next listing shows:

```
(gdb) help
List of classes of commands:

aliases -- Aliases of other commands
breakpoints -- Making program stop at certain points
data -- Examining data
files -- Specifying and examining files
internals -- Maintenance commands
obscure -- Obscure features
running -- Running the program
stack -- Examining the stack
status -- Status inquiries
support -- Support facilities
tracepoints -- Tracing of program execution without stopping the program
user-defined -- User-defined commands

Type "help" followed by a class name for a list of commands in that class.
Type "help" followed by command name for full documentation.
Command name abbreviations are allowed if unambiguous.
(gdb)
```

To quit gdb, type **q** and then press Enter.

gdb has a large number of commands, but you need only a few to find the cause of an error quickly. Table 1-4 lists the commonly used gdb commands.

Table 1-4	Commonly Used gdb Commands
This Command	*Does the Following*
`break` *NUM*	Sets a *breakpoint* at the specified line number (the debugger stops at breakpoints).
`bt`	Displays a trace of all stack frames. (This command shows you the sequence of function calls so far.)
`clear` *FILENAME:NUM*	Deletes the breakpoint at a specific line in a source file. For example, `clear xdraw.c:8` clears the breakpoint at line 8 of file `xdraw.c`.
`continue`	Continues running the program being debugged. (Use this command after the program has stopped due to a signal or breakpoint.)
`display` *EXPR*	Displays the value of expression (consisting of variables defined in the program) each time the program stops.
`file` *FILE*	Loads a specified executable file for debugging.
`help` *NAME*	Displays help on the command named *NAME*.
`info break`	Displays a list of current breakpoints, including information on how many times each breakpoint has been reached.
`info files`	Displays detailed information about the file being debugged.
`info func`	Displays all function names.
`info local`	Displays information about local variables of the current function.
`info prog`	Displays the execution status of the program being debugged.
`info var`	Displays all global and static variable names.
`kill`	Ends the program you're debugging.
`list`	Lists a section of the source code.
`make`	Runs the `make` utility to rebuild the executable without leaving `gdb`.
`next`	Advances one line of source code in the current function without stepping into other functions.
`print EXPR`	Shows the value of the expression *EXPR*.
`quit`	Quits `gdb`.
`run`	Starts running the currently loaded executable.
`set variable` *VAR=VALUE*	Sets the value of the variable *VAR* to *VALUE*.
`shell` *CMD*	Executes a UNIX command *CMD*, without leaving `gdb`.
`step`	Advances one line in the current function, stepping into other functions, if any.

(continued)

Table 1-4 *(continued)*

This Command	Does the Following
watch *VAR*	Shows the value of the variable named *VAR* whenever the value changes.
where	Displays the call sequence. Use this command to locate where your program died.
x/*F ADDR*	Examines the contents of the memory location at address *ADDR* in the format specified by the letter *F*, which can be o (octal); x (hex); d (decimal); u (unsigned decimal); t (binary); f (float); a (address); i (instruction); c (char); or s (string). You can append a letter indicating the size of data type to the format letter. Size letters are b (byte); h (halfword, 2 bytes); w (word, 4 bytes); and g (giant, 8 bytes). Typically, *ADDR* is the name of a variable or pointer.

Finding bugs by using gdb

To understand how you can find bugs by using gdb, you need to see an example. The procedure is easiest to show with a simple example, so I start with a rather contrived program that contains a typical bug.

This is the contrived program, which I store in the file dbgtst.c:

```
#include <stdio.h>

static char buf[256];
void read_input(char *s);

int main(void)
{
  char *input = NULL; /* Just a pointer, no storage for
    string */

  read_input(input);

/* Process command. */
  printf("You typed: %s\n", input);

/* ... */
  return 0;
}

void read_input(char *s)
{
  printf("Command: ");
  gets(s);
}
```

This program's `main` function calls the `read_input` function to get a line of input from the user. The `read_input` function expects a character array in which it returns what the user types. In this example, however, `main` calls `read_input` with an uninitialized pointer — that's the bug in this simple program.

Build the program by using `gcc` with the `-g` option:

```
gcc -g -o dbgtst dbgtst.c
```

Ignore the warning message about the `gets` function being dangerous; I'm trying to use the shortcoming of that function to show how `gdb` can be used to track down errors.

To see the problem with this program, run it and type **test** at the `Command` prompt:

```
./dbgtst
Command: test
Segmentation fault
```

The program dies after displaying the `Segmentation fault` message. For such a small program as this, you can probably find the cause by examining the source code. In a real-world application, however, you may not immediately know what causes the error. That's when you have to use `gdb` to find the cause of the problem.

To use `gdb` to locate a bug, follow these steps:

1. **Load the program under** `gdb`. **To load a program named** `dbgtst` **in gdb, type the following:**

```
gdb dbgtst
```

2. **Start executing the program under** `gdb` **by typing the** `run` **command. When the program prompts for input, type some input text.**

The program should fail as it did previously. Here's what happens with the `dbgtst` program:

```
(gdb) run
Starting program: /home/naba/rhls4e/dbgtst
Command: test

Program received signal SIGSEGV, Segmentation fault.
0x420632cc in gets () from /lib/tls/libc.so.6
(gdb)
```

3. Use the `where` command to determine where the program died.

For the `dbgtst` program, this command yields this output:

```
(gdb) where
#0  0x420632cc in gets () from /lib/tls/libc.so.6
#1  0x080483bc in read_input (s=0x0) at dbgtst.c:22
#2  0x0804837e in main () at dbgtst.c:10
#3  0x420154a0 in __libc_start_main () from
    /lib/tls/libc.so.6
(gdb)
```

The output shows the sequence of function calls. Function call #0 — the most recent one — is to a C library function, `gets`. The `gets` call originates in the `read_input` function (at line 22 of the file `dbgtst.c`), which in turn is called from the `main` function at line 10 of the `dbgtst.c` file.

4. Use the `list` command to inspect the lines of suspect source code.

In `dbgtst`, you may start with line 22 of `dbgtst.c` file, as follows:

```
(gdb) list dbgtst.c:22
17          }
18
19          void read_input(char *s)
20          {
21            printf("Command: ");
22            gets(s);
23          }
24
(gdb)
```

After looking at this listing, you should be able to tell that the problem might be the way `read_input` is called. Then you list the lines around line 10 in `dbgtst.c` (where the `read_input` call originates):

```
(gdb) list dbgtst.c:10
5
6           int main(void)
7           {
8             char *input = NULL; /* Just a pointer, no
    storage for string */
9
10            read_input(input);
11
12          /* Process command. */
13            printf("You typed: %s\n", input);
14
(gdb)
```

At this point, you should be able to narrow the problem to the variable named `input`. That variable should be an array, not a NULL (which means zero) pointer.

Fixing bugs in gdb

Sometimes you can fix a bug directly in gdb. For the example program in the preceding section, you can try this fix immediately after the program dies after displaying an error message. Because the example is contrived, I have an extra buffer named buf defined in the dbgtst program, as follows:

```
static char buf[256];
```

I can fix the problem of the uninitialized pointer by setting the variable input to buf. The following session with gdb corrects the problem of the uninitialized pointer (this example picks up immediately after the program has run and died, due to the segmentation fault):

```
(gdb) file dbgtst
A program is being debugged already.  Kill it? (y or n) y

Load new symbol table from "dbgtst"? (y or n) y
Reading symbols from dbgtst...
done.
(gdb) list
1       #include <stdio.h>
2
3       static char buf[256];
4       void read_input(char *s);
5
6       int main(void)
7       {
8          char *input = NULL; /* Just a pointer, no storage
    for string
*/
9
10         read_input(input);
(gdb) break 9
Breakpoint 1 at 0x8048373: file dbgtst.c, line 9.
(gdb) run
Starting program: /home/naba/rhls4e/dbgtst

Breakpoint 1, main () at dbgtst.c:10
10         read_input(input);
(gdb) set var input=buf
(gdb) cont
Continuing.
Command: test
You typed: test

Program exited normally.
(gdb)q
```

As the previous listing shows, if I stop the program just before `read_input` is called and set the variable named `input` to `buf` (which is a valid array of characters), the rest of the program runs fine.

After finding a fix that works in `gdb`, you can make the necessary changes to the source files and make the fix permanent.

Understanding the Implications of GNU Licenses

You have to pay a price for the bounty of Linux — to protect its developers and users, Linux is distributed under the GNU GPL (General Public License), which stipulates the distribution of the source code.

This does not mean, however, that you cannot write commercial software for Linux that you want to distribute (either for free or for a price) in binary form only. You can follow all the rules and still sell your Linux applications in binary form.

When writing applications for Linux, be aware of two licenses:

+ The GNU General Public License (GPL), which governs many Linux pro-grams, including the Linux kernel and GCC

+ The GNU Library General Public License (LGPL), which covers many Linux libraries

The following sections provide an overview of these licenses and some sug-gestions on how to meet their requirements. Because I am not a lawyer, however, don't take anything in this book as legal advice. The full text for these licenses is in text files on your Red Hat Linux system; show these licenses to your legal counsel for a full interpretation and an assessment of applicability to your business.

The GNU General Public License

The text of the GNU General Public License (GPL) is in a file named `COPYING` in various directories in your Red Hat Linux system. For example, type the following commands to read the GPL:

```
cd /usr/share/doc/gdb*
more COPYING
```

The GPL has nothing to do with whether you charge for the software or dis-tribute it for free; its thrust is to keep the software free for all users. GPL does this by requiring that the software is distributed in source-code form and by stipulating that any user can copy and distribute the software in source-code form to anyone else. In addition, everyone is reminded that the software comes with absolutely no warranty.

The software that GPL covers is not in the public domain. Software covered by GPL is always copyrighted, and the GPL spells out the restrictions on the software's copying and distribution. From a user's point of view, of course, GPL's restrictions are not really restrictions; the restrictions are really benefits because the user is guaranteed access to the source code.

If your application uses parts of any software the GPL covers, your application is considered a *derived work*. This means that your application is also covered by GPL, and you must distribute the source code to your application.

Although the GPL covers the Linux kernel, the GPL does not cover your applications that use the kernel services through system calls. Those applications are considered normal use of the kernel.

If you plan to distribute your application in binary form (as most commercial software is distributed), you must make sure your application does not use any parts of any software the GPL covers. Your application may end up using parts of other software when it calls functions in a library. Most libraries, however, are covered by a different GNU license, which I describe in the next section.

You have to watch out for only a few library and utility programs the GPL covers. The GNU dbm (gdbm) database library is one of the prominent libraries GPL covers. The GNU bison parser-generator tool is another utility the GPL covers. If you allow bison to generate code, the GPL covers that code.

Other alternatives for the GNU dbm and GNU bison are not covered by GPL. For a database library, you can use the Berkeley database library db in place of gdbm. For a parser-generator, you may use yacc instead of bison.

The GNU Library General Public License

The text of the GNU Library General Public License (LGPL) is in the file COPYING.LIB. If you have the kernel source installed, a copy of COPYING.LIB file is in one of the source directories. To locate a copy of the COPYING.LIB file on your Red Hat Linux system, type the following command in a terminal window:

```
find /usr/share/doc -name "COPYING*" -print
```

This command lists all occurrences of COPYING and COPYING.LIB in your system. The COPYING file contains the GPL, whereas COPYING.LIB has the LGPL.

The LGPL is intended to allow use of libraries in your applications, even if you do not distribute source code for your application. The LGPL stipulates, however, that users must have access to the source code of the library you use and that users can make use of modified versions of those libraries.

The LGPL covers most Linux libraries, including the C library (`libc.a`). Thus, when you build your application on Red Hat Linux by using the GCC compiler, your application links with code from one or more libraries the LGPL covers. If you want to distribute your application in binary form only, you need to pay attention to LGPL.

One way to meet the intent of the LGPL is to provide the object code for your application and a makefile that relinks your object files with any updated Linux libraries the LGPL covers.

A better way to satisfy the LGPL is to use *dynamic linking*, in which your application and the library are separate entities, even though your application calls functions in the library when it runs. With dynamic linking, users immediately get the benefit of any updates to the libraries without ever having to relink the application.

Chapter 2: Programming in C

In This Chapter

✔ Learning the basics of C programming

✔ Learning the features of the C programming language

✔ Taking stock of the standard C library

✔ Using shared libraries in Red Hat Linux applications

The composition of the C programming language — a sparse core with a large support library — makes it an ideal language for developing software. The core offers a good selection of data types and control structures while all additional tasks, including input and output (I/O), math computations, and access to peripheral devices are relegated to a library of functions. Basically, C allows you get to anything you want in a system. That means you can write anything from device drivers to graphical applications in C. In this chapter, I introduce you to C programming. I also briefly explain the importance of shared libraries and how to create one in Red Hat Linux using the C programming language.

The Structure of a C Program

A typical C program is organized into one or more source files, or modules (Figure 2-1). Each file has a similar structure with comments, preprocessor directives, declarations of variables and functions, and their definitions. You'd usually place each group of related variables and functions in a single source file.

Some files are simply a set of declarations that are used in other files through the #include directive of the C preprocessor. These files are usually referred to as *header files* and have names ending with the .h extension. In Figure 2-1, the file shapes.h is a header file that declares common data structures and functions for the program. Another file, shapes.c, defines the functions. A third file, shapetest.c, implements the main function — this is the function in which the execution of a C program begins. These files with names ending in .c are the source files where you define the functions needed by your program. Although Figure 2-1 shows only one function in each source file, in typical programs there are many functions in a source file.

```
shapes.h
/* File: shapes.h
 * Header file for data structures
 */
#ifndef _SHAPES_H
#define _SHAPES_H

enum shape_type {T_CIRCLE, T_RECTANGLE};
typedef struct RECTANGLE
{
  double x1, y1, x2, y2;
{ RECTANGLE;
typedef struct CIRCLE
{
  double xc, yc, radius;
} CIRCLE;
typedef struct SHAPE
{
  enum shape_type type;
  union
  {
    RECTANGLE r;
    CIRCLE C;
  } u;
} SHAPE;

/* Function protypes */
double compute_area (SHAPE *p_s);
#endif
```

```
shapes.c
/* File: shapes.c
 * Function that computes area of shapes
 */
#include <math.h>
#include "shapes.h"

double compute_area (SHAPE *p_s)
{
  switch(p_s->type)
  {
    case T_CIRCLE:
    {
        CIRCLE *p_c = &(p_c->u.c)
        return M_PI* p_c->radius * p_c -> radius;
    }
    case T_RECTANGLE:
    {
        RECTANGLE *p_r = r(p_s->u.r);
        return fabs  (p_r->x2 - p_r->x1)*
                     (p_r->y2 - p_r->y1)*
    }
  }
}
```

```
shapetest.c
/* File: shapes.c
 * Main program to test shapes.c
 */
#include <stdio.h>
#include "shapes.h"

int main(void)
{
  SHAPE s;
  CIRCLE c;
  s_type = T_CIRCLE;
  p_c->radius = 50.0;
  p_c->xc = p_c->yc = 100.0;
  printf("Area of circle = #f\n",
compute_area(rs));
  return 0;
}
```

Figure 2-1:
Typically, several source files make up a C program.

To create an executable program, you must compile and link the source files. The exact steps for building programs from C source files depend on the compiler and the operating system. For example, in Red Hat Linux, you can compile and link the files shown in Figure 2-1 with the following command:

```
gcc -o shapetest shapetest.c shapes.c
```

This command creates an executable file named shapetest, You can then run that file with the command

```
./shapetest
```

Here is the output the program displays:

```
Area of circle = 7853.981634
```

Declaration versus definition

A *declaration* determines how the program interprets a symbol. A *definition*, on the other hand, actually creates a variable or a function. Definitions cause the compiler to set aside storage for data or code, but declarations do not. For example,

```
Int x, y, z;
```

is a definition of three distinct integer variables, but

```
Extern int x, y, z;
```

is a declaration, indicating that the three integer variables are defined in another source file.

Within each source file, the components of the program are laid out in a standard manner. As the files illustrated in Figure 2-1 show, the typical components of a C source file follow a certain order if you were to scroll down through them on-screen:

1. The file starts with some comments that describe the purpose of the module and provide some other pertinent information, such as the name of the author and revision dates. In C, comments start with /* and end with */.

2. Commands for the preprocessor, known as *preprocessor directives*, follow the comments. The first few directives typically are for including header files and defining constants.

3. Declarations of variables and functions that are visible throughout the file come next. In other words, the names of these variables and functions may be used in any of the functions in this file. Here, you also define variables needed within the file.

4. The rest of the file includes definitions of functions. Inside a function's body, you can define variables that are local to the function and that exist only while the function's code is being executed.

Preprocessor Directives

Preprocessing refers to the first step in translating or compiling a C file into machine instructions. The preprocessor processes the source file and acts on certain commands (called *preprocessor directives*) embedded in the program. These directives begin with the hash mark (#) followed by a keyword. Usually the compiler automatically invokes the preprocessor before beginning compilation, but most compilers give you the option of invoking the preprocessor alone. You can utilize three major capabilities of the preprocessor to make your programs modular, more readable, and easier to customize:

✦ You can use the #include directive to insert the contents of a file into your program. With this, you can place common declarations in one location and use them in all source files through file inclusion. The result is a reduced risk of mismatches between declarations of variables and functions in separate program modules.

✦ Through the #define directive, you can define macros that enable you to replace one string with another. You can use the #define directive to give meaningful names to numeric constants, thus improving the readability of your source files.

✦ With directives such as #if, #ifdef, #else, and #endif, you can compile only selected portions of your program. You can use this feature to write source files with code for two or more systems, but compile only those parts that apply to the computer system on which you compile the program. With this strategy you can maintain multiple versions of a program using a single set of source files.

Including files

You can write modular programs by exploiting the #include directive. This is possible because the C preprocessor enables you to keep commonly used declarations in a single file that you can insert in other source files as needed. ANSI C supports three forms of the #include directive. As a C programmer, you should be familiar with the first two forms:

```
#include <stdio.h>
#include "shapes.h"
```

You use the first form of #include to read the contents of a file — in this case, the standard C header file stdio.h from the default location where all the header files reside. Put the filename within double quotes when the file (for example, shapes.h) is in the current directory. The exact conventions for locating the included files depend on the compiler.

Defining macros

A *macro* is essentially a short name for a reusable block of C code. The code can be as simple as a numerical constant or as complicated as many lines of detailed C code. The idea is that after you define a macro, you can use that macro wherever you want to use that code in your program. When the source file is preprocessed, every occurrence of a macro's name is replaced with its definition.

A common use of macros is to define a symbolic name for a numerical constant and then use the symbol instead of the numbers in your program. This improves the readability of the source code; with a descriptive name, you aren't left guessing why a particular number is being used in the program. You can define such macros in a straightforward manner using the #define directive. Here are some examples:

```
#define PI          3.14159
#define GRAV_ACC    9.80665
#define BUFSIZE     512
```

After these symbols are defined, you can use PI, GRAV_ACC, and BUFSIZE instead of the numerical constants throughout the source file.

Macros, however, can do much more than simply replace a symbol for a constant or some block of code. A macro can accept a parameter and replace each occurrence of that parameter with the provided value when the macro is used in a program. Thus, the code that results from the expansion of a macro can change depending on the parameter you use when running the macro. For example, here is a macro that accepts a parameter and expands to an expression designed to calculate the square of the parameter:

```
#define square(x) ((x)*(x))
```

If you use square(z) in your program, it becomes ((z)*(z)) after the source file is preprocessed. In effect, this macro is equivalent to a function that computes the square of its arguments — except you don't call a function. Instead, the expression generated by the macro is placed directly in the source file.

Conditional directives

You can use the conditional directives, such as #if, #ifdef, #ifndef, #else, #elif, and #endif, to control which parts of a source file are compiled and under what conditions. With this feature, you maintain a single set of source files that can be selectively compiled with different compilers and in different environments. (Another common use is to insert printf statements for debugging that are compiled only if a symbol named DEBUG is defined.) Conditional directives start with #if, #ifdef, or #ifndef — and may be followed by any number of #elif directives (or by none at all). Next comes an optional #else, followed by an #endif directive that marks the end of that conditional block. Here are some common ways of using conditional directives.

To include a header file only once, you can use the following:

```
#ifndef _ _PROJECT_H
#define _ _PROJECT_H
/*  Declarations to be included once */
/* ... */

#endif
```

The following prints a diagnostic message during debugging (when the symbol DEBUG is defined):

```
#ifdef DEBUG
    printf("In read_file: bytes_read = %d\n", bytes_read);
#endif
```

The following example shows how you can include a different header file depending on the type of system for which the program is being compiled. To selectively include a header file, you can use the following:

```
#if CPU_TYPE == I386
    #include <i386\sysdef.h>
#elif CPU_TYPE == M68K
    #include <m68k\sysdef.h>
#else
    #error Unknown CPU type.
#endif
```

The #error directive is used to display error messages during preprocessing.

Other directives

Several other preprocessor directives perform miscellaneous tasks. For example, you can use the #undef directive to remove the current definition of a symbol. The #pragma directive is another special purpose directive that you can use to convey information to the C compiler. You can use pragma to access the special features of a compiler — and those vary from one compiler to another.

C compilers provide several predefined macros (see Table 2-1). Of these, the macros _ _FILE_ _ and _ _LINE_ _ respectively refer to the current source filename and the current line number being processed. You can use the #line directive to change these. For example, to set _ _FILE_ _ to "file_io.c" and _ _LINE_ _ to 100, you say:

```
#line 100 "file_io.c"
```

Table 2-1	Predefined Macros in C
Macro	*Definition*
_ _DATE_ _	This is a string containing the date when you invoke the C compiler. It is of the form MMM DD YYYY (for example, Oct 26 2002).
_ _FILE_ _	This expands to a string containing the name of the source file.

Macro	Definition
_ _LINE_ _	This is a decimal integer with a value equal to the line number within the current source file.
_ _STDC_ _	This macro expands to the decimal constant 1 to indicate that the C compiler conforms to the ANSI standard.
_ _TIME_ _	This string displays the time when you started compiling the source file. It is of the form HH:MM:SS (for example, 21:59:45).

Declaration and Definition of Variables

In C, you must either define or declare all variables and functions before you use them. The definition of a variable specifies three things:

✦ Its *visibility*, which indicates exactly where the variable can be used (is it defined for all files in a program, the current file, or only in a function).

✦ Its *lifetime*, which determines whether the variable exists temporarily (for example, a local variable in a function) or permanently (as long as the program is running).

✦ Its *type* (and, in some cases, its *initial value*). For example, an integer variable x initialized to 1 is defined this way:

```
int  x = 1;
```

If you're using a variable that is defined in another source file, you declare the variable with an extern keyword, like this:

```
extern int message_count;
```

You must define this variable without the extern qualifier in at least one source file. When the program is built, the linker resolves all references to the message_count variable and ensures that they all use the same variable.

Basic data types

C has four basic data types: char and int are for storing characters and integers, and float and double are for floating-point numbers. You can define variables for these basic data types in a straightforward manner:

```
char   c;
int    i, j, bufsize;
float  volts;
double mean, variance;
```

You can expand the basic data types into a much larger set by using the long, short, and unsigned qualifiers as prefixes. The long and short qualifiers are size modifiers. For example, a long int is at least 4 bytes long, whereas a short int has a minimum size of only 2 bytes. The size of an int is system dependent, but it will definitely be at least as large as a short.

The unsigned qualifier is reserved for int and char types only. Normally, each of these types hold negative as well as positive values. This is the default signed form of these data types. You can use the unsigned qualifier when you want the variable to hold positive values only. Here are some examples of using the short, long, and unsigned qualifiers:

```
unsigned char mode_select, printer_status;
short     record_number; /* Same as "short int"    */
long      offset;    /* Same as "long int"     */
unsigned    i, j, msg_id; /* Same as "unsigned int"   */
unsigned short width, height; /* Same as "unsigned short int" */
unsigned long file_pos;   /* Same as "unsigned long int" */
long double  result;
```

When the short, long, and unsigned qualifiers are used with int types, you can drop the int from the declaration. You can also extend the double data type with a long prefix.

GCC comes with the predefined header files — limits.h and float.h — that define exact sizes of the various data types — and ranges of values — in those header files. You can examine these files in the /usr/include directory of your Red Hat Linux system to determine the sizes of the basic data types that the GCC compiler supports.

Enumerations

You can use the enum data type to define your own enumerated list — a fixed set of named integer constants. For example, you can declare a Boolean data type named BOOLEAN by using enum as follows:

```
/* Declare an enumerated type named BOOLEAN */
    enum BOOLEAN {false = 0, true = 1, stop = 0, go = 1,
                  off = 0, on = 1};

/* Define a BOOLEAN called "status" and initialize it */
    enum BOOLEAN status = stop;
```

This example first declares BOOLEAN to be an enumerated type. The list within the braces shows the enumeration constants that are valid values of an enum BOOLEAN variable. You can initialize each constant to a value of your choice, and several constants can use the same value. In this example, the constants false, stop, and off are set to 0, while true, go, and on are initialized to 1. The example then defines an enumerated BOOLEAN variable named status, which is initially set to the constant stop.

Structures, Unions, and Bit Fields

Use `struct` to group related data items together, and refer to that group by a name. For example, the declaration of a structure to hold variables of a queue may look like this:

```
/* Declare a structure */
struct QUEUE
{
    int  count;      /* Number of items in queue     */
    int  front;      /* Index of first item in queue */
    int  rear;       /* Index of last item in queue  */
    int  elemsize;   /* Size of each element of data */
    int  maxsize;    /* Maximum capacity of queue    */
    char *data;      /* Pointer to queued data       */
};

/* Define two queues */
struct QUEUE rcv_q, xmit_q;
```

The elements inside the `QUEUE` structure are called its *members*. You can access these members by using the member selection operator (`.`). For instance, `rcv_q.count` refers to the `count` member of the `rcv_q` structure.

A `union` is like a `struct`, but instead of grouping related data items together (as `struct` does), a `union` allocates storage for several data items starting at the same location. Thus, all members of a `union` share the same storage location. You can use unions to view the same data item in different ways. Suppose you are using a compiler that supports 4-byte `long` numbers, and you want to access the 4 individual bytes of a single `long` integer. Here is a `union` that lets you accomplish just that:

```
union
{
    long  file_type;
    char  bytes[4];
} header_id;
```

With this definition, `header_id.file_type` refers to the `long` integer, while `header_id.bytes[0]` is the first byte of that `long` integer.

Arrays

An *array* is a collection of one or more identical data items. You can declare arrays of any type of data, including structures and types defined by `typedef`. For example, to define an array of 80 characters, you would write the following:

```
char    string[80];
```

The characters in the string array occupy successive storage locations, beginning with location 0. Thus in this example, string[0] refers to the first character in this array, while string[79] refers to the last one. You can define arrays of other data types and structures similarly:

```
struct Customer          /* Declare a structure    */
{
  int id;
  char first_name[40];
  char last_name[40];
};

struct Customer customers[100]; /* Define array of structures */
int         index[64];   /* An array of 64 integers  */
```

You can also define multidimensional arrays. For example, to represent an 80-column-by-25-line text-display screen, you can use a two-dimensional array as follows:

```
unsigned char text_screen[25][80];
```

Each item of text_screen is an array of 80 unsigned chars, and text_screen contains 25 such arrays. In other words, the two-dimensional array is stored by laying out one row after another in memory. You can use expressions such as text_screen[0][0] to refer to the first character in the first row and text_screen[24][79] to refer to the last character of the last row of the display screen. Higher-dimensional arrays are defined similarly:

```
float coords[3][2][5];
```

This example defines coords as a three-dimensional array of three data items: Each item is an array of two arrays, each of which, in turn, is an array of five float variables. Thus, you interpret a multidimensional array as an "array of arrays."

Pointers

A *pointer* is a variable that can hold the address of any type of data except a bit field. For example, if p_i is a pointer to an integer variable, you can define and use it as follows:

```
/* Define an int pointer and an integer */
   int *p_i, count;

/* Set pointer to the address of the integer "count" */
   p_i = &count;
```

In this case, the compiler will allocate storage for an int variable count and a pointer to an integer p_i. The number of bytes necessary to represent a pointer depends on the underlying system's addressing scheme.

TIP

Don't use a pointer until it contains the address of a valid object.

The example shows p_i being initialized to the address of the integer variable count using the & operator, which provides the address of a variable. After p_i is initialized, you can refer to the value of count with the expression *p_i, which is read as "the contents of the object with its address in p_i."

Pointers are useful in many situations; an important one is the dynamic allocation of memory. The standard C libraries include functions such as malloc and calloc, which you can call to allocate storage for arrays of objects. After allocating memory, these functions return the starting address of the block of memory. Because this address is the only way to reach that memory, you must store it in a variable capable of holding an address — a pointer.

Suppose you allocated memory for an array of 50 integers and saved the returned address in p_i. Now you can treat this block of memory as an array of 50 integers with the name p_i. Thus, you can refer to the last element in the array as p_i[49], which is equivalent to *(p_i+49). Similarly, C treats the name of an array as a pointer to the first element of the array. The difference between the name of an array and a pointer variable is that the name of the array is a constant without any explicit storage necessary to hold the address of the array's first element. The pointer, on the other hand, is an actual storage location capable of holding the address of any data.

In addition to storing the address of dynamically allocated memory, pointers are also commonly used as arguments to functions. When a C function is called, all of its arguments are passed by value — that is, the function gets a copy of each argument, not the original variables appearing in the argument list of the function call. Thus, a C function cannot alter the value of its arguments. Pointers provide a way out. To change the value of a variable in a function, you can pass it a pointer to the variable; the function can alter the value through the pointer.

Type definitions

Through the typedef keyword, C provides you with a convenient way of assigning a new name to an existing data type. You can use the typedef facility to give meaningful names to data types used in a particular application. For example, a graphics application might declare a data type named Point as follows:

```
/* Declare a Point data type */
    typedef struct Point
    {
        short x;
        short y;
```

```
    } Point;

/* Declare PointPtr to be pointer to Point types */
    typedef Point *P_PointPtr;

/* Define some instances of these types
 * and initialize them */
    Point     a = {0, 0};
    PointPtr  p_a = &a;
```

As shown by the `Point` and `PointPtr` types, you can use `typedef` to declare complex data types conveniently.

Type qualifiers: const and volatile

Two type qualifiers, `const` and `volatile`, work this way in a declaration:

✦ The `const` qualifier in a declaration tells the compiler that the particular data object must not be modified by the program. This means the compiler must not generate code that might alter the contents of the location where that data item is stored.

✦ The `volatile` qualifier specifies that the value of a variable may be changed by factors beyond the program's control.

You can use both `const` and `volatile` keywords on a single data item to mean that, while the item must not be modified by your program, it may be altered by some other process. The `const` and `volatile` keywords always qualify the item that immediately follows (to the right). The information provided by the `const` and the `volatile` qualifiers is supposed to help the compiler optimize the code it generates. For example, suppose the variable `block_size` is declared and initialized as follows:

```
const int block_size = 512;
```

In this case, the compiler does not need to generate code to load the value of `block_size` from memory. Instead, it can use the value 512 wherever your program uses `block_size`. Now suppose you added `volatile` to the declaration and changed the declaration to:

```
volatile const int block_size = 512;
```

This says that the contents of `block_size` may be changed by some external process. Therefore, the compiler cannot optimize away any reference to `block_size`. You may need to use such declarations when referring to an I/O port or video memory because these locations can be changed by factors beyond your program's control.

Expressions

An *expression* is a combination of variables, function calls, and operators that results in a single value. For example, here is an expression with a value that is the number of bytes needed to store the *null-terminated string* str (that is, an array of char data types with a zero byte at the end):

```
(strlen(str) * sizeof(char) + 1)
```

This expression involves a function call — strlen(str) — and the multiplication (*), addition (+), and sizeof operators.

C has a large number of operators that are an important part of expressions. Table 2-2 provides a summary of the operators in C.

Table 2-2	Summary of C Operators	
Name of Operator	*Syntax*	*Result*
Arithmetic Operators		
Addition	x+y	Adds x and y.
Subtraction	x-y	Subtracts y from x.
Multiplication	x*y	Multiplies x and y.
Division	x/y	Divides x by y.
Remainder	x%y	Computes the remainder that results from dividing x by y.
Preincrement	++x	Increments x before use.
Postincrement	x++	Increments x after use.
Predecrement	−x	Decrements x before use.
Postdecrement	x−	Decrements x after use.
Minus	-x	Negates the value of x.
Plus	+x	Maintains the value of x unchanged.
Relational and Logical Operators		
Greater than	x>y	Value is 1 if x exceeds y; otherwise, value is 0.
Greater than or equal to	x>=y	Value is 1 if x exceeds or equals y; otherwise, value is 0.
Less than	x<y	Value is 1 if y exceeds x; otherwise, value is 0.
Less than or equal to	x<=y	Value is 1 if y exceeds or equals x; otherwise, value is 0.

(continued)

Table 2-2 *(continued)*

Name of Operator	Syntax	Result
Equal to	x==y	Value is 1 if x equals y; otherwise, value is 0.
Not equal to	x!=y	Value is 1 if x and y are unequal; otherwise, value is 0.
Logical NOT	!x	Value is 1 if x is 0; otherwise, value is 0.
Logical AND	x&&y	Value is 0 if either x or y is 0.
Logical OR	x||y	Value is 0 if both x and y are 0.
Assignment Operators		
Assignment	x=y	Places the value of y into x.
Compound Assignment	x O=y	Equivalent to x = x O y, where O is one of the following operators: +, -, *, /, %, <<, >, &, ^, or |.
Data Access and Size Operators		
Subscript	x[y]	Selects the yth element of array x.
Member selection	x.y	Selects member y of structure (or union) x.
Member selection	x->y	Selects the member named y from a structure or union with x as its address.
Indirection	*x	Contents of the location with x as its address.
Address of	&x	Address of the data object named x.
Size of	sizeof(x)	Size (in bytes) of the data object named x.
Bitwise Operators		
Bitwise NOT	~x	Changes all 1s to 0s and 0s to 1s.
Bitwise AND	x&y	Result is the bitwise AND of x and y.
Bitwise OR	x|y	Result is the bitwise OR of x and y.
Bitwise exclusive OR	x^y	Result contains 1s where corresponding bits of x and y differ.
Left shift	x<<y	Shifts the bits of x to the left by y bit positions. Fills 0s in the vacated bit positions.
Right shift	x>y	Shifts the bits of x to the right by y bit positions. Fills 0s in the vacated bit positions.

Name of Operator	Syntax	Result
Miscellaneous Operators		
Function call	x(y)	Result is the value returned (if any) by function x, which is called with argument y.
Type cast	(type)x	Converts the value of x to the type named in parentheses.
Conditional	z?x:y	If z is not 0, evaluates x; otherwise, evaluates y.
Comma	x,y	Evaluates x first and then y.

Operator Precedence

Typical C expressions consist of several operands and operators. When writing complicated expressions, you must be aware of the order in which the compiler evaluates the operators. For example, suppose a program uses an array of pointers to integers defined as follows:

```
typedef int *IntPtr;/* Use typedef to simplify declarations*/
IntPtr iptr[10];   /* An array of 10 pointers to int      */
```

Now suppose that you encounter the expression *iptr[4]. Does it refer to the value of the int with the address in iptr[4], or is this the fifth element from the location with the address in iptr? What you really need to know is whether the compiler is going to evaluate the subscript operator ([]) before the indirection operator (*) — or will it work the other way around? To answer questions such as these, you need to know the *precedence* — the order in which the program applies the operators.

Table 2-3 summarizes C's precedence rules. The table shows the operators in order of decreasing precedence. The operators with highest precedence — those applied first — are shown first. The table also shows *associativity* — the order in which operators at the same level are evaluated.

Table 2-3	Precedence and Associativity of C Operators		
Operator Group	*Operator Name*	*Notation*	*Associativity*
Postfix	Subscript	x[y]	Left to right
	Function call	x(y)	
	Member selection	x.y	
	Member selection	x->y	

(continued)

Table 2-3 *(continued)*

Operator Group	Operator Name	Notation	Associativity
Unary	Postincrement	x++	Right to left
	Postdecrement	x—	
	Preincrement	++x	
	Predecrement	—x	
	Address of	&x	
	Indirection	*x	
	Plus	+x	
	Minus	-x	
	Bitwise NOT	~x	
	Logical NOT	!x	
	Sizeof	sizeof x	
	Type cast	(type)x	
Multiplicative	Multiply	x*y	Left to right
	Divide	x/y	
	Remainder	x%y	
Additive	Add	x+y	Left to right
	Subtract	x-y	
Shift	Left shift	x<<y	Left to right
	Right shift	x>y	
Relational	Greater than	x>y	Left to right
	Greater than or equal to	x>=y	
	Less than	x<y	
	Less than or equal to	x<=y	
Equality	Equal to	x==y	Left to right
	Not equal to	x!=y	
Bitwise	Bitwise AND	x&y	Left to right
	Bitwise exclusive OR	x^y	
	Bitwise OR	x|y	
Logical	Logical AND	x&&y	Left to right
	Logical OR	x||y	
Conditional	Conditional	z?x:y	Right to left
Assignment	Assignment	x=y	Right to left
	Multiply assign	x *= y	
	Divide assign	x /= y	
	Remainder assign	x %= y	

Operator Group	Operator Name	Notation	Associativity
	Add assign	x += y	
	Subtract assign	x -= y	
	Left shift assign	x <<= y	
	Right shift assign	x >= y	
	Bitwise AND assign	x &= y	
	Bitwise XOR assign	x ^= y	
	Bitwise OR assign	x |= y	
Comma	Comma	x,y	Left to right

Getting back to the question of interpreting *iptr[4], a quick look at Table 2-3 tells you that the [] operator has precedence over the * operator. Thus, when the compiler processes the expression *iptr[4], it evaluates iptr[4] first, and then it applies the indirection operator, resulting in the value of the int with the address in iptr[4].

Statements

You use statements to represent the actions C functions will perform and to control the flow of execution in the C program. A *statement* consists of keywords, expressions, and other statements. Each statement ends with a semicolon (;).

A special type of statement — the *compound statement* — is a group of statements enclosed in a pair of braces ({ ... }). The body of a function is a compound statement. Such compound statements (also known as *blocks*) can contain local variables.

In the following sections — which are alphabetically arranged — I briefly describe the types of statements available in C.

The break statement

You use the break statement to jump to the statement following the innermost do, for, switch, or while statement. It is also used to exit from a switch statement. Here is an example that uses break to exit a for loop:

```
for(i = 0; i < ncommands; i++)
{
    if(strcmp(input, commands[i]) == 0) break;
}
```

The case statement

The `case` statement marks labels in a `switch` statement. Here is an example (here `interrupt_id` is an integer variable):

```
switch (interrupt_id)
{
    case XMIT_RDY:
        transmit();
        break;

    case RCV_RDY:
        receive();
        break;
}
```

A compound statement or block

A *compound statement* or block is a group of declarations followed by statements, all enclosed in a pair of braces ({ . . . }). Typical compound statements are the body of a function and the block of code following an `if` statement. In the following example, everything that appears within the braces — the declarations and the statements — constitute a compound statement:

```
if(theEvent.xexpose.count == 0)
{
    int i;
/* Clear the window and draw the figures
 * in the "figures" array
 */
    XClearWindow(theDisplay, dWin);
    if(numfigures > 0)
        for(i=0; i<numfigures; i++)
            draw_figure(theDisplay, dWin, theGC, i);
}
```

The continue statement

The `continue` statement begins the next iteration of the innermost `do`, `for`, or `while` statement in which it appears. You can use `continue` when you want to skip the execution of the loop. For example, to add the numbers from 1 to 10, excluding 5, you can use a `for` loop that skips the body when the loop index (`i`) is 5:

```
for(i=0, sum=0; i <= 10, i++)
{
    if(i == 5) continue;    /* Exclude 5 */
    sum += i;
}
```

The default label

You use `default` as the label in a `switch` statement to mark code that will execute when none of the case labels match the `switch` expression.

The do statement

The `do` statement, together with `while`, forms iterative loops with the following structure:

```
do
  statement
  while(expression);
```

where *statement* (usually a compound statement) executes until the *expression* in the `while` statement evaluates to 0. The expression is evaluated after each execution of the statement — thus a `do-while` block *always executes at least once*. For example, to add the numbers from 1 to 10, you can use the following `do` statement:

```
sum = 0;
do
{
    sum += i;
    i++;
}
while(i <= 10);
```

Expression statements

Expression statements are evaluated for their side effects. Some typical uses of expression statements include calling a function, incrementing a variable, and assigning a value to a variable. Here are some examples:

```
printf("Hello, World!\n");
i++;
num_bytes = length * sizeof(char);
```

The for statement

Use the `for` statement to execute a statement any number of times (basing that number on the value of an expression). The syntax is as follows:

```
for (expr_1; expr_2; expr_3) statement
```

where the *expr_1* is evaluated once at the beginning of the loop, and the statement is executed until the expression *expr_2* evaluates to 0. The third expression, *expr_3*, is evaluated after each execution of the statement. All three expressions are optional, and the value of *expr_2* is assumed to be 1 if it is omitted. Here is an example that uses a `for` loop to add the numbers from 1 to 10:

```
for(i=0, sum=0; i <= 10; sum += i, i++);
```

In this example, the actual work of adding the numbers is done in the third expression, and the statement controlled by the `for` loop is a `null` statement (a single `;`).

The goto statement

The `goto` statement transfers control to a statement label. Here is an example that prompts the user for a value and repeats the request if the value is not acceptable:

```
ReEnter:
    printf("Enter offset: ");
    scanf(" %d", &offset);
    if(offset < 0 || offset > MAX_OFFSET)
    {
        printf("Bad offset: %d Please reenter:\n",
            offset);
        goto ReEnter;
    }
```

The if statement

You can use the `if` statement to test an expression and execute a statement only when the expression is not zero. An `if` statement takes the following form:

```
if ( expression )  statement
```

The statement following the `if` is executed only if the expression in parentheses evaluates to a non-zero value. That statement is usually a compound statement. Here is an example:

```
if(mem_left < threshold)
{
    Message("Low on memory! Close some windows.\n");
}
```

The if-else statement

The `if-else` statement is a form of the `if` statement coupled with an `else` clause. The statement has the syntax

```
if ( expression )
    statement_1
```

```
else
     statement_2
```

where *statement_1* is executed if the *expression* within the parentheses is not zero. Otherwise, *statement_2* is executed. Here is an example that uses if and else to pick the smaller of two variables:

```
if ( a <= b)
     smaller = a;
else
     smaller = b;
```

The null statement

The null statement, represented by a solitary semicolon, does nothing. You use null statements in loops when all processing is done in the loop expressions rather than in the body of the loop. For example, to locate the zero byte marking the end of a string, you may use the following:

```
char str[80] = "Test";
int i;

for (i=0; str[i] != '\0'; i++)
                              ;   /* Null statement */
```

The return statement

The return statement stops executing the current function and returns control to the calling function. The syntax is

```
return expression;
```

where the value of the *expression* is returned as the value of the function. For a function that does not return a value, use the return statement without the expression as follows:

```
return;
```

The switch statement

The switch statement performs a multiple branch, depending on the value of an expression. It has the following syntax:

```
switch (expression)
{
     case value1:
          statement_1
          break;
     case value2:
```

```
            statement_2
            break;
                   .
                   .
                   .
        default:
            statement_default
}
```

If the *expression* being tested by switch evaluates to *value1*, *statement_1* is executed. If the expression is equal to *value2*, *statement_2* is executed. The value is compared with each case label and the statement following the matching label is executed. If the value does not match any of the case labels, the block *statement_default* following the default label is executed. Each statement ends with a break statement that separates the code of one case label from another. Here is a switch statement that calls different routines depending on the value of an integer variable named command:

```
switch (command)
{
    case 'q':
        quit_app(0);

        case 'c':
        connect();
        break;

    case 's':
        set_params();
        break;

    case '?':
    case 'H':
        print_help();
        break;

    default:
        printf("Unknown command!\n");
}
```

The while statement

The while statement is used in the form

```
while (expression) statement
```

where the *statement* is executed until the *expression* evaluates to 0. A while statement evaluates the expression before each execution of the statement. Thus, a while loop executes the statement zero or more times. Here is a while statement for copying one array to another:

```
i = length;
while (i >= 0)   /* Copy one array to another */
{
     array2[i] = array1[i];
     i--;
}
```

Functions

A *function* is a collection of declarations and statements. As such, functions are the building blocks of C programs. Each C program has at least one function — the *main function*, where the execution of a C program begins. The C library contains mostly functions, although it contains quite a few macros as well.

Function prototypes

In C, you must declare a function before using it. The function declaration tells the compiler the type of value that the function returns and the number and type of arguments it takes. Declare a function as a complete *function prototype*, showing the return type as well as a list of arguments. The `calloc` function in the C library returns a void pointer and accepts two arguments, each of type `size_t`, which is an unsigned integer type of sufficient size to hold the value of the `sizeof` operator. Thus the function prototype for `calloc` is the following:

```
void *calloc(size_t, size_t);
```

This prototype shows the type of each argument in the argument list. You can also include an identifier for each argument. In that case, you'd write the prototype as follows:

```
void *calloc(size_t num_elements, size_t elem_size);
```

Here the prototype looks exactly like the first line in the definition of the function, except you stop short of defining the function and end the line with a semicolon. With well-chosen names for arguments, this form of prototype can provide a lot of information about the function's use. For example, one look at the prototype of `calloc` should tell you that its first argument is the number of elements to allocate, and the second argument is the size of each element.

Prototypes also help the compiler check function arguments and generate code that may use a faster mechanism for passing arguments. From the prototype, the compiler can determine the exact number and type of arguments to expect. Therefore, the prototype enables the compiler to catch any mistakes you might make when calling a function, such as passing the wrong number of arguments (when the function takes a fixed number of arguments) or passing a wrong type of argument to a function.

The void type

What do you do when a function doesn't return anything nor accept any parameters? To handle these cases, C provides the void type, which is useful for declaring functions that return nothing and for describing pointers that can point to any type of data. For example, you can use the void return type to declare a function such as exit that does not return anything:

```
void exit(int status);
```

On the other hand, if a function doesn't accept any formal parameters, its list of arguments is represented by a void:

```
FILE *tmpfile(void);
```

The void pointer is useful for functions that work with blocks of memory. For example, when you request a certain number of bytes from the memory allocation routine malloc, you can use these locations to store any data that fits the space. In this case, the address of the first location of the allocated block of memory is returned as a void pointer. Thus, the prototype of malloc is written as follows:

```
void *malloc(size_t numbytes);
```

Functions with a variable number of arguments

If a function accepts a variable number of arguments, you can indicate this by using an ellipsis (. . .) in place of the argument list; however, you must provide at least one argument before the ellipsis. A good example of such functions is the printf family of functions defined in the header file stdio.h. The prototypes of these functions are as follows:

```
int fprintf(FILE *stream, const char *format, ...);
int printf(const char *format, ...);
int sprintf(char *buffer, const char *format, ...);
```

The C Library

The ANSI and ISO standards for C define all aspects of C — the language, the preprocessor, and the library. The prototypes of the functions in the library, as well as all necessary data structures and preprocessor constants, are defined in a set of standard header files. Table 2-4 lists the standard header files, including a summary of their contents.

If you're going to write applications in C, you have to become familiar with many of the standard libraries because that's where much of C's programming prowess lies. If you are writing graphical applications, you also must learn other libraries such as The GIMP toolkit.

Table 2-4	Standard Header Files in C
Header File	*Purpose*
`<assert.h>`	Defines the `assert` macro. Used for program diagnostics.
`<ctype.h>`	Declares functions for classifying and converting characters.
`<errno.h>`	Defines macros for error conditions, `EDOM` and `ERANGE`, and the integer variable `errno` where library functions return an error code.
`<float.h>`	Defines a range of values that can be stored in floating-point types.
`<iso646.h>`	Defines a number of macros that are helpful when writing C programs in non-English languages that may use character combinations such as & and ~ for other purposes.
`<limits.h>`	Defines the limiting values of all integer data types.
`<locale.h>`	Declares the `lconv` structure and the functions necessary for customizing a C program to a particular locale.
`<math.h>`	Declares common mathematical functions and the `HUGE_VAL` macro.
`<setjmp.h>`	Defines the `setjmp` and `longjmp` functions that can transfer control from one function to another without relying on normal function calls and returns. Also defines the `jmp_buf` data type used by `setjmp` and `longjmp`.
`<signal.h>`	Defines symbols and routines necessary for handling exceptional conditions.
`<stdarg.h>`	Defines macros that provide access to the unnamed arguments in a function that accepts a varying number of arguments.
`<stddef.h>`	Defines the standard data types `ptrdiff_t`, `size_t`, `wchar_t`; the symbol `NULL`; and the macro `offsetof`.
`<stdio.h>`	Declares the functions and data types necessary for input and output operations. Defines macros such as `BUFSIZ`, `EOF`, `SEEK_CUR`, `SEEK_END`, and `SEEK_SET`.
`<stdlib.h>`	Declares many utility functions, such as the string conversion routines, random number generator, memory allocation routines, and process control routines (such as `abort`, `exit`, and `system`).
`<string.h>`	Declares the string manipulation routines such as `strcmp` and `strcpy`.

(continued)

Table 2-4 *(continued)*

Header File	Purpose
`<time.h>`	Defines data types and declares functions that manipulate time. Defines the types `clock_t` and `time_t` and the tm data structure.
`<wchar.h>`	Defines data types and declares functions for working with wide character data types (`wchar_t`).
`<wctype.h>`	Defines data types and declares functions for classifying and converting wide character data types (`wchar_t`).

Shared Libraries in Red Hat Linux Applications

Most Red Hat Linux programs use shared libraries. At minimum, most C programs use the C shared library `libc.so.X`, wherein *X* is a version number. Using shared libraries is desirable because many executable programs can share the same shared library — you need only one copy of the shared library loaded into memory. Also, the *dynamic linking* (wherein a program loads code modules and links with them at runtime) is becoming increasingly popular because it enables an application to load blocks of code only when needed, thus reducing the memory requirement of the application.

When a program uses one or more shared libraries, you need the program's executable file, as well as all the shared libraries, to run the program. In other words, your program won't run if all shared libraries are not available on a system.

If you sell an application that uses shared libraries, make sure all necessary shared libraries are distributed with your software.

The subject of shared libraries is of interest to Red Hat Linux programmers because use of shared libraries reduces the size of executables. In this section I briefly describe how to create and use a shared library in a sample program.

Examining shared libraries that a program uses

Use the `ldd` utility to determine which shared libraries an executable program needs. Type the following `ldd` command to see the shared libraries used by a program (that was stored by GCC in the default file named `a.out`):

```
ldd a.out
```

Here is what `ldd` reports for a typical C program:

```
libc.so.6 => /lib/tls/libc.so.6 (0x42000000)
/lib/ld-linux.so.2 => /lib/ld-linux.so.2 (0x40000000)
```

A more complex program, such as The GIMP (an Adobe Photoshop–like program) uses many more shared libraries. To view its shared library needs, type the following command:

```
ldd /usr/bin/gimp
```

Here's the list displayed on my Red Hat Linux system:

```
libgtk-1.2.so.0 => /usr/lib/libgtk-1.2.so.0 (0x40025000)
libgdk-1.2.so.0 => /usr/lib/libgdk-1.2.so.0 (0x4016e000)
libgmodule-1.2.so.0 => /usr/lib/libgmodule-1.2.so.0 (0x401a6000)
libglib-1.2.so.0 => /usr/lib/libglib-1.2.so.0 (0x401a9000)
libdl.so.2 => /lib/libdl.so.2 (0x401ce000)
libXi.so.6 => /usr/X11R6/lib/libXi.so.6 (0x401d1000)
libXext.so.6 => /usr/X11R6/lib/libXext.so.6 (0x401d9000)
libX11.so.6 => /usr/X11R6/lib/libX11.so.6 (0x401e8000)
libm.so.6 => /lib/libm.so.6 (0x402c7000)
libc.so.6 => /lib/libc.so.6 (0x402e8000)
/lib/ld-linux.so.2 => /lib/ld-linux.so.2 (0x40000000)
```

In this case, the program uses quite a few shared libraries, including the X11 library (`libX11.so.6`), The GIMP toolkit (`libgtk-1.2.so.0`), the General Drawing Kit (GDK) library (`libgdk-1.2.so.0`), the Math library (`libm.so.6`), and the C library (`libc.so.6`).

Almost any Red Hat Linux application requires shared libraries to run.

Creating a shared library

Creating a shared library for your own application is fairly simple. Suppose you want to implement an object in the form of a shared library (think of an object as a bunch of code and data). A set of functions in the shared library represents the object's interfaces. To use the object, you would load its shared library and invoke its interface functions. (I show you how to do this in the following section.)

Here is the C source code for this simple object, implemented as a shared library (you might also call it a *dynamically linked library*) — save this in a file named `dynobj.c`:

```
/*-------------------------------------------------------------*/
/* File: dynobj.c
 *
 * Demonstrate use of dynamic linking.
```

```
 * Pretend this is an object that can be created by calling
 * init and destroyed by calling destroy.
 */
#include <stdio.h>
#include <stdlib.h>
#include <string.h>

/* Data structure for this object */
typedef struct OBJDATA
{
  char *name;
  int version;
} OBJDATA;

/*-----------------------------------------------------------*/
/* i n i t
 *
 * Initialize object (allocate storage).
 *
 */
void* init(char *name)
{
  OBJDATA *data = (OBJDATA*)calloc(1, sizeof(OBJDATA));
  if(name)
    data->name = malloc(strlen(name)+1);
  strcpy(data->name, name);

  printf("Created: %s\n", name);

  return data;
}
/*-----------------------------------------------------------*/
/* s h o w
 *
 * Show the object.
 *
 */
void show(void *data)
{
  OBJDATA *d = (OBJDATA*)data;
  printf("show: %s\n", d->name);
}
/*-----------------------------------------------------------*/
/* d e s t r o y
 *
 * Destroy the object (free all storage).
 *
 */
void destroy(void *data)
{
  OBJDATA *d = (OBJDATA*)data;
  if(d)
```

```
  {
    if(d->name)
    {
      printf("Destroying: %s\n", d->name);
      free(d->name);
    }
    free(d);
  }
}
```

The object offers three interface functions:

✦ init to allocate any necessary storage and initialize the object

✦ show to display the object (here, it simply prints a message)

✦ destroy to free any storage

To build the shared library named libdobj.so, follow these steps:

1. Compile all source files with the -fPIC **flag. In this case, compile the**
    dynobj.c **file by using this command:**

```
gcc -fPIC -c dynobj.c
```

2. Link the objects into a shared library with the -shared **flag, and pro-
    vide appropriate flags for the linker. To create the shared library
    named** libdobj.so.1, **use the following:**

```
gcc -shared -Wl,-soname,libdobj.so.1 -o libdobj.so.1.0
    dynobj.o
```

**3. Set up a sequence of symbolic links so that programs that use the
    shared library can refer to it with a standard name.**

For the sample library, the standard name is libdobj.so, and the symbolic links are set up by using these commands:

```
ln -sf libdobj.so.1.0 libdobj.so.1
ln -sf libdobj.so.1 libdobj.so
```

4. When you test the shared library, define and export the LD_LIBRARY_
    PATH **environment variable by using the following command:**

```
export LD_LIBRARY_PATH=`pwd`:$LD_LIBRARY_PATH
```

After you test the shared library and are satisfied that the library works, copy
it to a standard location, such as /usr/local/lib, and run the ldconfig
utility to update the link between libdobj.so.1 and libdobj.so.1.0.

These are the commands you use to install your shared library for everyone's use (you have to be `root` to perform these steps):

```
cp libdobj.so.1.0 /usr/local/lib
/sbin/ldconfig
cd /usr/local/lib
ln -s libdobj.so.1 libdobj.so
```

Dynamically loading a shared library

It's simple to load a shared library in your program and use the functions within the shared library. In this section, I demonstrate the way you do this. The header file `<dlfcn.h>` (that's a standard header file in Red Hat Linux) declares the functions for loading and using a shared library. Four functions are declared in the file `dlfcn.h` for dynamic loading:

✦ `void *dlopen(const char *filename, int flag);` — Loads the shared library specified by the filename and returns a handle for the library. The flag can be `RTD_LAZY` (resolve undefined symbols as the library's code is executed), or `RTD_NOW` (resolve all undefined symbols before `dlopen` returns and fail if all symbols are not defined). If `dlopen` fails, it returns `NULL`.

✦ `const char *dlerror (void);` — If `dlopen` fails, call `dlerror` to get a string that contains a description of the error.

✦ `void *dlsym (void *handle, char *symbol);` — Returns the address of the specified symbol (function name) from the shared library identified by the handle (that was returned by `dlopen`).

✦ `int dlclose (void *handle);` — Unloads the shared library if no one else is using it.

When you use any of these functions, include the header file `dlfcn.h` with this preprocessor directive:

```
#include <dlfcn.h>
```

Finally, here is a simple test program — `dltest.c` — that shows how to load and use the object defined in the shared library `libdobj.so`, which you create in the preceding section:

```
/*------------------------------------------------------------*/
/* File: dltest.c
 *
 * Test dynamic linking.
 *
 */
#include <dlfcn.h>  /* For the dynamic loading functions */
```

```
#include <stdio.h>

int main(void)
{
  void *dlobj;
  void * (*init_call)(char *name);
  void (*show_call)(void *data);
  void (*destroy_call)(void *data);

/* Open the shared library and set up the function pointers
   */
  if(dlobj = dlopen("libdobj.so.1",RTLD_LAZY))
  {
    void *data;

    init_call=dlsym(dlobj,"init");
    show_call=dlsym(dlobj,"show");
    destroy_call=dlsym(dlobj,"destroy");

/* Call the object interfaces */
    data = (*init_call)("Test Object");
    (*show_call)(data);
    (*destroy_call)(data);
  }
  return 0;
}
```

The program is straightforward: It loads the shared library, gets the pointers to the functions in the library, and calls the functions through the pointers.

You can compile and link this program in the usual way, but you must link with the -ldl option so that you can use the functions declared in dlfcn.h. Here is how you build the program dltest:

```
gcc -o dltest dltest.c -ldl
```

To see the program in action, run dltest by typing the following command:

```
./dltest
```

It should display the following lines of output:

```
Created: Test Object
show: Test Object
Destroying: Test Object
```

Although this sample program is not exciting, you now have a sample program that uses a shared library.

To see the benefit of using a shared library, return to the preceding section and make some changes in the shared library source file — `dynobj.c`. For example, you could print some other message in a function so that you can easily tell that you have made some change. Rebuild the shared library alone. Then run `dltest` again. The resulting output should show the effect of the changes you make in the shared library, which means you can update the shared library independently of the application.

Note that a change in a shared library can affect many applications installed on your system. Therefore, be careful when making changes to *any* shared library. By the same token, shared libraries can be a security risk if someone manages to replace one with some malicious code.

Chapter 3: Writing Shell Scripts

In This Chapter

✔ Trying out simple shell scripts

✔ Learning the basics of shell scripting

✔ Exploring Bash's built-in commands

Red Hat Linux gives you many small and specialized commands, along with the plumbing necessary to connect these commands. By *plumbing*, I mean the way in which one command's output can be used as a second command's input. Bash (short for Bourne Again SHell) — the default shell in Linux — provides this plumbing in the form of I/O redirection and pipes. Bash also includes features such as the `if` statement that you can use to run commands only when a specific condition is true and the `for` statement that repeats commands a specified number of times. You can use these features of Bash when writing programs called *shell scripts*.

In this chapter, I show you how to write simple *shell scripts* — task-oriented collections of shell commands stored in a file. Shell scripts are used to automate various tasks. For example, when your Red Hat Linux boots, many shell scripts that are stored in various subdirectories in the `/etc` directory (for example, `/etc/init.d`) perform many initialization tasks.

Trying Out Simple Shell Scripts

If you are not a programmer, you may feel apprehensive about programming. But shell *scripting* (or programming) can be as simple as storing a few commands in a file. In fact, you can have a useful shell program that has a single command.

While writing this book, for example, I captured screens from the X Window System and used the screen shots in figures. I used the X screen-capture program, `xwd`, to store the screen images in the X Window Dump (XWD) format. The book's production team, however, wanted the screen shots in TIFF format. Therefore, I've used the Portable Bitmap (PBM) toolkit to convert the XWD images to TIFF format. To convert each file, I've run two programs and deleted a temporary file, as follows:

```
xwdtopnm < file.xwd > file.pnm
pnmtotiff < file.pnm > file.tif
rm file.pnm
```

These commands assume that the xwdtopnm and pnmtotiff programs are in the /usr/bin directory — one of the directories listed in the PATH environment variable. By the way, xwdtopnm and pnmtotiff are two programs in the PBM toolkit.

After converting a few XWD files to TIFF format, I get tired of typing the same sequence of commands for each file, so I prepare a file named totif and save the following lines in it:

```
#!/bin/sh
xwdtopnm < $1.xwd > $1.pnm
pnmtotiff < $1.pnm > $1.tif
rm $1.pnm
```

Then I make the file executable by using this command:

```
chmod +x totif
```

The chmod command enables you to change the permission settings of a file. One of those settings determines whether the file is executable. The +x option means you want to mark the file as executable. You do have to mark it that way because Bash runs only executable files.

Now when I want to convert the file figure1.xwd to figure1.tif, I can do so by typing the following command:

```
./totif figure1
```

The ./ prefix indicates that the totif file is in the current directory — you don't need the ./ prefix if the PATH environment variable includes the current directory. The totif file is a shell script (also called a *shell program*). When you run this shell program with the command totif figure1, the shell substitutes figure1 for each occurrence of $1. (Note that $1 refers to the first option that the user types on the command used to execute the script.)

Shell scripts are popular among system administrators. If you are a system administrator, you can build a collection of custom shell scripts that help you automate tasks you perform often. If a disk seems to be getting full, for example, you may want to find all files that exceed some size (say, 1MB) and that have not been accessed in the past 30 days. In addition, you may want to send an e-mail message to all users who have large files, requesting that they archive and clean up those files. You can perform all these tasks with a shell script. You might start with the following find command to identify large files:

```
find / -type f -atime +30 -size +1000k -exec ls -l {} \; > /tmp/largefiles
```

This command creates a file named /tmp/largefiles, which contains detailed information about old files taking up too much space. After you get a list of the files, you can use a few other Linux commands — such as sort, cut, and sed — to prepare and send mail messages to users who have large files they should clean up. Instead of typing all these commands manually, place them in a file and create a shell script. That, in a nutshell, is the essence of shell scripts — to gather shell commands in a file so that you can easily perform repetitive system administration tasks.

Just as most Linux commands accept command-line options, a Bash script also accepts command-line options. Inside the script, you can refer to the options as $1, $2, and so on. The special name $0 refers to the name of the script itself.

Here's a typical Bash script that accepts arguments:

```
#!/bin/sh
echo "This script's name is: $0"
echo Argument 1: $1
echo Argument 2: $2
```

The first line runs the /bin/sh program, which subsequently processes the rest of the lines in the script. The name /bin/sh traditionally refers to the Bourne shell — the first UNIX shell. In Red Hat Linux, /bin/sh is a symbolic link to /bin/bash, which is the executable program for Bash.

Save this simple script in a file named simple, and make that file executable with the following command:

```
chmod +x simple
```

Now run the script as follows:

```
./simple
```

It displays the following output:

```
This script's name is: ./simple
Argument 1:
Argument 2:
```

The first line shows the script's name. Because you have run the script without arguments, the script displays no values for the arguments.

Now try running the script with a few arguments, like this:

```
./simple "This is one argument" second-argument third
```

This time the script displays more output:

```
This script's name is: ./simple
Argument 1: This is one argument
Argument 2: second-argument
```

As the output shows, the shell treats the entire string within the double quotation marks as a single argument. Otherwise, the shell uses spaces as separators between arguments on the command line.

This sample script ignores the third argument because the script is designed to print only the first two arguments. The script ignores all arguments after the first two.

Learning the Basics of Shell Scripting

Like any programming language, the Bash shell supports the following features:

✦ Variables that store values, including special built-in variables for accessing command-line arguments passed to a shell script and other special values.

✦ The capability to evaluate expressions.

✦ Control structures that enable you to loop over several shell commands or to execute some commands conditionally.

✦ The capability to define functions that can be called in many places within a script. Bash also includes many built-in commands that you can use in any script.

In the next few sections, I illustrate some of these programming features through simple examples. (I'm assuming that you're already running Bash, in which case you can try the examples by typing them at the shell prompt in a terminal window.)

Storing stuff

You define variables in Bash just as you define environment variables. Thus, you may define a variable as follows:

```
count=12  # note no embedded spaces allowed
```

To use a variable's value, prefix the variable's name with a dollar sign ($). For example, $PATH is the value of the variable PATH (this is the famous PATH environment variable that lists all the directories that Bash searches when trying to locate an executable file). To display the value of the variable count, use the following command:

```
echo $count
```

Bash has some special variables for accessing command-line arguments. In a shell script, $0 refers to the name of the shell script. The variables $1, $2, and so on refer to the command-line arguments. The variable $* stores all the command-line arguments as a single variable, and $? contains the exit status of the last command the shell executes.

From a Bash script, you can prompt the user for input and use the read command to read the input into a variable. Here is an example:

```
echo -n "Enter value: "
read value
echo "You entered: $value"
```

When this script runs, the read value command causes Bash to read whatever you type at the keyboard.

Note that the -n option prevents the echo command from automatically adding a new line at the end of the string that it displays.

Calling shell functions

You can group a number of shell commands that you use consistently into a *function* and assign it a name. Later, you can execute that group of commands by using the single name assigned to the function. Here is a simple script that illustrates the syntax of shell functions:

```
#!/bin/sh

hello() {
        echo -n "Hello, "
        echo $1 $2
}

hello Jane Doe
```

When you run this script, it displays the following output:

```
Hello, Jane Doe
```

This script defines a shell function named hello. The function expects two arguments. In the body of the function, these arguments are referenced by $1 and $2. The function definition begins with hello() — the name of the function, followed by parentheses. The body of the function is enclosed in curly braces: { . . . }. In this case, the body uses the echo command to display a line of text.

The last line of the example shows how a shell function is called with arguments. In this case, the `hello` function is being called with two arguments: `Jane` and `Doe`. The `hello` function takes these two arguments and prints out a line that says `Hello, Jane Doe`.

Controlling the flow

In Bash scripts, you can control the flow of execution — the order in which the commands are executed — by using special commands such as `if`, `case`, `for`, and `while`. These control statements use the exit status of a command to decide what to do next. When any command executes, it returns an exit status — a numeric value that indicates whether or not the command has succeeded. By convention, an exit status of zero means the command has succeeded. (Yes, you read it right: Zero indicates success!) A nonzero exit status indicates that something has gone wrong with the command.

For example, suppose you want to make a backup copy of a file before editing it with the `vi` editor. More importantly, you want to avoid editing the file if a backup can't be made. Here's a Bash script that takes care of this task:

```
#!/bin/sh
if cp "$1" "#$1"
then
    vi "$1"
else
    echo "Failed to create backup copy"
fi
```

This script illustrates the syntax of the `if-then-else` structure and shows how the exit status of the `cp` command is used by the `if` command to determine the next action. If `cp` returns zero, the script uses `vi` to edit the file; otherwise, the script displays an error message and exits. By the way, the script saves the backup in a file whose name is the same as that of the original, except for a hash mark (#) added at the beginning of the filename.

Don't forget the final `fi` that terminates the `if` command. Forgetting `fi` is a common source of errors in Bash scripts.

You can use the `test` command to evaluate any expression and to use the expression's value as the exit status of the command. Suppose you want a script that edits a file only if it already exists. Using `test`, you can write such a script as follows:

```
#!/bin/sh
if test -f "$1"
then
    vi "$1"
```

```
else
    echo "No such file"
fi
```

A shorter form of the `test` command is to place the expression in square brackets ([. . .]). Using this shorthand notation, you can rewrite the preceding script like this:

```
#!/bin/sh
if [ -f "$1" ]
then
    vi "$1"
else
    echo "No such file"
fi
```

Note: You must have spaces around the two square brackets.

Another common control structure is the `for` loop. The following script adds the numbers 1 through 10:

```
#!/bin/sh
sum=0
for i in 1 2 3 4 5 6 7 8 9 10
do
    sum='expr $sum + $i'
done
echo "Sum = $sum"
```

This example also illustrates the use of the `expr` command to evaluate an expression.

The `case` statement is used to execute a group of commands based on the value of a variable. For example, consider the following script, based on the `confirm()` function in the `/etc/init.d/functions` file in your Red Hat Linux system:

```
#!/bin/sh
echo -n "What should I do -- (Y)es/(N)o/(C)ontinue? [Y] "
read answer
case $answer in
    y|Y|"")
        echo "YES"
    ;;
    c|C)
        echo "CONTINUE"
    ;;
    n|N)
        echo "NO"
    ;;
```

```
    *)
      echo "UNKNOWN"
    ;;
esac
```

Save this in a file named `confirm` and type **chmod +x confirm** to make it executable. Then try it out like this:

```
./confirm
```

When the script prompts you, type one of the characters **y**, **n**, or **c** and then press Enter. The script should display `YES`, `NO`, or `CONTINUE`. For example, here's what happens when I type **c** (and then press Enter):

```
What should I do -- (Y)es/(N)o/(C)ontinue? [Y] c
CONTINUE
```

The script displays a prompt and reads the input you type. Your input is stored in a variable named `answer`. Then the `case` statement executes a block of code based on the value of the answer variable. For example, when I type **c**, the following block of commands is executed:

```
    c|C)
      echo "CONTINUE"
    ;;
```

The `echo` command causes the script to display `CONTINUE`.

From this example, you can see that the general syntax of the `case` command is as follows:

```
case $variable in
    value1 | value2)
    command1
    command2
    ...other commands...
    ;;

    value3)
    command3
    command4
    ...other commands...
    ;;
esac
```

Essentially, the `case` command begins with the word `case` and ends with `esac`. Separate blocks of code are enclosed between the values of the variable, followed by a closing parenthesis and terminated by a pair of semicolons (; ;).

Exploring Bash's built-in commands

Bash has more than 50 built-in commands, including common commands such as cd and pwd, as well as many others that are used infrequently. You can use these built-in commands in any Bash script or at the shell prompt. Table 3-1 describes most of the Bask built-in commands and their arguments. After looking through this information, type **help** *cmd* to read more about a specific built-in command. For example, to learn more about the built-in command test, type the following:

```
help test
```

Doing so displays the following information on my Red Hat Linux system:

```
test: test [expr]
    Exits with a status of 0 (true) or 1 (false) depending on
    the evaluation of EXPR. Expressions may be unary or binary. Unary
    expressions are often used to examine the status of a file. There
    are string operators as well, and numeric comparison operators.

    File operators:

      -a FILE    True if file exists.
      -b FILE    True if file is block special.
      -c FILE    True if file is character special.
      -d FILE    True if file is a directory.
      -e FILE    True if file exists.
      -f FILE    True if file exists and is a regular file.
      -g FILE    True if file is set-group-id.
      -h FILE    True if file is a symbolic link.
      -L FILE    True if file is a symbolic link.
      -k FILE    True if file has its 'sticky' bit set.
      -p FILE    True if file is a named pipe.
      -r FILE    True if file is readable by you.
      -s FILE    True if file exists and is not empty.
      -S FILE    True if file is a socket.
      -t FD      True if FD is opened on a terminal.
      -u FILE    True if the file is set-user-id.
      -w FILE    True if the file is writable by you.
      -x FILE    True if the file is executable by you.
      -O FILE    True if the file is effectively owned by you.
      -G FILE    True if the file is effectively owned by your group.
    (... Lines deleted ...)
```

Where necessary, the online help from the help command includes a considerable amount of detail.

Some external programs may have the same name as Bash built-in commands. If you want to run any such external program, you have to specify explicitly the full pathname of that program. Otherwise, Bash executes the built-in command of the same name.

Table 3-1	Summary of Built-in Commands in Bash Shell
This Function	*Does the Following*
`.` *filename* [*arguments*]	Reads and executes commands from the specified file using the optional arguments (works the same way as the `source` command).
`:` [*arguments*]	Expands the arguments but does not process them.
`[` *expr* `]`	Evaluates the expression *expr* and returns zero status if *expr* is true.
`alias` [*name*[=*value*] ...]	Defines an alias.
`bg` [*job*]	Puts the specified job in the background. If no job is specified, it puts the currently executing command in the background.
`bind` [-m *keymap*] [-lvd] [-q *name*]	Binds a key sequence to a macro.
`break` [*n*]	Exits from a `for`, `while`, or `until` loop. If *n* is specified, the *n*-th enclosing loop is exited.
`builtin` *builtin_command* [*arguments*]	Executes a shell built-in command.
`cd` [*dir*]	Changes the current directory to dir.
`command` [-pVv] *cmd* [*arg* ...]	Runs the command *cmd* with the specified arguments (ignoring any shell function named *cmd*).
`continue` [*n*]	Starts the next iteration of the `for`, `while`, or `until` loop. If *n* is specified, the next iteration of the *n*-th enclosing loop is started.
`declare` [-frxi] [*name*[=*value*]]	Declares a variable with the specified name and, optionally, assigns it a value.
`dirs` [-l] [+/-*n*]	Displays the list of currently remembered directories.
`echo` [-neE] [*arg* ...]	Displays the arguments on standard output.
`enable` [-n] [-all] [*name* ...]	Enables or disables the specified built-in commands.
`eval` [*arg* ...]	Concatenates the arguments and executes them as a command.
`exec` [*command* [*arguments*]]	Replaces the current instance of the shell with a new process that runs the specified command.
`exit` [*n*]	Exits the shell with the status code *n*.
`export` [-nf] [*name*[=*word*]] ...	Defines a specified environment variable and exports it to future processes.

This Function	Does the Following
`fc -s [pat=rep] [cmd]`	Re-executes the command after replacing the pattern *pat* with `rep`.
`fg [jobspec]`	Puts the specified job in the foreground. If no job is specified, it puts the most recent job in the foreground.
`getopts optstring name [args]`	Gets optional parameters (which are called in shell scripts to extract arguments from the command line).
`hash [-r] [name]`	Remembers the full pathname of a specified command.
`help [cmd ...]`	Displays help information for specified built-in commands.
`history [n]`	Displays past commands or past *n* commands, if you specify a number *n*.
`jobs [-lnp] [ jobspec ... ]`	Lists currently active jobs.
`kill [-s sigspec | -sigspec] [pid | jobspec] ...let arg [arg ...]`	Evaluates each argument and returns 1 if the last *arg* is 0.
`local [name[=value] ...]`	Creates a local variable with the specified name and value (used in shell functions).
`logout`	Exits a login shell.
`popd [+/-n]`	Removes entries from the directory stack.
`pushd [dir]`	Adds a specified directory to the top of the directory stack.
`pwd`	Prints the full pathname of the current working directory.
`read [-r] [name ...]`	Reads a line from standard input and parses it.
`readonly [-f] [name ...]`	Marks the specified variables as read-only, so that the variables cannot be changed later.
`return [n]`	Exits the shell function with the return value *n*.
`set [—abefhkmnptuvxldCHP] [-o option] [arg ...]`	Sets various flags.
`shift [n]`	Makes the *n+1* argument $1, the *n+2* argument $2, and so on.
`source filename [arguments]`	Reads and executes commands from a file.
`suspend [-f]`	Stops execution until a `SIGCONT` signal is received.
`test expr`	Evaluates the expression `expr` and returns zero if `expr` is `true`.
`times`	Prints the accumulated user and system times for processes run from the shell.

(continued)

Table 3-1 *(continued)*

This Function	Does the Following
`trap [-1] [cmd] [sigspec]`	Executes cmd when the signal sigspec is received.
`type [-all] [-type | -path] name [name ...]`	Indicates how the shell interprets each name.
`ulimit [-SHacdfmstpnuv [limit]]`	Controls resources available to the shell.
`umask [-S] [mode]`	Sets the file creation mask — the default permission for files.
`unalias [-a] [name ...]`	Undefines a specified alias.
`unset [-fv] [name ...]`	Removes the definition of specified variables.
`wait [n]`	Waits for a specified process to terminate.

Chapter 4: Programming in Perl

*W*hen it comes to writing scripts, the Perl language is very popular among system administrators, especially on UNIX and Linux systems. System administrators use Perl to automate routine system administration tasks such as looking for old files that could be archived and deleted to free up disk space.

Perl is a scripting language, which means you do not have to compile and link a Perl script (a text file containing Perl commands). Instead, an interpreter executes the Perl script. This makes it easy to write and test Perl scripts because you do not have to go through the typical edit-compile-link cycles to write Perl programs.

Besides ease of programming, another reason for Perl's popularity is that Perl is distributed freely and is available for a wide variety of computer systems, including Red Hat Linux and many others such as UNIX, Windows 95/98/NT/2000/XP, and Apple Macintosh.

In this chapter, I introduce you to Perl scripting.

Understanding Perl

Officially Perl stands for *Practical Extraction Report Language*, but Larry Wall, the creator of Perl, says people often refer to Perl as *Pathologically Eclectic Rubbish Lister*. As these names suggest, Perl was originally designed to extract information from text files and generate reports.

Perl began life in 1986 as a system administration tool created by Larry Wall. Over time, Perl grew by accretion of many new features and functions. The latest version — Perl 5.8 — supports object-oriented programming and allows anyone to extend Perl by adding new modules in a specified format.

True to its origin as a system administration tool, Perl has been popular with UNIX system administrators for many years. More recently, when the World Wide Web (or Web for short) became popular and the need for Common Gateway Interface (CGI) programs arose, Perl became the natural choice for those already familiar with the language. The recent surge in Perl's popularity is primarily due to the use of Perl in writing CGI programs for the Web. Of course, as people pay more attention to Perl, they discover that Perl is useful for much more than CGI programming. That, in turn, has made Perl even more popular among users.

Perl is available on a wide variety of computer systems because, like the Linux operating system, Perl can be distributed freely.

If you are familiar with shell programming or the C programming language, you can pick up Perl quickly. If you have never programmed, becoming proficient in Perl may take a while. I encourage you to start with a small subset of Perl's features and to ignore anything you don't immediately understand. Then, slowly add Perl features to your repertoire.

Determining Whether You Have Perl

Before you proceed with the Perl tutorial, check whether you have the `perl` program installed on your Red Hat Linux system. Type the following command:

```
which perl
```

The `which` command tells you whether it finds a specified program in the directories listed in the `PATH` environment variable. If `perl` is installed, you should see the following output:

```
/usr/bin/perl
```

If the `which` command complains that no such program exists in the current `PATH`, that doesn't necessarily mean you don't have `perl` installed; it may mean simply that you don't have the `/usr/bin` directory in `PATH`. Ensure that `/usr/bin` is in `PATH`; check by typing the following command:

```
echo $PATH
```

See if the output lists the `/usr/bin` directory. If `/usr/bin` is not in `PATH`, use the following command to redefine `PATH`:

```
export PATH=$PATH:/usr/bin
```

Now, try the `which perl` command again. If you still get an error, you may not have installed Perl. You can install Perl from the companion DVD by performing the following steps:

1. **Log in as** `root`.

2. **Insert the companion DVD-ROM in the DVD-ROM drive. If you are working in GNOME or KDE graphical environment, the DVD-ROM should mount automatically. Otherwise, mount the DVD-ROM by typing the following command:**

```
mount /mnt/cdrom
```

3. **Type the following command to change the directory to the location of the Red Hat packages:**

```
cd /mnt/cdrom/RedHat/RPMS
```

4. **Type the following** `rpm` **(Red Hat Package Manager) command to install Perl:**

```
rpm -ivh perl*
```

After you have installed Perl on your system, type the following command to see its version number:

```
perl -v
```

Here is typical output from that command:

```
This is perl, v5.8.1 built for i386-linux-thread-multi
(with 1 registered patch, see perl -V for more detail)

Copyright 1987-2003, Larry Wall

Perl may be copied only under the terms of either the Artistic License or the
GNU General Public License, which may be found in the Perl 5 source kit.

Complete documentation for Perl, including FAQ lists, should be found on
this system using `man perl' or `perldoc perl'.  If you have access to the
Internet, point your browser at http://www.perl.com/, the Perl Home Page.
```

This output tells you that you have Perl version 5.8, patch Level 1, and that Larry Wall, the originator of Perl, holds the copyright. (Remember, however, that Perl is distributed freely under the GNU General Public License.)

You can get the latest version of Perl by pointing your World Wide Web browser to the Comprehensive Perl Archive Network (CPAN). The following address connects you to the CPAN site nearest to you:

```
http://www.perl.com/CPAN/
```

Writing Your First Perl Script

Perl has many features of C, and, as you may know, most books on C start with an example program that displays Hello, World! on your terminal. Because Perl is an interpreted language, you can accomplish this task directly from the command line. If you enter

```
perl -e 'print "Hello, World!\n";'
```

Perl responds with the following:

```
Hello, World!
```

This command uses the -e option of the perl program to pass the Perl program as a command-line argument to the Perl interpreter. In this case, the following line constitutes the Perl program:

```
print "Hello, World!\n";
```

To convert this line to a Perl script, simply place the line in a file, and start the file with a directive to run the perl program (as you do in shell scripts, when you place a line such as #!/bin/sh to run the shell to process the script).

To try this Perl script, follow these steps:

1. **Use a text editor to type and save the following lines in the file named** hello.pl:

   ```
   #!/usr/bin/perl
   # This is a comment.
   print "Hello, World!\n";
   ```

2. **Make the** hello.pl **file executable by using the following command:**

   ```
   chmod +x hello.pl
   ```

3. **Run the Perl script by typing the following at the shell prompt:**

   ```
   ./hello.pl
   ```

   It should display the following output:

   ```
   Hello, World!
   ```

That's it! You have written and tried your first Perl script.

Notice that the first line of a Perl script starts with #!, followed by the full pathname of the perl program. If the first line of a script starts with #!, the shell simply strips off the #!, appends the script file's name to the end, and runs the script. Thus, if the script file is named `hello.pl` and the first line is `#!/usr/bin/perl`, the shell executes the following command:

```
/usr/bin/perl hello.pl
```

Getting an Overview of Perl

Most programming languages, including Perl, have some common features:

✦ **Variables** store different types of data. You can think of each variable as a placeholder for data — kind of like a mailbox, with a name and space to store data. The content of the variable is its value.

✦ **Expressions** combine variables by using operators. One expression may add several variables; another might extract a part of a string.

✦ **Statements** perform some action, such as assigning a value to a variable or printing a string.

✦ **Flow-control statements** enable statements to be executed in various orders, depending on the value of some expression. Typically, flow-control statements include `for`, `do-while`, `while`, and `if-then-else` statements.

✦ **Functions** (also called *subroutines* or *routines*) enable you to group several statements and give them a name. Using this feature, you can execute the same set of statements by invoking the function that represents those statements. Typically, a programming language provides some predefined functions.

✦ **Packages** and **modules** enable you to organize a set of related Perl subroutines that are designed to be reusable. (Modules were introduced in Perl 5.)

In the next few sections, I provide an overview of these major features of Perl and illustrate the features through simple examples.

Basic Perl syntax

Perl is free-form, like C. There are no constraints on the exact placement of any keyword. Often, Perl programs are stored in files with names that end in `.pl`, but there is no restriction on the filenames you use.

As in C, each Perl statement ends with a semicolon (`;`). A hash mark or pound sign (`#`) marks the start of a comment; the `perl` program disregards the rest of the line beginning with the hash mark.

Groups of Perl statements are enclosed in braces (`{ ... }`). This feature also is similar in C.

Variables

You don't have to declare Perl variables before using them, as you do in the C programming language. You can recognize a variable in a Perl script easily because each variable name begins with a special character: an at symbol (@), a dollar sign ($), or a percent sign (%). These special characters denote the variable's type. The three variable types are as follows:

+ **Scalar variables** represent the basic data types: integer, floating-point number, and string. A dollar sign ($) precedes a scalar variable. Following are some examples:

```
$maxlines = 256;
$title = "Red Hat Linux All-in-One Desk Reference";
```

+ **Array variables** are collections of scalar variables. An array variable has an at symbol (@) as a prefix. Thus, the following are arrays:

```
@pages = (62, 26, 22, 24);
@commands = ("start", "stop", "draw", "exit");
```

+ **Associative arrays** are collections of key-value pairs, in which each key is a string and the value is any scalar variable. A percent sign (%) prefix indicates an associative array. You can use associative arrays to associate a name with a value. You may store the amount of disk space each user occupies in an associative array, such as the following:

```
%disk_usage = ("root", 147178, "naba", 28547,
               "emily", 55, "ashley", 40);
```

Because each variable type has a special character prefix, you can use the same name for different variable types. Thus, %disk_usage, @disk_usage, and $disk_usage can appear within the same Perl program.

Scalars

A *scalar variable* can store a single value, such as a number or a text string. Scalar variables are the basic data type in Perl. Each scalar's name begins with a dollar sign ($). Typically, you start using a scalar with an assignment statement that initializes it. You even can use a variable without initializing it; the default value for numbers is zero, and the default value of a string is an empty string. If you want to see whether a scalar is defined, use the defined function as follows:

```
print "Name undefined!\n" if !(defined $name);
```

The expression (defined $name) is 1 if $name is defined. You can "undefine" a variable by using the undef function. You can undefine $name, for example, as follows:

```
undef $name;
```

Variables are evaluated according to context. Following is a script that initializes and prints a few variables:

```
#!/usr/bin/perl
$title = "Red Hat Linux All-in-One Desk Reference";
$count1 = 650;
$count2 = 238;

$total = $count1 + $count2;

print "Title: $title -- $total pages\n";
```

When you run the preceding Perl program, it produces the following output:

```
Title: Red Hat Linux All-in-One Desk Reference -- 888 pages
```

As the Perl statements show, when the two numeric variables are added, their numeric values are used; but when the `$total` variable is printed, its string representation is displayed.

Another interesting aspect of Perl is that it evaluates all variables in a string within double quotation marks ("..."). However, if you write a string inside single quotation marks ('...'), Perl leaves that string untouched. If you write

```
 print 'Title: $title -- $total pages\n';
```

with single quotes instead of double quotes, Perl displays

```
Title: $title -- $total pages\n
```

and does not generate a new line.

A useful Perl variable is `$_` (the dollar sign followed by the underscore character). This special variable is known as the default argument. The Perl interpreter determines the value of `$_` depending on the context. When the Perl interpreter reads input from the standard input, `$_` holds the current input line; when the interpreter is searching for a specific pattern of text, `$_` holds the default search pattern.

Arrays

In Perl, an *array* is a collection of scalars. The array name begins with an at symbol (@). As in C, array subscripts start at zero. You can access the elements of an array with an index. Perl allocates space for arrays dynamically.

Consider the following simple script:

```
#!/usr/bin/perl
@commands = ("start", "stop", "draw" , "exit");

$numcmd = @commands;
print "There are $numcmd commands.\n";
print "The first command is: $commands[0]\n";
```

When you run the script, it produces the following output:

```
There are 4 commands.
The first command is: start
```

As you can see, equating a scalar to the array sets the scalar to the number of elements in the array. The first element of the @commands array is referenced as $commands[0] because the index starts at zero. Thus, the fourth element in the @commands array is $commands[3].

Two special scalars are related to an array. The $[variable is one of them, and it's the current base index (the starting index), which is zero by default. The other scalar is *$#arrayname* (in which *arrayname* is the name of an array variable), which has the last array index as the value. Thus, for the @commands array, $#commands is 3.

You can print an entire array with a simple print statement like this:

```
print "@commands\n";
```

When Perl executes this statement, it displays the following output:

```
start stop draw exit
```

Associative arrays

Associative array variables, which are declared with a percent sign (%) prefix, are unique features of Perl. Using associative arrays, you can index an array with a string, such as a name. A good example of an associative array is the %ENV array that Perl automatically defines for you. In Perl, %ENV is the array of environment variables you can access by using the environment variable name as an index. The following Perl statement prints the current PATH environment variable:

```
print "PATH = $ENV{PATH}\n";
```

When Perl executes this statement, it prints the current setting of PATH. In contrast to indexing regular arrays, you have to use braces to index an associative array.

Perl has many built-in functions — such as delete, each, keys, and values — that enable you to access and manipulate associative arrays.

Predefined variables in Perl

Perl has several predefined variables that contain useful information you may need in a Perl script. Following are a few important predefined variables:

✦ @ARGV is an array of strings that contains the command-line options to the script. The first option is $ARGV[0], the second one is $ARGV[1], and so on.

✦ %ENV is an associative array that contains the environment variables. You can access this array by using the environment variable name as a key. Thus $ENV{HOME} is the home directory, and $ENV{PATH} is the current search path that the shell uses to locate commands.

✦ $_ is the default argument for many functions. If you see a Perl function used without any argument, the function probably is expecting its argument to be contained in the $_ variable.

✦ @_ is the list of arguments passed to a subroutine.

✦ $0 is the name of the file containing the Perl program.

✦ $^V is the version number of Perl you are using (for example, if you use Perl version 5.8.1, $^V will be v5.8.1).

✦ $< is the user ID (an identifying number) of the user running the script.

✦ $$ is the script's process ID.

✦ $? is the status the last system call has returned.

Operators and expressions

Operators are used to combine and compare Perl variables. Typical mathematical operators are addition (+), subtraction (-), multiplication (*), and division (/). Perl and C provide nearly the same set of operators. When you use operators to combine variables, you end up with expressions. Each expression has a value.

Here are some typical Perl expressions:

```
error < 0
$count == 10
$count + $i
$users[$i]
```

These expressions are examples of the comparison operator (the first two lines), the arithmetic operator, and the array index operator.

In Perl, don't use the == operator to determine whether two strings match; the == operator works only with numbers. To test the equality of strings, Perl includes the FORTRAN-style eq operator. Use eq to see whether two strings are identical, as follows:

```
if ($input eq "stop") { exit; }
```

Other FORTRAN-style, string-comparison operators include ne (inequality), lt (less than), gt (greater than), le (less than or equal), and ge (greater than or equal to). Also, you can use the cmp operator to compare two strings. The return value is –1, 0, or 1, depending on whether the first string is less than, equal to, or greater than the second string.

Perl also provides the following unique operators. C lacks an exponentiation operator, which FORTRAN includes; Perl uses ** as the exponentiation operator. Thus, you can write the following code in Perl:

```
$x = 2;
$y = 3;
$z = $x**$y;   # z should be 8 (2 raised to the power 3)
$y **= 2; # y is now 9 (3 raised to the power 2)
```

You can initialize an array to null by using ( ) — the null-list operator — as follows:

```
@commands = ();
```

The dot operator (.) enables you to concatenate two strings, as follows:

```
$part1 = "Hello, ";
$part2 = "World!";
$message = $part1.$part2;   # Now $message = "Hello, World!"
```

The repetition operator, denoted by x=, is interesting and quite useful. You can use the x= operator to repeat a string a specified number of times. Suppose you want to initialize a string to 65 asterisks (*). The following example shows how you can initialize the string with the x= operator:

```
$marker = "*";
$marker x= 65;   # Now $marker is a string of 65 asterisks
```

Another powerful operator in Perl is range, which is represented by two periods (..). You can initialize an array easily by using the range operator. Following are some examples:

```
@numerals = (0..9); # @numerals = 0, 1, 2, 3, 4, 5, 6, 7, 8 , 9
@alphabet = ('A'..'Z'); # @alphabet = capital letters A through Z
```

Regular expressions

If you have used any UNIX or Linux system for a while, you probably know about the `grep` command, which enables you to search files for a pattern of strings. Following is a typical use of `grep` to locate all files that have any occurrences of the string `blaster` or `Blaster` — on any line of all files with names that end in `.c`:

```
cd /usr/src/linux*/drivers/cdrom
grep "[bB]laster"  *.c
```

The preceding `grep` command finds all occurrences of `blaster` and `Blaster` in the files with names ending in `.c`.

The `grep` command's `"[bB]laster"` argument is known as a *regular expression*, a pattern that matches a set of strings. You construct a regular expression with a small set of operators and rules that resemble the ones for writing arithmetic expressions. A list of characters inside brackets (`[...]`), for example, matches any single character in the list. Thus, the regular expression `"[bB]laster"` is a set of two strings, as follows:

```
blaster    Blaster
```

Perl supports regular expressions, just as the `grep` command does. Many other Red Hat Linux programs, such as the `vi` editor and `sed` (the stream editor), also support regular expressions. The purpose of a regular expression is to search for a pattern of strings in a file. That's why editors support regular expressions.

You can construct and use complex regular expressions in Perl. The rules for these regular expressions are fairly simple. Essentially, the regular expression is a sequence of characters in which some characters have special meaning. Table 4-1 summarizes the basic rules for interpreting the characters used to construct a regular expression.

Table 4-1	Rules for Interpreting Regular Expression Characters
Expression	*Meaning*
.	Matches any single character except a newline.
x*	Matches zero or more occurrences of the character x.
x+	Matches one or more occurrences of the character x.
x?	Matches zero or one occurrence of the character x.
[...]	Matches any of the characters inside the brackets.
x{n}	Matches exactly n occurrences of the character x.
x{n,}	Matches n or more occurrences of the character x.

(continued)

Table 4-1 *(continued)*

Expression	Meaning
x{,m}	Matches zero or, at most, m occurrences of the character x.
x{n,m}	Matches at least n occurrences, but no more than m occurrences of the character x.
$	Matches the end of a line.
\0	Matches a null character.
\b	Matches a backspace.
\B	Matches any character not at the beginning or end of a word.
\b	Matches the beginning or end of a word — when not inside brackets.
\cX	Matches Ctrl-X (where X is any alphabetic character).
\d	Matches a single digit.
\D	Matches a nondigit character.
\f	Matches a form feed.
\n	Matches a newline (line-feed) character.
\ooo	Matches the octal value specified by the digits ooo (where each o is a digit between 0 and 7).
\r	Matches a carriage return.
\S	Matches a nonwhite space character.
\s	Matches a white space character (space, tab, or newline).
\t	Matches a tab.
\W	Matches a nonalphanumeric character.
\w	Matches an alphanumeric character.
\xhh	Matches the hexadecimal value specified by the digits hh (where each h is a digit between 0 and f).
^	Matches the beginning of a line.

If you want to match one of the characters $, |, *, ^, [,], \, and /, you have to place a backslash before the character you want to match. Thus, you would type these characters as \$, \|, *, \^, \[, \], \\, and \/. Regular expressions often look confusing because of the preponderance of strange character sequences and the generous sprinkling of backslashes. As with anything else, however, you can start slowly and use only a few of the features in the beginning.

So far, I have summarized the syntax of regular expressions. But I haven't yet shown how to use regular expressions in Perl. Typically, you place a regular expression within a pair of slashes and use the match (=~) or not-match

(!~) operators to test a string. You can write a Perl script that performs the same search as the one done with `grep` earlier in this section. Follow these steps to complete this task:

1. **Use a text editor to type and save the following script in a file named** `lookup`**:**

```
#!/usr/bin/perl

while (<STDIN>)
{
    if ( $_ =~ /[bB]laster/ ) { print $_; }
}
```

2. **Make the** `lookup` **file executable by using the following command:**

```
chmod +x lookup
```

3. **Try the script by using the following command:**

```
cat /usr/src/linux*/drivers/cdrom/sbpcd.c | ./lookup
```

In this case, the `cat` command feeds the contents of a specific file (which, as you know from the `grep` example, contains some lines with the regular expression) to the `lookup` script. The script simply applies Perl's regular expression-match operator (=~) and prints any matching line. The output should be similar to what the `grep` command displays with the following command:

```
grep "[bB]laster"
     /usr/src/linux*/drivers/cdrom/sbpcd.c
```

The $_ variable in the `lookout` script needs some explanation. The `<STDIN>` expression gets a line from the standard input and, by default, stores that line in the $_ variable. Inside the `while` loop, the regular expression is matched against the $_ string. The following single Perl statement completes the lookup script's work:

```
if ( $_ =~ /[bB]laster/ ) { print $_; }
```

This example illustrates how you might use a regular expression to search for occurrences of strings in a file.

After you use regular expressions for a while, you can better appreciate their power. The trick is to find the regular expression that performs the task you want. For example, here is a search that looks for all lines that begin with exactly seven spaces and end with a closing parenthesis:

```
while (<STDIN>)
{
    if ( $_ =~ /\)\n/ && $_ =~ /^ {7}\S/ )  { print $_; }
}
```

Flow-control statements

So far, you have seen Perl statements intended to execute in a serial fashion, one after another. Perl also includes statements that enable you to control the flow of execution of the statements. You already have seen the if statement and a while loop. Perl includes a complete set of flow-control statements just like those in C, but with a few extra features.

In Perl, all conditional statements take the following form:

```
conditional-statement
{ Perl code to execute if conditional is true }
```

Notice that you must enclose within braces ({...}) the code that follows the conditional statement. The conditional statement checks the value of an expression to determine whether to execute the code within the braces. In Perl, as in C, any nonzero value is considered logically true, whereas a zero value is false.

Next I briefly describe the syntax of the major conditional statements in Perl.

if and unless

The Perl if statement resembles the C if statement. For example, an if statement may check a count to see whether the count exceeds a threshold, as follows:

```
if ( $count > 25 ) { print "Too many errors!\n"; }
```

You can add an else clause to the if statement, like this:

```
if ($user eq "root")
{
    print "Starting simulation...\n";
}
else
{
    print "Sorry $user, you must be \"root\" to run this
    program.\n";
    exit;
}
```

If you know C, you can see that Perl's syntax looks quite a bit like that in C. Conditionals with the `if` statement can have zero or more `elsif` clauses to account for more alternatives, as in the following:

```
print "Enter version number:"; # prompt user for version number

$os_version = <STDIN>;        # read from standard input
chop $os_version; # get rid of the newline at the end of the line
# Check version number
if ($os_version >= 10 ) { print "No upgrade necessary\n";}
elsif ($os_version >= 6 && $os_version < 9)
                { print "Standard upgrade\n";}
elsif ($os_version > 3 && $os_version < 6) { print "Reinstall\n";}
else { print "Sorry, cannot upgrade\n";}
```

The `unless` statement is unique to Perl. This statement has the same form as `if`, including the use of `elsif` and `else` clauses. The difference is that `unless` executes its statement block only if the condition is false. You can, for example, use `unless` in the following code:

```
unless ($user eq "root")
{
    print "You must be \"root\" to run this program.\n";
    exit;
}
```

In this case, unless the string `user` is `"root"`, the script exits.

while

Use Perl's `while` statement for *looping* — the repetition of some processing until an existing condition becomes logically false. To read a line at a time from standard input and to process that line, you can use the following `while` loop:

```
while ($in = <STDIN>)
{
# Code to process the line
    print $in;
}
```

If you read from the standard input without any argument, Perl assigns the current line of standard input to the $_ variable. Thus, you can write the preceding `while` loop as follows:

```
while (<STDIN>)
{
# Code to process the line
    print $_;
}
```

Perl's `while` statements are more versatile than those of C because you can use almost anything as the condition to be tested. If you use an array as the condition, for example, the `while` loop executes until the array has no elements left, as in the following example:

```
# Assume @cmd arg has the current set of command arguments
while (@cmd arg)
{
    $arg = shift @cmd arg;  # this extracts one argument
# Code to process the current argument
    print $arg;
}
```

The `shift` function removes the first element of an array and returns that element.

You can skip to the end of a loop with the `next` keyword; the `last` keyword exits the loop. For example, the following `while` loop adds the numbers from 1 to 10, skipping 5:

```
while (1)
{
  $i++;
  if($i == 5) { next;} # Jump to the next iteration if $i is 5
  if($i > 10) { last;} # When $i exceeds 10, end the loop
  $sum += $i;      # Add the numbers
}
# At this point $sum should be 50
```

for and foreach

Perl and C's `for` statements have similar syntax. Use the `for` statement to execute a statement any number of times, based on the value of an expression. The syntax is as follows:

```
for (expr_1; expr_2; expr_3) { statement block }
```

expr_1 is evaluated one time, at the beginning of the loop; the statement block is executed until expression *expr_2* evaluates to zero. The third expression, *expr_3*, is evaluated after each execution of the statement block. You can omit any of the expressions, but you must include the semicolons. In addition, the braces around the statement block are required. Following is an example that uses a `for` loop to add the numbers from 1 to 10:

```
for($i=0, $sum=0; $i <= 10; $sum += $i, $i++) {}
```

In this example, the actual work of adding the numbers is done in the third expression, and the statement the `for` loop controls is an empty block (`{ }`).

The `foreach` statement is most appropriate for arrays. Following is the syntax:

```
foreach Variable (Array) { statement block }
```

The `foreach` statement assigns to *Variable* an element from the *Array* and executes the statement block. The `foreach` statement repeats this procedure until no array elements remain. The following `foreach` statement adds the numbers from 1 to 10:

```
foreach $i (1..10) { $sum += $i;}
```

Notice that I declare the array by using the range operator (`..`). You also can use a list of comma-separated items as the array.

If you omit the *Variable* in a `foreach` statement, Perl implicitly uses the `$_` variable to hold the current array element. Thus, you can use the following:

```
foreach (1..10) { $sum += $_;}
```

goto

The `goto` statement causes Perl to jump to a statement identified by a label. Here is an example that prompts the user for a value and repeats the request, if the value is not acceptable:

```
ReEnter:
print "Enter offset: ";
$offset = <STDIN>;
chop $offset;
unless ($offset > 0 && $offset < 512)
{
    print "Bad offset: $offset\n";
    goto ReEnter;
}
```

Accessing Linux commands

You can execute any Linux command from Perl in several ways:

✦ Call the `system` function with a string that contains the Linux command you want to execute.

✦ Enclose a Linux command within backquotes (`` ` ``), which also are known as *grave accents*. You can run a Linux command this way and capture its output.

✦ Call the `fork` function to copy the current script and process new commands in the child process. (If a process starts another process, the new one is known as a *child process*.)

✦ Call the exec function to overlay the current script with a new script or Linux command.

✦ Use fork and exec to provide shell-like behavior. (Monitor user input, and process each user-entered command through a child process.) In this section, I present a simple example of how to accomplish this task.

The simplest way to execute a Linux command in your script is to use the system function with the command in a string. After the system function returns, the exit code from the command is in the $? variable. You can easily write a simple Perl script that reads a string from the standard input and processes that string with the system function. Follow these steps:

1. **Use a text editor to enter and save the following script in a file named** rcmd.pl:

```
#!/usr/bin/perl
# Read user input and process command

$prompt = "Command (\"exit\" to quit): ";
print $prompt;

while (<STDIN>)
{
    chop;
    if ($_ eq "exit") { exit 0;}

# Execute command by calling system
    system $_;
    unless ($? == 0) {print "Error executing: $_\n";}
    print $prompt;
}
```

2. **Make the** rcmd.pl **file executable by using the following command:**

```
chmod +x rcmd.pl
```

3. **Run the script by typing** ./rcmd.pl **at the shell prompt.**

Here's a sample output from the rcmd.pl script (the output depends on what commands you enter):

```
Command ("exit" to quit): ps
  PID TTY          TIME CMD
  767 pts/0    00:00:00 bash
  940 pts/0    00:00:00 rcmd.pl
  945 pts/0    00:00:00 ps
Command ("exit" to quit): exit
```

You can also run Linux commands by using fork and exec in your Perl script. Following is an example script — psh.pl — that uses fork and exec to execute commands the user enters:

```
#!/usr/bin/perl

# This is a simple script that uses "fork" and "exec" to
# run a command entered by the user

$prompt = "Command (\"exit\" to quit): ";
print $prompt;

while (<STDIN>)
{
    chop;     # remove trailing newline
    if($_ eq "exit") { exit 0;}

    $status = fork;
    if($status)
    {
# In parent... wait for child process to finish...
        wait;
        print $prompt;
        next;
    }
    else
    {
        exec $_;
    }
}
```

The following sample output shows how the psh.pl script executes the ps command:

```
Command ("exit" to quit): ps
  PID TTY          TIME CMD
  767 pts/0    00:00:00 bash
  949 pts/0    00:00:00 psh.pl
  950 pts/0    00:00:00 ps
Command ("exit" to quit): exit
```

Shells (such as Bash) use the fork and exec combination to run commands.

File access

You may have noticed the <STDIN> expression in various examples in this chapter. That's Perl's way of reading from a file. In Perl, a *file handle*, also known as an *identifier*, gives a file a distinct identity while it's being read. Usually, file handles are in uppercase characters. STDIN is a predefined file handle that denotes the standard input — by default, the keyboard. STDOUT and STDERR are the other two predefined file handles. STDOUT is used for printing to the terminal, and STDERR is used for printing error messages.

To read from a file, write the file handle inside angle brackets (<>). Thus, <STDIN> reads a line from the standard input.

You can open other files by using the open function. The following example shows you how to open the /etc/passwd file for reading and how to display the lines in that file:

```
open (PWDFILE, "/etc/passwd"); # PWDFILE is the file handle
while (<PWDFILE>) { print $_;} # By default, input line is in $_
close PWDFILE;          # Close the file
```

By default, the open function opens a file for reading. You can add special characters at the beginning of the filename to indicate other types of access. A < prefix opens the file for writing, whereas a > prefix opens a file for appending. Following is a short script that reads the /etc/passwd file and creates a new file, named output, with a list of all users who lack shells (the password entries for these users have : at the end of each line):

```
#!/usr/bin/perl
# Read /etc/passwd and create list of users without any shell

open (PWDFILE, "/etc/passwd");
open (RESULT, ">output");      # open file for writing

while (<PWDFILE>)
{
    if ($_ =~ /:\n/) {print RESULT $_;}
}

close PWDFILE;
close RESULT;
```

After you execute this script, you should find a file named output in the current directory. Here's what the output file contains when I run this script on a Red Hat Linux system:

```
news:x:9:13:news:/etc/news:
```

Filename with pipe prefix

One interesting filename prefix is the *pipe character* — the vertical bar (|). If you call open with a filename that begins with |, the rest of the filename is treated as a command. The Perl interpreter executes the command, and you can use print calls to send input to this command. The following Perl script sends a mail message to a list of users by using the mail command:

```
#!/usr/bin/perl
# Send mail to a list of users

foreach ("root", "naba")
```

```
{
  open (MAILPIPE, "| mail -s Greetings $_");
  print MAILPIPE "Remember to send in your weekly report today!\n";
  close MAILPIPE;
}
```

If a filename ends with a pipe character (|), that filename is executed as a command; you can read that command's output with the angle brackets (<...>), as shown in the following example:

```
open (PSPIPE, "ps ax |");
while (<PSPIPE>)
{
# Process the output of the ps command
# This example simply echoes each line
    print $_;
}
```

Subroutines

Although Perl includes a large assortment of built-in functions, you can add your own code modules in the form of *subroutines*. In fact, Perl comes with a large set of these programs-within-programs. Here's a simple script that illustrates the syntax of subroutines in Perl:

```
#!/usr/bin/perl
sub hello
{
# Make local copies of the arguments from the @_ array
    local ($first,$last) = @_;

    print "Hello, $first $last\n";
}

$a = Jane;
$b = Doe;

&hello($a, $b);        # Call the subroutine
```

When you run the preceding script, it displays the following output:

```
Hello, Jane Doe
```

Note the following points about subroutines:

+ The subroutine receives its arguments in the array @_ (the at symbol, followed by an underscore character).

+ Variables used in subroutines are global by default. Use the local function to create a local set of variables.

✦ Call a subroutine by placing an ampersand (&) before its name. Thus, the subroutine `hello` is called by typing &hello.

If you want, you can put a subroutine in its own file. The `hello` subroutine, for example, can reside in a file named `hello.pl`. When you place a subroutine in a file, remember to add a return value at the end of the file — just type **1;** at the end to return 1. Thus, the `hello.pl` file appears as follows:

```
sub hello
{
# Make local copies of the arguments from the @_ array
    local ($first,$last) = @_;

    print "Hello, $first $last\n";
}
1;       # return value
```

Then, you have to write the script that uses the `hello` subroutine, as follows:

```
#!/usr/bin/perl
require 'hello.pl';   # include the file with the subroutine

$a = Jane;
$b = Doe;

&hello($a, $b);       # Call the subroutine
```

This script uses the `require` function to include the `hello.pl` file that contains the definition of the `hello` subroutine.

Built-in functions in Perl

Perl has nearly 200 built-in functions (also referred to as *Perl functions*), including functions that resemble the ones in the C Run-Time Library, as well as functions that access the operating system. You really need to go through the list of functions to appreciate the breadth of capabilities available in Perl. I don't have enough space in this book to cover these functions, but you can learn about the Perl built-in functions by pointing your Web browser to the following address:

```
http://www.perldoc.com/perl5.8.0/pod/perlfunc.html
```

This address connects you to the Perl 5.8.0 documentation page so that you can get an overview of the Perl built-in functions. On that page, click a function's name to view more detailed information about that function.

You can also read the Perl function manual on your Red Hat Linux system by typing the following command in a terminal window:

```
man perlfunc
```

This command displays the text `man` page for the functions. (I think you'll find the Web-based documentation much easier to use.)

Understanding Perl Packages and Modules

A *Perl package* is a way to group together data and subroutines. Essentially, it's a way to use variable and subroutine names without conflicting with any names used in other parts of a program. The concept of a package existed in Perl since version 4.

The package provides a way to control the *namespace* — a term that refers to the collection of variable and subroutine names. Although you may not be aware of this, when you write a Perl program, it automatically belongs to a package named `main`. Besides `main`, there are other Perl packages in the Perl library (these packages are in the `/usr/lib/perl5/X.Y.Z` directory of your Red Hat Linux system where X.Y.Z is the version number of Perl such as `5.8.1`), and you can define your own package, as well.

Perl *modules* are packages that follow specific guidelines.

Perl packages

You can think of a Perl package as a convenient way to organize a set of related Perl subroutines. Another benefit is that variable and subroutine names defined in a package do not conflict with names used elsewhere in the program. Thus, a variable named `$count` in one package remains unique to that package and does not conflict with a `$count` used elsewhere in a Perl program.

A Perl package is in a single file. The `package` statement is used at the beginning of the file to declare the file as a package and to give the package a name. For example, the file `timelocal.pl` defines a number of subroutines and variables in a package named `timelocal`. (Note that the `timelocal.pl` file has been superceded by the Time::Local module.) The `timelocal.pl` file has the following `package` statement in various places:

```
package timelocal;
```

The effect of this package declaration is that all subsequent variable names and subroutine names are considered to be in the `timelocal` package. You can put such a package statement at the beginning of the file that implements the package.

What if you are implementing a package and you need to refer to a subroutine or variable in another package? As you might guess, all you need to do is specify both the package name and the variable (or subroutine) name. Perl provides the following syntax for referring to a variable in another package:

```
$Package::Variable
```

Here `Package` is the name of the package, and `Variable` is the name of the variable in that package. If you omit the package name, Perl assumes you're referring to a variable in the `main` package.

To use a package in your program, you can simply call the `require` function with the package filename as an argument. For example, there is a package named `ctime` defined in the file `ctime.pl`. That package includes the `ctime` subroutine that converts a binary time into a string. The following simple program uses the `ctime` package from the `ctime.pl` file:

```
#!/usr/bin/perl -w

# Use the ctime package defined in ctime.pl file
require 'ctime.pl';

# Call the ctime subroutine
$time = ctime(time());

# Print the time string
print $time;
```

As you can see, this program uses the `require` function to bring the `ctime.pl` file into the program. When you run this program, it should print the current date and time formatted, as shown in the following sample output:

```
Sat Jul 26 14:54:25 2003
```

Note that the first line of this script uses the `-w` option. That option causes the Perl interpreter to print warning messages about any bad constructs in the Perl script. It's a good idea to include the `-w` option on the line that invokes the Perl interpreter.

Perl modules

Perl 5 took the concept of a package one step further and introduced the *module*, a package that follows certain guidelines and is designed to be reusable. Each module is a package that is defined in a file with the same name as the package but with a `.pm` extension. Each Perl object is implemented as a module. For example, the `CGI` object (for use in Web servers) is implemented as the `CGI` module, stored in the file named `CGI.pm`.

Nowadays Perl comes with many modules. You'll find these modules in the `/usr/lib/perl5/X.Y.Z` directory where `X.Y.Z` is the Perl version number.

For Perl version 5.8.1, the Perl modules are in the `/usr/lib/perl5/5.8.1` directory. Look for files with names that end in `.pm` (which stands for *Perl module*).

Using a module

You can call the `require` function, or the `use` function, to include a Perl module in your program. For example, a Perl module named `Cwd` (defined, as expected, in the `Cwd.pm` file) provides a `getcwd` subroutine that returns the current directory. You can call the `require` function to include the `Cwd` module and call `getcwd` as follows:

```
require Cwd;  # You do not need the full file name
$curdir = Cwd::getcwd();
print "Current directory = $curdir\n";
```

The first line brings the `Cwd.pm` file into this program — you do not have to specify the full filename; the `require` function automatically appends `.pm` to the module's name to figure out which file to include. The second line shows how you call a subroutine from the `Cwd` module. When you use `require` to include a module, you must invoke each subroutine with the *Module:: subroutine* format.

If you were to rewrite this example program with the `use` function in place of `require`, it would take the following form:

```
use Cwd;
$curdir = getcwd(); # no need for Cwd:: prefix
print "Current directory = $curdir\n";
```

The most significant difference is that you no longer need to qualify a subroutine name with the module name prefix (such as `Cwd::`).

You can call either `require` or `use` to include a module in your program. Just remember the following nuances when you use these functions:

✦ When you include a module by calling `require`, the module is included only when the `require` function is invoked as the program runs. You must use the *Module::subroutine* syntax to invoke any subroutines from a module you include with the `require` function.

✦ When you include a module by calling `use`, the module is included in the program as soon as the `use` statement is processed. Thus, you can invoke subroutines and variables from the module as if they were part of your program. You do not need to qualify subroutine and variable names with a *Module::* prefix.

You may want to stick to the `use Module;` syntax to include modules in your program because this lets you use a simpler syntax when you call subroutines from the module.

Using Objects in Perl

An *object* is a data structure together with the functions that operate on that data. Each object is an instance of a class that defines the object's type. For example, a rectangle class may have the four corners of the rectangle as data; functions such as one that computes the rectangle's area; and another that draws the rectangle. Then, each rectangle object can be an *instance* of the rectangle *class*, with different coordinates for each of the four corners. In this sense, an object is an instance of a class.

The functions (or subroutines) that implement the operations on an object's data are known as *methods*. That's terminology borrowed from Smalltalk, one of the earliest object-oriented programming languages.

Classes also suggest the notion of inheritance. You can define a new class of objects by extending the data or methods (or both) of an existing class. A common use of inheritance is to express the IS A relationship among various classes of objects. Consider, for example, the geometric shapes. Because a circle IS A shape and a rectangle IS A shape, you can say that the circle and rectangle classes inherit from the shape class. In this case, the shape class is called a parent class or base class.

The basic idea behind *object-oriented programming* is that you can package the data and the associated methods (subroutines) of an object so that they work like a *black box* — input generates output, without your having to specify every detail of how to get the job done. Programmers access the object only through advertised methods, without having to know the inner workings of the methods. Typically, a programmer can create an object, invoke its methods to get or set attributes (that's another name for the object's data), and destroy the object. In this section I show you how to use objects in Perl. With this knowledge in hand, you'll be able to exploit objects as building blocks for your Perl programs.

Understanding Perl Objects

Perl implements objects by using modules, which package data and subroutines in a file. Perl presents the following simple model of objects:

✦ An *object* is denoted by a reference (objects are implemented as references to a hash).

✦ A *class* is a Perl module that provides the methods to work with the object.

✦ A *method* is a Perl subroutine that expects the object reference as the first argument.

Object implementers have to follow certain rules and provide certain methods in a module that represents a class. However, you really don't need to know much about an object's implementation to use it in your Perl program. For practical purposes, all you need to know are the steps you have to follow when you use an object.

Creating and accessing Perl objects

An especially useful Perl object is the Shell object, which is implemented by the Perl module Shell.pm. That module comes with the Perl distribution and is in the /usr/lib/perl5/5.8.1 directory (for Perl version 5.8.1).

As the name implies, the Shell object is meant for running shell commands from within Perl scripts. You can create a Shell object and have it execute commands.

To use the Shell object, follow these general steps:

1. **Place the following line to include the Shell module in your program:**

```
use Shell;
```

You must include this line before you create a Shell object.

2. **To create a Shell object, use the following syntax:**

```
my $sh = Shell->new;
```

where $sh is the reference to the Shell object.

3. **Run Linux commands by using the Shell object and capture any outputs by saving to an appropriate variable. For example, to save the directory listing of the /usr/lib/perl5/5.8.0 directory in an array named @modules, write the following:**

```
@modules = $sh->ls("/usr/lib/perl5/5.8.1/*.pm");
```

Then you can work with this array of Perl module filenames (that's what *.pm files are) any way you want. For example, to simply go through the array and print each string out, use the following while loop:

```
while(@modules)
{
  $mod = shift @modules;
  # Do whatever you want with the module name
  print $mod;
}
```

How do you know which methods to call and in what order to call them? You have to read the object's documentation before you can use the object. The method names and the sequences of method invocation depend on what the object does.

Using the English module

Perl includes several special variables with strange names, such as $_ (for the default argument) and $! (for error messages corresponding to the last error). When you read a program, it can be difficult to guess what a special variable means. The result is that you may end up avoiding a special variable that could be useful in your program.

As a helpful gesture, Perl 5 provides the English module (English.pm), which enables you to use understandable names for various special variables in Perl. To use the English module, include the following line in your Perl program:

```
use English;
```

After that, you can refer to $_ as $ARG and $! as $ERRNO (these "English" names can still be a bit cryptic, but they're definitely better than the punctuation marks).

The following program uses the English module — and prints a few interesting variables:

```
#!/usr/bin/perl -w
# File: english.pl

use English;
print "Perl executable = $EXECUTABLE_NAME\n";
print "Script name = $PROGRAM_NAME\n";
```

Run this script with the following command:

```
./english.pl
```

When I run this script on Red Hat Linux, here's what I get as output:

```
Perl executable = /usr/bin/perl
Script name = ./english.pl
```

The English module is handy because it lets you write Perl scripts in which you can refer to special variables by meaningful names. To learn more about the Perl special variables and their English names, type **man perlvar** in a terminal window — or, better yet, point your Web browser to

```
http://www.perldoc.com/perl5.8.0/pod/perlvar.html
```

Appendix: About the DVD

In This Appendix

✔ **System requirements**

✔ **DVD installation instructions**

✔ **What you'll find on the DVD**

✔ **Troubleshooting**

System Requirements

Make sure that your computer meets the minimum system requirements shown in the following list. If your computer doesn't match up to most of these requirements, you may have problems using the software and files on the DVD.

- ✦ A PC with a 133 MHz Pentium-class processor (400 MHz Pentium II or better recomended for graphical mode)

- ✦ At least 64MB of total RAM installed on your computer for text mode and 128MB for graphical mode; for best performance, we recommend at least 256MB for graphical mode

- ✦ A DVD-ROM drive (if you have only a CD-ROM drive, use the included coupon to order Red Hat Linux on CD-ROMs)

- ✦ A graphics card and a monitor capable of displaying at least 256 colors

- ✦ A sound card

- ✦ Ethernet network interface card (NIC) or modem with a speed of at least 56 Kbps

- ✦ At least 650MB of free space on your hard disk for a minimal installation; 2.6GB recommended for a workstation class installation

DVD Installation Instructions

Installing Red Hat Linux from the DVD can be tricky, as some hardware on your PC is not supported by Red Hat Linux. Nevertheless, Red Hat Linux on the companion DVD already supports such a wide variety of hardware, so chances are good that all your PC's peripherals probably are supported.

To install Red Hat Linux from the companion DVD, follow these steps. (For the latest and greatest information, please refer to the README file located at the root of the DVD-ROM.)

1. **Gather information about your PC's hardware, such as graphics card, network card, and SCSI card, before you install Linux.**

2. **Use a partitioning program such as PartitionMagic or the FIPS program to create room on your hard disk for Red Hat Linux.**

   Skip this step if you plan to use Red Hat Linux as the sole operating system on your PC or if you plan to install it on an empty second hard disk.

3. **If your PC cannot boot from the DVD drive, create a Red Hat Linux boot disk.**

4. **Boot your PC with the DVD or by using the Red Hat Linux boot disk.**

   This step automatically runs the Red Hat Linux installation program. From this point on, respond to the questions and choices in a number of windows as the Red Hat installation program takes you through the steps. Here are some of the key installation steps:

   • Identify any SCSI adapters installed on your PC.

   • Prepare the hard disk partitions for Red Hat Linux. If you have created space by reducing the size of an existing DOS partition, this step enables you to create the partitions for Red Hat Linux.

   • Configure the Ethernet network, if any. You may have to specify parameters, such as the IP address and host name for your Red Hat Linux system.

   • Specify the local time zone and set the root password.

   • Install a boot loader program on your hard disk so that you can boot Red Hat Linux when you power up your PC after shutting it down.

   • Select the specific software packages that you want to install, such as the X Window System and the GNOME or KDE graphical desktop.

   • Configure the X Window System and enable the graphical login screen so that when you boot your Linux system, it displays a login dialog box and goes directly into the GNOME or KDE graphical desktop after successful login.

To install specific packages from the DVD to your hard drive, follow these steps:

1. **Log in as root.**

2. **Insert the DVD into your computer's DVD drive.**

3. **If you are using GNOME or KDE GUI, wait for the DVD to mount. Otherwise, open a terminal window and at the command prompt type**

```
mount /mnt/cdrom
```

4. **Choose Main Menu⇨System Settings⇨Add/Remove Applications.**

   The Add and Remove Software utility starts and gathers information about the status of packages installed on your system. After it sorts through the information about all the installed packages, the utility displays a list of all the packages. The left side of the window has two large buttons — Install Software and Remove Software. By default the Install Software button is selected.

5. **To install any uninstalled package, click the <u>Install</u> hyperlink next to that package.**

   A dialog box appears with details regarding what you're about to install and how much disk space the new packages require.

6. **Click Install Packages to install the selected package.**

7. **To remove the DVD from your DVD drive, type the following command at the command prompt:**

   ```
   umount /mnt/cdrom
   ```

What You'll Find on the DVD

This section provides a summary of the software and other goodies you find on the DVD. If you need help with installing the items provided on the DVD, refer back to the installation instructions in the preceding section.

Shareware programs are fully functional, free, trial versions of copyrighted programs. If you like particular programs, register with their authors for a nominal fee and receive licenses, enhanced versions, and technical support. *Freeware programs* are free, copyrighted games, applications, and utilities. You can copy them to as many PCs as you like — for free — but they offer no tech support. *GNU software* is governed by its own license, which is included in the folder of the GNU software. There are no restrictions on distribution of GNU software. See the GNU license at the root of the DVD for details. *Trial, demo,* or *evaluation* versions of software are usually limited by time or functionality (such as not letting you save a project after you create it).

You can find the following software on the DVD (for info on the directory organization of a DVD, refer to the README file located at the root of the DVD):

✦ Linux kernel 2.4.22 with driver modules for major PC hardware configurations, including IDE/EIDE and SCSI drives, PCMCIA devices, and CD drives and DVD drives

✦ A complete set of installation and configuration tools for setting up devices and services

✦ A graphical user interface based on the XFree86 4.3.0 package, with GNOME 2.4 and KDE 3.1 graphical desktops

✦ Full TCP/IP networking for Internet, LANs, and intranets

✦ Tools for connecting your PC to your Internet Service Provider (ISP) using PPP, DSL, or dial-up serial communications programs

✦ A complete suite of Internet applications, including electronic mail (`sendmail`, `mail`), news (INN), TELNET, FTP, DNS, and NFS

✦ Evolution 1.4.5 e-mail and calendar application

✦ OpenOffice.org 1.0 office suite with word processor, spreadsheet, presentation software, and more

✦ Apache Web server 2.0.47, to turn your PC into a Web server; and Mozilla 1.4, to surf the Net

✦ Samba 3.0 LAN Manager software for Microsoft Windows connectivity

✦ Several text editors (for example, GNU Emacs 21.3; `vim`)

✦ Graphics and image manipulation software, such as The GIMP, Xfig, Gnuplot, Ghostscript, Ghostview, and ImageMagick

✦ Programming languages (GNU C and C++ 3.3, Perl 5.8.1, Tcl/Tk 8.3.5, Python 2.2.3, GNU AWK 3.1.3) and software development tools (GNU Debugger 5.3, CVS 1.11, RCS 5.7, GNU Bison 1.875, flex 2.5.4a, TIFF, and JPEG libraries)

✦ Support for industry standard Executable and Linking Format (ELF) and Intel Binary Compatibility Specification (iBCS)

✦ A complete suite of standard UNIX utilities from the GNU project

✦ Tools to access and use DOS files and applications (`mtools` 3.9.9)

✦ Text formatting and typesetting software (`groff`, TeX, and LaTeX)

Troubleshooting

If you have difficulty installing or using the materials on the companion DVD, consult the detailed installation and troubleshooting instructions in Book I.

If you have trouble installing items from the DVD, call Customer Service at 800-762-2974 (outside the U.S.: 317-572-3993) or e-mail `techsupdum @wiley.com`. Wiley Publishing Inc. will provide tech support only for installation and other general quality control items; for tech support on the applications, consult the program's vendor or author.

Index

Symbols

. (dot)
  concatenation operator, 790
  `cp` command argument, 171
  file system navigation, 167
.. (dot dot)
  array initialization, 790
  file system navigation, 167
... (ellipsis), in C functions, 760
; (semicolon), comment indicator, 680
( ) (parentheses), null-list operator, 790
$0 (dollar sign, zero), Perl variable, 789
2> (two greater than), I/O redirection, 145
</...> (angle bracket, slash), HTML tags, 374
<...> (angle brackets), HTML tags, 374
* (asterisk)
  executable file indicator, 168
  wildcard, 145–148
@ (at sign)
  link indicator, 167–168
  Perl array names, 787
  Perl variables, 786
  in resource records, 680
@_ (at sign, underscore), variable, 789
` (back quote), Perl statements, 797
[...] (brackets), wildcards, 147–148
{...} (curly braces)
  in C statements, 754
  comment indicator, 678
  in Perl statements, 794
$ (dollar sign)
  Perl variables, 786
  zone file directives, 679

$< (dollar sign, less than), Perl variable, 789
$? (dollar sign, question mark), Perl variable, 789
$_ (dollar sign, underscore), Perl variables, 787, 789
$$ (dollar signs), Perl variable, 789
== (equal signs), equality operator, 790
! (exclamation mark)
  pattern matching, 662
  repeating commands, 148–149
/ (forward slash), root directory indicator, 161
> (greater than sign), I/O redirection, 145
(hash mark)
  , comment indicator, 652
  in C directives, 739
  in HTML anchors, 363
- (hyphen), permission indicator, 169
< (less than sign), I/O redirection, 145
% (percent sign), Perl variables, 786
? (question mark)
  in HTML anchors, 363
  wildcard, 146–148
/*...*/ (slash asterisk), comment indicator, 678
// (slash slash), comment indicator, 678
| (vertical bar), pipe character, 144, 800–801
=~ (equal, tilde), match operator, 792
!~ (exclamation mark, tilde), not-match operator, 793
~ (tilde), home directory indicator, 167

A

O

Notes

Notes

Notes

Notes

Notes

Notes

GNU GENERAL PUBLIC LICENSE

Version 2, June 1991
Copyright © 1989, 1991 Free Software Foundation, Inc.
59 Temple Place - Suite 330, Boston, MA 02111-1307, USA

Preamble

The licenses for most software are designed to take away your freedom to share and change it. By contrast, the GNU General Public License is intended to guarantee your freedom to share and change free software—to make sure the software is free for all its users. This General Public License applies to most of the Free Software Foundation's software and to any other program whose authors commit to using it. (Some other Free Software Foundation software is covered by the GNU Library General Public License instead.) You can apply it to your programs, too.

When we speak of free software, we are referring to freedom, not price. Our General Public Licenses are designed to make sure that you have the freedom to distribute copies of free software (and charge for this service if you wish), that you receive source code or can get it if you want it, that you can change the software or use pieces of it in new free programs; and that you know you can do these things.

To protect your rights, we need to make restrictions that forbid anyone to deny you these rights or to ask you to surrender the rights. These restrictions translate to certain responsibilities for you if you distribute copies of the software, or if you modify it.

For example, if you distribute copies of such a program, whether gratis or for a fee, you must give the recipients all the rights that you have. You must make sure that they, too, receive or can get the source code. And you must show them these terms so they know their rights.

We protect your rights with two steps: (1) copyright the software, and (2) offer you this license which gives you legal permission to copy, distribute and/or modify the software.

Also, for each author's protection and ours, we want to make certain that everyone understands that there is no warranty for this free software. If the software is modified by someone else and passed on, we want its recipients to know that what they have is not the original, so that any problems introduced by others will not reflect on the original authors' reputations.

Finally, any free program is threatened constantly by software patents. We wish to avoid the danger that redistributors of a free program will individually obtain patent licenses, in effect making the program proprietary. To prevent this, we have made it clear that any patent must be licensed for everyone's free use or not licensed at all.

The precise terms and conditions for copying, distribution and modification follow.

TERMS AND CONDITIONS FOR COPYING, DISTRIBUTION AND MODIFICATION

0. This License applies to any program or other work which contains a notice placed by the copyright holder saying it may be distributed under the terms of this General Public License. The "Program", below, refers to any such program or work, and a "work based on the Program" means either the Program or any derivative work under copyright law: that is to say, a work containing the Program or a portion of it, either verbatim or with modifications and/or translated into another language. (Hereinafter, translation is included without limitation in the term "modification".) Each licensee is addressed as "you".

   Activities other than copying, distribution and modification are not covered by this License; they are outside its scope. The act of running the Program is not restricted, and the output from the Program is covered only if its contents constitute a work based on the Program (independent of having been made by running the Program). Whether that is true depends on what the Program does.

1. You may copy and distribute verbatim copies of the Program's source code as you receive it, in any medium, provided that you conspicuously and appropriately publish on each copy an appropriate copyright notice and disclaimer of warranty; keep intact all the notices that refer to this License and to the absence of any warranty; and give any other recipients of the Program a copy of this License along with the Program.

   You may charge a fee for the physical act of transferring a copy, and you may at your option offer warranty protection in exchange for a fee.

2. You may modify your copy or copies of the Program or any portion of it, thus forming a work based on the Program, and copy and distribute such modifications or work under the terms of Section 1 above, provided that you also meet all of these conditions:

   a) You must cause the modified files to carry prominent notices stating that you changed the files and the date of any change.

   b) You must cause any work that you distribute or publish, that in whole or in part contains or is derived from the Program or any part thereof, to be licensed as a whole at no charge to all third parties under the terms of this License.

   c) If the modified program normally reads commands interactively when run, you must cause it, when started running for such interactive use in the most ordinary way, to print or display an announcement including an appropriate copyright notice and a notice that there is no warranty (or else, saying that you provide a warranty) and that users may redistribute the program under these conditions, and telling the user how to view a copy of this License. (Exception: if the Program itself is interactive but does not normally print such an announcement, your work based on the Program is not required to print an announcement.)

   These requirements apply to the modified work as a whole. If identifiable sections of that work are not derived from the Program, and can be reasonably considered independent and separate works in themselves, then this License, and its terms, do not apply to those sections when you distribute them as separate works. But when you distribute the same sections as part of a whole which is a work based on the Program, the distribution of the whole must be on the terms of this License, whose permissions for other licensees extend to the entire whole, and thus to each and every part regardless of who wrote it.

Thus, it is not the intent of this section to claim rights or contest your rights to work written entirely by you; rather, the intent is to exercise the right to control the distribution of derivative or collective works based on the Program.

In addition, mere aggregation of another work not based on the Program with the Program (or with a work based on the Program) on a volume of a storage or distribution medium does not bring the other work under the scope of this License.

3. You may copy and distribute the Program (or a work based on it, under Section 2) in object code or executable form under the terms of Sections 1 and 2 above provided that you also do one of the following:

   a) Accompany it with the complete corresponding machine-readable source code, which must be distributed under the terms of Sections 1 and 2 above on a medium customarily used for software interchange; or,

   b) Accompany it with a written offer, valid for at least three years, to give any third party, for a charge no more than your cost of physically performing source distribution, a complete machine-readable copy of the corresponding source code, to be distributed under the terms of Sections 1 and 2 above on a medium customarily used for software interchange; or,

   c) Accompany it with the information you received as to the offer to distribute corresponding source code. (This alternative is allowed only for noncommercial distribution and only if you received the program in object code or executable form with such an offer, in accord with Subsection b above.)

The source code for a work means the preferred form of the work for making modifications to it. For an executable work, complete source code means all the source code for all modules it contains, plus any associated interface definition files, plus the scripts used to control compilation and installation of the executable. However, as a special exception, the source code distributed need not include anything that is normally distributed (in either source or binary form) with the major components (compiler, kernel, and so on) of the operating system on which the executable runs, unless that component itself accompanies the executable.

If distribution of executable or object code is made by offering access to copy from a designated place, then offering equivalent access to copy the source code from the same place counts as distribution of the source code, even though third parties are not compelled to copy the source along with the object code.

4. You may not copy, modify, sublicense, or distribute the Program except as expressly provided under this License. Any attempt otherwise to copy, modify, sublicense or distribute the Program is void, and will automatically terminate your rights under this License. However, parties who have received copies, or rights, from you under this License will not have their licenses terminated so long as such parties remain in full compliance.

5. You are not required to accept this License, since you have not signed it. However, nothing else grants you permission to modify or distribute the Program or its derivative works. These actions are prohibited by law if you do not accept this License. Therefore, by modifying or distributing the Program (or any work based on the Program), you indicate your acceptance of this License to do so, and all its terms and conditions for copying, distributing or modifying the Program or works based on it.

6. Each time you redistribute the Program (or any work based on the Program), the recipient automatically receives a license from the original licensor to copy, distribute or modify the Program subject to these terms and conditions. You may not impose any further restrictions on the recipients' exercise of the rights granted herein. You are not responsible for enforcing compliance by third parties to this License.

7. If, as a consequence of a court judgment or allegation of patent infringement or for any other reason (not limited to patent issues), conditions are imposed on you (whether by court order, agreement or otherwise) that contradict the conditions of this License, they do not excuse you from the conditions of this License. If you cannot distribute so as to satisfy simultaneously your obligations under this License and any other pertinent obligations, then as a consequence you may not distribute the Program at all. For example, if a patent license would not permit royalty-free redistribution of the Program by all those who receive copies directly or indirectly through you, then the only way you could satisfy both it and this License would be to refrain entirely from distribution of the Program.

   If any portion of this section is held invalid or unenforceable under any particular circumstance, the balance of the section is intended to apply and the section as a whole is intended to apply in other circumstances.

   It is not the purpose of this section to induce you to infringe any patents or other property right claims or to contest validity of any such claims; this section has the sole purpose of protecting the integrity of the free software distribution system, which is implemented by public license practices. Many people have made generous contributions to the wide range of software distributed through that system in reliance on consistent application of that system; it is up to the author/donor to decide if he or she is willing to distribute software through any other system and a licensee cannot impose that choice.

   This section is intended to make thoroughly clear what is believed to be a consequence of the rest of this License.

8. If the distribution and/or use of the Program is restricted in certain countries either by patents or by copyrighted interfaces, the original copyright holder who places the Program under this License may add an explicit geographical distribution limitation excluding those countries, so that distribution is permitted only in or among countries not thus excluded. In such case, this License incorporates the limitation as if written in the body of this License.

9. The Free Software Foundation may publish revised and/or new versions of the General Public License from time to time. Such new versions will be similar in spirit to the present version, but may differ in detail to address new problems or concerns.

   Each version is given a distinguishing version number. If the Program specifies a version number of this License which applies to it and "any later version", you have the option of following the terms and conditions either of that version or of any later version published by the Free Software Foundation. If the Program does not specify a version number of this License, you may choose any version ever published by the Free Software Foundation.

10. If you wish to incorporate parts of the Program into other free programs whose distribution conditions are different, write to the author to ask for permission. For software which is copyrighted by the Free Software Foundation, write to the Free Software Foundation; we sometimes make exceptions for this. Our decision will be guided by the two goals of preserving the free status of all derivatives of our free software and of promoting the sharing and reuse of software generally.